A
KABUKI
READER

Japan in the Modern World

Series Editor: Mark Selden

This series explores political, economic, cultural, and strategic dimensions of Japan's modern transformations, with particular attention to their consequences for the peoples of Japan and the world.

A
KABUKI READER

HISTORY AND
PERFORMANCE

SAMUEL L. LEITER
Editor

An East Gate Book

M.E. Sharpe
Armonk, New York
London, England

An East Gate Book

Library of Congress Cataloging-in-Publication Data

A kabuki Reader: history and performance / edited by Samuel L. Leiter.
    p. cm. – (Japan in the modern world)
"An east gate book."
Includes bibliographical references and index.
ISBN 0-7656-0704-2 (alk. paper) – ISBN 0-7656-0705-0 (pbk.: alk paper)
    1. Kabuki—History. I. Leiter, Samuel L. II. Series.

PN2924.5.K3 K2358 2001
792′.0952—dc21   2001020301

To the memory of my dear friend, Peter Klemperer.

Contents

Part 3. Surveying the Field

Illustrations

Preface

The number of serious English-language essays dealing with Japan's *kabuki* theatre published before World War II is remarkably small. Most of what was published—although often interesting—was casual, anecdotal, and journalistic. Moreover, apart from Zoe Kincaid's *Kabuki: The Popular Stage of Japan* (1925), still a surprisingly useful tome, and Shutaro Miyake's *Kabuki Drama* (1938), a slim volume designed as a guide for foreign tourists and frequently reprinted after the war, no other prewar English-language books were devoted to *kabuki*, although one or two surveys, such as Frank Alanson Lombard's still worthwhile *An Outline History of the Japanese Drama* (1928), gave it respectful attention. The number of prewar *kabuki* play translations, too, was minuscule. Nor, to my knowledge, were there any prewar Ph.D. dissertations about *kabuki*. It was only after the war ended and the Occupation army entered Japan that the West truly discovered Japanese theatre. From 1952 to 1960, for example, at least a half dozen books solely about *kabuki* appeared. Several are still in print, a tribute to their usefulness. The first dissertation on *kabuki* appeared in 1953, followed over the next five decades by nearly a dozen.

The 1950s also saw the beginnings of more than superficial studies of *kabuki* in academic journals, from those devoted to Asian studies in general to those interested mainly in Japanese culture to those specializing in aesthetic or theatrical research. During the past five decades, then, a respectable body of English-language scholarship has accrued, although certainly nothing more than a blip compared to the amount published in Japanese during the same period. Yet, for all the value inherent in these scattered essays, no one before this has attempted to gather some of this material together in a single volume. With one millennium ending and another beginning, and with foreign interest in classical Japanese theatre burgeoning, now appears to be the perfect time for such a collection.

The twenty essays that compose this volume include fifteen representative works by most of the field's leading scholars writing in English. The earliest was published in 1955, the latest in 2000. The book also introduces five previously unpublished essays, one by a veteran expert in Japanese literature, the others by young scholars first making their reputations. The selection of materials for the project went through several phases, at one point including a much larger number of pieces by myself and James R. Brandon. However, I am now issuing a separate volume of my essays, and Professor Brandon is contemplating a similar project of his own. Thus each of us is represented by a single essay, which has allowed this book to offer a truly far-ranging selection of authors and subjects and to be considerably more representative of the field than I had originally envisioned.

As explained in more detail in the Introduction, the book is organized into three sections: *Kabuki* History, *Kabuki* Performance, and Surveying the Field. To a considerable extent, these categories are (pun unavoidable) purely academic, of course, as historical discussions pervade the performance and survey articles, while performance forms a major component of the essays in the other sections. My distinctions are based on how the treatment in any particular essay is balanced and on how specific essays contribute to the organizational sequence of the book. The Introduction will make clear how the essays are linked so that one may experience a sense of continuity by reading the book straight through; some, of course, may prefer to read what interests them in a more random fashion.

I have made an attempt to unify the essays in terms of orthography and have here and there corrected or revised punctuation or obvious misprints. Among the spelling changes made are the use of "n" before plosives instead of "m" (*shinbun* for *shimbun*, for example), and *nō* for noh, Noh, Nō, or their italicized versions. I have eliminated Chinese characters, which originally appeared in several essays, and have made extensive revisions and corrections to the original citations, including the provision of numerous translated titles. Many titles in the text have also been rendered in English. All notes that first appeared as footnotes, however, have been changed to endnotes. When necessary, I conferred with the authors about revisions; some of these based on my suggestions, while others come from the authors themselves. Thus most essays are not precisely as they first appeared. In many cases I have interjected in the text an editorial comment or reference by placing it in brackets [ ], with the comment followed by "Ed."

I wish to express my gratitude to all the authors who contributed to this work and, in the case of previously published essays, to the original publishers of those works for permission to reprint. The sources for all previously published essays are given in the notes to the introduction. Cambridge University Press granted permission for the essays taken from *Modern Asian Studies* and *Themes in Drama*. MIT Press granted permission for the essay from *The Drama Review*. Permission for the essays taken from *Asian Theatre Journal* was provided by the University of Hawai'i Press and the individual authors. All other journals listed either provided permission themselves or did so through the respective authors. Professor Kei Hibino of Seikei University, Tokyo, was an invaluable source for checking bibliographic data and answering various last-minute queries. And costume designer Rebecca Cunningham of Brooklyn College kindly helped with a costume-related item. To my wife, Marcia, love and kisses, as always.

Samuel L. Leiter

Introduction

Samuel L. Leiter

Since 1952, around thirty English-language books specifically about Japan's *kabuki* theatre have been published, not to mention more general surveys of Japanese theatre in which *kabuki* is described; a four-volume project in which nearly two dozen translators are rendering fifty-one previously untranslated *kabuki* plays into English is presently under way; English-narrated videos about the form are widely available from commercial distributors; a number of American colleges and universities have produced *kabuki* plays in English (often with directorial help from professional *kabuki* actors); graduate and undergraduate academic courses make it either their chief focus or an important component; workshops in *kabuki* performance are run regularly for foreigners in and out of Japan; pictures of *kabuki* have graced the covers of best-selling "introduction to theatre" texts; museum exhibits of *kabuki*-related art and practice are increasingly common; great international directors have openly avowed *kabuki*'s influence on them; the word *kabuki* is constantly invoked by journalists to describe what they (often mistakenly) believe to be suggestive of this theatre form; there are several *kabuki*-related Web sites, one even offering video and sound clips of authentic productions; and—judging by the number of e-mail requests for information I receive—even grade-school children are learning about *kabuki*. Enter *"kabuki"* in an Internet search engine and notice the word's amazing ubiquity—including its use as a restaurant name, bicycle brand, and popular comic book title.

Theatre lovers and artists around the world, especially those tired of primarily realistic and psychologically oriented drama, find in *kabuki* a universe of dazzling costumes, innovative scenery, virtuoso acting, imaginative conventions, and an array of visual and aural qualities epitomizing the notion of "total theatre." Moreover, despite its play texts being widely and somewhat unfairly considered primarily performance fodder rather than reading matter, they clearly offer insights into the thoughts and behavior of a people about whom, despite Japan's remarkable resurgence from the ashes of World War II, few in the West really know very much.

This first collection of disparate essays on *kabuki* has no particular agenda to address other than to bring together some of the best English-language writing focusing on this outstanding art form. Much of this book—the history portion, in particular—can be read straight through, as there is generally a clear progression from one essay to the next. That some of the material overlaps from one essay to another is an unavoidable by-product of such a collection, although most readers—regardless of the order in which they read the essays—will be grateful for such reiteration, which is always in a new context.

The essays will be found under three sections: *Kabuki* History, *Kabuki* Performance, and Surveying the Field. For each of these, the remainder of this introduction offers, first, "a brief outline" of the respective section, designed to convey a sense of the essays' continuity, and second, "a closer look" at the major purposes of that section's essays.

Kabuki History Essays: A Brief Outline

The history segment covers *kabuki* from the sixteenth century, in the years leading to its birth, and concludes with a description of the form's most current developments as it moves into the twenty-first century. The first essay, then, appropriately enough, offers an account of *kabuki*'s origins. It leads on to another "origins" essay, one that looks at the beginnings of *kabuki*'s important *aragoto* style. With *kabuki* established as an unusually popular new type of theatre, it was bound to run into various difficulties in the tightly regulated world of the new Tokugawa regime, and the third essay explains these legal problems, while also providing a detailed account of *kabuki*'s early and later growth pains. By the Genroku period (1688–1704), when *kabuki* was comfortably settled in as the people's theatre par excellence and its artistic qualities were flourishing under the impetus of brilliant actors, the previously described *aragoto* was competing for artistic dominance with another new style, *wagoto*, which, as the next essay points out, found a niche not only in the Kamigata area (Osaka/Kyoto) of its origins, but in Edo, birthplace of *aragoto*, as well. Acting styles were just one potential site for rivalry; another was the actors themselves, a subject taken up in the subsequent article. These rivalries, of course, were dependent on *kabuki*'s powerful fan base, and the following two essays investigate this very subject by looking at the fans of Edo and Osaka.

The history segment now moves out of the Tokugawa era into the Meiji period (1868–1912) and the twentieth century. Meiji was known for its reformist tendencies, and, as the next two essays make clear, *kabuki* faced its share of problems under the new regime. Some of these problems persisted well into the new century, leading one new company as described in the subsequent article to seek redress through a Marxist agenda. By the end of the century, according to the final essay in this section, a variety of new approaches to *kabuki* were being attempted by artists seeking to revivify an art that many believed was in need of a makeover. A more thorough survey of these contents ensues.

Kabuki History Essays: A Closer Look

By and large, as we are often reminded, *kabuki* is an actor's theatre and has been since its inception at the start of the seventeenth century, when a dancer named Okuni who may or may not have had Shinto shrine affiliations began doing her *kabuki* or "eccentric" dances publicly for profit. But Okuni did not appear in a vacuum. The path leading to *kabuki's* flowering had to be carefully prepared by numerous historical and artistic events, these being the subject of Andrew Tsubaki's "The Performing Arts of Sixteenth-Century Japan: A Prelude to *Kabuki*."[1] Tsubaki, professor emeritus of the University of Kansas, explains how earlier forms of drama, particularly *nō* and *kyōgen*, were becoming increasingly realistic and how a branch of *kyōgen* played a major role in the creation of early *kabuki*. A huge step forward came with the arrival of the shamisen, although its value to *kabuki*, says Tsubaki, would not be as immediate as some have thought. The presence of various minor forms of performance that have disappeared or linger on in altered form in out-of-the-way places also shaped *kabuki*. As this new form of theatre struggled to establish itself, Tsubaki reminds us, it witnessed a rivalry between companies dominated by women and others led by handsome adolescents, who actually may have been on the scene before the women.

Kabuki experienced such remarkable popularity during its first fifty years that the military government (*bakufu*), despite a token attempt at tolerance, was thrown for a loss. The theatre increasingly represented a clear and present danger to civil order, as seen by the riots that broke out when fans battled one another for actors' favors; sometimes the actors and their fan-patrons were of the opposite, sometimes of the same sex. Partly as a result of such disorder, women became the first victims of governmental anxiety and were excluded from *kabuki* by offical decree in 1629 (and several times thereafter), as Donald H. Shively, professor emeritus of Stanford University, observes in "*Bakufu* Versus *Kabuki*."[2] Shively's essay, based largely on contemporary legal documents, is the classic study of the long history of *kabuki*'s harassment by the government and of how *kabuki* producers, play-wrights, theatre builders, and actors continuously subverted the dictatorial power structure, finding ways to use the restrictions to make this theatre stronger and more attractive. One is reminded of parallels with the West in the restrictions imposed on theatres in London or Paris during the eighteenth and nineteenth centuries.

Kabuki had employed cross-dressing from its inception, with men play-ing women and vice versa, but the proscription of actresses practically legis-lated its necessity, as the theatre could not have survived without males playing females. As Shively notes, even males were banned in 1652, thereby briefly ending *kabuki*'s existence, but it was permitted to return as long as it adhered to certain restrictions. Although sex appeal continued to play a major role in their popularity, *kabuki*'s female-role specialists (*onnagata*) evolved from primarily exhibitionist performers into magnificent artists whose technique mingled realism with theatrical convention to create a gallery of beautifully realized female characters. The wide range of these characters is examined in my own essay, described below in the Performance section.

Kabuki acting methods are hereditary, and the major families possess their own artistic secrets for the roles in which they specialize. When an actor is considered sufficiently capable in the family's art, he will usually be rewarded with the name of an illustrious ancestor. The present Ichikawa Danjūrō is the twelfth to hold that name. Born in 1946, the son of the actor who later became Ichikawa Danjūrō XI, he started acting as Ichikawa Natsuo, was given the name of Ichikawa Shinnosuke in 1958, in 1970 became Ichikawa Ebizō X, and attained the name of Danjūrō in 1985. Danjūrō is *kabuki*'s most revered name, first used by an actor in the late seventeenth century. The Danjūrō line, Edo's dominant acting family, has been associated from its inception with the flamboyant *aragoto* style whose bravura theatrics are in direct contrast to the gentle, realistic *wagoto*. Laurence R. Kominz, of Portland State University, explains the difference between *aragoto* and *wagoto* in "Origins of *Kabuki* Acting in Medieval Japanese Drama,"[3] but his main task is to seek the origins of *aragoto* in pre-Edo-period religious practices, literature, and performance. Even *nō*, he suggests, contributed to the *aragoto* gene pool in its depiction of Soga Gorō, whose evolution as a dramatic character became indissolubly linked to this acting method devised by Danjūrō I. (Danjūrō I's godlike status in Edo is also taken up by C. Andrew Gerstle, whose essay is described below.)

As noted earlier, the Genroku period saw not only Edo's creation of *aragoto* but the Kamigata birth of *wagoto*. Kyoto's Sakata Tōūrō I (1647–1709) was the father of this gentle art just as Danjūrō I was of *aragoto*. However, it is often forgotten that Edo had its own great Genroku *wagoto* star, Nakamura Shichisaburō I (1662–1708). This actor's *wagoto* has not been widely discussed in English-language sources, but in her previously unpublished essay, "Nakamura Shichisaburō I and the Creation of Edo-Style *Wagoto*," Holly A. Blumner, a Ph.D. candidate in theatre at the University of Hawai'i, describes his important contributions, including his establishment of Soga no Jurō as a *wagoto* character in opposition to Danjūrō I's *aragoto* interpretation of Soga no Gorō. Blumner also emphasizes Shichisaburō's *wagoto* in the pivotal drama *Keisei Asamagatake* (The Courtesan and the Peak of Asama) of which she translates generous portions. Shichisaburō complicates the oversimplified stereotype depicting Edo as the town of uncouth samurai whose tastes did not extend beyond *aragoto*'s exaggerations, and Kamigata as the milieu for performative reason and realism.

Shively and others in this book often note the paradoxical condition of Edo-period actors as both social outcasts and social lions supported by powerful fan clubs who rallied at the theatre to encourage their favorites. Viewing the systematized nature of Japanese fan club activity at today's sporting events suggests something of what *kabuki* fans must have been like in the old-time theatre. With such support, it was inevitable that the big stars would become the center of fierce rivalries, and this indeed was true from the early years on. Annual books of criticism (*yakusha hyōbanki*) were published in the major cities, critiquing each player and giving him a ranking based on a detailed system that grew ever more complex. Fans must have devoured these works the way they now study seasonal sports statistics, and loved the opportunity to fan the flames of rivalry when two or more acting idols vied for their affections. Going to the theatre was not that much unlike going to a ball game except that one rooted for an actor rather than an athlete or a team. Spurring on these rivalries were not only the theatres, but the printmakers, who made a fortune in the sale of actor pictures, and all the other businesses that profited from box office booms. Among the greatest of these rivalries were those between nineteenth-century Osaka actors Nakamura Utaemon III (1778–1838) and Arashi Rikan I (1769–1821), and Utaemon and Edo actor Bandō Mitsugorō III (1773–1831). The former rivalry plays a large role in the late Charles J. Dunn's (University of London), "Episodes in the Career of the *Kabuki* Actor Nakamura Utaemon III, Including His Rivalry with Arashi Rikan I,"[4] which, like Blumner's essay, is valuable as one of the relatively few English-language biographical accounts of a premodern *kabuki* actor. Dunn covers many important actor-related conventions, such as the process by which an actor changes his name during his career, and reveals the fluidity with which actors from one city were able to play elsewhere, thereby intermingling the styles associated with one place or the other. Moreover, Dunn's description of a large, two-volume scrapbook of Utaemon-related materials introduces a potential gold mine for future research.

The multifaceted matrix in which theatrical performance occurred—the seasonal calendar, the popularity of actors' commercial endorsements, the sale of prints, the tours from town to town, the support of literary groups, the production of books and criticism, the publication of elaborate programs, the rise of amateur performing arts, and a host of other things reflective of a theatre-crazy society—is among the issues taken up by C. Andrew Gerstle's "Flowers of Edo: Eighteenth-Century *Kabuki* and Its Patrons."[5] Edo samurai were not legally permitted to attend *kabuki*, but their presence, as Gerstle demonstrates, was significant; those bitten by the *kabuki* bug were unable to stay away. The nature of *kabuki* fandom—wherein even feudal lords were avid patrons of the lowly actors—is also treated, but while Gerstle looks at Edo spectators, the late Susumu Matsudaira, of Sonoda University, Kobe, concentrates on Osaka in "*Hiiki Renchū* (Theatre Fan Clubs) in Osaka in the Early Nineteenth Century."[6]

Tokugawa-period *kabuki* clubs get their fullest treatment in Matsudaira's essay, which studies those that flourished in Osaka, where such groups were the most complex and had the longest history. Matsudaira recounts the special club hand-clapping and other rituals, the way fans welcomed actors to town on special boats, fan-actor banquets, gift-giving practices, fan costumes, and so on, emphasizing not only the incredibly powerful bond between theatregoers and artists, but the absolute necessity of an actor's having such patronage if he was to succeed. It might be noted that the connection between patrons and stars, while somewhat diminished under the circumstances of modern living, nevertheless survives, and actors' fan clubs still actively support their theatrical favorites.

The essays thus far mentioned all are concerned with *kabuki* during the Tokugawa period. Four history essays now move us from that formative period to the years of modernization and reform following the Meiji Restoration (1868). "*Kabuki* Goes Official: The 1878 Opening of the Shintomiza,"[7] by Yuichirō Takahashi, of Dokkyō University, Tokyo, takes up a subject touched on by several other essays in this book, but not in such great detail: how did *kabuki*, product of the Tokugawa era—a two-and-a-half- century stretch during most of which Japan was isolated from the rest of the world by a repressive dictatorship—manage in a matter of decades to make the transition into a society that was undergoing one of the most remarkable transformations in modern world history?

Obviously, such a transition required visionaries in every field. *Kabuki* was ready and waiting with one, the redoubtable theatre manager Morita Kan'ya XII (1846–1897), who immediately saw the possibilities of the new age and seized the main chance. Kan'ya transferred his family's venerable Morita-za management (soon renamed the Shintomi-za) out of the outlying district to which the government had segregated it and Edo's other theatres earlier in the century, and back into the maelstrom of what had now been renamed Tokyo. Moreover, he began to adapt his theatre's architecture to Western expectations and—as part of a reform movement urged by the nation's highest echelons—supported those who wished to revolutionize *kabuki*'s dramaturgy so as to make it respectable in foreign eyes. Unfortunately, all this reform activity—including the aesthetically misguided disruption of the intimate audience-actor relationship—tended to deprive *kabuki* of much of its vitality and began the increasing calcification against which twentieth-century *kabuki* was forced to fight an uphill battle that continues today. Takahashi's well-illustrated analysis clarifies the architectural revisions in playhouse construction demanded by Meiji's new requirements.

Takahashi's depiction of the architectural and dramaturgic reforms instituted at the Shintomi-za prepares the ground for Faith Bach's essay, "Breaking the *Kabuki* Actor's Barriers: 1868–1900,"[8] in which she describes how Meiji reforms affected the world of *kabuki* actors. Bach, of Kanto Gakuen University, Gunma Prefecture, describes how the deeply embedded rules and regulations of the actor's subculture, which flourished under the social constraints of the Tokugawa period, began to wobble when the new government came into power. She elucidates the licensing restrictions and managerial responses of the Tokugawa era, during which Edo maintained a bilevel system of production: major theatres (*ōshibai*) and minor theatres (*koshibai* and *miya shibai*), something like Broadway and Off Broadway, except with strict hierarchical codes concerning the theatres at which each actor was permitted to perform. The fact that, as Bach observes, Osaka had a somewhat different system from Tokyo's only complicated matters. When Meiji's more liberal licensing policies permitted the sudden growth of competition among playhouses, problems arose concerning the old limitations on where the actors could play, especially as the new theatres gave otherwise secondary actors—lacking pedigrees as sons of major players—a shot at stardom. At the heart of this "majors" versus "minors" rivalry is the story of what happened when one highly talented actor, Ichikawa Ennosuke I (1855–1922), challenged the old-time regulations and was expelled from the guildlike family group (*mon*) to which he belonged by its leader, Ichikawa Danjūrō IX (1839–1903). The problem and its resolution—part of which involved the activity of Japan's first actors' union—typify the confusion that the *kabuki* world encountered as it tried to cope with the tidal wave of modernization brought on by Meiji. Eventually, of course, actors could work wherever they pleased.

Bach also supplements Takahashi's account with material on the fostering by Danjūrō IX, playwright Kawatake Mokuami (1816–1893), and manager Kan'ya XII of a new type of *kabuki* play, called "living history" (*katsureki*), which aimed to provide accurate depictions of events, manners, and persons in history plays, unlike the often fantastical or highly theatricalized versions of such things in conventional *kabuki*. *Katsureki* proved a failure and fewer than a handful of its plays are still performed, but its appearance undoubtedly stimulated new trends in *kabuki* dramaturgy, especially the rise of the twentieth-century genre called *shin* (new) *kabuki*, in which traditional theatrical effects take second place to realistic staging and psychologically complex characters.

Even though the distinction between majors and minors was abolished, *kabuki*'s feudalistic family structures remained—as they still do—a stumbling block for actor advancement. The number of *kabuki* theatres and companies dwindled in the twentieth century, and opportunities were no longer as widely available as during the heyday of Meiji. One response was inspired by Marxism, which made such deep inroads in the 1920s in Japan that a new company of *kabuki* actors arose to greet it with open arms. In "Communist *Kabuki*: A Contradiction in Terms?"[9] Brian Powell, of Oxford University, first describes the actor-centered world of *kabuki* that grew up during the Tokugawa period. Then, touching on issues also mentioned by Bach, he ponders *kabuki*'s restrictive family guilds and the difficulties they placed in the path of many talented actors without the proper family patronage. He examines the conservative nature of the commercial matrix of Tokugawa *kabuki*, revisits the Meiji reforms (including *katsureki*), and explains the importance of the commercial control of *kabuki* acquired in the new century by the brothers who formed the joint-stock Shōchiku company. This organization brought modern managerial methods to *kabuki*, while retaining, for the most part, the existing feudal structure that dominated actors' lives. The powerful impact of Marxism on Japanese arts and letters in the 1920s, however, was felt in the theatre world as well, deeply influencing *shingeki* (modern drama) and inspiring the creation of two new *kabuki* troupes, the Taishū-za (1929) and its successor, the Zenshin-za (1931), which remains a major company, although no longer overtly polemical. Powell limns the story of the Zenshin-za, originally created as a combination *shingeki-kabuki* company under Kawarazaki (sometimes spelled Kawarasaki) Chōjūrō II (1902–1981), Nakamura Kan'emon III (1901–1982), and Kawarazaki Kunitarō V (1909-1990), all outstanding artists. Apart from Chōjūrō, who came from a well-established family, the others probably would never have achieved stardom under the traditional system. In their new troupe, everyone had equal status and ability counted more than name. After initial struggles, the Zenshin-za—whose members all eventually joined the Communist Party in 1949—flourished, on screen as well as stage, introducing an ensemble-based approach that contrasted with Shōchiku's star-oriented stagings. The Zenshin-za's frequent tours spread *kabuki* throughout the country, and the company fostered the career of leading *shin kabuki* playwright Mayama Seika.

Kabuki's evolution continues today. While Shōchiku still manages the best-known acting troupes much as it did for most of the century, *kabuki* has seen several radical new approaches to bringing it into the new millennium. Foremost among these, insofar as it was inspired by one of the most popular mainstream *kabuki* actors, is the so-called super *kabuki* devised by Ichikawa Ennosuke III (b. 1939) in the mid-1980s, which has produced half-a-dozen or so works in the new genre to date. These newly written, expensively produced historical epics, which employ state-of-the-art lighting, movable stages, pyrotechnics, trick techniques, music, and sound, may seem to some like a cross between Las Vegas and *kabuki*, and certainly have riled the feathers of purists, but they have been extremely successful with audiences. Ennosuke's work is briefly covered in Natsuko Inoue's "New (Neo) *Kabuki* and the Work of Hanagumi Shibai," originally written in 1997 as a master's thesis at Brooklyn College, CUNY, where I served as Ms. Inoue's adviser. I have adapted the much longer text for its appearance in these pages.

Inoue's principal task is to introduce a kind of *kabuki* that grew out of the "little theatre" (*shōgekijō*) movement of the 1960s, a *kabuki* created by playwrights, directors, and actors not associated with the traditional *kabuki* world. She discusses the rise of the movement, called either "new" or "neo" (the English words are used) *kabuki*, outlines its variations as represented by the chief companies, and then focuses on the major example, Hanagumi Shibai, and its leader, Kanō Yukikazu (b. 1960). Her account provides a historical overview of this unusual kind of *kabuki* and describes its performance methods. Here we have what is essentially a hybrid genre, experimenting with traditional *kabuki* methods while also struggling to establish an independent style of its own, and attempting all the while to avoid the label of being a *kabuki* parody. As it has grown from production to production, it has generated increasing interest and popularity amidst a growing contingent of theatregoers. Inoue's essay, as much about performance as it is about history, serves as an excellent bridge into the Performance section of the text.

Kabuki Performance Essays: A Brief Outline

The seven (broadly defined) performance essays do not, of course, follow as natural a progression as do the history ones, but some continuity can be discerned in them as well. The focus in the first four is on acting, which, as we have seen, also plays a crucial part in a number of the history essays. Here, however, while *kabuki* history is occasionally invoked, the emphasis is on what happens on stage rather than off.

The first essay is an account of how the *onnagata* turned the restriction of males being forced to play female roles into a positive inspiration and thereby developed a surprising variety of characterizations. The next two essays offer theoretical insights into understanding *kabuki* acting, one from the angle of viewing the multiple interrelationships that are played out among the actor, his role, and his role type, the other by viewing the actor as a virtual hieroglyph. The essay that follows looks at a specific acting technique, the rhetorical set-speech called *tsurane*, noting how it and the major play in which it appears represented an aesthetic weapon against overweening Tokugawa authority. The following two performance essays are also concerned with specific plays, *Kuzunoha* and *Shinrei Yaguchi no Watashi*. In the final essay, *kabuki*'s importance for non-*kabuki* theatrical uses is explored.

Kabuki Performance: A Closer Look

My essay, "From Gay to *Gei*: The *Onnagata* and the Creation of *Kabuki*'s Female Characters,"[10] explains something not often encountered in English-language accounts of *kabuki*, the range of strong, aggressive female characterizations in *kabuki* plays. I attribute the development of such stage women mainly to the artistry of the *onnagata*, whose many great artists created characters with which male and female audiences—but especially the latter—could happily identify in an age when offstage women were the victims of a powerful patriarchy that allowed them little freedom outside their households. The theatre served as an alternative reality in which women could identify with characters they could only dream of emulating, the irony being that these characters were the creation of male actors. The essay also discusses the use of cross-dressing as a dramaturgic device.

What, however, is the nature of the *onnagata*'s or, for that matter, any type of actor's relationship to his "character"? Barbara E. Thornbury, of Temple University, determines in "Actor, Role, and Character: Their Multiple Interrelationships in *Kabuki*,"[11] that *kabuki* actors do not bear the same relationship of actor to character as do actors in realistic Western theatre, because the former bring additional dimensions to their job—their family tradition, their role-type, their self-referentiality (or what many now call metatheatricality), and so on. The use of the conventions of doubling and disguising further complicates the nature of their art.

"*Kabuki*: Signs, Symbols, and the Hieroglyphic Actor,"[12] the first of two essays by Leonard Pronko, of Pomona College, is similarly preoccupied with the aesthetics of *kabuki* acting, and some of Pronko's notions can be fruitfully compared with those of Thornbury. Pronko is concerned with clarifying the distinction between signs and symbols in order to distinguish nonillusionistic, sign-dominated *kabuki* acting—which requires an audience able to read the signs—from Western realistic performance. He studies the nature of *kabuki* symbolism and seeks to understand the difference between analytical Western attitudes and intuitive Japanese ones. Pronko also draws comparisons between *kabuki* and symbolism as forms of theatricalist expression, and he sees various similarities between them because of *kabuki*'s reliance on suggestion over literalness. The nature of *kabuki* dancing and dramatic poses (*mie*) are essential factors in his decision to declare the *kabuki* actor a hieroglyph, not unlike a Chinese ideograph (*kanji*).

Katherine Saltzman-Li, of the University of California, Santa Barbara, offers a previously unpublished essay with "The *Tsurane* of *Shibaraku*: Communicating the Power of Identity." Those who have read the essays by Kominz and Gerstle, in which *aragoto* is explained, will further their appreciation of such acting when they encounter Saltzman-Li's analysis of the bombastic name-announcing speech delivered by Kamakura Gongorō Kagemasa in *Shibaraku* (Just a Minute!), the quintessential *aragoto* hero in the quintessential *aragoto* play. She explicates how this ostentatious piece's "social energy" has made it a perennial favorite and underlines the role played by the *tsurane*. Ideas familiar from essays like Shively's regarding the lowly status of actors will be helpful in comprehending Saltzman-Li's description of how actors often managed to flout regulations against them, and how actors of *Shibaraku*, in particular, wielded considerable psychological authority through their performances. Moreover, anyone who has ever wrestled with the conventions surrounding *kabuki* actors' names will benefit from her discussion of the value and import of names in Japanese society and theatre.

The two plays that form the basis of the succeeding essays, *Kuzunoha* (Lady Kuzunoha) and *Shinrei Yaguchi no Watashi* (Miracle at Yaguchi Ferry), are examined for different purposes. In "Conjuring Kuzunoha from the World of Abe no Seimei," independent scholar and translator Janet E. Goff recounts, in a previously unpublished essay, the way in which the popular play usually known as *Kuzunoha* evolved from earlier literary and dramatic examples. The essay allows us a glimpse of how *kabuki* and puppet theatre plays often represented an ongoing experimentation in the telling of familiar stories until they reached a final form. The play's title character is actually a transformed fox, and Goff offers insights into such shape-shifting, folklore-based creatures, whose ability to deceive human beings is the stuff of which many dramas were made.

Kuzunoha is, like so many others, a puppet play that was adapted by *kabuki*. The process by which such adaptation took place is the focus of Stanleigh H. Jones Jr., of Claremont Graduate School, in "*Miracle at Yaguchi Ferry*: A Japanese Puppet Play and Its Metamorphosis to *Kabuki*."[13] Jones, a major translator of puppet drama, has illustrated the process in the introductions to his various published translations, but he does so here in even greater detail, providing as well a translation of the play in question. His thorough analysis makes clear the differing dramatic requirements of the puppets, who need strong narrative content, and live actors, who depend on action and dialogue. Jones shows precisely what happens when one form is transmuted into the other and how *Yaguchi no Watashi* benefited from the procedure. Harking back to the history of Japan's puppet theatre in the eighteenth century, Jones also communicates the importance of *Yaguchi no Watashi* as a transitional work produced in late eighteenth-century Edo following the decline in Osaka's once-great puppet theatre.

One of the most productive areas of discussion stimulated by postwar familiarity with *kabuki* has been the application of this theatre's training methods and aesthetics to the production of Western plays. The chief academic figures in this discourse have been James R. Brandon and Leonard Pronko, the latter's article on actors as hieroglyphs having been mentioned earlier. Not only have both Pronko and Brandon brilliantly led the field in college productions of *kabuki* in English translation, they each have successfully written and produced their own *kabuki* scripts, Brandon's using Japanese backgrounds and Pronko's finding Western locales—such as the Wild West—that lend themselves to *kabuki* dramaturgy and performance. Pronko began his considerations of the possibilities of crossbreeding *kabuki* and Western theatre in his 1967 article, "*Kabuki* and the Elizabethan Theatre,"[14] reprinted here. He offers a very useful comparison of the similarities between *kabuki* and the theatre of Shakespeare's day and ponders the possibilities of using *kabuki* techniques as a potentially creative source for the staging of Elizabethan drama. This theme continues to be one of his principal concerns.

Surveying the Field

The book's closing section, Surveying the Field, offers two valuable chapters cast in the form of surveys. James R. Brandon, of the University of Hawai'i, offers in "*Kabuki*: Changes and Prospects: An International Symposium,"[15] a report on a major conference held in Tokyo in 1996. He summarizes in considerable detail the eighteen papers presented by Japanese and foreign scholars, providing an excellent idea of some of the leading issues in contemporary *kabuki* studies. Apart from the two keynote addresses, the symposium dealt with the overarching issues of *kabuki*'s confrontation with the West, its existence during the Tokugawa era, its place in the modern world, and actor training. Brandon's descriptions follow the order in which the talks were originally delivered.

We conclude with "*Kabuki* as National Culture: A Critical Survey of Japanese *Kabuki* Scholarship in Japan," by William Lee, University of Minnesota, Akita, Japan. This essay, published here for the first time, is a concise but thorough description of the kinds of *kabuki* research and publication done in Japan, where such scholarship, of course, dwarfs similar work in the West. Nothing like this has been published previously in English, and I hope it will prove as interesting and thought provoking for others as it has for me.

Conclusion

As this overview discloses, *kabuki* studies in English have provided a worthwhile corpus of documentation, analysis, and explication. However, there are numerous areas that remain relatively or completely untouched. For example, the lack of critical studies of *kabuki* texts is vividly apparent. Moreover, despite the forthcoming four-volume, fifty-one-play translation project that James R. Brandon and I are coediting, there still remain numerous classics that demand translation and explanation. Of course, the themes of English-language *kabuki* scholarship cannot hope to duplicate precisely those of Japanese scholars, such as the ones described by Lee. Scholars who write mainly for readers of English are dealing with a much smaller potential audience, one that often needs to be reintroduced to basic information if certain points are to be understood. Even specialists in Japanese literature and other forms of Japanese culture and history are not necessarily familiar with the essential historical or aesthetic background to Japanese traditional theatre. Thus scholars must always select their themes and issues with respect for this relative lack of preparation and with regard for what English readers— even Japanese-reading specialists—are likely to find worthwhile, useful, or interesting. Still, there remains a remarkably rich lode of material to be excavated and sifted through to bring *kabuki* ever closer to readers and audiences of the future.

Notes

1. Tsubaki, Andrew, "The Performing Arts of Sixteenth Century Japan." *Educational Theatre Journal* 29 (October 1977).
2. Shiveley, Donald H., *"Bakufu* Versus *Kabuki." Harvard Journal of Asiatic Studies* 18 (1955); reprinted in *Studies in the Institutional History of Early Modern Japan.* Ed. John W. Hall and Marius B. Jansen (Princeton: Princeton University Press, 1968).
3. Kominz, Lawrence R., "Origins of *Kabuki* Acting in Medieval Japanese Drama." *Asian Theatre Journal* 5 (Fall 1988).
4. Dunn, Charles J., "Episodes in the Career of the *Kabuki* Actor Nakamura Utaemon III, Including His Rivalry with Arashi R. Rikan I." *Modern Asian Studies* 18, no. 4 (1984).
5. Gerstle, C. Andrew., "Flowers of Edo: Eighteenth Century *Kabuki* and Its Patrons." *Asian Theatre Journal* 4 (spring 1987).

6. Matsudaira Susumu, "Hiiki Benchū (Theatre Fan Clubs) in Osaka in the Early Nineteenth Century." *Modern Asian Studies* 18, no. 4 (1984).

7. Takahashi Yuichirō, "*Kabuki* Goes Official: The 1878 Opening of the Shintomiza." *The Drama Review (TDR)* 39:T147 (fall 1995).

8. Bach, Faith, "Breaking the *Kabuki* Actors' Barriers: 1868–1900." *Asian Theatre Journal* 12 (fall 1995).

9. Powell, Brian, "Communist *Kabuki*: A Contradiction in Terms." In *Themes in Drama* 1, ed. James Redmond (Cambridge: Cambridge University Press, 1979).

10. Leiter, Samuel L., "From Gay to *Gei*: The *Onnagata* and the Development of *Kabuki*'s Female Characters." *Comparative Drama* 33, no. 4 (winter 1999–2000).

11. Thornbury, Barbara E., "Actor, Role, and Character: Their Multiple Interralationships in *Kabuki*." *Journal of the Association of Teachers of Japanese* 12:1 (1977).

12. Pronko, Leonard, "*Kabuki*: Signs, Symbols, and the Hieroglyphic Actor." In *Themes in Drama* 4, ed. James Redmond (Cambridge: Cambridge University Press, 1982).

13. Jones, Stanleigh H., Jr., "Miracle at Yaguchi Ferry: A Japanese Puppet Play and Its Metamorphosis to *Kabuki*." *Harvard Journal of Asiatic Studies* 38, no. 1 (1978).

14. Pronko, Leonard, "*Kabuki* and the Elizabethan Theatre." *Educational Theatre Journal* 19 (March 1967).

15. Brandon, James R., "*Kabuki*: Changes and Prospects: An International Symposium." *Asian Theatre Journal* 15 (fall 1998).

Part 1

Kabuki History

1

The Performing Arts of Sixteenth-Century Japan: A Prelude to *Kabuki*

Andrew T. Tsubaki

The 100 years beginning from the Onin wars of 1467 and ending with Oda Nobunaga's succession to power in 1568 were characterized by social and political uncertainties so vast that the period is called "the age of the country at war." Despite this strife, the energy of the people for maintaining the various performing arts remained high. With the temporary peace enjoyed during the reign of Toyotomi Hideyoshi, the populace seized the opportunity to formulate their own unique contribution to the performing arts. This art form, initiated by the shrine dancer Okuni, was a prelude to the *kabuki* theatre of later days.

The emergence of Okuni and her *kabuki odori* was no mere accident. From a historical perspective, we can now see diverse forces contributing to the process by which such an art form was molded, forces that were operating in the late Muromachi and Momoyama eras. This study will present a survey of the major forms that contributed to the formulation of *kabuki* forms such as *nō*, *kyōgen*, *ningyō jōruri* (puppet theatre, called also by its popular name *bunraku*), and certain kinds of folk theatre activities.

The Japanese performing arts of the sixteenth century were at a low point, as if in a valley surrounded by the two gigantic, surveyed peaks of the established theatre, the fifteenth-century *nō* drama and the seventeenth-century *kabuki*. The seeming inactivity of the performing arts in the sixteenth century, however, takes on new significance when carefully examined in the context of their contribution to the emergence of *kabuki*.

By the process called "*gekokujō*"—that is, the tendency of the lower class to displace the higher (typical of the samurai during "the age of the country at war") the newly emerging *kabuki* and the *ningyō jōruri* would replace the *nō* and the *kyōgen*, forms that were somewhat more refined in their style and appeal. In other words, the dynamic power that created *kabuki* was in the hands of amateurs, or common people, while the true professionals, the performers of the *nō* and the *kyōgen*, began to retreat behind the curtain of refinement.

The man who contributed most to the refinement of *nō* was Zeami Motokiyo (1364–1444), the second head of the Kanze School. His emphasis on *yūgen* (the beauty of gentle gracefulness) helped to raise the level of sophistication of the art to a great height. This tendency toward sophistication was in a sense motivated by Zeami's desire to cater to the interests of the shogun Yoshimitsu, who, as military governor of the Ashikaga family, was a great patron of the arts.

The main thrust of Zeami's creativity centered on the tragic heroine of noble birth, whose refined appearance was most suitable to enrich his performance with *yūgen* of the highest quality. This emphasis on *yūgen* resulted in a greater reliance on *buka* (dance and chant) than on *monomane* (mimicry). The latter term is used to indicate the representation of realistic movement, clearly defined conflict, and a carefully delineated characterization.

Zeami's strong inclination toward *yūgen* was not new. Inuō, an older contemporary performer, was known to have been extremely skilled in plays that revealed *yūgen*. Kannami, Zeami's father, also adopted the quality in his performance. But it was Zeami who refined the technique to its highest level in his performances of *nō*.

The well-placed emphasis on *buka* and *yūgen* was further observed by such masters as Onnami (1398–1467), the third head of the Kanze School and Zeami's nephew, and Komparu Zenchiku (1405–ca. 1470), Zeami's son-in-law. After Onnami, however, there was a series of rapid changes in the headship due to early deaths of successive heads. Masamori, the fourth head, died in 1470 at the age of forty-one. He was followed by Yūken (d. 1500), who inherited the position at an age just under twenty. Dōken (d. 1522) also succeeded at an early age, as did Sōsetsu, who became the head at the age of thirteen. Sōsetsu matured into a *meijin* (a great master) and was patronized by Tokugawa Ieyasu, initiating the long association of the Kanze with the Tokugawa shogunate. Ieyasu was the first shogun of the Tokugawa family, which reigned over feudal Japan for more than 260 years until the modernization of Japan forced its downfall in 1868.

During this critical period for the Kanze School, Kojirō Nobumitsu (1435–1516), the seventh son of Onnami, guided the two youthful heads as their regent and teacher. Nobumitsu's son Yajirō Nagatoshi (1488–1541) also functioned as teacher to Sōsetsu and contributed greatly to the preservation of the tradition.

Even more important than Nobumitsu and Nagatoshi's contributions to the Kanze School is their contribution to the art of playwriting. They expanded the scope of the *nō* play and intensified its dramatic impact. Without their contributions, *nō* would have remained a purely lyrical and highly elaborate storytelling art form. Their plays were an indication of the sensitivity to conflict and characterization, two elements of drama much prized in Western aesthetics. In their work there emerges the *geki nō* (dramatic piece)the earliest prototype of the *kabuki*.

There are fifteen plays by Nobumitsu still in the repertoire of *genkō-kyoku* (240 plays currently producible). Among them, the following are intensely dramatic and very popular even today: *Ataka* (The barrier at Ataka), *Funa Benkei* (Benkei in the boat), and *Momijigari* (The maple-viewing). Nine of the fifteen plays by Nobumitsu are of the *geki nō* variety. Only three of Nagatoshi's works remain in the repertoire and they are hardly ever performed today. Three others are cited as his works but are no longer performed. Two of these six fall into the category of the *geki nō*.

Geki nō are relatively more theatrical than earlier works. They have a high level of conflict, rich characterization, and a strong narrative quality. This contrasts with *mugen nō* (dreamy, impressionistic *nō*), with its otherworldly quality, where ghosts appear and where elegant dances and subdued chants reinforce the rich lyrical moods.

Nobumitsu's interest in the *geki nō* may be attributed to the following reasons: *nō* plays that emphasized *buka* and *yūgen* had quite possibly reached the peak of their development by this time. Kannami had written several plays that emphasized the realistic element of *monomane* with significant success. (Nobumitsu was to carry that form forward in such richly dramatic pieces as *Ataka* and *Funa Benkei*). Then, too, because of its character development and conflict-oriented situations, *geki nō* tends to be exciting and glamorous. Audiences may have begun to tire of *yūgen*. [See Kominz's essay, chapter 2. Ed]

Other more complex factors may have contributed to the evolution of the *geki nō*. Both Nobumitsu and Nagatoshi were obliged to provide interesting plays as vehicles for the young heads of their schools. Yet, in doing so, they had to deemphasize the *shite* (principal) roles performed by their comparatively inexperienced masters. Hence, the rise of the *geki nō* form witnessed a heightening of the importance of the *waki* (secondary) roles. Just as classical Greek drama gained in dramatic strength and complexity by the development of the deuteragonist, the *nō* gained significantly from the new emphasis of the *waki* role.

"Imaginatively weaving life into operatic dance drama,"[1] Nobumitsu successfully introduced a new form of the *nō* theatre. Since then, there have been no significant changes in the genre.

Research materials available on the early aspects of *kyōgen* are extremely limited. An early form of *kyōgen* primarily concerned itself with celebrating various festive occasions by means of dance and chant.[2] It seems reasonable to assume that during the time of Shirō Jirō and his successor Uji Yataro Masanobu a form of *kyōgen* appeared that revealed a more complex story line, a greater amount of conflict, and an increased taste for satire. Although we cannot be certain precisely when the shift occurred, we may safely assume that it took place sometime between the beginning of the sixteenth century and its mid-point.[3] The transformation of *kyōgen* may very well have paralleled that of *nō* by increasing the number of characters, developing dialogue among them, adding representational movement to enhance reality, and, in general, attempting to escape from the powerful grip of the *buka*-oriented style.

Through the writings of Zeami and others, we learn that as early as the mid-fourteenth century *kyōgen* plays were performed on the same program with *nō* plays. The *Tadasu-gawara Kanjin-Sarugaku* (Subscription performance at Tadasu dry-riverbed) of 1464, listing some twenty *kyōgen* plays by title, is our earliest record. Due to its spontaneous commedia-like nature, *kyōgen* resisted formalization until the mid-sixteenth century. Sometime during the Tenmon period (1532–1554), a Buddhist priest, Shōjō-shōnin of the temple known as Ishiyama Honganji, noted in his diary several titles of *kyōgen* plays he had seen.[4] There also exists a collection of synopses of over 100 *kyōgen* plays known as *Tenshō-bon*. This collection is dated "On an Auspicious Day of July in the Sixth Year of Tenshō,"[5] that is to say, 1578.

But the first solid record of *kyōgen* scripts does not appear until 1642, when an eight-volume anthology of *kyōgen* plays entitled *Kyōgen nō Hon* (A book of *kyōgen*) was compiled by Okura Toraakira (d. 1662), the thirteenth head of the Okura School. The anthology contains over two hundred plays, mostly in full versions, with a note that the plays, hitherto transmitted orally for many generations, were presented here for the first time in written form. Toraakira also left a treatise called *Waranbe-gusa* (A book for the youngsters), completed in 1651. This work transmits a secret tradition compiled for posterity. It contains many important materials relating to the history, art, theory, and criticism of *kyōgen* and is our single most important extant source on early *kyōgen*.

Aside from these two monumental works by Toraakira, we know of four other anthologies of *kyōgen* plays prepared between 1646 and 1660. This sudden burst of interest in committing plays to writing is apparently a reflection of the settled lifestyle of the performers of *nō* and *kyōgen*. The patronage of their art by the Tokugawa shogunate had lasted by now into the reign of Iemitsu, the third shogun. As the feudal system of the Tokugawa became well established, the activities of *nō* and *kyōgen* too became regularized, eventually to the most minute detail.

The gradual process of formalizing *kyōgen*, and the stabilizing of its position as the chosen art form under the patronage of the shogun, set it apart from the other performing arts, particularly from the *kyōgen* performers belonging to the school of Nanto Negi. The Negi are of special interest to us since, in a variety of ways, they participated significantly in the formation of early *kabuki*. Several references by Toraakira in *Waranbe-gusa* to the Negi performers show a clear disgust directed toward them on the part of the author. Through these references we can learn, if only indirectly, a great deal about what had taken place prior to 1651.

Referring to a then-popular play, *Tanuki nō Harazutsumi* (The badger's belly drumming), Toraakira disassociates himself completely from the play as follows. "Those *kyōgen* plays written in recent days by some not belonging to the four schools are not performed by our family. *Tanuki nō Harazutsumi* was said to be written by a man called Toppa of the Nara Negi. The *daimyō kyōgen* was presented first by a man called Sōsuke of the same Negi. The true author may have been someone else. I would not know that definitely, because it is not a matter associated with me. They are the ones who have performed these plays here and there."[6] The four schools mentioned here are the *nō* schools of Kanze, Konparu, Hōshō, and Kongō. The "legitimate" *kyōgen* actors attached themselves to one of these four schools to participate in their performances. The tone detected in Toraakira's statement indicates clearly that these plays of the Nara Negi were popular and that he was thoroughly disgusted by this fact. His further pronouncement, quoted below, reinforces this:

> Popular *kyōgen* today has no style; it is busy and noisy. It delivers empty words. It is perverse. Its actor twists his face, opens his eyes and mouth widely, makes his audience laugh by behaving outrageously, pleases those of the low class, but embarrasses those with discriminating minds. In the *kabuki* popular today he is what is called a clown. It is not the *kyōgen* of *nō*, nor can it be termed the *kyōgen* of *kyōgen*. Even if it is currently popular, the *kyōgen* of this kind is said to be the disease of *kyōgen* since the olden times. . . .
> . . . Thinking *kyōgen* to be something funny, both the actor and his audience alike believing this, the actor tries to make the other laugh while the latter claims he is still not amused. This is against the way it should be. Thus, the actor has no way but to become a clown. A clown is the one who is outside the norm. *Kabuki* is women who sing and dance.[7]

As a major figure in the conservative, professional *elite*, Toraakira must have felt considerable animosity toward this new, vibrant, performing art form which stirred up the common people. Although *kyōgen* had been born among the common people, it gradually increased its dependency upon the *nō*. Toraakira apparently felt himself too good to soil his hands with such a cheap form as *kyōgen*. He had expressed similar sentiments about the *kabuki*.

The people who were not afraid to support the development of *kabuki* were the Negi *kyōgen* actors. The Nanto Negi School was one of several minor schools of *kyōgen* existing from the end of the sixteenth century through the seventeenth. These groups were excluded from the main body of *kyōgen* actors belonging to the four *nō* schools mentioned above. Hattori Yukio states that a group of *kyōgen* actors, who were employed to perform in the service of Kasuga-jinja, an important Shinto shrine in Nara, made up the so-called Nanto Negi School. The originators of the school were believed to be two actors: Toppa and Sōsuke.[8]

After the middle of the sixteenth century, as the power of the shrines and temples declined, the Negi had to find a way to support themselves. They began leaving the Kasuga-jinja to engage in performance elsewhere and to establish themselves gradually as performers for the common people.[9]

In a diary known as *Goyudono no Kami no Nikki* (A diary of the Lord Goyu), there are many entries relating to performances by the Negi in the imperial palace. An important series of entries in the diary records their performances in May of 1598. The Negi *kyōgen* were invited as frequently as the *yayako odori* (performers of a popular contemporary dance). Hattori believes that the *yayako* dancers may already have established a liaison with the Negi *kyōgen* in order to perform together in the same program.[10] This familiarity between the Negi *kyōgen* and the *yayako* dancers developed later into a close professional relationship. The Negi provided the dancers with a dialogue-oriented scene with a touch of humor, while the dancers provided the Negi with an opportunity to earn their living by performing as part of the *yayako* dance program.

It is well known that the development of *ningyō jōruri* coincided closely with that of *kabuki*, and through the process of evolution each form greatly influenced the other. Early *ningyō jōruri* clearly precedes *kabuki*, although the details of its development are far less clear than those of *kabuki*. Before the skills of *ningyō jōruri* were forged into one unified performing art, each of its three basic elements followed its own process of development. The oldest element was a puppet show called *kugutsu*. This was a primitive form brought to Japan in the eighth century from central Asia after it had been introduced into China and Korea by a wandering tribe who eventually settled in Japan.

Biwa chanting has existed since the Heian period (794–1192), when many blind players of the *biwa* (a lute-like stringed instrument) sang the famous story of *Heike Monogatari* (Tale of the Heike) to entertain people of all classes in a manner similar to that of the European ballad singer of the Middle Ages. By the end of the fifteenth century, this form of popular entertainment had exhausted the interest of its audience. After 1525, there are several references to the term "jōruri," a new kind of chanted story accompanied by the *biwa* instrument. The most popular of these stories is the *Jōruri-hime Monogatari* (The story of Princess Jōruri), whose author and date cannot clearly be determined. It is known, however, that this famous twelve-act libretto had Ushiwakamaru (a boyhood name of the great general Minamoto Yoshitsune) as the hero, and the Princess Jōruri as the heroine; hence, the form came to be known as *ningyō* (doll or puppet) *jōruri* (from Princess Jōruri).

The last important element contributing to the popularity of *ningyō jōruri* was the use of the newly imported three-stringed instrument, the shamisen. The exact process by which it arrived in Japan is unclear, but it is generally said to have had its origin in Egypt. Sometime between 1558 and 1567 it came through China to the Ryukyus and eventually to Sakai (a part of modern Osaka). The skin covering the resonating chamber changed, in its travels, from sheep to snake, and, in Japan, to cat. Its novel, intricate, and complex musical tone captured the imagination of the Japanese, and its use quickly spread over the entire country in the brief period from 1565 to 1595.[11]

There are several accounts as to how *ningyō jōruri* actually came into being; however, in about 1595, someone put these three elements of puppetry, shamisen, and chanting together and succeeded in establishing a rich art form. That was just a few years before Okuni made her presence known in Kyoto.

Although the intense competition between *ningyō jōruri* and *kabuki* did not take place at this early stage in their mutual development, it is interesting to note that both art forms employed the shamisen as their principal musical instrument; *ningyō jōruri* had begun to use it shortly before *kabuki*. At the time of the earliest Okuni *kabuki*, it is fairly certain that no shamisen was employed. Records and paintings show the use of the shamisen on the *kabuki* stage after 1610, during the phase of *onna kabuki* (women's *kabuki*), but even here the shamisen seems more a hand property than a practical musical instrument.[12] The flute and drum accompaniment of the *nō* served as the usual accompaniment for the early *kabuki*. Only when *kabuki* reached the stage of *yarō kabuki* in the mid-seventeenth century (men's *kabuki*) do we see a shamisen player seated with the other musicians upstage center, clearly indicating his active participation.[13]

We have been examining the performing art forms that have been carried over into the present day. In varying degrees these forms have contributed to the formation of *kabuki*, but there were other groups of performing folk artists whose contributions were totally absorbed into *kabuki*, leaving only scattered traces behind today. A number of these groups, however, were of major importance to the nurturing of *kabuki*.

During the third quarter of the sixteenth century, and for several decades to follow, there was a tremendous fervor for folk dances among the common people. To strengthen their sense of unity in troubled times, to amuse themselves, and to help themselves forget the miserable reality of their lives, people craved the opportunity to watch enticing dances and to participate in dances as a group. As peace drew near, this inclination seems to have become even more intense. There were times when the common people utilized group dancing as a means of holding the samurai in check and of demonstrating their power.[14]

Before we proceed with the question of Japanese folk dancing, the difference between the terms *"mai"* and *"odori"* should be clarified. Both terms are translated as *dance* in English. But *mai* refers to a type of dance that employs gliding steps in its movement. It is characterized by a subdued mood and is abstract and restrained. Some of the best-known examples of this form are found in *nō*, *kagura* (shrine dance), and *bugaku* (court dance). *Odori*, on the other hand, is characterized by a rhythmic movement of the limbs. It is freer, more realistic, and more colorful than *mai*.

Ogasawara Kyōko states that originally *odori* was a form of dancing performed by the common people and was related to festive and animistic functions. It later grew specialized and was performed by professional dancers for the purpose of entertainment. *Mai*, on the other hand, was a refined art performed by specialists from the beginning.[15] I might add that in its earliest days *mai* was also performed in connection with festivals and for various religious purposes. The dances of *nō* epitomize most eloquently the quality of *mai*.

Since most of the dance forms of this sort were practiced in the sixteenth century, a brief review may be in order. From the end of the Heian period (794–1192), through the Kamakura period (1192–1333), to the Muromachi period (1333–1568), we observe that *ennen*, *dengaku*, and *sarugaku* were extremely popular.[16]

Ennen consists of a presentation at Buddhist temples of a variety of dances and dramatic performances on mythological themes. The performers are trained priests and child servants called *chigo*. A considerable influence from *bugaku* was exerted on *ennen*, as evidenced in the fact that *bugaku* was danced at the beginning of each program. Some of the more popular dance forms in the *ennen* included an act by a *chigo* imitating a woman dancer called *shirabyōshi*. In addition to pure *mai* programs, the performances at the temples contained dramatic portions that included an act called *furyū*, consisting of exchanges of dialogue and enactments of mythological legends.

Dengaku is a dance form that had, by the fourteenth century, quite possibly absorbed some aspects of the ancient indigenous dance *tamai* (field dance), which was itself an outgrowth of ritualistic acts related to the offering of prayers for a rich rice harvest. Some professional performers may have learned some of the theatrical elements of *tamai* and presented them under the name of *dengaku*. While *tamai* died away, *dengaku* became popular and gained the support of the populace and the patronage of the samurai, as welt as the priests. Although it was destined to be absorbed by a newly risen form, *sarugaku*, it remained in a limited way as a ritualistic event at certain temples and shrines. *Dengaku* continued to include acrobatic elements as a major part of its program, having taken them from the ancient *sangaku*, a dance imported from T'ang China. *Dengaku* developed a dramatic form called *nō* (*dengaku no nō*), and established a sound foundation for the later development of a similar form identified as *sarugaku no nō*. Because of *dengaku*'s exceptional popularity, it helped develop the folk performing arts, some of which still exist and continue to add richness to the local life.

The early form of the *nō* is known as *sarugaku no nō*. At that still vibrant stage of development, Zeami's father, Kannami, incorporated a dance form known as *kusemai* into the *nō*. By this innovation Kannami enriched the *nō* play. The *kusemai* had traditionally been performed by women, men, or children. It was essentially a dance performed by one or two dancers who chanted out a story with the accompaniment of a small hand drum.

Although there were several schools of *kusemai*, *kōwaka* (or *kōwakamai*), favored by Toyotomi Hideyoshi, came to represent all forms of *kusemai*.[17] *Kōwaka* tended to deal with stories having a martial theme and possessed a rather simple and forceful chanting style. It did not require the use of costumes or masks, and, for this reason, the production style was far simpler than that of *nō*. Together with *nō* texts, the *kōwaka* texts exerted a significant influence upon the development of *ningyō jōruri*.

After *sarugaku* (the old name of *nō*) had established its popularity, women were introduced into the form *onna sarugaku*, or women *sarugaku*, making their participation the main attraction. The existence and popularity of these female performers in *sarugaku*, *kusemai*, and even in the earlier *shirabyōshi* point out an important social condition. Okuni's emergence as a dancer and the founder of *onna kabuki* was in no way an unnatural event for the period. An atmosphere existed that was conducive to Okuni's appearance.

Today, it is commonly believed that Okuni created the *kabuki odori* on the basis of her experience with *furyū odori*.[18] This latter form had such diverse aspects that no one seems to have succeeded in giving a clear description of it. *Furyū* means to be elegant, refined, and beautifully attired.[19] In a specialized sense it also refers to an *odori* that was performed in a group with beautiful costumes, even in disguise, with a highly decorated large umbrella put up at the center of the encircling dancers. Many group dancing forms fall into this category.

As the common people grew rich, they began to promote group dancing at shrines and temples on festive occasions. The famous festivals, such as the Gion and Kamo Matsuri, are examples of *furyū*. Today we can still enjoy a parade of the *dashi* (huge, ornately decorated carriages) being pulled through the city of Kyoto every summer on the occasion of the famous Gion festival. This is one of the most representative forms of the extant *furyū*. Many *bon odori*, group-*odori* performed at the *bon* festival, are also good examples of these extremely popular *furyū*.

One famous *furyū* dance was the *nenbutsu odori* (a Buddhist prayer that dates back as early as the beginning of the Heian period). This was popularly believed to be the dance with which Okuni made her debut in Kyoto. Today that theory is losing ground. Okuni might have had such an act in her program; if so, however, it appears to have been added sometime after her appearance in Kyoto. Further, this *odori* seems not to have had much of a stage life at all, since even *onna kabuki* troupes, which imitated many aspects of the Okuni program, show no evidence of doing the *nenbutsu odori*.[20]

Today, in theories on the development of early *kabuki*, a view that is gaining support is that the *kouta odori*, sometimes called *yayako odori*, was a dance by young girls accompanied by a short song. The *kouta odori* absorbed various forms of the *furyū odori*, including the *nenbutsu odori*; at the same time, the *kouta odori* established a cooperative arrangement with the Negi *kyōgen* players and consequently succeeded in nurturing the *odori kyōgen* that possessed a slight dramatic structure.[21]

Records in 1603 show that Okuni from Izumo, who had once called her act a *yayako odori*, was identified with the *kabuki odori* at this time.[22] It is difficult to give a precise definition of *yayako odori*. The term "*yayako*" means "baby." The *yayako odori* may signify a dance to celebrate a baby turning into a girl. Thus it may be that the *yayako odori* is the same as the *musume odori* (girls' dance). The latter was performed frequently during the *bon* festival. Ogasawara Kyōko suggests that the dance had a song (*kouta*) at its core and a slow and elegant movement to match the quality of the song.[23] She explains that the *yayako odori* was performed by a small, itinerant troupe of women who did *kouta odori* as their main attraction and who were supported from approximately 1592 by male *kyōgen* players. The use of the name "*yayako*" is believed to be due to the fame they gained earlier, around 1580, by having young girls perform the *kouta odori*. They used the name *yayako* from that time on. At this stage of the *yayako odori*, dances and *kyōgen* were probably presented alternately without any artistic link between them. The *yayako odori* should be recognized not only as an early form of *kabuki* but also as an art form that transformed a group dance into a theatrical presentation by a small number of performers.[24]

It is interesting to note that today there are extant two kinds of dance known to be similar to *yayako odori*. One is called *ayako mai* and is found in Niigata Prefecture (the northwestern part of Honshū); the other is called *ayako odori* and is performed in Kagawa Prefecture (on Shikoku). There are some other folk art forms that contain songs similar to early *kabuki* songs, but these two have names that closely resemble *yayako odori*.[25]

The success of Okuni in establishing *onna kabuki*, beyond having included *kyōgen* in her program, was due to the creation of a dramatic scene in which a young man (played by a pretty woman) appears on his way to a teahouse; having arrived, he is entertained by *odori* in a drinking party scene. The term "*kabuki*" was first used as the name for this particular sequence of scenes.

Another success of Okuni consisted in her presentation of a scene in which there appears the ghost of Nagoya Sanza. This was not in itself a new idea. The plot in which a man is received from the underworld and, after revealing his identity, is entertained and sent back to the underworld is an old stage convention. What was new in Okuni's act was that she appeared as a priest who danced the *nenbutsu odori*. We can assume that she displayed a certain eroticism. By presenting herself as a priest who entertains a ghost, Okuni here assumes the characteristic role of a *waki*, an itinerant priest of a *mugen nō*. Okuni's act, however, differs from what one might expect to find in a *nō* play in that the ghost is only the spirit of a common man, reputedly Okuni's lover, and he is entertained in the teahouse rather than at a lonesome corner of a wild field or in a shabby hut on a deserted beach.[26]

After *onna kabuki* was established, its transition to *wakashu kabuki* (young men's *kabuki*) and then to *yarō kabuki* (men's *kabuki*) took place during the seventeenth century. In this well-known process, one common misunderstanding has long existed concerning the primacy of *onna kabuki*. As Ogasawara points out, by the fall of 1603, an early *kabuki*-style performance by young boys instead of women had already begun appearing in the records. This boys' version later came to be known as *wakashu kabuki*. The *odori* presentation by them had already come into existence four or five years earlier. We may assume that the boys' *odori* was staged much sooner than the girls', that the boys' program had more variety than the girls', and that the variety in later *kabuki* may well have had its origin in the performances of the boys' troupe.[27]

The remaining transitional processes in *kabuki* need not be discussed here. There is, however, one more aspect deserving our attention. The sixteenth century offered fertile ground for the emergence of *kabuki* and the puppet form *ningyō jōruri* in the following century. Yet the birth of these art forms cannot be understood without recognizing the vital relationship they have to *nō*.

In an early stage of its development, the *ningyō jōruri* attempted to win over the spectator from the *nō* by imitating cleverly the stage movement of *nō* actors. The *nō*, it will be recalled, is a rarefied form that denies, or negates, natural human movement. The grave miscalculation committed by the puppeteers was their failure to realize that puppets become a viable art form *only* to the extent that they take on living proportions in their appearance and their gestures. Eventually, this error was rectified and, in recovering the human naturalness denied by the *nō*, the *ningyō jōruri* became the representative art form of the new era.[28]

Like the *nō* theatre, the major element of Okuni's *kabuki* was *buka* (dance and chant). But Okuni's dance, possessing simple, natural movements and rhythms, must have borne a greater resemblance to the folk dance forms than to the *buka* of *nō*. Her chants were the equally simple *kouta*. Here we see, as with *ningyō jōruri*, a conspicuous contrast between the characteristics of *kabuki* and *nō*. The world of *kabuki*, as Tetsurō Watsuji puts it, is made up of a softness and a coquettishness that were completely foreign to the *nō*.[29] For eyes used to seeing a *nō* performance, a *kabuki* presentation must have appeared thoroughly outside the norm. The very word *"kabuki"* means beyond the norm, an irregular occurrence.

Okuni also succeeded in charming the audience by disguising herself as a man and by having men impersonate women. Sexual transposition is another of her unique contributions. The *nō* also had men impersonating women. *Nō* actors wear a female mask and costume, but they do not attempt a realistic impersonation of the female voice or movement. In Watsuji's opinion, Okuni's *kabuki* marks the beginning of the *onnagata* (female impersonator) tradition in *kabuki*. This view is acceptable on the whole, but giving sole credit to Okuni may be inaccurate. As Ogasawara points out, the specialized *onnagata* form may have started with *wakashu kabuki*, although this view has not been corroborated.[30] It is obvious, however, that Okuni's creative approach to *kabuki odori* brought attention to the form and that she was the center of the *onna kabuki* movement.

To submit an overall picture of the performing arts during the sixteenth century, a great number of details have been omitted from this study. Despite omissions in certain areas, I hope that this review has established clearly the significance of the sixteenth century as the foundation for the emergence in the following century of the *kabuki*, Japan's most popular and enduring traditional theatre form.

Notes

1. Kawatake Shigetoshi, *Nihon Engeki Zenshi* (Complete history of Japanese theatre). (Tokyo: Iwanani Shoten, 1959), p. 167.

2. Furukawa Hisashi, Kobayashi Seki, and Ogihara Tatsuko, eds., *Kyōgen Jitten* (*Kyōgen* encyclopedia). (Tokyo: Tōkyōdō, 1966), p. 484.

3. Ibid.

4. Koyama Hiroshi, *Kyōgen-shū* (*Kyōgen* collection). (Tokyo: Iwanami Shoten, 1960).

5. Ibid., p. 21.

6. Ōkura Toraakira, "*Waranbe-gusa*," in *Kokugo Kokubungaku Kenkyūshi Taisei* (Compilation of historical studies of Japanese literature), vol. 8: *Yōkyoku Kyōgen* (*Nō* and *Kyōgen* plays). Ed. Nishio Minoru et al. (Tokyo: Sanseidō, 1961), 514.

7. Ibid., pp. 517–518.

8. Hattori Yukio, *Kabuki Seiritsu no Kenkyū* (Study of *Kabuki's* formation). (Tokyo: Kazama Shobō, 1968), p. 377.

9. Ibid., p. 447.

10. Ibid., p. 452.

11. Kawatake, *Nihon Engeki Zenshi*, p. 435.

12. Gunji Masakatsu, *Kabuki: Yōshiki to Denshō* (*Kabuki:* style and tradition). (Tokyo: Gakugei Sharin, 1969), p. 305.

13. Ibid., p. 309.

14. Kawatake, *Nihon Engeki Zenshi*, pp. 227–228.

15. Ogasawara Kyōko, "Kabuki no Seiritsu" (The formation of *Kabuki),* *Kokubungaku* (Japanese literature) 20 (June 1975), 142.

16. See P.G. O'Neill, *Early Nō Drama* (London: Lund Humphries, 1958), for further information on each of these three forms.

17. See James T. Araki, *The Ballad-Drama of Medieval Japan* (Berkeley: University of California Press, 1964), for further information on *kōwaka*.

18. Ogasawara Kyōko, *Kabuki no Tanjō* (Birth of *Kabuki*). (Tokyo: Meiji Shoin, 1972), p. 6.

19. The term *furyū* is also read *fūryū* with the same meaning, although a performing art form is always referred to as *furyū*.

20. Hattori, *Kabuki Seiritsu no Kenkyū*, p. 180.

21. Ibid., p. 169.

22. Ogasawara, *Kabuki no Tanjō*, p. 73.

23. Ibid., pp. 76–77.

24. Ogasawara, "Kabuki no Seiritsu," p. 142.

25. Ogasawara, *Kabuki no Tanjō*, pp. 78–79.

26. Ogasawara, "Kabuki no Seiritsu," p. 143.

27. Ibid., p. 144.

28. Tetsurō Watsuji raises a fascinating philosophical issue concerning the opposing means and effects of the *ningyō jōruri* and the *nō*. In these two forms we find consummate skill applied either to celebrate or negate the dynamics of the living organism. This clash suggests a paradigm for some fundamental issues in Japanese aesthetics; see *Nihon Geinōshi Kenkyū* (Studies of Japanese performing arts history), vol. 1: *Kabuki to Ayatsuri Jōruri* (*Kabuki* and the puppet theatre). (Tokyo: Kazama Shobō, 1959), 36–49.

29. Ibid., p. 45.

30. Ogasawara, "Kabuki no Seiritsu," pp. 144–145.

2

Origins of *Kabuki* Acting in Medieval Japanese Drama

Laurence R. Kominz

Much of the appeal of Japan's *kabuki* theatre lies in its vivid contrasts and startling juxtapositions: the stylized sets, like woodblock prints, peopled by human actors who often move like puppets; the unsurpassable grace and femininity of the female impersonators; the wicked samurai, noble outlaws, and virtuous prostitutes who turn the social order upside down. Of *kabuki*'s contrasts none has been as consistently popular as the combination in a single play of two totally different male characters, the violent superhero and the meek, sensitive lover. These role types are known respectively as *aragoto* (rough business) and *wagoto* (gentle business), and plays based on the adventures of the two types of characters have been performed regularly from the Genroku period (1680–1704) until the present. The perfection of the two role types is credited to the two greatest actors in *kabuki* history, the Kyoto *wagoto* actor Sakata Tōjūrō (1647–1709) and the Edo (Tokyo) *aragoto* actor Ichikawa Danjūrō I (1660–1704). Both were superb actors and could carry a play alone, playing a *wagoto* or an *aragoto* role, respectively, but both recognized that the juxtaposition of character types added to the success of their plays. In many *kabuki* plays staged since their time, an *aragoto/wagoto* contrast is the core of the drama (figure 2.1).

What inspired these actors to devise characters with such long-lasting appeal? The answer to this question is complex and intriguing. Danjūrō and Tōjūrō drew on totally different contemporary performance traditions for inspiration and emulation. The roots of *wagoto* acting go back to the earliest recorded presentations of *kabuki* by women's troupes in the 1590s, includ-

Figure 2.1 **Sakata Tōjūrō in a languid pose as a wealthy young heir, the *wagoto* lead in *Keisei Mibu Dainenbutsu* (The prostitute and the great Buddhist ceremony at Mibu Temple). (Photo: Laurence R. Kominz.)**

ing those by the troupe of Okuni, the founder of *kabuki*. Women's *kabuki* consisted mostly of dance numbers, but two semidramatic skits were often performed. These scenes centered on activities in the pleasure districts and were called *keisei kai* (also *keisei gai* and *furo agari*) ("procuring courtesans" and "conversations with bath house girls"). The heroes in the scenes were stylish, handsome, young men (often played by women) and attractive, professional women of various statuses. [For more on *kabuki's* origins, see Tsubaki's essay, chapter 1. Ed.]

The *kabuki* as drama was born after women, and then young boys, were banned from the stage (in 1629 and 1652); in the 1650s and 1660s adult male actors developed the skills necessary to portray all sorts of characters in dramatic situations, with individual actors concentrating on specific character types. Arashi San'emon (1635–1690) is credited with pioneering the *yatsushi* (young lover) role, and several actors were noted as *wagoto* specialists before Tōjūrō emerged as the consummate master of the style. [See Blumner's essay, chapter 4, for further background on *wagoto*. Ed.]

Meanwhile, Danjūrō turned to Kinpira puppet plays and to ritual performances of certain popular religious sects for inspiration. Kinpira plays described the heroic exploits of four young warriors, with Sakata Kinpira as

Figure 2.2 **Danjūrō II in his debut at age nine as Fudō, top right. His father, Danjūrō I, plays the leading role, an** *aragoto* **portrayal of Soga Gorō, lower right. He fights Asahina (played by Nakamura Denkurō), who is throwing a horse in the river. Note the** *aragoto* **actors' long swords and the** *chikara suji* **(sinews of strength) painted on the arms and legs. (Photo: Laurence R. Kominz.)**

their leader. These plays fully exploited the use of puppets; heroes performed superhuman leaps and stunts, and combat scenes presented a mayhem of severed heads and limbs. Kinpira puppet plays were at the peak of their popularity in the city of Edo when Danjūrō began his career, and his first role was as the father of Sakata Kinpira, a demon-quelling samurai whose exploits had been told in stories and on the stage for six centuries.

Ritual religious performances had an even greater impact on Danjūrō's sense of the dramatic than did contemporary puppet performances. Danjūrō was a follower of *Shugendō*, and the patron deity of his sect was the Fudō. Fudō is the Buddha in fearsome aspect: "one eye glares downwards, the other squints upwards. His mouth is twisted into a snarl, revealing protruding fangs. He stands not on a lotus or animal mount, as do many Buddhist divinities, but on an immovable rock. Always he is ringed in fire" (Blacker 1975, 175). He carries a sword to smite demons and a rope to pull terrified believers into paradise. *Shugendō* contains elements taken from both Buddhism and Shinto. Its professional adherents are *yamabushi* (mountain ascetics), whose rituals include dances called *aramai* (Misumi 1975, 75). In the dances violent warriors and deities, including Fudō, stamp, glare, twirl, and do acrobatics. Swords and sticks are used to represent combat. Evidence linking the *kabuki* of the Ichikawa family with *Shugendō* practices and Fudō worship includes the following: (1) the movement in *aragoto* and *aramai* are similar; (2) the delivery of certain lines in *aragoto* plays seems to derive from *yamabushi* prayers (Misumi 1975, 129); and (3) Fudō is an important character in the *aragoto* repertory. Danjūrō I often played the role, and his son, Danjūrō II (1688–1758), debuted as Fudō (figure 2.2). Further, the dynamic and awesome appearance of certain Buddhist statues, the elements of including Fudō and other divinities important in *Shugendō*, provided the elements of a powerful visual model for *aragoto* actors: the *Niō tasuki* ("Buddhist Guardian King cords") that tie back an actor's sleeves during battle (Toita 1969, 33), the red and blue *chikara suji* (sinews of strength), the lines painted on an actor's face and limbs, and the defiant posture of treading on demons identified in *kabuki* by the actor's raised big toe (Toita 1969, 32) (figures 2.3, 2.4).

The origins of *wagoto* and *aragoto* acting are closely tied to specific actors working in different performance environments, but the juxtaposition between powerful, temperamental characters and meek, gentle ones has deep roots in Japanese literature. Perhaps the earliest *aragoto*-like character in the Japanese imagination was the god Susa no O, hero of myths in the *Kojiki* (Ancient chronicles), his sensitive counterpart being his sister, the sun goddess Amaterasu Omikami. The maturation of Japan's "national literature," originally oral literature transmitted by wandering minstrels (Ruch 1977), brought to the fore the contrast between the physical superhero and the gentle lover. Such contrasts were not important in the earliest accounts of the three great warrior-heroes, Yoshitsune and the two Soga brothers, central to the study of acting styles. By the fifteenth and sixteenth centuries, however, the main heroes of the enduring versions of *Gikeiki* (The tale of Yoshitsune) and *Soga Monogatari* (The tale of the Soga brothers) were clear prototypes of the *wagoto* and *aragoto* characters who would populate the thousands of *kabuki* and puppet plays based on the two tales (figures 2.5, 2.6).

Benkei is but one of the many faithful retainers in early accounts of the exploits of Yoshitsune. But in the *Gikeiki*, Benkei emerges as the rough-and-ready martial hero of the tale. Yoshitsune, by contrast having lost the martial bearing of his portrayal in *Heike Monogatari* (The tale of the Heike; recited by blind minstrels as early as the 1200s), by the mid-Muromachi period (late 1300s to 1400s) was known to all as the unjustly persecuted, gentle, and aristocratic lover of such famous ladies as Shizuka Gozen and the Princess Jōruri (McCullough 1971, introduction). In early versions of the *Soga Monogatori*, Jūrō and his younger brother Gorō are both strong, dedicated samurai who strive long and hard to kill their father's murderer. They succeed in the end, dying in the act. In *nō* plays also, written through the mid-

Figure 2.3 **A fearsome Guardian Deity that guards the entrance to the Buddhist temple of Daiganji at Itsukushima, near Hiroshima. The glaring expression, nearly crossed eyes, and strong musculature are features seen in** *aragoto* **acting poses. (Photo: James R. Brandon.)**

Figure 2.4 **A contemporary** *kabuki* **actor wearing costume sleeves designed to suggest musculature (***chikara suji***) that matches the red lines of the bold face makeup (***kumadori***). Red is an indication of strength. (Photo: James R. Brandon.)**

Figure 2.5 **Soga Gorō (Onoe Shōroku II), played as an *aragoto* character in the *kabuki* classic *Ya no Ne*. (Photo: Morita Toshirō.)**

1400s, the two brothers are both strong, virtuous samurai, and there is no striking difference between them in personality, appearance, or physical strength. But by the mid-sixteenth century, in the *rufubon* (popular version) of the Soga tale, Gorō appears as a superhuman strongman ever spoiling for a fight, and Jūrō as a cautious, sensitive man, best known for his love affair with the post station prostitute, Tora Gozen.

The Yoshitsune/Benkei juxtaposition and the two Soga brothers epitomize the new pattern of paired heroes with sharply contrasting personalities, so it is in plays about them written in the mid-1400s and later (in *nō* and *kōwakamai* ballad drama) that we would expect to find the beginnings of *aragoto/wagoto* contrasts on stage. *Nō* plays about Yoshitsune and Benkei include *Hashi Benkei* (Benkei on the bridge), *Funa Benkei* (Benkei in the boat), and *Ataka* (The Ataka barrier). In *Hashi Benkei*, Yoshitsune is still a youth, an acrobatic fighter, with few of the effeminate qualities of the mature

Figure 2.6 **Soga Jūrō (Onoe Kikugorō VII), played as a *wagoto* character in *Ya no Ne*. (Photo: Morita Toshirō.)**

(handwritten note in left margin: What about early history?)

Yoshitsune. In the source episodes for the latter two plays, Yoshitsune is a gentle aristocrat, but the authors of the *nō* plays were unwilling or unable to put such a character on an equal footing with the powerful Benkei. In both plays child actors take the part of Yoshitsune. The contrast in physical strength between Yoshitsune and Benkei is thus made very clear, but the romantic requirements of *wagoto* characters are absent. When the *shite* (principal role) character, Shizuka, expresses her love to the small child representing her lover in *Funa Benkei*, it is an incongruous scene. Yoshitsune is very much in the background in both plays.

Some fourteen *nō* plays were written about the Soga brothers in the Muromachi period (ca. 1330–1570). In one early play, *Youchi Soga* (The Soga night raid), written in the early to mid 1400s, Gorō is portrayed as more decisive than his brother and is given the combat scene in the play. The difference between the brothers is slight, however, and is overshadowed by

Figure 2.7 **The Soga brothers, Gorō, left, and Jūrō, right, in the *nō* play *Youchi Soga*. Notice that there is no difference in the brothers' costuming. (Photo: Laurence R. Kominz.)**

other events—crises in the brothers' relationship with their retainers, their sending keepsakes home to their mother, and Gorō's tragic fight in the shogun's camp (Kominz 1978, 447–59). Other Soga *nō* plays written about the same time resemble *Youchi Soga* in that the differences between the brothers are slight and subordinate to other thematic concerns (figure 2.7).

Three mid- to late-Muromachi period plays that point clearly toward the juxtaposition of *wagoto* and *aragoto* acting styles retell an episode added to the core of the Soga story in the late fifteenth or early sixteenth century (Araki 1977, 121), an episode that is found only in the popular version of the narrative. It is called "Wada Sakamori" (Wada's sake party) and describes one of Jūrō's narrow escapes from disaster. Jūrō goes to the town of Ōiso to visit Tora, reputedly the most beautiful courtesan on the Tōkaidō Road. The powerful warlord Wada Yoshimori arrives for a drinking party, accompanied by ninety-three retainers. He summons Tora to serve and entertain him, but she refuses to leave the inner room where she is conversing with Jūrō. Finally, Tora's mother and Jūrō persuade her to go out to Yoshimori. When Tora's mother asks her to serve sake first to the man she respects the most, she serves Jūrō, thereby offending Yoshimori. Yoshimori's retainers appear about to attack Jūrō when Gorō arrives and defeats Yoshimori's son, Asahina, in a test of strength, the famous armor-pulling contest. Yoshimori and his men are awestruck, allowing the Soga brothers to escape. The contrast between the brothers' personalities is part of the story, but more important is Tora's devotion to Jūrō and the struggle between the two legendary strongmen of the Kamakura period (ca. 1185–1330), Asahina and Gorō (*Soga Monogatari* 1966, 242–258).

The medieval play closest to the *rufubon* version of the episode is not a *nō* play, but *Wada Sakamori* (Wada's sake party), a play written for the *kōwakamai* ballad drama, a danced and chanted narrative genre that is not performed today (Araki 1964). Jūrō, who is present from the beginning of the play, exhibits many characteristics of later *wagoto* heroes: he weeps when he overhears Tora's mother threaten that she will never let Tora meet him again, and rather than argue he tries to get back in the woman's good graces by helping her persuade Tora to serve the important guest. Jūrō's heart is all aflutter when he sees Asahina draw his sword; Jūrō feels as if he were "staring down at an abyss, or walking on thin ice" (*Wada Sakamori* 1974, 474). Other scenes, however, show Jūrō as a brave samurai. Wearing armor, he makes a grand entrance into the banquet room and takes the seat of honor next to Yoshimori. And he drinks the sake offered him by Tora, knowing that to refrain would be cowardly, but to drink might well get him killed.

Gorō is much more clearly an *aragoto* character than Jūrō is a *wagoto* character. In fact, Shimazu Hisamoto singles out *Wada Sakamori* as *the* medieval prototype for *aragoto* acting (1933, 468). He bases his opinion on the test of strength between Gorō and Asahina:

> Asahina opened the lattice door with a slam. When he looked inside he saw a stranger a great robust man, seven feet tall. His great sword, more than five feet long, was pulled six or seven inches out of its sheath. He looked like he would be a dangerous foe if it came to a sword fight and even the demon-like Asahina stood with shaking knees. Asahina invited Gorō to join the party but Gorō refused. Saying, "You really won't join us?" Asahina ran up to Gorō, took hold of two or three plates of armor at the waist and pulled forward with an "Eiya!" Gorō didn't budge. One after another there appeared on Asahina's arms power sinews (*chikara suji*), evidence of his great strength. The power hair (*chikara ge*) that grew on his chest bristled like bronze needles from the surface of a *gō* board. The sinews on his body rose to his forehead. The sinews on his forehead moved down his body. It was a remarkable scene. Gorō stood in a powerful posture with knees bent and legs apart.[1] Asahina, his sideburns wildly awry,[2] pulled forward, "Eito!" and pulled backward, "Eitono!" and the armor plates ripped off. Gorō did not budge and stood as before. (*Wada Sakamori* 1974, 476–477)

It is a strong dramatic scene, and certain elements point directly to *aragoto*. The oversized sword is typical of *aragoto* characters, and

Figure 2.8 **The armor-pulling scene from** *Tsuwamono Kongen Soga***. Danjūrō I plays Gorō and stands on a *go* board. Dancing and acrobatic stunts performed on *go* boards were very popular in the Genroku period. Wada Yoshimori, Tora, and Jūrō look on from the right. (Photo: Laurence R. Kominz.)**

aragoto actors paint "power sinews" on their faces and limbs. Unfortunately, we have no idea how the above scene was enacted on stage. The total absence of information pertaining to the staging of *kōwakamai* makes a conclusive verdict on "the first *aragoto* play" an impossibility, but it is clear that the appeal of this scene was based on an exaggerated display of physical strength, exactly the appeal of *kabuki aragoto*.

Kōwakamai texts were published beginning in 1635 (Takano 1933, 473), and *Wada Sakamori* was presented as a puppet play in 1664 with a text virtually identical to the *kōwakamai* play. It was staged in the city of Edo during the period when Kinpira plays were popular, and its presentation was likely very dramatic. Danjūrō probably either read or saw later versions of the play. Scenes from *Wada Sakamori*, particularly the above scene, inspired numerous *aragoto* creations for *kabuki*, both dances and dramatic scenes. Danjūrō put the armor-pulling contest in his 1697 hit play, *Tsuwamono Kongen Soga* (The genesis of a Soga warrior) (figure 2.8).

A text for a *nō* play entitled *Wada Sakamori* still exists, but scholars are unsure of its authorship and date of composition. It was likely written a hundred years or more before *kabuki* began. Like the *kōwakamai* play, it is closely based on the popular version of the Soga tale, but it is considerably shorter than the *kōwakamai* of the same name. The test of strength, for example, is about one-tenth as long, although couched in dramatic language and replete with onomatopoeia—*eiya* for pulling, *battari* for bumping, *harari to* for ripping the armor cords, and *hata to* when Asahina falls backward to the ground (*Wada Sakamori*, 1911, 252). The relationships between Jūrō, Tora, and her mother are the same as in the *kōwakamai* play, but Jūrō no longer has two of the shows of bravado given him in the *kōwakamai*: he does not take the seat of honor and he tries, albeit unsuccessfully, to soothe Yoshimori's feelings before he drinks the sake served him by Tora. He is more consistently *wagoto*-like in the *nō* play.

Wada Sakamori is a very unorthodox *nō* play in terms of dramatic and musical structure. The *shite*, Gorō, appears only at the end of the play, and three *tsure* (companion actors to the *shite*, usually quite unimportant) who play Jūrō, Tora, and her mother each have more lines than Gorō. The *waki* and *waki tsure* (bystanders, foils to the *shite*) play Yoshimori and his retainers, making a remarkably large cast for *nō*. The play consists almost entirely of dialogue; there are only a few snatches of song and poetry before the concluding felicitous dance performed by Gorō and Asahina that demonstrates their reconciliation. The lyric sung for that dance is the only significant choral part in the play. The play uses none of the musical units normally employed to structure the flow of a *nō* play.[3] The reader of *Wada Sakamori* feels that the anonymous author has written a work that is not in fact a *nō* play, but that he described the roles in the terminology of the *nō* and made it about as long as most *nō* plays so that *nō* actors could perform it on a *nō* stage.

The *kōwakamai* and *nō* plays of *Wada Sakamori* are alike in that the struggle between the two superheroes overshadows the relationship between the two brothers. Jūrō and Gorō do not interact at all, except in each other's minds, until they are ready to leave the brothel together. Perhaps the first play in which the primary appeal is the contrast between a violent, martial character and a meek, sensitive one is the *nō* play *Hitsukiri Soga* (Soga slices the chest). *Hitsukiri Soga* is much more orthodox than the *nō* play *Wada Sakamori*, but it exhibits the inventiveness, delight in character contrasts, and novelty typical of *kabuki*.

We know the play was written no later than the early sixteenth century because it is mentioned in the document *Jika Densho*, compiled in the early 1500s from records of the Konparu school of *nō* (O'Neill 1958, 102). In it, *Hitsukiri Soga* is attributed to the playwright Miyamasu.[4] Although we know less about Miyamasu than any other important *nō* playwright, some scholars believe he was a contemporary of Zeami (1363–1443). The two playwrights are interesting in their contrast. Zeami wrote mainly *mugen nō* (spirit plays), where the main character is a ghost, spirit, or other supernatural being. Since

Zeami's time, spirit plays have been the most important and respected type of *nō* play. In contrast, all but two of the thirty-four plays attributed to Miyamasu are this-world plays (*genzai nō*), in which all the characters are living humans.

Miyamasu used the Soga legend in more plays than any other playwright. For many of his plays, Miyamasu invented entirely new scenes and inserted them into the traditional frameworks of stories he had read or heard recited. In many respects *Hitsukiri Soga* seems a typical Miyamasu play, but although no other author is cited in any source, some scholars dispute the attribution, and it seems likely that the play was written considerably later. In any case, the author of *Hitsukiri Soga* wrote the first *nō* play in which a violent male hero is paired with a gentle counterpart, and both are given, for *nō*, substantial character development.

A *wagoto* character in *kabuki* is not merely gentle and meek; invariably he is a sensitive lover, beloved of the most beautiful courtesan in the pleasure district. This is anticipated in *Hitsukiri Soga*. The first act is one of the most romantic scenes between a prostitute and her lover in *nō* drama. It is the only *nō* play with a love scene set in a brothel. The setting and the play's concern with the feelings of a prostitute neglected by the man she loves presage the locales and concerns of *kabuki*. Jūrō admits in his self-introduction that it is improper for a samurai committed to revenge to be distracted by an affair of the heart, and later he confesses the depth of his passion for Tora:

> The cares of the world are piled on my life, like faggots on a brushwood boat.
> Drawn to her, love chars my heart even before the fire is lit.[5]
> When will the flames in my breast die out,
> For I am stifling on the smoke. (*Hitsukiri Soga* 1957, 105)

Despite her resentment at his long absence, Tora invites Jūrō inside. A beautiful dialogue, replete with wordplay, represents the reconciliation Jūrō achieves by means of a gift of two silk robes and gentle words. The dialogue concludes with Tora and Jūrō speaking together:

> TORA: But words of love
> JŪRŌ: Dissolve our pain.
> TORA: If entangled
> JŪRŌ: In the twisted thread of love
> TORA: You come, then won't you stay with me?
> (*Hitsukiri Soga* 1957, 106)

Jūrō gently breaks the news to Tora that he must set out for the shogun's hunt, where he will likely die. He tells her, "How wretched I am, for tonight of all nights, how loath I am to leave you" *(Hitsukiri Soga* 1957, 108). Tora, like the brave and virtuous prostitutes of *kabuki* and puppet plays a hundred years later, bolsters her lover's flagging spirits.

A voice interrupts the intimate scene. Jūrō suspects that it is Kajiwara Kagesue, a minor villain of the popular version of the *Soga Monogatari.* Jūrō is worried and at a loss, so Tora, again reminding us of the resourceful prostitutes of Edo-period (1600–1868) *kabuki* drama, tells him to hide behind a large Chinese chest as she prepares to deal with the enemy single-handedly.

Finally, Gorō, the *shite*, enters. He expresses his suspicions of Tora, who is, after all, a prostitute, not a samurai woman, and whose pledges of loyalty are therefore untrustworthy. He glimpses someone darting away, and suspecting that Tora is harboring a traitor he storms into the room. The chorus sings:

> The lattice doors open with a slam,
> He kicks sake bottles and dishes in four directions,
> Then takes his ease, pulling his great sword three inches from its sheath.
> "Now. Tora Gozen, listen to me. Even though you are a prostitute,
> You made a vow of two lives with Jūrō. But all for nothing!
> I know someone's there, hiding behind the chest."
> And smoothly pulling his sword from his belt,
> He slices the chest in two with a clunk.
> It was a truly remarkable scene. *(Hitsukiri Soga* 1957, 109–110)

Gorō's quick anger, his harsh words, the violence he displays before he understands the situation, and his superhuman strength and oversized weapon are all typical of true *aragoto* characters in *kabuki.*

Neither *Hitsukiri Soga* nor *Wada Sakamori* is performed today, so we have to imagine how they were enacted in the Muromachi period. *Nō* acting has changed considerably since then, but the mimetic movements and dance now used to perform conflict-centered plays of the sixteenth century are significantly more explicit and dramatic than those used for the refined plays, in which actors seek to create a mood of *yūgen*.[6] Performance records indicate that in Muromachi times some actors staged *nō* in remarkably spectacular ways, on at least one occasion even using real horses on stage. It is safe to assume that when Gorō sliced the chest in two he would have done so with a large, dramatic stroke, and Asahina's pulling and tugging on Gorō's armor and his fall when the armor broke would have been energetically portrayed.

The well-developed *aragoto/wagoto* character prototypes are just two of several elements that mark *Hitsukiri Soga* as transitional drama, a *nō* play clearly pointing in the direction of *kabuki*. The division of roles is, as in *Wada Sakamori*, highly unorthodox. In no other play is the relationship between *waki* (Jūrō) and *tsure* (Tora) as important. Traditions in actor training and responsibilities necessitated this strange pairing—*waki tsure* simply do not wear masks, and a woman character needs to wear a mask. Gorō, the *shite*, is onstage for only one-third of the play. The play concludes with a pair dance for *waki* and *shite* together (this dance alone makes it almost impossible to stage the play today). Pair dancing is very rare in the *nō* and, in fact, it is found almost solely in Soga plays. The plot of *Hitsukiri Soga* is considerably different from the traditional "sake party" episode, but the concluding dance brings the situation back to the source story: the brothers leave the brothel together, bound for their mother's house to receive her blessing before setting out on their final journey

Hitsukiri Soga differs from *Wada Sakamori* in that the former is built of the musical units that form the structural framework of most *nō* plays. For example, *Hitsukiri Soga* opens with a poetic *shidai* song, followed by a prose *nanori* (self-introduction) by the *waki,* and then a *michiyuki* (traveling song) sung by the chorus as the *waki* walks around the stage once. Moreover, there is nothing unorthodox in the diction of the play. The images used to convey, for example, lack of control over one's destiny (a drifting boat), evanescence (smoke), and so on, are common to *nō* plays. In the first part of *Hitsukiri Soga*, there is more poetic wordplay than in almost any other Soga *nō* play.[7] The lovers are the focus of this section of the play, and the beautiful language emphasizes Jūrō's sensitivity. *Hitsukiri Soga* is clearly a *nō* play, albeit a transitional one, as opposed to *Wada Sakamori* which is in many ways an anomaly.

The chest-slicing scene, which establishes Gorō as an *aragoto*-like hero, is an invention not found in any previous work of Japanese literature. Theatre scholars have called it a *shukō*.[8] Normally the term is used to describe a bizarre and original plot twist invented by a *kabuki* or puppet playwright for a play set in one of the standard thematic *sekai* (worlds) of Edo drama. To use the word *shukō* in reference to a *nō* play is to imply that the author was working under one of the important constraints of Edo playwrights, namely, an audience that craves novelty and excitement. Many of the *nō* plays written in the late fifteenth and early sixteenth centuries suggest that such was the case, for that was when the most spectacular *nō* plays were produced.

The author of *Hitsukiri Soga* —whoever he was—shared with his intended audience complete familiarity with the popular version of the *Soga Mongatari*, and a major appeal of his *nō* play must have been its novelty. While the personalities of Jūrō, Gorō, and Tora correspond to the narrative tale, it would have been a new experience to see such a dramatic contrast in characters on stage. The plot would have been a total surprise. Jūrō's mistaking Gorō for

Kajiwara Kagesue does not exist in the traditional tale or in other medieval plays, nor do the brothers even come close to fighting each other. In *Hitsukiri Soga* Jūrō immediately forgives Gorō his impetuousness, so the conflict is over almost as soon as it begins, but the medieval audience would have been excited for a moment by new possibilities, before returning to the fraternal relations and standard plot of the story.[9] Problems of mistaken identity and conflicts between the brothers would be the earliest changes wrought in the Soga story by authors of the *kabuki* and puppet theatres.[10] As in *Hitsukiri Soga*, the drama of the conflicts between the Soga brothers would depend on their portrayal as drastically different personalities: Jūrō romantic and gentle, and Gorō strong and tempestuous.

Japanese theatre scholars have long been fascinated by the task of hunting for the sources of *kabuki's* great acting traditions. Most have approached *wagoto* and *aragoto* acting separately. Soon after Tōjūrō and Danjūrō established their reputations, each realized the effectiveness of including both types of acting in their plays, and most surviving classic history plays include both *aragoto* and *wagoto* parts. *Aragoto* acting itself may draw as much from popular religious performance as from professional theatre, but the conscious contrasting of tempestuous and gentle heroes was long the task of storytellers and playwrights, not priests and *yamabushi*. The theatrical origins of *kabuki* have been difficult to trace, obscured by the half-century of dance-dominated shows performed by women and young boys, and by the absence of texts from the first thirty years of men's *kabuki*. *Hitsukiri Soga*, the two versions of *Wada Sakamori*, and similar plays of late Muromachi period *nō* and *kōwakamai* show us that the impulse toward *kabuki* drama, not just *kabuki* dance, was very much alive in the sixteenth century, just before the birth of *kabuki*.

Notes

1. *Funjibatte tatta* indicates the basic posture of martial dance in *nō* and the martial arts, a stance with knees bent slightly and feet pointing outward.

2. "Sideburns awry" (*basshin o irarage*) describes the appearance of a warrior when his hair begins to come undone as a result of strenuous physical activity. One can see in *kabuki* wigs today that the hair sticks out to the sides of the head and then falls down in front of the shoulders.

3. See Hare (1986) for the best discussion in English of the musical structure of the *nō*.

4. Kitagawa (1957) accepts the attribution because no other author is cited and because the play exhibits many of the characteristics of plays more likely to be by Miyamasu. Amano (1978) rejects the attribution because of the chest-slicing scene. And the effective contrast of *aragoto*- and *wagoto*-like characters suggests that the play was written well after the time of Zeami and Miyamasu.

5. Wordplay in this passage, typical of *nō*, includes *engo* (related words)—brushwood faggots metaphorically lead to lighting a fire in Jūrō's heart—and *kakekotoba* (pivot words)—*kogareru*, to char, suggesting *akogareru*, to yearn or be drawn to.

6. *Yūgen* refers to a subtle, almost indescribable beauty, grace, or charm. In Zeami's later writings, the creation of an atmosphere of *yūgen* became the highest goal of his *nō*.

7. The only Soga *nō* play that is more poetic is *Kosode Soga* (The Soga and the wadded silk robe).

8. Amano (1978, 26) uses *shukō* to describe the plots of *Hitsukiri Soga* and *Fumisaki Soga* (The Sogas' Letter). I think his use of the terms is appropriate.

9. Although *Hitsukiri Soga* has an original plot, the author framed it within the traditional Soga story. Jūrō's opening line is very close to his opening line in the *nō* play *Wada Sakamori*, and the closing lines in *Hitsukiri Soga* indicate that the "Kosode" episode, in which the brothers receive their mother's pardon, should follow immediately after the events described in the play.

10. Mistaken identity scenes are important *shukō* in the first surviving Soga *kabuki* play, *Wakoku Fūryū Kyōdai Kagami* (A Japanese mirror of stylish brothers) (*e-iri kyōgen bon* [illustrated playbook] text, 1694), and in Chikamatsu Monzaemon's Soga *kabuki* plays *Soga Tayū Zome* (The Soga infatuation with courtesans) and *Daimyō Nagusami Soga* (A Soga play to entertain a *daimyō*), performed in 1696 and 1698, respectively. In pre-Chikamatsu puppet plays, such as Tosa no Shōjō's *Fūryu Wada Sakamori* (The up-to-date Wada's sake party), ca. 1680, the brothers are portrayed as on the verge of fighting with each other.

References

Amano Fumio. 1978. "Miyamasu Soga mono kō" (Thoughts on Miyamasu's Soga plays). *Geinōshi Kenkyū* 60: 18–34.

Araki, James. 1964. *The Ballad Drama of Medieval Japan*. Tokyo: Tuttle.

Araki Shigeru. 1977. "Sogamono no Kōwaka Bukyoku to *Soga Monogatari*" ("Soga ballad dramas and *The Tale of the Soga Brothers*"). In *Wakō Daigaku Jinbungakubu Kiyo* (Bulletin of the Wakō University Department of Humanities) 12: 117–130.

Blacker, Carmen. 1975. *The Catalpa Bow: A Study of Shamanistic Practice in Japan*. London: George Allen and Unwin.

Chikamatsu Monzaemon. 1927. *Soga Tayū Zome* and *Daimyō Nagusami Soga* (Two *kabuki* plays: The Soga infatuation with courtesans; A Soga play to entertain a *daimyō*). In *Chikamatsu Kabuki Kyōgen Shū* (Anthology of Chikawatsu's plays). Ed. Takano Tatsuyuki. Tokyo: Rokugokan.

Hare, Thomas B. 1986. *Zeami's Style: The Noh Plays of Zeami Motokiyo*. Palo Alto: Stanford University Press.

Hitsukiri Soga (Soga slices the chest). 1957. In *Bangai Yōkyokushū Zoku* (More *Nō* plays, continued). Ed. Tanaka Makoto. Tokyo: Koten Bunko.

Kitagawa Tadahiko. 1957. "Yōkyoku Sakusha Miyamasu Shiron" (An investigation of the *Nō* author Miyamasu). In *Kokugo Kokubun* (Japanese language, Japanese literature) 26 (May): 47–61.

Kominz, Laurence R. 1978. "The Noh as Popular Theater: Miyamasu's *Youchi Soga*." *Monumenta Nipponica* 33, no. 4: 441–459.

McCullough, Helen. 1971. *Yoshitsune.* Palo Alto: Stanford University Press.

Misumi Haruo. 1975. *Sasurai Bito no Geinōshi* (The performing arts history of itinerants). Tokyo: NHK Books.

O'Neill, P.G. 1958. *Early Nō Drama: Its Background, Character, and Development.* London: Lund Humphries.

Ruch, Barbara. 1977. "Medieval Jongleurs and the Making of a National Literature." In *Japan in the Muromachi Age.* Ed. John Hall and Toyoda Takeshi. Berkeley and Los Angeles: University of California Press, 279–309.

Shimazu Hisamoto. 1933. *"Kōwaka no Sogamono"* (Soga *Kōwakamai* plays). In *Kokugo to Kokubungaku* (Japanese language, Japanese literature) 10, no. 4: 111–122.

Soga Monogatari (The tale of the Soga brothers). 1966. Edited by Ichiko Teiji and Oshima Tatehiko. Nihon Koten Bungaku Taikei 88. Tokyo: Iwanami Shoten.

Takano Masami. 1933. *"Chikamatsu Sogamono Kō"* (An investigation of Chikamatsu's Soga plays). In *Kokugo to Kokubungaku* (Japanese language, Japanese literature) 10, no. 4: 123–150.

Toita Yasuji. 1969. *Kabuki Jūhachiban* (Eighteen famous *Kabuki* plays). Tokyo: Chūo Koronsha, Tosa no Shōjō. 1975. *Fūryū Wada Sakamori* (The up-to-date Wada's sake party). In *Tosa Jōrurishi* (History of Tosa's *joruri*). Ed. Torii Fumiko. Tokyo: Kadokawa Shoten.

Wada Sakamori (Wada's sake party). 1974. In *Kōwaka Bukyokushū.* (Anthology of *Kowaka* dance music). Ed. Sasano Ken. Tokyo: Rinsen Shoten.

Wada Sakamori. 1911. In *Yōkyoku Zenshū(ge)* (Complete collection of *Nō* plays). Tokyo: Kokumin Bunko Kangokai.

Wakoku Fūryū Kyōdai Kagami (A Japanese mirror of stylish brothers). 1925. In *Genroku kabuki Kessakushū* (Anthology of Genroku *Kabuki* masterpieces). Ed. Takano Tatsuyuki and Kuroki Kanzō. Tokyo: Waseda Daigaku Shuppanbu.

3

Bakufu Versus *Kabuki*

Donald H. Shively

The *kabuki* drama of the Tokugawa period was an art form that represented the taste and interests of the class of townsmen. Deprived of political and social opportunities, the townsmen tended toward grosser pleasures, evolving a theatre that was gaudy, graphic, and emotionally unrestrained. It contrasted with the drama of their social superiors, the military class of shogun, feudal lords, and upper samurai, who patronized *nō* drama: subtle, symbolic, a form already made static by tradition. Of all the lively forms of entertainment and art for which the culture of the townsmen is well known, none excited so much interest in all classes of society as early *kabuki*. Certainly there was none that ran so blatantly counter to the social and moral principles espoused by the Tokugawa government, the *bakufu*, nor which was more disruptive to the structure of Confucian relationships which the *bakufu* strove to maintain.

The traditional date for the first performance of *kabuki* is 1603, by coincidence the year Ieyasu received the title of shogun and the Tokugawa *bakufu* began officially. From the start, the government was appalled at the popularity of *kabuki* and its disruptive influence and took steps to control it. The running duel between the *bakufu* and *kabuki* lasted the entire 250 years of the Tokugawa period, the *bakufu* constantly thrusting with restrictive laws, the *kabuki* parrying with ingenious devices.

Of particular interest is the nature of these restrictions and the effect they had on the development of *kabuki* as a dramatic form. As might be expected, the harassing measures of the *bakufu* circumscribed *kabuki* in some respects, forcing it into some strange avenues. But most extraordinary, in some ways the effect was artistically beneficial.

A review of the origins of *kabuki* will help to explain the government's attitude. It began as open-air performances of dances and farces by women, who used it to advertise their secondary, if not primary, profession of prostitution. Among the most popular themes for the skits of the early period were those demonstrating techniques used by prostitutes in accosting clients or by clients in accosting prostitutes, and scenes of revelry in brothels,[1] all matters in which the actresses had professional competence. Contemporary notices leave no doubt that the dialogue was alive with indecent lines, the dances with suggestive movements. In most of the troupes of *onna kabuki* (women's *kabuki*) there were male actors, but distressingly enough, they often took the female roles while the actresses played the male roles, providing the opportunity for much improper pantomime. The young actors were involved in homosexual prostitution, which had become widespread in Japan during the campaigns of the medieval period, and particularly during the century and a half of intermittent warfare that ended in 1600. Among the early *kabuki* actors and promoters there were other dubious types: ruffians, gamblers, and panderers. The government seems to have been fully justified in considering those connected with *kabuki* an undesirable element in society.

The *kabuki* troupes were an immediate success, not only with townsmen, but perhaps even more with military personnel. With the close of the Korean campaigns and the restoration of peace after the battle of Sekigahara, the large numbers of men who had entered the military profession craved abandoned entertainment. And they had money to pay for it. The early *kabuki* performances, tailored to attract them, were crude and down-to-earth. As might be expected, the famous Confucian scholar Hayashi Razan (1583–1657) was not complimentary in his description of these shows:

> The men wear women's clothing; the women wear men's clothing, cut their hair and wear it in a man's topknot, have swords at their sides, and carry purses. They sing base songs and dance vulgar dances; their lewd voices are clamorous, like the buzzing of flies and the crying of cicadas. The men and women sing and dance together.[2]

An early seventeenth-century work provides a description of an actress-dancer's stage entrance in Edo:

> When a high placard was put up at Nakabashi announcing that there would be a *kabuki* by Ikushima Tango-no-kami, people gathered, and the high and the low thronged to it. After they had waited impatiently for her appearance, the curtain was flung up, the leading dancer appeared and came along the runway. She was gaily dressed, wore a long and a short sword

worked in gold, and had a flint-bag and gourd hung from her waist. She had Saruwaka as a companion. The figure, as it sauntered on in high spirits, did not appear to be that of a woman but of a truehearted man: it was indeed the image of Narihira,[3] who long ago was called the spirit of *yin* and *yang*. The people in the pit and in the boxes craned their necks and, slapping their heads, rocked about forgetting themselves. When she reached the stage, her face, which when seen more closely was even better, was indeed that of a Yang Kuei-fei. It was as though you could say that one of her smiles would throw the six imperial consorts into the shade. The outer corners of her eyes were like the hibiscus, her lips like red flowers. . . . Anyone who would not fall in love with such a beautiful creature is more to be feared than a ghost.[4]

Then fifty or sixty people danced on the stage, while the shamisen accompanied songs meant to arouse a desire for dissipation with such words as:

Be in a frenzy
In this dream-like floating world.
Even the thunder
That rumbles and rumbles
Cannot put you and me
Asunder.[5]

There is no doubt about the excitement that *kabuki* created during its early years. The same book says: "Although there are many different things that are popular in Edo now, there is nothing to compare with the *kabuki* women of Yoshiwara-chō."[6] A guidebook of Kyoto, *Kyō-warabe* (Child of Kyoto) (1658), describes the effect of the actresses on the audience at the height of women's *kabuki*:

They afflicted the six sense-organs of people, they captivated their hearts by appealing to their six senses. Men threw away their wealth, some forgot their fathers and mothers, others did not care if the mothers of their children were jealous. Day and night they had their hearts on [the actresses], and exhausted the money-boxes in their godowns. They did not tire of dallying as long as their wealth lasted. Although they concealed this from their parents and deceived their wives, it became known, [just as nothing escapes] the meshes of the many nets pulled up on the beach of Akogi. Because this was so disturbing to the country and an affliction of the people, the *kabuki* of prostitutes was banned.[7]

A guidebook to Edo, the *Edo Meishoki* (Famous sights in Edo), (1662), in reviewing the history of women's *kabuki*, says:

when theatres were built for the prostitutes to give *kabuki* performances, the impetuous eccentrics among the high and the low became infatuated with them and thronged and jostled one another in the boxes of the theatres. Still unsatisfied, they constantly engaged them, consummated their trysts, squandered their inheritances, and ruined their names. Some, engaging in brawls and arguments, were taken to court. Women's *kabuki* was banned because it disturbed the country, caused deterioration in various ways, and was the cause of calamities.[8]

Where the heavy-drinking, pleasure-bent veterans congregated, trouble was quick to flare up. These samurai, foot soldiers, and *rōnin* (unemployed samurai) were pugnacious and unruly. In the crowd around the stage, the accidental brush of sword scabbards or an unintentional touch with a foot might be enough to set off a brawl among the quick-tempered warriors. Heckling of a favorite actor often started quarrels. Sword fights broke out because of rivalries and jealousies over the attentions of actresses and young actors. Because *kabuki* performances so often led to disorder and even to bloodshed, Tokugawa Ieyasu himself ordered the troupes expelled from his base at Suruga in 1608.[9]

In other areas local reform measures were taken in the attempt to halt the subverting of public morals by actresses and actors. They were so much the rage in the capital that even court ladies were said to have been influenced by their style of behavior.

In 1608–1609 five ladies of the imperial court, of whom two were favorites of the emperor, went strolling about the city after the manner of prostitutes and *kabuki* actresses, and, holding a rendezvous with nine courtiers, drank and made love with them. The emperor was so displeased that he sent a messenger to Ieyasu, tasking him to punish the participants; the principals were executed or banished.[10]

In 1628 the *kabuki* dancer Azuma was ordered out of Edo when her performance resulted in a fight, and all women *kabuki* performers, women dancers, and women *jūruri* reciters were banned.[11]

When such local measures failed to solve the problem, and when women appeared in *kabuki* in Edo again the next year, in 1629 the Tokugawa government took the decisive step of prohibiting women's *kabuki* and banning all women from the stage.[12] At first this ban was not always strictly enforced, for there are reports of women appearing on the stage in Edo as late as 1642 or 1643.[13] This is also evident from the fact that the ban was repeatedly reissued, as in 1630, 1640, 1645, and 1646.[14] The next year, when women appeared again on the stage of Kasaya Sankatsu's theatre, the manager was thrown in prison.[15] After this time the ban was more rigorously enforced, and in effect, women were kept off the *kabuki* stage in the principal cities for 250 years until after the Meiji Restoration. Only in some provincial areas and around Ise did women continue to appear on the stage. Dancing girls were repeatedly proscribed in the principal cities, but the authorities were unable to check entirely their appearance for private entertainment.

More than a decade before women were banned from the stage, at least as early as 1612, there had appeared troupes composed entirely of young men, performing what was called *wakashū kabuki* ("youth's *kabuki*"). [An earlier date is suggested in Tsubaki's essay, chapter 1. Ed.] The popularity of the young actors is attested to by the *Kyō-warabe*:

> From the time that "youth's *kabuki*" began with youths beautifully gotten up, there was homosexual dallying. Still again [as in the instance of actresses] men had their souls so stolen by them that when they ate their meals they did not taste them. Moreover they became partners of the thighs and arms. Some young women asked to marry these beautiful youths, or were watchful for an arrow shot from Aizen's bow. How much more the monks of the various temples, who, wishing to get them, decided to use the *mameita* coins they received as offerings for theatre tickets, and gave these bewitching creatures as gifts the *chōgin* coins received as subscriptions.[16]

The description in the *Edo Meishoki* says:

> "[Y]outh's *kabuki*" began, with beautiful youths being made to sing and dance, whereupon droll fools again had their hearts captivated and their souls stolen. As they rapturously gave themselves up to visiting the youths in high spirits, the early depletion of even substantial fortunes was like light snow exposed to the spring sun. How much worse it was for those whose fortunes were slight to begin with. There were many of these men who soon had run through their fortunes and who, making for Nanbu Sakata, concealed their tracks; others became novice monks although their hearts were not in it, and clothing themselves in black robes, wandered about the various provinces. I have heard that men of the capital have also done this. . . . Even though the lineage of every one of the youths was extremely base, these beautiful youths were respected by the stupid; they flapped about like kites and owls and, going into the presence of the exalted, befouled the presence; and these were scoundrels who, saying insolent things as it pleased them, ruined men and held them in contempt; moreover, they polluted the highborn on the sly. This made them a canker twice over.[17]

It is said also that the sons and grandsons of the military heroes of the campaigns of Hideyoshi and Ieyasu had lost their interest in the martial arts and were not as familiar with the names of feudal lords as they were with those of actors and prostitutes. The passion of both the military and townsmen for the young actors so alarmed the authorities that in 1642 they banned all female impersonation from the stage.[18] In 1644, upon the petition of the theatre people, they relented to the extent of permitting female impersonations on condition that a clear distinction would be made between the actors who played female roles and those who played male, that the gender of their roles would be clearly made known, and that there would be no action on the stage that would confuse the audience as to this distinction.[19] In 1648 and repeatedly thereafter, decrees forbade homosexual practices by dancers and actors.[20] Although the government looked upon the theatre as an evil influence and upon the actors as little better than the pariah class, there was no denying the fascination they held. Occasionally troupes were even called to the shogun's castle for command performances, as in the ninth month of 1650 and three times early the next year, on each occasion receiving money and gifts as compensation for their services. However, with the death of the third shogun, Iemitsu (1604–1651), in the fourth month, the new regime under Ietsuna (1651–1680), as part of its sweeping reform movement, dealt severely with *kabuki*. The authorities were concerned not only with the effect of the young actors on the morality of the public at large, and on the morale of the samurai (which they considered to be waning from indulgence in luxuries and pleasures), but also with the fact that certain feudal lords and their retainers had become infatuated with the young actors.[21]

In 1652 the *bakufu* took steps considered second in importance only to the banning of women. "Youth's *kabuki*" was ordered stopped in the sixth month,[22] and in the twelfth month the more drastic action was taken of closing the twelve *kabuki* and puppet theatres in Edo."[23] As a result of repeated pleas by the troupe managers, a formula was worked out that enabled the theatres to reopen in the third month of the next year.

The chief concern of the *bakufu* seems to have been to reduce the attractiveness of the players of women's roles, the *onnagata*, and the key reform it required to this end was to shave the actors' forelocks and require them to dress their hair like men instead of women. To the society of that day, which took such interest in hairstyles and in which the dressed forelock could be highly alluring, apparently this was a change of major importance. This and lesser reforms were the basic agreement under which *yarō kabuki* (fellow's *kabuki* [also called "men's *kabuki*," "mature men's *kabuki*," etc. Ed.]), as it was thereafter called, was permitted to operate for over two centuries until the Meiji Restoration.

The effect of the shaven forelock evidently was most disenchanting: They [the actors] somehow looked precocious, as a man who, at forty, would wear a persimmon-color loincloth. The appearance of their faces was smooth and like cats with their ears cut off, and they were a sorry sight. It is said that these persons, sad, mournful, and plaintive, wept tears of blood. However true this was in the beginning, it seems that later they were not thought so ugly. They were accorded a welcome again, and they placed a wrap-around hood on their foreheads, arranging it so that they were not displeasing to look at, and so appeared on the stage.[24]

To hide their shaven forelocks when playing women's roles, the young actors began to wear scarves or small caps. At first scarves of cotton or silk were draped over their heads to appear like a casually placed kerchief; even this practice was at times prohibited.[25] Some wore brocade caps, and later a close-fitting patch of purple silk was placed over the shaven area to give the illusion of a woman's lustrous hair. Within a few years the actors surreptitiously began to use wigs in place of the disenchanting cloth patches. The hair wigs used in *kabuki* before this time had been only the crude ones taken from *nō* and *kyōgen*, such as the ones used for demon roles or the drab wigs used for the parts of old men and women. In the late 1650s, the cloth patches began to be replaced by crude hair wigs called *maegami-gatsura* (front hair wigs). The use of any hair wigs was forbidden in 1664, but it was conceded at that time that there would be no objection to the use of cotton caps or scarves.[26] That this order was not always strictly enforced is indicated by some contemporary woodblock prints which show actors wearing wigs. A book about Kyoto customs published in 1681 says: "Long ago when Ebisuya Kichirōbei and Ukon Genza were popular, they wore on their heads pieces of silk like hand-towels, and they called themselves *onnagata*. Now what actors do is to use helmets of copper on which hair is attached, and these are called wigs (*katsura*)."[27] The copper-lined *kabuki* wig developed from this time, and references to wigs in the literature and art thereafter suggest that they were probably in continual use.

To make themselves appear more feminine off the stage, the actors let their forelocks grow as long as they dared. There is even mention of *onnagata* of the early 1670s whose forelocks were unshaven.[28] Periodically the actors were required to appear at a government office to pass inspection to show that their forelocks were not more than a half-inch long.[29] There were orders issued from time to time, directing the actors to shave their heads more closely or to shave a wider area.[30]

In "fellow's *kabuki*" the old abuses continued, if less openly, and the madness of the audience for the youths remained unabated. Describing the performances, the Edo guidebook says:

When these youths, their hair beautifully done up, with light makeup, and wearing splendid padded robes, moved slowly along the runway, singing songs in delicate voices, the spectators in front bounced up and down on their buttocks, those in back reared up, while those in the boxes opened their mouths up to their ears and drooled; unable to contain themselves, they shouted: "Look, look. Their figures are like emanations of the deities, they are [?] heavenly stallions!" And from the sides others called: "Oh that smile! It overflows with sweetness. Good! good!" and the like, and there was shouting and commotion.[31]

A book on actors, entitled *Yarō Mushi* (Fellow bugs) (ca. 1660), gives us a satirical account of the young ones:

In these times in the capital there is a great number of what are called "fellow bugs" who eat away the bamboo and wood of the five monasteries and ten abbeys, the books of the learned priests, and even the purses of fathers and grandfathers. . . . "Fellow bugs" are about the size of a human being fifteen or sixteen years old; they are equipped with arms, legs, mouth, nose, ears, and eyes, wear a black cap on the head, fly around Gion, Maruyama, and Ryōzen, and have their eyes on people's purses. When I asked someone: "Are those not the young *kabuki* actors of Shijō-gawara?" he clapped his hands, laughed, and said: "You are right." These young *kabuki* actors have multiplied in number especially in the past year and this year. The handsome among the children of lowly outcastes and beggars are selected; and when, their faces never without powder, and dressed in clothes of silk gauze and damask, they are put on the stage to dance and sing, the old and the young, men and women, become weak-kneed and call out: "Gosaku! Good! good! I'll die!" Not only do they call to them, but seduced by their alluring eyes, after the performance they go with them to Higashiyama; borne away on woven litters and palanquins, they proceed in high spirits, calling: "Here, here! A palanquin, a palanquin." Ah! what grateful affection! Bilked of a large amount of gold and silver for one night's troth, the droll priests of the temples, their bodies wasting away day by day, desire only to engage the fellows. Having no money, they sell the treasures of paintings and tea ceremony utensils that have been handed down generation after generation in the temples, and if these do not suffice, they cut down the bamboo and trees, and with that money, engage fellows.[32]

The critical booklets on actors, the *yakusha hyōbanki*, give more attention to the physical attributes of the actors than to acting ability until the end of the seventeenth century; it was only by gradual stages that art gained ground on sex.[33] Those characteristics of early *kabuki* that were considered to have a corrosive effect on society and morals continued throughout the Tokugawa period, but were kept within certain limits by the intermittent harassing.

If the officials considered that *kabuki* constantly poured into society the poisons of immorality and extravagance, why did they not abolish *kabuki* outright? The attitude of the *bakufu* seems to have been that *kabuki* was, like prostitution, a necessary evil. These were the two wheels of the vehicle of pleasure, useful to assuage the people and divert them from more serious mischief. The document known as Ieyasu's legacy, a basic guide for *bakufu* policy, states:

> [C]ourtesans, dancers, catamites, streetwalkers and the like always come to the cities and prospering places of the country. Although the conduct of many is corrupted by them, if they are rigorously suppressed, serious crimes will occur daily, there will be punishments for gambling, drunken frenzies, and lasciviousness.[34]

Although *kabuki* and prostitution constituted social problems, if they were suppressed completely—if the professionals were thrown out of work and their patrons were disgruntled—still more serious social, if not criminal, results would follow. If Edo became the deadest town in Japan, the professionals and many others would move elsewhere. There were also economic and political reasons for not suppressing *kabuki* and prostitution. Instead, the government segregated and isolated them in certain quarters of the cities so that society as a whole would not be contaminated.

The government went beyond geographical segregation and attempted to draw and maintain distinctions between the professions of the prostitutes, dancers, and actors. As these professions were traditionally one, it was difficult to check their continual tendency to drift toward each other. It was also an innovation for the government to regard prostitution and homosexuality as evils. These had long been accepted in Japan and the attempt of the Confucian-inspired bureaucrat to curb them resulted in a tiresome repetition of laws of limited effectiveness.

The *bakufu*'s laws concerning *kabuki*, like so many of its laws, were ordinances primarily for the city of Edo, but they stood as models that other areas were encouraged to emulate. Some concluded with the phrase: "The above is ordered sent also to Kyoto and Osaka." In most cases, however, the commissioners in Osaka and Kyoto did not issue the Edo edicts at once, but waited for an opportune moment, when an incident occurred that would make the new restriction accepted with less discontent. In the same month of 1652 in which the forelocks of the Edo actors were ordered shaven, a sword fight in an Osaka theatre brought about the closing of the theatres there until the next year.[36] The Kyoto commissioner had to wait four years for an appropriate pretext; this was provided when a samurai, jealous over the favors of one of the actors, provoked a sword fight in a box of one of the theatres. It seems that the Kyoto theatres were closed longer than those of Edo and Osaka.[37] However, judging from the similarity of conditions in the *kabuki* theatres of the three cities, it is apparent that the prohibitions and the tacit permission were roughly the same.

The Tokugawa laws issued to the common people, known as *Ofuregaki*, were to a considerable extent hortatory. The government's attitude was that the townsmen were *gumin* ("stupid people") who had to be talked to like children. The officials summoned together all the theatre managers and actors once a year and read them the regulations. When the officials considered that the customary infringing of a law had become too blatant, another was issued to the same effect, prefaced with phrases such as: "There are rumors of violations. If these occur again, there will be swift and severe prosecutions." The leniency that the officials generally showed in enforcing the laws, preferring to issue warnings rather than to prosecute, is illustrated by a passage in another *Ofuregaki*: "as this is most improper, if an investigation were made it would call for strict punishment; but since all this is known by rumor, it will not be made a legal case this time"[38] One order concluded with the curious statement:

> In general, after there has been a prosecution, orders are issued; but in no time there are those who violate them, and it is not well that they have not been prosecuted. Since such has been the case, hereafter constantly and without remiss it should be kept in mind that investigations will be carried through.[39]

There is no comprehensive collection of these laws concerning the theatre, and most of them must have been lost. However, there are well over a hundred still to be found in the collections of Tokugawa laws or scattered through Tokugawa encyclopaedias, guidebooks, diaries, and miscellanea. Those already discussed were largely intended to curb prostitution and homosexual practices. The remainder fall into three general categories: first, those designed to segregate the theatre and its actors from the rest of society; second, sumptuary laws attempting to restrict the costumes and architecture of the theatre to an austerity appropriate to the townsmen class; and third, those forbidding subject matter in plays that would have a subversive political or moral influence. All were designed to preserve the morality of the state and its people, since political, social, and ethical morality were considered one, all subsumed under proper observance of human relationships, with particular stress on conduct appropriate to one's status. The Tokugawa official, then, would consider these to be not repressive but reform measures.

Fundamental to the segregation policy was the concentration of the large theatres in two quarters of the city. This was facilitated in Edo by the fires of the 1650s, especially that of 1657, which leveled large areas of the city. Thereafter the government required that all the main theatres be located in a quarter comprised of Sakai-chō and Fukiya-chō, or in Kobiki-chō.[40] The same occasion was utilized to concentrate the houses of prostitution farther from the center of Edo by moving the licensed quarter to Asakusa, where it became known as the New Yoshiwara. The number of ōshibai (large theatres) was restricted to four (not increased during the Tokugawa period), and there were allowed eight koshibai (small theatres) as well as those of temples and shrines [miya shibai or miyaji shibai. Ed.] which could put on performances for limited periods of time upon receipt of a permit from the machi bugyō (town commissioner). Punishment was threatened for the staging of unauthorized performances.[41] The number of actors in a troupe was also restricted, as in 1694 when each large theatre was limited to twenty actors and ten apprentice actors.[42]

The same procedures were followed in Kyoto and Osaka. In Kyoto the large theatres were restricted to Shijō-gawara and were gradually reduced in number, as opportunities permitted, from seven to three. In Osaka there were three theatres in Dōtonbori and one in Horie.[43] In addition there were some medium- and small-sized theatres in both cities.

In order to protect society at large from the corrupting influence of actors, great care was taken to separate them professionally and physically from the rest of society. Just as prostitutes were restricted to their respective quarters of the cities, actors were not permitted to leave the theatre quarters. They were required to live in the close neighborhood of the district, and could not reside in the homes of non-actors, nor allow those of other professions to live in their residences.[44] The authorities were interested primarily in preventing the actors from accepting invitations to entertain outside the quarter, particularly in the mansions of the daimyō (feudal lords) in Edo, or in the residences of samurai or wealthy merchants. It is evident that the actors were much in demand at private parties and that the attempt to keep them restricted was a continuous and largely unsuccessful battle. Countless arrests, imprisonments, and banishments seem to have been insufficient deterrents. That violations persisted is apparent from the fact that between 1648 and 1709 edicts ordering that actors should not leave the theatre quarters were issued so repeatedly that the texts of at least twenty can be found.[45]

It is evident that even the second of these, issued in 1655, had been preceded by many others:

Laws have been issued time after time that even if *kabuki* actors are invited to feudal lords' residences, they must not go. Of course they must not wear sumptuous costumes. . . . Minstrels, if invited to residences, must not do imitations of *kabuki*, nor imitate the Shimabara style. Even if one or two *kabuki* actors are invited to residences, they must not go nor perform imitations of Shimabara.[46]

The order of 1668 said:

After the actors of Sakai-chō and Kobiki-chō finish the plays on the stage, they must not meet government employees [i.e., samurai]; farmers and townsmen must not visit them indiscriminately and stay long.[47]

That of 1678 said:

We hear that actors go to the homes of samurai and townsmen and not only stay a long time, but also sometimes even stay overnight. This is most improper. Henceforth, even though they be summoned, they must not go.[48]

The edict of 1695 said:

It has been strictly forbidden by law over and over that *kabuki* actors, *rōnin yarō*, those with unshaven forelocks who do not appear as actors, women dancers, and homosexual youths, go out. It is hereby ordered that henceforth such people must not be sent out at all. We hear that recently there has been some going out, and that the above persons have also been sent out on boats. This is outrageous. Henceforth, more than ever before, it is prohibited to send the above persons anywhere. Of course they may absolutely not be sent out in boats. Anyone who violates this will, upon discovery, be arrested.[49]

There were also orders warning actors not to disguise themselves as ordinary townsmen in the attempt to slip out of the quarter to answer calls to residences. There were also numerous prohibitions against those not registered as actors to dress like them, or to put on performances, or to go to private residences to entertain. There were such prohibitions concerning not only youths but also women dancers.[50]

From time to time the government weeded out unauthorized entertainers, as in an order of 1689:

Hereafter, as the law on actors provides, only actors of Sakai-chō and Kobiki-chō, and with their forelocks shaved, are permitted to appear in theatres. As to the other youths, the money paid for them will be their master's loss, and they will be returned to their guarantor or parent. If they should be sold again, it will be an offense.[51]

An order of 1706 said:

Although it has often ordered over and over that women dancers must not be sent around, in recent years it has become rife, and this is outrageous. Hereafter women dancers are prohibited. Some word has been heard to the effect that they are being called "maids" and are being sent to feudal lords' mansions and townsmen's homes. The same applies to this as to the preceding.[52]

In 1703 the following was issued:

As offered repeatedly before, Sakai-chō and Kobiki-chō actors may not go out, but it is heard that recently there has been lax observation of the prohibitions against groups of townsmen who have entertaining skills going to feudal lords' mansions, and also the employing of women dancers and sending them about here and there. This is improper.[53]

The distinction between actors and the rest of society was emphasized by prohibiting any amateur dramatics, except at those two most important festivals, New Year and Bon.

In its efforts to enforce observance of laws concerning actors, the *bakufu* utilized informers and the devices of group and corporate responsibility on which it relied in much of its law enforcement. Most of the ordinances concerning the segregation of actors or prohibiting the keeping of female dancers and youths ended with clauses specifying the extent of responsibility, as for example:

The contents of the above is to be passed throughout the quarters (*chō*) to house-owners and renters and all those on their premises. Quarter representatives (*nanushi*), five-man groups, and house-owner groups should investigate, and should leave no one at all of the above types. From this [office] men will be sent around, and if there are such people, as soon as they see them or hear of them they will arrest them, and so this should be strictly observed. If there are those who violate this they should be reported at once. If they are concealed and we learn of them from other sources, the person in question, needless to say, and even the house-owner, five-man group, and quarter representative will be strictly prosecuted for the offense. Hence the purport of this should continue to be observed.[54]

Because of the attention the *bakufu* gave to proper relations between classes, it was most anxious to stop the type of fraternization implied by the visits of actors to the residences of lords and samurai. As each class had its own professions, its style of living and amusements, *kabuki* was not supposed to be a completely public theatre, but was intended only for townsmen. The theatre of the upper classes was *nō*, which was intended for them exclusively. When it was discovered that a special performance of *nō* was put on for townsmen in the Yoshiwara, those involved were punished. So that high personages could attend in secrecy, boxes were built in the Edo *kabuki* theatres in 1646, raised above the pit and screened with bamboo blinds. Three years later, and repeatedly thereafter, blinds and standing screens were prohibited.[55] The clever managers devised a means of slipping vertical lattices hastily in place to make sheltering partitions when a feudal lord or high-ranking samurai attended; they could be quickly dismantled when he left.

But men of such rank might lose status or even be punished for attending, and as *bakufu* surveillance increased late in the seventeenth century, they probably came rarely. The lords' wives, daughters, and ladies of the shogun's court were consumed with eagerness to have a glimpse of actors on the stage. Most did not have the nerve to go in, but stopped their palanquins in front of the entrance and had their footmen part the curtains so that they could have a glimpse. This practice became so common that there was a law forbidding it. Such was the envy of the upper classes for the townsmen's *kabuki*. The lower samurai, although forbidden to attend the theatre, seem to have gone quite openly when they could afford the price of proper seats, which was considerable.

Adjoining the theatres or in their close vicinity were many small establishments called *shibaijaya* (theatre teahouses). Here theatregoers could eat and drink, arrange for reservations at the theatres, check their wraps while they went to see the plays, or sit and visit with their friends. But "teahouse" was also a euphemism for a house of assignation. Since the actors were forbidden to leave the quarter, these establishments served as places to which their patrons could invite them. The furnishings of such teahouses became more and more luxurious, and the parties there were a concern to the authorities. They placed restrictions on the teahouses, but did not abolish them outright because they also had their legitimate functions, and eating and drinking were considered to be an important part of theatregoing. The actors were ordered not to meet patrons there, or backstage, or in the boxes, but such prohibitions were essentially unenforceable.[56]

The second category of prohibitions is related to the system of sumptuary laws by which the officials attempted to curb extravagance and conspicuous consumption by all classes. It specified for each class what sort of clothes, personal adornments, houses, and furnishings could be used. The government was particularly anxious to prevent any show of high living by the merchants that would excite the envy of the theoretically superior samurai.

Many of the sumptuary laws "governing" the *kabuki* forbade the use of expensive costumes. The love of expensive clothes is a dominating interest in traditional Japanese culture. Throughout Japanese literature from the *Genji Monogatari* (The Tale of Genji) on, there are minute descriptions of clothes, their style, color, and texture. This interest increased as the art of weaving developed in Japan after the immigration of Chinese weavers into Sakai late in the sixteenth century and the establishment by Hideyoshi of the Nishijin quarter of Kyōto as the major center of weaving. During the seventeenth century new developments in the arts of weaving and dyeing raised the interest in fine clothes to a passion.

Rich brocade and silk costumes were an essential part of *nō* drama and, as the only colorful and luxurious element, were heavily relied on for effect. But *kabuki*, as the theatre of the townsmen, was prohibited from using brocade or other expensive costumes. In addition to the sumptuary laws concerning the clothes townsmen could wear, specific orders were issued concerning *kabuki* costumes. In 1636 the manager and an actor of the Saruwaka-za were jailed for using costumes that were too sumptuous in a *kabuki* dance piece. The same year, when the manager of a puppet troupe, Satsuma Koheita, who had arrived in Edo advertising "the country's best, down from the capital," hung purple silk curtains bearing the crest of the Lord of Satsuma and used rich costumes on his puppets, he too was jailed.[57] The use of silk and other rich materials was forbidden repeatedly, as in 1649, 1650, 1655, 1662, and so on,[58] but it is evident that by 1668 the authorities were making concessions on this front also. The order of the third month of that year reads:

> 1. The shows in Sakai-chō and Kobiki-chō must not be extravagant. In general the actors may wear clothes of silk, pongee, and cotton, and on the stage, they may wear costumes of *hirashima*, *habutae*, silk, and pongee. Goods dyed to order, purple linings, red linings, purple caps, and embroidered articles are prohibited. Further, on the stage silk crepe and cotton curtains are permissible, but purple silk crepe is not permitted.
> 2. Puppet costumes must not be sumptuous. Gold and silver leaf must not be used on anything. But puppet generals only may wear gold and silver hats.[59]

Another order reads:

> [The observance of] what has been ordered over and over has lately become lax. Actors' costumes have gradually become more gorgeous. Gold and silver threads have been used to embroider all over. Chinese-style

weaving has been seen. It is improper for samurai costumes to use ceremonial kimono, long skirt and tunic, of course, and figured satin, *habutae*,
and crests, and to have long and short swords and other articles of intricate
work. . . . Actors' costumes should be of silk, pongee, and cotton, and
should not be gorgeous. Long and short swords and other articles of intricate work must not be used.[60]

Theatre managers were required to take oaths that they would not permit
any of the prohibited materials to be used, and periodically a number of
actors were given thirty days in jail for violations.[61] In certain periods there
were annual, semiannual, or even monthly inspections of the theatres and
their properties.[62] The managers seem usually to have had prior intelligence
of the inspection so they were able to conceal the proscribed items. The
officials, during most years, seem to have taken a generous attitude, not interpreting the law strictly. The inspection was an occasion to remind the
managers and actors about the prohibitions and to warn them of the intention
to give swift punishment for infractions in the future.

An example of the minuteness of the regulations is that realistic sword
blades could not be used; it was prohibited to cover the wooden blades with
silver foil or paper, but they could be painted.[63] Actors were forbidden to
ride in palanquins or litters of any kind (as were all townsmen) or on horses,
but the frequency with which this order was issued suggests the prevalence
of violations.[64]

Concerning the architecture and furnishings of the theatres, the *bakufu*
fought a protracted rearguard action against the shrewd theater owners. The
earliest *kabuki* was performed on a small, uncovered stage, the audience
enclosed by a bamboo paling or a bunting on four sides after the manner of a
sideshow tent without a top. Later just the stage was covered by a roof as in
the *nō*. A drawing of 1689 shows the audience sitting on matting spread on
the floor; overhead were installed reed blinds over which matting was placed,
so that performances could go on even in a light rain. Despite the disapproval of the authorities, the theatre and its appointments steadily developed
in size and elaborateness. A drawing of 1646 shows the bamboo paling replaced by a board fence.[65] Although the use of boxes, blinds, and screens
was repeatedly forbidden, even periodic inspections of the theatres failed to
halt completely the use of detachable partitions used to form boxes, or the
use of blinds; and at most times permanent boxes seem to have been in use.

After the fire of 1657, the Edo theatres were rebuilt on a more substantial
scale. In the next decade the evolution of longer plays with several acts led
to the development of different types of drawn and drop curtains to separate
acts and scenes, and to the designing of more elaborate stage sets. By 1677

the side *hashigakari* (runway) derived from the *nō* developed into the *hanamichi* (runway through the audience). A picture of 1677 shows actors making up, seated about on the second floor of the greenroom much as they do today. We see boxes equipped with screens and blinds extending on three sides of the pit. The area that a theatre was permitted to occupy was restricted by ordinances but, upon the petitions of the theatre managers, was gradually increased as the Tokugawa period progressed. At the front of the theatre stood a tower [*yagura*. Ed.] in which a drum was beaten from early in the morning on days when performances were to be given in order to draw a crowd. Townspeople were thus provided with a sort of weather forecast. This practice of drum beating was forbidden in 1679 and again in 1684.[66] By the end of the century, despite laws to the contrary, the theatre had a roof, three levels of boxes, three stories of dressing rooms, and luxurious theatre teahouses.[67] *Kabuki* was flourishing in defiance of the law when the greatest scandal in its history broke.

During the early years of the eighteenth century, the most talked-about actor in Edo was Ikushima Shingorō (1671–1743). A contemporary work on actors says that he specialized in love scenes, of which he was considered the founder, and that he played them "realistically" and provocatively.[68] Another book says he "presented love scenes on the stage, causing the ladies in the audience to be pleased."[69] He is said to have been extraordinarily handsome, and the women of Edo were wild about him. The one among them most smitten was Ejima (sometimes called Enoshima), one of the highest lady officials of the women's quarters of the shogun's castle, who served the mother of the seventh shogun, Ietsugu (1709–1716).

There are a number of differing accounts of the incident that brought this sensational affair to light, and they appear to have been so embroidered that the details of none of them are to be too seriously regarded. In essence what happened was that on the twelfth day of the first month of 1714, Ejima was ordered to make a proxy pilgrimage to the mausoleum at Zōjōji in Shiba, accompanied by a considerable number of attendants. The established precedent was that after they had attended to their duties, they would be feted in the abbot's quarters. However, on this day Ejima left the temple without stopping at the abbot's quarters and, with eleven others from the entourage, went to the Yamamura-za to see the plays. They called the actors to their box and drank with them. Among the actors was Ejima's lover, Ikushima Shingorō. News of the theatre party leaked out, and an investigation resulted in a full exposure not only of the party, but of the love affair between Ejima and Ikushima, which had been in progress for nine years. All those implicated in the affair and the party were given punishments ranging from banishment to death. The lady officials were placed in the custody of different lords, and

Ikushima was banished to Miyake-jima, where he remained eighteen years until he was pardoned the year before his death.[70] [Ejima was banished to Shinshū. Ed.]

The most serious consequence for the history of *kabuki* was that the Yamamura-za, which had been the most popular among the Edo theatres for more than a decade, was closed on the sixth day of the second month, the building demolished, and the assets confiscated. For the remaining 150 years of the Tokugawa period, there were three instead of four large theatres in Edo. All of the theatres were closed until the ninth day of the fourth month, when they were permitted to reopen under stringent conditions. The twenty-four leading actors of the Edo stage were required to submit written statements that they would not violate any of the orders of the *bakufu*. The regulations imposed upon the managers were set forth in a document of the ninth day of the third month:

> 1. The boxes of the theatres have been made two and three stories in recent years. As formerly not more than one story will be permitted.
> 2. It is prohibited to construct private passages from the boxes or to construct parlors for merry-making backstage, in the theatre manager's residence, or in teahouses and such places. Nothing at all should be done by the actors other than performing plays on the stage, even if they are called to the boxes or teahouses or the like. Of course pleasure-making patrons must not be invited to the actors' own houses.
> 3. In the boxes it is not permitted to hang bamboo blinds, curtains, or screens, and to enclose them in any way is prohibited. They must be made so that they can be seen through.
> 4. In recent years the roofs of theatres have been made so that even on rainy days plays can be performed. In this matter also roofs must be lightly constructed as was done formerly.
> 5. The costumes of actors in recent years have been sumptuous; this is prohibited. Hereafter silk, pongee, and cotton will be used.
> 6. It is strictly prohibited that plays continue into the evening and torches be set up. It should be planned so that they will end at 5 P.M.
> 7. Teahouses in the vicinity of the theatres should be lightly constructed, and parlor-like accommodations are entirely prohibited. Concerning those that are in existence at present, petitions should be submitted to the town commissioner's office, and upon inspection, a decision will be given.
>
> The above must be observed without fail. If there are violations, the principals, of course, and even the representative of that quarter and five-man group will be considered offenders.[71]

Four years later, in 1718, when the theatre owners pleaded that rainy days were bankrupting them, wooden shingle roofs were permitted over the stage and boxes.[72] Five years later, to reduce the fire hazard, the theatres were actually ordered to lay tile roofs and construct the outside walls of plaster.[73] The wily theatre managers pleaded that they could not afford this construction unless their income could be increased by the construction of a second tier of boxes on three sides around the pit, a request that was grudgingly granted. The same year the Nakamura-za was permitted to enlarge substantially the size of its stage and the length of its runway.[74] It is of course conceivable that the officials were encouraged to sanction these steps by gifts or entertainment provided by the managers.

Another restriction that the theatres encountered came in 1707 when they were instructed not to hold performances on days when the shogun proceeded out of the castle. In replies to pleas that this worked a financial hardship, the theatres were permitted, the next year, to begin performances after the shogun's return to the castle. On these occasions the program would last until after dark, and pine torches were used to illuminate the stage. Because of the fire hazard, by 1716 performances were permitted daily regardless of the movements of the shogun.[75]

The practice of using torches to light the stage must have been recurrent. In 1707 an order said that on days when the wind was strong, *kabuki* performances must be stopped to reduce the danger of fire.[76] After wooden roofs were permitted, it was no longer required to stop performances on windy days. An undated order complains that there were rumors of performances lasting until midnight. Because of the danger of fire as well as the impropriety of the late hour, the theatres were instructed to begin their performances early in the morning if necessary so as not to continue after dark.[77]

The third type of restrictive law forbade the introduction into plays of subject matter that would have an undesirable political or moral influence. The same restrictions were applied to playwrights as to other kinds of authors, that matters concerning the government must not be published, that the names of contemporary members of the samurai class and above must not be mentioned,[78] nor any incidents involving samurai occurring after 1600. In 1644 the order was issued: "In plays the names of contemporary persons will not be used."[79] By contemporary persons was meant, of course, the people who counted. It is believed that this order was issued as a result of a fight that broke out in the Yamamura-za earlier that year when a living person of importance was mentioned in a play. An order of the second month of 1703 read:

1. As ordered repeatedly before concerning unusual events of the times, it is prohibited still more henceforth to make them into songs or publish and sell them.

2. In the Sakai-chō and Kobiki-chō theatres also, unusual events of the times or [action] resembling them must not be acted out.[80]

This ban of 1703 was issued when dramatizations of the revenge of the forty-seven *rōnin* were performed within a few months of the event. [The most famous dramatization, *Chūshingura*, is described in the essays by Powell, chapter 10, and Inoue, chapter 11. Ed.] The playwrights were nimble in deceiving the censors, for they changed all the names and recast contemporary events in the Kamakura or Ashikaga period. It became a stock convention of the *kabuki* and puppet theatre that when Hōjō Tokimasa (1188–1215) appeared in a play he was really Tokugawa Ieyasu (1542–1616); Kamakura was substituted for Edo, the Inase River near Kamakura for the Sumida River, the Hanamizu Bridge near Kamakura for the Eitai Bridge in Edo, and so forth.[81] By such camouflage, some playwrights were clever enough to attempt political satire and get away with it. Of the several plays in which Chikamatsu Monzaemon (1653–1725) used this device, the most extensive use of contemporary materials was in his *Sagami Nyūdō Senbiki Inu* (The Sagami lay monk and the thousand dogs, 1714), in which he satirized Tokugawa Tsunayoshi (1646–1709) and his legislation protecting dogs.[82]

For moral reasons the *bakufu* disapproved of the too suggestive treatment of the gay quarters and their prostitutes. These quarters were the scene of much of the social life as well as entertainment of townsmen, and were much frequented by the samurai. They served as the setting of the most flowery scenes in practically all of the history plays as well as the domestic plays, providing the excuse to depict beautiful courtesans, romantic rivalries and intrigues, luxurious living, and riotous behavior. The types of action specifically proscribed were depictions of the style of walk and behavior of courtesans of the Shimabara quarter of Kyoto and episodes demonstrating the techniques of accosting and winning the favor of high-ranking prostitutes. Such miming had been an important part of *kabuki* from the time of the earliest skits, and despite the bans of 1655 and 1664 forbidding such scenes in any type of theatre, including the puppet stage,[83] they continued to be stock episodes in play after play. The effect of the ban seems to have been to prevent this action from becoming excessively salacious rather than to deny the audience the vicarious pleasure. Related to the sumptuary laws were the provisions that the houses of the gay quarters should not be made to appear luxurious. To make that life appear too glamorous would tend to undermine not only moral behavior but also the hierarchical social system.

Another favorite theme that was banned, but effectively only for a few years, was the double "love suicide." The sensational and romantic treatment of such suicides by playwrights like Chikamatsu seems to have been too suggestive to thwarted lovers. Rash young men and women anticipated that their deaths would be publicized, if not immortalized, in prose and drama. In addition to banning the publication of stories on this theme in 1723,[84] the *bakufu* attempted to discourage the acts by imposing punishments on those who survived unsuccessful attempts and by heaping dishonor on the corpses of those who succeeded. Within a few years, however, love suicide plays were again written and performed, and have continued to the present day to be a favorite theme of *kabuki* and the puppet theatre, nor did the disapproval of the Tokugawa government by any means eliminate from Japanese life the practice of committing double suicides.[85]

In the foregoing survey of the laws with which the *bakufu* attempted to reform or restrict the development of *kabuki*, the pattern that emerges is the tendency of the government to yield to the persistent pressure of the theatre interests. The officials were not only subjected to the pleas and petitions of the theatre managers, but were constantly faced with nonobservance of the laws, in varying degrees of flagrancy, not only by the managers, but by the actors, playwrights, and even the audience. Since the reason for permitting *kabuki* to continue to exist was to assuage and divert the lower classes, it was only during certain determined reform movements, when the leaders of the administration were attempting to restore the moral fiber of the country, that the laws were enforced as harshly as the letter might suggest. Because a more permissive attitude generally prevailed, it was difficult for the authorities to establish any specific line to hold against the constant pressure, motivated not only by commercial interests, but by the pleasure-loving, excitement-seeking propensities of the irrepressible townsmen. The government lost ground on almost every front: the increasingly substantial construction of the theatres, the luxurious teahouses, the elaborate staging, the use of wigs and rich costumes, and the introduction of "subversive" subject matter into the plays. The appeal of *kabuki* to all classes could not be checked. It is a symptom of the trend that by the early nineteenth century the women attendants of the lords' mansions and even of the shogun's castle were openly sent to the theatre to learn *kabuki* dances so that they could perform them for their lords.

If we are to assess the effect of the *bakufu*'s measures on the development of *kabuki*, we must give primary attention to the banning of women, as it led to the development of male players of women's roles, the *onnagata*. Incredibly skilled in impersonating women, they analyzed the characteristics of female motor habits and, abstracting the essential gestures, developed in their acting a peculiar type of eroticism never completely divorced from homosexualism. After women's parts had been played by *onnagata* for two and a half centuries, the conventions were so well established that the attempt to reintroduce actresses into *kabuki*, following the Meiji Restoration, was a failure. Actresses seemed less feminine, in part because of certain conventions that men hold about what makes women attractive, which women, of course, cannot be expected to understand. From the point of view of the aesthetics of acting, women seemed too natural and so were incapable of emphasizing the essential characteristics of women. This required a more detached order of understanding and execution. The extent to which the institution of *onnagata* has affected the development of *kabuki* can be illustrated by saying that if actresses were now to be substituted for *onnagata*, they would have to play their parts, not as women imitating women, but as women imitating *onnagata* imitating women.

An effect of the laws that was more clearly to the disadvantage of *kabuki* was that the actors were despised, at least officially. There had been some patronage by the second and third Tokugawa shoguns, notably in 1633 and 1650–1651, but because of scandalous incidents and the increasingly rigid attitude of the government toward ethics, this patronage ceased. In 1719 a *kabuki* troupe was invited to perform at the castle, but when an official protested, citing the Ejima affair of 1714, the invitation was withdrawn, and a puppet troupe was invited instead.[86] The official attitude was that actors were a social group lower than merchants and only a little above the pariah class. This type of social persecution prevented overt patronage by men of education and position, and gave the actors little opportunity or incentive to raise their art to levels that were potentially attainable.

The censorship eliminated any possibility of writing plays of real social or political significance. The isolated examples that touched on such subjects were intended more to electrify the audience with the playwright's daring than to influence it with his criticism.

It is futile to predict what the development of *kabuki* might have been without government interference, because this repression was present from the time of *kabuki*'s crude beginnings. We can only observe that the effect of the interference was beneficial in forcing *kabuki* to mature more quickly, that it separated *kabuki* from female prostitution, and that the continued supervision placed more emphasis, for lack of choice, on art. The *bakufu* must be given credit for accelerating or even causing the turn from vaudeville and burlesque toward dramatic art, from one-act dance pieces at best toward dramatically structured plays of five acts or more. The banning of women also quickened the development of makeup, costuming, and staging.

We lack the information to be able to evaluate what potentialities for development *kabuki* might have had if it had been unrestricted in the environment of Tokugawa culture, and to weigh them against the *kabuki* that actually developed and that was so profoundly affected by the repression. In the balance, it may be that the repression was beneficial to the development of *kabuki* as a dramatic form.

Notes

1. Takano Tatsuyuki, *Nihon Engekishi* (History of Japanese theatre), vol. 2. Tokyo: Toyōdo, 1948, 20, 39. All Takano references are to vol. 2.

2. *Razan Bunshū* (A collection of Razan's works [1662]), quoted in ibid., 23.

3. Ariwara no Narihira (825–880), whose amorous exploits are the subject of the *Ise monogatari* (Tales of Ise).

4. *(Keichō) Kenbunshū* (Keichō era chronicle) by Miura Joshin (Shigemasa) (1565–1644), vol. 5, in *Shiseki Shūran* (Collection of history books), vol. 10. Tokyo: Kondō Kappanjō, 1901; "*Sanrokurui*" (Collection of miscellaneous notes), no. 42, 144.

5. Ibid., 145.

6. Ibid., 143.

7. Nakagawa Kiun (1636–1705); in *Kyōto Sōsho* (Kyoto series), vol. 3 (Kyoto: Kyōto Sōsho Kankōkai, 1914), 7.

8. Asai Ryōi (d. 1709?); *Edo Meishoki*. In *Zoku Zoku Gunsho Ruijū* (Classified collections of Japanese classics: Second supplement), ed. Kokusho Kankōkai, vol. 8. Tokyo: Kokusho Kankōkai,1906, 756.

9. Ihara Toshirō [Seiseien], *Nihon Engekishi* (History of Japanese theatre), vol. 1. Tokyo: Waseda Daigaku Shuppanbu, 1904, 28–29.

10. Takano, *Nihon Engekishi*, 45.

11. Ihara, *Nihon Engekishi,* 29.

12. The law of the tenth month, 1629, reads: "In theatre performances we hear that heretofore men and women have been mixed. As this is improper, it will not be done henceforth." Cf. Ihara 30–31.

13. Takano, *Nihon Engekishi,* 45.

14. Sekine Shisei (1825–1893), *Tōto Gekijō Enkaku Shirō* (Edo theatre annals), vol. 1 (Tokyo: Chinsho Kankōkai, ed.) I (1916), 31b; Ihara, 87–88. The law of 1645 said: "Although notification was given during 1640 that it is a misdemeanor for men and women to appear together in *kabuki* dancing, lately not only were women dancers being employed and subjected to a bitter life [i.e., prostitution], but men and women were being mixed in *kabuki* performances, and consequently the employers and dancers were punished. Hereafter those who violate this law will receive severe punishment" (Ihara, 87).

15. Ihara, *Nihon Engekishi*, 88.

16. *Kyōto sōsho* 7. A silver mameita piece was 1 to 5 momme (which is 3.75 grams), and a *chōgin* was 43 *momme*.

17. *Zoku Zoku Gunsho Ruijū*, 8, 756.

18. Sekine, *Tōto Gekijō*, 32a. The order of the eighth month, 1642, read: "To call *kabuki* plays 'sarugaku,' and for the men to play as women and act voluptuously, is prohibited."

19. Ibid., 32ab. Ihara, 88, says 1643.

20. Ihara, *Nihon Engekishi*, 92.

21. *Tokugawa Jikki* (Records of the Tokugawa era), vol. 3. In *Zoku Kokushi Taikei*, (Supplementary compendium of Japanese history), vol. 11. Tokyo: Keisai Zasshisha, 1902, 55b.

22. Sekine, *Tōto Gekijō*, 34b–35a; cf. Takayanagi Shinzō and Ishii Ryōsuke, comp., *Ofuregaki Kanpō Shūsei* (Collected government regulations of the Kanpō era), no. 2685. Tokyo: Iwanami Shoten, 1934, 1239a. The government's edict was provoked, according to the *Tokugawa Jikki* (3.55b), by a fight that broke out in the Osaka residence of *daimyō* Hoshina Masasada (1588–1661), arising from a drinking affair involving a young actor. Another explanation says the order was issued by the Edo town commissioner when he found young actors at a banquet (Ihara, 93). Such explanations of what brought official action should be regarded more as symptomatic than as factual.

23. Ihara, *Nihon Engekishi*, 93–94. This is attributed to a certain lord's wife having had an affair with an actor, and the two planned to commit suicide together. It is also said that homosexual scandals were again prevalent.

24. Asai, *Edo Meishoki*, 756.

25. In the eighth month of 1641 Murayama Sakondayū appeared in a dance piece at the Saruwaka-za with a silk scarf draped over his head, carrying a branch of artificial flowers to which were attached poem cards. The performance was much applauded, but it was banned (Sekine 1.32a).

26. Ihara, *Nihon Engekishi*, 98, 436.

27. Quoted from *Miyako Fuzoku Kagami* (Mirror of customs in the capital [1682]) in ibid., 458.

28. Ibid., 100.

29. See, for example, one of the many orders of the fifth month, 1689, quoted in Ihara, *Nihon Engekishi*, 437.

30. 8/1694 and 1/1697, in ibid., 438 4/1699 in Shinzō and Ryōsuke, *Ofuregaki*, No. 2711.

31. Asai, *Edo Meishoki*, 757–758.

32. Quoted by Takano *Nihon Engekishi*, 57–58; facsimile ed., 1b-2b, in the Kisho Fukusei Kai Series, no. 3. Another account of the young actors, appearing in Asai, *Edo Meishoki* (756–757), seems to draw some of its material from the *Yarō Mushi*, to which it had referred earlier:

> While [the fellows] parade down the runway, they sing songs in voices like that of Kalavinka, said to be a bird in Paradise; the sight as they open their fans and perform a dance leads one to think that the fluttering of the sleeves of the feather robe of the heavenly maiden who descended from the sky at Udo Bay long ago must have been like this. The blind eccentrics, who think nothing of spending great amounts of money, consummate frequent rendezvous as their memories of the floating world. It is especially the exalted and noble monks of the various temples, and in addition, the acolytes of the various monasteries who, each and every one of then, are captivated and lured by these youths and go to visit them with their hopes pinned on a meeting. Each time they see them they feel as though the Three Holy Ones [Amida, Kannon, and Seishi] were coming to receive them. When they accomplish their end they feel like the carp of Lung-men who have leapt up the three-fold falls. Since they are still unsated, they go again and again. In the end, lacking the money with which to engage them, they sell their sutras and holy teachings to raise the fee; they pawn Buddhist utensils and their surplices, steal and carry away the age-old treasures of the temples, and present them to the youths to curry favor with them for a thousand-year troth. It is sad that on account of this they receive scandalous reputations, their virtue is damaged, and they are reduced to flight. Although I may not indicate who they are, there are among the *kabuki* youths of today those who are beautiful in face and form and resemble Narihira, but whose appearance when they take a fan and dance is like boars swimming. Or there are

those who are gentle in voice and speech but whose manners are coarse and movements unrefined like untrained, fledging falcons, or like calves newly muzzled. Again there are those who have a fearful look about the eyes, being cross-eyed. Then there are those whose mouths are large with thick lips, resembling rain-water jars. They are all as foul-tempered as starving dogs and in their greed for things they resemble cats guarding their food. Now the way of youth flourished in China and it has existed in Japan since ancient times, but the very name for the *kabuki* youths today is *onnagata* and in all ways they behave like prostitutes, having as their chief aim to seduce men and to take things. Furthermore, even though they contrive to sweeten their dispositions, their efforts easily fall apart and they are like inexperienced foxes disguising themselves as beautiful women. When they reveal their tales from time to time, ridiculous things happen. Nevertheless the devotees are blind to their good and bad points and indeed it is only after they have unswervingly spent everything that they finally awake from their dreams.

33. Takano, *Nihon Engekishi*, 57–59, 200–201, 304.

34. "Tokugawa Seiken Hyakkajō" (Tokugawa laws: 100 items). In *Tokugawa Kinrei Kō* (Collection of Tokugawa laws), ed. Shihō Daijin Kanbō Shomu-ka (Office of General Affairs, Ministry of Justice), vol. 1. Tokyo: Yoshikawa Kōbunkan, 1931, 88.

35. *Ofuregaki,* No. 2707.

36. Ihara, *Nihon Engekishi*, 95.

37. Ibid., 94–95. The precise year of the ban is in doubt. One tradition says the second month of 1656, another 1657.

Typical of the fanciful tales associated with Tokugawa-period literary and theatrical figures is the account that a Kyoto manager, Murayama Matabei, petitioned so earnestly and tenaciously for the reopening of the theatres that he remained ten-odd years in front of the town commissioner's office, never returning home, ignoring rain and dew, until his clothes were in tatters. Many of the actors went into other trades or moved to other areas, but those who remained in Kyoto took food to him, and he persevered until at last in 1668 his plea was granted. However, whatever the basis for this story, the *Kyō-warabe* describes the Kyoto theatres as in thriving condition; the *Yarō Mushi* (ca. 1659) mentions three theatres, and Asai Ryōi's *Tōkaidō Meishoki* (Famous sights along the Tokaidō [1662]), vol. 6, *Onchi Sōsho* (Things familiar series), ed. Kishigami Sō. Vol. 1 (Tokyo: Hakubunkan, 1891), 243–244, mentions a fourth. Cf. Takano, *Nihon Engekishi*, 356–357; also Tominaga Heibei, "Gei Kagami" (Mirror of art), in *Yakusha Rongo* (The actors' analects [1776]), in *Shin Gunsho Ruijū* (New classified collections of Japanese classics), ed. Kokusho Kankōkai, vol. 3. Tokyo: Kokusho Kanōkai, 1908, 6b.

38. Undated law in *Tokugawa Kinrei Kō*, vol. 5, 700–701.

39. 3/17/14. cf. *Ofuregaki*, no. 2733.

40. 12/1661: "Henceforth *kabuki* will not be performed except in Sakai-chō, Fukiya-chō [i.e., Upper Sakai-chō], and Kobiki-chō 5-chōme and 6-chōme." (*Ofuregaki*, No. 2690.) The former two were located northeast of Nihonbashi, the latter south of Kyōbashi.

41. 5/1708 (*Ofuregaki* No. 2726); in 1662 the "bamboo-grass walled theatres" at temples and shrines were ordered not to stage performances for more than 100 days a year. See Kitamura Nobuyo (1784–1856), *Kiyū Shōran* (Pleasurable viewing), vol. 5b (ca. 1830), in *Nihon Geirin Sōsho* (Japanese art world series). Tokyo: Rokugōkan, 1927–1929, 587.

42. Ihara, *Nihon Engekishi*, 438.

43. Ibid., 449.

44. Ibid., 437, gives 3/1678.

45. 2/1648 (*Tokugawa Kinrei Kō*, vol. 5, 521), 5/1655 (*Ofuregaki*, no. 2688), 1/1661 (Ihara, *Nihon Engekishi*, 436), 12/1661 (*Ofuregaki,* no. 2695), 1/1662 (Ihara, 436), 3/1668 (*Ofuregaki* no. 2695), 4/1671 (Ihara, 437), 3/1678 (ibid.), 5/1689 (*Ofuregaki*, no. 2704), 5/1689 (*Ofuregaki*, no. 2705), 5/1689 (*Ofuregaki*, no. 2706), 8/1695 (*Tokugawa Kinrei Kō* 5.695), 1/1697 (*Ofuregaki*, no. 2709), 4/1699 (*Ofuregaki,* no. 2711), 2/1703 (Ihara, 438), 4/1703 (*Ofuregaki*, no. 2716), 3/1706 (*Ofuregaki*, no. 2793), 3/1706 (Ihara, 438), 6/1706 (*Ofuregaki*, no. 2719), 6/1706 (*Ofuregaki*, no. 2720), 7/1709 (*Ofuregaki*, no. 2729).

46. *Ofuregaki*, no. 2688.

47. Ibid., no. 2695.

48. Ihara, *Nihon Engekishi*, 437.

49. *Tokugawa Kinrei Kō*, vol. 5, 695.

50. 6/1652 (*Ofuregaki*, no. 2658), 6/1666 (*Ofuregaki*, no. 2694), 5/1689 (*Ofuregaki*, no. 2703–2706), 5/1689 (*Tokugawa Kinrei Kō*, vol. 5, 694), 1/1697 (*Ofuregaki*, no. 2711), 4/1703 (*Ofuregaki*, no. 2716), 6/1706 (*Ofuregaki*, no. 2719), 6/1706 (*Ofuregaki*, no. 2720).

51. Ihara, 437–438.

52. *Ofuregaki*, no. 2720.

53. Ibid., no. 2716.

54. 6/1706 (*Ofuregaki*, no. 2720).

55. Ihara, *Nihon Engekishi,* 89; also law of 3/1668 (*Tokugawa Kinrei Kō*, vol. 5, 693).

56. 4/1671 (Ihara, *Nihon Engekishi,* 437).

57. Ibid., 89, Sekine *Tōto Gekijō*, vol. 1, 31b–32a.

58. 2/1649, 3/1650 (Ihara, *Nihon Engekishi,* 89), 5/1655 (*Ofuregaki,* no. 2688), 1/1662 (Ihara, 436), etc.

59. 3/1668 (*Ofuregaki*, no. 2695).

60. Undated (*Tokugawa Kinrei Kō*, vol. 5, 700–701).

61. In 9/1708, for example, four actors were jailed for thirty days for wearing prohibited costumes (Sekine, *Tōto Gekijō*, vol. 2, 82b).

62. 2/1726 (ibid., 100b).

63. 2/1704 (Ihara, *Nihon Engekishi*, 438). The incident that provoked the law against the use of real swords, however, was of another order. In that month the great actor, the first Ichikawa Danjūrō (1660–1704), was stabbed and killed on the stage during a performance by another actor who had a grudge against him (Takano, *Nihon Engekishi*, 258–259).

64. 3/1650 (Ihara, *Nihon Engekishi*, 89), 1665 (*Tokugawa Kinrei Kō*, vol. 5, 695–696) et al., 8/1695 (*Ofuregaki*, no. 2708).

65. Takano, *Nihon Engekishi*, 62.

66. Ihara, *Nihon Engekishi*, 454.

67. Miyako no Nishiki (l675?–1710) wrote in the *Genroku Taiheiki* (Great peace of the Genroku era [1702]): "The theatres of Edo, differing from those of Kyoto and Osaka, have three tiers of boxes, and are even more flourishing than has been heard. The ticket and seat charges are double those of Kamigata (Kyoto/Osaka), and you must even pay for fire for smoking." Cf. *Saikaku Zenshū* (The complete Saikaku), vol. 2. Tokyo: Hakubunkan, 1893),1019, vol. 24 in *Teikoku Bunko* (Imperial library) series.

68. *Yakusha za Furumai* (Actors' theatre conduct [1713]), quoted in Takano, *Nihon Engekishi*, 337.

69. *Yarō Nigiri Kobushi* (A man's clenched fist [1696]), quoted in ibid.

70. Ibid., 338–339. For a highly colorful, if undocumented, account of the Ejima-Ikushima affair, see Nagashima Imashirō and Ōta Yoshio, *Chiyoda-jō Ōoku* (The inner chamber of Edo castle), vol. 2. Tokyo: Chōya Shinbunsha, 1892, 69–106. This work (86–94) quotes an unnamed source for a description of Ejima's theatre party, which it claims included 130 persons:

> The aspect of this day was a hubbub that cannot be described. In the boxes were spread carpets, and the theatre owner, Nagadayū, Ikushima Shingorō, and Nakamura Seigorō, wearing *hakama* [divided trousers] and *haori* [jackets], were invited to be drinking partners. The uproar of the party was such that the sounds of the play could not be heard. . . . At this time in a lower box was a retainer of Matsudaira Satsuma no-kami, a person called Taniguchi Shinpei, watching the play with his wife. In the upper box, Ejima, quite intoxicated and not knowing what she was doing, spilled her sake, and it poured on Shinpei's head. He sent a messenger to the upper box. The *kachi-metsuke*, Okamoto Gorōemon, made the apologies, but this did not satisfy Shinpei. Gorōemon apologized over and over, and finally Shinpei accepted the apologies, and although it was about midday he and his wife left the theatre. Thereafter Gorōemon several times urged Lady Ejima to leave, but she would not consent, and instead became very angry. At 2 P.M. a passageway was installed from the second-floor box by which they went to Yamamura Nagadayū's house, and the capers of the many maids who went were beyond words. For the entertainment of Ejima, many actors, young actors, and youths were summoned to be drinking partners. . . . When it had become 4 P.M. they left Nagadayū's rooms and went to a teahouse on the street behind called Yamaya. On the second floor the maids and actors came and went and there was a great hubbub. . . . They finally left Kobiki-chō and returned by the Hirakawaguchi Gate [of the castle] at 8 P.M.

This account also says that some of the robes and money that had been intended as offerings to the Zōjōji were presented to the actors, youths, and teahouse people.

71. *Ofuregaki,* no. 2734; see also no. 2733.

72. Sekine, *Tōto Gekijō*, vol. 2, 87b; Takano, *Nihon Engekishi*, vol. 2, 340–341.

73. Ihara, *Nihon Engekishi*, 454–455. Because the Kobiki-chō theatres were situated near the Hamagoden [or Hamarikyū. Ed.], a detached residence of the Tokugawa family, they were directed in 1705 to have the buildings plastered and to cover the towers with copper sheeting as a fire-prevention measure.

74. Takano, *Nihon Engekishi*, 341.

75. Sekine, *Tōto Gekijō*, vol. 2, 81b–82a.

76. Ibid., 81b.

77. *Tokugawa Kinrei Kō*, vol. 5, 700–701.

78. 5/1673 (*Ofuregaki*, no. 2220).

79. Ihara, *Nihon Engekishi*, 90.

80. 2/1703 (*Ofuregaki*, no. 2668); see also 4/1703 (*Ofuregaki*, no. 2716).

81. Ihara, *Nihon Engekishi*, 458.

82. See the author's "Chikamatsu's Satire on the Dog Shogun," *Harvard Journal of Asiatic Studies* 18 (1955): 159–180.

83. 5/1655 (*Ofuregaki*, no. 2688), 1/1664 (Ihara, *Nihon Engekishi*, 436).

84. Twelfth month, Kyōho 7 [January 1723] (*Ofuregaki*, no. 2022).

85. On love suicide plays, see Serge Eliséev, "Le double suicide (Shinjū)," *Japon et Extrème-Orient* 9 (September 1924): 107–122; and the author's *The Love Suicide at Amijima* (Cambridge: Harvard University Press, 1953), esp. 18–29.

86. Ihara, *Nihon Engekishi*, 447.

4

Nakamura Shichisaburō I and the Creation of Edo-Style *Wagoto*

Holly A. Blumner

Sakata Tōjūrō I (1657–1709) is considered by most international scholars to be the greatest innovator of and contributor to the creation and development of the *kabuki* acting style called *wagoto*, a gentle, even delicate style associated with the playing of handsome young men. This Kamigata (Kyoto/Osaka area) actor's first step in the development of the style came in 1678, when he performed Izaemon, the spoiled young lover of the courtesan Yūgiri, in *Yūgiri Nagori Shōgatsu* (Yūgiri's farewell at New Year's). Yet there is another *wagoto* actor, not so often credited, who left an indelible mark on this type of performance. Along with Tōjūrō and Edo's Ichikawa Danjūrō I (1660–1704), Nakamura Shichisaburō I (1662–1708) was one of the three great actors of *tachiyaku* (male roles) during the Genroku era (1688–1704). He is the only one of the trio to have bridged the regional performance biases between Kyoto and Edo, competing for and winning the public's affection in each of those two great cities.

Tōjūrō developed his unique brand of acting in what were called *keisei kai* (courtesan buying; also spelled *keisei gai*) plays because they concerned the love affairs of young men who fell in love with courtesans and sought to raise money to redeem them from their contracts. Shichisaburō, meanwhile, was creating a similar style in Edo. Shichisaburō's *wagoto* contributions, as well as those of Tōjūrō, helped shape the standards of acting the romantic young male type known as *nimaime*, an important factor in the progress of the *wagoto* style. The term *wagoto*, it should be noted, was not widely used to identify the style with which it came to be identified until years later, in

Figure 4.1 **Nakamura Shichisaburō I. (Photo: Tsubouchi Memorial Theatre Museum, Waseda University.)**

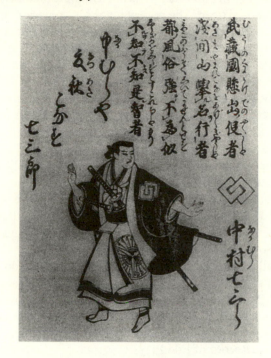

the mid-Kyōhō period (1716–1736), although the word itself (written with the characters for "soft thing" or "gentle thing"), made its first appearance in print in 1689. It went through several stages as the expression *yawarakagoto* (gentle thing) was gradually transmogrified into *wagoto* through revision in the way it was written with Chinese characters and syllabary letters. The component parts of *wagoto* were identified as *nuregoto* (love scenes), *keiseigoto* (scenes amidst courtesans), *kuzetsugoto* (lovers' quarrels), and *yatsushigoto* (scenes in which a samurai hero is forced by circumstances to assume a commoner's guise).

Unlike Tōjūrō, about whom nothing is known until 1676, Shichisaburō grew up in the theatre, his father said to have been the *tachiyaku* actor Amatsu Shichirōemon (dates unknown), a relative of well-known actor–troupe owner Nakamura Kanzaburō II (1647–1675). Shichisaburō's precise relationship to Kanzaburō has been disputed, but it is certain that Shichisaburō became the older man's student and performed under the surname "Nakamura" for his career on stage (figure 4.1).[1]

Shichisaburō debuted as an actor of adolescent boys (*wakashu*) and in his late teens turned to playing *wakaonnagata* (young women), specializing in the role category of *musume* (daughters), but also playing other related characters. His first entry in the annual *yakusha hyōbanki* (actor critiques) was in 1674, when he was sixteen. The review notes his "superior" looks and says, "he had too much erotic appeal to be playing a young woman." It also predicts that he will make a name for himself as he grows older.[2] Soon after, he began playing *tachiyaku*, including one of his most famous roles, that of Soga Jūrō, the older of the famous vengeance-seeking Soga brothers [see Kominz's essay, chapter 2. Ed.], for the New Year's performance of 1676. In this performance, he and Danjūrō I played the Soga brothers in the "Taimen" (encounter) scene of *Soga Ryōsha no Tamono* (Soga's two shrines of honor), produced at the Kanzaburō-za.[3]

In 1682, Shichisaburō made a creative decision that would change his life and alter the path of *kabuki* permanently. In the second month of 1682, he played Soga Jūrō in *Kōshoku Kamakura Gonin Onna* (Five women of lusty Kamakura).[4] Edo audiences loved seeing the legendary twelfth-century samurai, Soga Jūrō, and his brother, Soga Gorō, on stage. Although the situations featuring the Sogas varied from play to play, their characters remained constant through all. Both brothers were considered "sons of Edo" and typically were played in the bravura *aragoto* style associated with that militaristically oriented town. [See Kominz and Gerstle's essays. Ed.] In this particular performance, Shichisaburō decided to play Jūrō in the more natural *wagoto* style. His choice proved popular and the actor was written up in the *Edo Shibai Nendaiki* (Record of Edo Plays):

> Until now, the Soga brothers have both been played in the strong *aragoto* style. This time, Nakamura Shichisaburō, with a *genpuku* [a special type of young men's hairstyle], played Jūrō in a gentle way that was excellently performed. From that time forward, Jūrō has been played in the *wagoto* style.[5]

After the original 1682 production, Shichisaburō always played Jūrō in the gentle *wagoto* style. Other actors have adopted and continued the tradition to this very day, while the hotheaded Gorō typifies the flamboyant *aragoto* approach.

Wagoto became the trademark of Shichisaburō, an actor so handsome he was commonly nicknamed "Today's Narihira"[6] after the famous Heian poet Ariwara no Narihira (825–860), the object of desire in literary and dramatic works.[7] Though physically short, Shichisaburō possessed cool, clear eyes, abundant charm, and a definite sense of elegance. His natural acting and his skills in dance established his credentials as a *nimaime* actor.[8] There has been speculation that Shichisaburō's creation of the style was independent of Tōjūrō's, but recent research has demonstrated the influence of Tōjūrō on the Edo actor.[9] Moreover, there is evidence that *wagoto* was seen in Edo at the mansion of the *daimyō* Matsudaira Yamato no Kami. This *kabuki*-loving lord kept a now-famous diary of all his theatre experiences and recorded that he saw a production of *Yoshiwara Danrin* (Yoshiwara temple), a Yūgiri-Izaemon play, at his Edo residence in 1678, and had seen what was likely to have been *Yūgiri Nagori Shōgatsu* the previous year during his residence in Himeji. It seems highly possible that, with other actors, Tōjūrō's Osaka *wagoto* hit—or versions of it—was making its way eastward via Himeji to Edo, where Matsudaira had it played for him again.[10]

The following provides an account of the major highlights of Shichisaburō's career. A principal component recounts his significant stay in Kyoto at the end of the seventeenth century. To tell the story properly, I have translated several lengthy segments of *Keisei Asamagatake* (The courtesan and the peak of Asama), the crucial play in Shichisaburō's development of his Edo-style *wagoto*. I have also inserted representative examples of contemporary critiques of Shichisaburō's acting.

In 1686, Shichisaburō was featured in the dance play *Tanzen Sugata Kagami* (Mirror of a dandy at the *tanzen* bathhouse), in which he won acclaim for his *tanzen odori*, an exaggeratedly masculine type of dance. The play was a great success, and his performance elevated his popular status.[11]

In the autumn of 1698, when he was thirty-five, Shichisaburō was invited to perform with Yamashita Hanzaemon's (1650 or 1652–1717) company in Kyoto. In his debut there in the annual *kaomise* (face-showing performance) that opened the season, he experienced a dismal flop in *Miyako no Ehō Yome Iribunshō* (The lucky direction to Kyoto of the bride's letter). At the nearby Mandayū-za, Mizuki Tatsunosuke (1643–1745), recently returned from a sojourn in Edo, was performing with Tōjūrō. The dance play *Nanabake* (Seven spirits), written by Chikamatsu Monzaemon (1653–1725) and first performed in Edo, was a big hit in Kyoto. By comparison, Shichisaburō, performing with Hanzaemon, received poor reviews and small audiences.[12] So weak, apparently, was his art that the critique titled *Yakusha Daifukuchō* (The actor's account book) nicknamed him *"Shichisa Buta"* or "Shichisa the Boar."[13]

The New Year performances that welcomed 1698 saw Shichisaburō reprising the role of Koroku in one of his popular Edo plays, *Kantō Koroku Imayō Sugata* (Kantō Koroku's up-to-date figure), with the great *onnagata* (female-role specialist) Yoshizawa Ayame I (1673–1729) featured as the sister, Kane no Mae. At the Mandayū-za, Tatsunosuke continued to draw large crowds, while Shichisaburō reportedly brought in audiences of only two or three hundred. "Koroku is a hovering blowfly," said one review.[14] There was also a *kyōka* poem about Shichisaburō making the rounds: "Hanzaemon wanted to see Shichisaburō's beautiful eyelashes, so he went round to view the rear legs of the horse."[15] In *kabuki* theatre, a minor actor plays the hind legs of the two-man "horse." The poem poked fun at Shichisaburō, suggesting that he was no better than a horse's ass.

While local audiences were not impressed with Shichisaburō's acting, the famous *wagoto* star Tōjūrō did see a performance. According to an excerpt in the *Yakusha Rongo* (The actors' analects), Kyoto audiences may have been quick to ridicule Shichisaburō, but Tōjūrō recognized in him an outstanding performer.

> What stupidity! Kyoto audiences are thoroughly ignorant! Above all, Shichisaburō is one of the greatest actors of recent times: at the moment there is not one single one who stands higher than he does. If we exert ourselves, our art will be a little better during the year because he has come to Kyoto. Because we have done better than he has in the *kaomise*, he will be a far tougher opponent in the second program.[16]

Tōjūrō's prediction proved correct. On the twenty-second day of the first month of 1698, Yamashita Hanzaemon's company performed the aforementioned *Keisei Asamagatake*, featuring Shichisaburō as the *wagoto* character, Tomoenojō. The play featured three other well-respected actors in prominent roles: Troupe leader Hanzaemon played the loyal retainer Wataemon, Yoshizawa Ayame played Courtesan Miura, and Iwai Sagenta (dates unknown) was Courtesan Ōshū. The play was a huge success and ran for an unprecedented 120 days. Its overwhelming popularity left Tōjūrō and the rival Mandayū-za scrambling unsuccessfully to pull in audiences.[17]

The play—an *oiemono* or feudal house play—was staged to coincide with a *kaichō*, the unveiling of a Buddhist icon, in this case that of the deity Shinshū Asama Myōjin, brought to a local temple from nearby Higashiyama. Much of the play's success was owing to its intriguing plot line. At the House of Suwa, located in Higashiyama, the widow of the deceased lord has succeeded her husband as the head of the household, but she is not the rightful heir. As the play opens, the deceased lord's son, Tonegorō, is enamored of the courtesan Miura, but has bound her with rope because she refuses to give in to his desires. The lord's faithful retainer, Wataemon, enters the residence and hears Tonegorō's accusations. Unbeknownst to Tonegorō, Miura and Wataemon are in love and have a daughter together. Wataemon is working to ransom Miura from her brothel contract. He overhears Tonegorō's plot to usurp the family residence and murder Princess Otowa no Mae, the legal heir to the residence. He rescues Miura and the two flee the residence.

Kozasa Tomoenojō, Otowa no Mae's fiancé, has broken their engagement because he is love with the courtesan Ōshū. Having brought disgrace on his family, he has been disinherited. Cut off from family support, he takes a job as a palanquin bearer, calling himself Shichibei, and carries tourists up Mt. Asama to see the *kaichō*. Wataemon, using the name Sakubei, also takes work as a palanquin bearer, and the two become friends. One day, a *kamuro* (girl attendant to a courtesan) comes to ascend the mountain to the *kaichō*. After talking to Wataemon and Tomoenojō, she sings a song. Otowa no Mae, in a palanquin herself, overhears it and is touched by its beauty. Otowa no Mae is unaware that the nearby bearer, Shichibei, is actually Tomoenojō, her fallen fiancé.

A procession with a courtesan makes its way up the mountain. The *kamuro* bears a kimono of the mistress she serves. It has the same crest as that of Tomoenojō's love, Ōshū. The attendant is, in fact, Ōshū's *kamuro*. Suddenly, Otowa no Mae realizes that Shichibei is actually her Tomoenojō, and she reminds him of their mutual pledge. Confronted by Otowa no Mae, he agrees and decides he no longer needs the pledge and amulet given to him by Ōshū.

> *(TOMOENOJŌ flings the amulet into a nearby brazier and it immediately burns. Suddenly, a cloud of smoke rises from the brazier and the apparition of Ōshū appears. The apparition stands in the brazier, surrounded by flames, an expression of reproach on its face.)*
> PRINCESS OTOWA NO MAE, KAMURO, and ATTENDANT *(all see* ŌSHŪ*)*: How frightening! *(They fall down in a deep sleep).*
> TOMOENOJŌ: What is this? *(He looks behind him. When he sees* ŌSHŪ, *he is beside himself with surprise. He reaches for his long sword.)* Who are you?
> *(A musical passage in kouta style narrates* ŌSHŪ's *thoughts as she moves in response to the words.)*
> KOUTA SINGER: You ask me and I am pleased. You ask and I am shy. You replace me scandalously, and I stand by you. Darling sir, my true love. I want to give you all that's in my heart.
> TOMOENOJŌ: Oh! Is that you, Ōshū? What are you doing appearing around here?
> ŌSHŪ: My darling, I longed for you, yearned for you, to see you, to talk with you, that is why I came. *(This all seems like a dream to* TOMOENOJŌ.*)* What a pitiful figure.
> *(He tries to take her in his arms, but she mysteriously disappears, though her costume remains.* TOMOENOJŌ *stands in place looking at the spot where she has vanished, thoroughly amazed. The apparition appears again, as the song continues.)*
> KOUTA: "No resentment or love remains. I wonder if you have changed your heart? Why did you burn my vows of love? How spiteful. My heart blazes for you three times in the night, I long for you three times a day.

Compare this smoke with Mt. Asama.[18] Go look closely at Mt. Asama. The evil demon of lust tortures me. I can see my love at the top of the mountain of swords. Joyfully, I try to climb the mountain. My longing for you crushes my heart, how horrible it is. The figure of the flower gets weaker, weaker, weaker, I try to reach beyond, here I disappear." Like a misty moonlit night in spring, the apparition becomes vague, and slips away.

TOMOENOJŌ *(after* ŌSHŪ *has disappeared)*: Well, that must be the pledge of a determined soul. *(He rouses the three women.)* Hey, hey. A woman must not be obsessive like that!

PRINCESS OTOWA NO MAE: Listen, listen. That courtesan had such a strong longing for you that her spirit came forth to speak with you. If she has such feelings, you should redeem her contract, and let her serve you at your side.

TOMOENOJŌ: If you feel that way, I will ransom her. But first, I must take care of this child. Then, let us go pay a visit to the Lady of the House of Suwa.

(Everyone exits.)[19]

Soon after this, villainous Tonegorō and his companions appear under the guise of congratulating Tomoenojō and Otowa no Mae on their coming nuptials, but instead they try to force Tomoenojō to commit ritual suicide. After Tomoenojō defeats them in a swordfight, he and Otowa no Mae escape.

Wataemon learns that Tomoenojō owes a small fortune to the brothel for entertaining Ōshū and is trying to ransom her from her contract. Wataemon, a loyal retainer of the House of Suwa, decides to help his young master, the rightful heir to the Suwa household, by selling his sword to raise money to pay Tomoenojō's debts. While Wataemon is away from his residence, the evil *rōnin* (masterless samurai), Nikaidō Hyōsuke, steals the money received for the sword. Osan, Wataemon and Miura's thirteen-year-old daughter, witnesses the crime. When she questions Hyōsuke, he stabs her to death.

Tomoenojō, feeling responsible for Osan's death, is devastated and vows to commit *seppuku* (suicide by disembowelment). Wataemon discourages this. Tomoenojō visits Osan's grave and decides to become a priest. Meanwhile, Miura has decided to work extra diligently at the brothel to relieve Tomoenojō of his debts.

Tomoenojō pays a visit to the brothel to see Miura and is dismayed to run into Ōshū, who is ill, owing to Tomoenojō's long absence. Reluctantly, Tomoenojō enters the room to speak to Ōshū, who has already learned he is there to visit Miura. She is furious and throws a teacup full of medicine at him. Throughout this lovers' quarrel, Tomoenojō uses phrases that have a double meaning. As he argues (or tries to avoid arguing) with Ōshū, nearly everything he says relates to a strategy in the game of *go*.[20]

While Tomoenojō is with Ōshū, he learns there is serious talk of a customer wanting to ransom Miura. Tomoenojō, who is secretly in love with Miura, is devastated and professes to want to buy her first. He cuts off his own little finger to show his sincerity. When Wataemon appears and learns of his friend's actions, he is furious; in a fit of anger, he beats Tomoenojō with his sandal. Tomoenojō explains that he planned the previous scenario to rescue Miura from her other suitor. Hyōsuke appears in the brothel district, and he is slain by Wataemon and Tomoenojō in revenge for Osan's death.

In the final act, Otowa no Mae, Ōshū, and Miura are going to the temple to pay their respects. They bring a few locks of Osan's hair as an offering. They are surprised to see a young girl close to Osan in age and appearance. The prayers of the Buddhist deity Fugen Bosatsu have saved her. At a memorial service at the temple for twenty-five bodhisattvas, Tonegorō tries to kidnap Otowa no Mae, but he fails and is captured. Tomoenojō and Otowa no Mae are married, and the House of Suwa is restored to its original glory.[21]

As noted, this plot helped stimulate a long run and a consequent drop-off in business at the Mandayū-za. A reviewer lavished praise on Shichisaburō:

> The last review [of Shichisaburō] stated ten of his virtues, but that was hardly adequate. If you observe his performance, there are ten thousand things to praise. This time, the beginning of the play was so outstanding, no comment is needed. The middle of the play was miraculous. When Ōshū appears in a cloud of smoke, it is completely unexpected. The acting is so wonderful, there are no words to describe it. He has an innate ability for dance. Since ancient times there has never been a scene like the one where he begins to play *go*. There has not been a lovers' quarrel scene like this before, and no words can praise it highly enough. He really puts his heart into it. At the pivotal point, the spectators were nodding their heads in amazement. Next was the scene where he professes his love for Miura. No one could see what might happen next. . . . This man never speaks in long phrases, an advantage in [this] acting style. . . . He understands the heart of Kyoto style. . . . This is a splendid actor.[22]

The note about speaking concisely is a direct reference to Sakata Tōjūrō. Many critics complained that Tōjūrō's speeches were lengthy, laden with too many quotations from *waka* poetry. Shichisaburō's dialogue was succinct and to the point. Yet, as evident in the *go* scene with Ōshū, he could be direct and still use double entendres (figure 4.2).

Keisei Asamagatake featured all of the *wagoto* characteristics that Kyoto audiences loved. There was a typical *yatsushi* scene, one in which a fallen samurai appears in a lowly guise, with Tomoenojō's first appearance as the down-on-his-luck Shichibei. When Ōshū emerges from the brazier, Ōshū

Figure 4.2 **An anonymous 1698 print showing the angry spirit of the courtesan Ōshū rising from the brazier flames in** *Keisei Asamagatake*. **(Photo: Tsubouchi Memorial Theatre Museum, Waseda University.)**

and Tomoenojō performed a series of dance movements and gestures during the song sequences. Audiences were charmed by the lovers' quarrel because of the unprecedented *go* scene that added a deeper level to the play. As noted above, Tomoenojō uses game terminology during his lovers' quarrel with Ōshū.

(ŌSHŪ *is sleeping by herself on a futon as* TOMOENOJŌ *enters.*)

TOMOENOJŌ *(talking to himself)*: Miura, what made you bring me here to this large room by myself? (He looks around the room.) Oh! It's a sleeping courtesan. It looks like her guest has gone home. She must be worn out. *(He realizes who it is.)* Oh! That's Ōshū. *(He fumbles with her bedding, but she is oblivious to him and continues to sleep soundly.)* Poor thing, she is thinner. It looks like her illness hasn't gone away.

ŌSHŪ *(mumbling in her sleep to her child attendant)*: Mojino, please bring me some water.

TOMOENOJŌ *(hears her mumbling and looks around)*: If I mix some medicine in her medicine pot, she'll probably drink it. *(He pours the herb solution in a teacup, mixes it with water, and says a prayer to the Hotoke of healing.)* Please make her well, Physician of Souls, Amen.

(As he holds out the teacup, ŌSHŪ *wakens and her eyes widen in surprise. Resentful and angry, she throws the teacup. The medicine flies through the air and the teacup shatters into pieces. She settles back down under the bedclothes.)*

TOMOENOJŌ: What was that? A lovers' quarrel? Don't do this. What a hassle! I don't know my way around here very well, and I don't have anything else to do. I don't really want to have an argument. Well, perhaps they'll bring me a cup of sake. I'm lonesome and I want to amuse myself somehow. There was no need to do that to the teacup! Actually, these broken bits resemble go stones. I want to play a game of *go*. Courtesan, won't you play with me? *(He receives no answer.)* It's been so long since we've seen each other. If you are upset with me, it would be best to say something. Silence is no good. *(He goes to her side and she gestures with her foot for him to get away.)* This is no good either. (*He tries to stick his face in the bedclothes and is struck in the eye by the angry* ŌSHŪ.) Oh! That hurts! My eye is on fire! You smashed my eye! I don't care if you push me away, I'm going to play a game of *go*. Luckily, my haori jacket has a pattern like a *go* board. (*He removes his haori, which resembles a checkered* go *board on the back, and lays it out across his knees. He begins to set up the pieces of the broken teacup as* go *stones. A nō song is heard in the distance.)* I didn't even come here to see you, and you've gone and smashed my eye! While I was nearly blinded, you thought you'd kill me. Whatever you think of me, I've achieved what I came for,[23] and I won't die. You're a strong player and you can't stand a poor player like me. Recently I've heard that you have someone who plays better than me. You've been ill, and I've heard you have been calling him to the Izutsuya, for over 360 days, to cure your illness. After hearing that, I asked you if our relationship was over and you agreed. But I kept you in good health, and when I stumbled upon you by accident today, you made a strong play. Even though you tried to kill me, I have a winning strategy so I won't be beaten to death. I would like to play with you, but I don't have a strong position on the board and I've already lost. At any rate, I'm going home now. See you later.

(He stands up to leave, and ŌSHŪ, *who has remained silent, runs to him, trying to detain him by holding on to the back of his obi from behind.)*

ŌSHŪ: Here is the back gate, but if you have business, come around to the front.

TOMOENOJŌ: What is it now? *(He tries to pull away from her.)* Are you propositioning me? There was a time when your own Nishi no Tōin[24] was the pleasure quarter, but it's not trendy now.

ŌSHŪ: Why are you being so rude? *(She grabs hold of* TOMOENOJŌ's *thigh and bites it.)*

TOMOENOJŌ: Ow! That hurt! Do you think my thigh is your pheasant dinner? If you're hungry, go eat some tea on boiled rice. Biting was trendy a long time ago, now it's old. If you want to say something, say it.

ŌSHŪ: How long have you been keeping company with Miura?

TOMOENOJŌ: At the most, maybe sixty days.

ŌSHŪ: You're not even hiding it! I have been physically sick because of you, and you're off secretly meeting Miura.

TOMOENOJŌ: What? Oh that? Miura is a courtesan and she's here because of you. Now you listen and listen well. I still owe two *wan* and eight hundred *me* at the brothel for meeting you. I came to pay some debts today, so I would be spared the humiliation of wearing the bucket in public.[25] Miura is the wife of a loyal retainer. When this trouble came about, she agreed to work as a courtesan to help with my debts. Now, don't you agree, you're the reason for all of this? It's the truth. You'd probably want the three of us to talk about this, but there is no need. You've heard it directly and there is nothing that can be done. Praise her, but don't cry, crying is old. Do you have something to say?

*(*ŌSHŪ *listens but does not immediately respond.)*

ŌSHŪ: You don't let me say anything. *(She climbs back into the bedclothes.)* Well, are you joining me?

TOMOENOJŌ: Well, since you're asking, it sounds good to me.

(The two become intimate in the bedding.)[26]

The humor in this scene, as well as the plot and the production's acting, catapulted Shichisaburō into direct competition with Tōjūrō.

Another review of the day, *Mikuni Yakusha Butai Kagami* (The theatre mirror for actors of three countries), said of Shichisaburō: "Though a small man, he fills the stage. He is an Edo actor, and his mannerisms are funny. . . . His 'courtesan buying' scenes are as well done as Tōjūrō's."[27]

Although Shichisaburō received the most acclaim, he was, as noted, supported by a highly accomplished group of actors. Unlike many of the *oiemono* plays that tended to highlight the leading character at the expense of the other players, this play featured several main characters, and each had a prominent role.

Scholars such as Torigoe Bunzō and Tsuchiya Keiichirō have written about how *Keisei Asamagatake*—one of the standout works of its era—resembles similar scenes from the same time period. Although early scholarship credits Shichisaburō himself with creating the play, modern scholars conclude that Shichisaburō, Chikamatsu Monzaemon, Yamashita Hanzaemon, or even actor Nakamura Denshichi I (?–1725) might have written the play.[28] It seems unlikely that the play was written by Shichisaburō. If, in fact, he did write it, it is the only one with which he is credited.

Plays about Yūgiri and Izaemon, credited with being those in which Tōjūrō first introduced *wagoto* acting, introduced a genre—the *Yūgiri-Izaemon mono*—devoted to this romantic pair. Similarly, a new genre known as *Asama mono* came to life with Shichisaburō's performance in this work. The play had a great influence on both Chikamatsu and Tōjūrō. In the twelfth month of 1699, Tōjūrō experienced a career highlight as Umenaga Bunzō in Chikamatsu's *Keisei Hotoke no Hara* (The courtesan on the Buddha plain). This *oiemono* also coincided with a *kaichō* on Hotoke no Hara Mountain in Higashiyama. It features a *yatsushi* scene in which the *nimaime*, Bunzō, disowned by his family, appears in a *kamiko* (paper kimono). This popular convention for representing a once-wealthy young man's poverty, and is also seen in the Yūgiri-Izaemon plays. Bunzō has a lengthy dialogue with a courtesan named Ōshū. Tōjūrō captured Shichisaburō's comic sense in a scene in which he is unsuccessfully trying to hide at night in a garden. He ends up with a small lacquered tray of *kagamimochi* (ritual rice cakes) on his head, innocently placed there by an unsuspecting lady-in-waiting who thinks he is the wash basin.[29]

The same month that Tōjūrō was performing *Keisei Hotoke no Hara*, Shichisaburō performed to acclaim with Yamashita Hanzaemon's company in *Keisei Hanaikada* (The courtesan and the floral raft), playing the younger brother, Monosuke, to Hanzaemon's chief retainer. In the company's next production, he performed the title role, a samurai dandy, in *Nagoya Sanza*, which he originated in Edo.[30]

Each time a new play was introduced, Tōjūrō would observe it and praise Shichisaburō highly. In turn, Shichisaburō went to see Tōjūrō's performances and praised him with equal warmth. While Shichisaburō was in Kyoto, he and Tōjūrō met several times and they became friends, although they never performed together.[31] Shichisaburō performed with Hanzaemon and his company for two years before returning with his wife to Edo in the fall of 1699.[32]

Before Shichisaburō left Kyoto, he gave Tōjūrō a parting gift. Tōjūrō wanted to give Shichisaburō a gift in return, but wished it to be something meaningful, not something given pro forma. So he did nothing and Shichisaburō returned to Edo. Later, at the end of the year, six men appeared at Shichisaburō's house in Edo with a large gift and a letter. Tōjūrō, aware that a gift unique to Kyoto would have great meaning for Shichisaburō, had sent water from Kyoto's Kamo River in a special container, bidding Shichisaburō use it for his New Year's tea. Shichisaburō was overwhelmed by the thought that went into the gift. He is reported to have said, "After my meetings in Kyoto with Tōjūrō, I thought I had got to know him thoroughly, but I obviously had not. This present shows a sentiment that would be hard to measure."[33]

Although Shichisaburō returned to Edo, the aftereffects of his wildly popular play lingered in Kyoto. There were several new productions of it, as well as new "courtesan-buying" plays that incorporated its elements, including two starring Tōjūrō and written by Chikamatsu, *Keisei Mibu Dainenbutsu* and *Keisei Hangonkō* (The courtesan and the Hangon incense). Tōjūrō's reputation continued to soar.

Back in Edo, Shichisaburō appeared at the Yamamura-za. Though he no longer appeared together with Danjūrō I, they continued their rivalry. Unlike Danjūrō's Kyoto visit a few years earlier, Shichisaburō's two years had been a great success. He did not disappoint expectant Edo audiences. One of his most outstanding performances was in a new version of *Keisei Asamagatake*, staged in 1700. It had the old title, but the Soga brothers had been inserted into the heart of its plot, and Shichisaburō assumed his famous role as Jūrō. As a Soga brothers play, it included the stock characters from the Soga repertoire and also featured a spirit manifesting itself in smoke. Instead of Tomoenojō's Ōshū, Jūrō's lover, the courtesan Ōiso no Tora, suddenly appeared in the midst of a brazier's flames. The scene using a *haori* as a *go* board was also reprised. Shichisaburō continued to delight audiences with his unpredictable comic interludes. The play was a big hit in Edo.[34]

He performed yet another version in 1702, retitled *Keisei Asama Soga* (The courtesan, Mt. Asama, and the Soga brothers). The actors' critique *Yakusha Nichō Shamisen* (The actor's stringed shamisen) describes a few moments of Shichisaburō's performance:

> Shichisaburō portrayed Soga Jūrō. Returning from a ceremony at Lord Hōjō's residence, he appears on the *hanamichi* [audience runway], drunk on sake. His paper lantern dangles from the hilt of his sword. Hands tucked in his kimono, he walks unsteadily. He is very good. As he walks, he sees some *zeni* [coins] and a red silk loincloth along the road, carried to protect a man from

the evil of his forty-second year. He takes the *zeni* and puts them into his under-kimono. He holds up the red loincloth. A range of expressions crosses his face and he uses various physical gestures. There is no one else in Japan who performs like this. When he discovers what the loin-cloth is, he makes a face showing disgust. He throws it on the ground and walks away. But it still holds his interest. He walks back and picks it up again. It is funny even without words. The third time, he says, "It's prob-ably new," and sticks it in his kimono. The same scene with a few words added is amusing.

A vehicle appears and a forty-two-year-old man from Chichibu emerges. When he recovers his protection against possible evil, he is glad. He invites the man who recovered his talisman back to his residence where he has forty-two women waiting. Because Soga Jūrō has absorbed the evil spirits by handling the loincloth, the man suggests that he choose a woman from his forty-two at home, have her wear the loincloth, and sleep with her. That will release the evil spirits that have attached themselves to him.

When the man suggests that they leave, a look of great annoyance ap-pears on Shichisaburō's face and it is extremely funny. The man prepares to leave and the drunken Shichisaburō finally says, "Please forgive me, ladies." It was so funny [our] insides hurt.[35]

Once Shichisaburō returned to Edo, audiences constantly critiqued him and Danjūrō, trying to determine who was the better actor. Shichisaburō was praised for excelling in the Kyoto style, while Danjūrō's acting was consid-ered "coarse."[36] In *Genroku Kabuki Kō* (Thoughts on Genroku *kabuki*), Torigoe Bunzō illustrates numerous examples of individual *kata*, acting tech-niques a *tachiyaku* specialist was expected to perform, including *nuregoto* (love scenes), *shosagoto* (dance), *aragoto*, and *keisei kai*. While Danjūrō excelled at *aragoto*, he was not as skilled in the gentler *wagoto* style, a style essential to *nimaime* (young lover) performance.

Sakata Tōjūrō, on the other hand, was superior in all the *nimaime*'s skills, but could not do much else. He was criticized for his sword fighting, danc-ing, and the kind of bounding exit called *roppō*.[37] Shichisaburō showed a mastery of a wider range of acting skills than both Danjūrō and Tōjūrō.[38] He competed with the top two actors of two distinct regions and successfully held his own with each. No other actor in the Genroku era was able to ac-complish this feat.

Shichisaburō died fairly young, his popularity still strong. There are dif-fering accounts regarding his death. According to theatre historian Kawatake Shigetoshi, in 1708 Shichisaburō was reprising his role as Jūrō in *Keisei Arashi Soga* (The courtesan, the storm, and the Soga brothers). On the sec-ond day of the second month, he was performing a scene in which the hard luck Jūrō enters a rice cake shop. Suddenly, Shichisaburō's mood altered. The management immediately announced the play's conclusion. Shichisaburō returned to the dressing room and entered a deep sleep from which he never woke up, perhaps having suffered a cerebral hemorrhage.[39] Torigoe, however, suggests that Shichisaburō collapsed and died from an excess of alcohol.[40] He was forty-seven.

Shichisaburō's three most famous roles were Nagoya Sanza, Tomoenojō, and Soga Jūrō. All three were played in the *wagoto* style. Prior to his 1697–1699 visit to Kyoto, Nagoya Sanza was his most frequent role. When he returned to Edo, the Soga plays were his major preoccupation. Although *Keisei Asamagatake* is no longer performed, it is considered one of the most innovative Genroku-era plays. It influenced a new genre that inspired many of Chikamatsu's later plays, several of which remain in the repertory. Still, Shichisaburō's most enduring legacy is his creation of the *wagoto* interpretation of Soga Jūrō, an interpretation that continues to be the sole approach to playing this major role.

Notes

1. Kawatake Shigetoshi, *Nihon Engeki Zenshi* (Complete history of Japanese theatre). Tokyo: Iwanami Shoten, 1959, 362.

2. Kabuki Hyōbanki Kenkyūkai, ed. *Kabuki Hyōbanki Shūse* (Anthology of *kabuki* critiques), vol. 1. Tokyo: Iwanami Shoten, 1972, 192.

3. Ihara Toshirō [Seiseien], *Kabuki Nenpyō* (*Kabuki* chronology), vol. 1, rev. ed., Kawatake Shigetoshi and Yoshida Teruji, eds. Tokyo: Iwanami Shoten, 1973, 126. The Kanzaburōza was an early name of the long-lived Nakamura-za.

4. Ibid., 144.

5. Quoted in Kawatake, *Nihon Engeki Zenshi*.

6. Ibid.

7. See Taguchi Akiko, "Edo Wagoto no Tanjō" (Birth of Edo *wagoto*), *Ronshū Kinsei Bungaku* (Collection of essays on premodern literature) 2: 5 (1991), for a thorough analysis of the issues involved in the "birth of Edo *wagoto*." Among the interesting things Taguchi demonstrates is that early love scenes in Edo were primarily same-sex in nature and that it was not until 1692 and 1693 that male-female (*tachiyaku-onnagata*) love scenes began to be mentioned in the actor critiques, and then only because of the influence of Kamigata *onnagata* coming to play in Edo and thereby promoting the Kamigata *wagoto* approach.

8. Shinmura Izuru, *Kōjien* (Wide garden of words). Tokyo: Iwanami Shoten, 1993, 90.

9. Kawatake, *Nihon Engeki Zenshi*.

10. *Matsudaira Yamato no Kami Nikki* (Diary of Matsudaira Yamato no Kami), discussed in Taguchi, "Edo Wagoto no Tanjō," 46.

11. Ihara, *Kabuki Nenpyō*, 157.

12. Torigoe Bunzō, *Genroku Kabuki Kō* (Thoughts on Genroku *kabuki*). Tokyo: Kasami Shoin, 1967, 333.

13. *Kabuki Hyōbanki Shūsei*, vol. 4 (1972), 556.

14. Ihara, *Kabuki Nenpyō*, 212.

15. This quotation appears in Japanese in Torigoe, *Genroku Kabuki Kō*, 333. I have used Laurence R. Kominz's English translation from *The Stars Who Created Kabuki: Their Lives, Loves and Legacy.* Tokyo: Kodansha, 1997, 136.

16. Charles J. Dunn and Bunzō Torigoe, trans. and eds., *The Actors' Analects.* Tokyo: University of Tokyo Press, 1969, 133–135.

17. Ihara, *Kabuki Nenpyō*, 215–217.

18. Mt. Asama is actually a volcano.

19. Takano Tatsuyuki and Kuroki Kanzō, eds., *Keisei Asamagatake* in *Genroku Kabuki Kessakushū* (Anthology of Genroku *kabuki* masterpieces). Tokyo: Waseda Daigaku Shuppan-bu, 1925.

20. *Go* is similar in appearance to checkers, but is closer in strategy to chess.

21. The author is indebted to Tsuchiya Keiichirō for his synopsis of the plot of *Keisei Asamagatake* in Tsuchiya Keiichirō, *Genroku Haiyūden* (Genroku actor biographies). Tokyo: Iwanami Shoten, 1991, 80–87. A concise summary is also available in Samuel L. Leiter, *New Kabuki Encyclopedia: A Revised Adaptation of* Kabuki Jiten. Westport, CT.: Greenwood, 1997, 309–310.

22. This review appears handwritten on an illustration in Takano and Kanzō, *Kuroki Kabuki*, 393. Ikawa Mayuko transcribed it into regular characters for me.

23. Tomoenojō came to pay his debts at the brothel.

24. Nishi no Tōin was a licensed brothel district that was no longer considered fashionable.

25. As with the stocks in medieval England, people in Japan were publicly punished and humiliated by being forced to stand outside in a bucket.

26. Takano and Kuroki, *Genroku Kabuki*, 438–441.

27. Kabuki Kyōbanki Kenkyūkai, *Kabuki Hyōbanki*, vol. 2 (1972), 134.

28. See Torigoe Bunzō, *Genroku Kabuki Kō,* or Tsuchiya Keiichirō, *Genroku Haiyūden.*

29. Chikamatsu Monzaemon, *Keisei Hotoke no Hara* in *Chikamatsu Monzaemon Shū* (*Chikauatsu* Monzaemon anthology), vol. 15. Tokyo: Iwanami Shoten, 1983.

30. Ihara, *Kabuki Nenpyō*, vol. 1, 228.

31. Dunn and Torigoe, *Actors' Analects*, 133–135.

32. Ihara, *Kabuki Nenpyō*, vol. 1, 240.

33. Dunn and Torigoe, *Actors' Analects*, 133–135.

34. Ihara, *Kabuki Nenpyō*, vol. 1, 247–248.

35. *Kabuki* Hyōbanki Kenkyūkai, *Kabuki Hyōbanki Shūsei*, vol. 3 (1972), 224.

36. *Kabuki* Hyōbanki Kenkyūkai, *Kabuki Hyōbanki,* vol. 2 (1972), 418.

37. Torigoe, *Genroku Kabuki Kō*, 307–308.

38. Ibid., 331–332.

39. Kawatake, *Nihon Engeki Zenshi*, 366.

40. Torigoe, *Genroku Kabuki Kō*, 339.

5

Episodes in the Career of the *Kabuki* Actor Nakamura Utaemon III, Including His Rivalry with Arashi Rikan I

Charles J. Dunn

Introduction

The more spectacular incidents in the career of Nakamura Utaemon III (1778–1838) took place in Osaka. They include a fierce rivalry with the Arashi family, especially Rikan I (1769-1821), and a later career characterized by a marked reluctance to retire. In this account of his life, much use will be made of the "documentary" evidence of Osaka actor prints and also of *banzuke*, which are the programs of performances at a particular theatre. *Banzuke* come in various forms, including the illustrated ones called *e-banzuke*, more or less abbreviated ones such as those used apparently rather like fly-posters for circuses in England (*tsuji-banzuke*, put up at street corners), and the standard form that lists the roles and those who performed them, names of musicians, name of *zamoto* or manager, theatre, date, and so on. Many libraries have collections of these available for inspection, but I should like to mention here another source. In the Waseda University Theatre Museum there survives a sort of theatrical scrapbook, consisting of boxes of made-up books with materials from the 1620s to 1827, but in fuller detail for the period of the life of Utaemon III, which was of great interest to the compiler, thought to have been a wealthy Osaka ginseng merchant and *kabuki* fan called Yoshida Goun. He employed Hamamatsu

Utakuni, a well-known theatrical critic, to collect the material, order illustrations from artists, write explanatory pieces, arrange, and catalogue it. The result is two massive volumes of reproductions in *Nihon Shomin Bunka Shiryō Shūsei* (Collection of sources on Japanese popular culture), to which has been added an extra volume containing various indexes, among other materials. Like any scrapbook, this collection suffers from various defects. The compiler enjoyed cutting out with scissors figures from color prints and sticking them on sheets with other cut-outs and captions, without paying attention to the dating of the actual prints, but only to whether they illustrated the *banzuke* that form the basis of the collection and provide the solid, useful, dated evidence for historical study. An example of this is to be seen on pp. 1020-21, items 65-67. Item 65, a *banzuke* dated eighth intercalary month of Bunka 13 (1816) records that Ichikawa Ebijūrō had played the role of Tōken (? Karainu) in the play *Beni Murasaki Ōsaka Aide Someage* (Scarlet and purple Osaka-dyed) at the Kado no Shibai in Osaka. Item 66 is apparently a made-up print (possibly cut out from a triptych by Shinchō that is no. 39 in the Ikeda collection; see the bibliographical note at the end of this paper) of a scene from this play, which seems to have as an alternative title *Beni Murasaki Ōsaka no Aji* (Scarlet and purple Osaka flavor) or even *Ōsaka no Aji Beni Murasaki* (Osaka flavor of scarlet and purple). Item 67 includes a fine print by Hokushū (Ikeda no. 392), which, although the actor's name and role are not inscribed, is accepted as being Ebijūrō in the role mentioned above. However, the style of the drawing and the artist's signature clearly date the print later than 1816. Incidentally, it has been described by Susumu Matsudaira as a death-print and given a date appropriate to Ebijūrō's demise, which occurred on 16.7.1828 [sixteenth day of the seventh lunar month, 1828. Ed.]. The design of skulls and bones on the costume would seem to support this, but the poem by Hōrai Sanjin printed on the picture is cheerful and appropriate to spring, so that Matsudaira now considers that it is not in fact a memorial print, but was produced at some performance later than 1816.

This scrapbook is thus reliable for dated material, but doubtful for undated pieces. This rather long introductory diversion can be terminated by mentioning that the title of the collection is commonly read as *Kyota Kyakushoku Jō* (An abundance of dramatized items), although the first two characters would probably better be taken as *Amata*, by which abbreviated designation I shall refer to it in this paper.

The Careers of Utaemon and Rikan up to 1816

Nakamura Utaemon III

The Nakamura family goes back to the origins of Edo *kabuki* history and derives from the Saruwaka line of comic interlude players who are reported to have set up the Nakamura-za under Saruwaka (later Nakamura) Kanzaburō in 1622, thus establishing the tradition of dramatic acting, as distinct from the dance and spectacle of Okuni, in *kabuki*. A branch of this family was established by the father of the Utaemon of this paper, that is, Utaemon I, whose acting career in the late Edo period merits mention. He was born in Kanazawa, on the Sea of Japan, in 1714, the same year that Takemoto Gidayū, the chanter who worked with Chikamatsu Monzaemon, died, and was the son of a doctor, with the family name of Ōzeki. It seems that he was an ardent amateur of the theatre and started acting at the age of sixteen, first on tour in the district of Kanazawa (where there had long been a flourishing local theatre) and in Niigata. He subsequently appeared at the Furuichi-za, which formed one of the attractions of a pilgrimage to the Ise shrine and which rated high in the *kabuki* theatre hierarchy, not far below the theatre of Nagoya. He acquired a position among the students of Nakamura Genzaemon, a player of *kataki* (enemy) roles in the Kansai (Osaka/Kyoto area) region, and promotion to the Hayakumo-za in Kyoto with the name of Utanosuke. He was renamed Utaemon probably in the next year (1742). He had a distinguished career as a *jitsuaku* (true villain) player both in the Kansai and in Edo, where he and Ichikawa Danjūrō IV exchanged fraternal vows.

Our Utaemon was his real son, but, possibly because of the relatively long time that it had taken the father to establish himself in the large theatres, or for some other reason as yet unknown to us, he was unwilling to have his son take up an actor's career, and the name Utaemon went to an outsider, born in Kyoto in 1752. The second Utaemon's first recorded name was Mizuki Tōzō, which he received as a pupil of Mizuki Masano, a Kyoto actor, taking the name of Nakamura Tōzō when he became a pupil of Utaemon I. He gained critical acclaim in 1781 for his portrayal of Kamura Utaemon (spelled with different characters than the actor's name) in the play *Hinin no Katakiuchi* (The outlaw's revenge), and the following year saw him honored with the name of Utaemon II, his master assuming the name Kagaya Utaroku and, in fact, retiring from the stage in 1788.

Utaemon II does not seem to have maintained his artistic promise, and gave up his name (one wonders under what pressures) in 1790, reverting to the old one of Tōzō, which he kept till his death in 1798. One can imagine that his name had been taken from him for the use of his teacher's son. The latter had not been destined for an actor's career, but the legend goes that already at the age of six he got himself into the cast of one of the Osaka theatres that employed child actors [*kodomo shibai*, children's theatres. Ed.], and scored a considerable success. His father seems to have accepted the situation, and, having retrieved his name from Tōzō, presented it to his son in 1790.

It will perhaps be convenient to list here the various names that Utaemon III, as he now was known, used during his career, for he made full use of most of them at one time or another until his death. His father had not abandoned his original family name, and his son was known as Ōzeki Ichibei. The *yagō* (or *kagō*), that name corresponding to a merchant's house name that every actor still uses on occasion and that is shouted out by the admiring audience (or professional shouters) during performance, was used by both generations. It was Kagaya, and harks back to their Kanazawa origins in Kaga province. Incidentally, the outsider Tōzō had the *yagō* Yamatoya (sometimes Hirukoya). Utaemon III used Kagaya Fukunosuke as his first acting name, and much later he was to use Nakamura Tamasuke. His *haimei* [also *haimyō*. Ed.] (used in writing poetry) was Shikan, and later Baigyoku, and it was during his life that Shikan became also an actor's name. The late Utaemon (VI) was formerly Shikan, as is the second-ranking actor of his line. Another name that Utaemon III used, on unspecified occasions, was Hyakugien. Finally, like his father, he wrote some plays of his own, under the name of Kanazawa Ryūgyoku (figure 5.1).

Like many another understudy, Utaemon III, after playing for some years in small theatres in Osaka, won the opportunity of becoming a great popular figure when he took over the role of the bandit Goemon from Asao Tamejūrō at the Minamigawa Shibai (Southern Theatre, where the present Minami-za is) in Kyoto in 1801. He earned high praise, even though the month's season was apparently shorter than usual because of lack of audiences. In 1808 he went to Edo to the theatre long associated with his family name, the Nakamura-za, and played there the sort of performances for which he would remain famous, including Yojirō the monkey trainer in the *kabuki* version of the puppet play known from its main characters *as Oshun Denbei*, four roles in *Yoshitsune Senbon Zakura* (Yoshitsune and the thousand cherry trees), seven roles in *Kanadehon Chūshingura* (The treasury of loyal retainers), and a series of seven quick-change dances that formed a part of his repertory for years to come. A critical work of the period quoted in *Kabuki Nenpyō* (*Kabuki* chronology) says, "A great ball of fire has come to Edo from Osaka. [Ichikawa] Omezō [I] has been quite burned out, [Bandō] Mitsugorō [III] is in danger from the accompanying gale, [Matsumoto] Kōshirō [V] was quite disposed of." These actors worked at other theatres in Edo, and, in fact, it is recorded that so great was Utaemon's popularity at the Nakamura-za that audiences were small at the Ichimura-za, and some plays had to terminate early there.

The year 1815 seems to have been a particularly unfortunate one for Osaka actors working in Edo. For example, in the sixth month at the Ichimura-za the program had to be brought to a close and the theatre shut; Osaka actors

Figure 5.1 **Nakamura Utaemon III as Tadanobu in** *Yoshitsune Senbon Zakura*. **Painting by Utagawa Toyokuni I. (Photo: Courtesy of Tsubouchi Memorial Theatre Museum, Waseda University.)**

like Arashi Sangorō left Edo and seem to have filled in by appearing on provincial stages at Senda and Nagoya. Utaemon III himself played in the first month at the Nakamura-za, with multiple roles in the Soga play *Date Moyō Soga Hinaata* (A strikingly patterned Soga copy) but had had to retrieve poor houses with a new spectacular piece. During that year the Ichimura-za's fortunes did not improve, in spite of reduced prices, but Utaemon seems to have maintained his form and kept his theatre full. In the seventh month his performances were advertised as his farewell to Edo on his return to

Osaka. In fact, the *banzuke* issued on this occasion bear the phrase *isse ichidai*, normally reserved for retirement from the stage altogether; but it seems that he was drawing the best publicity he could from his withdrawal (for the time being) from the Edo stage. In fact, he remained there for a while and took part in successive programs also in the eighth, ninth, and tenth months, and when be arrived in Osaka he was greeted, as is described by Matsudaira in his paper on fan clubs [see Matsudaira's essay, chapter 7. Ed.], by a fine turnout of welcoming supporters in their boats. It was during this closing year of his stay in Edo that he seems to have established a relationship with the actor Ichikawa Ebizō [This appears to be a typo for Ebijūrō. Ed.], for a letter is preserved in *Amata* (p. 962) that is interesting for showing how actors carried on their affairs outside of the theatre. Utaemon III describes how in the fifth month Ichikawa Danjūrō VII handed over to Utaemon's care an actor who had up to then been Danjūrō's own pupil under the name of Ichinokawa Ichizō. Utaemon went, he says, to Danjūrō's and there was offered sake, in the presence of other Edo actors such as Kōshirō V, Iwai Hanshirō V, and Umezō [Omezō? Ed.]. Utaemon was impressed by the way in which all these paid respect to the young Danjūrō (who had the most eminent name on the Edo stage), calling him *oyakata* (master). There was a feast, souvenirs of the Ichikawa family were presented to Utaemon, and Ichizō was given the new name of Ebijūrō I, with also several significant gifts such as a sword formerly owned by Danjūrō II, another the property of Danjūrō IV, and costumes with the Ichikawa crest. Ebijūrō went to Osaka with his new teacher and founded an important career there.

One has not enough evidence to form a well-based theory on why Utaemon made his move at this time. Was he doing so well in Edo, at the expense of the other theatres, that the acting establishment there determined to get him to go away and to this end put up a scheme to persuade him to return to Osaka with this promising new pupil? Or was it rather that he thought that the Edo theatre was in decline and that it was time to get out? In any case, it was two months after his visit to Danjūrō that he started his series of "Farewell to Edo" performances, thus extracting from the circumstances the maximum publicity. In the eleventh month, at the Kado no Shibai in Osaka, at the *kaomise* when the actors for the new season "show their faces," he took the part of Yuranosuke and two other roles in a new version of the forty-seven *rōnin* story (*Kanadehon Chūshingura*). His new associate Ebijūrō I acted with him in the parts of Kanpei and Kudayū for the daytime performance, with extracts from *Imoseyama Onna Teikin* (Mt. Imo and Mt. Se: An exemplary tale of womanly virtue) in the evening. In face, perhaps, of this well-advertised competition, Arashi Kichisaburō II did not put on a *kaomise* at his Naka no Shibai in Osaka, but transferred for the eleventh-month performance at the Minamigawa no Shibai in Kyoto the program which his company had given in Osaka in the tenth month.

Arashi Kichisaburō II (Rikan I)

This actor was born in Osaka in 1769, the son of Kichisaburō I. The family's earlier surname was Takeda and it was connected with a Takeda family that had been puppet masters for Gidayū, had specialized at one time in automata [mechanized puppetry. Ed.], and in Takeda Izumo had provided the principal writer of the team which had put together *Kanadehon Chūshingura* and other famous pieces. Under the name of Kichimatsu, Kichisaburō II had appeared first at the Takeda Hama Shibai [Takeda Shore Theatre, later called the Takeda no Shibai: a mid-ranked theatre named for its location on the shore of the Dōtonbori canal. Ed.], but had moved then to Kyoto to study under Arashi Sangorō II. The Arashi family had been in the Kyoto/Osaka area since about 1670 when an actor, Nishizaki San'emon, acquired the nickname of Arashi from his fine performance of a passage including the word *arashi* (storm) and made it into his family name. The Kichisaburō line was thus a fairly recent recruit to it. Kichisaburō II was given his name in 1787 and from then on rapidly climbed to a top position in the grading of actors in Osaka. He spent his whole acting career there and in Kyoto, attracting a great deal of support from the public, especially, it is said, from his female fans, for he had inherited his father's good looks. He specialized in vigorous male roles and is reported to have had a remarkably fine voice. In 1815, when Utaemon came back to Osaka, Kichisaburō was recognized as the *hanagata* (top star) of the Osaka stage. His career had not been marked by any outstanding incident; it seems rather to have consisted of a rapid rise to, and maintenance of, the highest rankings.

The Rivalry

Apart from two seasons in 1818 and 1819, the rivalry between the handsome Kichisaburō and the allegedly ill-favored Utaemon was maintained. During the years mentioned, Utaemon went up to Edo and played in the Nakamura-za under the name of Shikan, his *haimei*. His reason for using this name was perhaps connected with his highly publicized departure from Edo in 1815, which he advertised as his farewell to that city. His protégé Ebijūrō continued to do well in Osaka, ranking second only to Kichisaburō II. The two large theatres in Osaka at the time were the Naka no Shibai and the Kado no Shibai (the Middle and the Corner); Kichisaburō played at the latter, so that their rivalry was also a rivalry between the two theatres. Actors who normally played in the large Osaka theatres would also, on occasion, perform in the Minamigawa no Shibai and Kitagawa no Shibai (Northern Theatre) of Kyoto and would also sometimes, if there was a particular reason, such as a fire in a large theatre, play in the various alternative small theatres in Osaka itself. Of these the Shinchi no Shibai (in the north of Osaka in the relatively newly developed areas around Umeda), the Takeda no Shibai, mentioned above, and the Horie no Shibai were examples. The Naka no Shibai and the Kado no Shibai were on the Dōtonbori canal, in a theatre and entertainment district that still exists, with theatres still more or less on the same sites. An instance of fire occurred in the second month of 1818, when a performance had been planned, and for which an actor print had been prepared (Ikeda no. 68). In the fifth month Kichisaburō played at the Horie theatre (also known as Ichi no Kawa). Utaemon returned to Osaka for the *kaomise* in the eleventh month of 1819, and from then on for two years the two actors were at something like war, waged not so much by the performers themselves as by their fan clubs and the publisher of actor prints. This war is nicely portrayed in a print reproduced on page 1010 of *Amata*, dated 1816, the year after Utaemon's first return from Edo, showing Utaemon and Kichisaburō indulging in *kubihiki*, a sort of tug-of-war, with a rope looped round their necks. They are attired in gorgeous costume, with flowery headgear. The umpire, who bears a fan, as in sumo, is the actor Ichikawa Monnosuke, and the two protagonists have supporters; Utaemon's is Ebijūrō, and Kichisaburō has Arashi Sangorō. The imitation *banzuke* mentioned in Matsudaira's paper, in which the *hiiki* (supporters) of the two rivals are themselves the objects of a grading, dates from this period.

There was possibly a movement working in the opposite direction, for in the ninth month of 1820 a print by Hokushū appeared (Pl. 3 in Keyes and Mizushima), technically a *mitate* (a term often translated as "parody," but implying an imaginary situation, such as did not represent an actual event, therefore better translated in my opinion as "imaginary scene"), in which Utaemon and Kichisaburō are shown in roles that they were playing, respectively, at the Kado and the Horie theatres. If this print was indeed part of a movement to bring them together, rather than show them in rivalry, it developed in the next year into an unquestionable attempt at rapprochement when a group of fans brought the two actors together on a boat on an Osaka river, on 26.6.1821, with a new Arashi Kitsusaburō II [son of Rikan I. Ed.] playing the role which his predecessor had been playing when he died. This new man had been born in Osaka in 1788 and had spent most of his early career there as a child actor and with the Takeda no Shibai. His teacher was Arashi Isaburō, and he was in Edo acting under the name of Arashi Tokusaburō when he was brought to Osaka by Utaemon and given his new name in the memorial performance. There are hints that Tokusaburō had inclined to be on Utaemon's side in the now past rivalry, and he had been playing at the Nakamura-za in Edo, so that any other candidates for what was now clearly the top position in the Osaka Arashi school would have failed for lack of Utaemon's support. In any case, the new Kitsusaburō II was recognized as a good actor, especially in realistic roles. His dancing was not highly regarded. His looks, however, were characterized by his large eyes, and he acquired the nickname of Metoku Rikan ("Rikan with the good eyes," a pun on his earlier name). He was later (1828) to change his acting name officially to Rikan II; he died in 1837.

There is a pair of prints by Hokushū (Ikeda no. 207) showing Utaemon III introducing the new man at the name-change ceremony. The introductory address and the reply are given. After management and the whole cast complimented the audience and thanked them for coming to the theatre on this auspicious occasion, Utaemon said that Tokusaburō was appearing in the theatre for the first time, having been in Edo, and that with the death of his mentor he was like a blind man without a stick. The anniversary of the sad event had now come round, and the whole cast had considered that a memorial performance was necessary. They were delighted to hear that Tokusaburō would be available, and it fell to Utaemon himself to organize the ceremony of the name-change. He therefore presented Tokusaburō to the public and trusted that they would give him the same support in the future as they had to his predecessor. An equally long speech by the new Kitsusaburō II related how grieved he was at the news of the tragedy, how he came to Osaka to pay his respects, with no thought of taking over the name, and how he gratefully accepted Utaemon III's kind offices, with many modest protestations. He concluded with a poem:

Shiratsuyu no	As it receives the benison of
Megumi o ukete	the white dew even the
Iroke naki	unattractive bush-clover
Hagi mo chigusa ni	can mingle with the
Majiru kono goro.	beauteous wildflowers.

In the prints, a circular vignette with the face of Ō-Rikan [Rikan I. Ed.] looks down on the two figures of Utaemon III and Kitsusaburō II. Ō-Rikan is shown in the role in which he died, now taken by his successor. The faces of the two Arashi actors are shown as virtually identical, and it is indeed difficult to differentiate between them in many prints that appeared about this time. A display of Ō-Rikan's costumes and personal props was put on at an Osaka temple at the time of the anniversary.

The Retirement of 1825

In the ensuing years, the rivalry between Utaemon III and the Arashi family seems to have died down, and the former seems to have been dominant. The next noteworthy event is Utaemon's widely publicized retirement plan, which appears in the prints in 3.1825. One in particular, by Hokushū (Ikeda no. 280), shows him onstage giving an address to the audience on the subject. His address is couched in the normally florid style of these *kōjō* (stage speeches), but is perhaps more informative than they usually are. It starts off fairly directly with the announcement that this is an *isse ichidai* (retirement) speech. He goes on to say that owing to illness he had had (at some unspecified date) to absent himself from a Kyoto *kaomise*; that later in Edo, when he was doing his nine quick changes, he had injured his left leg; and that, owing to the lack of Western-style doctors there, he had not completely recovered. Recently he had had to rest again. Many enquiries about his health had come from the public, and his relatives were showing signs of anxiety, particularly saying that his absence was unfair to the public. He still lacked two or three years of fifty and had not thought to go yet, but, ill as he was, he had decided to retire. In Edo there was an actor named Seki Sanjūrō II, who had become his pupil with the name of Nakamura Utasuke. Utaemon planned to hand on to him the name of Utaemon III and to give the name Shikan to Nakamura Tsurusuke. He himself would return to the name Kagaya Ichibei and leave the stage, so that if people wanted to enquire about his health in future they should say, "How goes it, Ichibei?" His colleague Ichikawa Ebijūrō asked Utaemon with tears in his eyes why the great actor had not consulted him first. There might also be some who would think that if he retired he would be back again in two or three years, but he certainly would not reappear in Osaka. He had forty or more pupils and begged his audience to support them in the future and also to patronize him during the remainder of his retirement performances.

In this month appeared a great number of prints labeled *isse ichidai*. Some were retrospective, showing famous roles; some are fan-shaped, made to be cut out and stuck on a flat fan; some are circular, of a size to be stuck on a sake cup or used as a model to be painted on a cup. The Ikeda collection has some thirty of these retirement prints of Utaemon, and they are often of high quality.

By the eleventh month, however, he was back again on the boards, admittedly not in Osaka, as he had promised, but in Kyoto, and under his old name. He felt obliged to defend himself in a speech, which has survived on a print by Ashiyuki (Ikeda no. 307). In this he relates the circumstances of the farewell appearances at Osaka, but states that so fervent has been the support from Kyoto audiences in the past that he felt obliged to appear before them again, and he prayed that their support should continue. In 3.1826 he gave what seems to be his second appearance since his Osaka retirement, this time in Sakai just to the south of that city. On 9.7.1826 he was back again on the Osaka stage, and the famous print of him in the role of Ishikawa Goemon by Hokushū (Ikeda no. 353) dates from this performance. He was obviously in business again, and there seems to have been no more talk of Sanjūrō II's taking over his name. Tsurusuke took the name of Shikan II in 11.1825, and in 11.1826 we find the trio (Utaemon III, Shikan II, and Sanjūrō II) playing together at the Kado no Shibai, the first time that Sanjūrō had been there for nineteen years.

The End of a Career

Until his death in 7.1839, Utaemon III seems to have used several names. When he passed on the name of Shikan in 11.1826, he adopted Baigyoku as his *haimei* and often acted under this name. Shikan II was renamed Utaemon IV in 1.1836, although this does not seem to have prevented his predecessor from still using the name on occasion, but he was also known as Tamasuke I. Ichikawa Ebijūrō had died in a great flurry of memorial prints in 7.1827. A print by Hokuei that appeared in 10.1835 (Ikeda no. 630) on the occasion of a performance at the Naka no Shibai, in which Rikan II, Shikan II, Baigyoku I, and Sanjūrō II played, shows six actors' heads, and it is noticeable that Utaemon (Baigyoku) is depicted as lined with age. Rikan II died in 6.1837, to be followed in the next month by his old friend. There is a memorial print by Hasegawa Sadanobu (Ikeda no. 665) to Utaemon III (Tamasuke) on which appear Shikan III and Nakamura Tomijūrō II, and a memorial speech in which Tomijūrō relates the sadness he feels at his loss "like a dark night when one's candle has gone out." While Tomijūrō was in this tearful state, two or three supporters and patrons came round to see him and said that no amount of weeping would bring Utaemon back. So the whole company decided that they would play some favorite piece of Utaemon's, something they had learned from him, however much it would be a mere shadow of his own performance. They were comforted by the thought of the pleasure that they were sure he would take in watching it from the other world.

So finished the picturesque career of one of Japan's most remarkable actors, who, in a profession that needs much publicity, seems to have sought it with more determination than most others.

Bibliographical Note

In the preparation of this paper I have consulted *Amata (Kyota) Kyakushoku Jō* (see my introduction), *Kabuki Nenpyō* (*Kabuki* chronology) by Ihara Toshirō, vols. 5 and 6 (Tokyo: Iwanami Shoten, 1960-61), and *The Theatrical World of Osaka Prints*, by Keyes and Mizushima (Philadelphia: Philadelphia Museum of Art, 1973). I have also used actor prints that I was allowed to study at the Hankyū Ikeda Bunko library, Ikeda, Japan. I would not, however, have got very far without the help of Susumu Matsudaira, a professor of Konan Women's University in Kobe [later of Sonoda University, Kobe. Ed.], who introduced me to the Ikeda collection, photographed selected items, read through inscriptions for me, and provided me with copies of his invaluable catalogues.

6

Flowers of Edo: Eighteenth-Century *Kabuki* and Its Patrons

C. Andrew Gerstle

At Tokyo's Kokuritsu Gekijō (National Theatre), *kabuki* plays conceived and premiered during the eighteenth and nineteenth centuries are performed today, yet the audience's experience is radically different from that of the period before 1868. Patrons of *kabuki* in Edo in 1770 would not have felt at all comfortable in having their theatre so close to the seat of government (in view of the Diet and Imperial Palace and next to the Supreme Court), nor would they have enjoyed the quiet, almost solemn atmosphere or the ban on eating and drinking in their seats. In short, they would be bored to tears at the exalted Kokuritsu Gekijō with its posh furnishings. They would feel a bit more comfortable at the Kabuki-za perhaps or would have at the old Shinbashi Enbujō recently demolished. [It was thoroughly reconstructed from 1979–1981. Ed.] If they wanted to get closer to eighteenth-century *kabuki*, they would have to leave Tokyo altogether and travel to the Naka-za [The Naka-za—the Edo period's Naka no Shibai—is presently being reconstructed for non-*kabuki* presentations. The nearby Shōchiku-za has become the chief Osaka *kabuki* venue. Ed.] in Osaka's Dōtonbori district or the Minami-za in Kyoto during the *kaomise* (face-showing) performance in December. Still they would be bored by the stiffness of the audience and performance. They would not be part of the show. It would not be a festival.

For Edoites of the Tokugawa period (1603–1868), commoner and samurai *kabuki* was one of the pillars of social and cultural life, an ongoing festival. The scholar Gunji Masakatsu (1969) uses the term *kyōen* (banquet) to describe *kabuki* theatre, and the author Shikitei Sanba ([1806] 1973, 468)

has a character say, "If you don't like Ichikawa Danjūrō's rough-style acting, Toraya *yōkan* sweets, and *katōbushi* singing, you're not a true Edokko."
Kabuki's "festival" was something in which Edo's residents participated vigorously throughout the year, as the *kabuki* calendar was arranged in bimonthly
programs following the rhythms of city life. Each program opened to coincide with the celebration of a festival: New Year, Dolls' (third month), Boys'
(fifth month), All Souls' or Obon (seventh month), and Autumn (ninth month),
with the special *kaomise* performance in the eleventh month. Jacob Raz (1983)
and Barbara Thornbury (1982) give, respectively, descriptions of the liveli-
ness of audiences and the year-long schedule of programs. A *senryū* (comic
poem) attests to the heights of *kabuki*'s smashing popularity: "A big hit /
Finally / Corpses all carted away" (Gunji 1956, 160).[1] There is no doubt that
Edo was a lively and creative place to be; most likely the largest city in the
world, it had a range of entertainment facilities rivaling any city. *Kabuki,* at
the center of this urban culture, to a certain extent embraced all levels of
society from the *hinin* (outcasts), who were allowed to enter free, to *daimyō*
(grand lords), who entered through doors other than the small *nezumi* (rat)
door at the front, namely the direct passages from adjoining teahouses. Because famous actors' names were used to advertise products, their fame extended into nearly every Edo home on kimono patterns, hairstyles, candy,
and cakes.

Further, through actor prints and touring companies, *kabuki*'s radiance
even penetrated far into the rural areas. Yet patronage of the theatre was not
confined to the masses. Most Edo writers also were fascinated by this distinctive world of fantasy, and many actors, conversely, took part in literary
groups as amateur poets. Ichikawa Danjūrō V (1741–1806), with the pen
name Hakuen, is a famous actor well known for his literary activities and
relations with writers of this period. Popular demand for information on theatre life was insatiable. *Banzuke* (playbills), *yakusha hyōbanki* (critiques),
ukiyoe (woodblock actor prints), as well as a continuous array of books on, or
set in, the theatrical world flourished nearly all through the eighteenth and nineteenth centuries, increasing as time progressed. Depending on one's moral perspective, the theatre, for better or worse, radiated into all corners of Edo life.

Of course not everyone in Edo society fully appreciated the breadth or
depths to which *kabuki*'s radiance permeated. For the conservative top ech-
elon of the *bakufu* (feudal government), *kabuki* was an unpleasant evil tolerated but pushed as far away from city life as possible. The government's
attitude toward *kabuki* is generally well known because of the research of historians. In English, there is the work of Donald Shively in such articles as "*Bakufu
versus Kabuki*" (1968) [included in this book, chapter 3. Ed.], "The Social
Environment of Tokugawa Kabuki" (1978), and "Tokugawa Plays on For-

bidden Topics" (1982). Especially in the period before 1720, the *bakufu* was continually banning or restricting all aspects of *kabuki*. According to Shively, "the official attitude was that actors were a social group lower than merchants, and only a little above the pariah class" (1968, 260). This attitude remained official policy as seen by the fact that actors were continually, throughout the Tokugawa period, restricted in where they could live and legally administered as beggars. They were considered male prostitutes, and accordingly the theatre district was eventually put near the Yoshiwara pleasure quarter far from the center of Edo. This does not mean that men of education or position did not patronize actors, however. In fact, samurai interest in *kabuki*, particularly in the mid-eighteenth century until the Kansei Reforms in the 1790s, seems to have been more widespread than is usually claimed. Though we imagine samurai (especially the young) in their large wicker hats stealthily making their way to the Yoshiwara pleasure quarter, the general view is that samurai and intellectuals had little love for *kabuki*. Gunji Masakatsu (1956, 10) emphasizes, however, that the distinction, first created in the Meiji period (1868–1912), between the brothel and theatrical worlds did not exist in the Tokugawa period. Commoners as well as the *bakufu* viewed these two spheres of entertainment as two sides of the same coin. The following *senryū* from the Kansei period (1790s) jokingly puts them in perspective: "Yoshiwara / *Kabuki* / The back and front of dice" (Gunji 1956, 10). For city dwellers these two areas were the worlds of pleasure and fun, a forbidden sphere outside restrictive society, often termed *akusho* (evil places) or *chikushō* (Buddhist realm of beasts), while the popular term was *gokuraku* (paradise).[2] [See Takahashi and Lee's essays, chapters 8 and 20, for more on the *akusho* concept. Ed.]

These contradictory attitudes toward *kabuki,* one of moral and social disdain versus the other of fascination and adulation, are an intriguing phenomenon. At least some actors seem to have been clearly aware of their official station. The source *Chūko Kejōsetsu* (On theatre of the past; 1805) records that Ichikawa Danjūrō II (1689–1758) was visited by a famous shamisen player and had him eat from a separate fire, showing explicitly that Danjūrō considered himself to be of the outcast class (Gunji 1956, 69). This humble attitude of Edo actors did not continue into the latter half of the eighteenth century, however, when records show actors visiting *daimyō* residences. Nor, ironically, does this humility seem to have been meant for the samurai class, because the same Danjūrō II was the creator of many of the most famous *aragoto* (rough-style) pieces that are defiant toward the samurai (figure 6.1). Whatever the official *bakufu* attitude was toward actors, their popularity was enormous and continued to grow throughout the Tokugawa period. During the latter half of the eighteenth century this fascination for the world of Edo *kabuki* fully matures, encompassing all levels of society. The tension between official disdain and popular adoration was always felt more acutely by actors in the city of Edo, who lived under close samurai scrutiny, than by their counterparts in Kyoto or Osaka. Perhaps this may help to explain the distinctive Edo *aragoto* tradition with its bombastic and rebellious style. Playwrights were conscious of the sharp distinction in styles. The author of the 1801 *Sakusha Shihō Kezairoku* (Treasury of rules for playwrights) compares *kabuki* in the three cities: the *kokoro* (heart) of Kyoto *kabuki* is a "beautiful woman"; Osaka, a "dandy"; and Edo, a "samurai" (*Kinsei Geidō Ron* 1972, 511). *Aragoto*, the essence of Edo *kabuki*, as described by Danjūrō I, is recorded in the important book *Kokon Yakusha Rongo Sakigake* (Past and present actors' analects, advanced, 1772):

> When invited to a *daimyō*'s residence, after sake was served, I was asked to show them *aragoto*. Therefore, to the chanting of the *nō* play *Kagekiyo*, I stripped to my underclothes and violently smashed the *shōji* and *fusuma* (sliding doors) with my feet. Whereupon, the patrons asked what are you doing? When I replied that this is *aragoto*, the *daimyō* was delighted and rewarded me well. Even in front of *daimyō* you must never be afraid, or it won't be *aragoto*. (*Kinsei Geidō Ron* 1972, 480)

The essence of *aragoto* is defiance toward the samurai. The actor must consider his audience to be samurai. Though most today imagine such defiance to be symbolic or abstract, I shall show that, in fact, during the eighteenth century, samurai were more intimately involved in *kabuki* life than previously thought.

Kabuki fans in Edo regarded the actors as godlike hero figures, and Ichikawa Danjūrō—whoever bore the name—was the king of this world; he was *Edo no hana* (the flower of Edo). During January 1982, in an interview with Ichikawa Ebizō X, whose father was Danjūrō XI and who has since become Danjūrō XII, I asked him to elaborate on his ideas of the past and present "Danjūrō" image. One reason for asking this question is that, on viewing a Danjūrō-type piece in the Edo *kabuki* repertoire for the first time, a spectator may be totally baffled by the ritualistic formality, the lack of action, and the grandiose exaggerations of the hero. In the famous and annually performed play *Shibaraku* (Just a minute!), almost nothing happens. The stage is filled with an array of red-bodied thugs, evil-looking villains, conniving priests, innocent victims, and beautiful princesses. The background to the story is a complicated power struggle for control of a family treasure, but in the scene performed nothing happens except for the grand entrance of Gongorō in an oversized outfit with a gigantic sword. After yelling *"Shibaraku!"* ("Just a minute!") from offstage to halt the villains' actions,

Figure 6.1 **Ichikawa Danjūrō II as Gorō in** *Ya no Ne*. **(Photo: Ichikawa Danjūrō Family Collection.)**

he then enters along the *hanamichi* (audience runway). He stops midway and announces his name and lineage, along with an assortment of hyperbole and humorous references to contemporary happenings. This kind of soliloquy, called *tsurane*, is famous in traditional Edo *kabuki*. [See Saltzman-Li's essay on the *tsurane* convention in chapter 15. Ed.] The play on first view may seem absolutely bizarre. During the Edo period, however, this was a magic moment in theatre. The contemporary Danjūrō's view (and sources support it) is that Danjūrō was considered a deity for the Edo *chōnin* (townsman), a god whose fierce look—like that of the guardian god Fudō Myōo at a temple—could exorcise evil and cure sickness.[3] Danjūrō was a superhero above the samurai and even above the shogun himself: "In all the world there's Danjūrō / And a spring morn" that is, in this world of Edo only Danjūrō matters, not the shogun (Gunji 1956, 65). Evidence from Danjūrō's letters to temples and shrines shows that he considered his performance to be inspired by the powers of this god: "My fame as the founder of *kabuki* is not due to human effort" (*Kinsei Geidō Ron* 1972, 690). Gunji Masakatsu takes a step further and suggests that Danjūrō's *aragoto* performances were "not just theatrics, but prayers" (*Kinsei Geidō Ron* 972, 690). Various references indicate that the myth of Danjūrō's relationship with Fudō was significant in the eighteenth century. The 1774 *Yakusha Zensho* (All about actors) states:

> Danjūrō I prayed to the Fudō at Narita temple and was blessed with a son, who later became Danjūrō II. Because of the circumstances of his birth Danjūrō II had, from his childhood days, deep faith in Fudō Myōo. Eventually he excelled and became a famous actor. The sacred mirror he presented to the temple is said to be still there. . . . During his lifetime he performed the Fudō role many times, always with great success. No other actor could charm audiences as he did in moments of nonacting. It was surely the power of Fudō Myōo. His eyes looked exactly like Fudō, frightening; the pupils would remain fixed for an extraordinarily long time. He was certainly inspired by the spirit of the god. (*Yakusha Zensho* 1973, 6: 122)

The earlier *Kabuki Jishi* (Origins of *Kabuki*, 1762) records a similar story. Danjūrō II was having a difficult time keeping his eyelids from blinking during the Fudō Myōo stare. He went to the Narita temple and pledged to pray continuously for seventeen days. After completing his pledge, "his eyes had exactly the fierce look of a Fudō, and could stay fixed in a stare. He surely was possessed by the spirit" (*Yakusha Zensho,* 1973, 6: 124). In a play like *Shibaraku* or *Fudō* the audience went to see its favorite actor as superman, the guardian of Edo's citizens (figures 6.2, 6.3, 6.4).

The third element central to the myth of *aragoto*—acting along with defi-

Figure 6.2 **Ichikawa Danjūrō I as Soga Gorō uprooting a bamboo in a print by Torii Kiyomasa dated 1697. (Photo: Tokyo National Museum.)**

ance of the samurai class and religious devotion—is the playboy image. Danjūrō, as an outlaw hero, swaggers boldly with flair and brashness, perhaps comparable to the "rebels" of modern film or rock music. Like them, Danjūrō was the rugged ladies' man, the sex idol of Edo. A short, fictional work gives us an insight into the popular legend. The 1782 *kibyōshi* (illustrated satirical fiction) *Ichikawa Sanshōen* (Ichikawa Danjūrō) refers to an oracle at the Narita Fudō temple who proclaimed a miracle drug called Ichikawa sanshōen, namely Danjūrō. "Listen folks, drink this potion three times, and pass through

Figure 6.3 **In a painting by Torii Kiyomasa, Ichikawa Danjūrō I plays Gongorō no Kagemasa in *Shibaraku*. (Photo: Ricar Museum.)**

the Yoshiwara gate; no courtesan will ever turn away from you again" (Hino 1977, 57; Mori 1972, 283). In Edo, one's reputation among courtesans was the touchstone for male sexual prowess. Edoites saw Danjūrō (or other actors) in the popular play *Sukeroku* (a character's name) as a virile, sexual powerhouse loved by all the courtesans of the Yoshiwara pleasure quarter. In the entrance soliloquy of that play, the actor gives a confident, egotistical, humorous self-introduction that brashly glorifies his role as the savior of the

Figure 6.4 **Ichikawa Danjūrō IX portraying Fudō Myōō. (Photo: Narita Shinshōji Temple.)**

Edo townsmen who lived beneath the sword of approximately 500,000 resident samurai. Edoites took pride in the actor Danjūrō, their number one *"Edokko."* Sukeroku is an especially intriguing role. Though really Soga Gorō, a samurai of the twelfth century, he is on the surface the townsmen's townsman—standing up to a samurai. As the contemporary Danjūrō remarks, however, for most people today that magic is gone. There are no longer official distinctions between tycoons and outcasts (figure 6.5).

97

Figure 6.5 Ichikawa Danjūrō VIII as Sukeroku in an 1850 print by Utagawa Kuniyoshi. (Photo: Tsubouchi Memorial Theatre Museum, Waseda University.

As for the *onnagata* (female-role specialists), famous actors were greatly influential in ladies' fashion in coiffure, kimono design, walking style, and a general sense of "femininity," extending from commoner homes through samurai residences all the way to the shogun's castle. Segawa Kikunojō II (1741–1773), also known as Rokō, was a particularly popular eighteenth-century *onnagata*, and the name Rokō came to be used as a brand-name for various products. Another *senryū* poem expresses Kikunojō's popularity and the wealth it brought him: "One glance / A thousand gold pieces / Kikunojō on the *hanamichi*" (Gunji 1956, 66). Rokō's fame extended even to the nether world. In Hiraga Gennai's *Nenashigusa* (Floating weeds); Enma, lord of the underworld, becomes infatuated with the actor after seeing a print and demands that his subjects bring Rokō in the flesh ([1763] 1961, 46–48).[4] His name adorned incense, hair oil, tea, hair ornaments, and the like—indeed, an incident in Shikitei Sanba's *Ukiyoburo* (Bath in a floating world), where a young girl persuades her mother to color her kimono with *rokōcha* dye, suggests the extent of actor adulation (Shikitei [1809] 1957, 187).[5] Most famous *kabuki* actors' names of the period adorned products, and adoring fans were loyal to their favorite actor's wares. Another *senryū* attests to the competition: "Face powder too / Chrysanthemum (Kikugorō) versus Peony (Danjūrō) / Patrons argue" (Gunji 1956, 81). Of course, *bakufu* officialdom frowned at such fawning over actors. Ironically, even courtesans, who had been the models for the development of the *onnagata* style—the basic role being the *keisei* (courtesan)—in the formative period during the seventeenth century, were in the eighteenth century, rather, imitators of *kabuki* actors. They looked to males acting as women for the ultimate in the arts of femininity. It is still a strong tradition, in Kyoto at least, that geisha are expected to attend the December *kaomise kabuki* (figure 6.6).

For townsmen, and samurai as well, the theatre district, with its restaurants and teahouses, provided a venue, like Yoshiwara, of complete freedom from the strictures of an officially moralistic Confucian society. The content of much eighteenth-century Edo *kabuki*, particularly the *Kabuki Jūhachiban* (Eighteen famous *kabuki* plays), is superhuman; most of the characters, Sukeroku, Kagekiyo, Gongorō, and others, are brash outlaw-heroes who stand in defiance of the samurai class. Theatre was a fantasy world and delicious, often ridiculous, fun, to some extent because of the official disfavor it continually received.[6] Perhaps people today would call it escapist art; an Edoite would not have disagreed. To what extent was the Edo preference for this type of drama (including later gangster-hero plays) influenced by an atmosphere in which "outcast" *kabuki* actors played for a mostly commoner audience in a city dominated by samurai? Certainly an unusual setting.

It is still generally thought that *kabuki* performances were directed at the commoner population of Edo while the samurai class kept its distance

Figure 6.6 **The *onnagata* performer Segawa Kikunojō II as the *shirabyōshi* dancer in *Musume Dōjōji*. Illustration by Torii Kiyomitsu dated 1756. (Photo: Tsubouchi Memorial Theatre Museum, Waseda University.)**

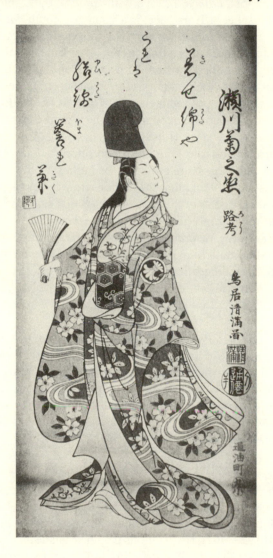

from the plebeian art. *Nō* drama was supposed to have been their theatre. Numerous references particularly, in the second half of the eighteenth century, clearly indicate, however, that these outcast *kabuki* performers had devoted fans, from low-level samurai retainers through high-ranking *bakufu* officials (*hatamoto*) to powerful *daimyō*.

Several works of fiction from the late eighteenth century make jest of the *daimyō* craze for *kabuki*. One, published in 1784, is *Kyōgen Zuki Yabo Daimyō* (literally, The boorish *daimyō* in love with *kabuki)*, by Kishida Tohō.[7] The character Umanosuke, or Horseface, is a young, uncouth *daimyō* whose retainers introduce him to *kabuki* for aesthetic training. Horseface is an impossible fool who follows all suggestions to the letter and has *kabuki* performed at his residence. After this exposure, he becomes so theatrical that he imagines his servant committing adultery with a salesman and accuses them in grand *kabuki* language. His retainers, worried that his histrionics may get out of hand, introduce him to the women of the pleasure quarter. They invite a group to his residence where Horseface has them put on a Soga *kabuki* play with himself in a leading role: courtesans and actors, a *daimyō*'s dream! This fictional work is a hearty satire aimed at the highest of the samurai class—especially robust considering that the author was a lowly picture framer.

From diaries and essays of the time we know that satire on *daimyōs*' love for *kabuki* was not simply idle fantasy. One *bakufu* official, Moriyama Takamori (1738–1815), records various current happenings, and in *Shizu no Odamaki* (Humble mutterings) he scornfully discusses eighteenth-century samurai love for imitating *kabuki* actors' speech and manners and putting on *kabuki* skits. Theatrical singing, *bungobushi* and *gidayū*, became popular during this time among samurai. He notes,

> The shamisen became extremely popular from 1740 to 1760. Eldest sons
> of good samurai families and even other sons all took lessons; from morn
> till night shamisen sounds were always to be heard. Eventually they began
> to perform other *kabuki* music and full dramas, and the like, and followed this
> depravity to the extent of performing amateur *kabuki* plays in residences.
> High *hatamoto* (banner men) officials mimicking riverbed beggars (actors),
> aping female impersonators and stage heroes! ([1802] 1929, 658)[8]

However, he adds: "But with the Kansei Reforms in the 1790s, all this ceased and society returned to normal."

In an earlier work, *Tōdai Edo Hyakkabutsu* (A hundred strange things in Edo), Baba Bunkō, also a *bakufu* official, discusses unusual characters in society ([1758] 1928, 402). He mentions that the Matsue *daimyō*, Matsudaira Munenobu (1729–1781), built a stage in his Edo residence for *kabuki* and invited merchants to see productions. He invited the actor Segawa Kikunojō II to perform and later, when he met Mizoguchi Naoatsu (1715–1780), the Shibata *daimyō*, he was thanked by Mizoguchi for being kind to his Kikunojō as if Kikunojō were a member of Mizoguchi's family. Mizoguchi thereafter acquired the nickname of "Foster Father." In *Nenashigusa*, Gennai expands this theme in satirical fiction, poking fun at samurai love for Kikunojō and other actors. Lord Enma can be seen as representing a *daimyō* or even the shogun. Consistent references in a variety of sources support a hypothesis that such activities were anything but uncommon. Ota Nanpo (1749–1823), a *bakufu* official, poet, critic, and fiction writer, records in *Hannichi Kanwa* (Idle chatter; 1927, 491) an incident in 1776 of a senior samurai official arranging seats on behalf of his *daimyō*'s wife for a *Sukeroku* performance at the Ichimura-za. Upon arriving, however, he discovers a mix-up: no seats are available. At that point, as an apology, the samurai commits *seppuku* (suicide) in the theatre teahouse. This all sounds rather fantastic, and Nanpo admits his doubts on the truth of the affair. True or not, we can be sure that *kabuki* was not completely alien to the warrior class in Edo (figure 6.7).

Our most authoritative source on this matter is a diary by a powerful *daimyō*, Yanagizawa Nobutoki (grandson of Yanagizawa Yoshiyasu). The piece is called *Enyū Nikki* (A banquet diary), compiled over the years 1773–1785 (and continued thereafter as *Shōkaku Nikki*).[9] This source, printed for the first time in 1977, confirms the fictional and other accounts of samurai interest in *kabuki* theatre. Nobutoki was such an avid fan that he kept a separate record of all performances attended. He describes in detail daylong excursions (with entourage) to the theatre district and speaks of collecting playbills and other materials from the theatrical world. His diary covers the years after retiring from active duty, but it is clear his interest did not emerge suddenly at the age of fifty.

Nobutoki was active in *haikai* poetry circles and other arts but was an extraordinarily devoted admirer of popular theatre. He patronized directly one actor only, Nakamura Nakazō I, but had indirect relations with other actors. His devotion to *kabuki* was zealous, his commitment perhaps unparalleled. He appears to have hired ladies-in-waiting according to their acting and dancing talents, and eventually he created a small *kabuki* troupe within his household (Koike 1980). Directed by Nobutoki and assisted by Nakazō, the women's troupe performed once or twice a year in a play written by the *daimyō* himself. He would take an old *ningyō jōruri* [puppet theatre. Ed.] play, rewrite it into *kabuki*, arrange cast and props, prepare playbills, and finally write his critique (*hyōbanki*) after the performance. For these shows he had a stage complete with *hanamichi* built within his residence. Certainly he was a fascinating *daimyō* who preferred the popular theatre of *kabuki* and *ningyō jōruri* over the austere *nō* and, as we have seen, was most likely not the only *daimyō* with such proclivities. The Kansei Reforms of the 1790s, however, suppressed this kind of open flirtation with the demimonde, and *daimyō* were obliged to pursue their theatrical pleasures more discreetly

Figure 6.7 **As both an actor and a poet, Ichikawa Danjūrō V, seen here in a print by Toyokuni I, was an important figure in Edo** *kabuki.* **(Photo: Tsubouchi Memorial Theatre Museum, Waseda University.)**

Nevertheless, *kabuki* was far more central to the life of all levels of Edo society than most historians admit.

Another substratum of Edo society for which *kabuki* was essential was the *gesaku* (popular fiction) writers and poets. For Utei Enba, Ota Nanpo, Hiraga Gennai, Santō Kyōden, and Shikitei Sanbato—to name but a few of the many samurai and commoner authors—*kabuki* was an important venue, particularly for the communal arts of *haikai* and *kyōka* (crazy poem) in which all the artists participated. *Kabuki* was not just a meeting place or common ground for them; actors often were poets who entered the writers' *bundan* (coterie) under poetic names. One actor, Ichikawa Danjūrō V (1741–1806), was a favorite among these writers and published *kyōka* with them under the name Hakuen. References from the writers themselves attest that Hakuen was friends with Nanpo, Enba, Kyōden, and others.[10] Hino Tatsuo has suggested that the *kyōka* world of fantasy was, for these writers, an imaginary utopia away from the restrictive society and that Hakuen stood as the pillar of this coterie (1977, 63–64). The fictional "Danjūrō" image was central to their fantasy world.

Along with this social contact with actors, fiction writers continually drew on the theatre for source material and inspiration to such an extent that a contemporary scholar of Edo fiction, Mizuno Minoru, complains about the theatrical world's grip on Edo fiction (1974, 59; also see Suwa, 1976, 187–193). *Gesaku* writers borrowed content and styles from *kabuki* and *ningyō jōruri* books, and certain writers—Kyōden and in particular Shikitei Sanba—seem to have kept their eyes on the theatre. Sanba wrote guidebooks on *kabuki* and used the *kabuki* audience as fictional settings for his works, which give us today a magnificent picture of *kabuki* audiences of the past. His *Kejō Suigen Maku no Soto* (Theatre on the other side of the curtain, 1806) shows the audience to be lively and riotous at times even causing performances to be halted briefly until calm could be restored. Popular fiction was part of the theatrical world. An awareness of this fact helps us to understand the context of Edo fiction, which has not been well received in the twentieth century in Japan.

For the common folk of Edo, popular theatre was a source of both festive entertainment and endless amateur activities. Shikitei Sanba's *Kakusha Hyōbanki* (A critique of audiences; 1811)[11] humorously delineates all types of lively fans—patrons, connoisseurs, actor worshipers, young ladies, loud-mouthed ruffians, boorish samurai, country folk, and tough old ladies. One of the most fascinating types is the actor mimic, who apes stage dress and actions all the time, even outside the theatre. These characters literally live an actor's life; art and life are reversed. Others specialize in mimicking monologues and spontaneously begin reciting during performances without care for those around them. This imitation of *kabuki* dialogue actually developed into a formal art, and practice texts for this *kowairo* hobby have survived. *Kabuki* fans today, as well, love to imitate the histrionic style of declamation, a style that certainly begs for mimicry (figure 6.8). [See Matsudaira's essay, chapter 7, on the activities of Osaka fans. Ed.]

Other amateur arts emerging from the theatre were *chaban* (skits), *zashiki kyōgen* (home *kabuki*), dance, and *gidayū* (puppet theatre) chanting. The first two arts were not formalized but were nevertheless very popular in Edo.

Figure 6.8 **A print by Toyokuni I illustrates the festive mood of *kabuki* patrons in the eighteenth century. (Photo: James R. Brandon; collection of the Museum of Fine Arts, Boston.)**

Chaban was the art of performing a *kabuki*-style skit when serving tea or food to a guest. In competitions, a theme would be given and the person had to improvise a skit. There are references to *chabanshi* (semiprofessional teachers), and numerous works of fiction contain episodes of *chaban* games.[12] *Zashiki kyōgen* was the more elaborate art of putting on *kabuki* plays in private residences. Evidence of the extent of the popularity of amateur productions is found in the 1774 book *Zashiki Kyōgen Haya Gatten* (The basic book of home *kabuki*), which explains the whole procedure and includes references to specialty shops in Edo for stage props and makeup. *Kabuki*-style dance became increasingly popular during the eighteenth century, when professional schools developed that still exist today. *Gidayū* chanting was a popular hobby for Edoites as well as Osaka city folk. Numerous records and fictional works attest to its popularity particularly among women.[13] In fact, female *gidayū* performers became such a craze that official edicts against public performances were issued frequently, but to no apparent avail. In Edo, *gidayū* puppet theatre flourished particularly from the 1770s, when Hiraga Gennai and others wrote new plays for Edo theatres, giving further impetus to amateur devotees.[14] Most *kabuki* singing styles (*tokiwazu, shinnaibushi, nagauta*) also matured and flourished from the mid-eighteenth century onward.

The fondness for things theatrical among the merchant class in Edo extended from the lowest clerk to the richest broker. In the records of crimes of male clerks in the huge Shirokiya department store, two reasons for theft stand out: the young men wish, first of all, to buy an expensive courtesan and, secondly, to spend a fortune on a lavish day of theatre.[15] Having both women and theatre, all their desires were satisfied. These young men were trying to imitate the eighteen grand-*tsū*—wealthy merchants who made an art of spending the money they had made as rice brokers and financiers for *hatamoto* samurai.[16] By the mid-eighteenth century, nearly all *hatamoto* were in debt to these *fudasashi* (official merchants and brokers) and were saved only by the cancellation of debts that came with the Kansei Reforms in the 1790s. All of these grand-*tsū* were *kabuki* fans and usually patrons of favorite actors. Some even had their own stages for private performances. Indeed, these imitators of *kabuki* became so successful in their attempts to emulate theatre life that Matsudaira Sadanobu, the architect of the reforms, called these wealthy men "*kabuki* actors" (Kitahara 1975). The Kansei Reforms, however, put an end to their overt extravagance.

Depending on one's viewpoint, theatre was either a source of depravity that corrupted the moral fiber of Confucian society or a source of life, imagination, fun, creativity—an escape from that same Confucian society. This tension, created by living directly under continuous official disfavor, certainly contributed to the rebellious tone of *kabuki* in Edo. Told that popular theatre was frivolous and immoral, eighteenth-century Edo actors and playwrights seem readily to have agreed (tongue in cheek), producing outlandish bombast with a vigor rarely matched in world theatre. What did it mean for actors in the mid- to late eighteenth century to find themselves the darlings of *daimyō* and intellectual society as well as idols in the popular mind? What did it mean to be idolized, to be taken seriously as artists, and, at the same time, officially to remain prostitutes of pleasure, wealthy but restricted to the outcast ghetto? Contact with sophisticated patrons surely affected their self-esteem as artists. This atmosphere, in which theatre thrived under such contradictory attitudes, must have affected the development of *kabuki* in Edo, which is strikingly different from that in Kyoto or Osaka. *Kabuki* was by and for the commoners of Edo, but actors could not, as they could in Kyoto and Osaka, ignore the samurai who were both their police and their patrons. Actors always had something before their eyes to react against, producing an irreverent flavor particular to Edo's popular culture. Further, *bakufu* policy toward *kabuki* fluctuated throughout this most crucial century—relaxed during Genroku (1690s to 1710s), strict during the Kyōhō Reforms (1720s to 1740s), relaxed during the Tanuma period (1750s to 1780s), and strict in the Kansei Reforms (1790s). With this history, Edo *kabuki* could hardly avoid being a bit twisted in its attitude toward the samurai class and its morality. Even with the overwhelming eighteenth-century influence of Osaka *ningyō jōruri* and *kabuki*, Edo *kabuki*, at its core, kept its "swaggering outlaw" image and amoral stance.

The role of the samurai class in Edo *kabuki's* development, therefore, should not be forgotten. In Danjūrō's words, *aragoto* is performed for *daimyō*: samurai were never out of sight for Edo actors. Though modern *kabuki*, clothed in artistic respectability, must suffer its fate of becoming representative of "national" culture, we must not forget its defiant past. *Aragoto* thrived on the tension implicit in the class structure of Edo society. I conclude with a comment by that great observer of Edo life, Shikitei Sanba, on the ambiguity of Edo *kabuki*'s position vis-à-vis its enemies and patrons:

> Theatre-lovers think theatre-haters fools.
> Theatre-haters think theatre-lovers fools.
> Theatre-lovers who think theatre is about morality are fools.
> Theatre-haters who think theatre has no morality are fools.
> Such fools know not that all morality is in theatre.
> Such fools know not that all theatre is in morality.
> Fools, fools, if you truly know morality
> and attend theatre,
> you'll realize theatre is morality.
> Ah! Theatre, thou art morality!

Sanba adds, however,

> This, too, is written by a fool,
> the chief priest of the Temple of Fun.[17]

Notes

1. See Nishihara Ryūu (1925) for *senryū* poems on *kabuki*.

2. There is a reference to the pleasure quarter as the "Western Paradise" (*saihō gokuraku*) in Ki no Kaion's play *Wankyū Sue no Matsuyama* (Wankyū and Mt. Matsuyama, 1708).

3. See Gunji (1969, chapter on *aragoto* style) and *Kabuki Jūhachiban Shū* (1965). See Watanabe (1975, 103–114) for information on the Narita Fudō. A verse by Kikaku, "Here inside / With Danjūrō / Demons driven outside" (quoted in *Yakusha Zensho* [1774] 1973, 218), expresses the popular image of Danjūrō as the protector.

4. In this work Gennai was parodying the fascination for actors of certain *daimyō*.

5. There are numerous references to Rokō fashion in fiction of the time. See *Yakusha Zensho* ([1774] 1973, 229–230) for a list of products with actors' names.

6. Eight of the eighteen plays are in *Kabuki Jūhachiban Shū*. There are translations of *Sukeroku*, *Kenuki*, and *Narukami* in Brandon (1975).

7. *Nenashigusa* (1763) by Hiraga Gennai has already been mentioned as a satire on *daimyō* love for *kabuki*. Satirical *kibyōshi* fiction has many examples of absurd characters imitating *kabuki*. Santō Kyōden's *Edo Umare Uwaki no Kabayaki* (1785) is a famous example; the fellow is a rich, young merchant.

8. Moriyama was a supporter of Sadanobu's reforms. In another work, *Ama no Yakimo Ki* ([1728] 1929, 706), Moriyama relates Sadanobu's attitude to the *kabuki*-like behavior and debauchery of samurai.

9. Printed in *Nihon Shomin Bunka Shiryō Shūsei* (1977, 13), *Shōkaku Nikki* was published in 1981; the text is a photocopy of the manuscript.

10. Hamada Giichirō (1942, 70–73) cites examples from Ota Nanpo's writing of his frequent contact with Ichikawa Danjūrō V. For Danjūrō I's relations with poets, see Ichikawa [1734–1747] 1972). [See also Laurence R. Kominz (1993). Ed.]

11. The text is in *Shomin Bunka Shiryō Shūsei* (1973, 6). See Jacob Raz (1980) for a summary of its contents.

12. Shikitei Sanba's *Chaban Kyōgen Haya Gatten* ([1824] 1915) gives all the basics of this amateur art.

13. *Jōruri Keiko Buri* (1777), by Saiza Sanjin, presents a picture of a woman giving *gidayū* lessons in Edo. The book attests to the increasing popularity of puppet theatre in Edo in the last thirty years of the eighteenth century.

14. Wakatsuki Yasuji (1943) outlines this development. See also Stanleigh H. Jones Jr. (1978).

15. Hayashi Reiko (1972,125–128) quotes from *Meikan Roku*, the Shirokiya store record of crimes by employees, to show the popularity of *gidayū* lessons and of *kabuki*.

16. There are numerous sources for the eighteen grand-*tsū* (*daitsū*), including *kibyōshi* and *sharebon* as well as nonfictional accounts. Their antics were extremely marketable products for book publishers. *Okuramae Baka Monogatari*, or *Jūhachi Daitsū*, by the popular dramatist and former *fudasashi* Mimasuya Nisōji (1784–1856), gives a history of these characters ([1846] 1928).

17. Shikitei ([1806] 1973, 478). He is perhaps echoing Hiraga Gennai's *Nenashigusa* ([1763] 1961, 61): "If you watch *kabuki* with a moral heart, then it becomes teachings or admonitions." He is also parodying a common style of exposition found in Buddhist sutras.

References

Adachi Yoshio. 1973. *Edo Senryū to Shomin Monshō Fūzoku* (Edo *senryū* and popular customs). Tokyo: Tōyōkan Shuppansha.

Baba Bunko. [1758] 1928. *Tōdai Edo Hyakkabutsu* (A hundred strange things in Edo). In *Nihon Zuihitsu Taisei* (Collection of Japanese essays), 2d series, vol. 1. Tokyo: Nihon Zuihitsu Taisei Kankōkai.

Brandon, James R. *Kabuki: Five Classic Plays.* Cambridge: Harvard University Press.

Chūko Kejōsetsu (On theatre of the past). [1805] 1907. In *Enseki Jisshu* (Enseki Collection). Tokyo: Kokusho Kankōkai.

Edo Chōnin no Kenkyū (Study of Edo townsmen). 1972. Edited by Nishiyama Matsunosuke. 4 vols. Tokyo: Yoshikawa Kōbunkan.

Edo Nanbyaku Nen (Three hundred years of Edo). 1975. Edited by Nishiyama Matsunosuke et al. 3 vols. Tokyo: Kōdansha.

Ema Tsutomu. [1921] 1976. "Kabukimono to Fukusō no Ryūko" (*Kabuki* actors and fashion). In *Ema Tsutomu Chosakushū* (Collected works of Ema Tsutomu), vol. 3. Tokyo: Chūo Kōronsha.

Gunji Masakatsu. 1956. *Kabuki to Yoshiwara* (*Kabuki* and Yoshiwara). Tokyo: Awaji Shobō.

———. 1969. *Kabuki: Yōshiki to Denshō* (*Kabuki*: Style and tradition). Tokyo: Kōdansha.

———. 1971. *Jishibai to Minzoku* (Country theatre and folk culture). Tokyo: Kōmeisha.

Haifū Yanagi Daru (Collection of comic poems) [1765] 1911. In *Kinsei Bungei Sōsho, Senryū* (Collection of literature: *Senryū*). 2 vols. Tokyo: Kokusho Kankōkai.

Hamada Giichirō. 1942. *Shokusanjin* (Ota Nanpo). Tokyo: Seigodō.

Hattori Yukio. 1970. *Kabuki no Kōzō* (Structure of *kabuki*). Tokyo: Chūo Kōronsha.

———. 1980. *Edo Kabuki Ron* (Study of Edo *kabuki*). Tokyo: Hōsei Daigaku Shuppankyoku.

Hayashi Reiko. 1972. "Edo Tana no Seikatsu" (Life of the Edo merchant). In *Edo chōnin no kenkyū* (Study of the Edo townsman), vol. 2. Tokyo: Yoshikawa Kōbunkan.

Hino Tatsuo. 1977. *Edojin to Yūtopia* (Edoites and utopia). Tokyo: Asahi Shinbunsha.

Hiraga Gennai. [1763] 1961. *Nenashigusa* (Floating weeds). In *Fūraisanjinshū* (Collection of works of *Fūraisanjin*). *Nihon Koten Bungaku Taikei* (Collection of classical Japanese literature), vol. 55. Tokyo: Iwanami Shoten.

———. [1789?] 1981. *Inaka Shibai* (Country theatre). In *Sharebon Taisei* (Collection of *Sharebon*) vol. 13. Tokyo: Chūo Kōronsha.

Hōseidō Kisanji. [1791] 1971. *Ukan Sandai Zue* (Edo's three theatres: Illustrated). Ed. Hattori Yukio. Tokyo: Kokuritsu Gekijō.

Ichikawa Danjūrō. [1734–1747] 1972. *Oi no Tanoshimi Shō* (The joys of old age). In *Kinsei Geidō Ron* (Collection of Edo-period art treatises). Ed. Nishiyama Matsunosuke. Tokyo: Iwanami Shoten.

Jones, Stanleigh, Jr. 1978. "Miracle at Yaguchi Ferry: A Japanese Puppet Play and Its Metamorphosis to *Kabuki*." *Harvard Journal of Asiatic Studies* 38, no. 1 (June): 171–224. [Included in the present volume; see chapter 17. Ed.]

Kabuki Hyōbanki Shūsei (Collection of *kabuki* critiques). 1972. 11 vols. Tokyo: Iwanami Shoten.

Kabuki Jishi (Origins of *kabuki*). [1762] 1973. In *Nihon Shomin Bunka Shiryō Shūsei* (Collection of sources on Japanese popular culture), vol. 6. Tokyo: San'ichi Shobō.

Kabuki Jūhachiban Shū (Collection of eighteen famous *Kabuki* plays). 1965. In *Nihon Koten Bungaku Taikei* (Collection of classical Japanese literature), no. 98. Ed. Gunji Masakatsu. Tokyo: Iwanami Shoten.

Kabuki Nenpyō (Chronology of *Kabuki*). 1956. Ed. Ihara Toshirō. 8 vols. Tokyo: Iwanami Shoten.

Kinsei Fūzoku Jiten (Dictionary of Tokugawa-period customs) 1967. Ed. Ema Tsutomu et al. Tokyo: Jinbutsu Ōraisha.

Kinsei Geidō Ron (Collection of Edo-period art treatises). 1972. Ed. Nishiyama Matsunosuke. Tokyo: Iwanami Shoten.

Kishida Tohō. [1784] 1926. *Kyōgen Zuki Yabo Daimyō* (The boorish *daimyō* in love with *kabuki*). In *Kibyōshi Nijūshū* (Collection of twenty *kibyōshi*). Tokyo: Nihon Meicho Zenshū Kankōkai.

Kitahara Susumu. 1975. "Fudasashi to Daitsūjin" (Fudasashi and great-*tsū*). In *Edo Sanbyakunen* (Three hundred years of Edo), vol. 2. Tokyo: Kōdansha.

Koikawa Harumachi. [1778] 1901. *Sanpuku Tsui Murasaki Soga* (The Soga brothers and Edo *kabuki*). In *Kibyōshi Hyakushū* (One hundred *kibyōshi*). Tokyo: Hakubunkan.

Koike Shōtarō. 1980. "*Daimyō* Nikki ga Egaku aru Edo Joyū" (An Edo actress as portrayed in a *daimyō*'s diary). *Rekishi to Jinbutsu* (History and individuals) vol.10, no. 11: 214–218.

Kokon Yakusha Rongo Sakigake (Past and present actors' analects—advanced). [1772] 1972. In *Kinsei Geidō Ron* (Collection of Edo-period art treatises). Ed. Nishiyama Matsunosuke. Tokyo: Iwanami Shoten.

Kominz, Laurence R. 1993. "Ichikawa Danjūrō V and *Kabuki*'s Golden Age." In *The Floating World Revisited*. Ed. Donald Jenkins, with Lynn Jacobson Katsumoto. Honolulu: Portland Art Museum and University of Hawai'i Press. Ed.]

Mimasuya Nisōji. [1846] 1928. *Okuramae Baka Monogatari* (Tale of Kuramae fools). In *Nihon Zuihitsu Taisei* (Collection of Japanese essays), 2d series, vol. 6. Tokyo: Nihon Zuihitsu Taisei Kankōkai.

Minami Kazuo. 1980. *Edokko no Sekai* (World of Edoites) Tokyo: Kōdansha.

Mizuno Minoru. 1974. *Edo Shōsetsu Ron* (Essays on Edo fiction). Tokyo: Chūo Kōronsha.

Mori Senzō. 1972. *Kibyōshi Kaidai* (Guide to *kibyōshi*). Tokyo: Chūo Kōronsha.

Moriyama Takamori. [1798] 1929. *Ama no Yakimo Ki* (Tale of fishermen burning seaweed). In *Nihon Zuihitsu Taisei* (Collection of Japanese essays), 2d series, vol. 11. Tokyo: Nihon Zuihitsu Taisei Kankōkai.

———. [1802] 1929. *Shizu no Odamaki* (Humble mutterings). In *Nihon Zuihitsu Taisei* (Collection of Japanese essays), 3d series, vol. 2. Tokyo: Nihon Zuihitsu Taisei Kankōkai.

Nihon Shomin Bunka Shiryō Shūsei (Collection of sources on Japanese popular culture). 1973. Vol. 6: *Kabuki*. Tokyo: San'ichi Shobō.

Nishihara Ryūu. 1925. *Senryū Edo Kabuki* (Edo *kabuki* and *senryū*). Tokyo: Shun'yodo.

Ota Nanpo. 1927. *Hannichi Kanwa* (Idle chatter). In *Nihon Zuihitsu Taisei* (Collection of Japanese essays), 1st series, vol. 4. Tokyo: Nihon Zuihitsu Taisei Kankōkai.

Raz, Jacob. 1980. "The Audience Evaluated: Shikitei Sanba's *Kakusha Hyōbanki.*" *Monumenta Nipponica* 35 (summer): 199–221.

———. 1983. *Audience and Actors*. Leiden: E.J. Brill.

Saiza Sanjin. [1777] 1980. *Jōruri Keiko Buri* (*Jōruri* lessons). In *Sharebon Taisei* (Collection of *sharebon*), vol. 7. Tokyo: Chūo Kōronsha.

Sakusha Shihō Kezairoku (Treasury of rules for playwrights). [1801] 1972. In *Kinsei Geidō Ron* (Collection of Edo-period art treatises), ed. Nishiyama Matsunosuke. Tokyo: Iwanami Shoten.

Santō Kyōden. [1785] 1958. *Edo Umare Uwaki no Kabayaki* (Broiled eels Edo-born dandy). In *Kibyōshi, Sharebon Shū* (Collection of *kibyōshi* and *sharebon*). *Nihon Koten Bungaku Taikei* (Collection of classical Japanese literature), vol. 59. Tokyo: Iwanami Shoten.

Santō Kyōzan. [1806] 1928. *Kumo no Ito Maki* (The spider's web). In *Nihon Zuihitsu Taisei* (Collection of Japanese essays), 2d series, vol. 4. Tokyo: Nihon Zuihitsu Taikei Kankōkai.

Seji Kenmon Roku (Record of current happenings). [1816] 1969. In *Nihon Shomin Seikatsu Shiryō Shū* (Collection of sources on Japanese life), vol. 8. Tokyo: San'ichi Shobō.

Shikitei Sanba. [1803] 1969. *Shibai Kinmo Zue* (Illustrated guide to the theatre). Tokyo: Kokuritsu Gekijō.

———. [1806] 1973. *Kejō Suigen Maku no Soto* (Theatre on the other side of the curtain). In *Nihon Shomin Bunka Shiryō Shūsei* (Collection of sources on Japanese popular culture), vol. 6. Tokyo: San'ichi Shobō.

———. [1809] 1957. *Ukiyoburo* (Bath in a floating world). *Nihon Koten Bungaku Taikei* (Collection of classical Japanese literature), no. 63. Tokyo: Iwanami Shoten.

———. [1811] 1973. *Kakusha Hyōbanki* (A critique of audiences). In *Nihon Shomin Bunka Shiryō Shūsei* (Collection of sources on Japanese popular culture), vol. 6. Tokyo: San'ichi Shobō.

———. [1811] 1901. *Kyōgen Inaka Ayatsuri* (Country puppet theatre). In *Kibyōshi Hyakushū* (One hundred *kibyōshi*). Tokyo: Hakubunkan.

———. [1814] 1901. *Shiroto Kyōgen Monkirigata* (Amateur theatre types). In *Kibyōshi Hyakushū* (One hundred *kibyōshi*). Tokyo: Hakubunkan.

———. [1824] 1915. *Chaban Kyōgen Haya Gatten* (All about *chaban* skits). In *Zatsugei Sōsho* (Sources on miscellaneous arts). Tokyo: Kokusho Kankōkai.

Shively, Donald. 1968. "*Bakufu* Versus *Kabuki.*" In *Studies in the Institutional History of Early Modern Japan*, ed. J.W. Hall and M.B. Jansen. Princeton: Princeton University Press.

———. 1978. "The Social Environment of Tokugawa Kabuki." In *Studies in* Kabuki, ed. J.R. Brandon, W. Malm, and D. Shively. Honolulu: University of Hawai'i Press.

———. 1982. "Tokugawa Plays on Forbidden Topics." In *"Chūshingura": Studies in Kabuki and the Puppet Theatre*, ed. James R. Brandon. Honolulu: University of Hawai'i Press.

Shōkado Hajō. [1771] 1974. *Shibai Nenjū Gyōji* (The theatre year calendar). In *Kyōgen Sakusha Shiryō Shū*. (Sources on *kabuki* playwrights). Tokyo: Kokuritsu Gekijō.

Suwa Haruo. 1976. *Edo: Sono Geinō to Bungaku* (Edo: Its theatre and literature). Tokyo: Mainichi Shinbunsha.

————. 1980. *Edokko no Bigaku* (Aesthetics of Edoites). Tokyo: Nihon Shoseki.
Terakadō Seiken. [1832] 1974. *Edo Hanjōki* (Splendors of Edo). 3 vols. Tokyo: Tōyō Bunko.
Thornbury, Barbara E. 1982. *Sukeroku's Double Identity: A Study in Kabuki Dramatic Structure*. Michigan Papers in Japanese Studies, no. 6. Ann Arbor: University of Michigan.
Wakatsuki Yasuji. 1943. *Ningyō Jōrurishi no Kenkyū* (A history of *Jōruri* puppet theatre). Tokyo: Sakurai Shoten.
Watanabe Shōkō. 1975. *Fudō Myōo*. Tokyo: Asahi Shinbunsha.
Yakusha Zensho (All about actors). [1774] 1973. In *Nihon Shomin Bunka Shiryō Shūsei* (Collection of sources on Japanese popular culture), vol. 13. Tokyo: San'ichi Shobō.
Yanagizawa Nobutoki. 1977. *Enyū Nikki* (A banquet diary). In *Nihon Shomin Bunka Shiryō Shūsei* (Collection of sources on Japanese popular culture), vol. 13. Tokyo: San'ichi Shobō.
————. 1981 *Shōkaku Nikki* (Shōkaku diary). 7 vols. Tokyo: Yumani Shobō.
Zashiki Kyōgen Haya Gatten (The basic book of home *kabuki*). [1774] 1915. *Zatsugei Sōsho* (Sources on miscellaneous arts). Tokyo: Kokusho Kankōkai.
Zuihitsu Jiten (Guide to Japanese essays). 1960. Edited by Shibata Shōkyoku et al. 5 vols. Tokyo: Tōkyōdō.

7

Hiiki Renchū (Theatre Fan Clubs) in Osaka in the Early Nineteenth Century

Susumu Matsudaira

Hiiki is the word commonly used for support given to a *kabuki* actor, or for the supporter or fan himself. It can be applied to other sorts of fans, such as one who follows a particular sumo wrestler. The derivation of the word is not certain, but it is generally taken as a lengthened form of *hiki*, with a meaning of "pulling" or "pulling together." The clubs themselves were known as *hiiki renchū*, the last element having the alternative pronunciation *renjū*. Throughout this paper, "*hiiki*," "supporter," and "fan" have been used interchangeably with the same meaning.

Kabuki has attracted many supporters from its earliest days until the present. In the Tokugawa period, especially in the eighteenth and nineteenth centuries, there were many such clubs in the three large cities of Kyoto, Osaka, and Edo, but those in Osaka had a long unbroken history and unique customs. They were the most remarkable examples of theatre fan clubs in the whole of Tokugawa Japan.

Gekijō Ichiran (The survey of the theatre, 1795) has the following passage:

> In the three cities, there are many fan clubs, and those of Osaka have a particularly long tradition. At *kaomise* (first performances of the season, in the eleventh month) they give presents to the actors. The eaves of the theatre teahouses are decorated with lanterns that bear the crests of the fan clubs. As the actors are introduced, the fans sing and perform extraordi-

nary and intricate clapping, to the astonishment of the audience. There is nothing that can be compared to them.

This description applies to Osaka, but much the same can be said for Kyoto.

In Osaka there were four main fan clubs, and their origins are set out in the work *Setsuyō Kikan* (The wonder of Osaka, 1833) by Hamamatsu Utakuni, as follows:

Name	Date	Founder
Sasa-se	1720	*Sasa*ya Kohei and *Se*tomonoya Denbei
Ōte	1770	Kawachiya Magobei and Yamatoya Hachirōbei living in *Ōte* street
Fuji-ishi	1770	*Fuji*wara (given name unknown), a timber merchant, and *Ishi*mura (same), a seller of shamisen
Sakura	1775	Fujiya Kisuke, living in Senba Midō

Another work, *Shibai Gakuya Zue* (Illustrated guide to theatre green rooms, vol.1, 1800, and vol. II, 1802), by Shōkōsai Hanbei, gives us much information about fan clubs, including the number of members of the six largest clubs out of a multitudinous list: Sasase, 25; Ōte, 41; Fujiishi, 37; Sakura, 21 (total of these four = 124); Zakoba, 23; Kōbai, 24. But the figures given in *Gekijō Ichiran* (1795) are: Sasase, 33; Ōte, 20; Fujiishi, 13; Sakura, 15 (total, 81). The increase of total membership probably indicates a general increase of enthusiasm for the theatre. Other club names that are known are Kanō-gumi, Shōnichi-kō, and Utsubo, and in Kyoto, Sasaki and Ōzasa. As we have seen, *Shibai Gakuya Zue* says that the clubs were multitudinous. Nevertheless, it is only about the four main clubs that we have detailed information, and they were known as the four great theatre clubs, or *teuchi-renchū* (clapping groups).

This *teuchi* was performed to celebrate the introduction of new actors at *kaomise*. It is thought that this sort of clapping started in Edo at the time of Danjūrō I (1660–1704), and the Edo style of clapping probably remained quite simple, but the Osaka style developed into something very different. *Kyōjitsu Satonamari* (The dialect of a gay quarter, 1794) states: "The *teuchi* group is a noted thing in Osaka, and its members are the leaders of the *suijin*." This term, which corresponds to *tsūjin* [or simply *tsū*; see Gerstle's essay, chapter 6. Ed.] in Edo, refers to those rich persons who enjoy frequenting the gay quarters and theatres, and admire actors, sumo wrestlers, courtesans, and the like.

Each club had its own unique tradition and was extremely proud of its own rules and customs. Naturally, each club kept tight control over admissions and resignations, by various regulations. In *Kinsei Fūzokushi* (Record of manners in the Edo period, 1853, by Kitagawa Morisada), we read:

> The members of the clapping clubs are the sons of wealthy citizens. All the year round they have to spend a great deal of money; so poor men cannot afford to join. Candidates must swear an oath to those who are already members, to obey the rules of the club even if disowned by their fathers. The clubs are extremely extravagant things. They are extraordinary institutions only to be found in Osaka and Kyoto, and such a thing does not exist in Edo.

What sort of things did they do? In brief, they joined in the various theatrical events that accompanied *kaomise*. At the beginning of the tenth month, *kabuki* theatres raised *maneki kanban* (preliminary notice-cards), and around the twentieth of the month the *kaomise banzuke* (list of new actors) was published. Exercise in clapping in each group had started by this time at specific teahouses in the Dōtonbori, which is still the theatre street of Osaka. In the meantime, officials of the theatre, such as *zamoto* (producers), *ginshu* (investors), and *omote-kata* (in charge of audience matters), went round the town (*machi-mawari*) visited the big fan clubs and Zakoba (fishmongers' association) [a major fan base. Ed.] to pay their respects and offer them gifts. At the end of the month the new actors arrived in Dōtonbori by boat, and people gathered along the banks and the bridges of the canal to welcome them. This event was known as *norikomi* (riding in). Sometimes club members fitted out *omukai-bune* (welcoming boats) and rowed out to meet actors. For example, in 1815, Utaemon III, the most famous name in Osaka *kabuki* at the time, came back from Edo after an absence of some years [see Dunn's essay, chapter 5. Ed.], and the scene of the arrival of his boat and the welcoming throng was said to be more magnificent than the Tenjin Festival itself, the greatest festival in Osaka. More than ten boats, including the Sakura-maru, Sasase-maru, and Ōte-maru, named after the fan clubs that were on board, sailed together with Utaemon's craft and resounded to the joyous clapping (*Yakusha Nazokake Ron* [Riddles on actors], 1816).

In the evening of the *norikomi* day, there was a banquet on the theatre stage. It was called *ōban-nari* (*ōban* shape) because the seated participants formed a shape like that of the *ōban*, the largest gold coin. The *zamoto*, the actors, and the club members all took part in the banquet. In the early part of the eleventh month, the *kaomise* took place. The most important element in this was the *zatsuki hikiawase* (introduction of the new members of the company). In the evening the actors donned their costumes and assembled in the green room. All the lanterns and candles in the theatre were lit simultaneously.

The members of the clapping group sat in the front row. The costume that they wore was very characteristic. *Setsuyō Kikan* says:

> Years ago, clapping groups wore simple costumes such as a black cotton kimono with a white silk sash, and a headgear (*zukin*) slightly embroidered with golden thread, bearing the scarlet crest of the club. Even so, the audiences of that time were astonished.

In this passage "Years ago" means, I think, the 1750s. Later on the club costume became magnificent and elaborate. According to *Kinsei Fūzokushi*, the costume employed the technique of *hikinuki*, that is, by the pulling out of threads sections of the costume could be removed instantaneously. [*Hikinuki* is one of *kabuki*'s best-known onstage instant costume change techniques. Ed.] The club members sat in the front row facing the actors and displayed dazzling costume changes by this technique.

Zatsuki hikiawase introduced the newly engaged actors to the audience and public of the town and celebrated their arrival. The fan club would put on the *zukin* with the club crest, and, as each actor's name was called and he appeared on the stage, they would strike together their *hyōshigi* (wooden clappers) and shout out "*Arya, arya.*" Formerly they had clapped their hands, but by this time *hyōshigi* made of wood (red sandalwood or ebony was used.) [*hyōshigi* (or *ki*) are the clappers used for various effects in kabuki performance. Ed.] were used. The rhythm of the clapping was extremely complicated and difficult to learn, and naturally there were good clappers and bad ones.

After the clapping, various gifts from the fan club to each actor were piled on the stage. The list of the gifts was read out loudly by one of the fans, from the *hanamichi* (runway). Since the late 1780s freshly composed songs had accompanied the clapping, and musical instruments such as the shamisen were played. Sometimes club members showed off their skills in performances of one sort or another, and superb set pieces or other ornamentations were lifted upon the stage. It can be said that the *zatsuki hikiawase* was already a sort of performing art in its own right.

The Edo actor Nakamura Nakazō III (1809–1886) wrote a diary, *Temae Miso* (Self-praise). He visited Osaka and Kyoto [It was begun in 1855 and published serially from 1885 to 1888. Ed.] and left a description of the *kaomise*. He reacted with astonishment to the scene at the Kyoto theatre when the *hiiki renchū* stalked proudly along the *hanamichi* and took their seats in the front rows. The members of Ōzasa and Sasaki, wearing gaudy costumes and *zukin,* walked deliberately on the *hanamichi* as if to say, "Look at me from now on!" Needless to say, the ritual of *teuchi* was a great honor for the actors, but at the same time it was something of a trial for them. The length and complication of clapping and singing were decided by the popularity and quality of the actors. So this was an elaborate but at the same time crude competition for popularity.

After the *teuchi* there came a special *kaomise* play that was a sort of light farce with dancing. The whole program was over by about six o'clock in the morning.

The fan clubs took charge of the decorations in and around the theatre auditorium. The stage curtain, which was renewed every year, was always presented to the two large Osaka theatres, Naka no Shibai and Kado no Shibai, for the opening of the New Year's performance. The hangings for the upper boxes were presented by the four main clubs, and the Kōkai group provided the lanterns for the pillars of these boxes. The fishmongers furnished awnings for the *yagura* (the turret erected over the entrance to the theatre), the small curtain at the entrance to the part of the stage then still called *hashigakari* [the passageway at stage right, which gradually expanded toward the audience until it was indistinguishable from the stage proper. Ed.], since it was a relic of the *nō* theatre, and the famous great lanterns that hung over the front entrance to the theatre. The rice-merchant group (Dōjima Ōrenchū) gave the hangings for the stage at the *zatsuki hikiawase*. On these hangings and lanterns were inscribed the name and crest of each actor. In front of the theatre, there arose piles of gifts, such as bales of charcoal and rice.

In front of the theatre teahouses (*shibaijaya*) were hung lanterns with the crests of the Ōte, Sasase, Fujiishi, and Sakura groups. Illustrations of all these traditional scenes are to be found in *Shibai Gakuya Zue*. The close concern of the fan clubs with the theatre had the inevitable result that it came to be more or less completely under their control.

Their members were sufficient for them sometimes to be able to interrupt an actor's performance. An anecdote is related about Nakajima Kunishirō, an Edo actor who came to Osaka and was abused by some of the *teuchi* people because of his Edo accent. This treatment of him continued for a few days, and Kunishirō, unable to perform, was at a loss to know how to extricate himself from the situation. At last, one night, he went to a well and poured water over himself while he prayed to Nichiren. Next day he went on the stage with a short sword concealed in his bosom. The abuse started as before, so he went to the front of the stage, and, stripping his arms for action, addressed the audience thus:

> I am an actor and so do not object to having my technique criticized, but abuse for my Edo accent I cannot accept. Do you insult the Governor of Osaka, who is sent here from Edo? You abuse not only me but also the people of Edo, and I can no longer be patient. Come up here. I will accept your challenge.

In spite of the strength of their earlier insults, there were none to answer this and silence fell. Then some important Osaka inhabitants and senior members of *teuchi* groups intervened, saying: "What Kunishirō has said is quite right. He is a very worthy man. I beg both sides in this dispute to calm down, for the sake of our honor." From then on Kunishirō was said to be a real man, and he acquired many fans of his own. On the next day piles of gifts for him began to form, even though he was really not a very good actor.

Up to now we have mainly seen the public side of the *hiiki* groups, but of course they were made up of individuals. The only source of information that I know for the identification of these is *Hiiki no Hanamichi* (Fandom's runway) (1815), a two-volume book of criticism of the *hiiki* of Nakamura Utaemon III, compiled by Hamamatsu Utakuni. Utaemon III has already been mentioned as a great *kabuki* star of the first half of the nineteenth century (also commonly referred to in the literature, and in this paper, as Nakamura Shikan I) who naturally attracted a great number of fans.

The style of the book is an imitation of that of *yakusha hyōbanki* (criticisms of actors), and it ranks the fans according to their enthusiasm for Shikan. This is perhaps the place to mention that fans were known by a name special to their *hiiki* activities, without use of their family names. The names mentioned in this paper are taken mainly from the sources mentioned, often without further identification.

The top position in the ranking was occupied by Nishimura of Dōjima, the second was Bokuri of Honmachi Bridge, and the third Hyakki of Nayachō. Other highly ranked men bore the names Umeoka, Kiyū, Baiki, Rishō, Sashi, Kyūro, Bukichi, Nigo, Haryū, Kochū, Masujin, Shibahei, Madoka, and Sumiji. There were also some women fans, such as Kano of Shimanouchi, Koito of Tenshō, Tatsu of Tsuruiya, and Kane of Orizuruya.

Similar information is to be obtained from a *mitate-banzuke* (imitation program, in this case, in imitation of a sumo ranking list), published in the same year. This compares the *hiiki* of the two top *kabuki* actors, their names being the aforementioned Utaemon III and Arashi Rikan I. One can see most of the highly ranked names that are found in *Hiiki no Hanamichi* in the rows of this *banzuke*, which would seem to indicate that the listings are objective.

The fans named in these documents are difficult to identify but there is some information about them in *Hiiki no Hanamichi*. Hyakki was the other name of Kazari'ya Jirōbei. The first element, Kazariya, indicates that he was the proprietor of a metal ornament shop or studio, probably both. At the same time he must have been a dilettante author, for he wrote *Shikan-Koku Ichiran* (A glance at the Shikan country; Shikan being Utaemon III's poet name [*haimei* or *haimyō*]). Nishimuraya must have been Nishimura Kiemon from Dōjima, a wealthy rice merchant. Hakujaku, mentioned in the *banzuke*, was also a rice merchant. Madoka probably owned a charcoal shop, and other businesses represented are a cake shop, restaurant, fish shop, tobacconist, *sushi* restaurant, and pharmacy. Shōhō was a well-known teacher of flower arrangement. The names on the *banzuke* include three actor-print artists, Ashikuni, Shunkō, and Shun'yō. The prints that they produced about this time survive in considerable numbers. The three are reported as having been amateur artists, but, regrettably, their profession is not recorded.

These representative individual *hiiki* belonged each to a certain group. For example, Juraku and Kyūro were members of the Ōte group and were called "masters of clapping." They had learned the art from one Tōsangen who was famed as a great master. Bokuri and Hayashima were named as "*Sewayaku* (senior consultants) of Ōte." Rojū belonged to Sasase and was said to be an "expert at clapping." Sento and Itchō are named as "current representatives of Sasase." Nigo and Haryū are members of the Zakoba group.

Hiiki no Hanamichi also has some information about a Shikan-kō group, which was, of course, exclusively devoted to Utaemon III. The group's members included Nishimuraya, Harumi, Shimakan, and others, and they had a monthly meeting at the Kawasaku teahouse on Dōtonbori, which was the residence of an Utaemon fan.

However, if one belonged to one of the principal large clubs, one had to join in corporate activities such as *teuchi*, and if one was a clapping leader one could not clap only for the actor of one's particular choice. Club representatives had to act not in support of a particular actor but for the whole of the Osaka theatre. *Hiiki no Hanamichi* has the following dialogue about Hayashima, a senior member of the Ōte group:

> A. Because he does not show partiality for an individual actor, sometimes he does not seem to be exclusively an Utaemon III fan. However, I think that he does not forget his duty to his club.
> B. If he did not belong to a club, he would be a very strong Utaemon fan.

Naturally, for ordinary members, the fan club was an exclusive group. It was thought to be against the rules to support two actors at the same time or visit the dressing room of an actor other than the one for which one was a fan. Such behavior was despised as a double-cross. As in the samurai code, the loyalty that demanded that one should not serve two masters was insisted on by club members and the actor himself. Ikka from Imabashi was suspected of duplicity when he produced a *surimono* [a type of engraving. Ed.] with a design of *tachibana* (wild orange) that formed the crest of Arashi Kichisaburō II [later Arashi Rikan I. Ed.], Utaemon III's great rival.

The ranking of the female fan Kane Ōrizuruya is designated as "not specified, for certain reasons" and the critical dialogue reads:

A. One cannot name her as an Utaemon fan, because she changed her support to that of Tanosuke.

B. I am aware of this report, so have given her ranking as "not specified."

A. Not merely a report. Even Utaemon himself saw it.

Sawamura Tanosuke I (1788–1817) was at the time at the top of the actors of young women's roles and was himself young and beautiful. Anyone who sees his portrait in an actor print can understand Kane's inconstancy. She was forgiven only on the condition that she begged pardon to the portrait of Utaemon III on a hanging scroll in her possession.

Another fan mentioned, Shibahei (alternate reading, "Shihei"), was formerly named Heishi, *shi* being written with the same character (*shiba*, as in *shibai*) as the first one in the name Shikan. Once he became a fan of Utaemon (= Shikan), he refrained from putting this character at the end (that is, the lower position when written vertically) of his name, so he renamed himself Shihei (Shibahei). He was so enthusiastic a fan that when Utaemon III was away performing in Edo, he went exclusively to see Nakamura Tsurusuke's *kabuki* performances. This Tsurusuke was Utaemon's favorite pupil and later became Utaemon IV (1796?–1852).

There were derivative taboos. The morning glory was a fashionable plant, and it was a widespread hobby to have pots of morning glory in one's garden. In 1814, two very popular stars, Tanosuke, mentioned above, and Arashi Kichisaburō II, Utaemon's great rival, performed the tearful love story *Asagao Nikki* (The diary of a morning glory—whose flower lasts only one morning). It was a great hit, not only in Osaka, but also in Kyoto. Because of this success, the morning glory flower became a symbol of support for Kichisaburō. As a result an Utaemon III fan named Rishō conceived a dislike not only for the wild orange, Kichisaburō's crest, but also for the morning glory, with sad results, for a maidservant of his household unwittingly brought home a pot of this flower and was immediately dismissed by her angry master.

The fan Madoka once won the first prize in a competition for showing the best morning glory. This was known to all, as *Hiiki no Hanamichi* had to defend him, saying: "He no longer has a single morning glory." [This was because the morning glory's association with support for Kichisaburō was considered an insult to Utaemon III. Ed.]

There was a group of people who were free from this sort of constraint—these were the actor portrait artists. They had to see many actors in order to draw their portraits, and in the *mitate-banzuke* Ashikuni, Shunka, and Shun'yō, although known as Utaemon fans, are classified as neither east (Kichisaburō) nor west (Utaemon), but in the neutral position at the bottom, as *sewanin* (go-betweens), because they were friendly with other actors.

Support for an actor sometimes involved parents, children, and whole families. Kiyū was Hyakki's son. Baiki and Baikō were the sons of Nishimuraya Baikyō. The young Bukichi, of whom much was expected for the future, was Bokuri's son. Daiyo, as I have mentioned above, owned a restaurant. In this establishment, any customer wearing a crest incorporating the wild orange (Kichisaburō II's emblem) was not served. Sumiji from Sonezaki had been a long and faithful supporter of Utaemon III, and his whole family, including the maids and the cooks, were also Utaemon's fans. The master of the famous restaurant Ukamuse made all of his family and employees wear uniforms of *shikancha* colors (literally, "Shikan-tea," a light chestnut color) when they went out shell gathering. *Shikancha* had been popular ever since Shikan I (Utaemon III) had worn a stage costume of this color.

One of Shikan I's crests was *tsuru-bishi* (a crane in a diamond-shaped background) and this, too, was used by his fans. The Nishimuraya family all had this crest on their purses, tobacco cases, and *furoshiki* [a cloth used to carry small items. Ed.]. Nishimuraya's favorite hobby was indoor archery, and all the equipment for this was decorated with this crest; the feathers of the arrows were *shikancha* in color. Hachiku from Nagahori put this crest not only on his small furniture but also his letter-paper. Merchants who came to Kiyū's shop to do business had to prepare a paper crest with the crane design and paste it over any wild orange crests that they had on them.

Fans often collected things associated with actors. The dark-colored costume that was used by Shikan I in the play *Keisei Tsurigane Zakura* (The courtesan and bell on the cherry tree) in 1814 was accepted in Nishimuraya's warehouse, and the brown costume worn by the same actor in the same play was given to Shōnen, who used to show it to visitors. Hayashima secretly kept a picture of a courtesan, with three short poems composed and written by Shikan I, Shinsui (the actor Bandō Hikosaburō III [1751–1828]), and Hajō (Nakamura Daikichi I). Bokuri once visited Shikan I when he was working in an Edo theatre, and as a farewell present received from the actor a short poem written in gold on a silk *fukusa* (a cloth used in the tea ceremony):

Furusato no mizu no natsukashi kakitsubata
(The iris misses even the water of its hometown)

The reference in *kakitsubata* (Japanese iris) was to the famous passage of the *Ise Monogatari* (Tales of Ise), in which the traveler writes a poem saying that he misses his wife left behind in Kyoto. In fact, Shikan I always tried to write something for his fans when requested, because he had been so advised by the famous Edo writer, Shokusanjin.

Needless to say, countless gifts were given to actors, and one or two examples can be given here. The play *Yadonashi Danshichi* (Homeless Danshichi) was performed in the fourth month of 1814 at the Naka no Shibai. Danshichi was a fish auctioneer and the opening scene was at the fish market (Zakoba). For this scene, every day, a large quantity of fresh fish was sent by the Zakoba to Shikan's dressing room. After being used in the scene on the stage, the fish were shared out among the personnel. *Hiiki no Hanamichi* says that the spirit of Zakoba was greater than the huge lanterns that they presented. Daiyo's present was barrels of sake such as are still to be seen piled up in front of *kabuki* theatres. The restaurant manager Sumiji often sent a tub of *sushi* to Shikan I's room. When Shikan was ill on one occasion, Shihei sent to him a doctor, attached to an important family, who successfully cured him. This was probably a very expensive gift. Often, in fact, when an actor was ill, his fans would visit him and also would go to a shrine to pray for him to be cured. This was often the Myōken shrine in Minō, a suburb to the north of Osaka, a visit to which was a half day's journey.

Another pleasure for members of fan clubs was to enjoy holiday trips with their actor. Yahachi of the Tsuruiya invited Shikan I from Edo to spend a week with him at Mount Minobu. This mountain was famous as a resort and also as the site of Kuon Temple, the headquarters of the Nichiren sect, to which Shikan belonged. A fan also enjoyed inviting an actor to his own home. Shikan did not drink sake, so Hayashima entertained him when he was his guest with his indoor archery. Chasing after an actor as he went on his journeys was a very hectic affair. Bokuri went as far as Edo to pay his respects to Shikan, but apart from the theatre, he visited only the Sumida River and the Thunder Gate (Kaminari Mon) to Asakusa Temple. This was because one of Shikan's hit roles was that of the fallen priest Hokaibō, whose activities took place at the Sumida River, and one of whose nine quick-change dance roles was that of Thunder.

I have already mentioned that Hyakki had published a book (*Shikan-Koku Ichiran*), so *hiiki* activities also included writing books. However, the most common production was *surimono*, woodblock prints designed and produced for special occasions and not for sale. Bokuri's son, Bukichi, was also known as an artist, a pupil of the famous artist Niwa Tōkei. A fan named Tōri was praised for a *surimono* showing a scarlet *shōki* (a mythical being who fought against the god of smallpox). Kokudō, Ashikuni, and Ikka were also said to be good *surimono* artists. Ikka made a *surimono* of a monkey climbing to the top of a wild orange tree, so that he was suspected of double-dealing. Sento, an important member of the Sasase club, had two further names, Kyōgen and Ahō Ōzeki, and produced a *surimono* on the subject of seven quick-change roles depicting the seven Gods of Good Fortune on their treasure boat, with eight short poems by Shikan I, Sento, Rojin, Karyū, and others. This *surimono* was very popular among the *hiiki*.

Another sort of event connected with *surimono* was a contest called *e-awase* (picture contest). A title was decided beforehand, and the contestants drew *surimono* to illustrate it. A description of an *e-awase* is found in *Hiiki no Hanamichi*: "The other day, the title *tomeru na tomeru na* (Don't stop, don't stop) was given out. The picture that won the most applause and was ranked first showed a monkey-trainer being wrested down by a lion dancer from Echigo province." The monkey trainer was Arashi Kichisaburō II's hit role, and the Echigo lion dance was Shikan I's favorite dance piece. The meaning of this picture was that Kichisaburō was beaten by Shikan, and the given title meant "Don't stop it," or, in other words, "Carry on playing," much to the delight of the Shikan supporters.

There is thus a clear connection between *surimono* and *hiiki*, and occasional inscriptions on actor prints mentioning Zakoba or *hiiki* suggest a similar relationship, but there is no certainty about this.

The activities of *hiiki* may have seemed stupid in other people's eyes, but it cannot be denied that there was in it an element of commercial publicity. *Dashi-busuma* was the name of a kind of sliding door that could be seen from the outside of a shop, and the one at Hiromaru the tobacconist's bore a humorous poem composed by Shikan I. Wakamatsuya's fresh cakes were named *Tsuru-bishi*, sold in a diamond-shaped box, and colored white and *shikancha*. The sliding door of shops of members of the Shikan-kō had painted on them various roles of Shikan by the famous artist Ashikuni. When all the family and employees of the Ukamuse restaurant wore *shikancha* uniforms it must have drawn publicity.

But people did not become fans of actors merely to advertise their trades. In a sense, being a *hiiki* was a big joke. Of course, they realized that it was all a game. Unless they could recognize their own lack of seriousness, they could not become *suijin* (connoisseurs). The reasons why there were not a great number of women *hiiki* must have been firstly economic and social, but secondly, the author of *Hiiki no Hanamichi* believed that it was difficult for women to be imbued with the spirit of game-playing. If one steps out of the rules of the game and becomes infatuated with an actor, one loses one's qualification to be a true *hiiki*.

Hiiki, then, while a part of the great publicity machinery that accompanied the acting profession, was at the same time a manifestation of the perverse spirit of fun and nonseriousness that was the characteristic of townsfolk in Japan, and especially those in Osaka.

8

Kabuki Goes Official: The 1878 Opening of the Shintomi-za

Yuichirō Takahashi

The Shintomi-za

When the new *kabuki* theatre called the Shintomi-za opened in 1878 it was one of the first theatres to be built in downtown Tokyo, following 1842's forced transfer of Edo's licensed theatres to the outlying district of Saruwaka-chō, close to the Sumida River on the city's eastern periphery. Although the Shintomi-za was a *kabuki* theatre, compared to Edo-period theatres, it had a distinctive architectural style. Its facade, now coated with white plaster intended to make it more fire resistant, had fewer decorative motifs. Gone were the *yagura* (drum tower) signifying its licensed status, and the *kido* (traditional entryways), while the amount of space formerly given to display of billboards was considerably curtailed. It also lacked the big thrust stage that characterized the Edo-era *kabuki* theatres. The Shintomi-za was the second theatre built by Morita Kan'ya XII (1846–1897), owner of one of the three licensed theatres (the Edo *sanza*) under the Tokugawa shogun's regime.

In 1872, after the 1868 takeover of the government, Kan'ya, whose family had managed theatres called Morita-za since 1660, had built a new one of that name in the Shintomi-chō section of Kyōbashi, near the Ginza; this marked the beginning of a significant transformation of the Japanese theatre structure. In 1875, the financially beleaguered Kan'ya relinquished ownership and reorganized the Morita-za into a new company, naming it the Shintomi-za. When the theatre burned down in 1876, production continued

Figure 8.1 **Morita Kan'ya XII. (Photo: Tsubouchi Memorial Theatre Museum, Waseda University; courtesy of Yuichirō Takahashi.)**

in a nearby makeshift house, and Kan'ya immediately embarked on rebuilding the theatre. The new theatre, the second Shintomi-za, was completed in 1878 and accelerated the transformation initiated by the Morita-za. With all the public attention it received, the Shintomi-za inaugurated a new era for *kabuki* theatres (figures 8.1, 8.2).

Seated today among an audience of 2,600 in Tokyo's Kabuki-za theatre, looking at a ninety-foot-wide stage lit in dazzling brightness, am I all alone in thinking that something is amiss? There is splendor, no doubt. Accomplished acting, colorful stage sets, and traditional chanters of the *jōruri*-style narration all combine to make a powerful impression on the spectator. But I cannot help thinking that despite its tremendous visual and aural appeal, *kabuki* was more fun when the spectators and the actors shared the same space in much smaller theatres, when the audience enjoyed smoking, eating,

Figure 8.2 **The Shintomi-za as it appeared in 1878. (Photo: Tsubouchi Memorial Theatre Museum, Waseda University; courtesy of Yuichirō Takahashi.)**

drinking, and chatting in their seats. The enjoyment of the *kabuki* audience was extended to the senses of touch, smell, and taste. The feeling of intimacy between the performers and the spectators is absent in today's oversized theatres.

Although the *hanamichi* (runway) still allows the actors to enter through the audience, and despite occasional *kakegoe* (shouts of encouragement), including the actors' *yagō* (a kind of family nickname), heard shouted from the third-floor gallery, an irreducible gap has opened up between stage and audience.

The popular fallacy of regarding *kabuki* as an art that has remained unchanged seems to die hard. During the summer of 1993 I attended a performance at the Kokuritsu Gekijō (National Theatre) in Tokyo that was part of the annual educational production for high school students—somewhat inappropriately titled *kabuki kanshō kyōshitsu* (*kabuki* appreciation school).[1] I noticed the following in the program notes: "*Kabuki* is a stage art created and nurtured by our ancestors and is still alive today. Like the other traditional performing arts of *nō* and *bunraku*, *kabuki* is a cultural heritage that Japan should be proud of" (Kawatake 1993, 1).[2] It is not difficult to read between the lines the conflicting desire of the writer and the producer to emphasize the tradition of *kabuki* while not wishing to preserve it as a museum piece.

Because the Japanese lifestyle is not what it once was, the ossification of *kabuki* is to some extent inevitable. Although its creative potential is undoubtedly alive, other forms of theatre more appealing to contemporary society have emerged. What I am concerned with, however, is the discourse that has "elevated" *kabuki* to high art. "*Kabuki* appreciation school" is a testimony to the popular notion that now one must study *kabuki* in order to appreciate it. This perception of *kabuki* as a high rather than popular art form developed sometime during the past 100 years.

As early as 1915, a writer complained in a *kabuki* magazine that the playgoer of his time had grown too intellectual. When he was young, he wrote, "nobody sought anything but fun out of a play. Whether it was true to life, or what philosophy it embodied, did not matter" (Tsukahara 1915, 238). A more recent observer, Koyama Akimoto, has noted that the hierarchy between actor and spectator has been reversed. In the past spectators were "allowed" to see *nō* or *gagaku* while they were "asked" to see *kabuki*. Now he feels they are also "allowed" to see *kabuki*. Koyama concludes: "The fall of the spectator to today's most miserable state began when he was banned from smoking in his seat. Next he was deprived of his lunch, of his liquor, and finally of the freedom to go in and out of the theatre" (Koyama 1975, 4–5). In 1956 Akimoto Shunkichi remarked: "people used to go to *kabuki* for enjoyment, but today people go to *kabuki* for instruction" (1956, 99).

The aestheticization of *kabuki*, with the emphasis on tradition and continuity, did not take place overnight. It seems indisputable, however, that the direction was laid out at the beginning of the Meiji period (1868–1912) when Japan set its course toward modernization, Westernization, and colonialism. The political changes of 1868 brought Japan face to face with the European powers whose cultural representations seemed inherently superior to the Japanese. The lives of the Edoites portrayed in *kabuki*, as well as their practice of theatregoing, were regarded as outdated as well as uncivilized. *Kabuki* could not have remained unchanged.

I consider the opening of the Shintomi-za as a historical node at which point the changes within *kabuki*—the introduction of a new theatre architecture, a new mode of theatregoing, and efforts to attain respectability—became perceptible. These changes reflected the cultural turmoil of the society, following the dissolution of the centuries-old feudal regime and Japanese exposure to totally alien civilizations. These changes—in the theatre and in society—drastically altered the actor-spectator relationship at the time of the Shintomi-za's opening.

The Opening Ceremony

On June 7, 1878, the opening of the Shintomi-za astonished Tokyoites with a dazzling display of Western amenities. Gaslights illuminated the facade of the theatre, spelling out its name. Covered with white plaster (for fire prevention), the building did not resemble the unpainted wooden exterior of older theatres. Likewise, the interior had gaslights, which were not yet allowed in private homes, and two chandeliers were hung from the ceiling. The traditional wooden boxes on the floor into which the floor was divided for seating (*masu*) were carpeted in red. Lanterns and flags embellished both the interior and the exterior of the theatre. The 1,000-plus invitees included Prime Minister Sanjō, high-ranking government officials, noble families from the imperial court, foreign legations, business leaders, and the press (figure 8.3).

In the ceremony, Kan'ya, the actors led by Ichikawa Danjūrō IX (1838–1903) and Onoe Kikugorō V (1844–1903), the playwrights led by Kawatake Mokuami (1816–1893), and the owners of the *chaya* (teahouses [also *shibai jaya*. Ed.]) came onstage in coattails at a time when Western clothes were still a novelty.[3] To those accustomed to seeing *kabuki* as Japan's traditional art, actors in Western clothes appeared strange. Even today, when *kōjō* (ceremonious announcements) are made onstage, *kabuki* actors wear formal Japanese clothes and speak sitting on the floor, not standing up (figure 8.4).

The ceremony took place in two parts, each completely different stylistically. Relegated to the second part was a *kabuki* adaptation of *Okina* (the name of a character), taken from *nō*, which had been the standard performance for celebrating auspicious occasions. The unprecedented first part began with Western band music, played alternately by the navy and army bands. Kan'ya made a bow when Kikugorō V read a speech for him. Danjūrō IX spoke on behalf of the actors. His speech, written by the scholar-financier Fukuchi Genichirō [later known as the playwright Fukuchi Ōchi. Ed.], was understood as a manifesto for theatre renovation. It admitted that *kabuki* had degraded itself by playing to the tastes of the populace, by portraying their manners and neglecting to honor righteous principles, and it declared that the opening of the new theatre put an end to *kabuki* as good-for-nothing amusement. The ceremony concluded with more band music.

The opening ceremony received wide press coverage. While most newspapers expressed admiration, the *Yomiuri Shinbun*, although allotting more than a full page, reported with a touch of sarcasm. The reporter began by describing the vicinity of the theatre on the day of the ceremony. He observed the huge crowd that had gathered and the many food and souvenir stalls that opened in anticipation of the crowd, "as if it was a festival day." The theatre, on the other hand, guarded by scores of policemen, was inaccessible to the jolly crowd. Only those with invitations, "who arrived in carriages and lacquer-coated rickshaws, were allowed in." A number of onlookers tried to force their way in but were threatened by police with batons and

Figure 8.3 **On its opening day, the exterior of the Shintomi-za was decorated with lanterns, flags, flower wreaths, and a gas-illuminated sign spelling out the name of the theatre. A crowd gathered to see the spectacle. Notice the couple in Western clothes on the lower right. (Photo: Courtesy of the Kokuritsu Gekijō.)**

turned away. Inside, he noticed, were many government officials accompanied by their wives or concubines. He also noticed that those in the first-class seats were served a Western-style dinner. The reporter concluded the article with a description of the area turning lively again after the ceremony, with

Figure 8.4 **At the opening ceremony of the Shintomi-za, the actors, dressed in Western clothes, listened to Danjūrō IX deliver a speech that is now regarded as a manifesto for theatre renovation. (Photo: Courtesy of the Kokuritsu Gekijō.)**

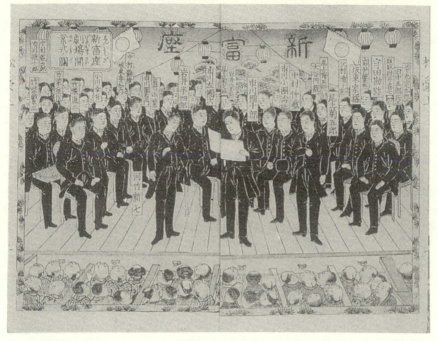

the crowd returning to see the illuminated theatre facade (*Yomiuri Shinbun* 1878).[4]

This account reveals the gap opening up between the two discourses concerning *kabuki*: one that sustained its vitality and had been embraced by the populace, and the other—an emerging discourse—now being granted official sanction. The festive aura of gathering crowds was replaced by the austerity of law enforcement and quelled by officers' batons. It was largely the merchant class of the cities of Edo, Kyoto, and Osaka who had patronized *kabuki*.[5] As the sarcasm of the above-cited article emphasizes, the traditional patrons of *kabuki* were now excluded. With the emergence of a new class of patrons—nobles, officials, and Westerners—*kabuki* was to go through subtle but significant changes.

The Structure of the Shintomi-za

To illustrate the changes initiated by the Shintomi-za, it is interesting to compare five *nishikie* (wood-block print) pictures depicting the mid-nineteenth-century theatres. Although the prints are by different artists, they reproduce the interiors of three theatres from more or less the same angle. Executed in the style of journalistic painting intended for circulation before the days of commercial photography, the illustrations maintain a certain degree of faithfulness to detail and accuracy. The comparison enables us to see the extent of changes made to the interior of *kabuki* theatres over a span of some twenty years at the time of the opening of the Shintomi-za.

Among the plates of the Shintomi-za in 1878, are two versions of the same picture, one with the curtain opened (figure 8.5) and the other with it drawn (figure 8.6). The titles suggest that figure 8.6 is a scene from the first commercial production after the opening of the theatre in June,[6] while figure 8.5 shows the audience gathered for Japan's first evening program in August of the same year.[7] Figure 8.7 is a picture of the Morita-za, the predecessor of the Shintomi-za. As noted above, it had been built in 1872 by Kan'ya as the first theatre to incorporate Western features. Figures 8.8 and 8.9, which bear the dates 1858 and 1859, represent earlier theatres built during the late Edo era.

Even on an impressionistic level, the earlier pictures (figures 8.8 and 8.9) convey a more vivacious air about the theatres. They show the performer and the spectator spaces intermingled and often indistinguishable. In the Shintomi-za, as in figures 8.5 and 8.6, the atmosphere is more reticent, with spectators who appear to be quietly watching the stage. The earlier theatres look more crowded and decorated to excess. The Shintomi-za, on the other hand, has a simple decor. A single unpainted banner with the crests of the Morita family adorns the ceiling. The ceiling banners of the earlier theatres are greater in number and more elaborately painted. In the Morita-za (figure 8.7), there seems to be no space left unpainted. While the earlier theatres look eclectic, almost baroque, the Shintomi-za, cleansed of superficial decorativeness, is simpler in design and gives an impression of the sparse utilitarianism that characterizes modern architecture.

The disappearance of eaves over the second-floor *sajiki* (side boxes), shown in the older theatre in figure 8.8, emphasizes this new sparsity. While *kabuki* was still performed outdoors [through the early eighteenth century. Ed.], only the stage and the *sajiki* were covered. The groundlings sat directly on the earth, braving the elements. When the theatre became covered,[8] the roofs over the *sajiki* were retained as a part for the traditional theatre interior and as a status symbol of those who could afford to sit there.

The most conspicuous change introduced in the Morita-za (figure 8.7) and retained in the Shintomi-za (figures 8.5 and 8.6) was the disappearance of the thrust stage. This had grave consequences for *kabuki*'s performer-spectator relationship. The thrust stage disappeared from Kyoto and Osaka theatres near the beginning of the nineteenth century (Yamazaki and Daikuhara 1990, 85). In Tokyo, where it remained until the political takeover of 1868,

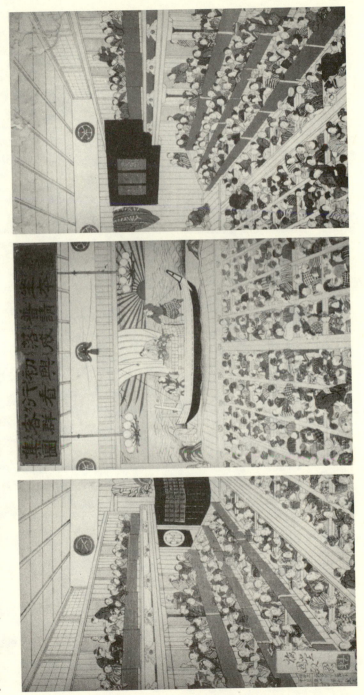

Figure 8.5 This print by Utagawa Toyokuni III illustrates the interior of the Shintomi-za at the time of its first commercial production. (Photo: Courtesy of the Kokuritsu Gekijō.)

132

Figure 8.6 The first evening *kabuki* performance at the Shintomi-za took place under chandeliers, as seen in this print by Utagawa Toyokuni III. (Photo: Courtesy of the Kokuritsu Gekijō.)

Figure 8.7 The predecessor of the Shintomi-za was the Morita-za, the first theatre built after the 1868 political takeover. Print by Utagawa Toyokuni III. (Photo: Courtesy of the Kokuritsu Gekijō.)

134

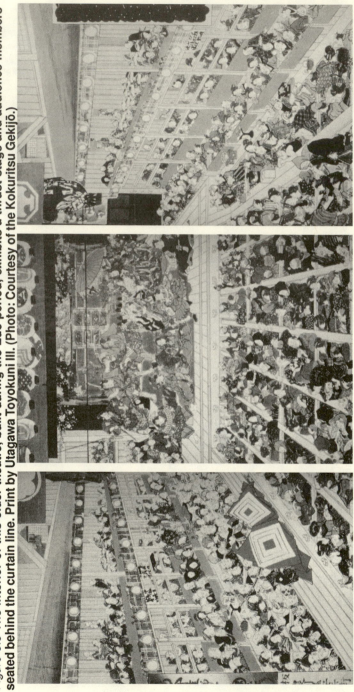

Figure 8.8 The interior of this older theatre, built during the Edo period, exhibits a thrust stage and audience members seated behind the curtain line. Print by Utagawa Toyokuni III. (Photo: Courtesy of the Kokuritsu Gekijō.)

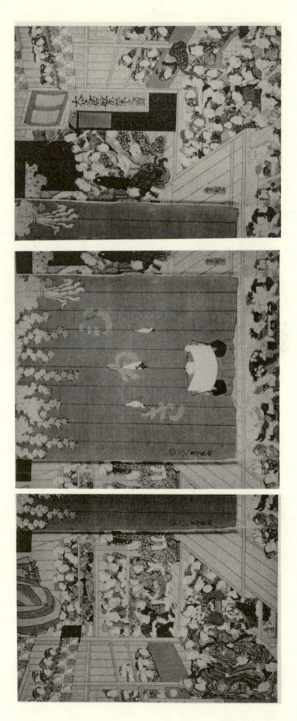

Figure 8.9 In one of the earlier theatres, built during the Edo period, the closed curtain covers only part of the stage as an announcement is being made. There are two onstage seating areas behind the curtain line. Print by Utagawa Toyokuni III.

the Morita-za and the Shintomi-za were the first theatres to do away with it. Their example was followed by all subsequent theatres, ending the tradition of viewing *kabuki* from at least three sides.

In figure 8.8, the actors are painted larger than life, as if they were not satisfied to occupy the small space allotted to them on the stage and were eager to transgress the space assigned to the spectators. In the Shintomi-za (figures 8.5 and 8.6), however, actors look smaller and are neatly contained within the picture frame of the proscenium arch. In the older theatres in Tokyo, the space that belonged to the actor and the space that belonged to the spectator were less strictly divided. As seen in figure 8.7, even in the Morita-za as late as 1872, a spectator could be ushered to her seat on the *kari* (secondary) *hanamichi* while the play was in progress. The *hanamichi* served both as an acting area and a gangway for spectators. It is out of the question for today's spectator to walk on the *hanamichi*; it has become sacrosanct.[9] In the Edo era, however, spectators were allowed not only on the *hanamichi* but also on the stage. Those who patronized *chaya* (teahouses) behind the theatre went in and out through the stage door and traversed the stage to reach their seats. Hasegawa Kanbei, a set builder, recalls how the work of the stagehands was disturbed by spectators who walked on the stage (Hasegawa 1928). The practice remained till Kan'ya banned it when he built the Morita-za (Kawatake 1959, 764).

In the eighteenth century the stage was also used as a viewing area. When the house was full and could accommodate no more spectators, the management allowed them on the stage, diminishing acting areas. Hattori Yukio cites instances from the journal of Danjūrō II in 1740 and from the *yakusha hyōbanki* (actor critiques) of 1756, when sets could not be erected because the stage had been narrowed by spectators (Hattori 1986, 15–16). A doggerel verse from the early nineteenth century reads, "Such a hit! The corpses are cleared away with difficulty" (17).

The *kabuki* spectator of the Edo era was different from today's docile and voyeuristic counterpart who is content to watch events unfold on the stage through the imaginary fourth wall. The actor-spectator exchange, the remnant of which is today observed in the practice of *kakegoe*, was more elaborate.[10] When a star actor appeared or made a pose in a climactic scene, the performance was occasionally stopped for a spectator—a representative of a *renjū* (or *renchū*) (a kind of actor's fan club) [see Matsudaira's essay, chapter 7. Ed.] to climb on the *hanamichi* or onstage to speak words of admiration for him. The practice was called *home kotoba* (words of praise). The actors, too, stopped the performance to reciprocate (see Gunji 1954, 51; Raz 1983, 184). Spectators were also involved in the action of a play. In one play, when a child prince was pursued by the army of an evil enemy, the actor guarding him would hand the child actor playing the prince to the front-row spectators; they would hide him while the stage was ransacked (Hattori 1993, 66).

In the older theatres (as in figures 8.8 and 8.9), spectators were seated on both sides of the thrust stage. The two narrow viewing areas that formed between the stage and *sajiki* boxes on the sides were called *takotsubo* (octopus pots) because their shape resembled pots used to catch octopuses. The occupants of these seats most intimately shared the space with the actors. When the curtain closed, these spectators disappeared from the view of the other spectators. Scene changes were done before their very eyes.[11] Hasegawa Kanbei recalls that, unless the show was excessively popular, these seats were sold cheaply because the curtain brushed the spectators' heads and dust fell off the stage.

In addition to the octopus pots, figures 8.8 and 8.9 show two other seating areas behind the curtain line, called the *rakandai* and the *yoshino*; they were located on the stage. The downstage right area, previously occupied by the *nō*-derived *hashigakari* runway at stage right and used for the entrance of the actors, lost its significance as an acting area after the addition of the *hanamichi*. In the middle of the eighteenth century, these provisional viewing areas were added when audience numbers surpassed the theatre's capacity.[12] The new seating allowed its occupants to see the actors only from behind. It was called the *rakandai* (Hattori 1986, 12) after *rakan*, a collective name given to lesser disciples of the Buddha. The 500 *rakan* who gathered to hear the Buddha's sermon was a popular subject for Buddhist sculpture. The spectators huddling together behind a balustrade at one corner of the stage resembled the small clay or wooden figures of the *rakan* commonly found in Japanese Buddhist temples. Later, a second layer was added on top of the *rakandai* and called the *yoshino*, after the mountain range famous for cherry blossoms.[13] Spring scenes in *kabuki* are often played beneath artificial cherry blossoms thrust from above. This gallery promised the best view of the cherry blossoms but not of the stage. The *rakandai* and the *yoshino* offered the cheapest seats in the theatre.

Hattori thinks it was those seats that the real connoisseurs frequented. Referring to another old doggerel verse, "*Rakan* knows which actor is to come onstage next," he points out that the spectators in the *rakandai* had a view of the offstage area where actors warmed up. He thinks it possible that they shared a pleasure with their Brechtian counterparts in that they were able to observe the actors getting in and out of character (Hattori 1986, 14).

When the thrust stage was removed, the *rakandai* and the *yoshino* disappeared.[14] Figure 8.7 indicates a small section of the *yoshino* retained by the Morita-za. With some half-dozen spectators, its size was much reduced. The absence of the *rakandai* below makes it appear unbalanced. Its new triangular shape, although it may have improved the sight line, meant its occupants were no longer face to face with the rest of the audience. The *yoshino* now served as an extension to the second-floor side gallery. In the Shintomi-za (figures 8.5 and 8.6) no seating is found on the stage.

Changes are also discernible in the placement of the musicians. The *geza* music, which is today played offstage, had been played onstage. Figure 8.9 shows the musicians upstage left, in full view of the spectators. The Shintomi-za took advantage of a development that first appeared in Edo *kabuki* theatres during the 1850s, namely, the placement of the musicians in a black room, fronted by a rattan screen, at stage right, near where the *rakandai* formerly had been. This convention persists to the present day.

Without the spectators in the *rakandai* and the *yoshino* on stage right and the musicians on stage left, the Shintomi-za stage was uncluttered. While the stages of earlier theatres served other functions—seating and walking areas for spectators—the Shintomi-za stage was reserved for performing. The change is indicative of, among other things, *kabuki*'s transition from an eclectic and amalgamated experience for the spectator to an art confined to the stage space. The actor-spectator exchange diminished as the acting area expanded and was bounded. To maintain a shared space between the actor and the spectator, it was imperative that spectators be seen by other spectators. When some were seated behind the curtain line, they viewed not only the stage and the actors but also other spectators. The role of the spectator was to be seen as well as to see. The disappearance of the thrust stage and confrontational seating turned the spectators into passive viewers.[15] Further altering the spectators' physical relation to the performance was Kan'ya's introduction in his two theatres of Western chairs, now standard in all Japanese theatres. Chairs diminished the significance of the *hanamichi* and minimized the possibility of environmental staging for *kabuki*. Sitting on a floor, spectators could easily turn around to look in many directions, but in fixed chairs facing the stage spectators must contort their position even to look sideways in the direction of the *hanamichi*.

Hattori believes that the Shintomi-za was Japan's first proscenium theatre (1974, 109), although, as it lacks the massive arch of the European theatres, its designers had no clear idea of what a proscenium arch was.[16] With the opening of this theatre, Edo *kabuki* receded behind the stage opening, except for what was performed on the *hanamichi*. Figure 8.8 indicates that the thrust stage, when it still existed, provided the principal acting area, while the stage behind it, between the *rakandai* on stage right and the musicians on stage left, provided a background. In the Shintomi-za (Figure 8.5), both the set and the performers are seen contained behind the stage opening.

The difference is greater between figures 8.6 and 8.9, both of which depict a theatre at the moment before the curtain goes up. In figure 8.9 an announcement, possibly about the play or about the cast, is being made on the stage, with the curtain covering only a part of it. Even when the curtain is closed, spectators have a partial view of the sets and whatever is going on behind it. The spectators in the side seats, as well as those in the *rakandai* and the *yoshino*, have an unrestricted view of behind-the-curtain activities. The curtain here functions as a marker signifying a beginning or an interruption of a play, and does not have to conceal the scenery. In the Shintomi-za (figure 8.6), on the contrary, the curtain hides everything except a stagehand holding *tsuke* (wooden clappers). In the earlier theatres, no effort was made to induce the "suspension of disbelief" by insulating the fictional stage—a need first recognized in *kabuki* staging during the two decades separating the two pictures (figures 8.6 and 8.9).

According to Gunji Masakatsu, two things were responsible for the "degradation," as he puts it, of the Japanese theatre: one was the loss of the participatory role of the spectator, and the other was the enlargement of the stage (1991, 72). The significance of the Shintomi-za, or of its predecessor, the Morita-za, is clear: the stage size set a standard for the theatres to come. The width of the early *kabuki* stage, when it used the square *nō* stage, was 3 *ken* (about 5.5 m). In 1688, the Ichimura-za widened it to 5 *ken* (about 9 m; Kawatake 1943, 171). In 1725, the Nakamura-za, the most innovative of the three licensed theatres in Edo, widened the stage to 6.5 *ken* (about 12 m) and built a roof to cover the entire theatre. The size of the stage remained more or less the same for about 150 years, until Kan'ya's Morita-za embarked on the first major enlargement of the theatre after the 1868 government takeover (Kawatake 1943, 174; Fujinami 1988, 85).[17] Its total building area increased by 50 percent, with the stage now measuring 8 *ken* (about 15 m; Kawatake 1959, 765).[18] A comparison of figures 8.7 and 8.8 confirms the enlargement. While figure 8.8 shows seven vertical rows of *masu* boxes between the two *hanamichi*, in figure 8.7 there are ten. In the Shintomi-za, the stage was further widened to 11 *ken* (about 20 m). The stage frontage had increased by 70 percent in less than ten years. The seating capacity of the Shintomi-za was reported to be 1,965.[19] Although there is no definitive study on the capacity of theatres in the Edo era, it has been estimated to be between 1,000 and 1,300 (Hattori 1980, 159).[20] The Shintomi-za nearly doubled the capacity.[21] The theatre enlargement was a combined result of the lifting of the regulations that limited its size and the commercial motivation of entrepreneurs to draw larger audiences. But the enlargement continued. The Kabuki-za of 1889 had a stage frontage of 12 *ken* (about 22 m). The present Kabuki-za, rebuilt in 1952, has the largest stage at 13 *ken* (about 27 m), with a seating capacity of 2,600. Its stage is roughly twice as big as the standard *kabuki* stage of the Edo era. The Kokuritsu Gekijō, opened in 1966, has a stage twelve meters in width. There is no denying that the enormous size of today's *kabuki* theatres is responsible, if not for degradation as Gunji suggests, at least for the further separation between the stage and the audience.

The Reforms in the Early Meiji Period

The renovations made to the structure of the Shintomi-za reflect the theatre policy of the fledgling government as well as the ambition of the young entrepreneur, Morita Kan'ya.[22] The theatre that he had inherited was the smallest of the three licensed theatres and the least prestigious. He had been also in constant debt. When the old laws that bound theatre business seemed moribund, his ambition soared with the dream of a new theatre.

The government, intent on modernizing the nation, had a dual objective in laying out its theatre policy: assigning to the theatre a pedagogic role in the education of the populace, and adding social respectability to attract Westerners. The policy was made manifest in February 1872 when the owners of the three licensed theatres, as well as the playwrights under their contracts, were asked to report to the Tokyo metropolitan government. They were advised that "since the nobles and the foreigners now frequented theatres, such licentious acts that parents dared not show their children must be avoided" (Matsumoto 1974, 23). In April, Kan'ya and the playwrights were again told to stress moral righteousness. Under the government's guidance—which gradually approached censorship—plays in which the good always triumphed were encouraged.[23] They were also expected to stop telling lies and to adhere to historical truth.[24]

In August, the Ministry of Education issued a decree that included the following: (1) theatre must not portray emperors and must avoid themes that might do them an injustice; (2) moral righteousness must be a theatre's first concern; a theatre must improve public morality, not degenerate it with indecency; and (3) as actors are no longer considered *ningaimono* (outcasts, or those who do not belong to the class system), they must display high moral conduct in keeping with their new status (Matsumoto 1974, 84; Osasa 1985, 21).

In the Edo era, theatres and brothels were called *akusho* (evil places).[25] [See Lee's essay, chapter 20, for more on *akusho*. Ed.] For the people whose freedom was curtailed by the strictures of the class system and by the moral codes of samurai society, they promised a moment of release and freedom. Occasional visits to the theatre were condoned and their existence was considered a necessary evil. *Akusho* formed isolated communities that were culturally marked and that developed unique practices by annulling the social order outside. These changes extended to uses of language that were observed only within the boundaries of the *akusho*. The business inside was not permitted to filter into the "normal" world outside. *Akusho* maintained a system of values that was upside down; located on the periphery of a city, the brothel and theatre districts formed margins of the unreal on the edge of mundane reality. But when their influence on the popular consciousness became too great in the eyes of the rulers, sumptuary laws were passed to curb them. The *akusho* were sites of negotiation between the subordinate classes seeking freedom and the ruling classes trying to impose control.

The Meiji government's emphasis on morality assigned a contradictory role to the theatre. Education was recognized as a vehicle for modernization. The new rulers saw the theatre as a pedagogical tool that could be used to correct the tastes and the manners of the people. Their attitude is well reflected in an 1874 magazine article entitled "The Employment of Actors in Teaching Professions," in which theatres are equated with classrooms (in Kawatake 1959, 758). The article argues that an actor, with his popularity and accomplished skill in evoking emotions, is better suited to a pedagogical role than a preacher, who is only capable of prosaic speech. The leading playwright of the day, Kawatake Mokuami, complied with the government edicts by writing a new play for the Shintomi-za entitled *Shusse Musume Hisago no Kanzashi* (The rising young woman and the gourd hair ornament). In a long speech by one character, he acknowledged the pedagogical role of the *kabuki* texts and denounced the sexual language found in older works. This character proudly announces that the *kabuki* of his time is not at all what it was ten years before, concluding his speech with the exclamation, "dirty scenes that make parents and children blush with shame will never be seen on the stage of the Shintomi-za" (Toita 1978,16).

The reform of *kabuki*, however, was intended not only for the populace. It was deemed necessary because "the nobles and the Westerners now frequented the theatres." The advocates of reform comprised those who had studied or toured in Europe and in the United States and had perceived in the theatre of the West, and particularly in opera, the refined tastes of the upper classes. The urgent diplomatic goal of the government was to revise the treaties signed by the shogun's regime that allowed the Western powers extraterritoriality and limited Japan's autonomy in the area of tariffs. It was naively but quite insightfully thought that to stand on equal footing with the West at the negotiating table, Japan needed a cultural representation of equal renown. In 1883, the government built an imitation European mansion called Rokumeikan, where balls were held in strict compliance with European decorum. Theatre was called upon to provide similar Western-style sophistication.

The emulation of Western culture was skin-deep; the time was not ripe for a sophisticated appreciation of Western culture. Everything Western was recommended, while things Japanese were considered backward, irrational, and superstitious. A hypothetical value judgment based on what a Westerner might think and do became the criterion for action. The *kabuki* of the first half of the nineteenth century displayed a predilection for decadence, reflecting the social instability under the weakening shogun's government. Grotesque subject matter and contorted plot structures were favored. Onstage violence and true-to-life portrayals of sex were the standard fare. Evil was idolized. Such trends were censured according to the new criteria; they were not what the hypothetical Westerner would find acceptable.[26] A Tokyo *Nichinichi Shinbun* article on February 22, 1872 sums up this view, pointing out that without reform foreigners might confuse the indecency of plays with the national character (in Kobitsu 1988, 47).

During the 1870s, when *nō* was in danger of extinction with the disappearance of its patrons (the samurai class), *kabuki* was the only form of theatre in Japan that could compare in size and complexity with Western opera. The people who sought diplomatic salons in theatres had nowhere else to turn. Thus reform of *kabuki* became a government mandate. The new rulers sought a theatre that could fulfill the role of the Western opera houses and national theatres. This is where Morita Kan'ya, in his efforts to obtain a license for his new theatre by seeking contacts among the government circles, appeared on the scene. Infused with the ideas of a Western theatre through his new government acquaintances, Kan'ya first added a viewing area for Westerners in his 1872 Morita-za. At the front edge of the second-floor gallery, some twenty tables and "good-looking chairs" were installed (Kimura 1943, 304; Kawatake 1959, 764).

In 1878 Kan'ya produced *Okige no Kumo Harau Asagochi* (Morning east wind clearing the clouds of the southwest), a play based on the recent uprising of Saigō Takamori.[27] Following the government's mandate on historical accuracy, Kan'ya intended the play to be Japan's first onstage reportage and proceeded to interview a number of the officials who had taken part in the campaign. One was Komyōji Saburō, a devoted fan of the Western theatre who had spent six years in France. He confided in Kan'ya the plan for a national theatre and infused in him the ambition to be its first director (Satō 1971, 194–196; Ihara 1933, 236). Kan'ya tried to strengthen his government ties by lavishly entertaining his new friends.[28] Although the plan for a national theatre was aborted, Kan'ya's Shintomi-za came to be seen as the government's official theatre.

The unprecedented opening ceremony was in line with the new government policies. A *Chōya Shinbun* article reported that "the opening of this theatre would light a new light in civilizing the nation and its people" (in Satō 1971, 196). The Shintomi-za was used on a number of occasions to entertain state guests, and when a visit was announced Kan'ya would cancel the regular performance for a day and mount a special program comprised of a short play and a colorful dance number. The Shintomi-za entertained its first state guest, Prince Henry, the seventeen-year-old grandson of the German emperor, on June 4, 1879, followed a week later by John Hennesy, the British governor in Hong Kong (Kimura 1943, 573–575; Kokuritsu Gekijō 1984, 700–702). The most celebrated personage to visit the theatre, however, was the former U.S. president, Ulysses S. Grant. After having served two terms as president, Grant set off on a world tour in 1879. Although in retirement, he was the first Western head of state to visit Japan. The government took his visit very seriously and used the occasion to publicize a "civilized" image of Japan to the rest of the world. During the two months Grant stayed in Japan, every possible effort was made to please him and his retinue. For Kan'ya, Grant's visit to the Shintomi-za marked the pinnacle of the manager's career. He did not hesitate to spend a fortune to welcome the former president.[29] Kan'ya had Mokuami write a new play, set in medieval Japan, that contained scenes translated from Grant's experiences during the Civil War.[30] As it was hot on the evening of Grant's visit, Kan'ya placed blocks of ice in the auditorium and ordered ice cream (both a rarity in 1879 Japan) from a dealer in Yokohama for his guests.[31] A Western-style fan (another rarity) was placed behind the general's seat. Grant seemed to have enjoyed the last part of the show—a dance by some seventy geishas wearing kimonos with a design of the Stars and Stripes—more than the play based on his life. As a token of his appreciation, he later presented a curtain to the theatre.

An eyewitness record of the evening survives in the diary of Clara Whitney, the daughter of an American accounting professor. Then age eighteen, she saw the show from Grant's box:

> We cantered down in the carriage behind Mr. Sanjō's [the prime minister] elegant barouche to the Shintomiza Theater. It was all a blaze of light, and crowds of people . . . had assembled outside and peered anxiously into every carriage to get a glimpse of notables. . . . And indeed every celebrated person in Tokyo was there. It was a grand show of nobility and power. (Whitney 1979, 258–259)[32]

As Whitney wrote, Grant's visit to the Shintomi-za was a "grand show of nobility and power." But we must take care not to oversimplify matters and conclude that the events that took place at the Shintomi-za in the late 1870s faithfully reflect the general trend of Japanese culture at the time. The proposed reform of *kabuki*, like numerous other "reforms" conducted in the same period, was something imposed from above by the government and the business leaders as part of the overall design of the nation. The display of Western representa-

Figure 8.10 **This cartoon by George Bigot depicts theatregoers of the 1880s, when it was still acceptable for common workers to enter the theatre in their street attire. (Photo: Shimizu Imao; Courtesy of Iwanami Shoten.)**

tions at the Shintomi-za appealed mainly to the minority that made up the new ruling class.

The average theatregoer still appreciated the kind of *kabuki* that had been popular before 1868, in its familiar setting. If theatre were to change under its own momentum, it had to be accompanied by changes in the lives and attitudes of the common people of the city, the theatre's true patrons. In other theatres, and even in the Shintomi-za, when reform experiments or official programs were not scheduled, the traditional *kabuki* repertory attracted the crowds. One of the most popular shows at the Shintomi-za in 1878 was *Chūshingura* (The treasury of loyal retainers), the famous vendetta play from the early eighteenth century.[33] Kan'ya's venture in 1879 to employ Western performers for a play-within-a-play in a *kabuki* production failed as it received a cold reception from the popular audience.[34] The comment by the *Tōkyō Nichinichi Shinbun* (January 23, 1888) reflects the public sentiment: "The object of theatre is to please the senses. To seek morality where pleasure is offered, is like ordering medication at a good restaurant" (in Kōbitsu 1988, 437). An 1883 etching by French cartoonist Georges Bigot (figure 8.10) shows a husband and wife watching a play. Judging from their unpretentious style, the theatre depicted is not one of the larger theatres, such as the Shintomi-za, where admission was high. Nevertheless, it is testimony that in the early 1880s it was still acceptable for a common worker to go about the streets in summer with only his loincloth on; enter the theatre in that attire; and with his family, enjoy food, pipe, and tea.

The opening of the Shintomi-za signifies the addition of the official discourse to the viewing of *kabuki*. The new class of audience raised the social status of the actor. In 1887, Kan'ya's troupe—*kabuki* actors who, under the previous regime, had been despised as riverbed beggars—gave a performance in front of the emperor, whose position, like that of the actor, was being raised in the official discourse of the period.[35] The emperor was being made into a living god. Although the reception of *kabuki* at this higher stratum of society was at first separate from its popular reception, in the course of time it has left an indelible mark on *kabuki*'s character. In the past hundred years or so, *kabuki* has been gradually absorbed by high culture. In exchange for an official sanction, *kabuki* lost its vitality as a marginal but popular art form.

In 1966, some ninety years after the opening of the Shintomi-za, Kan'ya's dream came true: the National Theatre of Japan (Kokuritsu Gekijō)opened. But the patrons of *kabuki* in Edo "would not have felt comfortable at all" with this new theatre (Gerstle 1987, 52). It was built in the heart of Tokyo's government district, next door to the massive granite structure of the Supreme Court of Justice, the seat of judicial authority.

Notes

1. The 1993 production ran from July 4–25. A half-hour lecture on *kabuki* conventions preceded the one-and-a-half-hour play, *Hikosan Gongen Chikai no Sukedachi* (A vow's assistance at the Mt. Hiko shrine), with Danjūrō XII playing the main role. With two shows staged daily, about 68,000 students saw the program.

2. Unless otherwise noted, all translations from the Japanese are by the author.

3. License was taken by the painter of figure 8.4 in portraying everyone on stage in Western clothes. In reality, *onnagata* (actors in female roles) wore Japanese clothes. The choreographer Hanayagi Jusuke, because he was reluctant to cut his *chonmage*, the traditional topknot, joined the ranks of the *onnagata*. Kawatake Mokuami, who hated Western clothes, was persuaded to wear them by Kan'ya. He never wore a Western garment again in his life (Kimura 1943, 533). Some accounts maintain that frock coats, not tailcoats, were worn for the occasion. According to Kimura Kinka, the actors wore tails and the owners of *chaya* wore frock coats. To coax Mokuami to wear Western clothes, Kan'ya let him wear tails, suggesting that his greatness as a playwright was equal to the fame of Danjūrō and Kikugorō, the most famous actors of the day (Kokuritsu Gekijō 1978, 12).

4. The reporter also remarked on the audience's bored expression during the long *Okina*, commenting that the *daimyō* (feudal lords in the Tokugawa era) learned such dances to digest the expensive food they had eaten—they did not need to work and thus had nothing else to do.

5. Osasa Yoshio suggests that whenever a new class emerged in Japan, a performance genre unique to that class also developed. The class associated with *kabuki* was the merchant class, which became prominent in the sixteenth century (Osasa 1985, 22).

6. *Matsu no Sakae Chiyoda so Shintoku* (Flourishing pines and the divine power of Chiyoda) ran for forty-two days and attracted, according to the report submitted by the Shintomi-za to the police department, a total of 49,000 people, an average of 1,170 per performance (Ihara 1962, 237).

7. The first evening program in August 1878 was *Butai Akaruki Meiji no Yoshibai* (The well-lighted evening stage of our day) (Ihara 1962, 238).

8. The roof over the entire theatre was not allowed until 1718 (Goto 1925, 40).

9. Recently, after a performance at the Kabuki-za in Tokyo, I saw a spectator put a camera on the *hanamichi* while he tied his shoelaces. The camera was swiftly snatched up by an usher and handed back to the spectator even before he finished tying his shoelaces.

10. Active participation by the audience came to be considered contrary to the manners of a genteel, educated society. When Prince Henry of Germany visited the Shintomi-za in 1879, Kanagaki Robun noticed there was no *kakegoe* uttered by the spectators. In the article he wrote for *Kanayomi Shinbun*, he offered tongue-in-cheek praise for their improved manners (in Kokuritsu Gekijō 1984, 701).

11. It is not clear from these pictures, however, how many people were accommodated in the narrow side areas. In a study conducted on an earlier theatre, the Ichimura-za of the Bunka-Bunsei period (1804–1830), the project team of Obayashi-gumi speculates that there were three rows of *masu* (boxes) on each side of the stage. This would make the number of boxes behind the curtain twenty-one. As the same study indicates, the size of the box at this period was 1.40 meters by 1.21 meters, large enough to accommodate five people, enabling about 100 people to be seated behind the curtain line (Obayashi-gumi Project Team 1979, 17–24). Hasegawa testifies that a total of eighteen *masu* boxes went behind the curtain (1928, 193).

12. The addition of the *rakandai* was traced by Kimura (1934, 245) to the Kyōhō period (1716–1736); by Hattori (1986, 12) to the Hōreki period (1751–1764); and by Kawatake (1943, 192) and Yamazaki and Daikuhara (1990, 83) to the Meiwa period (1764–1772).

13. Kimura (1934, 250), Hattori (1986, 14), and Yamazaki and Daikuhara (1990, 83) all agree that this addition took place in 1793.

14. It is possible, however, that a number of *takotsubo* seats were retained in the Shintomi-za. The seating plan of the Shintomi-za printed in the journal *Kabuki Shinpō* in 1879, and another plan that survives from 1881, show them on stage left, but figure 8.2, of the Morita-za six years earlier, and another picture of the Shintomi-za show no evidence of it. The plans of the theatres that were built after the Shintomi-za—the Saruwaka-za, built in 1882 (Kokuritsu Gekijō 1992, 64), and the Chitose-za, built in 1885 (144)—however, indicate their continued presence.

15. The related issue here is the diminishing significance of the *hanamichi*. What makes the performance on the *hanamichi* interesting is the presence of the spectators on the other side of it. The *hanamichi* leaves little room for illusionism or the suspension of disbelief, because the performance takes place not in front of a stage set but in front of the audience in raised *sajiki* side boxes. What the spectators see are the faces of the other spectators. The actors, instead of inhabiting the fictional world of a play, are forced to share a space with the spectators. In the Kokuritsu Gekijō, opened in

1966, however, the side boxes were abolished: there is now only a bare wall where the *sajiki* used to be on the other side of the *hanamichi*. Most other theatres in Japan at which *kabuki* continues to be performed, however, retain the side boxes.

16. Yamazaki and Daikuhara (1990, 87) and Kawatake (1959, 1144) take the same view. Fujinami, however, disagrees. He thinks that the first theatre equipped with a proscenium arch was the Kawakami-za, built in 1896 (1988, 235). The people who built the Shintomi-za possessed no direct knowledge of the Western theatre. Therefore, Fujinami argues, a real proscenium could not have been built before Kawakami Otojirō—the first Japanese professional actor to tour the West (1899)—returned to Japan [See Lee's essay, chapter 20, on Kawakami's performances in Germany and Switzerland. Ed.] I believe, however, that the stage opening of the Shintomi-za, if it did not fulfill the requirements of the proscenium arch of the European tradition, served well its purpose of segregating the fictional space of a play from the real space occupied by the audience.

17. When the Nakamura-za expanded the stage by a *ken* (about 3.9 m) in 1798, the change was not welcomed by the actors. After persistent complaints from the principal actors, such as Matsumoto Kōshirō V and Bandō Hikosaburō III, the theatre restored the stage to its former size (Fujinami 1988, 86; Gunji 1990, 359–60).

18. Some researchers maintain that it was 11 *ken* (about 20 m) wide (see for example, Suda 1957, 351; Yamazaki and Daikuhara 1990, 87).

19. There were 285 in *sajiki* side boxes; 1,039 in the orchestra; 347 in other cheaper areas; and 294 standing (Kokuritsu Gekijō 1978, 13).

20. Hasegawa recalls that although the capacity of the three licensed theatres of Edo was 1,000 spectators, 1,400 to 1,500 were occasionally admitted (1928, 197–198).

21. Curiously, despite the widening of the Shintomi-za stage, its height has remained unchanged. For a wooden theatre—which already had two levels of galleries—an increase in stage height was not called for in order to increase the audience capacity. By keeping the height unchanged, Kan'ya avoided expensive scale readjustment of stage sets. This eventually led to today's strangely elongated rectangular stage. The proportion between the height and the width of the stage in today's *kabuki* theatres has reached the staggering figure of one to three (Hattori 1974, 97).

22. Kan'ya was twenty-two in 1868 at the time of the government takeover. He had a penchant for all things new. His craze for European civilization reached such an extent that for a while he preferred to eat *sashimi* (raw fish) with salt and pepper and not with soy sauce as the Japanese did. As a boy of twelve, when the port of Yokohama was opened for overseas trade, he ran away from home with a dream of becoming a millionaire by doing business with Westerners. Unfortunately, he was caught by the shogun's police and sent back home (Kawatake 1959, 761).

23. This time, the theatre owners and playwrights were summoned by Tokyo's First Ward Office (Matsumoto 1974, 36; Kawatake 1959, 757).

24. In the Edo era, topics related to the shogun or his government could not be dramatized. To dodge government censorship, contemporary topics were set in different historical periods and characters were given fictional names. The new government saw this practice as irrational falsification and demanded that the texts be true to history.

25. For the link between theatre and prostitution, see Gunji (1956) and Shively (1978).

26. In *Japan Day by Day*, Edward S. Morse, an American natural historian who

taught at the Imperial University of Tokyo, records his visit to a *kabuki* theatre. He noticed that acting was "exceedingly realistic" and was repelled by some "shocking" scenes. He describes a *harakiri* scene he witnessed:

> All the details are shown: the baring of the abdomen, the cut from left to right with a short knife, the handle and blade held in the two hands; the blade passes along, the cut appears as a blue line followed by a red fluid; the actor then throws his head forward and a friend starts to strike it off with a sword, but turning away in agony drops his weapon, which another quickly picks up, and terminates the sad tragedy. It is like a juggler's trick, for in the excitement you are not aware that some of the actors pass in front of the victim, so that the sword really seems to come down on the neck of the man, who has in the meantime, like a turtle, drawn his head within his loose robes. Be that as it may, a head with a bloody stump rolls out, which is gathered up, placed in a tray, and conveyed to the judge or daimyo, who, recognizing the features, knows that the act has been accomplished. (Morse 1990, 1:404)

Such grotesque realism is absent from the *kabuki* today. Surprisingly, the theatre mentioned here seems to be the Shintomi-za, since Morse describes it in other places as being new and the best and largest in Japan, lighted by two gas chandeliers. The play he saw about the "history of an early shogun" was perhaps *Matsu no Sakae Chiyoda no Shintoku*, which portrayed the life of the first Tokugawa shogun, Tokugawa Ieyasu. It was the first commercial production in the Shintomi-za, in June 1878. The episode indicates that even a play produced with the clear goal of reform had retained the bloodthirsty imagery of the previous era,

27. The use of contemporary subject matter, the graphic depiction of battle scenes (which used fireworks onstage), and the popular sympathy for the defeated hero all contributed to the enormous success of the play, which ran for eighty days (Kawatake 1959, 772).

28. Fukuchi Genichirō later commented that "there are many who buy geisha and prostitutes, but it is Kan'ya alone who buys the government officials with money" (in Kawatake 1959, 773).

29. Beyond the 3,000-yen budget allotted by the Grant welcoming committee, Kan'ya spent 10,000 yen to produce the show and an additional 5,000 yen for the geisha (Kimura 1943, 578, 582). For comparison, the price of a box for four at the Shintomi-za in the same year was 3 yen and the total construction cost of the theatre was estimated at 23,000 yen (Kokuritsu Gekijō 1984: 680–681).

30. The play was *Go Sannen Ōshū Gunki* (A chronicle of the latter three year campaign in the far provinces). For a description of the evening, see Kimura (1943, 125).

31. Kan'ya paid 300 yen for the ice cream and sweets alone (Kimura 1943, 582).

32. Whitney's description of the geisha dance is also of interest:

> What made the blood rush with a thrill through the hearts of the Americans? What in the appearance of these girls made thousands of sweet memories and patriotic thoughts arise in our minds? Ah, the old flag, the glorious Stars and Stripes! What else could produce in an American such feelings! Each girl was dressed in a robe made of the dear old Stars and Stripes, while upon their heads shone a circlet of silver stars. It made the prettiest costume imaginable. The stripes constituted the over-robe itself while one sleeve slipped off from one shoulder revealed a sleeve of stars below, their girdles were dark blue, sandals, red and white, and presently they

took out fans having on one side the American and upon the other the national flag. The surprise was complete. We looked with strong emotion upon this graceful tribute to our country's flag and felt grateful to our Japanese friends for their kindness displayed not only to General Grant but to our honored country. (1979, 260–261)

33. Although produced for the November *kaomise* (the season-opening show in which all the leading players of the troupe took part) of 1878, *Chūshingura* ran till January the following year, due to its popularity (Kimura, 545–546; Ihara 1962, 239).

34. The play was *Hyōryū Kidan Seiyō-geki* (Wanderers' strange story: Foreign *kabuki*). The poor acting of the Western performers and the incomprehensible language, likened to roosters being strangled, caused its failure. Kan'ya's loss, which amounted to more than 20,000 yen, led to his eventual downfall (Kimura 1943, 585–588; Kawatake 1959, 780–781).

35. *Nō*, which had been the official theatre of the shogun's government and considered to be a superior art form, was performed in front of the emperor in 1876 and again in 1880. The viewing of *kabuki*, because of the actors' status under the previous regime, was strongly opposed by the imperial household and did not occur until 1887 (Kimura 1943, 752–753: Kawatake 1959, (809–815).

References

Akimoto, Shunkichi. 1956. "Kabuki Audiences, Past and Present." *Japan Quarterly* 3: 99–104.

Ando, Hiroshige III. 1984. *Shintomi-za Kaigyō Hanagasa Zu* (Shintomi-za decorated with flowers for the opening) Tokyo: Kokuritsu Gekijō.

Fujinami, Takayuki. 1988. *Dentō Geinō no Sai Hakken* (Rediscovery of the traditional performing arts). Tokyo: Hakushisha.

Gerstle, C. Andrew. 1987. "Flowers of Edo: Eighteenth-Century *Kabuki* and Its Patrons." *Asian Theatre Journal* 4, no. 1 (spring): 52–75. [Reprinted in this volume, chapter 6. Ed.]

Goto Keiji. 1925. *Nihon Gekijōshi* (History of Japan's theatres). Tokyo: Iwanami.

Gunji Masakatsu. 1954. *Kabuki: Yōshiki to Denshō* (Kabuki: Style and tradition). Tokyo: Nara Shobō.

———. 1956. *Kabuki to Yoshiwara* (*Kabuki* and the Yoshiwara). Tokyo: Awaji Shobō.

———. 1990. *Kabuki Mon: Gunji Masakatsu Santeishū* (*Kabuki* gate: Selected works of Gunji Masakatsu), 1. Tokyo: Hakusuisha.

———. 1991. *Henshin no Sho: Gunji Masakatsu Santeishū* (Song of transformation: Selected works of Gunji Masakatsu), 4. Tokyo: Hakusuisha.

Hasegawa Kanbei. 1928. "Saruwaka-chō no Omoide" (Remembrances of Saruwaka-chō) *Engei Gahō* (Theatre illustrated) 22, 11 (November): 192–198.

Hattori Yukio. 1974. *Kabuki no Genzō* (The phenomenon of *kabuki*). Tokyo: Asuka Shogo.

———. 1980. *Edo Kabuki Ron* (Edo *kabuki* discussions). Tokyo: Hosei University Press.

———. 1986. *Ōoinaru Koya* (Great theatres). Tokyo: Heibonsha.

———. 1993. *Edo Kabuki*. Tokyo: Iwanami Shoten.

Ihara Seiseien [Toshirō]. 1926. "Shintomi-za no Zenshin" (Advances of the Shintomi-za). *Kabuki Kenkyū* (*Kabuki* studies) 6: 687–699.

Ihara Toshirō [Seiseien]. 1933. *Meiji Engekishi* (History of Meiji theatre). Tokyo: Waseda University Press.

————. 1962. *Kabuki Nenpyō* (*Kabuki* chronology), vol. 7. Tokyo: Iwanami Shoten.

Kawatake Shigetoshi. 1943. *Kabukishi no Kenkyū* (Studies of *kabuki* history). Tokyo: Tōkyōdō.

————. 1959. *Nihon Engeki Zenshi* (Complete history of Japanese theatre). Tokyo: Iwanami.

Kawatake Toshio. 1993. *Program for Kabuki Kanshō Kyōshitsu*. Tokyo: Kokuritsu Gekijō.

Kimura Eijirō. 1934. *Gekijō oyobi Eigakan* (Theatres and movie houses). Tokyo: Private Publication.

Kimura Kinka. 1943. *Morita Kan'ya*. Tokyo: Shin Otsukasha.

Kōbitsu Matsuō. 1988. *Nihon Shingeki Rinenshi: Meiji Zenki hen: Meiji no Engeki Kairyō Undō to Sono Rinen* (History of Shingeki ideas: Early Meiji: The Meiji theatre reform movement and its ideas). Tokyo: Hakusuisha.

Kokuritsu Gekijō (The National Theatre of Japan). 1978. "Tōkyō no Gekijō" (Tokyo theatres). Unpublished report by Enjōji Kiyōomi. Tokyo: Kokuritsu Gekijō.

————. [1917] 1984. *Tōtō Gekijō Enkakushi* (Annals of Edo's theatres). Tokyo: Kokuritsu Gekijō. Reprint of Shisei Sekine, *Tōtō Gekijō Enkaku-shi*. Tokyo: Engeki Tōsho Dōkōkai.

————. 1990. *Kokuritsu Gekijō Shōzō Shibai Hanga to Zuroku IV* (National Theatre theatrical prints and illustrations, vol. IV). Tokyo: Kokuritsu Gekijō.

————. 1992. *Nishikie ni Miru Edo, Meiji no Gekijō* (Seeing Edo and Meiji theatres in woodblock prints). Tokyo: Kokuritsu Gekijō.

Koyama Akimoto. 1975. *Kankyaku no Geidan* (Audience comments on acting art). Tokyo: Chuō Koron.

Matsumoto, Shinko. 1974. *Meiji Zenki Engeki Ron shi* (Complete history of early Meiji theatre ideas). Tokyo: Engeki Shuppansha.

Morse, Edward S. 1990. *Japan Day by Day*, 2 vols. Atlanta: Cherokee Publishing.

Obayashi-gumi Project Team. 1979 "Bunka-Bunsei-ki Ichimura-za Fukugen no Kokoromi" (Attempts to restore the Bunka-Bunsei era Ichimura-za). *Kikan Obayashi* 4: 17–24.

Osasa, Yoshio. 1985. *Nihon Gendai Engekishi: Meiji Taishō Hen* (Modern Japanese theatre history: Meiji and Taishō periods). Tokyo: Hakusuisha

Raz, Jacob. 1983. *Audience and Actors: A Study of Their Interaction in the Japanese Traditional Theatre*. Leiden: E.J. Brill.

Satō Yūji. 1971. *Dentō Geijutsu no Inochi* (The life of the traditional arts). Tokyo: Keiryūsha.

Shimizu Isao. 1992. *Zoku Bigot Nihon Sobyō-shū* (Collection of Bigot's Japanese sketches, continued). Tokyo: Iwanami.

Shively, Donald H. 1978. "The Social Environment of Tokugawa *Kabuki*." In *Studies in Kabuki*, ed. James R. Brandon et al., 1–62. Honolulu: University of Hawai'i Press.

Suda Atsuo. 1957. *Nihon Gekijōshi no Kenkoyū* (Studies in the history of Japanese theatres.) Tokyo: Sagami Shoten.

Toita Yasuji. 1978. Kabuki *Kono Hyakunen* (This 100 years of *kabuki*). Tokyo: Mainichi Shinbun.

Tsukahara Seiseien. 1915. "Mukashi no Kenbutsu to Ima no Kenbutsu (Old-time theatregoing and today's theatregoing." *Engei Gahō* (Theatre illustrated) 9, no. 1 (January): 237–239.

Utagawa Kunisada III. 1872. *Morita-za Ōiri no Zu* (Pictures of Morita-za hits). Courtesy of Kokuritsu Gekijō.

———. 1878a. *Shintomi-za Honbushin Kōgyō Kankyaku Gunju Zu* (The crowd gathering at the reconstructed Shintomi-za). Courtesy of Kokuritsu Gekijō.

———. 1878b. *Shintomi-za Honbushin Rakusei Yoshibai Kankyaku Gunju Zu* (The crowd gathering at the completed reconstructed Shintomi-za for the evening performance). Courtesy of Kokuritsu Gekijō.

Utagawa Toyokuni III. 1858. *Odori Keiyō Edoe no Sakae* (Dance illustrating the glamor of Edo). Courtesy of Kokuritsu Gekijō.

———. 1859 *Ōshibai Hanei no Zu* (Picture of a prosperous large theatre). Courtesy of Kokuritsu Gekijō.

Whitney, Clara A. 1979. *Clara's Diary: An American Girl in Meiji Japan*. Edited by William M. Steele and Ichimata Tamiko. Tokyo: Kodansha International.

Yamazaki Yasutaka and Daikuhara Jun. 1990. "Dentō Geinō Kūkan no Kenshō: Sono Rekishi to Tokuchō" (Inspection of traditional performing arts spaces: Their history and characteristics). In *Kyōto Minami-za no Kiroku: Yawarakai Gekijō Ron* (Record of Kyoto's Minami-za: Gentle theatre discussions), ed. Kyōto Minami-za no Kiroku Shuppan Iinkai, 73–106. Tokyo: Rokuyōsha.

Yomiuri Shinbun. June 9, 1878.

9

Breaking the *Kabuki* Actors' Barriers: 1868–1900

Faith Bach

Ever since its inception at the beginning of the seventeenth century, the traditional popular theatre of Japan, *kabuki*, had been subject to minute surveillance by a hostile military government, most stringently in Edo (old Tokyo), where the Tokugawa shoguns had their seat. Government restrictions on *kabuki* were both artistic and social. Censorship curtailed the scope of subject matter. Sumptuary edicts limited materials, styles, and even colors in costumes and properties. Women were banned from the stage in 1629 and youths in 1652. Theatre buildings were restricted in size and facilities, as well as in number, confined to certain sections of the city, and finally banished altogether to the suburban outskirts, next to the pleasure quarters. Actors and managers were frequently arrested for transgressions. In 1714 an entire theatre was closed down and all its assets sold at public auction when its leading actor was discovered to have been conducting a love affair with a high-ranking lady in the shogun's household.[1] [See Shively's essay, chapter 3, for details on *kabuki's* battles with the government. Ed.]

In Tokugawa Japan, where relations between the social classes were strictly circumscribed, actors were relegated to a caste so low that they were not permitted surnames and were listed as *hinin* (nonpersons) in the census. They were officially prohibited from fraternizing with the citizenry and were periodically required to wear *amagasa* (basket hats) in public to conceal their faces from their fans. Although enjoying great support from the populace as well as influence upon its styles and customs, actors as a class were oppressed from above and legally ostracized from society at large. Thus they were bound to found their own social sphere within the isolated theatre world. Indeed, this specialized society developed a system of hierarchical structures comparable to those from which actors were excluded. It was not until the middle of the Meiji period (1868–1912) that these structures finally crumbled. They were eroded not only by direct interference by the new progressive bureaucrats who had overthrown the shogunate but also by the liberalizing influence of the new civilian population that poured into Tokyo from the provinces to replace the departing warlords.

The very first directive to the Tokyo theatre world from the new Meiji government upon assuming power in 1868 was an order obliging all three licensed theatres [the *sanza* or "three theatres." Ed.] to move out of the Saruwaka-chō entertainment district in suburban Asakusa.[2] On the whole, theatre managers were loath to give up the land they had been occupying since 1842, when the death of the liberal shogun Ienari had enabled a conservative backlash to banish the theatres thither. The only manager to see in the new directive any real benefit for his theatre was young Morita Kan'ya XII (1846–1897), a progressive visionary who would become one of the leading theatrical innovators of his era. Occupying the remote northern corner of the Saruwaka-chō district, his theatre was the youngest of the *sanza* and had always been the weakest. Kan'ya was determined to reverse his theatre's fortunes, and, in October 1872, he opened his new Morita-za at Shintomi-chō in Tsukiji, not far from the foreign settlement. It was an immediate success. Increasing conventional audience capacity by 25 percent, it offered such innovations as a fire-resistant roof and solid ceiling, enhanced acoustics, toilet facilities in the theatre proper, and chairs in the stalls for the convenience of patrons in Western dress. For his actors, Kan'ya expanded the backstage and dressing room areas and planned vacation days into the runs for the first time in *kabuki* history. [The story of this theatre's early days is told by Takahashi in chapter 8. Ed.]

The first of the *sanza* to reopen uptown, the new Morita-za symbolized the edge of the wedge in the dissolution of *sanza* hegemony in the theatre industry that had prevailed unchallenged for nearly three centuries. For Kan'ya's venture represented a rupture in *sanza* solidarity and a subsequent rebalancing of power within it. Time-honored custom fostered *sanza* solidarity by requiring a manager to secure permission from his two fellow managers for any major operational changes he wished to make. Although government sanction had been given Kan'ya's move earlier in the year, he was next obliged to get approval from the *sanza* elder, Nakamura Kanzaburō XIII, whose ancestor had established the first theatre in Edo in 1624. Kanzaburō met Kan'ya's initial approach with a classic Japanese method of expressing disapproval: manifesting concern for the hardship the proposal would cause the proposing party. Kan'ya countered that continued occupation of remote Saruwaka-chō would eventually spell the collapse of the *sanza*'s grasp on the industry in the face of inevitable urbanization, and he offered himself as first martyr to the *sanza* cause in risking the transfer to the city. Kanzaburō and the third *sanza* manager, Ichimura Uzaemon XIV (then Ichimura Kakitsu V), were trapped by this logic into giving Kan'ya their blessing.

The collapse that Kan'ya predicted came with unexpected force. It enfranchised free market competition unprecedented in the theatre world, against which Kan'ya's foresight had already placed him in a position of advantage. Shortly before the new Morita-za's opening, the Tokyo government issued a ruling under which *sanza* hegemony was all at once destroyed: "For theatres under prefectural jurisdiction, the *sanza* and others: for those who have heretofore been operating free of tax, it is now required to obtain permit and license; for those already in operation, application for permission must be resubmitted" (Ihara 1975, 23). By clearly implying, with the words "*sanza* and others,*" that license applications from new theatres would be considered, the relicensing edict did away with the longstanding Tokugawa restriction of the number of legitimate theatres to three and amounted to a "theatre liberation order" (Akiba 1955, 6).

The Tokyo *sanza* system can be said to have begun forming with the founding of the Nakamura-za in 1624 and was fully developed by 1660 when the Morita-za was first established.[3] The theatres were at first run by actors whose licenses to produce as *zamoto* (managers) were hereditary and passed down through their families. In later years, some members of a managing line might cease to act. Kan'ya, for instance, although of an acting family, was not himself an actor. Nonetheless, the fortunes of these managers were inextricably bound up with certain actors of their own or traditionally connected families. Thus licensed theatre management continued to remain the sole province of a few powerful acting families; moreover, all actors were required to sign seasonal contracts restricting their employment to one *sanza* theatre for a full year's season beginning with the eleventh month *kaomise* (face-showing) performance. In 1735 an unlicensed playhouse, the Kawarazaki-za [also Kawarasaki-za. Ed.], was given government permission to hold the license of the Morita-za temporarily and stage its plays while the latter was unable to do so, thus becoming the first *hikae yagura* (auxiliary or alternate) theatre. Soon the Miyako-za and the Kiri-za affiliated in this fashion with the Nakamura-za and Ichimura-za, respectively. The *hikae yagura* was permitted to mount productions for a period not exceeding ten years whenever its parent *sanza* theatre was obliged by debt or disaster to close its doors.

As might be imagined, disputes inevitably arose between parent and auxiliary over the lucrative rights to the single license they were forced to share. The exertion of pressure of dubious legality upon the parent theatre by its *hikae yagura* could sometimes force the closure of the former for extended periods. Such was the case with the Morita-za, for example, from 1837 to 1855, due to the underhanded methods of its *hikae yagura* manager, Kawarazaki Gonnosuke VI. More commonly, disputes resulted in both theatres closing temporarily until their differences were settled. During these closures it was not only managers who suffered but also the actors, forced by the seasonal contract system into compulsory unemployment. With the revolutionary 1872 relicensing directive, the *hikae yagura* saw the chance to emerge from their marginal and occasional existence. The Kawarazaki-za and Kiri-za promptly applied for and received permission to reopen under independent license.

Although the *sanza* system kept control of the legitimate theatre world in the hands of certain families by limiting mainstream theatres to three, there had always been small, unlicensed playhouses catering to the lower orders through attachment to temple fairgrounds and similar entertainment centers. These playhouses had long been known by the pejorative epithet *donchō shibai* (drop-curtain theatres) from the fact that, among other numerous and sundry restrictions imposed by the government, only the *sanza* were permitted to use the elegant curtain that is still drawn from side to side in *kabuki*. Drop-curtain theatres were tolerated by the authorities within certain limits—among them severely restricted periods of operation confined to a few fixed days per year, usually coinciding with festival seasons. Only the *sanza* were allowed to remain in continuous production, or as continuous as their finances and legal disputes would permit. The 1872 directive offered, through licensing, equal commercial freedom to all, consequently enabling even smaller theatres to offer competitive employment conditions to actors.

The first drop-curtain manager to apply for enfranchisement was one Bandō Muraemon, owner of the Muraemon no Shibai in the Ryōgoku entertainment district along the Sumida River. A license was granted him to reopen under the name Nakajima-za, which he did on April 21, 1873. He was soon joined by two of his neighbors, the Haruki-za (which survived as the Hongō-za until 1930) and the Kishō-za (since 1893 the Meiji-za). This pioneering group became known as the "Ryōgoku *sanza*." Although the distinction between *ōshibai* or *daigekijō* (major) and *koshibai* or *shōgekijō* (minor) theatres was not officially systematized until 1890, prior to that all theatres first licensed under the 1872 directive are normally considered "minors."

Their early history is bound to be obscure. With the exception of the Haruki-za, a large theatre listed with some regularity, inclusion of the minors in *kabuki* chronologies is sporadic.[4] Name changes and troupe regroupings were frequent, suggesting vigorous competition among them. But while their position in the 1872 market was new, all had been functioning as drop-curtain theatres for considerable periods prior to relicensing, so they already had commercial experience and established custom. It is safe to assume that they were solvent, since they were able immediately to hire troupes. They thereby opened up a world of unprecedented opportunity for the Tokyo actor.

It had always been the rule throughout *kabuki* history that a mainstream actor played the *sanza* and nowhere else (except *hikae yagura* when they took over *sanza* productions). He could never under any circumstances play an unlicensed house without immediately forfeiting all future right to play *sanza*. The strict discrimination between *sanza* and drop-curtain theatres thus produced two classes of actor. Drop-curtain actors were nominally members of one or another mainstream acting *mon* (guild or "family") wherein they had learned or copied their craft from *mon* masters or, more likely, their apprentices. [See Powell's explanation of *kabuki* acting-family hierarchies in chapter 10. Ed.] *Mon* affiliation granted the actor onstage use of a prestigious acting surname, access to the masters and their vast networks of professional associates, and the vital *shihanjō* (teaching license).[5] This license authorized the bearer to teach dance, music, and other performing arts under the *mon* aegis—a respectable trade that had always catered to a lucrative amateur market and no doubt supported many actors' families through the lean drop-curtain seasons. In a society that still considers one's group to be one's primary identification, estimable *mon* affiliation was crucial to an actor of either class, and for the most part it was only an accident of birth—remote or nonsanguinous connection—that separated the drop-curtain actor from his more purely pedigreed *sanza* colleagues. For the repertoire in both worlds was the same, as was, presumably, the level of talent—judging from the drop-curtains' large fan followings and the career epithets attached to popular drop-curtain actors like "Tuppenny Danjūrō" and "Kikugorō of the Park" that identified them with the highest-ranking mainstream actors. Although within the *sanza* world certain plays, roles, costumes, styles, and even performance "bits" were zealously guarded by their creators' descendants as family monopolies, the same were freely played in drop-curtain houses with *sanza* sufferance. A drop-curtain manager and his leading actor might appear at the home of the *sanza mon* master whose "property" their next show was and officially request indulgence, but never do the records show that indulgence was withheld or that the request itself was much more than a formality. The drop-curtain houses were a world apart and tolerated by the *sanza* as beneath their notice.

All this changed with the 1872 relicensing, which threw the two worlds into competition. It may be said to have generated a third world, as well, the members of which would prove instrumental in the eventual dissolution of the traditional actors' barriers. For in the event, the class of actor most benefited by the newly enfranchised minor theatres was that middling group of talented but not highly pedigreed *sanza* men who were relegated by custom to a career of lesser roles in the troupes of ranking *mon*. A great many of these actors during 1873 turned their backs on limited prospects in the *sanza* to join the minor troupes and become part of what history calls the *dassōgumi* (deserters' brigade) (Kimura 1943, 405). While those who became deserters entertained a certain risk, they had no reason to believe that their careers would be second-rate. Many of them, despite extreme youth, became *zagashira* (troupe leaders) immediately upon joining a new minor theatre, as did Yamazaki (later Ichikawa) Ennosuke I for the Nakajima-za at the tender age of eighteen. And although the deserters were obliged to forfeit their places in the *sanza* hierarchy, joining the minors did not itself constitute a break with their original *mon*. Though propriety prevented all of them from continuing to use their masters' family crests and most their masters' surnames, the deserters could expect to retain the basic *mon* privileges that had always been accorded even drop-curtain actors. While *sanza* masters cannot have been pleased to lose promising apprentices to the minors, very few cases of discord over the issue are on record, and in none is severance with the *mon* indicated. The word *hamon* ("broken *mon*," meaning excommunication) is a precise one signifying a very serious event and is a matter of public record when it occurs.

Like all new movements, the rising minors were writing their future, and their pioneers held hopes of success. There is no evidence, however, that their hopes at the outset went beyond the sphere of individual ambition for increased artistic and economic prospects. It is apparent that for many, such hopes were quickly realized. Evidently the success of the new minor theatres was initially self-contained. There is nothing to suggest, for instance, that it in any way seriously affected the *sanza*. In fact, the *sanza*, catalyzed by Kan'ya's vision and encouraged by new Meiji audiences, embarked upon a new phase of prosperity, overcoming the recession that had plagued the entertainment industries during the social and political upheavals of the 1860s. It is possible to argue that both the *sanza* and the minors would have gone on occupying their own separate worlds, had it not been for the singular career of one man.

Ennosuke I (1855–1922) joined the Nakajima-za on May 2, 1873, not two weeks after its opening. Despite a relatively humble birth (as grandson of an Edo gold-leaf merchant who had taken to the stage), his career in the *sanza* was not at all unpromising. After doing his earliest adult acting work in the Keihan [also called Kamigata or Kansai. Ed.] (Kyoto/Osaka) area, where his father was contracted as a *tateshi* (fight choreographer), he was "scouted" by Tokyo's most powerful actor oligarch, Ichikawa Danjūrō IX (1838–1903). Greatly favored by the master, to the extent of being given roles disproportionate to his rank, Ennosuke could reasonably have expected a steady rise in status, perhaps even eventual stardom, under Danjūrō's patronage. He opted instead to join the deserters. Although Danjūrō above all deplored this trend, Ennosuke remained in the *mon* throughout 1873. The following January he became the first actor in history to be excommunicated over an artistic issue. Without leave from his master, to whose name the role traditionally belonged, Ennosuke at the age of nineteen played Benkei in *Kanjinchō* (The subscription list). Examination of Ennosuke's life suggests that this was a calculated career decision.[6] He spent the next several years as a top actor for the Ryōgoku *sanza* before going back to Keihan to emerge as a full-fledged star.

Far from the shogunal seat and its strict surveillance, the Keihan theatre world had developed a system quite different from Edo's. Theatre polity in Keihan overall had always been less elitist and stratified. Management was less a hereditary right than a moneymaking enterprise and had historically been entrusted by the acting families to that class of impresarios and actors' agents peculiar to Keihan: the *shiuchi*. Theatre classifications were less strictly enforced, as well. Actors from major and minor theatres regularly appeared on the same bill. These bills often ran at a *chūshibai* (middle theatre), a popular institution unique to Keihan that had no counterpart in Tokyo.[7] It provided a platform not only for "mixed" bills but also for younger actors' recital-style runs in starring roles, for visiting or *kodomo shibai* (children's troupes), for untried plays or stagecraft—in short, for whatever the market would bear. In Keihan, furthermore, actors were not constricted by a seasonal contract system but could negotiate employment freely on a per-run basis. This policy allowed Keihan actors to make lucrative guest appearances in Tokyo, all the more popular for their brevity, not only at the *sanza* but at the minors as well. Keihan's high-ranking Kataoka Nizaemon XI (then Gatō, 1857–1934) played with great success periodically at the Nakajima-za and Haruki-za in the 1880s.

Ennosuke's career flourished in the more democratic environment of Keihan with the initial help of the *shiuchi* San'ei [these individuals typically used one name. Ed.], who also managed Keihan's top master of popular *keren* (stunt) art, Jitsukawa Enjaku I (1831–1885). The first hit San'ei engineered for Ennosuke was in a *keren* role tailor-written for him in *Kawanakajima* [Kawanaka Island. Ed.]: that of a *ninjutsu-tsukai* (black magician). Revolves and traplifts figured prominently as Ennosuke executed quick changes, sleights of appearance, tree climbing, roof stunts, tumbling, and rafter-hangs and finished with a *tachimawari* [choreographed fight scene. Ed.] battle of immense proportions. During his seven years in Keihan, Ennosuke further honed those *keren* skills for which he had first developed a reputation at the Ryōgoku *sanza*. He frequently repeated such popular successes as *Shiranui* (The Shiranui story), *Hokaibō* (The priest Hokaibō), various enchanted-fox pieces, and a spectacular "thunder and lightning" *raimei chunōri* (aerial stunt) in a *henge* (transformation) monster role. He also played more classical roles, such as Benkei, to acclaim. At the end of 1886, Ennosuke returned to the Tokyo minors to press fanfare with a homecoming performance as Matagorō Fox in *Meoto Gitsune* (Mr. and Mrs. Fox).

The Tokyo mainstream to which Ennosuke was returning was rather different stylistically from the mainstream he had left over a decade earlier. Although such grassroots arts as *keren* still flourished in Keihan, in Tokyo they had fallen out of fashion. During the 1880s a distinct movement for theatre reform, discouraging the more florid stage conventions and idealizing modernization and progress, had begun to take hold.[8] It culminated in the establishment of the Engeki Kairyōkai (Society for Theatre Reform) under the leadership of activist Suematsu Kenchō with the support of the literati and of statesmen such as Itō Hirobumi. [See Lee, chapter 20, for more details on the Society for Theatre Reform. Ed.] The society's activities reached a peak in October 1886 with the gala staged reading of its first "reformed" script, *Yoshino Shūi Meika no Homare* (Praise of famous poems gleaned at Yoshino), which was attended by such theatre luminaries as Danjūrō and Kan'ya (who declined, however, to produce it). The movement gained great ground among government leaders, intellectuals, and a new breed of self-styled playwrights, critics, and scholar-consultants from outside the traditional theatre world who began to infiltrate it as outside specialists. Kan'ya, lobbying for subsidy as a national theatre, was a friend of the reformers, and Danjūrō was their leading onstage light. Danjūrō's naturally sober style and preoccupation with the past made his art compatible with the ideals of the reformers, who advocated a "naturalistic" renovation of style and content more appropriate to Japan's emerging national cultural consciousness. With their encouragement, he had embarked on a career of creating serious, historically accurate, *katsureki* (living history) plays.[9] These plays transformed well-loved stage heroes with authentic costume, locution, and blocking even down to forfeiture of famous *mie* (dramatic poses).[10]

The congruity of Danjūrō's concerns with those of the reformists gained him even greater standing within the theatre polity than was already his by right. He was held in high esteem by the ruling classes and invited to star in private shows for officialdom and visiting foreign dignitaries, as well as to represent the theatre world by addressing reformist functions. In some con-

Figure 9.1 **Ichikawa Danjūrō IX, left, as Benkei, and Onoe Kikugorō V, right, as Togashi, in** *Kanjinchō*. **(Photo: Tsubouchi Memorial Museum, Waseda University.)**

trast was the situation of his counterpart and traditional "rival," the high-ranking star Onoe Kikugorō V (1844–1903), a hereditary champion of *keren* and populist art. Kikugorō was snubbed by reformist and government elements and his art devalued as counterprogressive. This treatment resulted in management's disrespect (perhaps best symbolized by his being made redundant by Kan'ya in 1885) and a consequent loss within the theatre polity of authority that was his by hereditary right. Many other traditional-minded actors fared the same. Thus the fabric of *kabuki*'s traditional hierarchy was fundamentally rent by ruling-class intervention in such strong support of Danjūrō and disregard of his more orthodox colleagues (figure 9.1).

While it is arguable that in a certain sense these external incursions into the *kabuki* polity contributed in the long run to its ensuing democratization, they had the immediate effect of inflating Danjūrō's personal authority, already considerable, to great proportions. He continued to insist on actors' segregation, refusing to recognize minor theatres as legitimate platforms for "major" art. Both Danjūrō's art and his politics were in direct antithesis to those of his renegade apprentice, Ennosuke, and his personal power was immense. Yet it was this authoritarian figure whom Ennosuke managed to appease—becoming the first and only ranking actor to recross the traditional actors' boundary and reenter the major theatre world from the minors. He achieved this not long after his return to Tokyo, when in October 1890 he shared the stage with Danjūrō for the first time in nearly twenty years.

Tokyo *kabuki* had never made official provision for boundary-crossing at any cost. It is highly significant that the new actors' union, with Danjūrō as president, did so for the first time in history at its inaugural session in 1889.[11] That negotiations for Ennosuke's return to Danjūrō's *mon* were already under way at this time is known.[12] This invites speculation that Danjūrō had Ennosuke's accommodation specifically in mind when establishing the regulation. It must be noted that along with this groundbreaking ruling, however, the actors' boundary itself was reinforced by another formal union regulation requiring forfeiture of major status by any actor taking employment at a minor theatre. This policy was strengthened by Danjūrō's personal promise to boycott any theatre employing boundary-jumping actors. On the whole, the passage of both statutes might be taken to indicate the union's attempt to exercise control over a phenomenon it no longer felt able to hold off entirely, for since the rise of the minors the old order had been coming under pressure. When as late as 1887 the major actors Sawamura Tosshi, Ichikawa Yaozō [later Ichikawa Chūsha VII. Ed.], and Ichikawa Kyūzō [later Ichikawa Danzō VII] had opened the new minor theatre Azuma-za with *Yoshitsune Senbon Zakura* (Yoshitsune and the thousand cherry trees), they were immediately blackballed by Danjūrō from subsequent major-theatre appearances. The redoubtable Kyūzō, who had earned a great sum for his role of Tomomori, replied to Danjūrō's public scolding by pointing out that as his character died out of sight of the audience, he had no way of knowing whether the curtain had been dropped or drawn. This incident attracted great publicity, and public sympathy was clearly on the side of the three actors. At the same time Kan'ya, due to a speculative venture of his own involving minor theatres, urged leniency and in fact campaigned, albeit unsuccessfully, for the inclusion of minor actors into the new union.

The new boundary-crossing ruling laid down by the union stipulated that a minor-theatre actor petitioning name status in the majors, or a major actor who had played the minors but wished to return to the majors, had first to appear in three major productions in *nadaishita* (subname) walk-on roles.[13] This stipulation included adherence to the strictly delineated backstage behavior that went along with the lowly subname rank. Ennosuke was required, for example, to leave his vehicle some distance away and to be seen entering the theatre on foot. In October 1890 he played a tumbling warrior in Kikugorō's corps at the new Kabuki-za; playwright Okamoto Kidō recalled decades later how sorry he had felt for the actor while watching the show (Okamoto 1922, 25). Ennosuke did two more subname roles in succeeding months and then in March 1891 formally reentered the *mon* as Ichikawa Ennosuke. Danjūrō himself gave the onstage *kōjō* (ceremonial address). For this, his first appearance under *kabuki*'s most illustrious acting surname, Ennosuke played a version of his signature enchanted-fox character in the "Sashi Kago" (Raising high the palanquin) scene of *Kuzunoha* (a character's name).

The wealth of references to Ennosuke's boundary-crossing ascent to major status leave no doubt that in contemporary opinion it was a unique event and worthy of unanimous praise. In fact there is a great deal of sentiment adhering to the reports. Ennosuke was considered a star in the Tokyo minors and had maintained a high profile in the Keihan majors. Thus his perseverance through the humbling transition regulations took on heroic qualities in the eyes of his public and colleagues. Furthermore, the old order was soon to crumble; Ennosuke was both the first and the last to endure such initiation rites. This imbued him with that sacrificial aura, always heroic in Japanese eyes, surrounding the end of an era; for, concurrent with Ennosuke's crossing, the second set of theatre control regulations (*gekijō torishimari kisoku*) generated radical changes in the theatre world and paved the way for the final dissolution of actors' segregation.[14]

The theatre control regulations, promulgated by the Tokyo government, drew an exclusively physical distinction between major and minor theatres. The implication was that any house able to conform to major physical standards as delineated could be licensed as a major theatre—as indeed the Ryōgoku *sanza* thereafter were. Although minors were still forbidden the use of draw-curtains, the discriminatory epithet "drop-curtain theatre" was officially replaced by *shōgekijō* (literally, small theatre), a term that until then had only had occasional and unstandardized usage. The total number of theatres permitted in the city was set at twenty-two. Apart from the lifting of the age-old prohibition on men and women sharing the stage, no rulings pertinent to actors or their status were included. This was a remarkable omission in a document that so transformed existing standards in the theatre world—and gives rise to the argument that the regulations contributed to undermining actors' segregation simply by not having reinforced it. Faced with the official position that the major/minor distinction was now to be regarded only as a physical one, the theatre world itself was encouraged to redefine that distinction. And indeed the regulations led to energetic debate on this topic in the press among specialists and the public. Danjūrō, however, continued to hold firm against the *daraku* (decay) of the major actors' art upon association with the minors (Ihara 1975, 702). As late as June 1891, just weeks after Ennosuke's epoch-making advancement, several actors from

Kikugorō's *mon* who had played a run at the minor Misaki-za were struck from the major actors' roster in accordance with union policy. Danjūrō even resigned as union president in protest, evidently in a fit of pique over Kikugorō's characteristic refusal to prevent the incident or even to discipline his wayward actors. At this dramatic juncture, minor theatre managers, with sympathy from the press, organized and began to campaign against the existing policy of actors' segregation, claiming that it put their theatres at a competitive disadvantage. Ironically, it was Danjūrō himself whose bending of the rules at last provoked the final collapse of the old order.

Although major actors were prohibited from appearing in minor theatre productions, the minor houses themselves were freely available for rental as venues for private or special performances if certain conditions were met. A major troupe, for instance, could rent a minor house for a special show or recital on the stipulation that they pay major tax rates for the run. In September 1892, Danjūrō rented such a house: the Fukuroku-za in Asakusa, which he renamed briefly for the occasion the Keiko-za. Under the aegis of his Mimasu-kai, a reform-oriented society of *mon* members, Danjūrō staged what he called a *keikō shibai* (rehearsal play) made up of scenes performed by his name actors and younger actors together; it was meant to be the first in an enlightened series to provide training and exposure for the young actors. They starred in such classics as *Kurumabiki* (Pulling the carriage apart) and *Domo Mata* (Matahei the stutterer), sharing the bill with senior actors like Ennosuke, who played Chūya in *Keian Taiheiki* (Keian-era chronicle of the the great peace).[15]

The production was well received by fans but caused uproar in the industry. Attention seems initially to have been attracted by the presence in the cast of that same Yaozō who had been blackballed by Danjūrō for a minor theatre appearance in 1887. Although Danjūrō's side argued that the Keiko-za production was just a staged "rehearsal" offering public access, technically Yaozō's presence made the show a cooperative venture between major and minor actors. Above all, it was discovered that Danjūrō had paid minor tax rates on the rental. The press protested vigorously, recalling the Misaki-za incident. Agitation began among lower-ranking major actors for the right to similar rentals at reduced rates. Danjūrō's "rehearsal play" series ended there, but the following spring, when the major Ichimura-za was damaged by fire, its *zashū* (owner) Nakamura Zenshirō took the opportunity to rent the minor house Sawamura-za as a venue for his continuing major troupe productions. As these were standard commercial ventures rather than private recitals, technicalities required the troupe to be registered as a minor company. These Zenshirō ignored, contracting his minor venues by discreet arrangement to protect his actors' status (Ihara 1975, 703). In November his rental of the notorious "Keiko-za" brought Zenshirō's arrangements to public and union attention. His actors were disciplined by the union but retained their status, and antidiscriminatory agitation in the theatre world increased. In the spring of 1894, minor theatre managers petitioned the Tokyo government for action. Representatives of both the major and minor worlds met for discussions with the authorities, which continued throughout the year. In February 1895 the Tokyo theatre world was notified by the government as follows:

> Although theatres are categorized by the appellations major and minor (*daishōgekijō*) according to their size, this is not for the object of dividing actors also into two classes. The segregation, regardless, of actors into two major and minor classes . . . has in the event produced no small number of regulatory abuses. In view of this fact, henceforward these two major and minor classes shall be considered one body. [Ihara 1975, 704]

With this order, all discrimination among actors was abolished. Theatre managers were directed by the authorities that all actors were free to take employment as it suited them. Tax brackets based on actors' incomes were recalibrated. The actors' union, which had never accepted minor actors, was disbanded. A new one was formed that included all actors and had for its president Ichikawa Sumizō. The vice president was Ennosuke.

At the dawn of the new century, the theatre control regulations were again amended to obliterate all remaining vestiges of major-minor theatre discrimination. In January 1900 the theatre world was advised by the authorities that thereafter any house that so desired was free to install a draw-curtain.

Notes

1. This was the notorious Ejima-Ikushima Incident, named after the lovers in question. Relations between their widely separated social classes were strictly proscribed. The actor Ikushima Shingorō, a popular romantic star, was exiled to distant Miyakejima along with the manager of his theatre, the Yamamura-za. Other staff from the theatre and its teahouses were variously punished and banished, as were members of Lady Ejima's family and entourage, and she herself was exiled to Shinsha. Pardoned after thirty years, Shingorō returned to his home in the theatre district, where he died a few months later at the age of seventy-two. [See Shively's essay, chapter 3. Ed.]

2. Tokyo governmental directive of September 24, 1868 (Ihara 1975, 9).

3. Originally there were four licensed theatres; in 1714 the Ejima-Ikushima Incident reduced their number to three.

4. The earliest full *banzuke* (playbill) discovered, for example, for the Nakajima-za by minor-theatre historian Abe Yūzō is for February 1875, nearly two full years after its establishment (Abe 1970, 26). Abe and other sources, however, can identify a few earlier troupes and plays.

5. The *shihanjō* license is extinct in *kabuki*. Today it is retained only in the dance

world, where it is given by the *ie no moto* [or *iemoto*. Ed.] (head of the artistic house) to students of certain ability and seniority.

6. Ennosuke claims to have been resigned to becoming *rōnin* (masterless) from the outset; still, as a "defense for the future," he played the *hamon* Benkei without the important dance "Ennen-no-Mai" (Ichikawa 1908, 36). Under the circumstances, performance of this dance, traditionally considered the soul of Benkei's role, would have been an enormous violation. The following year, at the same theatre, the dance was included in the role by another Danjūrō apprentice, Yamazaki Sakimatsu, who was immediately excommunicated. No more is known about him.

7. The term *chūshibai* is occasionally used loosely by Tokyo chroniclers to refer to those minor houses that employed actors classified by the first actors' taxes in 1875 as *chūtō* (mid-rank), according only to their salaries without regard to hierarchical standing) or to those larger minor theatres that were reclassified as majors in 1890. The Nakajima-za and Haruki-za are often referred to in this way. Authentic *chūshibai* flourishing in Osaka at the beginning of Meiji were the Takeda no Shibai, Chikugo no Shibai, and Wakatayū-za.

8. *Fūzoku no kairyō* (reform of manners) was a popular force in Meiji society from the beginning of the period, when progressivist Fukuzawa Yukichi's treatise *Katawa Musume* (Disfigured misses) helped abolish the customs of blackened teeth and shaved eyebrows for women. Many of the arts were affected. The most radical theatre reformers advocated removing from *kabuki* such integral elements as the *hanamichi* (runway), *kurogo* (onstage assistants), *onnagata* (female-role specialists), and narrative accompaniment. By the end of the 1880s many reformist theories found accommodation in the rising *shinengeki* (modern drama) genres, which thereafter provided the major outlet for reformist energies. [See Takahashi's essay, chapter 8, for details on these reforms. Ed.]

9. The invention of the term *katsureki* is usually credited to Japan's first prominent professional drama critic, Kanagaki Robun, in his review of what is historically considered Danjūrō's first true *katsureki* play, *Nichō no Yumi Chigusa no Shigedō* (A double-stringed, multibraided bow) in 1878 (Tamura 1922, 214). However, the word *katsureki* was first coined in a *Nichinichi Shinbun* editorial of April 13, 1872, reacting to a government directive urging the use of historically accurate names onstage (Matsumoto 1974, 168). Danjūrō's *katsureki* can in fact be traced back stylistically as far as his seminal *Sangoku Musō Hisago no Gunsen* (The battle fan with the gourd: Peerless in three realms) in October 1872.

10. The *mie* is the highly stylized, stop-motion pose struck at climactic moments. It is eagerly awaited and hailed with *kakegoe* (encouraging shouts) by connoisseurs in the audience. *Katsureki* not only replaced *kabuki*'s traditionally stylized aesthetic elements with more authentic and "naturalistic" ones but also altered well-known stories in the interest of historical realism. (In his 1884 version of *Tōeizan Nōfu no Negaisho* [The peasant's petition at Mt. Tōei]), for example, Danjūrō eliminated the rebel farmer Sakura Sōgorō's heroic final confrontation with shogunal authority on the grounds that Sōgorō's low status would not have permitted him to address the highest power in the land directly. Argument from both management and the playwright, Kawatake Shinshichi III, failed to move him, and the playwright temporarily retired in humiliation.) *Katsureki* was at first a critical success and accepted by the new Tokyoites, who had come from the provinces for the benefit of Meiji civilization and tended on the whole to support progress. But traditional audiences were alienated, and by the mid-1880s box-office pressure forced Danjūrō to return to the classics of his heritage. Only two *katsureki* pieces

remain in the repertoire, primarily as curiosities: *Takatoki* (The shogun Takatoki) (1884) and *Sakai no Taiko* (Sakai's drum) (1881).

11. The "union" is now a relatively tame body known as the Haiyū Kyōkai, literally "Actors' cooperative society." It is responsible for a charity benefit system for needy actors, arbitration of casting disputes among actors, and nominal "protection" of the actor's image. (Prior to any publication of stage photos, for example, photographers and authors must secure the Kyōkai's permission by submitting a draft of the manuscript. The actor in question is not always consulted. Frequently an author's request for a specific actor is turned down and a photo of a different actor—of higher rank—in the same role is substituted. The only actor in *kabuki* today who circumvents this system is the present Ennosuke [III. Ed.], *kabuki*'s only actor-manager and head of his own troupe. Ennosuke gives his photos to authors as it suits him.) From Meiji times until the beginning of the militaristic 1930s, the union was known by the proper term for labor union, *kumiai*, reflecting its somewhat wider political scope.

12. Ennosuke himself credits the intervention of his wife, Koto (1862–1930), an influential proprietor in the licensed quarters whom he married in 1886 (Ichikawa 1908, 44). Although Ennosuke's formal verbal apology for the *hamon* Benkei took place in 1890, negotiations actually began with his private reacceptance by Danjūrō in 1886, immediately after the two men met for the first time in two decades on the emotionally charged ground of the funeral of Danjūrō's younger brother Ebizō VIII, who had died at the age of forty.

13. *Nadai* (name) actors in *kabuki* are billed; subname actors are not. There are also other distinctions having to do with dressing-room facilities, salaries, and the like. (The terms as such were first formally standardized by Kan'ya's theatre in 1878.) Today any actor aspiring to name status is required to pass a strict audition judged by high-ranking members of the various *mon*.

14. The first regulations were promulgated in February 1882 and had much to do with safety standards and censorship under police control (Ihara 1975, 452 ff.). The second were promulgated in August 1890 (Ihara 1975, 698 ff.).

15. Significantly, however, Ennosuke himself never became a member of the Mimasu-kai, a fact that was clearly reflected in his billing whenever he appeared with them.

References

Abe Yūzō. 1970. *Tōkyō no Koshibai* (Tokyo's little theatre). Tokyo: Engeki Shuppansha.

Akiba Tarō. 1955. *Nihon Shingekishi* (History of Japanese modern drama). Tokyo: Risōsha.

Ichikawa Ennosuke I. 1908. "Ichikawa Ennosuke." *Engei Gahō* (Theatre illustrated).

Ihara Toshirō. 1975. *Meiji Engekishi* (History of Meiji theatre). Tokyo: Hō Shuppan.

Kimura Kinka. 1943. *Morita Kan'ya*. Tokyo: Shintaishūsha.

Matsumoto Shinko. 1974 *Meiji Zenki Engeki Ronshi* (History of early Meiji: Theatre ideas). Tokyo: Engeki Shuppansha.

Okamoto Kidō. 1922. "Hajimete Danshirō o Mita Toki." (The first time I saw Danshirō). *Engei Gahō* (March).

Tamura Nariyoshi. 1922. *Zokuzoku Kabuki Nendaiki* (Second supplement to *kabuki* chronology). Tokyo: Ichimura-za.

10

Communist *Kabuki*:
A Contradiction in Terms?

Brian Powell

On March 7, 1949, the members of a *kabuki* company called Zenshin-za with their families—over seventy people in all—joined the Japan Communist Party. It is this company to which the words "communist *kabuki*" in the title refer and about which the question is asked. The three ideographs used for the name "Zenshin-za" mean "Forward Advance Company," a rather cumbrous name in English. While the Japanese is certainly incongruous, especially in traditional *kabuki* circles, it is not cumbrous, so the Japanese name will be used in this essay.

It is a truism in Japan that *kabuki* is "feudal." To answer the question in the title, one needs only to list the "feudal" characteristics of *kabuki* in order to conclude that of course communist *kabuki* is impossible in any meaningful sense. Zenshin-za must therefore be either a freak or a fraud. In practice, however, the situation is more complicated. Zenshin-za's contribution to the development of modern Japanese theatre in the widest sense has been great and its achievements considerable. Others may say that Zenshin-za represents neither *kabuki* nor communism, but such statements depend on a definition of those terms. Formally at least, Zenshin-za was for many years a company of mainly *kabuki*-trained actors many of whom were full members of the Japan Communist Party.

The institutions of the *kabuki* theatre may be broadly divided into two categories: first, those connected with the actors who appeared in any given performance, and second, those involving the externals of the performance, especially the theatre management.

The acting world of eighteenth- and nineteenth-century Japan was organized in families. It became almost impossible to embark on an acting career
if one happened not to have been born into one of the established acting
families; and, conversely, it was almost impossible not to become an actor if
one had been born the son and heir of an acting family. Not all acting families were equal by any means. Although in most cases the members of an
acting family could usually be assured of working for much of the time, the
type of role that would be given was rigidly controlled by a conventional
hierarchy among the families. A few families, such as the Ichikawa, achieved
fame and position because of the brilliance of their heads at an early stage of
kabuki development. The leading roles were always played by the members
of these few families. Actors in other families always played the subordinate
roles, and members of the lowest class of acting families were condemned
permanently to walk-on parts. In the circumstances of Japanese society during this period, a hierarchical system of this kind, even in an artistic sphere,
was generally accepted by those who were part of it; we should not automatically imagine that the bit-part actors were deeply discontented at what
would seem to us to be injustice. There was a modicum of flexibility, in that
an obvious nincompoop born to a famous actor could be persuaded to turn
his hand to other things and might be replaced, by means of adoption, by a
bright scion of a low-class acting family. In general, however, the system
ensured that the mediocre actor would be the star provided he had been born
appropriately, and the genius who had not might spend a lifetime carrying
spears. The system had the positive effect of imparting a sense of security to
members of a notoriously insecure profession and to members of a class in
Japanese society that was constantly subject to interference. From above, it
had a negative effect in that power and influence inside the theatre inevitably
accumulated in the hands of the famous acting families, who therefore had a
strong vested interest in preserving the *status quo*.[1]

There was also a strict hierarchy within single acting families. The eldest
son was expected to succeed his father. One should also include in the families of famous actors the sons of other, often lower-class, acting families
who had been accepted as disciples of the master. The personal relationships
among these various family members were, as one might expect, vertically
organized and strictly controlled. The master's word was law and could not
be challenged. Blood relatives spent many hours in practical training. The
disciples, when they were not fulfilling some menial duty for the master,
often had to be content with learning by silently watching the master in rehearsal or performance. Meaningful dialogue between the master and his
pupils about the interpretation of a given role or scene was almost unknown.

Japanese society from 1615 to 1868 was officially divided into four classes.

These were, in descending order of precedence, the samurai, the peasants, the artisans, and, at the bottom, the merchants. *Kabuki* actors were regarded as belonging to a class so low that it was not included in the official classification. Of the four official classes, the merchants enjoyed a prosperity and financial influence out of all proportion to the low social position accorded them by the samurai rulers. There were thriving business communities in all the main towns, and in the course of time a distinctive merchant culture came into being. It was in this cultural milieu that *kabuki* (and the woodblock print) developed, and it is therefore not surprising to find a strong element of commercialism in this form of theatre.

The financing of a theatre was in the hands of the owner of the theatre or his agent, and the actors depended on these functionaries for their livelihood. Once funds had been raised for a season of productions, contracts were signed by the actors, usually of a year's duration. Money to back a season of plays was as hard to find in Japan as it has been anywhere. Unless a sympathetic backer with an interest in the theatre could be found, the terms on which money had to be borrowed were very hard. Everything had to be done to maximize the commercial success of a theatre. Much pressure was put on the actors to perform what the public wanted to see. It must be said that in general the actors responded readily to these pressures. Apart from the obvious fact that commercial success was in their interests, too, in the case of failure the theatre owner or manager might simply disappear, leaving the debts to be shouldered by the actors.

The commercialism of *kabuki* had two important consequences. First, it became the custom to perform only selected scenes from plays, usually the scenes that showed off the leading actors' talents to best advantage. This custom confirmed the subordinate position of the playwright, who worked as one of a team creating plays at the specific behests of the actors. Second, commercialism reinforced the traditional idea of the theatre as a place for social gathering. Theatregoing was not only, or perhaps even mainly, to watch and appreciate the play. People almost always went in a large group and, as a full program took most of the daylight hours, they needed various other services such as food and drink, toilets, and, if it was an all-male party, perhaps some feminine company. These were provided, not by the theatre itself, but by nearby teahouses (*shibai jaya*) which, when the authorities allowed it, were linked to the theatre by covered passages. The teahouses would delegate one of their employees to look after a certain group of patrons, and throughout the performance these stewards would bring food and especially drink to their customers in the theatre or conduct them out of the theatre for a period of relaxation at the teahouse. [See Shively's essay, chapter 3, for more on theatre teahouses. Ed.]

In the course of time, clearly understood relationships developed between those who ran these ancillary services on the one hand and the theatre management and the actors on the other. Once these relationships had been established, they were difficult to break, even if the financial advantage shifted sharply either one way or the other. A whole nexus of such relationships developed that fully integrated the theatre into merchant society during the Edo period.

Thus, although *kabuki* has rightly been described as a lively theatre form, the institutional framework within which it pursued its sometimes inspired artistic aims was essentially conservative and naturally tended to perpetuate itself as such.

This then was the situation in 1868 when, after two and a half centuries of seclusion, during which the country was officially closed to the outside world, a transfer of power (the Meiji Restoration) took place and the new government opened Japan to Western culture. The years 1868 to 1912 are referred to as the Meiji period (the reign name chosen by the emperor), and during these forty-four years Japan modernized herself economically and culturally at an astonishing rate.

In Japanese writings comparing Meiji Japan with the West, one often comes across a number of words for "logic" or "reason." Many Japanese at the time perceived the difference between the Japanese and the Western traditions in terms of structures based on or ignoring logic. If certain premises were given, certain consequences followed logically from them. The Western theatre was seen as eminently logical compared with *kabuki*. Given that a play had a certain theme, the development of the plot and the characters and the emphasis of the acting would be a logical expression of it. Since drama was an art form, those who went to watch it would do so because, logically, they wished to see a performance of a play. This type of argument has many ramifications that cannot be examined here, but even at this level of superficial generalization one can see that it could have considerable force when applied to the situation in the theatre in immediate post-Restoration Japan. Japanese travelers were soon visiting the West and observing its "logical" theatre. Would they be satisfied with Japanese "illogical" theatre—*kabuki*—when they returned home?

They were not, and *kabuki* was subject to reforms of three kinds during the Meiji period. First was the movement, begun in the 1870s, and led by actor Ichikawa Danjūrō IX and playwright Kawatake Mokuami, toward increasing *kabuki's* historical accuracy, which culminated in the ultimately unsuccessful new genre called *katsureki* (living history) plays. Second was the Engeki Kairyō Undō (Theatrical Reform Movement) of the late 1880s, in which Danjūrō, theatre manager Morita Kan'ya, and various important political, business, and intellectual leaders tried to alter *kabuki* to make it worthy in the eyes of the West. [See the essays by Takashashi, Bach, and Lee, chapters 8, 9, and 20, respectively, for details on these two kinds of theatrical reform. Ed.]

The third type of pressure toward change exerted on *kabuki* came from the new big business of Meiji Japan. In particular, two energetic brothers, Shirai Matsujirō (1877–1951) and Ōtani Takejirō (1877–1969), realized that entertainment organized along the lines of the new joint-stock companies could be very profitable indeed. In 1892 these two brothers formed a company that was later known by the name of Shōchiku. Their company quickly took over the main theatres in the Kyoto-Osaka region and in the decade from 1905 to 1915 also gained almost complete control of all Tokyo theatres.[2] Under Shōchiku, *kabuki* was certainly organized along eminently "logical" Western lines.

What effect did these changes have on traditional *kabuki* of the pre-Meiji period? The audiences did not like Danjūrō's "living history plays," and during the last years of his life he reverted to classical *kabuki* performed in the time-honored way. Only historians of the theatre remember most *katsureki* plays today. The Theatrical Reform Movement certainly succeeded in confirming the social acceptability of *kabuki*. Later historians, however, have credited the movement with little else. Its discussions were mainly confined to peripheral matters, such as seating arrangements or lengths of performances, and *kabuki* theatres came to adopt many aspects of Western theatre architecture. In itself, however, the Theatrical Reform Movement only scratched the surface of *kabuki* tradition.

As the Shōchiku company established its near monopoly position, the question whether *kabuki* would fundamentally change or not inevitably depended on the management policy of its new commercial masters. Shōchiku's policy, still followed today, can be summed up briefly as having three main elements: to mount programs consisting of excerpts rather than complete plays, to have the lead parts played by star actors, and to encourage group theatregoing by offering special terms to organizations wishing to give their employees a treat.

The new commercialism reaffirmed the old commercialism of the pre-Meiji period. The acting families remained preeminent and conservative. The audiences showed that they did not approve of change. To be sure, they now sat in numbered seats, but they still ate from their lunch boxes and wandered in and out at will during the performance. The institutions of *kabuki* remained essentially what they had been before the Meiji Restoration. Progress still depended on the occasional actor of brilliance and initiative, but Danjūrō's experience had shown what limited scope even such an actor had.

It was in these circumstances that a group called Taishū-za (Theatre of the Masses) was formed in 1929 by a number of *kabuki* actors. The group was closely linked to the Marxist arts movement, and one of its leaders has subsequently suggested that it was not unconnected with the illegal Japan Communist Party.[3]

Until the formation of Taishū-za, the term "communist drama" could be used in only relation to the development of *shingeki* (new drama). During the Meiji period, while *kabuki* was responding at best only partially to the new age, various attempts were made to foster the growth of an independent modern drama—antitraditional and anticommercial. In 1924 these efforts came to fruition with the formation of the Tsukiji Shōgekijō (Tsukiji Little Theatre). This company of young actors and actresses had their own very modern, Western-style theatre, where they performed a varied repertory of Western drama in translation and, from 1926, plays by contemporary Japanese playwrights.[4]

Tsukiji Shōgekijō was supported mainly by progressive young intellectuals who were ecstatic in their welcome of its performances of German Expressionist plays. Most of those who patronized Tsukiji Shōgekijō were caught up in the craze for Marxism that had swept a large section of the Japanese intelligentsia off its feet. It was not only social scientists and historians who were affected. Novelists and poets and other creative artists saw in Marxism the solution to the problems that they faced in building a twentieth-century Japanese culture. Although one does not immediately think of poets and playwrights as good organizational material, it was felt necessary to set up elaborate organizations—societies, leagues, federations—to coordinate the activities of Marxist and Marxist-inclined writers and artists.[5]

The first national league of such writers was established in November 1925, and one of its sections was concerned with drama. The years 1926 and 1927 were times of great debate about Marxism, and they also saw the formation of legal left-wing political parties and the increased visibility of the still illegal Japan Communist Party. Many splits and realignments took place among the various political groupings, and the arts, including drama, were also subject to this tendency. By the end of 1926, all artists who wished to be acknowledged by the left-wing arts federation had to show their "consciousness of a [Marxist] objective" in their works. Playwrights emerged who tried to accomplish this. After the mass arrests of suspected communists and sympathizers in March 1928, some unification was achieved in the left-wing drama movement, and in 1929 a federation for drama alone, called PROT in the conventional abbreviation of its Esperanto name *Proletarea Teatoro* (Proletarian Theatre), was formed. By this time the political requirements imposed on proletarian writers (as they may now be called, following Japanese usage) had been narrowed, and "proletarian realism," which enjoined seeing the world from a strictly communist viewpoint, was the creative method to be followed. In 1929 and early 1930, proletarian drama achieved some notable successes, and its influence rapidly spread. Proletarian drama was now being performed by a large number of *shingeki* groups throughout Japan, including the larger of the two groups into which Tsukiji Shōgekijō had split in 1929. It would not be an exaggeration to say that proletarian drama almost monopolized the Japanese modern drama movement at this time. Late in 1930, the Japan Communist Party was successful in establishing total control over PROT and initiating a new form of "agit-prop" drama whose object was strictly political. In 1932 a bold, but misguided, declaration of the movement's international links with Moscow brought on the intensified police drives that finally smashed the PROT organization completely in 1934.

The positive results of the proletarian drama movement are usually recognized in Japan only by those who share its ideology. It cannot be denied that Marxism has deeply influenced all *shingeki* since the 1920s, for better or for worse. In 1934 the organization for left-wing drama was smashed, but the idea lived on. The sometimes heroic, sometimes circumspect attitudes of the artistic Left in the militarist later 1930s ensured that all subsequent playwrights would have to define their ideological position against the yardstick of Marxism.

During its heyday proletarian drama achieved some important successes, if its activities are seen in the context of the development of a modern drama. It brought people into the modern (as opposed to the commercial) theatre who had never been there before. In addition, a brief but substantial unity was achieved among all the human elements of a stage production: the playwright, actors, audiences, and critics, something unknown in *shingeki* previously. The immediate negative effect of communist domination of *shingeki* is clear. Progressively from late 1930 onward, the artistic character of drama was subordinated to political aims to such an extent that much dramatic writing became unrecognizable as plays in any previously accepted definition of the term.

The *kabuki* actors who founded Taishū-za in 1929 were all young and most came from lower-class acting families. There had been a general slump in the entertainment business in 1929, and these actors had been the first to suffer. They had been forced by Shōchiku to accept salary cuts and even redundancies. They formed a society to protect themselves and then broke away from commercial *kabuki* altogether by founding Taishū-za. Soon afterward the new company was strengthened by the addition of actors from another group that had just disbanded. This was the Kokoro-za (Soul Theatre, a name inspired by the work of Russian playwright–theorist Nikolai

Evreinov), which had been a partly *shingeki*, partly *kabuki* group since its inception in September 1925. It had been linked closely with the proletarian drama movement. Its leading member had been a *kabuki* actor named Kawarazaki [or Kawarasaki. Ed.] Chōjūrō II, who had traveled to the Soviet Union in 1928 and returned an admirer of it. Chōjūrō had close connections with several of the leaders of the *shingeki* movement. Taishū-za thus became a mixed *kabuki* and *shingeki* group, with professional *kabuki* and semiprofessional *shingeki* actors. It continued Kokoro-za's links with the proletarian literary movement and performed both modern and period plays. At about the same time the famous acting family headed by Ichikawa Ennosuke II also broke away from Shōchiku and formed a company of its own. This was Shinjū-za (Spring and Autumn Company), but its first production, of a Soviet play by Sergei Tretyakov, was a failure, and the venture collapsed soon afterward. Ennosuke himself and a number of the other leading actors returned to the Shōchiku fold. The remainder joined with Taishū-za to form Zenshin-za in May 1931. It had thirty members at its foundation.[6]

The three acknowledged leaders of Zenshin-za were Kawarazaki Chōjūrō II (1902–1981), Nakamura Kan'emon III (1901–82), and Kawarazaki Kunitarō V (1909–1990). Chōjūrō was the only one from a major *kabuki* family. Chōjūrō might in his own right have been expected to become a famous actor. Kan'emon and Kunitarō were different. Kan'emon was the scion of a minor acting family and, though genius was seen in him at an early age, within the traditional *kabuki* system he would only ever have played small parts. Kunitarō was the son of an artist, and as an outsider trying to make his way in *kabuki* would similarly have had to be content with insignificant roles.

At the founding meeting of the new company the following resolutions were passed:

1. The company's finances should be open and the actors' salaries, conventionally secret, should be decided in general meetings.
2. The status system of [traditional] *kabuki* should be abolished.
3. The equal rights of all members as human beings should be recognized. That is to say, the organization of the company should be rationalized and members should help each other whatever the task in hand.

Zenshin-za mounted its first program in June 1931. Three plays were performed, all newly written. The first was entitled *Kabuki Ōkoku* (The kingdom of *kabuki*) and was a satirical description of the contemporary world of *kabuki*. The audiences for this first production were very poor, sometimes numbering fewer than the actors. Every single member of the group was mobilized to distribute advertising material around Tokyo, but audiences for the second production in July were not much better. A subsequent tour to Okayama did not produce improved results. Financial difficulties and the problems associated with them caused many internal tensions during the first months. True to its declaration, Zenshin-za held frequent and sometimes very protracted meetings of the whole company to discuss the various issues.

Toward the end of 1931, Zenshin-za began to realize that, to survive, it would have to compromise its principles to some extent. A backer was found for a December production, but he wanted Zenshin-za members to appear in a play on a war theme. This was to be a joint production with a company that specialized in such plays. The leader of this second company, an actor famous for his performances of military heroes, was to head the cast. Needless to say, such an arrangement was anathema to many members of Zenshin-za. A general meeting was held, and the issues were very clear. Either Zenshin-za would not appear at all and would risk going out of existence or it would have to swallow its principles. In the end a compromise was reached. Both the war play and a famous proletarian play were performed in the same program. According to one of Zenshin-za's main actors, the war play ended with a rendering of "*Kimi ga yo,*" the Japanese national anthem (whose title suggests the imperial reign), and the proletarian play with the "Internationale."[7]

Once Zenshin-za had accepted the need for survival if it were to achieve anything at all, the way was open for the next compromise, this time of a more fundamental nature. There was a possibility of a long-term arrangement with the Ichimura-za, one of the three "Edo theatres" [Edo *sanza*; see the essays by Takahashi, Bach, and Saltzman Li, chapters 8, 9, and 15, respectively. Ed.], with a history dating back to 1651. But the Ichimura-za management made various demands. The first was that traditional *kabuki* star billing should be restored. Up to this time, on posters and advertising material the Zenshin-za actors had been listed in strict alphabetical order in accordance with the principles laid down at the founding meeting. The second demand was that Zenshin-za should perform *Chūshingura* (The treasury of loyal retainers).[8] *Chūshingura* was written in the mid-eighteenth century and since that time has enjoyed unbroken popularity. In the modern period there have been numerous adaptations for film and television. The theme, which was based on a historical event, is the vengeance taken by forty-seven samurai on the man who had caused the disgrace and death of their lord. Because of the precautions taken by their future victim, nearly two years pass before the revenge is finally achieved, but during this time the forty-seven never lose sight of their goal. Sustained by their feelings of loyalty toward their dead lord, they sacrifice all that is dear to them in order to accomplish their object. The play ends with the burning of incense before the spirit of the lord who is now avenged, but historically there is a sequel to the episode that adds significance to the narrative. By exacting vengeance, these samurai have placed themselves outside the law and should be executed as common criminals. The military ruler of the time and his advisers, however, taking account of their selfless and steadfast loyalty to their dead lord, grant them the honor of *seppuku* or *harakiri* (self-inflicted death by disembowelment). Glorification of the samurai virtues and the concept that a criminal act may be condoned if it is carried out in a spirit of loyalty and absolute sincerity have unpleasant associations with militarism in modern Japan, and there was uproar in Zenshin-za when the Ichimura-za's demand was made known.

But *Chūshingura* was performed, with great success, and star billing was reintroduced. Zenshin-za soon became famous for its performances of *Chūshingura*, and at least one classical *kabuki* play was included in all future programs. By the end of 1932, plays with left-wing content had become rare, but Zenshin-za seemed to be firmly established. In October 1932 it managed to pay its actors a salary for the first time, everyone's salary being decided at a general meeting. An acting school was organized and a monthly magazine published.

Zenshin-za started 1933 with a policy statement. It had four headings: rationalization of *kabuki* plays; providing a stimulus for *kabuki*; training of progressive theatre people; and productions of progressive plays. Four slogans were adopted for 1933: "Zenshin-za to the masses with all speed"; "From individualism to collectivism"; "Face problems square on"; and "Once we decide on something, let's do it at once."

Productions continued. Zenshin-za now had a national reputation, and requests from provincial theatre managements for visits started coming in. Classical *kabuki* and new plays were performed. One of the latter was a piece written especially to incorporate the latest popular hit song. In July Zenshin-za signed a contract with Shōchiku, the very company that the members had been execrating for the previous five years at least. In September the first Zenshin-za film was made, and contracts with two big film companies followed in 1935. Zenshin-za was making a lot of money.

Toward the end of 1933, it drew more attention to itself by disregarding a hallowed *kabuki* tradition. It decided to perform *Kanjinchō* (The subscription list) in spite of the fact that the leading role, Benkei, was regarded by the main Ichikawa family as its monopoly. Chōjūrō performed the role without obtaining permission or paying royalties. [See Bach's essay, chapter 9, on what happened when Ennosuke I did the same in the Meiji period. Ed.] The production was a triumphant success and ironically confirmed Chōjūrō's position as a member himself of a leading acting family. Zenshin-za was now generally recognized in the *kabuki* world. To round the year off, Zenshin-za performed an adaptation of Schiller's *The Robbers*.

By now Zenshin-za's repertory fell regularly into three categories—*kabuki*, *shingeki*, and *taishūgeki* (popular drama), a pattern that was to remain throughout the 1930s and early 1940s.

Notwithstanding the low position in the traditional hierarchy that its actors had originally occupied, Zenshin-za built up a high reputation for superlative productions of classical *kabuki*. The company became known for a certain style of acting, referred to as *aragoto* (rough stuff), which had been the hallmark of Edo (Tokyo) *kabuki*, as opposed to the more realistic, even effeminate *wagoto* style of western Japan, during the premodern period. The leading actors of male roles in the main Ichikawa family were the principal exponents of this style, and in 1840 Ichikawa Danjūrō VII had established a corpus of plays whose leading roles required a high level of *aragoto* technique. These were known as the *Kabuki Jūhachiban* (Eighteen famous *kabuki* plays), which became the exclusive preserve of the main Ichikawa family. *Kanjinchō* (one of the corpus) had been performed without permission, but in 1936 the Ichikawa accepted the realities of the situation and gave its approval for a Zenshin-za production of a second play from the corpus. During the following years, some of Zenshin-za's most successful productions were of other plays from the *Kabuki Jūhachiban*.

Most of the *shingeki* plays that Zenshin-za performed were written by playwrights who in the 1920s had been associated with the proletarian drama movement. In the circumstances of late 1930s Japan, as expansionism abroad continued and the military tightened its hold on the government, plays with overtly left-wing themes could no longer be written and many left-wing playwrights turned to historical subjects. Fujimori Seikichi (1892–1977), famous in Japan for his earlier proletarian plays, was one such playwright, and from this period he wrote plays regularly for Zenshin-za. In the early 1940s the company had a close association with the playwright Mayama Seika (1878–1948). Mayama, who had been writing plays and working in the commercial theatre for over thirty years, had never himself been connected with the proletarian drama movement, but as a writer he was interested in historical personages whose lives had been governed by strong beliefs and convictions. Mayama and Zenshin-za seemed ideally suited to each other, and Zenshin-za benefited greatly from its association with him.

The "popular drama" section of Zenshin-za's repertory was represented by both plays and films. It was the theatrical counterpart of *taishū-bungaku* (mass literature), a term coined in the 1920s to describe the literature produced to meet the demands created by the new mass-communications media. Popular drama in Japan was like popular drama anywhere in the West, highly commercialized, mostly superficial, and usually melodramatic, but occasionally redeemed by a playwright of distinction. One such was Hasegawa Shin (1884–1963), whose swashbuckling but sympathetic gangland heroes found appropriate expression in the very successful productions of Zenshin-za.

Zenshin-za also made films during this period. Ten were shot between 1935 and 1940 under contract to Japan's two largest film companies, Nikkatsu (four) and Tōhō (six). Twice Zenshin-za films were judged to be among the best ten films made during a certain year.

Not surprisingly, Zenshin-za was now financially secure. From the foundation of the group there had been hopes of one day creating an artistic community that would not only act together but also live together. In 1937 this was achieved by the construction of a large-scale study center, including rehearsal rooms, offices, and living accommodation. This was enlarged in 1940 and 1942. A community life was established in which everything was decided by general debate. It is said that at the beginning even the leaders of the group had to accept the standard of accommodation laid down as appropriate to the size of their families. All facilities for normal life were available at the study center, and everyone, including the wives and children, partook collectively in the activities of the company.

Internally, however, the years 1938 and 1939 were a time of great stress for Zenshin-za, partly caused by the general circumstances of the theatrical world. After the China Incident of July 1937 (the start of Japan's war in China), *kabuki* went into such serious decline that the newspapers began to speculate on its complete collapse. *Shingeki*, on the other hand, began a remarkable run of success that lasted well into 1938. This situation posed some problems for Zenshin-za. From the beginning it had performed *shingeki* plays and it included among its membership a number of actors and actresses who were trained only in *shingeki* technique. But Zenshin-za was still essentially a company of *kabuki* actors, and the great majority of the *shingeki* plays that it performed were set in the premodern period. The problem was complicated by the fact that, despite the vigilance of the censors, the successes that the *shingeki* companies were currently enjoying were mainly productions of plays that could be considered left-wing in inspiration. Apart from the content of the plays themselves, attendance at performances given by *shingeki* companies formerly linked with the proletarian drama movement was regarded by intellectuals as the only form of protest against militarism open to them. Encouraged by the indirectly expressed but genuine revival of the Left, the *shingeki* group within Zenshin-za increased its resistance to classical *kabuki* and reactionary themes and was successful in forcing the abandonment of a planned production of a Mayama Seika play concerning a famous modern Japanese general. Flushed with this success, the group subsequently opposed the production of an eighteenth-century *kabuki* domestic drama, but this time Chōjūrō asserted his leadership and the play was performed very successfully. Several members of the *shingeki* group then resigned. Zenshin-za had acknowledged itself as primarily a *kabuki* company.

One may describe Zenshin-za's record during Japan's wars in China and in the Pacific as either patriotic or time-serving. Given the company's left-wing history and associations, perhaps the latter description is more appropriate. In 1939, with government support and encouragement, it performed a dramatization of a novel advocating Japanese immigration into occupied Manchuria. This production was subsequently made into a film. Much of the film version was shot on location in Manchuria, where a smiling Chōjūrō was photographed by the press shaking hands with a local Japanese official. Later the same year (1940), just after the two large *shingeki* companies had been forced to disband by the authorities, who disapproved of their political coloration, Zenshin-za identified itself ever more strongly with the militarist government by performing a play as part of the celebrations to mark the 2,600th anniversary of the founding of the Imperial Japanese State. The performance won a prize.

During the last few months of the war, several Zenshin-za members were called up and the rest were evacuated to the country, where they played to local communities. This experience was useful to Zenshin-za when it found that within two years after the end of the war no Tokyo theatre was interested in full-length Japanese plays. There was more money to be made showing American films to the Allied Occupation forces. Zenshin-za took to touring, specializing in playing Shakespeare to audiences of young people in school auditoriums. The aim of this Youth Theatre Movement, as it was called, was to enable as many young people as possible to appreciate great works of world literature. In this Zenshin-za was highly successful. It is estimated that the total audience for its production of *The Merchant* of *Venice* eventually reached a million.

And so to March 7, 1949, when, after three days and three nights of almost continuous discussion at a general meeting, the members of Zenshin-za decided that they would all join the Japan Communist Party (now, under the Occupation, legal for the first time in its existence). It was, Chōjūrō said at the time, a harder decision to take than the one that had resulted in the group being formed eighteen years previously. The event caused a sensation and much speculation about the motivation behind the decision. Some said that it was based on hard commercial calculation. The stronger of the two labor union federations was communist-backed and it could mobilize large numbers of members to watch Zenshin-za performances. This would probably be more profitable than continuing the school performances. It is true that the left was riding high at the time and such considerations may well have played a part. However, audience numbers could hardly have been the sole topic of a three-day and -night discussion. The slogans adopted by the company for 1949 had already included a reference to worker audiences, and it is likely that in the new atmosphere of freedom of speech Zenshin-za was moving to resurrect its early left-wing idealism. Perhaps also the linking of the company with the Communist Party in such a spectacular way was intended to compensate for what many saw as its collaboration during the war.

As predicted, joining the Japan Communist Party opened some doors for Zenshin-za but closed many others. On the one hand, touring performances (often linked with appearances in political demonstrations) attracted wide support from workers and their families in areas where the Communist Party was strong. On the other, most headmasters would have nothing more to do with Zenshin-za, and police harassment began to increase. After the first heady few years of Occupation encouragement of democracy, the "Reverse Course" had started and American policy made the rebuilding of Japan as a strong economic power the first priority. Communism, although still legal, came under pressure again, and as in the 1920s the authorities regarded with especial concern the power of professional actors to influence audiences. Kan'emon was particularly pursued by the police in Hokkaidō and a number of (in retrospect) amusing incidents occurred. Makeup is a useful disguise for a hunted actor. The police were chagrined to discover on two occasions that they had arrested a musician in mistake for Kan'emon; even more humiliating was to be told that Kan'emon was actually appearing on stage, but to fail to capture him and then to arrest an actor playing the same part who was not Kan'emon at all. Kan'emon created a sensation by fleeing secretly to Peking, and the early 1950s, while he was there, was a difficult period for Zenshin-za.

By this time, however, the company had a wealth of experience in many different types of theatre: in large-scale performances of classical *kabuki* and modern plays, in films, and latterly in touring. In the later 1950s and the 1960s, this experience was used to good effect. Touring remained, and remains, central to Zenshin-za's activities: five groups would be performing in different parts of Japan at any one time. Performances by the whole company in major urban theatres were not neglected, and a new mass audience was created through appearances on television. The repertory remained much the same as before, with some slight shift of emphasis toward domestic dramas in the *kabuki* productions. In 1974 Zenshin-za, apart from its usual touring activity, performed in five major Tokyo theatres, appeared on three different television channels, and started three new projects in children's and study theatre. In 1981 it celebrated its fiftieth anniversary, and it continues to be a significant presence in Japanese theatre.

To return to the title of this article: Is the "communist *kabuki*" created by Zenshin-za a contradiction in terms?

Kabuki has been defined here as an art form that is fundamentally conservative. The institutional conservatism of the premodern period has been carried over into the modern age. Artistically *kabuki* was, and is, also conservative, but in the past century, as in the premodern period, artistic innovation and creativity have been possible when an actor of genius has appeared.

The use of the word "communist" in the title is inexact in one sense. Although the joining of the Japan Communist Party by Zenshin-za *en masse* was a sensational event, the group's ideological stand did not change significantly at that time. Historically Zenshin-za grew out of the proletarian arts movement of the 1920s. Whatever one may say about the ideological shifts of this movement, its members were always united in the belief that art should be closely connected with a Marxist *Weltanschauung*. The ideological differences between those Marxists who actually joined the Japan Communist Party in the 1920s and those who did not seem minor to a non-Marxist. Ideologically, the Left in Japan has been almost totally Marxist. Practically, to become a member of the Japan Communist Party during its history of nearly eighty years has been both very difficult and very easy. In the late 1920s, such a step meant an underground life or certain imprisonment and possibly torture. In 1949 it was a limited act of faith that many people in all walks of life took. The circumstances of prewar and postwar Japan are so different that it would be almost meaningless here to limit the definition of communism to membership in a communist party. Here it should be taken to refer to an ideological commitment to Marxism on the part of creative artists.

Marxism in the 1920s, however, had a further significance for Japanese intellectuals and writers. It was a stage, perhaps the final triumphant stage, in a modernization process. Japanese proletarian literature developed at such an amazing speed that most of the West—excluding, of course, the USSR—was left trailing behind. In this respect Japan had become more modern than the Western countries that she had been emulating. Now logic was on Japan's side. Japanese Marxist writers of the 1920s considered the literature that they were writing to be more logical than anything comparable in Western capitalist societies. Left-wing literature and arts were ahead of contemporary society, which was developing much more slowly There was an element of idealism in the attitude of the writers toward their work and what they hoped to achieve by it.

The question in the title of this chapter must now be rephrased as two questions: Can a highly developed and deeply conservative premodern art form be subjected to changes based on a modern ideology and still flourish in a society that has itself been rather slow to change? And is the resulting art product recognizable as being both progressive and traditional, or is this impossible?

The answer to the first of the two new questions is not difficult. If one accepts that Zenshin-za art fits the description given, then one cannot deny that this art has flourished and still flourishes in modern Japanese society. Not only has Zenshin-za performed *kabuki* successfully in large urban theatres; it has proved over seventy years that high-quality performances of *kabuki* plays can attract audiences from a great variety of different social groups. Through Zenshin-za, *kabuki* has flourished in Japanese society more widely than ever before.

The answer to the second question—whether Zenshin-za's art is a successful fusion of communism and *kabuki*—is more complex, requiring that *kabuki* again be considered in its two main aspects, artistic and institutional. As has already been mentioned, *kabuki* art was essentially the art of the actor. In the 1970s Kan'emon became Zenshin-za's main spokesman on acting technique, writing a number of books on the subject. In one work the following sentence occurs: "It is required of the actor that he pay particularly careful attention to polishing his technique of movement (what the audience sees) and delivery (what the audience hears), so that he can be seen and heard in every corner of the theatre."[9] Elsewhere in this book Kan'emon lays emphasis on ensuring that the audience obtains what it has paid for. These seem rather obvious points to make, but Kan'emon's practical approach is very different from much of the writing on *shingeki*, which has been highly theoretical. His ideas are in the long *kabuki* tradition of serving the audience as opposed to involving, leading, or educating it, and in this respect Zenshin-za has been credited with standards as high as one would expect from commercial *kabuki* companies.

Kan'emon also tried to go beyond this perspective, and Stanislavsky's theory of acting exerted a considerable influence on his thinking. He sees a danger that traditional *kabuki* technique alone can lead on the one hand to mannerisms and on the other to forced delivery and movement which may interrupt the smooth flow of the action. He hopes that the internalized psychological training of the Stanislavsky system will prevent these shortcomings.

Perhaps more significant than these notions is the way in which Zenshin-za has attempted to change some of the institutions of *kabuki,* enabling them to be reevaluated as part of the artistic aspect of the form. For example, the strict system of the acting families was abolished, and to a large extent casting is done according to individual talent (it is also a matter for corporate discussion and decision). A corollary of this change in casting procedures has been that dominance of the production by the performances of one or two actors has been restricted. It would be difficult to claim that it has been completely eliminated, as Chōjūrō, Kan'emon, and Kunitarō [all now deceased. Ed.] usually played the lead parts, but Zenshin-za is renowned for its ensemble playing, something almost unknown in commercial *kabuki*. This has been a natural by-product of breaking down the traditional relationships that have always existed between acting families and of establishing corporate life in their place.

Kawatake Shigetoshi, Japan's most eminent theatre historian, singles out the establishment of communal life as the most significant reform of Zenshin-za.[10] It was a goal set by the company within a short time of its foundation and fought for hard. On the many occasions during the 1930s and 1940s when principles were heavily compromised, the justification was often given that by this means alone the financial basis of communal life could be made secure. By the simple fact of a group mainly of *kabuki* actors living together and attempting to establish a community based on equality and cooperation, the conservative aspects of *kabuki* art were bound to undergo some change. A change has certainly taken place. It is very tempting to suggest that it is a change for the better—that a performance by a company of actors cooperating in conveying the meaning of the play is somehow superior to a performance in which the lesser actors are only foils to the self-important and domineering lead actor. This would be a Western view, but it is one that Japanese theatre critics have increasingly come to adopt. Not only has there been this qualitative change in *kabuki* performances as a result of Zenshin-za beliefs, but more Japanese than ever before are watching *kabuki* plays as plays rather than spectacles.

Zenshin-za's left-wing stance has affected its general approach to *kabuki* in several ways. The logical left-wing position must be that *kabuki* is feudal, has no place in modern Japan, and cannot therefore be allowed to stay as it is. *Kabuki* actors traditionally have altered plays to suit themselves. Why not rewrite the plays in one's repertory in order to give them a left-wing interpretation? This is an extreme position, which was, briefly and unsuccessfully, adopted by Zenshin-za in the 1950s. A more moderate variation of this position is to give scenes of ordinary life in the premodern period a more realistic representation than in traditional performances. These are the scenes that commercial *kabuki* would usually omit, as there would be little scope for the lead actors to display their special talents. Zenshin-za has often adopted this middle course, earning the praise of critics who have admitted to gaining a new insight into the play as a whole. A third approach is to see *kabuki* historically as an art form produced in a feudal age by the creative energy of the social class most oppressed during that age (in Japan, officially at least, the merchants were at the bottom of the scale). *Kabuki* should thus be regarded as an expression of the resistance of that class to the oppressive feudal authority. As socialists Zenshin-za's artists can justify themselves in performing this drama if they can recreate it as it was. So they study the circumstances in which a play, perhaps 200 years old, was originally created and performed, and try to mount a new production that is historically accurate. Thus, in a curious way, the need to reconcile an artistic belief with a political ideology has brought about a reexamination of classical *kabuki* and an attempt to rediscover the original significance of its plays as works of art.

The preceding paragraph may sound like chop logic, but such theoretical problems have always been taken seriously in Japan. There has been a degree of youthful idealism in the Japanese left that can appear to have a cynical aspect when an encounter with reality forces compromise. Zenshin-za has had this idealism in good measure. Compromises were certainly made, but it was because Zenshin-za was left-wing that communal life was established, equality practiced, and new productions of theatrical classics brought to millions of people. Zenshin-za's "communism" has shown itself able to reform *kabuki* without destroying it.

Notes

[With the author's permission, I have made several cuts in this essay to avoid excessive duplication of similar discussions in other essays. Ed.]

1. There are exceptions to all generalizations. In the mid-nineteenth century, the son of a theatre tobacco-stall-holder succeeded through dogged determination in becoming a star actor (Ichikawa Kodanji IV, 1812–1866), but such men were very rare.

2. Ishizawa Shūji, *Shingeki no Tanjō* (The birth of new drama) (Tokyo: Kinokuniya Shinsho, 1964), 80 ff.

3. Toita Kōji, ed., *Taidan Nihon Shingekishi* (Dialogues on the history of Japanese new drama) (Tokyo: Seiabō, 961), 185.

4. Although several have subsequently appeared, at the time of writing there was only one book in English concerning *shingeki*: J. Thomas Rimer, *Kishida Kunio: Toward a Modern Japanese Theatre* (Princeton, NJ: Princeton University Press, 1974). See also A. Horie-Webber, "Modernisation of the Japanese Theatre: The *Shingeki* Movement," in W. G. Beasley, ed., *Modern Japan* (London: Allen and Unwin, 1975), 147–165. For Tsukiji Shōgekijō, see Brian Powell, "Japan's First Modern Theatre: Tsukiji Shōgekijō and Its Company, 1924–26," in *Monumenta Nipponica* 30: 1 (1975), 69–85.

5. See George Tyson Shea, *Leftwing Literature in Japan* (Tokyo: Hōsei University Press, 1964).

6. Information concerning Zenshin-za is taken mainly from Sakamoto Tokumatsu, *Zenshin-za* (Tokyo: Ōdosha, 1953).

7. Kawarasaki Kunitarō, *Engeki to wa Nani ka* (What is drama?) (Tokyo: Popurasha, 1974), 86–87. This incident is not mentioned by Sakamoto.

8. The full title *is Kanadehon Chūshingura*. There are several English translations, including Donald Keene, *Chūshingura: The Treasury of Loyal Retainers* (New York and London: Columbia University Press, 1971).

9. Nakamura Kan'emon, *Kabuki no Engi* (*Kabuki* technique) (Tokyo: Miraisha, 1974), 6. My translation.

10. Kawatake Shigetoshi, *Nihon Engeki Zenshi* (A complete history of Japanese theatre) (Tokyo: Iwanami Shoten, 1959), 950.

Further Reading

There are many English-language books about Japanese theatre in which *kabuki* is treated along with other genres. The principal English-language books dedicated to *kabuki* exclusive of the other genres include James R. Brandon, trans. and ed., *Kabuki: Five Classic Plays* (Cambridge, MA: Harvard University Press, 1975; reprinted, University of Hawai'i Press, 1992); James R. Brandon, William P. Malm, and Donald H. Shively, eds., *Studies in Kabuki: Its Acting, Music, and Historical Context* (Honolulu: University of Hawai'i Press, 1978); Ronald Cavaye, *Kabuki: A Pocket Guide* (Tokyo and Rutland, VT: Tuttle, 1993); Charles J. Dunn and Bunzō Torigoe, trans., *The Actors' Analects* (New York: Columbia University Press, 1969); Earle Ernst, *The Kabuki Theatre* (New York: Grove Press, 1956); Gunji Masakatsu, *Kabuki*, rev. ed., trans. John Bester and Jant Goff (Tokyo: Kodansha, 1985); Gunji Masakatsu, *The Kabuki Guide*, trans. Christopher Holmes (Tokyo: Kodansha, 1987); Aubrey S. Halford and Giovanna M. Halford, *The Kabuki Handbook* (Tokyo and Rutland, VT: Tuttle, 1961); Yonezo Hamamura et al., *Kabuki* (Tokyo: Kenkyusha, 1956); Kawatake Shigetoshi, *Kabuki: Japanese Drama* (Tokyo: Foreign Affairs Association of Japan, 1958); Toshio Kawatake, *Japan on Stage: Japanese Concepts of Beauty as Shown in the Traditional Theatre*, trans. P.G. O'Neill (Tokyo: 3A Corporation, 1990); Zoe Kincaid, *Kabuki: The Popular Stage of Japan* (London: Macmillan, 1925); Laurence R. Kominz, *Avatars of Vengeance: Japanese Drama and the Soga Literary Tradition* (Ann Arbor: Center for Japanese Studies, University of Michigan, 1995); Laurence R. Kominz, *The Stars Who Created Kabuki: Their Lives, Loves and Legacy* (Tokyo: Kodansha, 1997); Samuel L. Leiter, *New Kabuki Encyclopedia: A Revised Adaptation of Kabuki Jiten* (Westport, CT: Greenwood Press, 1997); *The Art of Kabuki: Five Famous Plays* (Mineola, NY: Dover, 2000; orig. publ. Berkeley: University of California Press, 1979); Matazō Nakamura, *Kabuki: Backstage, Onstage* (Tokyo: Kodansha, 1990); A.C. Scott, *The Kabuki Theatre of Japan* (Mineola, NY: Dover, 1999; orig. publ. London: George Allen and Unwin, 1956); Ruth Shaver, *Kabuki Costume* (Tokyo and Rutland, VT: Tuttle, 1966); Barbara E. Thornbury, *Sukeroku's Double Identity: The Dramatic Structure of Edo Kabuki* (Ann Arbor: Center for Japanese Studies, University of Michigan, 1982); Toita Yasuji, *Kabuki: The Popular Theatre* (Tokyo: Kodansha, 1982); Shōyō Tsubouchi and Jirō Yamamoto, *History and Characteristics of Kabuki, The Japanese Classical Drama*, trans. Ryōzo Matsumoto (Yokohama: Heiji Yamagata, 1960).

11

New (Neo) *Kabuki* and the Work of Hanagumi Shibai

Natsuko Inoue

Beginning amid—and partly inspired by—the student activism of the late 1960s, the experimental *shōgekijō* (little theatre) movement saw wave upon wave of growth, development, success, and failure. Several generations of outstanding theatre companies and artists have come and gone during that period, and some of the work—like that of directors Suzuki Tadashi and Ninagawa Yukio—has gained worldwide renown. Although the *shōgekijō* movement met with various critical setbacks during the last decade of the twentieth century, one of its most effective and interesting outgrowths has been a kind of contemporary *kabuki*, variously called "new" or "neo" *kabuki*, which arose in the 1980s.

It is not clear who came up with the anglicized name "new *kabuki*" and it is difficult to define the term distinctively. To borrow critic Ei Norio's words, new *kabuki* is "a form of theatre that dramatizes *kabuki* themes or presents theatrical works by using *kabuki* techniques and devices. Namely, it is a parody of *kabuki* themes and techniques."[1] He also defines it as "theatre staging adaptations of *kabuki* or using *kabuki* acting techniques and other stage devices."[2] As he himself later points out, these definitions are not enough to define new *kabuki*. *Shingeki* (modern drama) troupes also have drama-tized *kabuki* themes and staged modern adaptations of *kabuki*. Director Suzuki Tadashi presented several *kabuki*-influenced experimental works.[3] *Kabuki* actor Ichikawa Ennosuke III has directed performances by combining tradi-tional acting techniques with modern stage devices. He calls these produc-tions "Ennosuke *kabuki*" or "super *kabuki*." A number of other actors have performed parodies of *kabuki*. However, these approaches should be distinguished from new *kabuki*.

In order to outline its characteristics, I would like to introduce four major companies known for new *kabuki* and clarify the difference between new *kabuki* and earlier approaches, and also to examine the future prospects of new *kabuki*. Following an overview of new *kabuki*, I will offer a close view of the principal exemplar of the genre, the company called Hanagumi Shibai.

New *Kabuki*: Survey of Companies

There are three major companies known for new *kabuki*: Hanagumi Shibai (Flower group theatre), Gekidan Chōjū Giga (Caricature of birds and beasts company), and Super Ichiza (Super company). [4] Among these three, Hanagumi Shibai is first in scale, reputation, and popularity. The company was founded by Kanō Yukikazu in 1987 with the aim of creating what he called "neo *kabuki*." [5] Since its foundation, the company has made constant efforts to revitalize the energy of *kabuki*. Hanagumi Shibai's chief contributions will be discussed in detail later in this essay.

Gekidan Chōjū Giga is another of the major companies referred to as new *kabuki*. Chinen Masabumi founded it in 1975 in order to create original musicals that combine modern and classical, Western and Japanese styles. Chinen named the company after *Chōjū Giga*, an illustrated narrative hand-scroll of the mid-twelfth century. "*Giga*" means pictures drawn in jest—that is, pictures showing entertaining comical stories, like cartoons. The word is also used to refer to pictures drawn just for entertainment. *Chōjū Giga* is an amusing scroll that illustrates birds and beasts frolicking happily. These humorous pictures give full play to our imaginations. Like *Chōjū Giga,* the company aims at creating an amusing entertainment without being bound by a conventional idea. The company has created a variety of musicals that parody movies, Shakespeare, and *kabuki,* as well as straight plays.

Since adapting Ihara Saikaku's seventeenth-century novel *Kōshoku Gonin Onna* (Five Women Who Loved Love) in 1981, Chinen has revived a number of classical works and has devoted all his energy to "*kabuki* musicals." He scripted and directed *Kōshoku Ichidai Otoko* (The life of an amorous man) in 1982 and created a *kabuki*-style musical with *Shiranami Gonin Otoko* (Five bold bandits) in 1984. Since then, the company has been known for its *kabuki* musicals. The shows, with their speedy scene changes, comic devices, and witty humor, have attracted young audiences.

Super Ichiza is not as big as Hanagumi Shibai and Chōjū Giga in scale and popularity, but it also has pleased young audiences. The company was founded in Nagoya in 1979 by Iwata Shinichi, its producer-director, who has created a unique form of performance with his entirely original concept of "rock *kabuki*." This contemporary *kabuki* comically dramatizes *kabuki* themes using the same stylized acting forms and period costumes as traditional *kabuki*, but accompanies them with live rock music rather than the traditional instruments.

Since its first performance in 1979, a comedy called *Ehon Benkei-ki Gohiiki Kanjinchō* (A pictorial life of Benkei, or great favorite subscription list), Super Ichiza has produced a new play (modern adaptations and parodies of *kabuki*) every year. Starting with a rock *kabuki* version of *Macbeth* in 1984, the company has given about two hundred performances in eight countries overseas, mostly in Europe. Its rock *kabuki* version of *King Lear*, performed in Holland and Belgium in 1987, received international acclaim.

New *Kabuki*: Characteristics

The approaches to *kabuki* of these three groups vary in style and concept, so it is hard to find common characteristics in their activities. I would, though, like to examine the major differences between these new *kabuki* groups' activities and previous efforts to modernize *kabuki*.

Stressing the importance of theatricality and pure entertainment, each company tries to attract general audiences, especially young ones who are not familiar with traditional *kabuki*. Mainstream star Ennosuke III, known for his experimentation and spectacular performances, also contributed to the popularization of conventional *kabuki* for general audiences with his unique, new approach. Insisting on the importance of "attract[ing] today's audience by creating a stage with free ideas, new interpretations, and various ways of expression,"[6] he created his original "super *kabuki*" in the mid-1980s. In order to create visually entertaining shows to cater to the masses, he used speedy action and stunning acrobatics. He boldly employed classical staging techniques, such as *hayagawari* (quick changes) and *chūnori* (flying through the air), that had rarely been used since the Meiji period (1868-1912). He also made daring adaptations of the classics and sometimes introduced Western costumes and music. His modernized, spectacular *kabuki* was especially successful in opening up conventional *kabuki* to younger audiences.

In the sense that his shows engage audiences by combining *kabuki* with modern and Western techniques, super *kabuki* is similar to new *kabuki*. The first and chief difference is that Ennosuke is a reformer within the traditional *kabuki* system. Although he makes bold modern adaptations, adopts high-tech stage devices, and opens the conventional *kabuki* world to outsiders, he does not intend to change the system or the traditional acting style. His concern is not to alter the *kabuki* system but to pass on the great tradition of *kabuki* over to the young generation by educating young performers in the traditional style. With *Ibukiyama no Yamato Takeru* (Yamato Takeru at Ibuki Mountain) in 1986 as a start, he established Nijūisseiki Kabukigumi (Twenty-first century *kabuki* group) with the aim of training young actors who are not from *kabuki* families. He has trained these actors by stressing the importance of inheriting the systematic *kabuki* acting style. Ennosuke directs classics as well as original works so that the actors can learn the traditional techniques and apply them to new plays. [7] Thus Ennosuke's concern is to deepen interest in *kabuki* by introducing original ideas, new interpretations, and modern staging techniques.

Second, unlike *shingeki* troupes, the emphasis in new *kabuki* performance is on acting. New *kabuki* groups stage existing *kabuki* scripts or adaptations, but they do so in a way that differs from the *shingeki* approach to modernizing *kabuki*. *Shingeki* broke a way from *kabuki* by staging translated Western drama and training actors according to Western acting techniques, which stressed realism. But after World War II it realized the value of reinterpreting *kabuki* plays in a modern way. A few *shingeki* actors were trained in *kabuki* acting, but basically they performed in a realistic style. Three new *kabuki* companies focus on bringing the actors' energy to the stage; they regard actors as their priority and try to make their performances as theatrical as possible. In this sense, they inherit the position of the *shōgekijō* groups of the 1960s, which criticized *shingeki's* text-oriented presentations and sought to privilege performance over script.

The third and most significant difference between new *kabuki* and *shingeki, shōgekijō,* and the work of Ennosuke III is that new *kabuki* groups do not create their works based on special performance theories or methods. Ennosuke III directs performances strictly based on traditional acting techniques, and *shingeki* troupes stage their modern adaptations of *kabuki* within the framework of a realistic acting style. A number of *shōgekijō* groups, especially those that emerged in the 1960s, created theatre founded on an original theory or concept; for example, many directors found inspiration in traditional performance and tried to regain its power in their productions.

The director Suzuki Tadashi has been the most successful at utilizing traditional performance methods on the modern stage. He "was not only criticizing the West-oriented realism of *shingeki* and shallow avant-garde modernism, but also revitalizing the tradition-bound possibilities of *nō* and *kabuki*." [8] He did this not simply by imitating traditional theatrical forms such as *nō* and *kabuki*; instead, by capturing the essence of their unique quality, he developed his renowned "Suzuki method" of acting.

New *kabuki* groups also attempt to create new acting styles or forms in order to create unique and original works. Unlike Suzuki and others, however, these companies pay little regard to creating works based on a specific methodology. They seem to use *kabuki* only for their convenience, playing with it, and using whatever elements they want in order to entertain audiences rather than to create performances rooted in a specific theory. Ennosuke, on the other hand, has a firm mission to reform and open up conventional *kabuki* to more people. *Shingeki* troupes looked at *kabuki* academically for the purpose of studying its tradition. Suzuki attempted to change the consciousness of people who inclined toward Western-oriented performance.

A general lack of performance theory, method, or serious sense of mission was one of the characteristics of *shōgekijō* activity in the 1980s and 1990s. Their productions were often criticized for their shallow interpretations and amateurism, but the popularity of new *kabuki* reveals that it is such an entertainment-oriented approach that continues to attract younger audiences who grew up over the past two decades.

New *Kabuki*: Prospects for the Twenty-First Century

I would like to consider here the future prospects of new *kabuki* through observing the companies' current activities. These companies either started their activities with the idea of *kabuki* as the essence of their creativity or discovered *kabuki* as a way of expression after being founded. Hanagumi Shibai and Super Ichiza belong to the former type and Chōjū Giga belongs to the latter. [9]

Kanō Yukikazu of Hanagumi Shibai has been enthusiastic about *kabuki* since his childhood. He founded the company with the aim of creating "neo *kabuki*." Since its foundation, *kabuki* has been the very essence of Hanagumi's creation. As Kanō himself says, "Our performances are always *kabuki* no matter what texts, forms, and techniques we use." [10]

Like Kanō, Iwata Shinichi of Super Ichiza has seen productions by *jishibai* (local *kabuki*) theatre troupes since his childhood. He was stunned by their performances, full of wild and primitive energy, and their bold and entirely free expressiveness. To bring out this feeling of excitement and entertainment, he has created productions based on *kabuki* themes with rock music and other contemporary devices.

Chinen Masafumi (playwright, director, choreographer, and actor), on the other hand, did not have *kabuki* in mind when he started Chōjū Giga. While studying at Waseda University, he was active as an actor in the Gekidan Shibaraku (Just a Minute Theatre Company), where he directed and acted in Tsuka Kōhei's early plays. Later, he worked at the Tsuka Kōhei Jimusho (Tsuka Kōhei Studio) but left to found Chōjū Giga with the aim of creating original works. After a long struggle, Chinen finally realized that he could use *kabuki* techniques as a device for creating original musicals. His primary object, however, was not creating works based on *kabuki* but producing new Japanese musicals. In *kabuki*, he discovered the great energy that empowers professionally trained actors. In order to energize his musicals, he has trained actors in *nihon buyō* (classical Japanese dance) as well as in Western acrobatics and jazz dance. His actors are also trained to play the classical shamisen and *kabuki's nagauta* music.

Thus Hanagumi Shibai and Super Ichiza have constantly produced shows with "New *kabuki*" as a slogan, while Chōjū Giga employs *kabuki* merely as a creative method. The current activities of the three companies reinforce this distinction. Chōjū Giga has continued to produce "*kabuki* musicals," but, since its primary concern is not creating *kabuki,* the company does not stick to new *kabuki*. Its current activities include performing at schools and in children's theatre, producing family concerts, and creating original domestic dramas and musicals with themes based on current Japanese social issues. It also promotes a number of events for TV and radio. Super Ichiza started its activities to produce its unique rock *kabuki*, but the company no longer offers such productions.

Unfortunately, the current activities of these companies show that new *kabuki* has not yet been established as a genre. It is a form of theatre that emerged by taking advantage of the "*kabuki* boom" and the "*shōgekijō* boom" of the 1980s, and its unique performances have attracted young audiences. But Hanagumi Shibai now seems to be the only troupe operating under a policy of creating neo *kabuki*. One can say that new *kabuki* has attracted public attention because of Hanagumi Shibai's great accomplishment. Whether new *kabuki* ends up a flash in the pan or realizes its potential of being established as a genre, depends on the achievement of Hanagumi Shibai. In the following section, I would like to look more closely at the new *kabuki* of Hanagumi Shibai.

Hanagumi Shibai

Kanō Yukikazu (b.1960) founded Hanagumi Shibai in 1987 with the aim of creating original and contemporary "*kabuki*" [11] theatre and to contribute to a "restoration of *kabuki* culture" in today's society.[12] Following the "artistic *kabuki*" [13] of the post-Meiji era, the "academic *kabuki*" [14] of the postwar generation, and the "Japanesque *kabuki*" [15] that has characterized efforts to preserve *kabuki* since the 1980s, Kanō's Hanagumi Shibai represents a new direction in Japanese theatre through his effort to "revitalize the *kabuki* spirit" for the contemporary stage.[16] In order to differentiate his own approach from the "new *kabuki*" of others, Kanō refers to Hanagumi Shibais production as "neo *kabuki*."

Kanō has set the goal of developing neo *kabuki* capable of transcending the existing *kabuki* system. While Kanō appreciates the well-preserved, centuries-old *kabuki* tradition, he observes that its system has been strictly operated only within families with a traditional lineage, thus excluding outsiders, no matter how talented. [17] Because Kanō has sought to develop his neo *kabuki* independently of the existing *kabuki* system, Hanagumi Shibai represents a direct confrontation with that system.

Kanō's neo *kabuki* can also be seen as an attempt to go beyond both the style-centered post-Meiji "artistic *kabuki*" and *shingeki*'s text-oriented "academic *kabuki*." Neo *kabuki* also faces the task of surpassing Ennosuke's "Japanesque *kabuki*," which popularized *kabuki* as entertainment mainly by modernizing it through the introduction of high-tech devices.

Thus intending to go beyond other twentieth-century approaches to *kabuki*, Kanō started Kanō Yukikazu Jimusho (Kanō Yukikazu Studio) in 1984 and presented several works modeled after *kabuki*, using only new actors in his casts. Kanō decided to establish a repertory company in order to create his own style of *kabuki*.

Kanō's Challenges

Kanō has revealed three key challenges for the development of his neo *kabuki*. [18] First, neo *kabuki* must find a way to revive the wild and primitive spirit that inspired traditional *kabuki's* development. Second, it must find a way to achieve unity between performers and audiences and thus greater social relevance for contemporary Japanese society. And finally, it must develop an original theatre style, transcending any superficial attempt to update or parody traditional *kabuki*.

In order to reinvent *kabuki* as neo *kabuki*, Kanō has sought to rediscover the energy that produced traditional *kabuki*. Kanō observes that although *kabuki* has been preserved as a rich tradition for nearly three hundred years, this tradition is burden that makes it slow and stuffy for today's audience. [19] Now that it has become so systematized and refined, it lacks the spontaneity needed to surprise and upset that it once possessed. In order to revive that vital energy, Kanō demands that his actors evoke an aura of thrills, tension, and the unexpected.

The Chinese characters presently used to write *"kabuki"* are a combination of *"ka"* (music), *"bu"* (dance), and *"ki"* (dramatic action). [During the Tokugawa period, the character for *"ki"* was usually another one, meaning "prostitute." Ed.] But at the turn of the seventeenth century, the word carried a different meaning. [See Shively's essay, chapter 3. Ed.] Originating from the verb "*kabuku*" (literally, "to incline" or "to tilt"), "*Kabuki*" signified the unusual, unconventional, and excessively unorthodox in relation to social trends or conventional rules of the time. This nonconformity also involved a certain lavishness and eccentricity in dress and behavior, so that "*kabuki*" also hinted at "fashionable" and "in vogue." *Kabuki* actors were called *kabuki mono* because they acted recklessly and their outrageous fashions shocked people. Analogous to the hippies of the 1960s, the *kabuki mono* in the seventeenth century were people who defied the established order by dressing up in highly unusual and shocking ways.

It is this "*kabuki* spirit" that Kanō aims to embody. Hanagumi Shibai's neo *kabuki* defies current ethics and common sense by exaggerating flamboyant manners and fashion. Hanagumi Shibai thus aims to shock and excite audiences used to seeing conventional performances.

Kanō's second challenge has been to confront the apparent lack of social relevancy in traditional *kabuki*. At the time of its original development in the seventeenth century, *kabuki* was a part of people's everyday lives; a performance was a shared experience between the audiences and the performers. However, this unity has been fractured, because rather than being the people's ordinary entertainment, *kabuki* has become limited largely to scholars, connoisseurs, and others who are well informed about it. Thus it can hardly attract general audiences, especially young ones, who find it difficult and boring. In order to restore public interest in *kabuki* as exciting theatre, Kanō introduces overt entertainment values. He brings in contemporary humor, dance, music, sets, and costumes. But more than simply updating texts and stage devices, Kanō combines classical *kabuki* elements with contemporary entertainment in order to achieve audience-performer unity.

Rather than *kabuki*'s technical aspects, such as acting technique and stage devices, Kanō strongly believes that it is the powerful unity between the audience and actors that vitalizes *kabuki*. For example, Kanō points to the stylized *mie* (pose) at climactic moments. At this heightened point, the feeling of the audience is unified with the actor's as if they were breathing together. Kanō believes no other art form can show such a high vitality as *kabuki,* and he wants to bring that powerful energy on stage.[20]

Finally, Kanō has challenged himself to develop originality in his neo *kabuki,* rather than mere imitation or parody. To those conservative critics, who think that Hanagumi Shibai is mocking real *kabuki*, Kanō insists that, he is experimenting to find a way of presenting *kabuki* performance with a wider vision. By trying out various styles and devices, Hanagumi Shibai tests the limits and possibilities of neo *kabuki* as vital and contemporary performance.

Indeed, in conservative Japanese society, it takes plenty of time and labor to change a single system, so it is very difficult to cultivate something new, particularly in the *kabuki* world where the old system has been so well maintained. However, as an outsider to the *kabuki* family, Kanō aims to reform *kabuki*, not by criticizing or changing the existing system itself but by offering his original approach as a supplementary system of its own.

The following discussion is based upon scripts, videotapes, and articles from the clipping file at Hanagumi Shibai. Because of space restrictions, the analysis is limited to two scripts, *Za Sumidagawa* (The Sumida River) and *Tenpesuto: Arashi-nochi-Hare* (Tempest: Storm—later fine); and three videotapes of performances of *Za Sumidagawa, Tenpesuto Arashi-nochi-Hare*, and *Izumi Kyōka no Tenshu Monogatari* (Izumik Kyōka's story of Himeji castle).[21]

Kanō's Dramaturgy

While Kanō's writing seems to reveal no special dramaturgical formulae, his technique resembles that of *kabuki* playwright Tsuruya Nanboku IV (1755-1829), who was famous for writing bizarre scripts with multiple-layered plots and themes. *Kabuki* plays were usually written within a *sekai* (dramatic world), a well-known dramatic context, such as the story of the forty-seven faithful samurai. Frequently, more than two familiar *sekai* were combined to meet the demand for novelty. Nanboku mastered this technique, called *naimaze* (mixture), sometimes using up to five *sekai* to create a new play with fantastically interwoven plots. His *naimaze* was not just a reinterpretation of existing plays or a patchwork of scenes, characters, and dialogue, but a novel concoction of distinct forms, styles, and genres, even mismatched ones.

Like Nankobū, Kanō uses *naimaze* to combine a number of *kabuki* themes; he selects numerous plays as sources, deconstructs scenes, chooses elements and characters he likes, and reconstructs them as if creating a collage. Kanō takes inspiration not only from Nanboku's technique but also from his own interpretation of "*kabuki* spirit," spurring himself on to destroy the established style in order to produce a new one. Just as Nanboku deconstructed the established *kabuki* world and writing in ways that may have been uncomfortable for audiences familiar with conventional plotting, Kanō makes odd and mismatched combinations, often creating surprises by placing unexpected happenings between well-known episodes. Kanō seeks to deconstruct the world of existing plays and reconstruct them, mixing various forms and genres to create his original *kabuki* world in a contemporary context.

Texts and Structure

Kanō always uses existing *kabuki* scripts or classical or contemporary plays and novels as sources. However, his plays are original in that he not only combines existing plays, but creates his own world by layering various genres.

Kanō's earlier plays, such as *Za Sumidagawa* (1987), *Iroha Yotsuya Kaidan* (ABC ghost story of Yotsuya, 1987), and *Sakura-hime Akebono Zōshi* (Story book of Princess Sakura, 1988), were written by combining scenes from a number of *kabuki* plays. *Kaitan Shintokumaru* ("Monster-birth" Shinto-kumaru, 1988) is an adaptation from a 1773 puppet play, *Sesshū Gappō ga Tsuji* (Gappō and his daughter Tsuji), later adapted for *kabuki*. Kanō also writes plays combining *kabuki* themes with Western works, such as *Kabuki-za no Kaijin* (Phantom of the Kabuki-za, 1989), based on Andrew Lloyd Webber's *Phantom of the Opera*, and *Okujochūtachi* (The maids, 1992), inspired by Jean Genet's *The Maids*.

For the most part, Kanō's plays keep to the language of the original text and story, suggesting at first glance that these plays are patchworks or parodies of existing works. However, Kanō achieves originality in many ways: the plays are fast moving and full of a modern sense of humor with contemporary gags and surprising ironies; serious scenes are often interrupted by funny ones or jokes referring to modern events. Thus Kanō's adaptations allow audiences familiar with the original plot to enjoy the performance as parody, while at the same time reaching new audiences unfamiliar with the classical language and themes through incorporation of modern vernacular and ideas.

Kanō does not consider the text primary. His main concern is not to give new interpretations to the classical plays or to deliver messages. Rather, Kanō regards *kabuki* as an actor's theatre and the scripts only as pretexts for actors. Thus the structure of a Hanagumi Shibai production is sometimes altered during rehearsals. Kanō constructs the main plot, but minor scenes and dialogue are edited and adapted as actors' ideas are tested and then incorporated. Kanō is mostly concerned about how he can keep actors interesting on stage.

In order to observe how Kanō's plays embody his vision for neo *kabuki*, it is useful to examine his approach to texts and structure. For example, *Za Sumidagawa* demonstrates Kanō's effort to revive classical *kabuki* themes, characters, and language through skillful use of *naimaze*. Kanō wrote *Za Sumidagawa* based on *Sumidagawa mono*, a series of puppet theatre and *kabuki* stories about an event that occurred near the Sumida River.[22] [These form a *sekai* of their own. Ed.] Kanō chose four of the stories as his sources: *Futago Sumidagawa* (Twins at the Sumida River) by Chikamatsu Monzaemon (1653–1725),[23] *Sumidagawa Gonichi no Omokage* (Latter-day memories of the Sumida River) by Nagawa Shimesuke (1754-1814),[24] *Nagare no Shiranami* (Flowing bandits) by Kawatake Mokuami (1816-1893),[25] and *Sumidagawa Hana no Goshozome* (The floral-dyed silk and the Sumida River) by Tsuruya Nanboku IV.[26]

In order to make his neo *kabuki* version purposeful for today's audiences, Kanō modernizes the characters so the audiences can better identify with them. Kanō's *Za Sumidagawa* opens with Hanjo, the heroine of the *nō* play *Sumidagawa,* who appears wearing traditional *nō* costume and introduces a treasure of her family, the Yoshida, a scroll with a picture of a carp. But in Kanō's version, Hanjo, a sixteenth-century, middle-aged woman who has lost her only son, Matsuwaka, is transformed into a young, single, female tour guide who flirtatiously introduces the scroll to a group of high school students making a school trip to the Sumida River. Like a typical Japanese tour guide, she poses for souvenir photos with the students.

One mischievous student draws eyes on the illustration carp for fun, despite his twin brother's warning. The carp comes alive and jumps from the scroll into the river. A series of legends on the Sumida River comes to life on stage. As the two high school students experience the world of Sumida legends in the form of the twin Yoshida brothers, Matsuwaka and Umewaka, the audience experiences the classical world of the play with a sense of intimacy.

Kanō draws his audience in further with humor by comically depicting Hanjo, the tour guide who, using a funny mixture of classical and modern language. With similar effectiveness, Matsuwaka, a wicked nobleman in the original play, becomes a wicked high school student, and Sōta, a robber, shows up as a college student who mugs tourists.

Kanō's skillful use of *naimaze* reemerges in the next scene, which begins with the famous episode from *Futago Sumidagawa* about a number of events surrounding the Yoshida family's disputes. Yoshida Matsuwaka loses the scroll through carelessness and the Yoshida family is abolished. In order to find the lost scroll and restore his family, Matsuwaka disguises himself. Kanō here weaves the play *Sumidagawa Hana no Goshozome,* which consists of two famous *sekai* called *Onna Seigen* (Female Seigen)[27] and *Kagamiyama* (Mirror Mountain), into the action. *Onna Seigen* is an episode about Matsuwaka's fiancée, Hanako, who, upon receiving wrong information about Matsuwaka's death, becomes a nun (named Seigen) to mourn for him. Later, she meets her younger sister's fiancé, who resembles Matsuwaka. (He is actually Matsuwaka disguised as a nobleman in order to search for the lost scroll. In Kanō's *Za Sumidagawa,* he disguises himself as his younger twin brother Umewaka.) Realizing later that he is really Matsuwaka, Seigen (formerly Hanako) becomes mad from jealousy, which drives her to wickedness.

Adding to these multiple layers, Kanō interweaves three famous scenes from the famous *kabuki* play *Kagamiyama*: "Zōriuchi," "Nagatsubone," and "Okuniwa." In "Zōriuchi" (Sandal beating) the evil court lady Iwafuji has been plotting to swindle the shogunate for some time; because her secret message has been picked up accidentally by Lady Onoe, Iwafuji beats the lower-ranking Onoe with her *zōri* (sandal), an extreme form of disgrace. The maidservant Ohatsu avenges her mistress Onoe by killing Iwafuji. The cruel insult pushes Onoe to suicide. Kanō next weaves in dramatic action from "Nagatsubone" (Lady-in-waiting): The deeply humiliated Onoe returns to her room, describes Iwafuji's evil deeds in a suicide note, and takes her own life. Her maid Ohatsu vows to take revenge on Iwafuji. In "Okuniwa" (The inner court), Ohatsu kills Iwafuji, Iwafuji's coconspirators are found out, and Ohatsu is rewarded by being given the name of Onoe II.

Kanō keeps to the original plot and characters for the most part except for transitional elements needed to connect new scenes with the previous plot development. (In Kanō's version, Iwafuji schemes to get hold of the Yoshidas' property.) But he uses two popular characters who appear often in *kabuki* plays: Hokaibō and Shinobu no Sōta. The disgraceful and amorous priest, Hokaibō, a popular comic villain in *Sumidagawa Gonichi no Omokage*,[28] appears as a party to Iwafuji's conspiracy. He plots to poison Onoe at Iwafuji's urging. An amorous Hokaibō also barges in on Hanako and, after she rejects him, kills her. Shinobu no Sōta, a robber-hero in one of the Sumida plays, also appears as a conspirator with Iwafuji. Requested by Iwafuji to find the scroll, he kills Umewaka (who happened to find the scroll) by mistake.

Kanō's choice of comically juxtaposing all these characters transforms the heavy tone of the play into one more playful. Kanō ends the play with material taken from *Futago Sumidagawa*. Matsuwaka disguises himself as Hanako, kills Sōta, and gets the scroll back. Umewaka, who was thought dead, comes back. Matsuwaka pulls out the eyes of the carp to restore it to the scroll, tears the scroll down, and throws it into the Sumida River. As everything sinks, the two students come back to reality. Thus well-known scenes and characters from *Sumidagawa mono* are cleverly intermingled in *Za Sumidagawa* and modernized in order to delight contemporary audiences.

Since Kanō keeps much of the language and plot of the original story, the play might seem to be a simple parody or haphazard collage of scenes and characters. Kanō has said that some people may enjoy the play as parody if they know the originals, but it is not his intention to write *kabuki* parody or give new interpretations to these plays. Rather, his intention is to create his own original play by selecting scenes and characters to entertain, surprise, and excite.

Kanō frequently inserts contemporary gags and humor between *kabuki* episodes so the audience can feel at home in the world of the play and enjoy the play not only intellectually, as parody, but also casually, as entertainment. Serious scenes are often interrupted with elements of comedy. For example, the "Zōriuchi" is tragic in the original but in Kanō's adaptation is depicted as slapstick.

The scene where Onoe commits suicide is traditionally depicted poetically, but it can seem excessively melodramatic and lengthy for impatient modern audiences. In Kanō's lighter, more swiftly paced version, Iwafuji, who has no patience to wait for Onoe to take this last tragic action of her life—writing her suicide note while eating her favorite soft round rice cake and lamenting the sorrow of death—chokes her to death from behind. Iwafuji's rushing Onoe's death provides the scene with comic relief.

Kanō also meets his goal of surprising audiences by making unexpected things happen. In the scene where Hanako performs a solemn ritual to become a nun, the carp that has escaped from the scroll breaks into the ceremony, while all the play characters appear on stage trying to catch it. Matsuwaka, disguised as Hanako, barges in on Sōta in order to get the scroll back and is found out to be a man. Moreover, Sōta turns out to be a bisexual and Matsuwaka becomes his lover.

Thus, in *Za Sumidagawa*, Kanō revived the classical world of *kabuki* by incorporating modern elements to make it relevant. *Za Sumidagawa*, nevertheless, left a number of critics as well as spectators with the impression that it is a revival or parody of classical *kabuki*. From this perspective, Kanō had not yet developed *kabuki* themes to create his own world.

In order to break through people's misconceptions of neo *kabuki* as parody or imitation, Kanō sought with his next neo *kabuki* play to approach *kabuki* themes in a more pertinent and original way. He constructed his original contemporary characters and dramatic worlds by reviving classical archetypes within contemporary contexts. In *Iroha Yotsuya Kaidan* (ABC ghost stories of Suya) (1987), Kanō broke through twentieth-century *kabuki*'s previous limitations by incorporating modern Japanese social and family contexts into the traditional *kabuki* world context, thereby creating his own new world.

As with *Za Sumidagawa*, Kanō wrote *Iroha Yotsuya Kaidan* by using *naimaze*, incorporating scenes from two popular *kabuki* plays, *Kanadehon Chūshingura* (The treasury of loyal retainers) by Takeda Izumo II (1691–1756) and *Tōkaidō Yotsuya Kaidan* (The ghost stories at Yotsuya on the Tōkaidō) by Nanboku IV.

Chūshingura is one of the best-known *jidaimono* (history plays) in Japan. The play is based on a famous vendetta that occurred at the beginning of the eighteenth century: *Daimyō* Asano Naganori (Enya Hangan, in the play), unable to control his anger toward the feudal lord, Kira Yoshinaga (Kō no Moronao), attacked him. Accused of violating the feudal code, Asano was sentenced to commit *seppuku* and the Asano family was abolished. In the second month of 1703, forty-seven Asano *rōnin* (masterless samurai), with Ōishi Kuranosuke (Ōboshi Yuranosuke) as their leader, raided Kira's mansion, slew him, and avenged the honor of their lord. They were sentenced to death, but, in consideration of their noble motives, given the honor of committing *seppuku*. Their sense of loyalty made them national heroes. Many puppet and *kabuki* plays were written about them. The most eminent of all, *Kanadehon Chūshingura*, originally written for the puppets, is Japan's greatest revenge drama.

Tōkaidō Yotsuya Kaidan is one of the most popular plays in the *kizewamono* category (nineteenth-century dramas about contemporary lower-class characters). It is *kabuki*'s best-known ghost play. The play has close connections to *Chūshingura* because Tamiya Iemon, a *rōnin* of the Enya Hangan family, is the main character. He lives in poverty with his sick wife, Oiwa. Oume, a granddaughter of Itō Kihei, a high official, falls deeply in love with him. Hoping to marry her to Iemon, Kihei sends medicine to disfigure Oiwa. Iemon, horrified at Oiwa's resulting deformity, divorces her to marry Oume. Realizing that she is a victim of their conspiracy, Oiwa dies with a grudge against Iemon. Iemon kills his servant Kohei and arranges their bodies so that they appear to have been lovers who have committed a double suicide. He nails them to opposite sides of a door, which he throws into the river. At Iemon's wedding ceremony, Oiwa's ghost appears, leading Iemon to kill Oume and her father by mistake. He is haunted by Oiwa's ghost and finally killed.

Kanō keeps to the original story and language for the most part and leaves the characters' names unchanged. Also, as in *Za Sumidagawa,* he modernizes the original text by trimming slow-moving scenes, making the action faster, contemporizing the characters, and inserting timely and appropriate humor. But what distinguishes Kanō's *Iroha* from *Za Sumidagawa* is that his theme and characters are more up to date. Convinced that *Yotsuya Kaidan* can be more persuasive today as a modern drama about Iemon's family, and *Chūshingura* as a modern drama about the corporate battles of Japanese businessmen, Kanō interprets *Iroha* as a drama illustrating family relationships and the modern Japanese business world. While *Chūshingura* dramatizes warriors' loyalty and faithfulness to feudal authority and *Yotsuya Kaidan* dramatizes human love, hatred, and betrayal as seen in the ordinary lives of the Edo period's lower classes, Kanō's *Iroha Yotsuya Kaidan* dramatizes the modern characters' relationships, contemporary themes of homosexual love triangles, the desire for success and promotion, and a character's deep-seated grudge.

Kanō has designed the characters as stereotypical Japanese in order to enhance the audience's sense of intimacy with them. In the original *Chūshingura*, Kō no Moronao is Enya Hangan's superior. After making an unsuccessful pass at Enya's wife, the lecherous Moronao taunts Enya, who strikes him. Enya is then forced to commit *seppuku* and his family's fief is confiscated. But in *Iroha,* the men are business partners who have a homosexual relationship, and Moronao kills Enya out of jealousy. Ōboshi Yuranosuke, a loyal businessman who works at Enya's office, later leads the vendetta against Moronao. In *Yotsuya Kaidan,* Iemon (a former retainer, although an unfaithful one, of Enya) becomes a *rōnin* after the abolition of the Enya family and endures many hardships with his sick wife, Oiwa, and his mother, Okuma. But in *Iroha,* he is shown as a typical Japanese businessman who becomes unemployed after his office goes bankrupt and as a conventional Japanese husband with a mother complex. Okuma is a typical Japanese mother who dotes on her son and ill-treats her daughter-in-law. Oiwa, like many Japanese wives troubled by their husbands' capriciousness, commits adultery with Kohei, who forces his attention on her. Afterward, she agrees to elope with him. Itō Kihei, Moronao's feudal master, appears as the president of a big corporation who has the authority to force Iemon to marry his granddaughter, Oume.

For entertainment purposes, serious scenes are often interrupted or turned into comical ones. While the scene in *Yotsuya Kaidan* where Iemon kills his faithful servant Kohei creates a ghostly and horrifying atmosphere, in *Iroha,* this is shifted to comedy: Kohei's penis is cut off and Kohei dies in agony, holding his member in his mouth. The farcical performance style makes this potentially gruesome action funny. The following scene, where Oiwa and Kohei's dead bodies are nailed together to the door and thrown into the river, is one of the most grotesque but horrifyingly beautiful scenes in the original drama, but in Kanō's version, it lacks seriousness. The wedding scene, where Oiwa's ghost curses Iemon, is also supposed to create a haunting atmosphere but, in *Iroha,* Kohei appears as a cute angel in a loincloth and dances to the wedding music with the sexily dressed Oiwa, interrupting the solemn mood of the wedding. The scene suddenly becomes chaotic when several businessmen led by Ōboshi arrive to take revenge on Moronao, who is attending, and a battle takes place. The wedding is interrupted by a crowd of partygoers celebrating the coming Christmas holidays. Thus the scene ends with dancing, musical performance, and a cabaret show. Iemon is possessed by Oiwa's ghost and dies in agony in the original, but in *Iroha,* Oiwa and Iemon are stunned by the crowds and remain standing in the street with little hope for their future.

Kaitan Shintokumaru[29] is based on the puppet play *Sesshū Gappō ga Tsuji.* Kanō set his version in the Indian kingdom of God and designed the characters as Indian deities. By introducing unusual juxtapositions of dance and comic scenes, Kanō made this play amusing; by dramatizing traditional themes of love and morality as family relationships, he made the classical theme appropriate for contemporary spectators. Similarly, *Romio to Jurietto* (1990), an adaptation of Shakespeare's *Romeo and Juliet*, is a domestic comedy about an interoffice love affair and the competition between two big business enterprises. Thus, by using non-*kabuki* material, Kanō experimented with further possibilities for his neo *kabuki*.

Kanō did not seem to develop his vision of neo *kabuki* in plays written after *Iroha*. In his later productions, he staged plays by others. These included Yamada Shōichi's (b. 1925) adaptation of Shakespeare, *Tempesuto: Arashi-nochi-Hare* (Tempest: Storm—later fine), and plays by Izumi Kyōka (1873–1939), such as *Izumi Kyōka no Kusameikyū* (Izumi Kyōka's Kusameikyū, 1991), *Izumi Kyōka no Yashagaike* (Izumi Kyōka's Yashagaike, 1995), and *Izumi Kyōka no Tenshu Monogatari*.[30] In these experiments, Kanō seems to have used texts as subtexts for the development of a neo *kabuki* acting style.

Production

Kabuki is an actor-centered theatre that places greater emphasis on performance than on dramatic context or theme. Its conventional staging methods, called *kata* (form or pattern of acting), have been perfected over generations. In Kanō's view, *kabuki* has become so beautifully stylized and stabilized that it lacks the novelty and surprise that once inspired its development. As a result, because of its slow action and lack of current relevancy, traditional *kabuki* may seem dull and its actors lacking in the requisite showmanship.

Yet Kanō does not intend to establish a systematized acting style or method. While professional *kabuki* performers have been strictly trained to perform *kata* passed down from generation to generation, the actors in Hanagumi Shibai are not encouraged to have *kata* training. This is partly because they are not descendants of *kabuki* families and partly because Kanō believes that systematized forms lack the spontaneity necessary to startle and disturb viewers. In Kanō's view, actions and movement patterns that spring spontaneously or intuitively from each actor can produce more powerful energy. He has found that amateur *kabuki* groups often give unexpectedly exciting performances because they perform freely under no method or rule.[31]

Hanagumi Shibai's productions are powerful because Kanō makes full use of the actors' "little theatre" energy. Kanō writes with certain images of the characters in mind; he conserves the main structure and dialogue but allows the actors to express themselves and move as they like. As previously mentioned, some scenes are created in the rehearsal process through impro-visation and spontaneous reactions to the script. The company members ex-change their ideas and sometimes create new scenes inspired by the rehearsal process, discussions, and even casual conversation. Moreover, with Kanō's encouragement, his actors aim to surprise, shock, and excite by acting reck-lessly or outrageously.

The acting style for neo *kabuki* is often a unique concoction, a range of action and movement from the classical to the burlesque. The productions also introduce American musical styles that are familiar to younger audi-ences, including modern, jazz, disco, and hip-hop.

An Example of Kanō's Neo *Kabuki* Style

Space limitations allow me to describe only one of Hanagumi Shibai's out-standing productions, *Izumi Kyōka no Tenshu Monogatari*, performed in 1997 to celebrate the company's tenth anniversary. It is the best example of Hanagumi Shibai's achievement in creating a truly original theatrical style, one that builds on previous experiments and shows the company at its ripest. As in earlier works, Kanō retains traditional *kabuki* elements in acting, cos-tumes, and music, but he also succeeds in developing a neo *kabuki* style that does not mimic any existing performance styles.

In *Tenshu*, Kanō's actors embody his idea of neo *kabuki* by staging a non-*kabuki* play. The production follows faithfully the original text by Izumi Kyōka: A beautiful princess, Tomi, lives in the tower of Himeji Castle, the secret realm of an illusory woman. One day, a handsome hunter, Zusho-no-suke, comes in search of his lost falcon and is slowly drawn into Tomi's world of supernatu-ral beauty. Kanō changes the classical setting of the Edo-period castle to a modern one, the top floor of a high-rise commanding a distant view of the night scene of a chaotic megalopolis.

He uses dance both for its own aesthetic charms as well as to vary the pace and mood. *Tenshu* is a concoction of various acting and dance forms, such as *nihon buyō* (classical Japanese dance), Japanese folk dance, disco, jazz dance, and hip-hop, as well as *kabuki*-like movement. However, rather than simply juxtaposing the dance forms, Kanō creates an original style by splicing them together. For example, in the scene where Princess Kame (Prin-cess Tomi's monster friend) and Tomi's monster lover, Shu no Banbō (Prin-cess Kame's bodyguard), enter Himeji castle dancing with two little girls, Kanō introduces elements of disco and hip-hop into a traditional folk dance. In the next scene, Princess Tomi and her maidservants perform a vivid group dance to upbeat disco music to welcome Princess Kame. The style resembles *nihon buyō* but it is oddly fused with an amusing cheerleader's dance, creating a happy and welcoming mood. Thus Kanō choreographs movements that suggest accepted forms of dance without directly quoting them. By modulating the elements of existing forms, he creates an abstract vocabulary of movements that is original to himself, yet flexible enough to extract meaning from the existing forms.

A closer examination of Kanō's use of music in *Tenshu* supports a similarly original effect. Referring to *Tenshu* as a rock musical, Kanō uses electric guitar, bass, and traditional Japanese instruments—*taiko, shō, hichiriki, biwa*, and *koto*—to create a novel amalgamation of jazz, techno-rock, upbeat electric disco music, and traditional Japanese folk music. Kanō again creates a unique style by splicing them together.

In the costumes, Kanō integrates traditional elements with modern ones to offer up the world of classical theatre to the modern audience. The overall design incorporates elements that allude to classical theatre, monstrosity, and modern technological waste. Princess Tomi appears in a beautiful, colorful traditional kimono reconstructed to emphasize her hybrid identity as a monstrous creature and social outcast. The sleeves of the kimono have been altered in such a way as to evoke the wings of a monstrous mothlike being. The traditional *kanzashi* (hair ornaments) are mimicked by an arrangement of objects that appear to be discarded from the technological age. The ear ornaments resemble deathly skulls.

Thus in *Tenshu,* Kanō succeeds in reviving Kyōka's classical world by fusing the modern elements with classical ones and creating his own. The scene in which Princess Tomi first appears is especially interesting. She wears a kimono and a *mino* (straw raincape), hiding her face with a sedge umbrella. Heavy-metal music fused with the sound of *hichiriki* and *shō* is played at full volume. The odd fusion of colorful traditional kimono, contemporary megalopolis, and rock music embodies the chaotic modern world as well as the fantastic and chaotic classical world of Kyōka's play. Kanō's interpretation suggests that this is not only a classical story set in Himeji Castle in the feudal era but also a story about people driven out of the modern social system. The tower of Himeji Castle can be interpreted as a place isolated from reality and the resident, Tomi, as an outcast from modern society. Thus, by blending classic with contemporary elements, Kanō creates a neo *kabuki* world transcending time and space. In *Tenshu,* Kanō has developed an original style imbued with great potential for transcending conventional attempts to update traditional *kabuki*.

The company's future direction seems to be suggested by *Tenshu;* it is likely that Hanagumi Shibai will develop its most original style as it moves further away from dramatizing *kabuki* themes. As critic Senda Akihiko says,

Kanō's choice of staging the non-*kabuki* play is correct.[32] *Kabuki* texts were written to embody its dramatic world through stylized acting. As long as Kanō dramatizes *kabuki* themes, his neo *kabuki* cannot overcome the impression of *kabuki* parody because he cannot move away from *kabuki* style to embody the *kabuki* world. *Tenshu* is a symbolic play that transcends time and space so it enables Kanō to develop his original neo *kabuki* style by transcending *kabuki* without restriction.

Tenshu also suggests that Kanō may further seek to revitalize "*kabuki* spirit" without using *kabuki* acting. In *Tenshu,* Kanō has succeeded in creating an original style by fusing contemporary and traditional elements. The play's success suggests that in order to transform "*kabuki* spirit," Kanō has to divorce himself from the technical aspects of *kabuki*.

Conclusion

Kanō has aimed to create an original, contemporary *kabuki* and contribute to a "restoration of *kabuki* culture" in today's Japan. Ever since its creation, Hanagumi Shibai and its unique neo *kabuki* have built a reputation for an irreverent and excitingly experimental *kabuki*, which has become especially popular among a new generation of theatregoers unfamiliar with the traditional form. Hanagumi Shibai has revealed the potential to represent a new direction in *shōgekijō* through Kanō's efforts to revitalize the "*kabuki* spirit" for the contemporary stage.

Kanō faced three key challenges for the development of his neo *kabuki*: to revive the wild, primitive spirit that inspired traditional *kabuki* development; to achieve unity between performers and audience, and thus greater social relevance; and to develop an original neo *kabuki* style, transcending any superficial attempt to update or parody traditional *kabuki*. As noted above, he has succeeded in meeting the first two challenges, but his neo *kabuki* has had to struggle to overcome the impression of parody or imitation. To solve the problem, Kanō adapted plays and novels based on non-*kabuki* as well as *kabuki* themes. But after *Iroha,* by focusing more on the development of originality in acting, he succeeded in finding an original performance style capable of transcending the image of parody.

However, Kanō's neo *kabuki* reveals several limitations. For example, despite his success at charming audiences, he has sometimes damaged the dramatic quality of the originals by turning tragic and melodramatic scenes into comedy, and he has not completely eradicated the image of *kabuki* parody because he has kept traditional *kabuki* elements in texts and productions.

In order to develop his goal of revitalizing "*kabuki* spirit," Kanō must transcend the company's image of imitating *kabuki*. In his view, traditional *kabuki* acting style has been refined to present the Japanese body beautifully and powerfully, but for modern Japanese actors there must be more suitable physical expression capable of transforming their energy more directly and powerfully to a contemporary audience. Kanō has said that his objective for the company's twentieth anniversary in 2007 is to establish a "Hanagumi style" totally different from that of *kabuki* but uniquely Japanese and Hanagumi's.[33]

Notes

1. Ei Norio, "*Kabuki* wa Dare no Mono?—New *Kabuki* no Tōjō ga Imi Suru Koto" (*Kabuki* is for whom?—what emergence of new *kabuki* means), *Subaru* (October 1988). (Clipping file, Hanagumi Shibai.)

2. Ei Norio, "'New *Kabuki*' to Chinen Masabumi no Shire" ("New *kabuki*" and Chinen Masabumi's future), *Teatoro* (Theatre) (December 1987). (Clipping file, Hanagumi Shibai.)

3. Suzuki directed the series of experimental works "Gekiteki naru-mono-o-Megutte" (In search of whatever is dramatic) in the 1960s and the early 1970s. In Number Two of that series, the insane heroine, confined in a room by her family, acts out several roles of heroines from classic *kabuki* and *shinpa* (new school) pieces in her fantasies. Suzuki found that Shiraishi Kayako, the actress who played the heroine, was perfect at embodying his developing acting method based on Japanese body movements. This method is now known as the "Suzuki method."

4. A group named Chikamatsu Shibai (Chikamatsu Theatre), founded in 1987 within the company known as Bungaku-za, and centered on experiments with the puppet plays of Chikamatsu Monzaemom lasted only a brief time and is no longer active.

5. Kanō names his company's original *kabuki* "neo *kabuki*" to differentiate it from "new *kabuki*."

6. Nomura Akira, *Heisei no Kabuki* (*Kabuki* in the Heisei [1989–] period) (Tokyo: Maruzen, 1994), 185.

7. Kani Rika, *Nijūisseiki Kabukigumi Sanjō!* (Here comes the twentieth-century *kabuki* group) (Tokyo: Bungei Shunjū, 1996), 9–16.

8. Takahashi Yasunari, "Suzukis Work," in *Suzuki Tadashi no Sekai* (Suzuki Tadashi's world) (Tokyo: SCOT, 1991), 21.

9. Ei, "Kabuki wa Dare no Mono?"

10. Ibid.

11. Here Kanō uses a Chinese character meaning "to tilt," although the characters *ka* (to sing), *bu* (to dance), and *ki* (to act) are generally used to describe *kabuki*.

12. Ei Norio introduces the company's proposal for the play *Iroha Yotsuya Kaidan* (1987) in "Kabuki wa Dare no Mono?"

13. Starting in the late 1880s, *kabuki* has been gradually recognized as a national theatre of modern Japan and has been preserved as a cultural property. Kanō claims that people have been devoted to preserving only *kabuki*'s artistic beauty while its wild "*kabuki*" spirit has disappeared.

14. After World War II, many *shingeki* troupes, which staged translated Western realistic drama, started to modernize *kabuki* by interpreting the text in modern ways. Kanō criticizes this intellectual approach as "academic *kabuki,*" which made *kabuki* merely an object of study for scholars.

15. Kanō calls Ichikawa Ennosuke's contemporary *kabuki* "Japanesque *kabuki.*" According to him, today's *kabuki* emphasizes Japanism too much in order to attract an audience by its exotic elements. Ichikawa Ennosuke's "super *kabuki,*" which exaggerates *kabuki*'s exotic visual appeal, is a typical example of this Japanism. Kanō thinks that Ennosuke's *kabuki* approaches the unconventional and the modern by using high-tech stage devices, but it attracts the masses (and many foreigners) because it looks Japanese.

16. Ei, "Kabuki wa Dar no Mono?"

17. Kanō Yukikazu, *Haikei Kabuki-za no Kaijinsama* (Dear phantom of the Kabuki-za) (Tokyo: Kindai Bungeisha, 1994), 12.

18. This analytical framework is my own, based on information from an interview with Kanō and from promotional material.

19. Kanō, *Haikei Kabuki-za.*

20. Ibid.

21. Additional materials were not available from the public library and archives because the company does not publish its scripts and videotapes.

22. *Sumidagawa mono*: The original story is told in the *nō* play *Sumidagawa,* written in the fifteenth century. Later, several playwrights wrote plays modeled after this story. *Kanazōshi* (a kind of novel) *Sumidagawa Monogatari,* written in 1656, became the origin of puppet and *kabuki* versions. Further details are in Moriya Shigeo, *Tsuruya Nanboku "Naimaze no Sekai"* (Tsuruya Nanboku: "The world of his *Naimaze*") (Tokyo: Sanichi Shobō, 1993), 173–188.

23. In 1720, Chikamatsu Monzaemon wrote this puppet play based on *Kanazōshi Sumidagawa Monogatari.* It has no direct connection with a number of *kabuki* adaptations of the original *nō* play. In his version, Hanjo appears as the mother of twin brothers, Umewaka and Matsuwaka. The story is about the twins and the Yoshida family's various feuds over the family treasure.

24. The play premiered in 1784. This prominent farce about the Yoshida family's treasured scroll and a triangular relationship involving Hokaibō is commonly known as *Hokaibō.*

25. This play is one of the *shiranami mono* (bandit plays) category, popular in the mid- to late nineteenth century. Sōta is a robber-hero in it. The play is commonly known as *Shinobu no Sōta* [Sōta disguised. Ed.].

26. Since the Tenmei era (1781–1788), *Sumidagawa mono* have been used in *naimaze* plots. The play was premiered in 1814. Nanboku IV mixed up the worlds of *Sumidagawa mono,* *Seigen mono,* and *Kagamiyama* and created his own world. This play is usually called *Onna Seigen.*

27. Seigen, originally a male role, is here transformed into a woman for the sake of novelty. This was a common nineteenth-century dramaturgic device designed to find new life in old scripts.

28. Hokaibō often appears in *Sumidagawa mono.* He commits all sorts of evil deeds, such as dirty tricks, theft, and murder.

29. An Indian Buddhist tale became a source of the *sekkyōbushi* version of *Shuntoku* and the *nō* play *Shuntoku. Sekkyōbushi* is an old type of narrative performance, offering morally uplifting tales.

30. Izumi Kyōka was a novelist and playwright whose works are known for their supernatural and fantastic themes. He wrote for *kabuki* and *shinpa*.

31. "Kanō Yukikazu wa Ima Nani o Kangaete Iru ka?" (What is Kanō Yukikazu thinking now?), *City Road* (December 1993). (Clipping file: Hanagumi Shibai).

32. Senda Akihiko, "Hanagumi Shibai-ban *Tenshu Monogatari*" (Hanagumi Shibai version of *The Story of Tenshu*), *Musical* (March 1997): 47.

33. Hanagumi Shibai, producer, and Kanō Yukikazu, director, *Izumi Kyōka no Tenshu Monogatari,* 150-minute videotape (Tokyo: Hanagumi Shibai and Jiyū Kōbō, 1997).

Part 2

Kabuki Performance

12

From Gay to *Gei*:
The *Onnagata* and the Creation
of *Kabuki*'s Female Characters

Samuel L. Leiter

From 1629 to 1877, women were officially forbidden to act in Japan's *kabuki* theatre, which—under the leadership of a former shrine priestess named Okuni—they had founded in 1603. From 1629 on, male actors, the *onnagata*, played women's roles. The reasons for the banning of actresses have been frequently recounted elsewhere and need not be reexamined here in detail. [See, for example, Shively's essay, chapter 3. Ed.]

At the time, Japanese urban culture was largely under the influence of Confucian ethics and Buddhist religious practice, both of which—albeit with some degree of overstatement and inaccuracy—have been considered anti-female systems. Whereas, despite endemic misogyny, ancient and medieval Japan had had many women of accomplishment, such women were exceedingly rare during the Tokugawa period (also called the Edo period, 1603–1868). For example, Chieko Irie Mulhern's anthology, *Heroic with Grace: Legendary Women of Japan,* jumps from the death of Hōjō Masako in 1225 to the birth of Hani Motoko in 1873. Mulhern insists on "the absence of women accorded a legendary stature in the positive sense" during these years, although she admits that a very few women did stand out in one way or another.[1] One such woman, in fact, was Okuni, *kabuki*'s founder. Women of the time may have been more socially and commercially active than is commonly supposed,[2] but it is clear that Tokugawa women were, by and large, second-class citizens. People were to behave in this world according to their given place in it. When the dictatorial military government, the *bakufu*, determined that *kabuki*'s women had overstepped their bounds, it banned them from the stage.

In 1652, it did the same to the youths in the homosexual boys' *kabuki*, who had replaced the women and who were eliminated for much the same reasons. *Kabuki* would have died had not increasingly believable instead of merely pretty female characters begun to appear in the mature male *kabuki* that emerged in the 1650s and took its first important artistic steps in the following decade. At this point, *kabuki* witnessed a transition from gay theatre to *gei* theatre, *gei* being Japanese for "art," including "acting art." Only actors past their adolescence could perform, and they were forced by law to reduce their physical attractiveness, principally by shaving off the beautifully coifed forelocks that boys wore before celebrating their accession to adult status.

The English theatre, by introducing actresses, opened the door to an emphasis on the commodification of women. On the other hand, since *kabuki*'s mature males were required to radically tone down their glamour, one might have feared that the presumably desexed *kabuki* was not long for this world. But *kabuki* not only managed to turn the new restrictions to its advantage, it also was able to guarantee that sex remained a fundamental component. Moreover, it served to commodify men as sex objects, regardless of which gender they portrayed. Eros remained primary, and the actors, while continually striving to achieve lifelike portraits of the women they depicted, were always alert to maintaining the proper level of *iroke* (sex appeal).

From the mid-seventeenth to the late nineteenth century, playwrights and actors successfully created a rich panoply of female roles and types. Sue-Ellen Case has identified two basic images in Western dramatic depictions of women, the positive, which shows "women as independent, intelligent, and even heroic," and the misogynist, "commonly identified as the Bitch, the Witch, the Vamp, and the Virgin/Goddess."[3] *Kabuki* has its share of bitches, witches, and vamps—its virgins are positive, not negative figures—but they are in the minority and most *kabuki* women actually occupy the first category. Although she somehow overlooks *kabuki*, Case correctly notes that female characters in all-male theatres surely offer a gender depiction denying real women representation in favor of a fictional construct favoring patriarchal values. The appropriateness of her perspective will be apparent during the following survey of *kabuki*'s women (many of them first created for *bunraku* puppet plays, later adapted for *kabuki*).[4] I will also demonstrate that, despite the obvious persistence of patriarchal attitudes, *kabuki* was surprisingly fair to and respectful of women characters, quite possibly because the actors playing/inspiring their creation were men whose artistic status was dependent on the authenticity with which they captured the truthful essence of another gender for an audience in which women generally outnumbered men.[5] Finally, I will describe the exploitation of cross-dressing as a dramaturgical device of this all-male theatre.

Women of the Tokugawa Period

The actual women of the Tokugawa period were the victims of a mighty patriarchy, which relegated them to a position of relative powerlessness. As Basil Hall Chamberlain observes, a Tokugawa woman was subject to "the three obediences": "obedience, while yet unmarried, to a father; obedience, when married, to a husband and that husband's parents; and obedience, when widowed, to a son."[6] From the early eighteenth century, nearly every properly brought up woman was inculcated with the popularized teachings of Confucian-based moral tracts that stressed woman's lowly place, most notable of these "women's bibles" being *Onna Daigaku* (The greater learning for women) by Kaibara Ekken (1631– 1714). Ekken advises families to raise their daughters so that they humbly submit to the demands of their husbands and parents-in-law; too much parental tenderness will make a young woman self-willed and unable to bear the yoke of marital obligations. Women must honor virtue over beauty. "The only qualities that befit a woman are gentle obedience, chastity, mercy , and quietness." Females must be shielded from all glimpses of impropriety, maintain an appropriate distance from all men (including brothers and husband), and have no friends unless so "ordered" by family superiors. All this will require that she "harden her heart like rock or metal." She must never question her husband, regardless of the circumstances, and never leave his house. She may be divorced—the ultimate shame—for disobedience to her in-laws, failure to have children, lewdness, jealousy, leprosy, talkativeness, or stealing. She must honor her in-laws over her birth parents, even when they abuse her horribly; consider her husband her lord above all others; be always "courteous, humble, and conciliatory"; revere her husband's siblings; show no resentment of her husband's debauchery and unfaithfulness; do her housework unflaggingly, no matter how many servants she has; refrain from fondness for theatre or music; resist praying to the gods or relying on diviners; avoid extravagance; be unobtrusive; and remain on guard against a woman's "five worst maladies"— "indocility, discontent, slander, jealousy, and silliness."[7]

At the turn of the twentieth century, Lafcadio Hearn, famed for his interpretations of Japanese culture, described women of the premodern era in terms resembling the *Onna Daigaku*. He called the Japanese woman a being working only for others, thinking only for others, happy only in making pleasure for others,—a being incapable of unkindness, incapable of selfishness, incapable of acting contrary to her own inherited sense of right,—and in spite of this softness and gentleness ready, at any moment, to lay down her life, to sacrifice everything at the call of duty; such was the character of the Japanese woman.[8]

Chamberlain similarly notes: "These delicate-looking women have Spartan hearts. Countless anecdotes attest their courage, physical as well as moral." [9]

The ideal for men—emulated to some extent even among commoners—was *bushidō*, the way of the samurai, while for women it was *teijidō*, the way of the virtuous woman. Similarly, the ideal of femininity was summed up in the expression *Yamato nadeshiko*, "gentle woman of Japan." In a society where such an ideal of femininity was worshiped, one would expect to see this image reflected in *kabuki*.

Case, referring to Western examples of all-male theatre, says, in words that could as easily apply to Japan: "This practice reveals the fictionality of the patriarchy's representation of the gender. Classical plays and theatrical conventions can now be regarded as allies in the project of suppressing real women and replacing them with masks of patriarchal production." [10] *Kabuki* women often exemplify such masks, yet the range of characters is quite wide and it is worth looking at some of them to see how they differ from or correspond to the conventional images. There are many meek and submissive women in *kabuki* but there are also many who oppose their social bonds and demonstrate considerable independence of action and thought. One of the theatre's functions has always been to act as a subversive outlet for people's repressed desires, and the many women who attended *kabuki* must certainly have wanted to see characters who transcended their own restricted lives and actions. Nevertheless, when feminine independence is expressed, it is almost invariably in the form of a crucial sacrifice made on behalf of a man.

The Courtesan as Icon

If any *kabuki* character may be said to typify the ideal woman, it is certainly not Hearn's compliant housewife, nor is it the virginal young miss not yet subjected to a husband's dominance. Instead it is the courtesan (*keisei*, among other terms), fabled in song, story, art, dance, and theatre. In fact, Japan's prostitutes belonged to a hierarchically organized profession, with multiple ranks and levels ranging from walk-ons to superstars. And most of these figure in *kabuki*, although the most respected ones are those who dominate the pleasure quarters, which appear as dramatic locales in one play after the other.

In a sense, we might conclude that there really never was a total ban on actresses because the top-ranking courtesans stepped in to fill the gap. These women, whose rise to national fame paralleled *kabuki*'s development, created a fantasy of feminine appeal and desirability within the prototheatrical world of the quarters. There they attained skills in music, poetry, the tea ceremony, flower arrangement, dance, conversation, and the like, providing the actress-deprived public with an image of woman certainly not to be found in anyone's actual home. Many courtesans, writes Mark Oshima, were "women [of good backgrounds] who entered the licensed pleasure quarter in order to raise money for their lord or family."[11] They remind us of the demimondaines of mid-nineteenth-century France, who, Lesley Ferris declares, "were cultivated by aristocratic backgrounds and education but impoverished by the loss of their fathers and acceptable suitors in the many wars of the Empire."[12] French courtesans, adds Ferris, offered their wealthy clients "intellectual and cultural amusements beyond the expected sexual liaison,"[13] and so did Japan's.

Through the media of *kabuki*, popular literature, woodblock prints, and guidebooks that described and even ranked their beauty and accomplishments, courtesans were famous everywhere, known even by those who never set foot in the quarters. In reality, they were indentured slaves, but the social construction of them was of superbly accomplished women who were sexually available only to those with bottomless pockets and, even then, only after being wooed in an elaborate system of artificial courtship. They were on display, however, for all social classes, rich and poor, for they paraded daily, dressed and made up to the nines, occasionally altering their walk by dragging the inside edges of their foot-high clogs in a sweeping *hachimonji* (figure eight). The necessity of slightly opening the almost always pressed-together legs for this movement had powerful erotic overtones. The images they projected were replicated in *kabuki* by the *onnagata*, who expressed the courtesans' famed sense of pride, their spirit, and—ironically for sellers of sex—their faithfulness to a particular lover. Since many of these *kabuki* "emblems of feminity"[14] were based on actual women, even their actual names being used, the courtesans' renown clearly made them the female movie or rock stars of their day.

Kabuki women are constantly being sold or selling themselves into whoredom for self-sacrificing reasons, Omatsu in *Kamiko Jitate Ryōmen Kagami* (Mirror of the two-sided paper kimono, 1768) even attempting to do so to enable her husband to redeem his prostitute sweetheart from the quarters. Many *kabuki* heroes either have a prostitute mistress or hope to gain one.

Although prostitutes were notorious in real life for their insincerity, those in *kabuki* are typically dignified, pure of heart, deeply sincere, and faithful to the death on behalf of the man they love. The renowned courtesan Yatsuhashi in *Kagotsurube* (A sword named Kagotsurube, 1888) is so devoted to her jealous lover that when another man promises to buy her contract she reluctantly refuses her freedom, publicly insulting the man, for which he eventually slays her. An exception to the selfless courtesan is the selfish Miyokichi in *Chijimiya Shinsuke* (Silk salesman Shinsuke, 1860), whose creation is representative of the mid-nineteenth-century decline in courtesan standards.

Confucianists frowned on romantic love outside of marriage but romantic love is pervasive in *kabuki*, although it constantly leads to one catastrophe or another. Courtesans could not afford to fall for a client, and they could be ransomed by anyone with the price, but they were human, after all, and the conflict between love for a man who cannot afford to buy out their contract and the attempts to stifle someone who can forms the action of many dramas. When all else fails, such women often choose to commit suicide with their lover in the hope of achieving happiness in the other world. This act of defiance signaled possible relief to so many repressed copycat lovers that such plays—powerful signs of theatre's subversive power for the emotionally oppressed—eventually were banned.

An invariable pattern is for the courtesan to save her lover from some imminent danger of which he is usually unaware. Her only recourse is to deny him, which she must do publicly in a letter or *aisozukashi* (speech of denunciation), even though it breaks her heart; the woman disguises her true feelings in the interests of the presumed greater good and—like Armand Duval being rejected by Marguerite Gautier—the man remains innocent of her motives. Such scenes of *enkiri* (divorce) have been extremely common since being introduced by playwright Namiki Gohei I (1747–1808) in the mid-1790s, although always provided with a new twist, and an all-too-frequent result is that the lover, completely misreading the woman's intentions, kills her in revenge. The example of Yatsuhashi in *Kagotsurube*, mentioned earlier, is a variation of this pattern, with the real lover being the cause for the would-be lover's rejection.

Kabuki prostitutes could also show a defiance and backbone worthy of drama's most strong-willed women, perhaps the best example being the dazzling Agemaki in *Sukeroku Yukari Edo no Zakura* (Sukeroku: Flower of Edo, 1713). This powerful figure adamantly refuses her services to her lover's wealthy but evil samurai rival, castigating him in a scathingly biting putdown. Unlike Yatsuhashi, Agemaki truly does despise this suitor, and she is not killed for her defiance.

According to Yoshizawa Ayame I (1673–1729), the greatest early *onnagata*, the courtesan was the basis for all female-role acting. "The reason for this," he said, "is that, since he is basically a man, he possesses, by his nature, a faculty of strong action, and he must carefully bear in mind the softness of the *keisei* and her feminine charm."[15] In other words, the *keisei* is the antithesis of masculinity, being soft instead of hard, gentle instead of rough, delicate instead of strong. At the time, *kabuki* had not yet developed such important women as townsmen's wives and respectable daughters (although they were beginning to appear in the puppet theatre), but many of these would before long require similarly feminine qualities, although expressed in different patterns. But the *keisei* clearly was the basis on which such later forms of theatrical womanhood were established. The *keisei*, after all, was then the most visible woman available for regular observation, most others being carefully secluded from the public gaze.

As the development of female characters proceeded, actors had to find ways to remain sexually interesting yet not to confuse the qualities of one role type with another. Even a virgin had to have sex appeal, so different types of charisma had to be constructed. As the *onnagata* Nakamura Utaemon V (1865–1940) wrote:

> The distinction between a woman who has a lover and one who doesn't is a bit difficult: the virgin consistently acts with a sense of embarrassment as her fundamental quality. She keeps her head bent and eyes lowered, and she must have a full emotional complement of sexuality. For example, when the man she loves is near her, much as she seems as though she would fly to him, it would be disgraceful to appear so, yet her feelings must be completely and unflaggingly directed toward him. Her acting uses her sleeves in insinuating ways but everything is done in moderation. In the case of the *keisei*, this is business, so she must *seem* embarrassed. Instead, she acts with the sense that she takes pride in her manner.[16]

The sleeves are another source of difference between *keisei* and other women. Manipulation of the hanging sleeves—whose length varies according to the character type—can suggest an extraordinary range of feelings, and they are of particular use when wiping away one's tears. The *keisei*, however, normally dabs her tears with a wad of paper always seen protruding from her breast fold; one paper can also serve a variety of other important purposes, such as fanning herself or repairing the thong on a sandal.

Closely aligned to the prostitute are the geisha, entertainers who came on the scene in the mid-eighteenth century, but did not sell sex, at least not overtly. One interesting difference between geisha and prostitutes derives from the way they hold their skirts, although today's actors often ignore the distinction. An old name for the female geisha (there were male geisha, too) is *hidarizuma* (left skirt), which derives from the tradition of her holding up her kimono skirt with her left hand, while the prostitute does so with her right, providing the term *migizuma* (right skirt). Critic Tobe Ginsaku reports that the skirts open wider with the right grip, thereby being more revealing, as suits a sexual professional, while the modest left grip permits a more graceful manner of movement.[17] Although their circumstances differ somewhat from those of the prostitutes, geisha are embroiled in similar love problems, and, because they, too, were indentured, they often face comparable situations.

Taking Matters into Their Own Hands

Like Antigone and Clytemnestra, many *kabuki* women are not shrinking violets but choose to take action with their own hands when the life or well-being of their husband or lover is at stake, when a family member must be avenged, when a political objective must be gained, or when the woman has been cruelly wronged. Such cases mirror the comments by Hearn and Chamberlain about delicate women behaving with remarkable fortitude; as will be seen, some of these women ware not as delicate as the stereotype suggests. Not only samurai women, but commoners also could demonstrate single-minded dedication, bravery, and resourcefulness when tragedy threatened. Frequently, they make enormous sacrifices to raise money for an endangered lover or an important cause. Or their devotion drives them to what Edo-period Japanese considered ultraheroic acts of subversion, perhaps the most fabled being performed by Greengrocer Oshichi, of *Yagura Oshichi* (Oshichi and the fire tower, 1773). She is so desperate to be reunited with her lover Kichisaburō that she commits a capital crime by banging the fire tower drum when there is no fire in order to rouse the neighborhood and hopefully bring Kichisaburō back to her. Such things were not likely to happen to the average woman in this oppressive society, of course, but she could see them enacted on the stage and understand how even she, were the circumstances similar, might rise to heroic heights.

Women in Dance

In the *onnagata*'s early years, roles of such power went to male-role actors while dance was the *onnagata*'s specialty. The early dances may have reflected folk beliefs in woman's fearsome sexual powers. Thus many dances—perhaps serving as exorcistic channels through which dangerous female energy could be dispelled—concerned the release of the central demons in the form of madness. A typical means of expressing this was through *shishi* (a creature often translated as "lion") dances inspired by earlier sources, such as the *nō* play *Shakkyō* (Stone bridge), in which the gentle lion of the first half, played as a young girl, goes mad and returns in all its crazed frenzy. Others dances allowed the dancer to play an actual maiden who is overcome by jealousy, as in the innumerable dances exemplified by *Musume Dōjōji* (The maiden at the Dōjō Temple, 1753). The *onnagata*'s dance monopoly was not successfully challenged until the late eighteenth century. But even the later *onnagata* dances (as well as dramas) often featured the female character as the anthropomorphic embodiment of unknowable forces, such as the spirits of plants and animals.

Also reminding us of the importance of females in dance are the many numbers shared with a male, such as *michiyuki* (travel dances), in which there is a passage of lamentation called *kudoki*, usually expressing the woman's love for her man. During these sections, sung by the onstage musicians, the man generally sits quietly while the woman expresses her deepest feelings choreographically. *Kudoki* are also found in dramas and are the emotional highlights for females, in which they may chastise someone, say farewell to a beloved, wail over a dead child, and so on. These passages are very important to the usually sedate *onnagata* because he can allow his emotions to rip in a musically balanced sequence replete with weeping and expressive gestures.

Jealous Women

Jealousy—about which the *Onna Daigaku* has many cautionary things to say—is the most common of a *kabuki* woman's unattractive traits. It is so frequently seen that there is even a term for the acting in such plays, *shittogoto* (jealous business). One jealousy drama that should send feminists on a rampage is *Banchō Sarayashiki* (The chamberlain and the china mansion)—a 1916 adaptation of a once popular 1741 puppet play adapted by *kabuki*—in which a jealous woman decides to test her fiancé's love by smashing one of his prized heirloom plates. He is willing to forgive her when he thinks it an accident but drowns her in a well when he discovers that she doubted his fidelity. She is so happy to learn that he is faithful that she willingly takes the plunge. Jealousy can also affect women regarding their relative status in a *daimyō*'s inner court. One of the greatest dramas with a mainly female-role cast, *Kagamiyama* (Mirror Mountain, 1782, among several versions), is about just that. And in *Karukaya Dōshin Tsukushi no Iezuto* (Karukaya Dōshin and the souvenir of Tsukushi, 1735), jealousy is horrifically manifested when two women fall asleep while playing a board game and their hair turns into snakes that bite at each other.

Female Purity Inspires Female Strength

Jealous or not, princess or not, most young women in *kabuki* epitomize the purity of youthful beauty and innocence. Unmarried young women may be noblewomen, countrywomen, or townswomen. From the latter two groups come those known as *musume* (daughters), while from the former come the upper-class girls called *hime* (princesses). These maidens, coming as they do from the most protected environments, are extremely delicate, gentle, modest, and retiring. With their entire existence resting on an unsullied but tragic love, they shamelessly elicit audience sympathy. Such women are *kabuki*'s quietest, using their sleeves and skirts to communicate embarrassment, happiness, sorrow, laughter, and the like, and so holding their *furisode* (long, voluminous sleeves) that one can barely discern their hands within them.

Kabuki critics call the three most challenging of such roles the *sanhime* (three princesses), just as they similarly designate the *sannyōbō* (three wife roles) and the (*sanbābā*) (three old lady roles), although, for some reason, perhaps the sheer abundance of the field, there are no "three courtesans." One of the reasons for these selections is that, despite their reticence and physical frailty, these women express considerable independence of mind and action. Princess Toki in *Kamakura Sandaiki* (Record of three generations at Kamakura, 1781) breaks convention by begging her betrothed to spend one night with her before he goes off to battle and, despite her having been raised with absolutely no domestic skills, determines to prepare dinner no matter what the cost. In some cases, their desires are strong enough for supernatural forces to be induced to aid them. Princess Yuki in *Kinkuji* (The golden pavilion, 1757) is so set on rescuing her lover that, when bound with ropes to a cherry tree, she becomes capable of willing the cherry blossoms at her feet to turn into rats who chew her free. The sexually naive Princess Yaegaki in *Honchō Nijūshikō* (Japan's twenty-four paragons of filial virtue, 1766) wishes to reach her endangered lover so greatly that magic foxes appear to help her cross a frozen lake. To convey the abnormal power of these latter two climactic transformations, *kabuki* has both Yaegaki and Yuki perform them in *niangyō buri* (puppet movement) style, with black-robed manipulators seeming to control their movements. Critic Tsuda Rui tells us that, for the oppressed women of the day, who had little freedom of thought or action, such heroines were their alter egos, their dreams come true.[18] They acted as a momentary release, a liberating force, in their struggle for freedom and their overturning of convention to fight for the perfection of their love.

Commoner girls are similarly devoted to their men, of course, as we saw in the story of Greengrocer Oshichi. Ofune, a rural girl in *Yaguchi no Watashi* (The miracle at Yaguchi ferry, 1770), substitutes her body for her lover's on an enemy sword and, mortally wounded, further aids him by climbing a tower to bang a drum and raise a siege. [This play is translated and discussed in Jones's contribution, chapter 17. Ed.] In fact, a considerable number of plays have women who willingly substitute their bodies for those of their loved ones. In *Hashi Kuyō Bonji no Mongaku* (The memorial service at the bridge, 1883), a faithful wife deceives an enemy samurai into thinking he is killing her sleeping husband while she puts herself in her spouse's place.

Women and the Aesthetic of Cruelty

Because of the delicacy of the average *kabuki* woman, any threat to her physical or mental well-being should bring shudders, a consideration actors and writers exploited by finding ways to threaten her safety in melodramatic scenes of torture. These "Perils of Pauline"–like scenes form a crucial part in *kabuki*'s so-called *zankoku no bi* (aesthetic of cruelty), a highly aestheticized, even fantastical world where the inherent sadism is muted by artistic techniques. In "snow tortures," the woman is tied up and punished in the freezing cold. She invariably escapes at the last moment, just as in many Western melodramas. In the most aestheticized "torture" scene, the courtesan Akoya, in the play of that name (1732), is tested as to whether she is lying when she denies knowing the whereabouts of her fugitive lover. The test requires her to play three different musical instruments—a sort of artistic polygraph—while her interrogators determine by her playing whether she is lying. No matter how conventionalized, these scenes clearly play to male fantasies of domination and aggression.

Another way to wring audience tears is to have a beautiful woman go blind from grief, forcing her to earn her living as a beggar, or be horribly disfigured by poison or a physical attack. The *onnagata* created a number of vivid makeup conventions to depict scarred or mutilated features, none more awful than the grotesque effect of purpled skin and drooping eye worn by Oiwa after her husband poisons her in *Tōkaidō Yotsuya Kaidan* (The ghost stories of Yotsuya on the *Tōkaidō*, 1825). In a heartrending moment, this once proud beauty combs her long black hair only to see it come out in bloody clumps. But because nothing is more noble than a self-sacrificing woman, what could be more dramatic than to have such a woman, renowned for her beauty, deliberately mar her own appearance? This happens in *Natsu Matsuri* (Summer festival, 1745), when the married Otatsu, to prove that she can be trusted alone with the handsome young Isonojō, places a red-hot iron against her cheek, branding herself with a frightful scar. "Do you still find me alluring?" she inquires.

Another form of self-mutilation, the severing of a finger, is meant as a sign of devotion, still practiced by the *yakuza*, Japan's Mafia-like gangsters. One *kabuki* example is in *Kirare Otomi* (Scarface Otomi, 1864), when Otomi pledges her love, while another example stems from a different type of devotion. In *Yoshibei Ume no Yoshibei* (Plum blossom Yoshibei, 1796), Koume, realizing that the bitten-off pinky in the mouth of her dead brother is her husband's, and that her husband must have killed him, assumes responsibility for the crime by slicing off her own digit and then committing suicide.

Sex and the *Kabuki* Woman

Patriarchal attitudes are at their most rampant in the treatment of women who have been raped. In a number of plays the rape actually comes as a pleasant surprise to the previously inhibited victim, as it reveals to her pleasures of which she has been ignorant. In *Sakura-hime Azuma Bunshō* (The scarlet princess of Edo, 1817), for example, the high-class title character has been raped in the dark by Gonsuke and is unable to forget the experience. She even gets a tattoo like the one she glimpsed on his arm, so when Gonsuke inadvertently appears before her she recognizes his tattoo, jumps into bed with him, throws away her glossy lifestyle, and willingly descends into degradation in order to be with him. Such nineteenth-century plays reflect a general social decadence, among the effects of which are characters like Sakura, who—despite their fulfillment of male rape fantasies—deliberately flout accepted social standards and carve out individualistic lives based on their own personal needs. Such roles also give the actor an enormous range of possibilities as he goes from ultrarefined to increasingly uncouth speech, actions, and appearance.

Although prostitutes are in the business of selling sex, some of *kabuki*'s most sensually aggressive women are not prostitutes at all. Sakura's bedroom scene with Gonsuke is franker than anything that could have been viewed in the West at the time and, considering that it is played by two men, still evokes a frisson at its daring today. In the "Sushiya" scene from the classic *Yoshitsune Sembon Zakura* (Yoshitsune and the thousand cherry trees, 1747), the shopgirl Osato, believing that she will be marrying the supposed clerk Yasuke, boldly invites him to sleep with her. And the flirtatious behavior of the virgin princess Yaegaki toward her lover in *Honchō Nijūshikō* always elicits laughter because of the way her unabashed forwardness contrasts with her essential innocence.

Mothers and Wives: Society's Role Models

Far more sedate than the women we have touched on are *kabuki*'s wives, both samurai and commoner, but principally the latter. Their principal purpose is to support the desires—no matter how selfish—of their husbands. These often shallow and unworthy men squander their money at the brothels, but the wives—as the *Onna Daigaku* instruct—show no jealousy and in every way are models of domesticity. When a crisis threatens, these quietly intrepid women do all in their power to avert it, even at the cost of divorcing their spouse or dying on his behalf.

Such characters were modeled on the townswomen of the day. They epitomize virtuous behavior, so even the suggestion of adultery carries shock value. Chikamatsu Monzaemon (1653–1725) wrote three adultery plays that were later adapted from the puppets for *kabuki*, but in each case the woman is a passive victim of circumstances and her essential virtue remains intact. It was extremely difficult for a married woman of the time to engage willfully in adultery because her life was so circumscribed and because chastity was so highly revered. One of the few important plays written directly for *kabuki* and centered on adultery is *Kagatobi* (The Kagatobi fire brigade, 1886), in which a proud fireman's wife is unfairly suspected of infidelity, leading to her attempts to clear herself of the charge. Because of its late date, it is vaguely possible that Western models, such as *Othello*, influenced this play. In general, *kabuki* wives exemplify fidelity, while their husbands often epitomize the double standard.

A woman's sexual passion can also be illicit in other ways, and incest plays a role in several works, although usually unintended and discovered only after the act has been discovered. Here the writer's objective is to uncover the unexpected workings of karma. The Phédre-like heroine of *Sesshū Gappō ga Tsuji* (Gappō and his daughter Tsuji, 1773), however, deliberately pursues her stepson, and only when her behavior causes her imminent death does she reveal her noble motives. No sooner does a woman seem truly lewd than the convention of *jitsu wa* (in reality) intrudes and the altruistic truth comes out.

Samurai wives are best represented by the women of the inner court known as *katahazushi*, a term which reflects the off-centeredness of their hairstyle. Among *katahazushi* heroines are some of the most dignified and tragic of characters. One of the greatest is Masaoka in *Meiboku Sendai Hagi* (Precious incense and the autumn flowers of Sendai, 1777, and later versions), a governess who, to protect the child of her lord, must sit impassively as her own child is brutally slain before her eyes. Only when she is alone can she erupt with pent-up grief. Such roles challenge the actor's emotional capacities and his ability to make the extremes his character suffers believable to a contemporary audience.

Mothers, in particular, strain a Japanese audience's heartstrings. One might argue that the relationships between so many weakling heroes and nurturing courtesans reflect a pervasive Japanese male fixation, but plays with actual mothers in emotionally wrenching situations are common. These include those where a mother must react unflinchingly to the death of a child, to her parting from one forever, or to her search for a kidnapped child. Like so many other situations, the first two of these complications stem from conflicts between a character's obligations and duties under the Confucian codes and her personal inclinations. When *giri* (social duty) wins out over *ninjō* (human feelings), the audience reaches for its hankies. Still, as scholar Kintō Tamao has noticed, the preeminent mothers are tragically prevented by dramatic circumstances from openly expressing their maternal feelings, making this fundamental human relationship a victim of social ethics.[19] In such a world, he thinks, Sadaka's killing of her own daughter in *Imoseyama* (Imose Mountain, 1771) so that the dead girl can join her lover in the afterworld is the ultimate expression of maternal love. *Kabuki* also has a Medea-like mother in *Shusse Kagekiyo* (Kagekiyo victorious, 1685): Akoya, Kagekiyo's jealous mistress, murders their two sons before his eyes when the recalcitrant hero rejects her pleas for forgiveness and says the boys are no longer his.

Female Versions of Male Roles

Perhaps the most distinctive sign that *kabuki* is a theatre of men playing women is the phenomenon of plays originally written for male-role actors being revised to accommodate the *onnagata*'s talents. This is not the same as an actress playing Hamlet as a man; it is Hamlet conceived of as a woman, with all the attendant transformations this requires in the other characters. In *Narukami* (1742), the beautiful Princess Taema visits the priest Narukami at his mountain lair in order to seduce him. If she is successful, she will be able to end a drought by releasing a dragon god the priest has imprisoned. In *Onna Narukami* (Female Narukami, 1696), Narukami is a nun seduced by a handsome young lord. The most exaggeratedly masculine hero is Gongorō Kagemasa in *Shibaraku* (Just a minute! 1697), yet even he was transmogrified into a strange hybrid when played by an *onnagata* in *Onna Shibaraku* (Female just a minute! 1745?/1746?). When the character makes her exit on the *hanamichi* (runway), she begins in the bounding male style (*roppō*) but then, realizing that she is, after all, a woman, becomes embarrassed and runs off in typical female fashion.

It is a standard part of all *onnagata* roles in which the character somehow displays qualities associated with masculinity for her to constantly catch herself up short and revert to more feminine behavior. The expression of embarrassment when she realizes how far she has wandered from the actions expected of her character's gender is almost always good for a laugh. The audience's knowledge that it is actually a man playing the role only intensifies the humor. When these moments occur, the entire fabric of constructed gender behavior is illuminated and the artificiality of the *onnagata*'s art shines forth. The most obvious examples are in the grouping of roles called *onna budō* (female warriors), in which the samurai heroine displays amazonian propensities. In *Keya Mura* (Keya village, 1786), Osono is disguised as a Zen priest, fights off a band of robbers, and battles with an enemy while holding a child in her arms. However, she sharply drops her mannishness to demonstrate ladylike bashfulness when she discovers that her opponent is her never-before-seen betrothed. Another superwoman is Hangaku in *Wada Kassen* (The Wada dispute, 1736), who has to smash down a gate. The eighteenth-century actor Arashi Koroku II (dates unknown), criticized for lacking femininity in his roughhouse scene, only gained approval after first holding a handkerchief against the gate to soften the effect, and this became the standard business.

Hell Hath No Fury Like a *Kabuki* Woman Scorned

As we have seen, *kabuki* women are mainly sincere, self-sacrificing, demure even when robust, gracious, and so on. We have also noted that women can start out all these things and then descend into the mire of decadence and disgust, but with it all, such women rarely display overt evil. One of the chief ways in which women who have been trampled on become empowered is to turn into vengeful spirits after they have died. The entire world of selfish, unfaithful husbands and lovers must take cover when one of these women comes back from the other world to seek revenge on those who have wronged her.

In more earthly revenge dramas, women are mainly brave pillars of support for their retribution-seeking spouses, although they may have to commit suicide to help bring the action to a successful conclusion, as in *Goban Taiheiki* (*Go* board record of the great peace, 1706). But plays in which the living avengers are women do exist, most notably *Go Taiheiki Shiroishi Banashi* (The tale of Shiroishi and the Taihei chronicles, 1780), based on an actual 1723 vendetta accomplished by a pair of teenage sisters, here depicted for typical *kabuki* contrast as a country bumpkin and her citified courtesan sibling.

To return, though, to the depiction of women who exude viciousness, the relatively few who exist are generally confined to two types. One is the mean-spirited court women who live secluded from most men and fill out their time with intrigues and backbiting. Such murderous creatures are considered too treacherous for pure *onnagata* to play and are almost always cast with *tachiyaku* (male-role actors) to underline their uglier qualities. In a sense, this represents cross-gender casting within a one-gender theatre. Other distasteful women are heartless mothers-in-law and stepmothers, who appear in history plays as well as those of contemporary life. In *Shinjū Futatsu Haraobi* (The double suicide of two sashes, 1722), a notably brutal stepmother kicks her pregnant daughter-in-law out of the house. She has no redeeming features, but the abusive Otaki in *Kama ga Fuchi* (The Kama depths, 1737) reveals as she dies that her bullying behavior was intended to drive her stepson away in order to protect him from potential disgrace. There are also some terrifically hateful women in plays of contemporary life who do not fit any particular pattern, but whose realistic meanness (like the deliciously bitchy Manno in *Ise Ondo* [The Ise dances], 1796) can still rile an audience.

But pure *onnagata* relish the ability to play *kabuki*'s other bad women, the *akuba* or *akujo* (evil women), also known as *dokufu* (poison ladies). These characters, sometimes originating in low-class backgrounds, sometimes fallen from the nobility, like Princess Sakura, came on the scene at the turn of the nineteenth century and took *onnagata* acting in a completely unfamiliar direction. These tough women of the backstreets, who lord it over their men, are often obsessed with thoughts of revenge on someone who wronged them. They bear nicknames like "Crescent Moon" Osen, "Riverside" Oroku, "Fed Up" Omatsu, and "Scarface" Otomi; speak the slangiest of dialects; and engage in gambling, blackmail, theft, whoring, and murder. They can be calculating, cruel, and defiant, yet, like most *kabuki* women, beneath all the bravado and forbidden activity, they reveal a sharp streak of sentimentality that explains their behavior as being on behalf of the man they love. This was an absolutely necessary concession to audience tastes, which required such tradition-breaking heroines to have traditional redeeming qualities.

Plays featuring the *akuba*, especially those by Tsuruya Nanboku IV (1755-1829), reflected a growing tendency toward a theatricalized naturalism focused on the lives of society's outcasts, and her depiction represented a sharp move from idealization to gritty, if conventionalized, actualism; however, with an abundance of such roles, standardization set in and the *akuba* developed into yet another iconographic woman. Nevertheless, she represents a major step away from the excessively feminized woman of the past toward a potently independent character happy to demolish the stereotype of women as the victims of a suffocating patriarchy. And she was not simply a theatrical fiction, as there were a number of actual women who closely fit the description.

Cross-Dressing and the *Kabuki* Woman

As one might expect in a form employing all-male casts—and in a culture that Leupp demonstrates was increasingly enthralled with androgyny,[20] especially in the nineteenth century, when gender distinctions began to blur—

kabuki has its share of characters who cross-dress both to complicate the plot and to create a degree of sexual titillation. But such situations are relatively few when compared to the proportion of them in Shakespeare. *Kabuki* cross-dressing is mainly a matter of men dressing as women rather than the reverse. Ultimately, it is an excuse for allowing the actor to display his versatility at playing male and female versions of the same role. Cross-dressing, down to hairstyles and makeup, however, did occur in actual Japanese life, although outlawed, and appears to have been a particularly effective way for nineteenth-century con men to maneuver themselves into compromising situations, which they could turn to their advantage. This device is represented in two popular plays, *Sannin Kichisa* (The three Kichisas, 1860) and *Benten Kozō* (1862). In the first, the thief Ojō Kichisa masquerades as the stage character Greengrocer Oshichi, mentioned above, in order to facilitate his crimes; in the second, Benten Kozō dresses as a samurai maiden shopping for her trousseau in order to deceive a shop owner as part of a robbery scheme. At the climax, Benten's ruse is revealed and, to the delight of audiences ever since, he disrobes on stage and switches from demure young miss to arrogant hoodlum, his female robes loosely draped about his tattooed torso, while he retains his female makeup and hairstyle. The vision of this androgynous hybrid remains one of the most telling images of the mid-nineteenth-century fascination with the grotesque.

Men required by other plot complications to dress as women include Sangobei in *Satsuma Uta* (Song of Satsuma, 1704), who disguises himself as the court lady Hayashi, a device to help him find his father's murderer; Miyake Hikoraku in *Keisei Mibu Dainenbutsu* (The courtesan and the farce performed at Mibu Temple, 1702), who happens to be dressed as a woman while performing a *kyōgen* farce and overhears a dangerous plot, which leads him to get in on the conspiracy by pretending to be his own wife; and Matsuwakamaru in *Sōta no Shinobu* (Sōta in disguise, 1854), whose situation is the most complex. [The neo *kabuki* version of this play is discussed in Inoue's essay, chapter 11. Ed.]

Matsuwakamaru, the heir of the troubled Yoshida clan, disguises himself as the beautiful geisha Hanako as a ruse to help him uncover the clan's missing seal and scroll. A former clan retainer, Sōta, who also wants to regain these things for Matsuwakamaru, becomes Hanako's steady customer, drawn to her by her resemblance to his former lord. The complications grow thicker as Hanako—known for her unwillingness to take lovers—becomes the target of someone else who wishes to ransom her. She rushes for help to Sōta's house where she soon agrees to marry him so long as they do not sleep together until certain plot conditions are met. However, taking advantage of Sōta's night blindness, Hanako reveals herself to be the male bandit Kiritarō, whose henchmen soon loot Sōta's place. But, of course, she is really

Matsuwakamaru, the henchmen are Yoshida retainers, and the theft is carried out in an attempt to obtain the missing seal. Later, after Hanako—wearing female clothes but behaving as Kiritarō—retrieves both the seal and scroll, she drops both guises to become Matsuwakamaru again. Attacked by the police, who are after Kiritarō, he doffs his female clothes onstage, retaining his woman's red under-kimono and revealing his man's coiffure, thereby creating a marvelously androgynous image as he nonchalantly fights off his attackers while eating a bowl of rice and drinking tea. This is a rare case of a single male character being divided into three parts, one of them female.

Benten's cross-dressing is part of a tradition of admittedly homosexual male characters whose gender flexibility is part of their charm. Lesbianism, however, is barely hinted at in *kabuki*, although there is a scene in a play called *Ōgiya Kumagai* (Kumagai and the fanshop, 1730) in which the handsome Atsumori, who must go into hiding, dresses as a woman and takes refuge at a fan maker's home. The fan maker's daughter, knowing him to be a man, falls in love with him, but the love scene between the two, with the man dressed as a woman, definitely conveys a touch of forbidden desire.

Kabuki also has examples of women who dress as men, most interestingly in *Onna Shosei* (The female student, 1877), written during the early years of Westernization and inspired by a real incident. Suggestive of Isaac Bashevis Singer's *Yentl*, it tells of a country girl brought up as a boy. Her hair is cut short in the new fashion and, passing as a male, she goes to study in Tokyo, is forced by circumstances to commit a crime, and has sex with a lout who threatens to blow her cover. When the man against whom her crime was committed discovers her true gender, he arranges for her to become his mistress. Among the plot complications, another woman falls for her in her male guise and tries to drown herself on learning the truth. Other women dressed as men include Miyokichi, who dresses in a male dancer's festival costume in *Chijimya Shinsuke*; Mankō, an elderly woman who passes herself off as a samurai in order to reach her supposedly wayward son in *Sukeroku* [see Thornbury's essay, chapter 13. Ed.]; and, most dramatically, "Demon" Omatsu in *Shinpan Koshi no Shiranami* (Newly published superbandit, 1780), a wife who teaches fencing as a front for her activities as a cross-dressed bandit leader; after being captured, she is slain by her husband, who does not recognize her in her male guise.

There are, of course, numerous other outstanding and unusual female characters in *kabuki*—some of them truly grand and heroic, others depraved and immoral—and numerous other ways of looking at the ways they were conceived for this all-male theatre. The survey presented here hopefully provides a picture of the Japanese woman's infinite variety within *kabuki*'s severely restricted boundaries. It might also serve as a starting point for more critical and historical examinations of the ways in which, once *kabuki* had progressed from gay to *gei*, the actor grappled with the problems of female representation.

Notes

1. Chieko Irie Mulhern, ed. *Heroic with Grace: Legendary Women of Japan* (Armonk, NY: M.E. Sharpe, 1991), xii.

2. Gary Leupp, *Male Colors: The Construction of Homosexuality in Tokugawa Japan* (Berkeley: University of Hawai'i Press, 1995), 185.

3. Sue-Ellen Case, *Feminism and Theatre* (London: Macmillan, 1988), 6.

4. For reasons of space, the discussion does not cover the important category of old women. Most play titles mentioned in the text are based on the abbreviated versions by which plays are popularly known. Plays typically have at least one formal title and several popular ones, making their identification problematic. For more information on the plays mentioned, see Samuel L. Leiter, *New Kabuki Encyclopedia: A Revised Adaptation of Kabuki Jiten* (Westport, CT: Greenwood, 1996).

5. A brief, but excellent look at issues relating to the presence of the *onnagata*, as seen from an anthropological perspective, is in Jennifer Robertson, *Takarazuka: Sexual Politics and Popular Culture in Modern Japan* (Berkeley: University of California Press, 1998), 53–56.

6. Basil Hall Chamberlain, *Japanese Things: Being Notes on Various Subjects Connected with Japan* (Tokyo: Tuttle, 1971; orig. pub. 1904), 500. Chamberlain translates the entire *Onna Daigaku*.

7. Ibid., 502–508.

8. Lafcadio Hearn, *Japan: An Attempt at Interpretation* (New York: Macmillan, 1935; orig. pub. 1904), 396–397.

9. Chamberlain, *Japanese Things*, 500.

10. Case, *Feminism and Theatre*, 7.

11. Mark Oshima, "The Keisei as a Meeting Point of Different Worlds," in *The Women of the Pleasure Quarter: Japanese Paintings and Prints of the Floating World*, ed. Elizabeth de Sabato Swinton (New York: Hudson Hills Press, in association with Worcester Art Museum, 1995), 101.

12. Lesley Ferris, *Acting Women: Images of Women in Theatre* (New York: New York University Press, 1989), 89.

13. Ibid.

14. Elizabeth de Sabato Swinton, "The Artistic Vision," in *The Women of the Pleasure Quarter*, 130.

15. Yoshizawa Ayame, "The Words of Ayame," in *The Actors' Analects,* ed. and trans. Charles J. Dunn and Bunzō Torigoe (Tokyo: University of Tokyo Press, 1969), 50.

16. Nakamura Utaemon V, quoted in Tobe Ginsaku, "Onnagata no Gihō to Seishin" (The *onnagata*'s technique and mentality), *Kabuki* 12 (1971): 140–41.

17. Ibid., 143.

18. Tsuda Rui, *Edo Kabuki no Shūhen* (The environment of Edo kabuki) (Tokyo: Perikansha, 1990), 71.

19. Kintō Tamao, "Subete Yasashii Haha Oyatachi" (All gentle mothers), *Engekikai* (Theatre World) 29:2 (February 1971), 68.

20. Leupp, *Male Colors*, 172–178.

13

Actor, Role, and Character: Their Multiple Interrelationships in *Kabuki*

Barbara E. Thornbury

Kabuki is a grand display of theatre, very appealing to anyone's sense of a good show. But the significance of *kabuki* lies more deeply than this, and serious theatregoers will inevitably be disappointed unless they can discover this significance through a workable critical approach. This means viewing *kabuki* in terms of dramatic art, as something that can be understood by applying theories of the art form.

At present, how far has criticism of *kabuki* come? To begin, there is a substantial amount of information—mostly in Japanese, some in English and other languages—on the origins and history of *kabuki*, as well as on the kind of costumes and makeup, music and sound effects, and styles of acting that are used. Research has been done on playwriting and play structure, categorizing, and to some extent analyzing the function of various dramatic and theatrical techniques and conventions.

In evaluating the plays and analyzing what happens during a performance, however, there has been a tendency, especially among critics familiar with both Western and Japanese theatrical traditions, to describe *kabuki* simply by comparing it to Western theatre. At best we are told that *kabuki* is a kind of total theatre, in the sense that it uses many devices of theatrical presenta-

This article is a revised version of a paper read at the Association of Teachers of Japanese meeting (literature panel) held in Washington, DC, November 28, 1975.

tion (including some that are rarely or never seen on the Western stage). At worst, we are told that it is a rather formless array of music, dancing, and posturing by actors—a kind of poor version of the American musical.

In effect, criticism of *kabuki* has swung between the overadoration of those impressed by an exotic spectacle and the underrating of those who have not been able to see further than the spectacle. This predicament was summed up by the film director Eisenstein, who wrote the following in 1928, after a troupe of *kabuki* actors had visited Russia on one of their first trips outside of Japan: "We have been visited by the *kabuki* theatre—a wonderful manifestation of theatrical culture. Every critical voice gushes praise for its splendid craftsmanship. But there has been no appraisal of what constitutes its wonder."[1] In general, Eisenstein's evaluation still holds true today, even though many years have passed and *kabuki* has received increasing worldwide exposure.

In is not easy to adequately describe the nature of any dramatic art without getting caught in a web of overly simplified comparisons. We must find instead an approach that is workable from the standpoint of universal dramatic theory; one that appears particularly interesting and suitable for our purposes is a study of the interrelationship between actor, role, and character.

With this approach in mind, we may begin by looking into a charge that is often leveled at *kabuki*: that it is actor-centered, but without meaningful dramatic context.[2] This is to say that the plays have value only as vehicles for the actor's skill, but on the whole are not significant in their artistic conception. That *kabuki* should be labeled actor-centered is natural: All theatre is. But the notion that it is without meaningful context only reflects failure to understand its nature as a dramatic art.

If a play has a meaningful context, from what is it derived? Is it from the plot? The characters? In the *Poetics,* Aristotle designates six separate parts of tragedy, plot and character being foremost. It should be made clear that Aristotle separates plot and character for purposes of analysis, not because they really can be separated in the process of a play. As Santayana has noted, "character can never be observed . . . except as manifested in action."[3] And what we call plot, after all, is the way we describe that action; it is an outline of the dramatic action.

But, then, how does character manifest this action? When we talk about the characters in a play we are not talking about isolated beings, but about beings that interact. Hamlet would not be Hamlet without Ophelia, without Gertrude—in short, without the interaction of the other characters.[4] With the present popularity of psychoanalytic theory, there is the temptation to analyze a play by isolating characters from the play as a whole and treating them as if they were distinct psychological entities. But as Bentley has said in his chapter on character in *Life of the Drama*:

While we have been brought up to believe that what interests us in the life shown on stage is the character of separate individuals, a factor that probably does more to hold us fascinated is the spectacle of a more adequate kind of communication with others, hence of relationship with others, than we can find in life.[5]

Assuming that the interest of a play does lie in the interactions of the characters, in what way are actors related to these characters? In the modern realistic tradition the actor's duty is to serve a play with direct and faithful representations of character. This means, *ideally*, that the audience is concerned with the actors not as individuals, but as agents who manifest character. The actor's job is to step inside a play, as it were, and take on a new identity—that being the character portrayed. This is essentially how Stanislavsky viewed acting, his primary concern being how the actor can most effectively enter into the character being played.

Can the task of the *kabuki* actor be looked at in the same way? Is the audience's interest in *kabuki* limited only to certain character interrelations within a play? The answer appears to be no. The *kabuki* actor has a multiplicity of roles, both inside and outside the conventional limits of a play. Thus the meaningful dramatic context must even extend beyond any written script. And indeed, it is often said that *kabuki* scripts are not meant to be read. (One is reminded that the first publication of *kabuki* plays came as late as the Meiji era, playwriting having started some two centuries earlier.[6]) [Most earlier publications of *kabuki* scripts were in the form of illustrated texts providing only selections of the dialogue. Ed.]

Here we find an important feature of *kabuki*. Whereas we think of many—if not most—plays in the Western tradition as having both a theatrical and a purely literary appeal (meaning that we see them as works to be produced in the theatre as well as to be read in the library), *kabuki* is a more exclusively theatrical art. This is not true however, of other classical Japanese theatre forms. For example, many more people read *nō* plays than attend performances of them. Although reading *kabuki* plays is not without value, the basic script is incomplete because it cannot reveal all of the special multiple interrelationships between actor, role, and character that are so central to *kabuki*.

It is these multiple interrelationships and some of their implications that I wish to discuss in the remainder of this chapter. In order to give concrete examples, I will focus mainly on *Sukeroku Yukari no Edo Zakura* (Sukeroku: Flower of Edo), commonly called *Sukeroku,* one of the most popular plays of the repertoire.

The *kabuki* actor works simultaneously on three different levels: the actor as *yakusha,* the *yakusha* as *yakugara,* and the *yakugara* as *yaku.*

Since *yakusha* is usually translated into English as "actor," it may seem redundant to call the first level "the actor as *yakusha*." In fact, however, the word *yakusha* as it is applied to *kabuki* implies a great deal more than just individuals who happen to find themselves on the stage. In a 1962 production of *Sukeroku*,[7] Sukeroku was played by Ichikawa Danjūrō XI, Agemaki by Nakamura Utaemon VI, and Ikyū by Bandō Mitsugorō VIII. Danjūrō, Utaemon, and Mitsugorō are all, of course, historical stage names, indicating that the actors who were accorded these names had after many years of training and practice attained a certain level of skill and esteem in the *kabuki* world. Recognition of the individual actor takes the form of a number along with the name (for example, Jūichidaime Ichikawa Danjūrō—Ichikawa Danjūrō XI), but what really is at issue is the symbolic value of names like Danjūrō and Utaemon (figure 13.1).

Individuals may die, but the spirit of the great stage names continues. Audiences who come to see these actors perform already have certain expectations apart from any play per se. This is important because, in a very real sense, Danjūrō, for example, already has a dramatic function before one even considers Sukeroku or any other particular part he may be playing. This point is best illustrated in a discussion of the second level, *yakusha* as *yakugara*.

Yakugara may be translated "role" or "role type." The Danjūrō line of actors, for instance, is known for its portrayal of the *tachiyaku*, the great male hero roles, consummate source of the *aragoto* (rough business) style of Edo *kabuki*. Utaemon VI, on the other hand, is an *onnagata*, a player of women's roles. There are many subdivisions of role types within the more general categories. Danjūrō as Sukeroku is a kind of *otokodate*, or "chivalrous commoner." Utaemon as Agemaki is a *tayū*, a high-ranking courtesan. Mitsugorō as Ikyū is a *jitsuaku*, a bad guy. This kind of role type categorization can be done for all the actors who appear in *Sukeroku* or any other *kabuki* play.

There are few examples in world theatre where role types are so central to the dramatic art and developed with such complexity as they are in *kabuki*. The best example that comes to mind is the *commedia dell'arte*, which flourished in Europe from about the middle of the sixteenth to the middle of the eighteenth century. Like *kabuki* the *commedia dell'arte* had well-developed role types, but that is as far as its development reached. When *commedia dell'arte* actors performing roles such as the phlegmatic doctor, the wily lawyer, the harsh father, the beautiful daughter, the handsome suitor, and the evil rival met on stage, many dramatic situations could and did arise. But in order for a theatrical tradition to grow—and thus survive—interesting and well-conceived dramatic characters derived from a substantial repertoire of plays is prerequisite. The *kabuki* had the plays and survived; the *commedia dell'arte* did not and died.

Figure 13.1 **Ichikawa Danjurō XI as Sukeroku in the play of that name. (Photo: Courtesy of Samuel L. Leiter.)**

Even before character is considered, it should be said that although particular actors may be identified primarily with certain *yakugara,* the art of *kabuki* gains much from the skillful versatility of its major actors. It is fascinating to see actors with the ability to move between and among role types and in certain instances to instantly transform themselves on stage from one role type to another, depending on the particular characters the actor is playing. This, then, brings us to the third level on which the actor works: the *yakugara* as *yaku.*

Yaku are the particular characters in a play, and it is at this level that the concept of multiplicity in the interrelationship between actor, role, and character is fully developed.[8] Although instances of actors playing more than one character in a play can be found in the European tradition—as in Shakespeare's *Much Ado About Nothing,* Yeats's *The Words upon the Window Pane*, and Genet's *The Balcony*—there is generally a one-actor-to-one-character relationship in the course of a play. This is not the case in *kabuki*. On the contrary, one *kabuki* actor may play several characters—and roles—in the same play, often with very interesting results.

There are two techniques by which an actor can enter a multiplicity of role and character interrelationships in a play. One is to play a single character and also that character in disguise. The other is for the actor to double his parts by playing different characters—characters who, apart from their not appearing on stage with one another at the same time, have no dramaturgically necessary relationship to each other except that they appear within the framework of the same play. These two techniques are, in short, disguising and doubling.

Sukeroku provides what is perhaps the archetypal example of disguising in *kabuki*. In the 1962 production that has been referred to, Danjūrō plays the warrior hero Soga Gorō, who has disguised himself as a commoner named Sukeroku. What is most curious is that the real Soga Gorō lived in the twelfth century. By being represented as Sukeroku, he is then catapulted by a special kind of theatrical time machine into the eighteenth century.[9] Historically, it is illogical, but theatrically it is acceptable—and workable for generations of *kabuki* audiences.

Time is not the only element that is theatricalized for the purpose of a disguise. At the beginning of the play, Sukeroku's mother, Mankō, disguised as a samurai, has set out to find her son. The actor portraying Mankō is an *onnagata,* a male actor who plays women's roles. In order to carry out Mankō's samurai disguise, he must play a woman in the role of a man. Thus, in effect, the actor is at a double remove from reality. It is only in the theatre where the process of time can be bent to human will and where a woman who is not a woman can pretend that she is a man. [Similar situations can, of course, be found in Western drama, especially Shakespeare. Ed.]

Other instances of disguising can be found in *Sukeroku* and throughout the whole repertoire as well. Hanako as Kiyohime in *Musume Dōjōji* (The maiden at the Dōjō Temple) and Benten Kozō in his numerous disguises— including a woman's role—in *Benten Kozō* are noteworthy examples. Although disguises exhibit varying degrees of complexity [see Leiter's essay, chapter 12, for a play in which a man is disguised as a woman, which disguise is in turn perceived as being that of yet another male character. Ed.], in order for the technique of disguising to be effective the same actor must play all parts of the disguise. It will not work if Sukeroku and Soga Gorō, for example, are played by different actors.

Similarly, if different actors play the different roles, then doubling, as such, does not exist. While a play may be written for disguising, it will not require doubling, which is not built into the dramatic structure and is, essentially, an actor's—or a director's—choice.

In the *kabuki* version of *Funa Benkei* (Benkei in the boat), the beautiful Shizuka Gozen and the monstrous Tomomori are traditionally played by the same actor. Doubling not only is pleasing as a display of the actor's versatility, but it also can create or clarify new—and often ironic—character interrelations for the audience. While Shizuka and Tomomori have no particular relationship to each other, they are both related in an almost opposite way to Yoshitsune. One is Yoshitsune's lover; the other is the incarnation of his mortal enemy. When the two characters are played by the same actor, a transformation of lover into enemy is necessitated. Although the role of lover is distinct from the role of enemy, at least in *Funa Benkei*, in the world of men the line that separates "lover" and "enemy" may be thin indeed, and it is this kind of fluid contrast that the actor achieves through the technique of doubling. The same results would not be possible if the parts were played by different actors.

There are a number of variations of disguising and doubling, two examples of which I will briefly mention here. One is the type used in the play *Chūshingura* (The treasury of loyal retainers). As is commonly known, the play, written in the mid-eighteenth century, depicted a recent incident. Because of government restrictions at that time on the dramatization of contemporary events, however, all of the characters and action in the play are "disguised" within the world of fourteenth-century Japan. The disguise is never revealed except in the mind of the audience. The other example is that most theatrical of all disguises and doublings: the moment when actors seemingly reverse the artistic process and suddenly step out of character to take the role of "plain" actors. They may pause to sip tea, chat with the audience, or congratulate or sympathize with fellow actors. The most flamboyant of such occasions is when a play is brought to a halt for the formal introduction of a child actor new to the stage or the announcement that a veteran player has been promoted to a new stage name and rank. Although the actors who make the announcements and those who are the objects of the accolades remain very much in character as actors, in effect they bring the world of the stage closer to the everyday world of the audience. Success here absolutely requires that a play in progress be brought to a halt and then restarted. This reminds everyone watching that many levels of disguise form the core of theatrical art.

Kabuki, as dramatic art, gives expression to the complexities of human nature and society. The artistic process is based on the actor, who functions through a multiplicity of role and character interrelationships in a play: *yakusha*, *yakugara*, and *yaku*. In sum, *kabuki* begins with the *yakusha,* the great Danjūrō, Utaemon, and others, whose artistic heritage gives them immediate and significant dramatic stature. The activity of the *yakusha* is based on generalized *yakugara* (the *tachiyaku* and *tayū*, for example) and finds final expression in specific *yaku* (Sukeroku and Mankō, for example). These interrelationships are multiplied by disguising and doubling, highly theatrical techniques that enhance the enjoyment and meaning of a play.

Having followed this approach, we can conclude that the dramatic complexity of *kabuki* stems in large part from the actor in his richly varied dimensions of role and character. It is a complexity that cannot be entirely appreciated by reading only the script of a play. Moreover, it is a complexity that adequately fulfills the critic's search for artistic significance or, in other words, meaningful dramatic context in *kabuki*.

Notes

1. Sergei Eisenstein, "The Unexpected," in E.T. Kirby, ed., *Total Theatre: A Critical Anthology* (New York: E.P. Dutton, 1969), p. 178.

2. Kawatake Toshio, *A History of Japanese Theater II, Bunraku and Kabuki* (Tokyo: Kokusai Bunka Shinkōkai, 1971), p. 63.

3. George Santayana, from *The Sense of Beauty,* quoted in Eric Bentley, *The Life of the Drama* (New York: Atheneum, 1964), p. 62.

4. J.L. Styan, *The Elements of Drama* (Cambridge: Cambridge University Press, 1960), pp. 174–175.

5. Bentley, *Life of the Drama*, p. 67.

6. Gunji Masakatsu, *Kabuki,* trans. by John Bester (Palo Alto: Kodansha International, 1969), p. 33. Although the publication of *jōruri* (puppet theatre) plays began in the early seventeenth century, the first *kabuki* play to appear in print was Kawatake Mokuami's *Kanzen Chōaku Nozoki Garakuri* (A peepshow morality tale) (1891). *E-iri kyōgenbon,* summaries of *kabuki* plays in pamphlet form, date from the late seventeenth century. See also Ted Takaya, *An Inquiry into the Role of the Traditional Kabuki Playwright* (New York: Ph.D. diss., Columbia University, 1969), pp. 19 and 152 ff.

7. Entire performance, with accompanying script and descriptive notes, Victor Records, SJ-3001-3.

8. "Role" is a broader and more abstract concept than "character." As can be seen from examples already given, roles are labeled in generalized terms: the hero, the chivalrous commoner, the courtesan, and so on. Characters, on the other hand, are usually given proper names: Sukeroku, Agemaki, and so on.

9. See the section "Gikyoku no hassō" (The conception of drama) in Gunji Masakatsu, *Kabuki no Hassō* (The conception of *kabuki*) (Tokyo: Kōbundō, 1959), pp. 68–80, for a discussion in Japanese terms of matters related to disguising and doubling.

14

Kabuki: Signs, Symbols, and the Hieroglyphic Actor

Leonard C. Pronko

Signs and Symbols

When we speak of symbols in theatrical production, we are most often referring to what Jung called signs. In his *Symbols of Transformation* he made the classic distinction between the two: "A symbol is an indefinite expression with many meanings, pointing to something not easily defined and therefore not fully known. But the sign always has a fixed meaning, because it is a conventional abbreviation for, or a commonly accepted indication of something known."[1]

In addition to the things signed or symbolized, signs and symbols have, of course, a fundamental reality, whether this be a word in a poem, the paint in a painting, a person or an object on the stage. Realism tends to prefer this fundamental reality, presenting it as an end in itself. In a naturalistic drama, a trash can is offered simply as a trash can, a tree as a tree, each adding something to our understanding of a milieu, but meant to represent little beyond itself. Characters, too, are of interest in themselves, as particular cases, and not as representatives of humanity in general. The actor's own reality is, ideally, hidden behind that of the character, the actor as sign disappearing.

Nonrealistic drama, by contrast, deals largely in signs. The great theatres of the past—and even the mediocre ones—presented actors as actors disguised as characters in a presentational, nonillusionist manner. The actor as sign, and his stylized performance of conventionalized scenes that also acted as signs (monologues, soliloquies, narratives, murder scenes, duels, spying, etc.), evolved within a staging made up of signs: fixed décors masquerading as forests, battlefields, palaces; costumes with conventional colors to indicate character, race, function.

Although the texts of nonrealistic theatre may use symbols, most Western theatre before the end of the nineteenth century did not use symbols in its production techniques. Those techniques we call symbolic, like the mansions of the medieval stage, were actually conventions that were commonly understood and possessed none of the vagueness or suggestiveness of symbols. Shakespeare's rich suggestiveness lies in his texts, not in the performances of his day—for the so-called symbolic areas were in fact signs of "a balcony," "a battlefield," and the entire audience understood this.

Most theatre, then, uses signs. Realism prefers the solid reality (or rather, illusion, mistaking the sign for the fundamental reality). The symbolist theatre of Villiers de l'Isle-Adam, Maeterlinck, and others and more recent drama that inherited symbolism's aesthetic (or parts of it) uses theatrical symbols with great frequency. The great dramatists who stand at the beginning of modern drama all present symbolic elements in their plays, and the resulting ambiguity is one mark of their modernity. The doors in *Hedda Gabler*, real in their solidity, suggest something more than a mere entrance. The tree in *Waiting for Godot*, a bona fide symbol, is as mysterious as any swan or reed pipe in Mallarmé's poetry.

The oriental theatre, like traditional nonrealistic theatre in the West, is rich in signs, never masking them beneath an illusion, but instead allowing the double experience of actor and character that has been the theatrical experience since the beginning. Realism, in this regard, is an upstart heresy of recent manufacture. The *kabuki* theatre, like other Asian forms, uses signs at every level of the performance and occasionally turns to symbols.

Just which elements are signs and which symbols must be determined by the attitudes of the Japanese audience, because signs, at least, are the result of common consent, a general acceptance. What are clear signs for the *kabuki* connoisseur may appear as symbols to the uninitiated outside, for, when crossing cultures, signs and symbols slip about. What is conventional for one culture may seem fresh and poetic in another. In Japan the view of cherry blossoms (or the word alone) suffices to set off automatic associations. For centuries, in poetry, prose, and painting, cherry blossoms have been used to evoke a sense of ephemerality, of the evanescence of human life. For a Westerner, however, such an association is not immediate, and the blossoms may appear to be somewhat symbolic since we are free to interpret them in a number of ways.

Some objects have different conventions depending upon the culture. For the Westerner, peonies and butterflies suggest something light, lovely, perhaps even feminine. In Japan they are inevitably associated with the strong *shishi*, a mythical beast usually called a lion in English, but combining attributes of dragon, dog, and other animals. A Japanese therefore does not automatically think "feminine" at the mention of butterflies. Instead he may think "masculine" or "heroic."

An outsider is often tempted to read more into foreign signs and symbols than the average enlightened native might. The analytical Western tradition delights in explanations and equations, ever seeking to understand. The Japanese, aided by the very nature of the language, is often content to live an experience in a more integrated way without constant recourse to intellect and analysis. Viewing, for example, the dedicatory dance *Sanbasō*, the Japanese accepts it simply as that and does not wonder why the dancer uses a tree-shaped bell-prop and a fan, sometimes hitting them together. Granted, the bell-tree, or *suzu*, is shaken in such a way as to represent the sowing of seeds to the four corners, but there the Japanese association with fertility will probably stop. The Westerner, bred on Freud, does not take long to see the bell and fan as signs of male and female sexuality. There is every indication that this is indeed their function in the *Sanbasō* dances, but for the Japanese spectator they are more symbols than signs, suggesting perhaps a variety of meanings, but not tied down specifically to the sexual dimension that is so striking for the Westerner.

Kabuki's rich use of signs and symbols is to be expected in a traditional nonrealistic form of theatre. The highly ritualized Japanese way of life encouraged it, as did the earlier performing arts that contributed to *kabuki*'s rich heritage, and most notably the aristocratic *nō* theatre, highly symbolic and ritualized both in text and performance. That signs are more numerous than symbols in *kabuki* is not surprising either, for *kabuki* is a popular form, and the popular audience demands an instant understanding. It is the elite audience of *nō*, of Maeterlinck and Beckett, that thrives on ambiguity.

Astonishingly, this popular theatre—so popular that for almost three hundred years in Japan the word for "play" (*oshibai*) simply meant *kabuki*—lies close to the ideals of the elitist symbolist theatre. Like the Wagnerian music drama, so admired by the French symbolists, *kabuki* uses a synthesis of the arts in a nonrealistic form based largely on legend, myth, or folktale. In Wagner, however, music is the major focus, and one rarely sees a performance in which movement and acting match the caliber of the voices. *Kabuki*, however, offers a true synthesis. The visual impression appears most important to the foreigner because the visual force of the performance is easy to appreciate and understand, whereas the words are difficult or incomprehensible and the music is perhaps totally foreign. But even without understanding the words, the Westerner should be able to appreciate the immense impact of the sounds, music, and vocal intonations, including shouts, whines, grunts, and occlusive vocalizations. Indeed, attending *kabuki*, one is often reminded of Artaud's admonitions regarding the nonintellectual use of words and sounds in his idealized concept of total theatre.

In fact, intellectualization is as rare in *kabuki* as it is in symbolist drama and literature. Eschewing direct expression, both use suggestion, connotation, association. "To name an object, Mallarmé wrote, is to destroy three quarters of the enjoyment of the poem." (*Réponse à une enquête*, 1891).[2] Earle Ernst, in his superlative study of *kabuki*, sounds curiously Mallarméan when he writes that it is "characteristic of Kabuki to present to the audience not the thing itself, but the designed impression of the thing."[3]

Stylized, often larger than life, *kabuki* rarely delivers a precise message. Instead, by indirect means, it suggests perceptions. Like the forest of symbols described by Baudelaire, a *kabuki* performance seems to be speaking a forgotten language of the senses. The supreme satisfaction experienced by anyone who surrenders totally to this experience derives perhaps from some intuition of what David Gascoyne has called the poetic landscape of Eden.[4] In the sensual *kabuki* world we recapture as adults something of the paradise of childhood: "Instinct has not yet been completely outlawed by reason. Sensation is still vivid and feeling unrestrained."[5] In the total theatre of *kabuki* we find again the past moment in which we once operated as a unity.

No wonder a Japanese critic once described *kabuki* as the nearest possible approach to a paradise on earth.[6] Without the *conscious* idealism of Western symbolism, without the planned program of the Wagnerian and Artaudian total theatre, *kabuki* offers us something like the realization of the symbolist ideal.

It is in the *kabuki* actor, the absolute focus of a *kabuki* performance, that we best see this ideal realized. In all aspects of *kabuki*, signs abound: in décor, music, sound effects, costume, wig, makeup, props. It would require dozens of pages to set forth the impressive usage found in any single performance. The *kabuki* actor, however, midst all these signs, occupies a very special place: he is reality (actor), sign (character), and symbol (visual and aural resonances) all at once. E.T. Kirby, following the lead of such illustrious predecessors as Sergei Eisenstein and Antonin Artaud, calls him a hieroglyph, "intersection of more than one mode of knowing or more than one medium of communication."[7]

Words written phonetically (as in letters of the alphabet) can only with difficulty, if at all, suggest something other than what they denote. Their appeal is largely to the intellect. This is one of the major problems of symbolist poetry and explains why Mallarmé constantly reduced the words in his poems and would finally have ended with a blank page. It also explains why the symbolists wanted to find the musical values of words and "take back poetry's own from music."[8] Hieroglyphs, unlike phonetically written words, offer a physical presence which, at the same time that it indicates a precise conventional meaning, speaks directly to our visual sense and suggests much beyond what it actually signifies. A circle with a dot in it, the sun for the ancient Egyptians, and a square with a line through its center, the sun for the modern Japanese, also carry a secondary meaning of "day." They can be used phonetically, but the sign of the eyelike sun, looking up at us from the page, carries overtones impossible with a phonetic writing system. The hieroglyph—physical reality, convention, and symbol all in one—exemplifies synesthesia as phonetic writing cannot.

If the symbolists had been able to write with hieroglyphs, many of their problems would have been solved. As a matter of fact, they did what they could to make hieroglyphs of phonetic signs by disposing the words suggestively on the page, as Mallarmé did in *Un coup de dés*. And one of symbolism's immediate heirs, Apollinaire, wrote a number of poems (calligrams, he called them) in the shapes of objects.

In the theatre, realistic actors in everyday clothing correspond to the phonetically written word. They have for us the literalness of such writing and little of the suggestiveness of the hieroglyph. Nor can they extend themselves gesturally in graphically suggestive ways. It is difficult to take symbolically a man in a business suit, particularly if he is only doing the things normally done in a coat and tie and is handling such unsuggestive objects as cocktails, cigarettes, and money. This is one of the stumbling blocks of modern poetic drama, over which Ibsen triumphed magnificently in his last plays, but one that has stymied most would-be creators of poetic contemporary drama in the twentieth century.

Actors in period costume can be suggestive. They are even more so if they are clad in a leotard or some neutral garb allowing maximum freedom of movement and possessing a minimum of specific denotation. The actor can then assume almost any posture and take on the suggestiveness of pictograms, eschewing the literalness of dry words. People and objects used in works of art necessarily take on the value of signs. Realism militates against this fundamental vitality of art, attempting to deny the sign-value and convince us that the thing we see is the thing itself. Realistic drama is most successful if we forget the actor and recognize only the character. Hollywood and television seem most often to take just the opposite tack: we are conscious instead of the actor who forever plays the same role. Great traditional theatre has always dealt with the double identity of the actor as actor and as sign. In modern Western theatre, because of its realistic bias, its phonetic limitations so to speak, the actor can rarely go beyond the role as sign to become a symbol. Dancers easily achieve symbolic status because they are not tied to words and are rarely limited to specific characters or situations. Moreover, they may use their bodies pictorially. Since the 1960s we have seen liberating experiments, but by and large the dominant form of acting today is illusionistic and not much bigger than real life. Indeed, in film and television it is sometimes even smaller.

The Hieroglyphic Actor

The *kabuki* performer, dancer-singer-actor, in violent contrast to his Western counterpart, is permitted to use all his bodily and vocal resources, disciplined according to traditional patterns. Clad in nonrealistic costumes, often highly fanciful, with generous padding, platform shoes, immense wigs, colorful makeup, the actor moves in carefully designed, dynamic patterns in order to suggest the essence of a character. Speaking in a deep voice, or in falsetto, or on the break between the two, rising to a high pitch, falling to a low, interspersing words with grunts, muffled sounds, the actor creates the aural *impression* of his character rather than an imitation. "Intersection of more than one mode of knowing or more than one medium of communication," he is indeed a hieroglyph. Blending voice, shape, color, pattern, movement, and precise gestures, he appeals to the spectator through eyes and ears at both conscious and unconscious levels. As a certain character in a certain play, he is a sign. As a famous actor portraying that character, he is his fundamental reality—in *kabuki* almost always apparent through pounds of costume, wigs, and makeup. But, like a true hieroglyph, his extravagant visual or aural impact causes the spectator to feel there is more, something mysterious, vague perhaps, but meaningful, beyond what is apparent and signaled by the conventions of the role. Perhaps this theatre of essences suggests somehow a fleeting glimpse of the Absolute—the experience yearned for by the symbolist poets and summed up in Mallarmé's mad cry, *"L'azur! L'azur! L'azur! L'azur!"*

The "archetype of hieroglyphic expression,"[6] in Kirby's words, is the *mie*, that dynamic pose that, summing up the emotions of a peak moment, gathers all the energies of the actor at one focal point, then lets them explode in a carefully balanced display of controlled tensions. Like the great Buddhist guardian deities that may have inspired the *mie* (although its origin is ultimately unknown), the actor performing (or cutting, as the Japanese has it) a *mie* may dispose his limbs in a number of ways, but he always expresses immense controlled energy. Although one or more limbs may move away from the body, the final feeling is that of returning to center, as the actor ends the pose by sinking low, pelvis perfectly centered, head moving in an arc, then settling with chin pulled in.

The synesthetic-kinesthetic experience of the *mie* is accentuated by the sharp sound of wooden clappers accompanying it in a stylized rhythm. The piercing whack attacks us through all five senses, drawing their attention to this supremely expressive moment. Standing there like "some huge insects full of lines and segments drawn to connect them with an unknown natural perspective,"[9] as Artaud might have said, *kabuki* actors at this moment represent the hieroglyphic actor at his zenith: actor, sign, and symbol. As actor, his art is vocally appreciated by the spectators, who now shout their approbation, often using his *yagō* (clan or "shop" name). Clearly in evidence then is his fundamental reality as an actor whose skill is being judged and enjoyed. As sign, he stands for the character he is portraying, decked out in costume, wig, and makeup, which contain yet other signs.

In the central *mie* from Kumagai's narrative in *Kumagai Jinya* (Kumagai's battle camp) as performed by the late Matsumoto Kōshirō VIII (1910–1982), we observe the easily recognized features of one of contemporary *kabuki*'s most impressive performers. Disguised by the contours of a wig, strong makeup, and a massive costume, this major actor of heroic roles is still easily distinguished (figure 14.1). The richness of the costume, its bold pattern, and the breadth of the winglike upper garment indicate his rank and strength as a warrior. The strong but elegant line of his wig again signals his rank, as does his shaved head. Some actors of this role wear a wig with a mixture of human hair and bear's hair, which is thought to give more body and strength to the wig. Around the top inner edges of the wig there is a small amount of curly hair, also a sign of strength. The makeup again stresses the heroic power of Kumagai, eyebrows and lips stronger than for ordinary mortals, eyes and forehead stressed with heavy brown lines, nostrils similarly reinforced. The pose, with the entire body firmly centered and the right fist held before the chest, suggests solidity, strength, self-assurance (figure 14.1).

All these elements may be considered signs, but Kumagai's pose possesses symbolic elements also. What, for example, is meant by the inverted fan held in the left hand? Why precisely is his right hand clenched at his chest? Although this clenched fist is used in many *mie*, its meaning may differ somewhat, determined by the context of the pose. Kumagai is recounting his fight with a young warrior whom he killed. The warrior's mother, to whom he is deeply indebted, is listening. What Kumagai does not tell her is that, in reality, he substituted his own son, in order to repay his debt of gratitude to the mother. The spectator is free to view this fist as an indication of frustration and anger or as an effort on the part of Kumagai to restrain his own emotions. The inverted fan is usually interpreted as representing the mountain referred to in the accompanying narrative text. At this point in his tale Kumagai has urged the young warrior to flee, but the boy refuses, insist-

Figure 14.1 **Matsumoto Kōshirō VIII as Kumagai in *Kumagai Jinya*. (Photo: Courtesy of Leonard Pronko.)**

ing he should die honorably. Kumagai, unable to draw his sword, hesitates when he hears the voice of a fellow warrior urging him to strike. "Then I heard!" chants the Narrator, temporarily speaking for Kumagai, "From the mountaintop behind me, routed Hirayama cried out!!" The actor opens his fan and assumes the pose in the photograph. We may feel the fan is purely decorative, or we may prefer to think of it as standing for the mountain. The narrative movements are not precise enough to require a single meaning here, but combined with the rich accoutrements, and the rapt concentration of the crossed eyes, they are deeply suggestive. The icon-like pose even intimates that Kumagai, because of his sublime sacrifice (incomprehensible and grisly perhaps in Western terms, but a standard device in *kabuki*), attains a divinity-like stature.

Some *mie* are more patently iconographic. In *Narukami*, when the epony-mous seduced priest discovers he has been betrayed, he transforms himself into a demon to pursue the princess who seduced him. Stopped by his aco-lytes, he fights against them, striking a series of *mie*, many of which have names and specific connotations, though they, too, like most movements, are

suggestive. Tearing the sacred sutras in two, he tosses the ends to two aco-
lytes and holds two ends to his chest, thus creating diagonal lines resembling
a mountain, with himself at the peak. The pose is known as the Fuji *mie*.
Later, he leaps onto the backs of his acolytes, his feet forward, his hands
clasped before him, in what is known as the Riding in the Clouds *mie*. Mount-
ing a hillock, he grasps a rope in one hand and a sacred object in the other,
and holds them before him, one to each side, in a pose reminiscent of the god
Fudō in Buddhist iconography and hence called the Fudō *mie*.

Although the figure of Kumagai may not strike the Western observer as
realistic in any way, it represents a *comparatively* realistic style in *kabuki*.
The role of Tadanobu in *Yoshitsune Senbon Zakura* (Yoshitsune and the thousand cherry trees) is an example of high stylization in which the fanciful
dominates. Figure 14.2 shows Onoe Tatsunosuke I (1946–1987) playing
Tadanobu, a fox that has taken on human shape in order to accompany Princess Shizuka, who has in her possession a keepsake drum made with the
skins of the fox's parents. In the photograph, Tadanobu has just vanquished
a number of warriors and places his foot victoriously on the back of one.
Holding the precious drum in his extended left hand, he raises his right hand
toward his mouth. As the *mie* reaches its climax, he slowly brings his right
hand up and out to the right. Tadanobu utters a dry, snarling sound representing his fury. Finally, as in the picture, the right hand comes to his chest in a
fist, much like Kumagai's; he moves his head in an arc, draws in the chin,
and crosses his eyes as the clappers deliver a loud whack.

Tadanobu's signs are many and complex. He is both fox and samurai, and
his makeup indicates this double nature. The shaved head of the samurai, the
strong black lip line, and red circular lines over the temples are often used
for strong warriors in the *aragoto* (roughhouse) tradition. The eyebrows,
however, with their broken lines, are distinct indications of an animal nature
and are meant to suggest the flickering flames of supernatural foxfires. The
arm and leg decorations (formerly painted, now worn on a cotton garment),
like the temple lines, are indications of heroic strength, emphasizing the bulg-
ing blood vessels of an irate warrior. The braided rope around the shoulders
is another indication of *aragoto*-style strength, as is the dark, plain-colored
obi that ties at the back in a huge, stuffed, rope-like bow known, because of
its shape, as a dragonfly obi. The wig is particularly strong with its light blue
forepart of metal to represent the shaved area of the pate. Made of lacquered,
slightly curly hair, it gives an impression of force and is used for supermen
characters in several plays. Tadanobu's two swords indicate that he is a samurai, since commoners were allowed only one. His fringed garment indicates
his squire's rank, and the wheel-like crest on his costume might well be
interpreted as representing the crest of his master, Yoshitsune, who belongs

Figure 14.2 **Onoe Tatsunosuke I as Tadanobu in *Yoshitsune Senbon Zakura*. (Photo: Courtesy of Leonard Pronko.)**

to the Genji clan. The Genji wheel, however, was also the crest of the puppet theatre narrator who first chanted this play, and it is for this reason that the design is used here.

Tadanobu, cutting across the boundaries between the human and the supernatural, is a particularly rich hieroglyph. His signs point toward both the world of everyday reality and that of magic and animals. His visible manifestation suggests a world of hidden possibilities. When he snarls, as in the photograph, he is both human and animal, as he is when he makes his dazzling exit *roppō*, a magnificent, stylized, flying dance. Accompanied by the strong rhythms of drums and flutes and the sharp percussion of the clappers, casting his limbs in all directions in varied patterns, he presents the spectacle of a moving hieroglyph, mysterious, suggestive, yet meaningful and dramatic within the specific context.

Dance as Symbolist Poetry

Tadanobu's *roppō* also reminds us that the *kabuki* actor is a dancer. In a later act of the same play he will perform an entire scene in dance, speaking only a few lines of dialogue. It is in such moments, when the *kabuki* actor is most clearly performing as a dancer, that his acting becomes most symbolic. Within the framework of any play, especially the highly stylized *jidaimono* (period plays), an actor may revert to dance to express his emotions, as Kumagai does when he performs his battle narrative. Like the poetic moments of Western drama, these moments of visual poetry—of what Cocteau might have called "poetry of the theatre"—normally occur at emotional climaxes within *kabuki* plays that are not specifically dance plays. Other pieces, known as *shosagoto* (posture pieces) or *buyō geki* (dance plays), use dance throughout to portray emotion, character, and actions, sometimes with no dialogue, sometimes with a good deal. It is in these pieces, particularly those with little speech, that *kabuki* most clearly achieves the ambiguity of symbolism. Choreographed, according to old traditions, by living dance teachers, rather than being passed on within the *kabuki* families, these dances are invariably accompanied by a song, which the movements are meant to illustrate to some degree. One might say that they stand in the same relationship to a long *kabuki jidaimono* as a poem of Mallarmé stands in to a play of Shakespeare. Concentrated, pared to essentials, often performed by a single dancer, they present, like most verbal poetry, a fundamental meaning, secondary resonances, and a wide margin of ambiguity. Like poetry, dances use rhythm, music, decorations, allusions, and of course synesthesia. But the synesthesia available to the *kabuki* dancer is necessarily more complex than that of verbal poetry, since he blends the words of a poem with music and the visual appeal of movement, color, design.

To the visual and aural elements in Tadanobu's poses and exit we must add a rich network of gestures tied, now closely, now only tenuously, now not at all, to the words of the accompanying song. One Japanese choreographer, sounding very much like a modern poet, claimed, "We make a dance, but we don't explain it." As in symbolist poetry and its posterity, part of the pleasure arises from this area of ambiguity that allows us our own interpretation beyond the specific meanings either given by tradition or made clear by gestures that work as signs rather than symbols.

In Japanese dance, the vocabulary of gesture and movement may be seen as falling into two fundamental categories, not always mutually exclusive: concrete or mimetic gestures, which carry a specific meaning; and abstract gestures, which are used decoratively, or for accent, or as "pure" dance. Since the dance is always performed to words, an understanding of the text will give meaning to gestures that otherwise might appear to be quite abstract or will at least suggest a way of interpreting otherwise "decorative" gestures.

Among the gestures with specific meanings, there are imitative, evocative, and grammatical expressions. Imitative gestures are stylizations of real-life movement, like laughing, weeping, drinking, or gazing with eyes shaded by one hand. With such gestures there is usually no difficulty of interpretation. Evocative gestures are usually just as comprehensible: They include movement that is not strictly imitative, but suggests objects or natural phenomena, often with a fan or a towel as a hand prop. The fan held open vertically and gently fluttered may represent falling snow, rain, or blossoms, depending on the style of movement (and the words of the song). Large waves, ripples, swords, halberds, pipes, umbrellas, and so forth may all be suggested by various uses of the fan.

Grammatical gestures may derive from natural gestures, as when one says "I" and points to oneself (one's nose, in Japan) or indicates a negative by waving the hand back and forth at about waist level, a normal, everyday Japanese gesture simply stylized in the dance. Other grammatical gestures are signs requiring some acquaintance with the conventions of dance: A small vertical slice of the hand, moving from left to right, is an indication of time, "once," "someday," "forever." A male character holding the hand to the chest with elbow protruding glances down at his elbow, where presumably his crest would be, as an indication of "I/me," "myself," "my identity."

An example of these and other mimetic gestures: in *Gojōbashi* (Benkei at the bridge), Benkei does the following:

Text	Movement
As for me, he thinks aloud,	*Right hand to chest, looks at crest.*
	Left hand to chest, looks at crest.
None can match	*Waves hand in sign of negation, shakes*
My peerless strength.	*head. Strokes beard with hand.*
I would like to have at hand,	*Stamps right foot and thrusts right*
Ah! A worthy foe.	*hand forward. Laughs.*

Nonmimetic gestures are often used to create an atmosphere or suggest an emotion. Often they are decorative, and whether they bear a precise meaning will depend upon the context in the dance, words, music, surrounding movement. The gesture known as "tying the obi," for example, could be used to indicate that the character is really adjusting his or her sash and in this case would be considered mimetic. Often, however, the gesture gives the feeling of girding the loins for action, getting ready for whatever one must accomplish. The hands rise close to the face, palms in, then turn palms out and circle in a wide arc around to the back of the dancer's waist—

the style is, of course, different for male and female characters, as in all phases of *kabuki* dance.

Stamping plays a large part in all *kabuki* dance, but the stamps are rhythmic devices, normally decorating the performance rather than adding meaning. However, a character who is angry might well stamp rhythmically to indicate his fury, in which case we are once again witnessing mimetic movement. By and large, however, the so-called *hyōshi* or stamping and clapping rhythms are pure dance, used most often in the flamboyant finale section known as the *odoriji*, which usually has less meaning than other sections of a dance.

The *mie* is used to accentuate the dances of strong male characters, but it could also indicate that one is looking, or glaring, at one's enemy. Similarly, the gentle *mitsuburi* (three-part head movement) used in women's dances could show a woman glancing coyly at her lover, but often it simply serves as a way to give a feeling of finality to a phrase or section of a dance.

Whether concrete or abstract, dance movement may be allusive as well. Like the allusions of verbal poetry, these moments, usually poses, refer us to other works in which similar characters or emotions are exhibited. Or they might suggest some occasion, some season, that is connected with the performance at hand. Many allusions are recondite and understood only by the most learned of connoisseurs of the dance, just as the allusions of, say, *The Wasteland* or "*La chanson de mal aimé*" will be understood by a small number of readers. For those sensitive to them, however, they add layer upon layer to the meaning of the poem or the dance.

In *Ame no Gorō* (Gorō in the rain), for example, the young hero, who frequents the pleasure quarters, but also must remember it is time to avenge his father's murder of some eighteen years ago, strikes a number of poses that are taken from earlier *kabuki* plays based on the same theme. In one pose, he extends his left hand at an angle before his body, the hand upright, and places his right hand at his right chest, elbow extended and hand upright—this pose reminds us of a fiery old *aragoto* piece in which the young hero goes on New Year's Day to the home of his enemy and tells him officially that he intends to seek revenge. During the course of the old play *Kotobuki Soga no Taimen* (The Soga brothers confront their enemy), young Gorō strikes the pose at least eight or ten times, so it is intimately identified with this particular play (although it occurs in other plays as well).

Another incarnation of Gorō occurs in the celebrated play, *Sukeroku*. Here we see the dandified behavior of the young man as he struts among the courtesans of the pleasure quarter. In Sukeroku's famous entrance dance, he poses holding his umbrella overhead and looking off at the mountains. *Ame no Gorō*

alludes to this aspect of Gorō's character, and adds the multiple association of the heroic dandy, Sukeroku, by including several of his poses in
its choreography.

The early play *Kotobuki Soga no Taimen* itself contains a famous allusive pose of a different nature. Since it is usually performed in January
(when the events of the play take place), it is fitting that the final pose be
of an auspicious nature. Accordingly, at the finale we see the following
tableau: at stage left on a platform stands the powerful villain, Kudō. He
holds his sword in his left hand extended straight out left, and in his
right hand a fan held against the chest with the fan pointing at the audience. With his beak and wing he is understood to represent a crane, a
sign of longevity. At stage right, near center, are grouped Gorō, his brother
Jūrō, and their friend Asahina. Gorō stands in the middle of the group,
his hands extended in the manner described above, suggesting his anger
toward Kudō. Kneeling to his left, his brother holds up his right hand to
restrain the fiery Gorō. To the right, Asahina, his knees bent, crouches
low, extending his hands also, wrists broken in comic effect. This group
is meant to represent Mount Fuji. The entire tableau, a crane flying over
the sacred mountain, is auspicious indeed.

Whether this or the other allusive poses are signs or symbols will depend
upon the understanding of the spectator. For the cognoscenti they are signs
with precise characteristics; for the uninitiated, however, they possess the
ambiguity of the true symbol. Even for the initiate, they add layers to the
meaning of the dance and, like true symbols, possess a power of endless
expansion. Like the allusion to Andromaque, for example, in Baudelaire's
"*Le cygne*," these visual reminders do not make us stop at the association
between exiled swan and exiled queen, between young Gorō as Gorō-at-his-
enemy's-mansion or Gorō as Sukeroku-in-the-gay-quarters. Instead, they add
to our aesthetic enjoyment of poem and dance the multiple associations of
the Trojan War and of Greek culture, on the one hand, and the rich world of
eighteenth-century pleasure quarters and of twelfth-century Kamakura, on
the other.

If anything, the symbolic possibilities of the dance are richer than those of
poetry because they are not impeded by the rational function of the word,
which, despite associative values, equates word with concept, because that
is the function of words. In order to escape this limitation, Mallarmé kept
paring down, attempting to avoid the precise word in order not to limit the
possibilities of meaning. Defeat in such a struggle was, of course, inevitable.
In dance, however, the true symbolist poem can be realized. Associated with
words because he performs to a text, yet endlessly suggestive and multiva-
lent because his vocabulary is that of movement, color, pattern, and sound,

the *kabuki* actor escapes the limitations of the word. A living hieroglyph, constantly moving, changing, he is, at precious moments, actor, sign, and symbol.

Notes

1. Carl G. Jung, *Symbols of Transformation*, trans. R.F.C. Hull (Princeton, NJ: Princeton University Press, 1956), 124.
2. Stéphane Mallarmé, *Oeuvres Complètes* (Paris: Bibliothèque de Pleiade, 1956), 869.
3. Earle Ernst, *The Kabuki Theatre*, 2d ed. rev. (Honolulu: University of Hawai'i Press, 1974), p. 178. All of Ernst's book can be consulted with great benefit. He treats at length many of the questions that can only be hinted at here.
4. Dowid Gascoyne in conversation with Robin Skelton in Robin Skelton, *The Poetic Pattern* (Berkeley and Los Angeles: University of California Press, 1956), 222.
5. Skelton, *The Poetic Pattern,* 172.
6. Hamamura Yonezo et al., *Kabuki* (Tokyo: Kenkyusha, 1956), 45.
7. E.T. Kirby, *Total Theatre: A Critical Anthology* (New York: E.P. Dutton, 1969), xxix.
8. Ibid., xxx.
9. Antonin Artaud, *The Theatre and Its Double*, trans. Mary Caroline Richards (New York: Grove press, 1958), 64. Much of what Artaud says of the Balinese dancers might well apply to *kabuki*, and one can only lament that Artaud never witnessed a *kabuki* performance. He, too, alludes to the dancers as "living hieroglyphics," 61.
10. James R. Brandon, *Kabuki: Five Classic Plays* (Cambridge, MA: Harvard University Press, 1975; reprinted, University of Hawai'i Press, 1992.), 195.
11. See Cocteau's preface to his *Les Mariés de la Tour Eiffel* (1921) in Jean Cocteau, *Theatre,* vol. 1 (Paris: Grasset, 1957), 5.

15

The *Tsurane* of *Shibaraku*: Communicating the Power of Identity

Katherine Saltzman-Li

The Edo period was in some ways like our own in the flood of information available to people at many levels of society. The expansion of nationwide networks of communication and the publication industry led to the creation and availability of a great deal of information—political, economic, and cultural, and the increase in literacy rates meant that there were people interested and able to consume such information. Where we travel on the so-called information superhighway, Tokugawa-era people had access to an information highway system that gradually came to connect large cities and small villages throughout Japan. As Constantine Vaporis points out, "A well integrated system of major post roads made possible the steady growth of communications."[1] In the cultural sphere, this fact contributed to the possibility of sharing, borrowing, or being influenced by cultural activities based in locales not one's own. In the case of *kabuki,* we note that while Kamigata (Osaka/Kyoto) *kabuki* and Edo *kabuki* retained region-specific characteristics, the cross-borrowing of techniques, practices, and even actors occurred with increasing frequency and impact as the Tokugawa period progressed. Nonetheless, certain styles and tendencies were so rooted in one of these two areas that they remained strongly in evidence there throughout the period, little affected by influences from outside the region.

In this essay, I will examine the play *Shibaraku* (Just a minute!), an example par excellence of Edo-style *kabuki.*[2] Stephen Greenblatt writes in

Shakespearean Negotiations, "the social energy encoded in certain works of art continues to generate the illusion of life for centuries. I want to understand the negotiations through which works of art obtain and amplify such powerful energy."[3] I will focus on the *tsurane*, or introduction speech, of the main character as a way to understand the "social energy" encoded in this play and the intense appeal it has always carried for audiences. I will seek explanations in dramatic, literary, and social contexts. The expansion of literacy and publishing in Tokugawa Japan led to an increased appreciation of and interest in various kinds of information, and the Japanese had long been in the habit of compiling and leaving records for later generations. The *tsurane* provide information and present a record, and in these ways they partake of the broader conditions of contemporary communication. However, as I shall explore, their communicating functions are much more complex than the simple circulation of information.

Shibaraku

Shibaraku is a *kabuki* play that was performed annually throughout most of the Tokugawa period; it provides one of the most popular and representative opportunities for display of Edo-style *kabuki*. The complex of beliefs and practices out of which it formed and to which it tied itself was a significant part of the foundation of Tokugawa-period *kabuki*, particularly in Edo. It was a quintessential part of Edo *kabuki* in the primary connection it had to the Fudō worship and bravura *aragoto* acting tradition of the Ichikawa Danjūrō acting line[4] highlighted by its early placement as part of the *kaomise* or (face-showing) production that began the Edo *kabuki* calendar year.[5] [See the essays by Kominz and Gerstle, chapters 2 and 6, for more on these matters. Ed.] In its link to the *kaomise* production, *Shibaraku* offered a kind of advertisement for the entire year of productions to come, showing off the company's newly contracted actors for the coming year and heralding the new season in a familiar yet somehow novel way.

Following the "godless" tenth month,[6] the eleventh-month beginning of the *kabuki* calendar year coincided with the winter solstice. The renewal of natural life was tied to the return of divine presence and the reinvigoration of theatrical activity: With the return of the gods came the return of the actors. The word *kaomise* was most commonly written with three characters literally meaning the "showing of faces." However, in Edo, *kaomise* was often written with a different third character, so that, while the pronunciation stayed the same, the meaning changed to the "vigorous showing of faces."[7] The Edo *kaomise* dramatized the vigor of the actors' (re)appearance. As an important Edo *kaomise* hero, the hero of *Shibaraku* presents the power of the sun, which after the winter solstice begins to show itself more fully each day: darkness, in the person of the villain, may not be eliminated, but it cannot obliterate the increasing presence and significance of the sun, in the person of the hero.[8] *Shibaraku* presents us with a coming-of-age story: as the sun dispels the darkness of winter, as winter yields to spring, old age must yield to youth. The *aragoto* (roughhouse) hero was to be acted so as to show the vigor and brashness of a youth in his late teens. In *Shibaraku* authority is challenged, the authority of the play's older villain as well as that of the society outside of the theatre.

The roots of the play go back to performances of Ichikawa Danjūrō I (1660–1704), who first performed a version of it in 1692. Current productions are based on a play of 1697 performed by this Danjūrō. Danjūrō II (1688–1758) inherited it as part of the *ie no gei* (family art) of the Danjūrō line. Following his great success in the *kaomise* play *Banmin Daifukuchō* (The great ledger of the people), performed in the eleventh month of 1714, it became customary to present *Shibaraku* as the third act in *Kaomise* productions.[9] Productions of the last 100 years have been based on the script from an 1895 performance by Danjūrō IX (1838–1903), in which the hero is named Kamakura no Gongorō Kagemasa; previously, the hero's identity varied with each production (figure 15.1). The script presented a particular situation that could be worked into whatever longer play was being enacted; thus the hero's name was not always the same. Pre-Meiji versions can be summarized better by their general idea than by their plot: Evil designs and their perpetrators are undone by the sudden appearance of a brash *aragoto* hero about eighteen years old. His identity is unknown until he introduces himself. He then exposes the villains and puts an end to both their plans and their power.[10]

The main character's entrance is announced from the back of the *hanamichi* (runway) when he calls a halt to the onstage villainy with the word "*shibaraku*" (just a minute!). The artful elongation and repetition of this word, which became the act's title when Danjūrō VII (1791–1859) collected together the Ichikawa family's *Kabuki Jūhachiban* (Eighteen famous *kabuki* plays), dates from a specific performance of the early eighteenth century. As Danjūrō II explains it in *Kokon Yakusha Rongo Sakigake* (Pioneering analects from past and present actors), a 1772 treatise by Kinjinsai Shinō containing anecdotes from actors and information on actor evaluation:

> When I first came from the Yamamura-za to settle in at the Nakamura-za after my coming of age, the play *Shibaraku* was to be performed. Yamanaka Heikurō I, who used to appear in plays with my father, Danjūrō, despised being paired with me because of my youth. I was supposed to come out

Figure 15.1 **Ichikawa Danjūrō IX as Kamakuro no Gongorō Kagemasa in** *Shibaraku.* **(Photo: Courtesy of Samuel L. Leiter.)**

with "Just a minute!" at the point when Heikurō touches the ledger, but Heikurō wouldn't give the cue. Because of this, I remained behind the curtain without calling out. People came from the dressing room four or five times, but it would have appeared weak to give in, and after only a little of this waiting, the play began to drag. Finally, realizing he had no choice, Heikurō touched his forehead, at which point I entered with "Just a minute!" This made a strong impression.[11]

The daring inherent in Edo *kabuki,* its denial of constrictions, its assertion of self, are all embodied in this anecdote. The same is found in the *tsurane*, a highlight that is delivered on the *hanamichi* just after the hero's entrance.

The *Tsurane*

The delivery of the *tsurane* from the *hanamichi* underscores its importance, as only the most meaningful characters were sanctioned to announce themselves on this passageway. In the 1895 *Shibaraku*, the *tsurane* is as follows:

We learn from the Chinese Han scholar Enanji that heaven bestows its blessings impartially, no matter what the amount, no matter what the purpose. The Genji samurai of the East have always purified and emboldened themselves in the dewdrops of the Tama River, that same river where I, Mimasu of the ninth generation, hail from. Called Kamakura no Gongorō Kagemasa by most, I am here this year in the winter-peony makeup which recalls the many *kaomise* of old. Ready to appear again in this play for which my forebears have been famous, my coat is the color of the persimmon, its puckery flavor the refinement of the technique which has been transmitted to me. I take my turn and clumsily display my skills as an *aragoto* specialist. *Aragoto* is the height of Edo acting and the fame of my family. Permit me to show you. I speak with all due respect.[12]

Tsurane is one type of *kabuki* speech, usually delivered—as in *Shibaraku*—as a self-introduction by an *aragoto* hero on the *hanamichi* in conjunction with his entrance.[13] The term probably came from a performance practice of *ennen* and *sarugaku* (pre-*nō* performing arts that developed from imported Chinese traditions) known as *tsurane goto*. *Tsurane goto* means "linked or connected things" and refers to some sort of performance centered on elocutionary skill. In *kabuki*, *tsurane* first appear in early *yarō kabuki* (mature men's *kabuki*), which succeeded the 1652 ban on *wakashu kabuki* (youth's *kabuki*). [See Shively's essay, chapter 3, for information on this period. Ed.] *Tsurane* became particularly popular in the Genroku period (1688–1704). The *tsurane goto* idea of linkage was carried forward through the punning connection of words and the associations emphasized among the character, the actor, his acting lineage, and the places and attributes associated with that lineage.[14] Like the earlier *tsurane goto*, *kabuki tsurane* are also centered on elocutionary skill. Verbal features include the use of *kake kotoba* (pivot words, which allow phrase-ending syllables to carry meanings referring to both the previous and the following phrase), what we might refer to in Japanese as *naninani zukushi* (the tradition of exhaustive punning), the frequent use of *shichigochō* (alternating verse lines of five and seven syllables respectively), and a generally musical and rhythmic declamatory style.

The *tsurane* was rewritten for each new production of *Shibaraku* by the actor who would deliver the lines or, increasingly, by a *sakusha* (playwright) writing under the actor's name.[15] The actor's task was to introduce himself as actor while proclaiming his entrance as character. This double intention defines, in some ways, the relationship between the *kabuki* actor and his audience. The double interest of spectators in the actor as character and in the actor as actor/person was nowhere more in evidence.[See Thornbury's essay, chapter 13. Ed.]

The immediate pleasures of the *Shibaraku tsurane* for the audience are the presence of the actor and his voice, both projected in a massive and grand manner. The enactment of the *tsurane*, in all its aspects, celebrates abundance and copiousness. The great, thick, oversized costume, the extra long sword, and the striking *sujiguma* (makeup) worn by the actor are matched at this moment by his voice, presented forcefully in the mostly uninflected, continuous delivery style often used for major speeches of *aragoto* heroes. The exaggeration of the costume finds support from the tumbling words and the complete way in which the speech's material is treated. The satisfaction in pulling the most out of a theatrical moment is intensified by the Edo delight in getting the most out of a verbal subject. In this respect, the *tsurane* offers bravura variation on traditional literary wordplay. Furthermore, the *tsurane*'s rhythmic, often poetic language stands out from the surrounding dialogue rhetorically and in the heightened delivery and expectation surrounding its presentation on stage. The great pleasure taken in words and in their construction into works of art throughout Japanese literary history was inherited by the Tokugawa period; with the increase in literacy and shared literary practices, this pleasure was made more widely available. The words with which the hero of *Shibaraku* announced and introduced himself were anxiously awaited. They were written by men with the skills needed to produce both the necessary verbal qualities and the dramatic fire which the scene inevitably ignited.

Tsurane are representative examples of the Edo literary spirit, which found enjoyment in a renewal—through moderate additions, deletions, or changes— of preserved, recognizable elements of particular forms. Most literary forms were created through the choice, arrangement, and integration of used and new phrases and stories. Such literary practice mirrored a cultural theme of renewal that manifested itself in such concrete forms as festivals and ritual, as well as other creative practices. The recurring yet changeable elements of the *Shibaraku tsurane* included the way in which it was embedded in the scene, the ways in which it began and ended, the possible common use of a particular theme around which the exhaustive punning revolved, and the interweaving of name/place/attributes of the actor and character.

Two types of openings are most common: One works spatially to locate the actor's time, place, and, often, performance with telescopic focus, moving rapidly from reference to the cardinal directions to a more specific placement in the actor's home neighborhood or the particular performance underway, and the other situates the actor on intellectual terrain. In the latter case, a *tsurane* might start with, "Chuangtze said" or, as in the case of the example quoted above, "We learn from the Chinese Han scholar Enanji. . . ."

The ending of the *tsurane* is generally *to/te, ho ho uyamatte mōsu* (I speak with all due respect).[16] Within the frame of these conventionalized opening and closing elements is a string of numerous references to the actor. Included are his name or names ("I, Mimasu of the ninth generation . . . [c]alled Kamakura no Gongorō Kagemasa"[17]), where he lives, where he worships, the references to nature in his crests and costume (winter-peony makeup and a coat "the color of the persimmon"), his acting specialty (*aragoto*), aspects of the character he is portraying, and references to the *kaomise* production and the new year ("I am here this year in the winter-peony makeup which recalls the many *kaomise* of old"). Together, these elements define the form and offer the building blocks for the annual re-creation of the *Shibaraku tsurane*.

Legal Regulations

For whom do these speeches speak—the actor himself, his acting line, the entire *kabuki* community, or some combination of these? A look into the legal restrictions on the actors' freedom and identity within Tokugawa society at large will help us answer this question.

Regulations of the Kansei era (1789–1801) concerning the management of the Edo *sanza* (three major) theatres make clear the restricted position that actors held. Their artistic power was their only means to breaking through confines set by both the *bakufu* (shogunate) and the theatre managers in pursuit of control over the financial rewards of entertainment. In 1794 and again in 1837, concerns with the proper status of actors and the organization of theatrical business are voiced through regulations drawn up by theatre managers for judicial approval. Actors are accused of making unreasonable salary demands and of leaving without permission for lucrative, independent provincial tours when such demands were not met, "with the result that the power of the theatre-proprietors has become very small, while that of the actors is great; which is quite the opposite of the usual relation of employee and employer."[18] The regulations drawn up in 1794 to control this perceived imbalance were ineffectual, so an official reconsideration of the same problems was again necessary in 1837. Once again we find the hope that, "if the willfulness of the actors can be controlled, the theatre-proprietors and employees will possibly recover their former power and be able to continue their business, as well as to control the actors properly."[19] [See Shively, chapter 3, for a thorough account of Edo-era *bakufu* regulations. Ed.]

Among the regulations listed in the 1794 document we find the following three: Number16, a warning against presenting "vividly the events, whether happy or unhappy, of recent days or to treat realistically the life of the present time"; Number 17, a warning against actors displaying extravagant clothing or manners outside the theatre "lest their mode of life tend to be too ostentatious owing to the nature of their occupation, and to influence unduly the young men and women of the town and thus create undesirable customs among them"; and Number 18, a "warning against drinking too much or acting in an unseemly manner" at parties, which actors should attend only if obliged for professional reasons, "for the purpose of entertaining their financial backers or other townsmen whom they have good cause to entertain."[20] The regulations also sought to put a cap on actors' salaries, curtail provincial travel, and otherwise control actors for the benefit of the financial concerns of the theatre manager and the social purposes of officials.

These restrictions attempt to control every aspect of an actor's life—freedom of movement; personal financial control; and freedom of expression, onstage and off—through material and behavioral means. Not only *bakufu* officials but theatre managers as well worked to suppress actors. On the one hand, the managers show concern for the many people working in the theatres who, together with "their families, will come to be deprived of their livelihood" should the top actors continue to demand ever-increasing salaries.[21] On the other, the managers' self-interest clearly permeates the regulations.

In spite of official backing, why was the enforcement of these regulations so unsuccessful as to require restatement and reissue in 1837? The broader answer to this question can be found in studies concerning general responses of Tokugawa-era Japanese to laws governing behavior. These studies have found that such laws, while upholding basic codes of behavior and social expectations, often could not be enforced. For example, Anne Walthall has studied commoner protest in the eighteenth century. She documents rising numbers of protests as the century draws to a close and changes in the ways in which people viewed and expressed what they hoped to obtain from such acts: "repeatedly during the 1780s, peasants and townspeople said things deemed inexcusable or outrageous by their lords. Regardless of what and how rulers expected their subjects to communicate, commoners did precisely what they felt was necessary."[22] In his study of travel in the Edo period, Constantine Vaporis also finds

> a great disjunction between government regulations on travel and the social reality at which they were aimed. Countless persons from all social ranks defied governmental authority by traveling without official permission despite the volumes of legislation intended to regulate or restrict movement. Such legislation appears to have been merely a reaction to the social reality that existed and thus, in a sense, was little more than sumptuary legislation. The social, economic, and political implications of this interpretation necessarily recast our view of Tokugawa society.[23]

Vaporis shows "the limits of the state's ability to impose its will."[24] He gives examples of the ways in which commoners eluded official restrictions as well as official reaction to such evasive behavior, which—as Walthall explains regarding government reaction to protests—was to try to steer a middle course between suppression and appeasement.[25]

Kabuki and the Regulations

The history of *kabuki* is not only full of similar cat-and-mouse interactions, it is at least partially made in reaction to them: At various points, the government set controls on who was allowed to act and on what could be portrayed and how, but a disjunction between regulations and reality, similar to the one Vaporis finds in the case of travel, often obtained in the theatre.[26]

One of the vexing issues for the *bakufu* was the mixing of classes. Top actors not only interacted with samurai and even *daimyō*, but often lived lives of luxury that rivaled or surpassed those of their betters. Historically, the actors' access to opulence and their ability to associate above their station were tolerated at times when the *bakufu* had little other trouble on its hands; however, crackdowns—either personally affecting particular troupe members or affecting what could be enacted—occurred at turbulent intervals throughout *kabuki* history. The exact circumstances leading to these crackdowns are not usually clear. It might have been an unacceptable play title or theme, an actor or a manager who was too daring generally or in a particular instance, or a violation of sumptuary laws.[27]

While the *bakufu* encountered defiance of its rules and regulations from various quarters of society, a significant reason for infractions against the *kabuki*-governing regulations outlined above was the great star power of top actors, which led both to the actors' ability to demand troubling salaries and to the general inability of managers and officials to control the actors. The popularity of top *kabuki* actors of the eighteenth and nineteenth centuries, in particular, was comparable to that of Hollywood movie stars of the twentieth century: Face and name recognition were so great that fans crowded around at any opportunity, and products offered under a famous actor's name were guaranteed a healthy sale. Pinup woodblock prints of actors' portraits served a similar function as the star posters of today. Fans eagerly followed the particulars of the performances and careers of favorite stars in the *yakusha hyōbanki* (actor critique booklets) and other sources. Society's adoration of these stars allowed them a sense of freedom that did not in fact exist legally.

In spite of star power, however, the top actors must have lived in great awareness of the restrictions imposed upon them. Legal control meant that, at any given time, government officials could curtail the actors' activities onstage and off. Whatever else this meant to them, one outlet for the reactions it must have engendered was found in the enactment of certain roles and situations onstage. *Shibaraku*'s hero is one such role, providing an opportunity for the actor and his equally restricted audience members to promote themselves—in actuality or vicariously—in ways otherwise not allowed. The self-identification articulated in the *tsurane* (rather than identification conferred by others) became an act of defiance and rebellion, especially when its narration was highlighted verbally, vocally, and materially (through the actor's exaggerated physical appearance), as in the case of *Shibaraku*.

Names

An examination into names and naming practices in Tokugawa Japan, and especially in *kabuki*, allows us to further grasp the meanings of these speeches. Their identity-conferring function can be more fully comprehended with reference to the many practices and regulations concerning names that governed a *kabuki* actor's life. A name is ontologically linked to the individual's self in Japanese cultural understanding; therefore, "revealing a name stirs or shakes up the power or *tama* of the referent."[28] Naming things "was an ancient means available to man to bring them under his control"; not naming them was the flip-side means of denying access to power and control. Thus names were used to demarcate society and to integrate or exclude people from the sociopolitical order.[29] On the practical level, this "animistic" view of names led to strict control by those in power over the use of names from Japan's earliest history and into modern times. Since names were considered claims to authority, political leaders sought to restrict the proliferation of surnames.

Within *kabuki* troupes, the bequeathing or announcing of new stage names was taken with utmost seriousness. At each stage of his career, an actor took on a name that in effect told the world what could be expected of him. An inherited name represented the actor to the world as a practitioner with certain skills and qualifications, indicating the level of respect due him by the community of fellow professionals and spectators. For example, when we read of an actor with the name Ebizō, we know that he is in the Ichikawa Danjūrō acting line and that he is most likely an actor of promising talent who is only a stage away from receiving the Danjūrō name and reaching the pinnacle of his career.[30] Ceremonies for announcing newly bestowed names preceded or interrupted performances, and the weight of meaning the names conveyed was of great importance to everyone involved with *kabuki*. The conferring of a name was like the awarding of a diploma: it acknowledged a certain level of skill and licensed certain professional possibilities.

Name-announcing ceremonies aimed toward more than secular benefit.

Just as parents of a newborn bring their baby to the local shrine to present the baby and its name to the *kami* (deity), actors were presenting their new selves to both the community and the gods in a ritual request for both secular and divine patronage. As Hattori Yukio points out, even the announcing of play titles carried a ritual significance of informing the gods and thereby requesting their support toward the success of the production.[31] Revealing a name unleashes possibilities and initiates relationships, and its careful handling is essential if all is to go well.

Official regulations against the use in plays of the names of important contemporary figures also point to the power names were believed to hold. These concerns inform Regulation Number 16, mentioned above, the warning against the realistic portrayal of contemporary events and life onstage. They are related, as well, to the official withholding of the right of actors (and others of low status) to have surnames[32]: The power of names is evident when their utterance is seen as a proper venue for official control.

Communicating the Power of Identity

In returning to the *tsurane* of the *Shibaraku* hero, we must ask, "What does the *tsurane* do for the actor?" Apart from providing the opportunity to display oratorical eloquence and other performance skills, and apart from the dramatic force it offers the play, the *tsurane* allows the actor a declaration of his identity. Through the *tsurane*, freedom of control over his existence, denied in significant ways in life, is enacted in the most pronounced and material way: The actor wears the most extraordinary clothing, he displays himself in the most flamboyant way, and he dares to proclaim—loudly, clearly and in all possible variations—his name and the ways in which it connects him to the worlds within and outside the theatre. Knowing that the absence of a name locates a person at the periphery of society, Danjūrō "overnames" himself—as Mimasu of the ninth generation, as Kamakura no Gongorō Kagemasa, as the one who appears in the persimmon coat, as the current representative of a line of actors famous for the role he currently enacts, and as the repository of an acting style—in an attempt to secure undeniable position in each of his intersecting worlds.

We might see the *tsurane* self-introduction as a kind of permit for the traveler/actor setting out on his journey/professional mission. Vaporis lists the usual information included on a typical travel permit in Tokugawa Japan: (a) number of travelers, (b) purpose of journey, (c) destination, (d) request for safe passage, (e) name of permit issuer, (f) date of issuance, and (g) name of *sekisho* (transit barrier) for which the permit was issued.[33] The *tsurane* contains much of this same information. In the order of information just listed, we learn that: (a) the number of travelers is one, but one who follows a path trodden by his forebears; (b) the purpose is to show *aragoto* acting, the "fame" of his family; (c) the "destination" is an excellent, well-received performance; (d) the request for safe passage is phrased, "Permit me to show you"; (e) the permit issuer is none other than the actor himself with the sanction of his troupe and inheritance; (f) the "date of issuance" is this year's *kaomise*; and (g) the "transit barrier" he must cross is that of acceptance by audience and fans. The actor/hero supplies all the pertinent information, but he has not received official permission for his journey: The fact that the permit issuer is the "traveler" himself is one indication of the audacity and defiance displayed through the *tsurane*. Yet at the same time, by so boldly and conspicuously naming himself, the actor places himself in a precarious position. Although revealing oneself through names allows access to greater control and power, it also opens up the danger of putting oneself in the power of others. Danjūrō faced two "others," the audience and the Tokugawa authorities. This willingness to risk so much fed the excitement, energy, and sense of importance of the *tsurane* delivery.

The *tsurane* becomes a kind of speech ad, a "performative"[34] making certain promises and drawing its power from the accumulation of its earlier enactments. What is being performed and promised? Simply that the skill of the present Danjūrō represents the skill of Edo's grandest master of the *aragoto* style. The present master is the human repository of something larger than his personal talents, so that the real promise is that the present Danjūrō is worthy of carrying on the traditions bequeathed and taught him, that he is not only Edo's current greatest *aragoto* master but also represents Edo's grandest tradition of masters from its beginnings. Judith Butler's queries regarding the "performative" underscore these points:

> If performativity requires a power to effect or enact what one names, then who will be the "one" with such a power, and how will such a power be thought? . . . Does the "one" who speaks the term cite the term, thereby establishing him or herself as the author while at the same time establishing the derivative status of that authorship? Is a community and history of such speakers not magically invoked at the moment in which that utterance is spoken?[35]

When Danjūrō says, "I take my turn and clumsily display my skills as an *aragoto* specialist. *Aragoto* is the height of Edo acting and the fame of my family. Permit me to show you. I speak with all due respect," he is merged with his line. His personal accomplishments are his own, but they are only meaningful in their connection to the accomplishments of a line, and that line is formed by its geographic and human context. "The art (*gei*) of Danjūrō II was not simply his individual art, but the art of his line (*ie no gei*), Edo's art."[36] It is the power of the line that energizes the personal performance and supports the possibility of enacting the performative of representing "Edo's foremost and grandest."

The repetitions of the *Shibaraku tsurane* through time and generations are repetitions with a difference, in which previous enunciations are cited and then revised. They are marked by being from the Danjūrō line, with the cumulative group voice cited more strongly than any individual articulator within it. In the excitement of the moment it is the individual who speaks, but the power of the message and the force of his claim receive their support and strength from the accumulation of voices that have come before.

We should recall that the *tsurane* continued to be considered the creation of the actor even after the rest of the play's composition was taken over by the playwright and even when the *tsurane* was in fact the work of a playwright. It was too important and too central to *kabuki* as a social statement and as a vehicle for personal statement for its star deliverer to relinquish acknowledged ownership. Hattori Yukio explains this phenomenon as follows:

> The *tsurane* (a long prayer-like speech) delivered by Ichikawa Danjūrō during the *Shibaraku* scene of the *kaomise* was presented as though written by Danjūrō himself. In reality it was written by the lead *sakusha*, but it was necessary to believe that this particular speech was actually created by Danjūrō. If it weren't, it was thought that the magical power contained in the *tsurane* would lose its efficacy. The audience, while understanding the true situation, considered it as the work of Danjūrō.[37]

The magical power of the *tsurane* related to its naming and identifying ability, and the force of this power was strengthened because it named that which had been deemed officially unrecognizable. The actor was here claiming for himself some of the power conferred by names and naming in Tokugawa cultural practice. This daring usurpation was bolstered by the actor's display of fearsome power through fierce expression and exaggerated appearance, both based in the Danjūrōs' worship of Fudō and their assumption of some of the manifestations of Fudō's awesomeness. The "prayer-like" recitation of the *tsurane*, and everything in the performance that reinforced its intended effect, emphasized the import and message of the actor's claim to an unauthorized power.

The *tsurane*, through the cleverly embedded recital of the actor's name and lineage, is a self-proclamation, a declaration of the actor's importance, contrary to the social plan. However, there is more: the actor's claim of name power is simultaneously used to declare his existence as significant and to activate his performance, to highlight him as actor/person and to highlight him as character. His claim results, that is, both in his proud self-proclamation and in the display of the fearful energy he manifests before the audience. As the character is making himself known, the actor is insisting, "I am," "I can," "I thrive" in spite of all restrictions imposed from various authorities. The incredible energy that supported this declaration was inspired by the act of making an unsanctioned claim, amassed as though from the denial of the energy's daily expenditure. The audience's anticipation of the moment of performance, and the rapturous approval that accompanied it, further supported these affirmatives in a powerful and undeniable way.

Notes

1. Constantine Nomiko Vaporis, *Breaking Barriers: Travel and the State in Early Modern Japan* (Cambridge, MA: Council on East Asian Studies, Harvard University Press, 1994), 12.

2. While *Shibaraku* is actually a scene that formed part of longer dramas during the Edo period, it now stands on its own and will be referred to as a play.

3. Stephen Jay Greenblatt, *Shakespearean Negotiations* (Berkeley: University of California Press, 1988), 7.

4. For more on the connection of Fudō worship, *aragoto* heroes, and Danjūrō, see Laurence R. Kominz, "The Power of Fudō Myōo: Ichikawa Danjūrō and His Soga Gorō Character in the *Kabuki* Play *Tsuwamono Kongen Soga* " (The genesis of a Soga warrior), in *Currents in Japanese Culture: Translations and Transformation*, ed. Amy Vladeck Heinrich. (New York: Columbia University Press, 1997), 81–98. See also the chapter on Danjūrō I in Kominz, *The Stars Who Created Kabuki: Their Lives, Loves and Legacy* (Tokyo: Kodansha, 1997).

5. The *kabuki* calendar year opened with the *kaomise* production in the eleventh month, which was customarily followed by bimonthly program changes.

6. So called because the gods were believed to be away during this time.

7. See Furuido Hideo, *Bunka Ninen Jūichigatsu Edo Sanshibai Kaomise Kyōgenshū* (Collection of *kaomise* plays at Edo's three theatres in the eleventh month of 1805) (Tokyo: Kokusho Kankōkai, 1989), 463.

8. Ibid., 466.

9. As the *mitateme* (or *jomaku*). The *mitateme* corresponded to the first act of the main play on a full-day program in Edo. [*Shibaraku* was shown in this position in the 1714 *Kaomise* mentioned in the text. Ed]

10. *Shibaraku* performances are actually divided into three groups, *shin* (true or orthodox), *gyō* (popular), and *sō* (vulgar). The latter two developed from the performances of actors other than those of the Danjūrō line. Those of the *sō* group can be considered as further from the *shin* group than those of the *gyō* group. For example, the *sō* group includes *Onna Shibaraku* (Female just a minute!), in which the protagonist is played by an *onnagata*. I am concerned here only with the *shin* group.

11. In *Kinsei Geidō Ron* (Discussions of premodern art), Nishiyama Matsunosuke, ed. (Tokyo: Iwanami Shoten, 1972), 486.

12. Hattori Yukio, *Kabuki On-Suteeji* (*Kabuki* onstage), vol. 10 (Tokyo: Hakusuisha, 1985), 9.

13. Not all self-introduction speeches are called *tsurane*. For example, Sukeroku's self-introduction, which shares aspects of *Shibaraku*'s *tsurane* but which also has conspicuous differences, is called *nanori*. (See James R. Brandon, trans., *Kabuki: Five Classic Plays* [Cambridge, Mass.: Harvard University Press, 1975; reprinted, University of Hawai'i Press, 1992], 71–72, for Sukeroku's *nanori*.)

14. Not all of these associations show in my translation of the 1895 *tsurane*. For example, what I have translated as "this play for which my forebears have been famous" comes from a reference to the *Kabuki Jūhachiban* of the Ichikawa Danjūrō acting line. In the Japanese, the line reads *kotoshi koko ni jūhachiban*, ([performing] the *jūhachiban* here this year). The word *jūhachi* (eighteen) is also meant to refer to the age of the hero, a significant age for *aragoto* heroes.

15. *Sakusha* were men who worked on writing and otherwise preparing plays. Their work was not limited to playwriting, but the term is usually translated as "playwright." Fukuchi Ōchi helped with the preparation of the 1895 *tsurane* translated here. See Hattori, *Kabuki On-Suteeji*, 202.

16. An exception is found in the *tsurane* of *Onna Shibaraku*, in which the protagonist is a woman. [See Leiter, chapter 12, on this play in the context of *kabuki*'s female roles. Ed.] While *Onna Shibaraku* is not in the orthodox group of *Shibaraku* plays, the added feminine touch in the last line is still valuable from a comparative point of view. It reads *"to, ho ho uyamatte, ō hazukashii,"* literally, "Respectfully offered with great embarrassment," and is close to the idea of, "With all due respect, please forgive my intrusion." See Iizuka Tomoichirō, *Kabuki Saiken* (A close look at *kabuki*) (Tokyo: Daichi Shobō, 1926), 691.

17. This and the following quotes are taken from the *tsurane* example translated above.

18. John Henry Wigmore, ed. *Law and Justice in Tokugawa Japan: Materials for the History of Japanese Law and Justice under the Tokugawa Shogunate, 1603–1867,* Part III-B (Tokyo: Japan Foundation, 1983), 98.

19. Ibid.

20. Ibid., 96.

21. Ibid., 86.

22. Anne Walthall, *Social Protest and Popular Culture in Eighteenth-Century Japan* (Tucson: University of Arizona Press for the Association of Asian Studies, 1986), xiii.

23. Vaporis, *Breaking Barriers*, 5.

24. Ibid., 257.

25. Walthall, *Social Protest*, 224.

26. See Shively's *"Bakufu* versus *Kabuki,"* chapter 3, for more on this subject.

27. Donald Shively, "The Social Environment of Tokugawa *Kabuki*," in *Studies in Kabuki: Its Acting, Music, and Historical Context*, James R. Brandon, William P. Malm, and Donald H. Shively, eds. (Honolulu: University of Hawai'i Press, 1978), 28.

28. Herbert Plutschow. *Japan's Name Culture* (Kent, UK: Japan Library, 1995), 198, 25.

29. Ibid., 32, 204.

30. There are exceptions. For example, Danjūrō V (1741–1806) resumed the name Ebizō upon retirement from acting, and Danjūrō VII became Ebizō only after giving the name Danjūrō to his son, Danjūrō VIII (1823–1854).

31. Hattori Yukio, *Edo Kabuki* (Tokyo: Iwanami Shoten, 1993), 236.

32. Actors were officially forbidden to have surnames, but they were known by names such as Ichikawa, Nakamura, and others. *Daimyō* were known in the Tokugawa period and before to bestow names on peasants, artisans, and performers out of gratitude for loyalty or admiration for skills (Plutschow, *Japan's Name Culture*, 165.) These private surnames could receive wide currency, though not in official proceedings. By the end of the Edo period, most peasants had at least private surnames which they publicly displayed on their graves (ibid., 179), and the same is true of others officially denied surname use.

33. Vaporis, *Breaking Barriers*, 143. These were the main possibilities. However, as Vaporis points out, permits became more abbreviated as the period progressed.

34. The performative "is a sentence whose utterance itself, when executed under appropriate institutional and other conditions, accomplishes the state of affairs that it signifies. Examples are 'I now pronounce you man and wife'; 'I apologize'; 'I call this meeting to order'; 'Let spades be trumps'; 'I bet you a dollar Ohio State will beat Michigan tomorrow.' " See M.H. Abrams, *A Glossary of Literary Terms* (New York: Holt, Rinehart and Winston, 1971), 240.

35. Judith Butler, *Excitable Speech: A Politics of the Performative* (New York: Routledge, 1997), 49. Butler's concern is with injurious words, such as racial slurs. She ends this quote by asking, "And if and when that utterance brings injury, is it the utterance or the utterer who is the cause of the injury, or does that utterance perform its injury through a transitivity that cannot be reduced to a causal or intentional process originating in a singular subject?" If we replace the word "injury" with the more general notion of "effect," her line of inquiry is clearly related to the questions being asked in this essay.

36. Tsuchiya Keiichirō, "Shizen to Gei, Oedo Katagi no Danjūrō" (Nature and art: Danjūrō's Edo spirit)," *Gendai Shisō* (Modern thoughts) 14: 10 (1986), 137.

37. Hattori, *Edo Kabuki*, 257–258.

16

Conjuring Kuzunoha from the World of Abe no Seimei

Janet E. Goff

In the highly competitive seventeenth- and eighteenth-century Japanese theatre world, the ability to rapidly produce new crowd-pleasing plays was critical
to a theatre company's commercial viability. Playwrights kept close track of
the latest fashions and capitalized on technological innovations. They followed and flouted dramaturgical conventions, plucked ideas from hit plays,
and constructed new parts to showcase star performers.

These trends are reflected in the genesis of *Ashiya Dōman Ōuchi Kagami*
(A courtly mirror of Ashiya Dōman), a five-act puppet play by Takeda Izumo
(d. 1747) that made its debut at Osaka's Takemoto-za in 1734 and was transferred to the *kabuki* stage a few months later. Today, Izumo's play is best
known for its depiction of Kuzunoha, the white fox of Shinoda Forest who
gave birth to Abe no Dōji, eventually famous as the yin-yang diviner Abe no
Seimei.

Nō and *kyōgen* had already produced memorable fox characters that were
warmly embraced by the world of *kabuki*. Kuzunoha, however, was the product of a new age. Although the character sprang from the world of Abe no
Seimei, a superhero renowned for his occult powers, the story of her separation from her son (*kowakare*) and journey (*michiyuki*) to her home in Shinoda
Forest still draws audiences, whereas the once-popular world that nurtured it
has receded into the background. The play thus makes an interesting case
study of changing expectations among audiences in the Edo period and today. The purpose of the present essay is twofold: to place Kuzunoha's story
within the evolving world of Abe no Seimei, which culminated in *Ashiya*

Dōman Ōuchi Kagami, and to examine the treatment of the character Kuzunoha in *kabuki* today. The material is organized according to the story's development as represented in five texts, one from the early Edo period and four from the years 1662, 1074, 1699, and 1734.

The *Hoki-shō*

Stories about foxes turning into beautiful women, marrying, and bearing children abounded in Japanese culture, dating back to the early ninth century. Although an enormous body of lore celebrating the magical exploits of Abe no Seimei already existed in the middle ages, the convergence of the fox-wife motif and Seimei's story can be traced back with certainty only to the early Edo period, when a popular commentary on the medieval astrology book *Hoki-shō* (Sacred vessel) was published.

Some editions of *Hoki-shō* are prefaced by a series of legends about the sources of Seimei's supernatural powers.[1] The legends introduce a number of elements that later shaped *Ashiya Dōman Ōuchi Kagami*. One concerns the provenance of the astrology book *Kin'u Gyokuto Shū* (The golden crow [sun] and jeweled hare [moon]), another name for *Hoki*. The commentary states that *Kin'u Gyokuto Shū* was taken from India to China by a wizard named Hakudō. During an eighth-century Japanese embassy to China, Kibi Daijin's life was saved when he passed a test of knowledge, aided by the spirit of Abe no Nakamaro, a member of a previous embassy who never succeeded in returning to Japan. The grateful Kibi returns to Japan with the astrology book and gives it to Nakamaro's descendant, Abe no Dōji (Seimei's childhood name), in Nekoshima, a village in Hitachi province in eastern Japan. (The historical Seimei and Abe no Nakamaro were, in fact, unrelated.)

Another legend recounts how Seimei (Dōji) received a pair of magical objects (a stone box and medicine) in the realm of the dragon king. The medicine enables him to understand bird language and learn why the emperor has fallen ill. As a reward for curing the emperor, Dōji receives a court position and the name Seimei.

The commentary further states that Dōji's mother was "a supernatural being" who came to Nekoshima disguised as "a woman of the road" (*yūjo ōrai no mono*). The text tersely states that she lived there with somebody for three years and gave birth to Seimei. When he was three, she composed the following poem and disappeared:

> *koishiku wa* [or *koishikuba*]   If you long to see me
> *tazune-kite miyo*   come to visit
> *Izumi naru*   in Izumi's

Shinoda no mori	Shinoda Forest
urami kuzunoha	the kudzu leaves whose backs are visible.

When Dōji went to the capital, he recalled his mother's poem and paid a visit to Izumi province. While he was praying in the sacred precinct at Shinoda Forest, the deity of Shinoda appeared before him as an aged fox and revealed that she was his mother.

The commentary also contains legends involving a rival diviner, Ashiya Dōman, whose enmity for Seimei created occasions for the latter to demonstrate the nature of his supernatural powers. One legend had to do with a test to divine the contents of a box. Another recounts that Dōman was able to secretly copy the *Kin'u Gyokuto Shū* while Seimei was studying under the wizard Hakudō in China. As a result, Dōman was able to best Seimei in a divination contest and kill him. Hakudō came to Japan and brought Seimei back to life with a magic ritual. Seimei killed Dōman and recovered the book, which he transmitted to posterity.

At this point, the only distinguishing features possessed by Seimei's mother are her fox identity as the deity of Shinoda and her parting poem. The poem remained a core element of her story; in time, the last line—*urami kuzunoha*—would provide her name.

The conventional pairing of *urami* and *kuzunoha* (kudzu leaves) in *waka* poetry derived from the fact that wind reveals the distinctive pale white back of the vine's leaves. *Urami* (seeing the back) is a homophone with a word meaning "resentment" or "bitterness"; it also suggests "telling the future." Thus its meaning can vary considerably, depending on the context. ("The kudzu leaves whose backs are visible" in the above translation merely attempts to strike a neutral note.)

The connotation of anger or resentment in *urami* is brought to the fore in a brief sketch of Seimei's life contained in a collection of short tales centering on *waka*. The collection dates from roughly the same period as *Hoki-shō* and may in fact be older.[2] Seimei is described as the son of a low-ranking courtier and as a student of the diviner Kamo no Yasunori (actual historical facts). "His mother was not a human being," we are told. The text adds, "When Seimei was three she composed a poem and disappeared, angry or bitter (*uramite*) because the boy's father had formed a liaison with another woman."

Seimei's father goes to Shinoda Forest in Izumi province out of curiosity and encounters an aged fox (said to be an incarnation of the shrine deity) that acknowledges having composed the poem. The role of the deity in Seimei's life is further clarified when he goes there at the age of thirteen and receives a crystal-like jewel that enables him to understand the language of birds and beasts.

Abe no Seimei Monogatari

Seimei's mother is depicted in greater detail in *Abe no Seimei Monogatari*
(The story of Abe no Seimei) (1662), a popular prose work consisting of an
account of Seimei's life, followed by disquisitions on astrology and physi-
ognomy. The sections on his life shape the raw material in *Hoki-shō* into a
more sustained narrative.[3] Seimei's previously anonymous father is now
known as Yasuna, and he is depicted as a farmer living in Abeno, a village
near Shinoda Forest in Izumi province, rather than in Nekoshima (eastern
Japan). A beautiful woman suddenly appears at his house and asks him to
marry her. She bears Dōji and assiduously helps with the farming, bringing
prosperity to his home. Then one summer day she writes a poem on the *shōji*
and vanishes.

Although the last line of the poem has *shinobi shinobi ni* ("secretly, secretly") instead of *urami kuzunoha*, the business about writing it on the *shōji*
became an essential part of the story—one that is fully exploited by *kabuki*
actors today. The remainder of the chapter fleshes out the first part of the
poem, by depicting the journey of the distraught father and son to Shinoda
Forest looking for the boy's vanished mother, who is identified as a fox in
Shinoda.

Shinodazuma Tsurigitsune (tsuketari) Abe no Seimei Shusshō

This new aspect of Seimei's story is further developed in the earliest extant
play. Known as *Shinodazuma Tsurigitsune (tsuketari) Abe no Seimei Shusshō*
(The Shinoda wife, fox trapping, and the birth of Abe no Seimei), the play
falls under the category of *kojōruri* (old puppet dramas), that is, puppet plays
created before 1684, when Takemoto Gidayū established the *gidayū bushi*
style of chanting.

Although *Shinodazuma* first appeared in 1674, roughly a decade after
Abe no Seimei Monogatari, the question as to whether the playwright drew
upon the earlier prose piece is a matter of dispute.[4] One scholar, Watanabe
Morikuni, argues that *Abe no Seimei Monogatari* served as a bridge between
Hoki-shō and the play. He criticizes other scholars for ignoring the interaction between dramaturgy and literary genres in the Edo period.[5] The more
widely held view presumes the existence of a precursor to *Shinodazuma* in
the world of *sekkyōbushi*, a type of religiously oriented narrative chanted to
shamisen music and performed with puppets that flourished in the sixteenth
and early seventeenth centuries. The appeal of this theory is attested by the
inclusion of the *kojōruri* as a substitute for the absent text in a prominent
collection of *sekkyōbushi*, despite the lack of any concrete evidence in the

form of texts or performance records that a *sekkyōbushi* version of *Shinodazuma* ever existed.[6]

The five-part play is written in a crisp, quickly paced style. It employs a third-person narrative, interspersed with dialogue, which strings together self-contained episodes linked by verbal cues such as "turning now to," which alert the audience to a change of scenes. The emphasis on visual effects (frequent fight scenes, flamboyant gestures, and strong emotions) reflected the nature of the puppet theatre as a medium.

While *Shinodazuma*, too, sets out to examine Seimei's origins, it simplifies the story and economically weaves key motifs from previous works into the central, linear plot. For instance, Yasuna's father is introduced in Act I as an inhabitant of Abeno, whose family owned an astrology book that had been handed down from their ancestor Abe no Nakamaro. Instead of going to the dragon realm to obtain a box and jewel (as in *Abe no Seimei Monogatari*), Dōji receives them from his fox mother in Act III.

The events involving Seimei and Dōman in *Hoki-shō* and *Abe no Seimei Monogatari* are placed in Acts IV and V. Hakudō is inserted in Act IV, when Dōji, now more than ten years old, is beginning to manifest brilliance as a student, thanks to the magical gifts bestowed by his mother. Identified as a supernatural being who had met Dōji's ancestor Abe no Nakamaro in China long ago, Hakudō descends from heaven and presents him with the astrology book *Kin'u Gyokuto Shū*. As a reward for discovering the cause of the emperor's illness by means of the magic jewel, Dōji is appointed head of yin-yang divination and given the auspicious name Seimei. Dōman is introduced as a famous court diviner who is driven by jealousy to challenge him to a test of skill, which Seimei wins by miraculously transforming the contents of a box from oranges into rats. In Act V, Dōman orders his men to kill Yasuna at Ichijō Bridge. On the way home from court, Seimei finds his father's corpse and restores him to life, using the ritual taught him by Hakudō. At court he lays a life-or-death wager with Dōman about whether Yasuna is dead or alive. When Yasuna appears, the loser, Dōman, is beheaded. Seimei is appointed head of the divination bureau and master of astrology and enjoys endless prosperity.

Shinodazuma's greatest point of departure from *Abe no Seimei Monogatari*, not to mention *Hoki-shō*, is that it seeks to explain why the fox weds Yasuna and why she has to leave. The groundwork is laid by the introduction of a new villain in Act I: Dōman's younger brother, Ishikawa Akuemon, who uses Dōman's political power to acquire a government post near Shinoda. Advised by Dōman that the liver of a white fox would cure his gravely ill wife, Akuemon goes hunting in Shinoda Forest in Izumi province, where many foxes live.

While Yasuna is visiting Shinoda Shrine, a pair of foxes race past him, followed by a young fox that runs up to him as though seeking help. When Akuemon and his hunting party show up, Yasuna rejects their demand to surrender the fox. During the fierce fighting that ensues, Yasuna is captured, but just as he is about to be killed, a fox disguised as the priest in charge of Akuemon's family temple appears and saves him.

In Act II, Yasuna rescues a beautiful maiden from drowning in a river. She invites him to her humble cottage nearby. Worried by his absence, his father, Yasuaki, sets out to look for him and is killed by Akuemon. Yasuaki's attendant, Mitani no Zenji, chases after Akuemon, who unwittingly seeks refuge at the cottage where Yasuna is staying. Yasuna kills him. Unable to return home after losing his father and killing Akuemon, Yasuna lives in obscurity in a village near Shinoda Forest with the maiden, whom he has wed.

Act III opens when their son Dōji is seven years old. In a homely domestic scene, Yasuna's wife dotingly watches over her son and weaves while Yasuna is away tilling the fields. All of a sudden, she becomes so enchanted by the chrysanthemums growing in the garden that she reveals her true shape, frightening her son when he awakens from his nap. Returning to her senses, she breast-feeds him and puts him to bed while lamenting that she must bid farewell to him now that he knows her true identity. She leaves Yasuna a letter explaining that she is a fox living in Shinoda Forest and that she had married him to repay him for saving her life. After writing the *kuzunoha* poem on the *shōji*, she disappears.

The reason she must leave her beloved child was inspired by a traditional association of foxes with chrysanthemums that goes back to a famous couplet by Po Chü-i:

> The owl calls out in branches of pine and cassia;
> the fox hides amid orchid and chrysanthemum leaves.

Like *Abe no Seimei Monogatari*, *Shinodazuma* depicts Yasuna's longing for his wife and Dōji's longing for his mother; they heed her poem and seek her out in Shinoda Forest. But the play also dramatizes the last line of the poem by recounting the fox's painful regrets (*urami*) as she returns to her home in the forest.

The poignant journey of Dōji's mother back to Shinoda Forest through the fields departs from *Abe no Seimei Monogatari* in another important regard: it takes place in autumn rather than summer. Her feelings are heightened by time-honored images from the poetic tradition, such as the cries of insects and the autumn wind, that reflect the melancholy season, which is conventionally associated with longing and separation.

The transformation of Dōji's mother into a fox is cleverly orchestrated using elements from the fox-trapping scene in the *kyōgen* play *Tsurigitsune* (Fox trapping) (a strategy foreshadowed by *Shinodazuma*'s subtitle, in which the words "fox trapping" appear). In the *kyōgen*, when a fox disguised as a human comes across fox traps, it decides to change back to its animal form. Similarly, when Dōji's mother draws near the forest, she grows fearful of the fox traps that are lying about. In a twinkling, the woman wearing a kimono and broad-brimmed hat turns into a fox.

While Yasuna and his son, overcome by longing, are wandering in the wood looking for her, the fox suddenly appears in her previous shape as the boy's mother and bestows on him a golden box containing a talisman that provides universal knowledge and a crystal-like jewel that renders the speech of birds and beasts intelligible.

Superhuman heroes, stock villains, and divine intervention are staple fare in *kojōruri*, and *Shinodazuma* is no exception. Its five-act structure depicting the triumph of good over evil also follows a common pattern. A case in point is the birth of the hero and his fox-mother's reluctant departure in Act III, which typically deals with self-sacrifice that tilts the scales in favor of virtue.

Shinodazuma

Later puppet theatre and *kabuki* playwrights expanded and refined central elements of Seimei's story. The name Kuzunoha was first bestowed on the fox-wife in the *kabuki* play *Shinodazuma*, which premiered in Kyoto in 1699.[7] The play also invented new characters and eliminated others or endowed them with new attributes, providing a vehicle for the comic antics, love scenes (*nuregoto*), and realism that were hallmarks of Genroku-period (1688–1704) *kabuki*.

The play is framed by the fox hunt and the separation scene and reunion at Shinoda Forest. In other words, Ashiya Dōman's role has been eliminated; his brother Ishikawa Akuemon, however, is his usual evil self. Mitani no Zenji is now Yasuna's retainer and, it is he rather than Yasuna who rescues the fox at Shinoda Shrine in the opening scene.

The comic, *kabuki*-like twist given to familiar elements of the story is exemplified by the opening scene, in which Akuemon offers *kagura* (ritual shrine music) at Shinoda Shrine, where a fox is worshiped as the deity's messenger. After trying unsuccessfully to bully the shrine priest into procuring a white fox to cure his ailing wife, Satsuki no Mae, Akuemon goes off into the hills to hunt a fox. Meanwhile, Mitani no Zenji comes to pray at the shrine. When a fox fleeing from Akuemon and his hunters runs up, Zenji hides the fox by covering it with his *haori* coat and sitting on it. The suspicious Akuemon looks under the coat and finds only a rock. When Zenji looks, there is a fox. Later we learn that Satsuki no Mae is secretly in love with Zenji and is merely feigning illness to avoid Akuemon, whom she detests.

In the penultimate scene, Abe no Yasuna's evil younger brother, Dakaku no Suke, feigning madness, embraces Kuzunoha and threatens to kill Dōji if she does not give in to him. He starts to leave with her on his back, but when he looks up, he notices that her face has turned into that of a fox. Her true nature having been revealed, she can no longer remain in Yasuna's home, so she bids farewell to the sleeping Dōji, writes the *kuzunoha* poem on the *shōji*, and disappears. Noteworthy is the fact that Kuzunoha writes the poem on the *shōji* with her tail. This feat may have inspired the practice by *kabuki* *onnagata* of holding the brush with their teeth while writing the poem, a trick discussed in greater detail below.[8]

In the final scene, the cook Kisuke and Dōji meet up with Yasuna at Shinoda Forest: They are all looking for Kuzunoha. When the fox-Kuzunoha, originally played by the famous *onnagata* Mizuki Tatsunosuke I (1673–1745), finally appears, Yasuna persuades her to resume her human shape and return home. The role of the cook, first played by Yamatoya Jinbei II (d. 1704), an actor known for his comic roles and dancing, was a new element that satisfied the taste for everyday realism in *kabuki*. It is conjectured that the role was created to provide a vehicle for Jinbei. In the final scene, Jinbei mimes fox trapping in the manner of the fox in *Tsurigitsune*, a role for which he was famous.

Ashiya Dōman Ōuchi Kagami

In 1713, the Shinoda story returned to the puppet stage in a five-act history play called *Shinoda no Mori Onna Urakata* (Female divination in Shinoda Forest) by Ki no Kaion (1663?–1742). The play draws heavily on the plot and language in the *kojōruri Shinodazuma*, while incorporating elements of the 1699 *kabuki* version. It in turn provided Takeda Izumo with material for *Ashiya Dōman Ōuchi Kagami*.[9]

As suggested by the title, a dynastic struggle forms the overarching theme of *Ashiya Dōman Ōuchi Kagami*. The fight for control of the court is linked to ownership of the *Kin'u Gyokuto Shū*. Ashiya Michitaru (Dōman) and Abe no Yasuna are cast as the chief disciples of the late court diviner Kamo no Yasunori, the owner of *Kin'u Gyokuto Shū*, which had been passed down from the Chinese wizard Hakudō. Michitaru and Yasuna are members of opposing factions headed, respectively, by Sadaishō Tachibana no Motokata and Sangi Ono no Yoshifuru, the fathers of Crown Prince Sakuragi's favorite concubines, Miyasudokoro and Rokunokimi. Although Yasunori had intended to marry his adopted daughter, Sakaki no Mae, to Yasuna and give him the astrology book, he has died suddenly without doing so.

Stylistically and musically, the prologue follows common dramaturgical practice by opening with a densely allusive passage that extols the wondrous nature of the fox and intimates the birth of the brilliant diviner Abe no Seimei, whose knowledge of the workings of heaven contributes to a peaceful world.

Act I presents a dispute at court between Motokata and Yoshifuru over the recent occurrence of a strange lunar phenomenon suggesting disorder in the realm. When Sakaki no Mae is summoned for advice, she reveals that her father's astrology book cannot be consulted because it has been locked away, ownerless, at the Kamo mansion since his death. The senior retainers of Motokata and Yoshifuru—Iwakura Jibu no Tayū and Sakon Tarō—are ordered to draw lots at the Kamo mansion the next day to determine through divine will who should receive the book, Michitaru or Yasuna.

The late diviner's widow steals the book by copying Sakaki no Mae's key. Conspiring with her brother, Jibu no Tayū, to frame Yasuna, she accuses Sakaki no Mae of giving the book to Yasuna. When Sakaki no Mae accepts the blame and commits suicide to protect her beloved Yasuna, he loses his mind and wanders off. The plot is exposed when the duplicate key is discovered. Following a typical pattern in five-act history plays, a fight scene brings the act to a close, as Yasuna's attendant, Yokanbei, kills the widow and hurries after Yasuna, taking Sakaki no Mae's robe.

In the first half of Act II, the Motokata faction plots to use the astrology book to seize political control. Trying to ensure that Miyasudokoro wins the race to produce an heir to the throne, Jibu no Tayū gives his son-in-law, Ashiya Michitaru, the stolen book and asks him to divine a way to enable Miyasudokoro to become pregnant. Michitaru's advice is to procure the liver of a white fox and perform a special rite. Jibu no Tayū orders his minion, Ishikawa Akuemon, to kill Miyasudokoro's rival, Rokunokimi, and asks Michitaru to provide a magical spell to lure her out of the house. Michitaru is forced to comply when Jibu threatens to take back the book and Tsukubane, his wife. Akuemon succeeds in abducting Rokunokimi late at night, but just as he is about to drown her in a pond, she is rescued by what the text calls a *hinin*—perhaps a beggar or an outlaw—and vanishes.

The second half of Act II draws upon the events at Shinoda Shrine in the first act of *Shinodazuma*. In a sequence commonly known as the *kosode monogurui* (kimono madness), Yasuna comes to the shrine after wandering derangedly through the fields carrying Sakaki no Mae's robe over his shoulder. Catching sight of her younger sister, Kuzunoha, who looks exactly like her, he hallucinates that he has found his beloved, but Kuzunoha's words restore him to sanity. When her parents arrive, Yasuna asks permission to marry her, a wish that cannot be granted because her villainous cousin, Ishikawa Akuemon, has already demanded her hand.

Just then, an aged white fox races up, pursued by Akuemon and his men, and vanishes between Kuzunoha and Yasuna. Thwarted in his hunt for the fox, the villain tries to flee with Kuzunoha, but is fought off by Yasuna and his attendant, Yokanbei. After the latter leads Kuzunoha and her parents away, Yasuna continues to fight until Akuemon escapes. Just as Yasuna is about to kill himself in despair, fearing that Kuzunoha has been captured by Akuemon, she suddenly runs up and stops him. The couple goes off to hide from the world in Abeno.

Act III deals with the consequences of Rokunokimi's abduction. Jibu no Tayū orders her execution when he finds her hiding at the home of Michitaru (her rescuer). His order unleashes a complex chain reaction that forces Michitaru and others around him, bound by conflicting obligations imposed by birth and marriage, to choose between love and duty to parent, spouse, and lord. In a case of *migawari* (mistaken identity), Michitaru unwittingly kills his father, who had sought to take responsibility for the abduction. Discovering Michitaru's honorable intentions and her father's treachery, Tsukubane kills her own father, Jibu no Tayū, when he returns to Michitaru's house the next day to confirm Rokunokimi's death. Michitaru renounces his warrior status and changes his name to Dōman, vowing to devote himself to divination. He is extolled as a model of loyalty. His transformation from an archvillain into a hero is completed in the next act, when he bestows the name Seimei on Dōji and gives him the astrology book.

The restoration of the honor of someone who has been treated in legend and history as a villain—a strategy prefigured in the epithet *ōuchi no kagami* (mirror of the court) in the play's title—followed a trend in puppet theatre in Izumo's day. Although the complex calculations of love and duty in Act III also resonated with contemporary audiences, the act did not enjoy lasting success, unlike the following act, which begins with the famous *kowakare* (child separation) scene.

Echoing Act III of *Shinodazuma*, Act IV opens at Yasuna's house, where the fox, disguised as Kuzunoha, is weaving and tending to the five-year-old Dōji while Yasuna is away at Sumiyoshi and Tennōji praying for the boy's future. Her true identity is unmasked when the real Kuzunoha and her parents suddenly come to visit. The fox-Kuzunoha must bid a painful farewell to her son. Taking him in her arms, she explains that she is really a fox that had been rescued from hunters by Yasuna at Shinoda Forest and then took human form. After telling him to look upon the real Kuzunoha as his mother, she disappears, leaving behind the *kuzunoha* poem on the *shōji*.

A two-part *michiyuki* (travel scene) follows. The first part, which depicts the fox-Kuzunoha's sad journey back to Shinoda Forest, is often performed. Echoing *Shinodazuma*, chrysanthemums form an important motif, and fox-

Kuzunoha's language and movements recall the *kyōgen* play *Tsurigitsune*, such as when she looks at her image in a pool of water. The poignant autumnal images and language also hark back to the earlier play. In the second part, Yasuna, Dōji, and the real Kuzunoha wander through Shinoda Forest, pushing aside the chrysanthemums, as they search for Dōji's mother. Suddenly she appears in her erstwhile form as Kuzunoha. Before turning into a century-old white fox and disappearing again, she vows to cast off her earthly attachment but promises to protect Dōji. When Yasuna, Kuzunoha, and Dōji suddenly come upon Ashiya Dōman, who is traveling back to his home, she appears and disappears among the chrysanthemums, offering support during Dōman's test of Dōji's knowledge, which qualifies the boy to receive the *Kin'u Gyokuto Shū*.

In the final scene, sometimes called "Ninin Yakko" (Two attendants in Shinoda Wood), Akuemon reappears and tries to abscond with Kuzunoha and her son to use as bait in his attempt to capture Yasuna. They are saved by Yasuna's servant, Yokanbei, and his double, a white fox (Yakanbei).

Akuemon's dual role as a member of the Motokata faction and as Kuzunoha's cousin and suitor for her hand provides a crucial link between the world of the court and the Shinoda story. As her suitor and the oppressor of her father, he also provides a convenient obstacle that prevents her marriage to Yasuna, paving the way for the fox-Kuzunoha. Akuemon continues his villainy at the start of Act V by killing Yasuna at Ichijō Bridge. Seimei's rite at court restoring Yasuna to life completes the downfall of the evil faction led by Motokata. Seimei and Dōman are hailed as peerless diviners, and peace and prosperity are restored to the realm.

The weight attached to *henshin* (transformation) as a guiding principle in *kabuki* and the puppet theatre translated into a predilection for plots that featured mistaken identities and disguises, quick costume changes (*hayagawari*), and special effects (*keren* and *karakuri*). The magical world of Abe no Seimei was clearly conducive to treatment in such an environment. So was the traditional Japanese view of foxes as shape-shifters and tricksters.

Takeda Izumo's creation of identical human and fox characters in Act IV proved to have lasting appeal. His depiction of the fox-Kuzunoha's wifely and motherly attributes draws upon conventional role types of *sewa nyōbo* (domestic–play wives). Indeed, this aspect of her character is already present in the *kojōruri*. What sets apart his depiction of Seimei's fox mother is the idea that love for human beings causes foxes to lose their supernatural powers.[10] To help her son, she must return to her own world. Her refusal to surrender to her love for her child and return to Abeno parallels the conflict between love and obligation in Act III, but ironically portrays that conflict in a much more realistic way.

The poignant *kowakare* scene in Act IV in which the fox-Kuzunoha bids farewell to her son was often staged independently in the Edo period. When the play made its debut, however, it was surpassed in popularity by the "Ninin Yakko" scene at the end of the act. The roles of Yokanbei and Yakanbei earned the play a special place in puppet theatre history, for tradition has it that they were the first roles in which three operators were assigned to one puppet, an innovation that made the puppets more lifelike.

Today, Act IV is the only part of the play that is usually performed. Some *kabuki* programs present the *kowakare* scene alone or in combination with the fox-Kuzunoha's journey back to Shinoda Forest; others include the fight scene at the end of the act.[11] Two *shosagoto* (dance plays) inspired by *Ashiya Dōman Ōuchi Kagami* are also part of the repertoire: *Yasuna* draws upon the *kosode monogurui* sequence in Act II; *Kuzunoha* on the fox-Kuzunoha's *michiyuki* in Act IV. Both dances derive from early nineteenth-century *henge buyō* (transformation dances), dance sequences performed by a single actor featuring multiple characters and quick costume changes. In *kabuki*, the ability to shift characters abruptly and convincingly is a measure of an actor's skill. The performance by an *onnagata* of both Kuzunoha and the fox-Kuzunoha, a tradition started by Nakamura Baigyoku III (1875–1948) in 1894, is one such test.[12]

The fox-Kuzunoha's farewell to her child in the *kowakare* scene is unusually demanding, for it requires an actor to convey her grief while performing the difficult feat of writing the *kuzunoha* poem on the *shōji*. In the puppet theatre, the poem is simply discovered on the *shōji* after Kuzunoha disappears.[13] *Kabuki* performances, however, add dialogue to the sequence in which the fox-Kuzunoha bids farewell to her child, and she writes the poem on the *shōji* while cuddling him in her arms. *Onnagata* have devised different strategies for performing this passage to convey the character's fox nature and her feelings for her child. In the following version used by Nakamura Ganjirō I (1860–1935), Kuzunoha begins *koishikuba* (if you long for me) normally, but writes the last three syllables (*shi-ku-ba*) upward from the lower part of the screen. After she writes *tazune-kite miyo* (please come to visit), Dōji runs up calling her name, so she holds him on her lap with her left arm around him. Her grief at having to part from him causes her to write *Izumi naru* (in Izumi's) backward. Shifting Dōji to her right side, she writes *Shinoda no mori no* (Shinoda Forest) with her left hand. She then puts both arms around him, forcing her to write the last line, *urami kuzunoha* (the bitter kudzu leaves), holding the brush with her mouth (figure 16.1).[14]

Kabuki performances alter the original puppet-theatre text in other ways that affect Kuzunoha's characterization. Performances that delete Akuemon's

Figure 16.1 **An 1831 woodblock print showing Mimasu Gonnosuke as Yasuna and Nakamura Shikan II as Kuzunoha during the scene in which Kuzunoha writes her farewell poem on the *shōji* with the brush held in her teeth. (Photo: Courtesy of Samuel L. Leiter.)**

role, for instance, intensify the emotional impact of her parting from her child; likewise, the excision of references to events beyond the immediate story, such as Dōji's future service at court, sharpens the focus.

Actors have a well-stocked bag of tricks to draw upon to depict the vulpine nature of Dōji's mother. Unusual speech rhythms and the pronunciation of *kitsune* (fox) without the *su* sound, for instance, are also used for the fox roles in *Yoshitsune Senbon Zakura* and *Tsurigitsune*. The performance of both Kuzunoha and the fox-Kuzunoha by the same actor places a premium on the quick costume changes for which *kabuki* is famous. During the travel scene, a fox mask hidden in the *onnagata*'s sedge hat quickly transforms Kuzunoha into the fox-Kuzunoha. On other occasions, bits of dialogue are added to facilitate the actor's exit and quick reentrance.

Although the above elements, honed by long practice, are basic building blocks in the creation of Kuzunoha's character on stage, an actor's skill ultimately is judged by his ability to subordinate them to higher aesthetic and thematic goals. Similarly, our understanding of the character Kuzunoha depends upon our grasp of the world that produced her. Knowledge of *Ashiya*

Dōman Ōuchi Kagami and the cultural tradition from which it sprang is an essential part of that process.

Notes

1. My summary of *Hoki-shō* is based on Watanabe Morikuni, "Hoki-shō izen: Kitsune no Ko Abe no Dōji no Monogatari" (Pre-*Hoki-Shō:* The story of the fox-child Abe no Dōji), *Kokubungaku Kenkyū Shiryōkan Kiyō* (Bulletin of the Library of Japanese Literary Research) 14 (1988): 63–124.

2. The collection, *Tsuki no Karumo Shū* (Seaweed gathered in the moonlight), is located in *Zoku Gunsho Ruijū*, vol. 33-a (Tokyo: Zoku Gunsho Ruiju Kanseikai, 1923) 63–65. The poem is the same as the one in *Hoki-shō* except for *tazunete mo toe* (visit me and ask) in the second line. See Kaga Keiko, "Kojōruri Shinodazuma no Shinoda: Sandanme no Haikei" (The *Kojōruri Schinodazuma no Chinoda:* Background to act III), *Kabuki: Kenkyū to Hihyō* (Kabuki: Research and criticism)18 (1996): 92–104.

3. *Abe no Seimei Monogatari*, in Asakura Haruhiko, ed., *Kanazōshi Shūsei* (Kanazōshi anthology), vol. 1 (Tokyo: Tōkyōdō Shuppan, 1980), 363–469.

4. My discussion of *Shinodazuma* is based on the text in *Kojōruri Shōhon Shū* (Anthology of *kōjōruri* plays): 357–87, 578–80, and 645; and Araki Shigeru and Yamamoto Kichizō, eds., *Sekkyōbushi*, Tōyō Bunko 243 (Tokyo: Heibonsha, 1973), 275–306. See also Watanabe Morikuni, " 'Kitsune no Kowakare: Bungei no Keifu (Fox child-separations: The literary tradition)," *Kokubungaku Kenkyū Shiryōkan Kiyō* (Bulletin of the Library of Japanese Literary Research) 15 (1989): 135–65.

5. Watanabe, "Kitsune no Kowakare," 139.

6. The volume in question is Araki and Yamamoto *Sekkyōbushi*; see note 4 above. Kaga Keiko, "Kojōruri Shinodazuma no Shinoda: Sandanme no Haikei," *Kabuki: Kenkyū to Hihyō* (Kabuki Research and Criticism) 18 (1996): 92–104, suggests that an earlier *katarimono* (recited narrative) set in a different part of Japan served as a common ancestor for both *Abe no Seimei Monogatari* and the *kojōruri Shinodazuma*.

7. Yūda Yoshio and Torigoe Bunzō, eds., *Kamigata Kyōgenbon 4* (Kamigata plays), in *Koten Bunko* (Classical library. Ed.) 246 1968): 179–228; Shuzui Kenji, "Shinodazuma Kō: Kyōgenbon to Rokudanbon to" (Shinodazuma: The *Kabuki* playbook and the six-act joruri text), in *Shuzui Kenji Chosaku Shū* (Collected writings of Shuzui Kenji), vol. 1 (Tokyo: Kasama Shoin,1976), 328–43.

8. Shuzui, "Shinodazuma Kō," 333–34.

9. My discussion is based on the text in Takeda Izumo, Namiki Sōsuke, *Jōruri Shū* [Takeda Izumo, Namiki Sōsuke: *Joruri* anthology. Ed.], Tsunoda Ichirō and Uchiyama Mikiko, eds., vol. 93 of *Shin Nihon Koten Bungaku Taikei* (New compendium of Japanese classical literature) (Tokyo: Iwanami Shoten,1991), 4–137.

10. Ibid., 96, *n.* 6.

11. The puppet theatre program at the Kokuritsu Gekijō (National Theatre) in August 1984, for instance, included the first and last scenes in Act I, the *monogurui* scene in Act II, and the *kowakare*, *michiyuki*, and Shinoda Forest fight scene in Act IV. My discussion of the treatment of Kuzunoha in *kabuki* is based on the text in Toita Yasuji et al., eds., *Meisaku Kabuki Zenshū* (Complete

collection of *kabuki* masterpieces), vol. 2 (Tokyo: Tōkyō Sōgensha, 1968). A translation of the *kowakare* scene and the fox-Kuzunoha's journey back to Shinoda Forest, including a detailed description of their performance, can be found in Cody Poulton, "Lady Kuzunoha," in *Brilliance and Bravado: Kabuki Plays On-Stage, 1697–1766,* James R. Brandon and Samuel L. Leiter, eds. (Honolulu: University of Hawai'i Press, forthcoming).

12. Poulton, "Lady Kuzunoha."

13. The eighteenth-century play script in Kabuki Daichō Kenkyūkai, ed., *Kabuki Daichō Shūsei* (Anthology of *kabuki* scripts), vol. 2 (Tokyo: Benseisha, 1983), 227–314, indicates similar staging in *kabuki*.

14. Theatre program, Kabuki-za, Tokyo, March 1996, 28.

17

Miracle at Yaguchi Ferry: A Japanese Puppet Play and Its Metamorphosis to *Kabuki*

Stanleigh H. Jones Jr.

A large proportion of the plays in the Japanese *kabuki* theatre are *maruhon mono*: that is, plays originally written for and performed by the puppet theatre. Indeed, though *kabuki* boasts masterworks of its own, it would be far poorer without the contributions of the puppet theatre. It is not surprising that puppet works have been so freely borrowed by the actors. Up through the middle years of the eighteenth century, Japan's greatest playwrights for the popular theatre were, by and large, those who devoted their talents to the dolls. While there are obvious similarities between the two theatres, they differ precisely because one is based on a long-standing narrative tradition adaptable to puppets, whereas the lifeblood of the other has always been the skill of great families of actors.

The differences between the two theatres become most apparent, of course, through performances on their respective stages, where the conventions and demands of each form make for variations that are readily apprehensible to the spectator. Stage techniques aesthetically appropriate or dramatically feasible for the puppets may be discarded by live actors who in turn may add elements that an actor portrays more convincingly. Particularly famous scenes of a play will generally be given the same careful attention by both puppets and actors, but the latter may occasionally make relatively minor characters or scenes considerably more dramatic and important than the original. A good example of this is seen in Act V of *Chūshingura* (The treasury of loyal retainers), where *kabuki* developed and emphasized the role of the highwayman Sadakurō well beyond its scope in the original puppet version.[1] Alterations will vary in nature and extent from play to play, or they will take shape according to the peculiar genius of a given actor or adapter. The result is usually a compromise in which ingenuity and a search for the dramatically viable combine to produce a play that works on the *kabuki* stage, often in ways it would not for the puppets.

Shinrei Yaguchi no Watashi (Miracle at Yaguchi Ferry) is one of the many puppet plays that have found their way into *kabuki*. A *jidaimono* (historical play) that first went on the boards in Edo on the sixteenth day of the first month in 1770, *Yaguchi* was written by a newcomer to the ranks of puppet playwrights, Fukuchi Kigai—the theatrical nom de plume of a man better known to history as Hiraga Gennai (1728–1780).[2] Hiraga's play proved to be such a success that certain parts of it were brought to the stage again in the eleventh month of the same year. By the 1860s, one or two acts had been performed by the puppets at least a dozen times. In 1794 the play was adapted to the *kabuki* theatre. Since that time it has become part of the permanent repertory of both the *kabuki* and puppet theatres, though it is offered nowadays more frequently in *kabuki*. As a rule, puppet and *kabuki* plays tend to be preserved on stage mainly as famous acts or scenes from longer works. Though originally written in five acts, *Yaguchi* is never performed in its entirety today; only the long scene in Act IV, entitled "Tonbei Sumika" (Tonbei's House) has achieved theatrical longevity.

The metamorphosis that *Yaguchi* underwent in its transposition from a theatre of puppets to one of actors will probably give a fair idea of the process in general as it might apply to other plays. My objectives here are to describe some of the ways in which *Yaguchi* was changed to make it a suitable vehicle for *kabuki* actors and to provide a translation of the *kabuki* version of that part of the play that is still performed. Some initial notes on the background of the play, however, may be useful.

The circumstances of *Yaguchi*'s success are of importance historically and deserve some notice. Prior to the Edo première of *Yaguchi*, Osaka was the traditional home of the puppet theatre. From the middle years of the eighteenth century, however, a decline had begun to set in. Many of the great playwrights and other artists of the puppet theatre had either died or retired, and there appeared to be little talent in Osaka to take their place. Official harassment, never distant from any plebeian enterprise, also hurt the theatre. An example was the imprisonment late in 1761 of Takeda Ōmi IV, manager of the famous Toyotake-za and one of its chief playwrights. His offense was giving a lavish party that was, in the eyes of class-conscious feudal officials, grossly unbecoming to his social station as a commoner. The Toyotake-za was also plagued by fire: two years running—1761 and 1762—the playhouse was reduced to ashes. Finally, in 1765, after sixty years of operation, hard times obliged the Toyotake to sell out to a *kabuki* troupe. Half a dozen years later, the doors closed at the rival Takemoto-za puppet theatre, which claimed an even longer history and in which the famous dramas of Chikamatsu Monzaemon (1653–1725) had stirred audiences during the early years of the eighteenth century.

Although the puppet theatre was deteriorating in Osaka, it was about to enjoy a modest renaissance in Edo. Once a stodgy town dominated by the Spartan mores of the military class, Edo (with a population of well over a million by 1750) and its rapidly rising standard of living had fostered a greater sophistication in popular tastes. During the 1730s and 1740s, when leading members of the Osaka puppet troupes had toured the city, Edo citizens saw the puppet theatre at its best and gave their visitors an enthusiastic welcome. Soon Edo was adding new puppet theatres to the few already in existence there and luring away from Osaka many of its finest performers. Before the eighteenth century ended, Edo had clearly emerged as the intellectual and cultural hub of the country. It was perhaps symbolic of the decline of the Osaka puppet theatre and its concomitant revitalization in Edo that the last play to be produced (in 1771) in the Takemoto-za and the first play to grow out of a distinctly Edo environment were one and the same: *Shinrei Yaguchi no Watashi*.

The influx of theatrical talent from Osaka to Edo contributed an important element to the success of *Yaguchi*. Among the newcomers late in 1767 were Takemoto Sumidayū (d. 1806) and Yoshida Kanshi (1732–1790). Sumidayū, already celebrated as a superb narrator in his native Osaka, was to be one of the leading figures in the Edo puppet theatre for nearly forty years after his arrival. During the opening run of *Yaguchi,* his narration of the last part of Act IV (translated here) won him particular acclaim, and he thereafter made it one of his specialties. Indeed, a number of puppet plays subsequently written by Edo playwrights were fashioned expressly to suit Sumidayū and his style. Yoshida Kanshi, successor to the great innovator in the puppet theatre, Yoshida Bunzaburō, was celebrated both as an expert in manipulating the dolls and as a skilled playwright. Yoshida not only collaborated in the writing of *Yaguchi*, but also was acknowledged by the author, Hiraga Gennai, as the man who first suggested to him the idea of writing a puppet play. Though *Yaguchi* is essentially the product of Hiraga's own versatile talents, it is probably safe to assume that such seasoned veterans as Sumidayū and Yoshida, familiar with the varied conventions of the puppet theatre, made important contributions to the play's success.

The unusual reputation of the author of *Yaguchi* doubtless acted as an additional attraction. A man of roving and eclectic curiosity, Hiraga Gennai compressed a remarkable array of activities into a relatively brief lifetime. His countrymen today remember him as the first Japanese to conduct rudimentary experiments with electricity and as the man responsible for introducing into the mainstream of Japanese art the materials and techniques of Western-style oil painting, but his genius went well beyond these accomplishments. Originally a student of medicinal herbs, he spent a great deal of his time traveling about Japan gathering herb specimens and prospecting for mineral deposits. He wrote most of *Yaguchi*, in fact, during the hours he was not supervising operations at an iron mine he had discovered some miles north of Edo. Hiraga also took an avid interest in the scientific and technological advances of the West, and he is usually counted among that small but influential band of intellectuals who, through their study of *Rangaku* (Dutch learning), laid important groundwork for Japan's later spectacular modernization.

Hiraga's literary efforts included a number of humorous novelettes and short stories that often lapsed into outspoken polemical attacks against broad segments of his society that he felt were intellectually stagnant and imitative. Although these critiques were his forte, he also managed to write nine plays for the puppet theatre. Of these only *Yaguchi* survives on stage today.

While the success of *Yaguchi* derived in part from a set of favorable circumstances that were in many ways fortuitous and outside the control of the playwright, in the end the play's popularity depended primarily on those features over which the playwright did exercise an important measure of control. *Yaguchi* offered audiences many time-honored dramatic elements: there were stirring battles and romantic intrigues, paragons of samurai loyalty and conniving traitors, the pathos of self-immolation, slapstick farce, and finally a miraculous rescue—the perennial stock-in-trade of the puppet and *kabuki* theatres that never failed to stir Japanese audiences. One of the most memorable features of the play was the role of Tonbei the ferryman, the dominant personality in the present translation. Greedy and cold-blooded, he is unredeemed by any virtue; but the very vigor of his incorrigible character, depicted first by the puppets and later by *kabuki* actors in the extravagant *aragoto* (roughhouse) acting style, was instantly popular among Edo audiences.[3] Tonbei was originally intended to be just one particular villain in a play already filled with villains. But Tonbei's callous self-interest made him unique, and he captured the stage from the other more stereotyped characterizations. Eventually, through the spirited interpretation of the famous actor Ichikawa Danjūrō VII (1791–1859) in 1831, the portrayal of Tonbei achieved the status of a major *kabuki* role.

Yaguchi possessed one other special attraction to the audiences who first saw it. This was its unmistakable Edo quality. It was only natural that the puppet theatre, which had matured in the popular milieu of Osaka and Kyoto, would bear the particular stamp of that region. As a result, the settings and local color of the plays often derived from the Osaka-Kyoto environment, and there was a tendency for the language of the plays to be the softer western dialect. *Yaguchi*, however, presented a noticeable contrast: much of the setting was in the immediate vicinity of Edo and thus familiar to an Edo dweller; the manners and customs were those of Edo; and, though difficult to suggest in translation, the brash and distinctive language of Edo pervaded the entire play. Moreover, the playwright himself lived in Edo. The result was a specifically Edo flavor, which not only appealed to the regional esprit of that city but also gave *Yaguchi* the historical importance of ushering in the era of the Edo puppet theatre.

A historical incident recorded in a fourteenth-century war tale, the *Taiheiki* (Chronicle of the great peace), provided the material from which the plot of *Yaguchi* was woven. The tale relates the military exploits and death in 1358 of a famous general named Nitta Yoshioki, a loyal supporter of the Southern Court during the half century of disunion (1336–1392) known as the period of the rival Northern and Southern courts. According to the *Taiheiki*, it was through the machinations of one Takezawa Yoshihira and the ferryman of Yaguchi Ferry that Yoshioki was trapped on a sinking boat at the Yaguchi crossing. Rather than suffer the dishonor of falling into the hands of his enemies (the troops of Ashikaga Takauji), Yoshioki and several of his retainers committed suicide.[4]

Most historically based puppet and *kabuki* plays elaborate on their material with abandon. In the *Taiheiki,* Yoshioki's death is recounted rather laconically, and the villain is merely a nameless boatman at Yaguchi Ferry. The full-blown development of both the details of the event and the distinctive character of Tonbei is completely the product of the playwright's literary and dramatic license. What results is the typical "great scene," as in most traditional popular plays, which has become essentially an independent play in itself. Though in the course of "Tonbei's Sumika" there is enough explanation of prior events for the scene to possess a basic dramatic integrity in itself, it will be useful to outline the preceding action in order to explain certain references and characters and to indicate the place of "Tonbei's Sumika" in the overall continuity of the play.

With the opening of Act I, Nitta Yoshioki, commander of the troops loyal to the Southern Court in Yoshino, is obliged, against his better judgment, to attack the enemy forces of the Ashikaga. Before setting out to do battle, he entrusts to the care of his younger brother, Yoshimine, two treasured arrows, which are family heirlooms. Yoshimine, meanwhile, has become attached to a beautiful Kyoto courtesan named Utena, and during his clandestine visits he has fallen into the company of Takezawa Kenmotsu, an unscrupulous man who is secretly an agent of the enemy general Takauji. Yoshimine persuades Yoshioki to take Takezawa into his service. Shortly after Yoshioki, accompanied by Takezawa, has set out on his campaign, Yoshimine is robbed of the precious arrows he was supposed to protect.

Act II depicts the battle between Yoshioki's loyalist troops and the Ashikaga forces led by Eda Hangan. By prearrangement with Takezawa, Eda and his army pretend to be routed. Yoshioki, though warned by his senior retainer against any rash action, gallops off in pursuit. The scene then shifts to the Nitta castle in the north, where, the wives of Yoshioki and several of his retainers await news of the battle. A soldier arrives to report Yoshioki's imminent victory. The company is about to celebrate with a toast when in dashes another soldier, mortally wounded. He describes in a dramatic monologue how Yoshioki has been betrayed and defeated. Takezawa, he gasps, has been in league with Eda Hangan, and they have brought into their conspiracy the ferryman of Yaguchi Ferry on the Rokugō River. He tells how Yoshioki and a handful of retainers had ridden ahead of their main force in pursuit of Eda and boarded the ferry at Yaguchi. In midstream the boatman scuttled the boat and jumped overboard. Instantly a large body of enemy troops under Takezawa appeared on one side of the river, while Eda and another contingent appeared on the other, showering the boat with arrows. Trapped helplessly, Yoshioki and his men all committed suicide. The rest of Yoshioki's army has been annihilated. The messenger breathes his last, and the shouts of Takezawa's men are heard as they storm the castle. In the ensuing melee, Yoshioki's wife and son and several others manage to escape to safety.

Act III traces the adventures of the several persons who escaped from the Nitta castle. With the exception of a brief scene in which Takezawa makes an appearance, none of the characters of Act IV appear, and the story is sufficiently distinct from the remainder of the play that a synopsis of it may be omitted here.

As the fourth, act opens, Yoshimine, now a hunted fugitive, and his mistress Utena are traveling north where they hope to be sheltered by friends. They arrive at Namamugi Village, where a priest named Dōnen hides them from ruffians bent on collecting a reward for turning them over to Takezawa. Following their escape from Namamugi Village, Yoshimine and Utena continue their flight to friends in the north. The scene now changes to the house of Tonbei, the ferryman at Yaguchi crossing. (The accompanying translation begins at this point.) Tonbei has become rich from the reward money he received for his role in defeating Yoshioki and causing his death. At the edge of the river Tonbei has built a comfortable house with a pavilion constructed over the water. His wealth has helped him become a successful gambler and he now lives in leisure, but he hopes to acquire further rewards through the capture of any stray Nitta adherents who might happen by. Should any appear, arrangements have been made for Tonbei to fire a rocket calling for reinforcements. The beating of a drum hanging in the pavilion of Tonbei's house will signal that the fugitives have been caught and that help is not needed. As the scene opens we see Rokuzō, Tonbei's servant and henchman, and Tonbei's attractive daughter, Ofune. Rokuzō is grumbling about his menial chores. Three gambling cronies arrive to see Tonbei, who, in the conversation that follows, describes how he became rich. After the gamblers depart, Tonbei is called away by a village runner. No sooner is he gone than Rokuzō, who has long courted Ofune, starts making advances, but she repulses him. In the midst of his clumsy amours, Rokuzō too is summoned away.

While Ofune is alone in the house, Yoshimine and Utena arrive, seeking lodging for the night. Reluctant at first, Ofune becomes completely infatuated when she sees the handsome young Yoshimine. She is visibly disappointed, however, when she catches sight of Utena. A few moments later, when she is alone with Yoshimine, Ofune questions him about Utena. Yoshimine, careful not to arouse suspicions about his identity, says that she is his sister. Ofune is beside herself with joy and presses herself upon the young man. As they embrace, however, they both fall into a faint. Utena rushes in and tries to revive Yoshimine. Then, remembering the Nitta banner he carries in the fold of his kimono, she takes it out and unrolls it. Instantly the pair regain consciousness. Utena and Yoshimine quickly retire to an inner room, but not before Ofune has seen the banner and realized the identity of her guests.

Meanwhile, Rokuzō has returned and observed the scene from outside. He debates with himself whether to go for help or attempt single-handedly to capture the fugitives and thus receive the reward. Avarice wins out, but just as he is about to go in Ofune stops him. Coquettishly wheedling and cajoling Rokuzō with the prospect of becoming his wife, she finally persuades him to go and summon her father. As the elated Rokuzō dashes off, Ofune locks the gate and reenters the house.

A short time has passed and it is dark. Stealthily, Tonbei and Rokuzō appear, swords drawn. Leaving Rokuzō to guard the gate, Tonbei breaks into the lower part of the house and picks his way through the darkness to a place beneath the inner room where he believes Yoshimine is sleeping. He plunges his sword up through the floor. There is a scream, and Tonbei runs outside and up the steps. He throws open the doors to the room and discovers not Yoshimine but his own daughter, Ofune, mortally wounded. She confesses that she has helped Yoshimine escape because she loves him and because he has promised her that if she will atone for her father's murder of Yoshioki she will be his wife in the next world. Furious, Tonbei beats the girl mercilessly. He then shoves her aside, leaps down from the house, and fires the signal rocket in the yard. Then he rushes off in pursuit of Yoshimine.

Ofune is in despair. She then remembers that beating the drum will cancel the alarm signaled by the rocket. Painfully she drags herself to the pavilion and, her strength ebbing, begins pounding the drum. Rokuzō hears the sound and rushes in to stop her. They struggle, but she manages to draw his short sword and stab him, and he falls into the river. Using her last bit of strength, Ofune beats the drum with Rokuzō's empty scabbard. As she falls dead, Tonbei is seen furiously rowing a small boat across the river. He is approaching the further bank when suddenly an arrow (one of the stolen heirlooms, as it turns out) flies in from nowhere and strikes him in the chest, killing him. (The scene ends here in *kabuki*. For the ending as it occurs in the original puppet play, see both the description below and the translation of the puppet version following the *kabuki* translation.)

The fifth and final act is typically a congratulatory scene in which a shrine at Yaguchi is about to be dedicated to Yoshioki in order to placate his wrathful ghost, which has been causing fearful thunder to roll over the Ashikaga headquarters in Kamakura and Kyoto. Present are Yoshimine, the priest Dōnen, an imperial emissary, and others. Just as Eda Hangan and two other villains involved in the treachery attempt to enter the shrine, the great crossbar on the gateway mysteriously tumbles down and crushes them. Yoshioki's terrible vengeance is now complete, and the play ends.

It has been said that historically the integrity of the texts of puppet plays has been better respected than those of *kabuki*, where actors often call for extensive revisions of a playwright's work and where plays have been written mainly as vehicles to suit the special talents of a great actor. Yet this penchant for rewriting plays and creating texts especially suited to the style of a particular performer is far from unknown in the puppet theatre. The great plays of Chikamatsu Monzaemon still appear regularly on the puppet stage, and yet virtually none of them are produced today just as he wrote them; in fact, many were rewritten only a few years after his death in 1725 in order to satisfy changing conditions in the puppet theatre. And both Chikamatsu and later playwrights wrote texts designed specifically to give full play to the individual styles of leading narrators. With such practice already well established, and in view of the fact that *Yaguchi* was being transposed from the puppet milieu to *kabuki*, it was to be expected that the play would undergo a certain metamorphosis. Some changes were dictated by the differing demands of a theatre of actors; others represented a difference between the dramatic potential of *kabuki* and that of the puppets. And doubtless some alterations were made in order to suit the tastes of adapter and actor.

One of the first modifications affected the narrator. The vitality of the puppets depended in large measure on a narrator who not only spoke all the dialogue but also sang and intoned descriptive passages. In a theatre of actors capable of great subtlety and variety of body movement, facial expression, and voice modulation, the need for a narrator is markedly reduced, and his part is sometimes eliminated altogether. In the *kabuki* adaptation of *Yaguchi,* the narrator is retained, partly perhaps as a reminder of the play's puppet origins, but also for utilitarian reasons and for the dramatic effect he contributes in several places. His overall role, however, is considerably reduced, most of his long narrative passages becoming unnecessary as actors make situations clear through their performance and through a certain amount of new dialogue written into the play.

The narrator remains useful in the *kabuki* version for introducing and sometimes briefly characterizing new personalities as they come on stage. For example, he introduces Ofune ("a peacock born of a crow") and Rokuzō at the beginning of the play, the three gamblers when they come to visit Tonbei, and shortly thereafter Tonbei himself ("a scowling face flushed scarlet and set into a beard so white it might be taken for snow. Greed and villainy glint in his eyes"). In the scene where Tonbei reviles and beats the dying Ofune for allowing the fugitives to escape, the narrator serves to heighten the dramatic intensity and to give the performer (Ofune) a breathing space during a long speech by trading lines back and forth with the actor. Of course, this alternation of lines does not occur in the puppet play. In *kabuki*, the narrator is also useful in describing action that is mimed on stage, for instance, the scene in which Tonbei creeps about in a darkened house. Further, he is effective in providing a semipoetic recitative for scenes of emotional intensity, such as those describing Ofune's infatuation with Yoshimine. In these two latter instances, however, the narrator's role, and in fact his lines, are much the same in *kabuki* as they are in the puppet play.

The narrator's presence in the *kabuki* version of *Yaguchi* is not the only element recalling the play's puppet origins. The scene in which Ofune has been left alone after Yoshimine and Utena, to whom she has just offered lodging, have entered the inner room of the house is often performed in a manner known as *ningyō buri,* or "puppet style." As Ofune first rhapsodizes over Yoshimine's charms, then voices her apprehension about Utena, she performs with an expressionless face in the jerky fashion of the puppets, while other actors or stage assistants "manipulate" her from behind as though she were indeed a puppet. This type of performance is not unique to *Yaguchi*; it also occurs occasionally in other *kabuki* adaptations from the puppets.

To a greater extent than in the puppet original, the *kabuki* adaptation provides a lively interchange of dialogue between characters, thus heightening the dramatic quality of the play and often injecting a more natural and logical sequence into the action. Rokuzō's first utterances in the puppet play, for example, are two questions:

"Ofune, is supper ready? The master still at his nap?" In the *kabuki* version the dialogue runs as follows:

ROKUZŌ: Ofune, is supper ready?

OFUNE: Stop worrying about my duties, Rokuzo. Hurry up and put things away.

With this exchange, the two characters come alive and react to each other, and in Ofune's reply we get an early hint of her attitude toward Rokuzō.

Another instance of this greater tension in the dialogue is the entrance of the three gamblers. In the puppet play, the narrator, of course, delivers all the lines:

NARRATOR: . . . in troop Shikkari Sorobei, Mikami no Jūji, and Kara no Pinsuke.

GAMBLERS: (*Together*) The boss at home?

NARRATOR: They come boldly in the door and squat cross-legged on the floor.

OFUNE: Oh, come right in.

NARRATOR: All hospitality, she brings out a tobacco tray.

OFUNE: Father is still napping. If you have some business with him, I'll wake him up.

NARRATOR: In the next room Tonbei hears her voice and yawns.

TONBEI: Hum, I'll come in there and see them.

The result of this interchange is that the gamblers remain rather colorless, and Rokuzō, who is still onstage, is left out entirely. In the *kabuki* version each of the gamblers as well as Rokuzō joins in the conversation, considerably enlivening the stage:

NARRATOR: . . . in crowd Shikkari Sorobei, Mikami no Jūji, and Nizoro no Pinsuke.

TOGETHER: The boss at home?

NARRATOR: They come in the door and squat cross-legged on the floor.

ROKUZŌ: Oh, welcome, all three of you. Now, what did you want with the boss?

SOROBEI: You see, the three of us here have got some business, so . . .

JŪJI: We've come together like this.

PINSUKE: Listen, young lady, is the boss at home?

OFUNE: Father is in there napping just now.

SOROBEI: The sun is already sinking, . . .

JŪJI: So if he's taking a snooze, that's too bad, but . . .

PINSUKE: Could you please wake him up for us?

OFUNE: It's already time for him to wake up. Oh Father, three gentlemen have come to see you.

NARRATOR: In the next room Tonbei hears her voice and yawns.

TONBEI: Hmm, I'll come in there and see them.

The division of what is essentially a single line so that it is spoken sequentially by several characters is a common stylized practice in *kabuki*, especially for enlivening groups of lesser figures on stage; but for the one-man narrator the device would be difficult and in any case much less effective.

It is characteristic of *kabuki* that greater attention is given to secondary characters than in the puppet theatre. In the puppet theatre, these supernumeraries are often simple one-man puppets instead of the far more complex and expressive dolls manipulated through the coordinated efforts of three men. An actor, however, by his more animated entrance and presence on stage demands a greater degree of vitality. Accordingly, the boatman Hachisuke, who has little more than a perfunctory role in the puppet version as he interrupts Rokuzō's clumsy advances to Ofune, is given much fuller treatment in *kabuki,* both in dialogue and in action. In the puppet play he is introduced by the narrator, and then:

HACHISUKE: Hey, Rokuzō. You said you had some private matter to attend to and asked me to take over the ferry for you. Now you've left it all to me while you're up here flirting. If the boss hears of it you'll really be in trouble. Come on.

NARRATOR: He pulls him away.

ROKUZŌ: (*To Hachisuke*) I've still got some unfinished business. Wait just a little longer.

HACHISUKE: No, I can't wait. How can you expect anyone to feel romantic with a face like yours! You're a perfect clod at this sort of thing.

In *kabuki,* Hachisuke is immediately drawn into the action as Rokuzō, blindly pursuing Ofune about the stage, embraces Hachisuke instead, producing an exchange that takes full advantage of the scene's potential.

HACHISUKE: Rokuzō, what's going on?

ROKUZŌ: Oh, is that you, Hachisuke?

HACHISUKE: Look here, Rokuzō, you asked me to take your place ferrying people across the river because you had work to do at home. What do you mean? Is this the kind of work you have to do? If the boss finds out about it, he'll be furious. Now, now, come on, come on.

ROKUZŌ: I've got some unfinished business. Wait a minute.

HACHISUKE: Oh, no, I'm not waiting for you. You can't make love with a face like yours; it's like being romantic with an old pumpkin, you melon-head!

ROKUZŌ: You've got a lot of cheek! Now I've still got a little . . .

HACHISUKE: A little what, I wonder. Oh, come on.

ROKUZŌ: Just wait a minute.

HACHISUKE: Damn it, let's go!

Rokuzō is essentially a comic figure in both the puppet and *kabuki* versions of *Yaguchi,* but this aspect of his role is given considerably greater attention in *kabuki.* As Tonbei's ruffian henchman, he assisted in the deed that brought Tonbei his fortune, but Rokuzō is unhappy with his own lot. He is also a bumblingly unsuccessful suitor of Ofune. As he eavesdrops on the scene in which the Nitta banner is revealed and Yoshimine confides to Utena his suspicions about Tonbei's house, Rokuzō realizes that the visitors are fugitives whose capture means a reward. In the puppet play, he reviews his options and makes his decision in the following brief monologue: "Shall I send up the signal rocket? No, no! I won't get any credit if I call in an attacking party to catch them. I'll get in there first, and the reward money will be mine. Good! Good idea!" To the *kabuki* adapter, the situation opened up great possibilities for comedy and for developing Rokuzō's avaricious character. Faced with a risky but potentially rewarding opportunity, Rokuzō's instinct for calculating odds comes into play. First he thinks of the signal rocket, but hesitates: "The credit won't go to me. I won't even get first or second place in the reward. Huh! I will have worked for nothing! I can't just send up that rocket without giving it a little thought, can I?" Then, his excitement growing as he considers capturing the fugitives single-handed, he is carried away by the multiplying prospects of reward: "First of all, I'll be made a samurai. At the least I'll get a salary of one measure of rice, or two measures, or three measures—maybe a bushel even, or two bushels! I'll be a samurai with I don't know how many bushels! Pretty soon the boss, Tonbei, will be getting old, and when he drops dead his daughter will be mine! Meanwhile Utena in there can be my concubine. Great! With money *and* women, I don't know if I'll be able to stand it!" Again he hesitates as he contemplates his adversary: "If I fight with a boatman, man to man, I won't get beaten. But Nitta Yoshimine, even if he is weak and withered, is probably a good fighter. If I make a mistake he could chop my head clean off!" Rokuzō wavers. Is he doing it for love, or for money? Finally, concluding his one-man debate, he makes up his mind: "Well, I guess I'll do just as everyone else does; let's make it for money and I'll do the job alone!"

As the foregoing has already suggested, most of the changes wrought in the adaptation of *Yaguchi* to *kabuki* worked to improve the play as a dramatic vehicle. In many instances characters were more fully developed, situations were more thoroughly exploited for their comic or dramatic potential, and a more natural effect was achieved by rearranging or augmenting the dialogue. The *kabuki* treatment of the ending of the play, however, fails to improve on the original and in fact is less satisfying in several respects.

In the *kabuki* version, Tonbei, after striking down the mortally wounded Ofune, sends up the signal rocket and races off in pursuit of the fugitives. His exit is a vigorous and exciting performance (known as *roppō*) in which powerful leaps and an animated flailing of arms highlight the actor's movement along the *hanamichi* (runway), which extends through the pit from the stage to the rear of the theatre. The play ends when, in the final scene, Tonbei is killed by a mysterious arrow as he rows across the river. The music is exciting, and the scene is lively and theatrically effective, but we are left with unanswered questions: What about Yoshimine and Utena? Where did the arrow come from? How has vengeance been satisfied?

The ending of the play in its original puppet version not only answers these questions but also provides some spectacular scenes omitted in *kabuki*.

In his struggle with Ofune, Rokuzō is wounded and falls into the river, but he swims on in pursuit of the fleeing pair. Meanwhile, Tonbei reaches the far bank, where he is confronted by Yoshimine and the two engage in a spirited sword fight. Tonbei slips, and just as Yoshimine is about to kill him, Rokuzō enters dragging Utena and threatening to kill her if Yoshimine does not release Tonbei. As the villains then set about beating their captives, they are suddenly cut down by two mysterious arrows. The arrows, it is explained when Yoshimine examines them, are none other than the precious heirlooms stolen from him earlier (Act I) and now sent in his moment of need by the ghost of his brother Yoshioki. The appearance of the arrows is of course nothing more than a *deus ex machina*, but their return serves several purposes. Part of the plot of *Yaguchi* involves the search for these stolen treasures, and their appearance at this point concludes the quest. At the same time, they are the instruments that miraculously rescue Yoshimine and Utena and partly consummate the vengeance of Yoshioki. Moreover, it is appropriate that the two arrows kill Rokuzō and Tonbei, the two men most directly responsible for Yoshioki's death. In the *kabuki* version, only one of the arrows is accounted for, but its source and significance are not noted even though reference has been made to the arrows earlier in the scene. The *kabuki* version thus omits several dramatically desirable and technically feasible elements and fails to tie up several loose ends.[5]

With the death of Tonbei, the recovery of the arrows, and the safety of Yoshimine and Utena, it would seem that all issues in the plot of *Yaguchi* have been resolved. There is, however, another important villain to be accounted for: the treacherous Takezawa, through whose pretended loyalty Yoshioki was led into the fatal ambush at the Yaguchi crossing. Takezawa is mentioned several times in both versions of the play, and it is clear that he is the man to whom Tonbei reports when fugitives are in the vicinity. Tonbei, one might say, represents the physical threat to Yoshimine, but Takezawa represents the brains behind the plot to capture him. In the final scene of the puppet play, Takezawa decides to continue the pursuit in spite of the drum signaling that the fugitives have been caught. He and his men board a small boat and set out across the river. In midstream a fierce storm arises, shattering the boat and drowning all but Takezawa. Suddenly the mounted ghost of Yoshioki emerges from the clouds. Calling Takezawa to his doom, Yoshioki reaches forth and crushes him. The play ends as Yoshioki intones, "Now I am revenged," and peace once again settles over the heaving waters.

Though the scene provides a fine dramatic cap concluding the play, it is easy to see why it is not performed in *kabuki*. In the puppet theatre, an acceptance of the puppets themselves as performers leads naturally to the acceptance of situations that would be contrived, even ludicrous, if attempted by actors. *Kabuki* is not without its ghosts and miraculous happenings, but Yoshioki's appearance on horseback in the clouds and his destruction of Takezawa may well have created a major technical problem in *kabuki*.

The modification of *Yaguchi* to the *kabuki* stage is probably characteristic of similar *kabuki* adaptations of other puppet plays: The strengths of *kabuki* have been emphasized, frequently at the expense of the distinctive features marking a puppet play. The requirement of a performer in *kabuki* that he *act* in order to impart vitality to the text and its story results in a sharply diminished reliance on the narrative-descriptive aspect of the puppet play. New lines have been inserted and situations enlivened with expanded dialogue and action, with the result that character often develops dimensions only adumbrated in the puppet version. Spectacular effects viable in the realm of the puppets frequently disappear in the world of human performers, but to a certain extent there is compensation through skillful utilization of well-developed features of the *kabuki* theatre. The *hanamichi*, for instance, serves as an acting area of dramatic potential in both theatres [although only minimally in the puppet theatre. Ed.], but an adroit actor energizes this zone with an electricity beyond the capability of any puppet. Tonbei's vigorous *roppō* exit after he has beaten Ofune is one example: A puppet performing the same exit would hardly impart the concentrated sensation of dynamic power and vitality achieved by an expert actor. Indeed, because the puppets appear to less advantage on the *hanamichi*, it is rarely used, most entrances and exits being made through the wings. As a result, one often misses in puppet performances that tingle of dramatic tension generated by the frequent movement of actors along this runway in close proximity to the audience.

Apart from the important changes already noted, the metamorphosis of *Yaguchi* into a successful vehicle for the *kabuki* stage also involved various minor alterations, such as slight changes in wording and occasional shifts of lines from one place to another, but these produce no significant difference from the original puppet version. When the complete range of modifications is considered as a whole, however, *Yaguchi* emerges as a more effective theatrical experience in its *kabuki* transformation. Skilled actors unarguably bring an enormous range of subtlety and expressiveness to their performances. This should not blind one, though, to the unique charm of the Japanese puppet theatre. The combined effect of dolls that themselves are works of art, puppet handlers expert at a great variety of manipulative techniques, and the often spectacular virtuosity of a seasoned narrator infuses plays and their characters with compelling vitality. Like many other plays in the popular theatre of Japan, *Shinrei Yaguchi no Watashi* enjoys a kind of double life— enlivened with bold highlights and etched in poignant delicacy in two vital theatrical traditions.

A translation of the *kabuki* version of the play follows. Appended to it for comparison is a translation of the ending in the original puppet version.

MIRACLE AT YAGUCHI FERRY[6]

Cast of Characters (in order of appearance)

OFUNE, Tonbei's daughter
ROKUZŌ, Tonbei's chief henchman
SHIKKARI SOROBEI, gambler
MIKAMI NO JŪJI, gambler
NIZORO NO PINSUKE, gambler
TONBEI, ferryman at Yaguchi crossing
RUNNER from the village headman's house
HACHISUKE, a boatman
YOSHIMINE, scion of the Nitta family
UTENA, Yoshimine's sweetheart, a former courtesan
TAKEZAWA KENMOTSU, traitor in league with the Ashikaga family
YOSHIOKI (appears as a ghost), Nitta general

The Stage: A thatch-roofed building stands somewhat right of center stage, its floor about three feet above ground level. It is open toward the audience; a stairway leads to the interior. In front of the house stands a gate. At stage left, on posts sunk in the water, is an open-frame thatched pavilion, its floor somewhat higher than that of the main house, to which it is joined by a stairway. Hanging from the ceiling of the pavilion is a large drum. Below the pavilion, in the water at stage left, is a skiff. At far stage right is a hedge; near it is an upright post bearing the inscription "Yaguchi Ferry." As the curtain opens, music suggesting flowing water is heard, and the musical narration begins.

NARRATOR: Rokugō River[7]: nowadays it boasts a ferry,
But travelers in ancient days, bound eastward from the capital,
Were obliged to take the longer circuit—arc of a strung bow—
To the ferry known as Yaguchi.
On its upper waters,
Like morning dew upon a fence
Where woven cloth hangs bleaching in the sun—
Boats upon the flowing Tama River.[8]
Tonbei the ferryman: deep are his innermost thoughts,
Less fathomable than the depths of the current that tosses the boats.

His house, strange to say, extends out over the water.
With its curious pavilion, uncommon for one of Tonbei's trade,
It is a pretentious affair:
The proverbial "stairs of agate, emerald crusted curtains."
And is that Princess Oto of the Dragon Palace?[9] Is that she?

(*Ofune emerges from within the house. She wears a kimono with long flowing sleeves and clasps a doll.*)

That's Tonbei's daughter Ofune, a peacock born of a crow.
A seductive girl, she is; too good for these backwoods.
There comes the servant Rokuzō,
Bringing back water pails upon a shoulder pole.

(*Water music as Rokuzō appears from stage right, balancing across his shoulders a pole holding a water bucket. His clothes are rather shabby.*)

ROKUZŌ: Ofune, is supper ready? (*He enters the house, disposes of the bucket.*)

OFUNE: Stop worrying about my duties, Rokuzō. Hurry up and put things away.

ROKUZŌ: I will, I will. The master still at his nap? It's hard to believe that it's true. Tonbei, a ferryman, is now probably the richest man in the whole country. But he treats his servants so badly that they can't stand it here more than three days, and you, his own daughter, you have to tend the kitchen. You poor thing. When I think of your hands getting so rough, what a pity, what a pity. I could shed tears for you—tears of blood, big as cherries. And I, Rokuzō, respected as his chief lieutenant, his head clerk; whenever I'm not out rowing the ferry, then it's splitting firewood or carrying water. I'm sick of it. Things would be easier if this house had neither master nor ferry.

OFUNE: Stop grumbling, Rokuzō, and finish with the water. If you don't tend to the ferry, you'll get a tongue-lashing from father.

NARRATOR: And just as she is restraining him, in crowd Shikkari Sorobei, Mikami no Jūji, and Nizoro no Pinsuke. (*They enter downstage right, music suggesting waves.*)

TOGETHER: The boss at home?

NARRATOR: They come in the door and squat cross-legged on the floor.

ROKUZŌ: Oh, welcome, all three of you. Now, what did you want with the boss?

SOROBEI: You see, the three of us here have got some business, so . . .

JŪJI: We've come together like this.

PINSUKE: Listen, young lady, is the boss at home?

OFUNE: Father is in there napping just now.

SOROBEI: The sun is already sinking, . . .

JŪJI: So if he's taking a snooze, that's too bad, but . . .

PINSUKE: Could you please wake him up for us?

OFUNE: It's already time for him to wake up. Oh Father, three gentlemen have come to see you.

NARRATOR: In the next room Tonbei hears her voice and yawns.

TONBEI: Hum, I'll come in there and see them.

NARRATOR: In comes the master, Tonbei, still wobbly of leg,
A scowling face flushed scarlet
And set into a beard so white it might be taken for snow.
Greed and villainy glint in his eyes.
Arrayed in a wide-sleeved undergarment
And modishly tailored outer coat,
Down he sits with a thud!

(*He brings with him a tobacco pouch, sits on the floor.*)

THE THREE GAMBLERS: Boss, did you just wake up?

TONBEI: Ah, glad all of you came. How's your luck been?

SOROBEI: Luck? Out of the question. Everything has been one complete mess.

JŪJI: All the money, among the three of us, we lost it all.

PINSUKE: We had shameful luck.

TONBEI: So you've had a bad time of it, eh? Well, never mind. It stands to reason you lose some and win some. But just because you lost a bit, don't make a big fuss like a tinker going to mend a temple bell. Well, now it's time we had a game. Daughter, bring me some money from the back room.

OFUNE: No need to go back there. This morning Mangorō from Shinagawa came and brought some money he said you had lent him the other day. It's right here in the drawer of your writing box.

TONBEI: How fortunate. In that case bring it to me.

OFUNE: At once, at once. (*She brings him his writing box. From a drawer Tonbei takes out six packets of money wrapped in white paper. Each packet contains 100 ryō*[10] *in gold.*)

TONBEI: Ah, good. There are six packets here. That makes two hundred *ryō* apiece. If that isn't enough, shall I lend you a little more?

NARRATOR: The three men are dumbfounded.

SOROBEI: Did you hear that! Now there must be plenty of rich men around, but six hundred ryō just sitting in a writing box as though it were a mere pittance! There's a limit to good things!

JŪJI: Well, now, there's an old saying that money and ghosts don't exist. But ghosts still appear, don't they? What's gone nowadays is money.

PINSUKE: That's right! When I occasionally take in a play for relaxation, I don't know why, but nowadays whatever the occasion, it's talk about money.

SOROBEI: In such stingy times as these, where there is any money, it's this much?

JŪJI: Say, how does one go about making such a pile as this?

PINSUKE: Master Tonbei, explain that to us . . .

ALL THREE: Please!!

NARRATOR: With a tap-tap, Tonbei knocks his pipe against the tray.

TONBEI: Aw, you've all got the wrong idea. That's why you can't lay hands on what money is around. They say that if you pile up enough dust you can make a mountain, but while you are piling it up the wind may blow it all away. If you scatter two coppers here, four there, you'll get nowhere. Now, if you are trying to be a success in life, there's speculating, or prospecting, and of course there's gambling. But lately people have gotten sharper and there haven't been so many easy marks around who can be fleeced in a game. So

I, Tonbei, hit upon an idea.[11] The "banker" general Ashikaga Takauji and his high-bidding opponent Yoshioki recklessly wagered high stakes against each other at Kamakura. Then in their "big game" held at the "gambling house" of Musashino, Takauji, though he had the greater resources, fairly lost his shirt. "This is only the first shuffle," he shouted and withdrew to the "dice boards" of Kamakura. "Villain," cried Yoshioki in complete abandon, "Your fate hangs on a roll of the dice!" and followed him to Kamakura. But there were some under-the-table dealings and when the situation got out of hand, that eager old plunger Takezawa Kenmotsu and Eda Hangan[12]— he's a small-time player—sent a man to me. He told me they wanted to give me the "banker's cut" and pleaded with me to think of a plan for killing Yoshioki. I wasn't worried about how this would affect my eventual salvation. After all, I was doing the job for somebody else. But I knew I'd better not underestimate my man, so I got the idea of boring a hole in Yoshioki's boat. Then I had Rokuzō pull out the plug. The reward for this task of seeing to it that Yoshioki drowned in the river was Tonbei's. With Lord Takauji's backing I was to be made a baron. But I just wouldn't feel easy in that role—I couldn't gamble as I was fond of doing. So I gave up the baron's fine fare, and I told him that the noodle soup I was accustomed to eating as a ferryman suited me quite well. "In that case, choose what you want," he told me. Well, I said, a good pile of money would do just fine, and that became my fortune. It was quite a game, and I really won big.

A millionaire? That's me. Even the fancy way I had this house built was to keep me from forgetting the past. Just as you see over there in the alcove—a sculling oar and a straw raincoat.[13] Those decorations are the story of how I came up in the world.

NARRATOR: The doubts of the listeners are dispelled.

SOROBEI: Now I get it. Here, I have an idea. Why don't we try something wild?

JŪJI: We don't have a boat to bore a hole in, but now if we drill a hole in a dice cup and put in a piece of glass . . . how about that, Pinsuke?

PINSUKE: Oh, no. What I'd like better than that is to do a little hole-boring here in Ofune's bottom.[14]

SOROBEI: Huh! Why do you say such stupid things?

JŪJI: Well, we'd better be going.

TONBEI: Well then, have a good game! (*The three move toward the front gate.*)

THREE: We'll see you again tomorrow, boss.

NARRATOR: The three leave together. (*Music suggesting waves, as they exit on the* hanamichi.) Suddenly in comes a village runner. (*From the* hanamichi. *He goes to the front gate.*)

RUNNER: Master Tonbei, Master Takezawa wants to talk to you about some wanted men. Would you come with me for a moment to the village headman's house?

TONBEI: What's that? Wanted men? Oh, it's probably about arresting Nitta fugitives. If that's the case, I don't need to go. No matter where they come from, there is only one road, and they will have to cross at this ferry. Master Takezawa and I have already made our plans. Once any Nitta fugitives come here that's the end of them. When I set off the signal rocket, horns will be blown in all the villages, and a constable will set out from Master Takezawa's place. If we should capture or kill the fugitives, then we will inform him by beating on that drum hanging up there in the pavilion that we need no assistance, and the villagers who are surrounding the fugitives will know that they are to go home. The village headman is just putting on airs for himself. I'm sick of all of his tedious explanations.

OFUNE: Still, Father, he's a messenger from the village headman. You'd better go along.

RUNNER: I don't know what he wants to see you about. He just instructed me to summon you. Please come along.

TONBEI: All right, then, I'll go and see what he wants. Hey, Rokuzō, if you see anybody who looks suspicious, don't forget the arrangements for the rocket and the drum. Daughter, bring me my short sword.

OFUNE: Yes, Father. (*She brings it from inner room*; *Tonbei puts it into his sash and then dons his outer coat.*)

TONBEI: Daughter, look after the house.

NARRATOR: He thrusts his broad-blade sword into his sash and goes off with the runner. (*Water music, as Tonbei and the runner exit along the* hanamichi.) When he is gone, Rokuzō lowers his voice and snuggles up to Ofune.

ROKUZŌ: Oh, Ofune, you're heartless.

OFUNE: There you go flirting again as soon as Father is away. You're always doing that. I'm disgusted with it.

ROKUZŌ: [15]I'm not just flirting! I've been in love with you for a long time, but no matter how much I plead with you, you pay me no more heed than you would a bean wobbling about on a door plank! I'm so hard up that I've worn myself out roaming the forbidden pleasure quarters from the Cold River District to Susotsugi Tower, to Korean Tenements, Sharkbridge, and Radishfield, not to mention the Nezu and Otowa districts.[16] But there's no one in all of Edo *as* pretty as you and that famous beauty Osen of Kasamori.[17] I beg you, please give in to me. I tell you, I'm one of those fellows who's easily aroused, and I just can't stand it any longer! (*He sidles up to her, she pushes him away.*)

OFUNE: If you talk like that, I'll tell Father!

ROKUZŌ: That would be cruel! (*Ad-libbing his speech, Rokuzō pursues Ofune about the room. The hired hand, Hachisuke, enters downstage left, his kimono hitched up in back. He enters the front gate quite unaware. Rokuzō, blindly pursuing Ofune, mistakenly embraces Hachisuke.*)

HACHISUKE: Rokuzō, what's going on?

ROKUZŌ: Oh, is that you, Hachisuke?

HACHISUKE: Look here, Rokuzō, you asked me to take your place ferrying people across the river because you had work to do at home. What do you mean? Is this the kind of work you have to do? If the boss finds out about it, he'll be furious. Now, now, come on, come on.

ROKUZŌ: I've got some unfinished business. Wait a minute.

HACHISUKE: Oh, no, I'm not waiting for you. You can't make love with a face like yours; it's like being romantic with an old pump-kin—you melon-head!

ROKUZŌ: You've got a lot of cheek! Now I've still got a little . . .

HACHISUKE: A little what, I wonder. Oh, come on.

ROKUZŌ: Just a minute.

HACHISUKE: Damn it, let's go!

NARRATOR: Hachisuke pulls him away against his will, and they hurry to the boat landing while Ofune remains behind talking to herself. (*Hachisuke drags the reluctant Rokuzō off. They exit stage right.*)

OFUNE: Every time Father is away, that fellow gets unpleasant. Now he's gone and messed up my hair, and I just had it fixed this morning. That nasty Rokuzō! (*Preening her hair and grumbling to herself, she enters the house.*)

NARRATOR: Murmuring to one another, in come the inseparable lovers, Yoshimine and his mistress Utena. Through Dōnen's[18] loyalty, Yoshimine has finally fled from Namamugi Village, hoping to cross at Yaguchi Ferry and head north to the Nitta family castle.

(*A bell sounds, tolling the hour. Nitta Yoshimine enters along the* hanamichi. *He is clad in a dark kimono and wears straw sandals. Twin swords are thrust into his sash. Behind him, dressed more colorfully as befits a courtesan, follows Utena. They pause on the* hanamichi, *about one third of the way from the stage.*)

YOSHIMINE: Here, Utena, this is Yaguchi Ferry where my brother Yoshioki died. Ah, bitter are the depths of these waters.

NARRATOR: Facing the river he clasps his hands in prayer.

YOSHIMINE: I pray that your spirit may find release from this world of life and death, and gain the enlightenment of Buddha. Namu Amida Butsu, Namu Amida Butsu.

NARRATOR: Mingled for a moment with his dreamlike prayers are bitter tears; Utena too speaks in a sob-choked voice.

UTENA: Your grief at this place is only natural, but let us hurry on to Nitta and tell your family our story. Then you can search for the arrows[19] and take vengeance on your brother's enemies.

YOSHIMINE: You are right; but if we request a ferry now they will surely tell us that they don't put the boats out after dark. It must be a strain for you with your cough. We can probably ask a night's lodging at that house over there. Come along.

NARRATOR: They approach the gate.

YOSHIMINE: Excuse me, is anyone at home?

NARRATOR: From within, Ofune runs out. (*She carries a lamp.*)

OFUNE: I don't know who you are, but the ferry crossing is just down there a bit further.

YOSHIMINE: We are travelers seeking lodgings for a night.

OFUNE: Oh, no. This is the ferryman's house, not an inn.

YOSHIMINE: I know this is not an inn, but we are weary with walking, and it has grown so late that there are no boats. We really do not know what to do. This is indeed a rude request, but I beg of you to allow us to remain here this one night.

OFUNE: Having heard this, I should like to give you lodging, but my father is away, you see, and I . . .

NARRATOR: As she speaks, she opens the gate and studies his graceful and noble face. (*Ofune opens the gate, looks at Yoshimine. Their eyes meet; a pose to show she is impressed.*)

OFUNE: The lodgings are for yourself, my lord?

YOSHIMINE: Yes, for myself.

OFUNE: Then, the lodgings are for yourself? Well, then, for you, if it is for you, my noble lord, we can surely find a place.

YOSHIMINE: Then I am indeed grateful to you.

OFUNE: Well, please come in.

YOSHIMINE: In that case, with your permission . . .

NARRATOR: Bowing, he passes into the house, and Ofune sees who follows behind him. (*Yoshimine enters; Utena prepares to follow. Ofune now becomes aware of Utena. She registers surprise.*)

OFUNE: Oh, excuse me, are you his companion?

UTENA: Yes, I am.

OFUNE: Oh, well then, please come in. (*Mood music by shamisen. Yoshimine and Utena move to stage left. Ofune begins to heat water for tea.*)

OFUNE: You must be tired. Forgive me, this is a poor house, but over there in the pavilion, there is a fine view. Please rest there.

YOSHIMINE: Ten thousand times we are grateful to you. This night, so fortunate for us, a night preceding lovers' parting.[20]

UTENA: When day breaks, good fortune, since this is the house of a ferryman, . . .

OFUNE: The crossing you seek is here, and here in my heart, . . .

YOSHIMINE: In her breast, desire smolders with the thin smoke of passion.

UTENA: Then, our kind hostess, . . .

OFUNE: My honorable guests, . . .

YOSHIMINE: We beg you to excuse us. (*The two exit, Yoshimine helping Utena, who is suffering spasms of coughing as they ascend the half flight of steps to the pavilion.*)

NARRATOR: Yoshimine and Utena enter the inner room together. Behind, gazing after them, remains Ofune. (*Melancholy strains of shamisen music. As she puts charcoal in the stove, Ofune poses pensively.*)

(*During the following monologue, Ofune performs in puppet style,* ningyō buri, *appearing to be manipulated from behind by another actor or stage assistant.*)

OFUNE: Can one merely say he is handsome? That he is charming? Whatever the case, if one is born a woman, that is the sort of fine gentleman one would wish to marry. But, first of all, that woman—if she is his sister, fine, but if she is his wife—I don't know what I shall do.

NARRATOR: Entangled as the fine threads of the pampas grass
Are the young girl's guiltless thoughts,
So evident her single-minded love. (*Ofune poses.*)
From the neighboring room emerges Yoshimine.

YOSHIMINE: Excuse me, young lady; oh, young lady.

OFUNE: Yes, is there something you need? (*Caught off guard, she hustles about, straightening a mirror stand, and other things.*)

YOSHIMINE: By some strange fate we find ourselves here this

night, and we are most grateful. There is something I must tell you: my companion is suffering rather severely from a cough she contracted some time ago, and I would like to give her some medicine. Could I trouble you for some hot water?

OFUNE: Yes, of course. What a pleasure it is to have you here. Oh, was it hot water that you wanted? I'll get some ready right away. My, what a pleasure it is to have you here. Oh, I have something I would like to ask you. Would you be so kind as to let me speak?

YOSHIMINE: I cannot imagine what you might wish to ask, but you have shown us much hospitality. Please make your request and I will try to comply.

OFUNE: Then, will you hear me?

YOSHIMINE: By all means.

OFUNE: Truly?

YOSHIMINE: Yes; now what is your request?

OFUNE: It's only this: ahhh, the lady who accompanies you, is she your sister or is she your wife?

YOSHIMINE: Ah, my lady companion. (*Pose.*) Truly, she is my younger sister. She has been ill for some time, and so we are taking the opportunity of making a pilgrimage together to the Kannon Temple in Asakusa[21] to pray for her health.

OFUNE: Oh, then she is not your wife!

YOSHIMINE: Most certainly, she is not.

OFUNE: Oh, wonderful! How relieved I am to hear that! My lord, please stay in my house ten days, even ten years, a hundred years! Other than my father there is no one here whom you need consider, so. . . . If you are going to pray to the goddess Kannon, please take me with you . . . so she is truly your sister!? But here, you just let me do all the talking. I wish you'd pay some attention to me.

NARRATOR: All about him she hovers, drawn
Like dust to an amber rod, like a needle to a lodestone.
Now coy, now artless, at one and the same time,
As confusion grows upon bewilderment.
Pity shows on Yoshimine's face.

(*Ofune ladles hot water into a cup and places it on a tray, then brings it to Yoshimine, bowing.*)

YOSHIMINE: They say that the shadow of a single tree, the flowing of a single river, even the chance brushing together of two people's sleeves, is foreordained by a previous existence. Since it is here that I sought lodging, how much closer our relationship. In repaying your kindness, in everything, I hope you will understand that it is because of our karma. But since we are on a journey now, I shall have to add this obligation to many others, and repay you later.

NARRATOR: He is about to enter his room, but she holds him back. (*Ofune restrains him, pulling at his sleeve.*)

OFUNE: Oh, that is too heartless! So deeply have I fallen in love with you, it would be most cruel of you not to answer me. Even though I was born in the country, consider that it was my fate to fall in love with you, . . .

NARRATOR: (*Speaking for Ofune*) and your misfortune to be loved by me. Even in the shade of trees flowers bloom, and the water that gathers in the crevices of rocks is still clear. As a memento to this world in which I live, I wish you would grant my request and . . .

OFUNE: (*Resuming her lines again*) say just one word.

NARRATOR: She clings to the hem of his sleeve,
But like the glittering frost that falls so freely
From the untouched bamboo grass,[22]
Unwooed she has been won.
Hopeless, though, this road of love.
Yet Yoshimine is not disdainful of these feelings.

(*During the narrator's monologue, Ofune looks at Yoshimine, poses. Yoshimine, gazing tenderly at Ofune, poses.*)

YOSHIMINE: The hopes which you feel so strongly are not, I think, entirely in vain. But we have barely met, and so you cannot speak of love. You have spoken thus, but I have important business I must attend to. If I didn't . . .

OFUNE: Then you will grant my wish?

YOSHIMINE: You need not worry on that account.

OFUNE: Oh, I am so happy.

NARRATOR: Deep within her eyes, she holds the lock and key of
love.
They clasp each other in embrace,
But this beginning love-thread, tinged by the quickly fading
Hue of the wild moon-grass, is destined to be torn. (*They embrace.*)
But now, how strange!
Both Yoshimine and the girl are turning pale.
Suddenly both tremble, and all at once
They sink down, gasping.

(*The lights dim, a sinister roll of drums sounds as the two fall into a
faint.*)

Startled by the sound, in rushes Utena,
Only to be bewildered by the scene before her.

UTENA: What has happened? My lord, what have you done? (*She
takes water in a dipper and makes Yoshimine drink.*)

NARRATOR: She ministers to him, calls out to him,
To no avail, it seems.
She is desperate what to do. But then
The astute Utena realizes what has taken place.

UTENA: Yoshimine! My lord Yoshimine! You have been beguiled
by this girl's charms. Have you now put a blot upon your heart, a
stain upon your banner?

NARRATOR: She thrusts her hands in the folds of cloth at
Yoshimine's breast,
And there unfurls the very banner[23] he has carried with him.
Instantly the unconscious pair wakes as from a dream.
Outside the gate, Rokuzō returns with stealthy steps.
Inside, Yoshimine surveys his surroundings.

(*As all of this is taking place, Rokuzō steals in from downstage right,
goes to the gate, and observes.*)

YOSHIMINE: Utena.

UTENA: You've come to your senses?

YOSHIMINE: (*Nodding*) When I looked around after we stopped
here, I didn't think about how magnificently this house was built, or
how out of keeping with its owner's calling. Nor did I notice its

appearance or location. I thought I might take advantage of this young lady's confession of her love to get an explanation. But when she came up to me, this is what happened. And there is indeed something strange about the interior of this house. Come, Utena.

NARRATOR: He rolls up the banner and puts it into his kimono. (*They exit into the inner room.*) Rokuzō, who has been waiting out front, gets the sword hidden in the woodshed and thrusts it into his sash. (*He poses at gate as he considers the situation.*)

ROKUZŌ: Here's an unexpected development. From what I can hear, they are real Nitta fugitives. This is great! Looks like the God of Wealth has just dropped in on me. Shall I let everyone know by sending up the signal rocket?

NARRATOR: He starts to go, then stops. (*He dashes to the* hanamichi, *then comes to a halt. A pose, his face indicating that a thought has come to him.*)

ROKUZŌ: Wait a minute, wait a minute. If I go and set off the signal and then all of us break in on them, we'll capture them all right, but the reward will be split up among everyone. The credit won't go to me. I won't even get first or second place in the reward. Huh! I will have worked for nothing! I can't just send up that rocket without giving it a little thought, can I?

NARRATOR: He cocks his head to one side, thinking.

ROKUZŌ: If I capture them single-handed, I'll turn them over to Takezawa, and the reward will all be mine. First of all, I'll be made a samurai. At the least I'll get a salary of one measure of rice, or two measures, or three measures—maybe a bushel even, or two bushels! I'll be a samurai with I don't know how many bushels! Pretty soon the boss, Tonbei, will be getting old, and when he drops dead his daughter will be mine! Meanwhile Utena in there can be my concubine. Great! With money *and* women, I don't know if I'll be able to stand it! If all goes well on both scores, fine, but. . . . Well, at any rate, let's start with the fugitives.

NARRATOR: He starts to return to the house, then pauses a moment.

ROKUZŌ: If I fight with a boatman, man to man, I won't get beaten. But Nitta Yoshimine, even if he is weak and withered, is probably a good fighter. If I make a mistake, he could chop my head clean off! Huh, I'll still have gone to a lot of trouble and for nothing! Looks like I can't do it this way either without giving it some thought. Wouldn't it be better, though, to let the whole village know he's here? But if I do it alone, I get the reward, the girl falls into my hands, and Utena becomes my concubine. But first of all, I've got to make up my mind: shall I do it for money or shall I do it for love? Love, or money? Money, or love? Well, I guess I'll do just as everyone else does; let's make it for money and I'll do the job alone!

NARRATOR: He nods in approval. But there stands Ofune, blocking his dash into the room.

OFUNE: Rokuzō, wait! What do you intend to do to these travelers?

ROKUZŌ: Eh? You know very well what I'm going to do! Just a while ago I was watching very closely. He's got a banner with the Nitta crest on it. He must be the Nitta fugitive, Yoshimine. Your father and I planned it all last year. When we bored that hole in the bottom of the boat and killed Yoshioki, he made me help with all the risky work. Then when the reward money was received, he was the one who got rich. Rokuzō here was just as he is now, empty-handed. This time I'm going to capture the brother Yoshimine, and I'll make a name for myself. Your father won't stand for your getting in the way.

NARRATOR: He is uncontrollable in his resolution. Ofune resolves to make of her love a protective barrier and determines to get rid of Rokuzō.

OFUNE: Wait, Rokuzō.

ROKUZŌ: Wait for what?

OFUNE: Just bear in mind, he's a warrior. He's not likely to make any mistakes.

ROKUZŌ: And so?

OFUNE: Oh, Rokuzō, wait!

ROKUZŌ: Wait for what?

OFUNE: You're not listening to anything I have to say. Are all those things you've said to me lies?

NARRATOR: Rokuzō is taken aback.

ROKUZŌ: What! You really mean that? Oh, no! You plan to stop me because you've taken a fancy to that fellow in there. Well, you won't get away with it so easily.

OFUNE: Wait, Rokuzō!

ROKUZŌ: Wait for what?

OFUNE: Oh, I understood how you felt about me. But I've been thinking it over, and I haven't given you an answer until now. But if you doubt me, then go ahead and do as you please.

NARRATOR: Rokuzō begins to sulk. Then comes a chill, a flush, in his head a jet of steam.

ROKUZŌ: If you've seen how I really feel about you, have you made up your mind?

OFUNE: Well, if we are going to be man and wife, that makes you Father's child, doesn't it? You shouldn't leave Father out of it and capture them by yourself. You'd better talk it over with Father when he gets back from the village headman's house.

NARRATOR: She speaks with wild abandon, stalling for time,
Guiding her words as she would the rudder of a boat.
It works! What luck, like having a boat at a ferry crossing.[24]
And the easily hoodwinked Rokuzō has climbed right on board!

ROKUZŌ: Well! It has been a long time since the dice rolled so well for me! All right. I'll hurry over to the headman's house and bring your father back. Don't let those birds in there get away.

OFUNE: Of course not.

ROKUZŌ: Well, then, keep an eye on things while I'm gone. I'm off; Ofune, I mean, my dear wife.

OFUNE: My dear husband.

ROKUZŌ: Take care.

NARRATOR: Off hurries the great lover in a confusing fluster and flourish.

(*After a pose, Rokuzō exits down the* hanamichi. *Ofune closes the gate.*)

Ofune remains behind, dejected, listless, speechless.
Her head hanging pensively, she is like a rudderless ship
Bobbing aimlessly on the ocean.
Hunting for some shrewd stratagem,

Her mind drifts first one way, then another,
As though deep in some fathomless sea.

OFUNE: Oh, shall I warn him of what awaits him? No, no, no. If I
did, Father would . . .

NARRATOR: If she does nothing
And fails to warn him of impending peril,
Then her beloved Yoshimine faces grave danger.
Whatever she may do, duty to her father
And steadfastness to her love
Are twisted into a single strand that draws her,
Like the guide rope on a sail, into a channel of meditation.
At length, her indecision takes anchor in firm resolve.

(*In Ofune's face, confusion gives way to determination. She goes
inside the house.*)

Meanwhile . . . it has grown late.
The ten o'clock moon of the twentieth
Appears and shines with brilliance
Across the winter night's sky.
Bong, bong, the peal of a distant temple bell,
The ceaseless murmur of the river water—eerie sounds.
Suddenly, in the dense and sinister thicket by the gate,
Tonbei appears. At a whistle that all is ready,
His underling Rokuzō emerges from the shadows of the wall.

(*A deep bell tolls. Music suggests stealth. Pushing aside the thicket
at downstage right, Tonbei comes out, looks about, then blows softly
on a whistle. Rokuzō comes out.*)

ROKUZŌ: Boss! (*Tonbei looks about. Pose.*)

TONBEI: Hey, Rokuzō. If Ofune wakes up and gets in the way it's
going to complicate things. I'm going to slip in quietly by myself.
You keep an eye on the front here. If they try to escape, kill them!

ROKUZŌ: I understand.

TONBEI: (*Whispering*) Go on then.

NARRATOR: Rokuzō gives a nod, and silently he hides himself
Back in the shadows. Tonbei pulls at the gate.
Impatient when it does not open,
He draws his sword and slashes through the wall.

He enters the house, but the wind sweeping in from the river
Blows out the light, plunging the room into darkness.
His own house, he knows it well,
But Tonbei's mind is clouded by his greed,
And though he tries to hide his presence, beneath his heavy body
The floor gives with a creak, creak.
At the sound of his own footsteps, he pauses,
Catches his breath, and advances toward the next room.
Bang! He stumbles on the tobacco tray.

(*Tonbei takes his short sword. After hacking his way through the downstage right wall of the house, he enters, looking about cautiously. At an opportune moment a half moon appears in the sky. The groping Tonbei stumbles, poses.*)

TONBEI: Damn!

NARRATOR: His anger rises, but gently he shoves the tray aside.
Crash! He slams into the sliding door.
"Ouch!" he cries, but this does not deter him.
Creeping up the ladder, he moves toward the room
Two steps, three steps . . .

TONBEI: Wait a minute. If that fellow is a member of Yoshioki's family, he'll be tough to handle.

NARRATOR: Nodding to himself, he quietly creeps back down
And gropes for a place beneath the chamber above.
Even in the darkness black as pitch his sword flashes
As he plunges it through the floor of the upper room.
From within, a cry of shock!
With a shout of triumph, Tonbei wrenches back his blade
And wipes away the warm blood.
Up the ladder he dashes to the floor above,
Kicks open the sliding panels.
He pulls away the bedclothes, and there in the moonlit shadows
Revealed to his astonished eyes

(*From under the house he thrusts his sword upward into the floor above. Stage assistants remove the* shōji *panels, revealing Ofune wounded.*)

TONBEI: What! My daughter? Ofune?

OFUNE: Father!

TONBEI: Where have Yoshimine and that woman gone? Tell me the truth! Out with it!

NARRATOR: His eyes are wild, his voice loud with rage. Ofune, her expression wistful, gazes at him bitterly.

(*Flute music. Ofune poses, clings to Tonbei's robe.*)

OFUNE: Oh, Father!

TONBEI: What is it?

OFUNE: You . . . you. . . . (*Plaintive music accompanies her speech.*) Of all the people born into this passing world, there are none who do not know greed, but such a grasping man as you . . . Others may die, fall into ruin, but you don't care as long as all is well with you. How can there be such selfishness, such avarice and injustice? You deceived General Yoshioki and killed him without the slightest remorse. The punishment of heaven for that crime is on your child. It never entered my mind that the traveler who stopped here this evening

NARRATOR: (*Speaking for Ofune*) was Yoshimine, but he was so fine a gentleman that—it's difficult to tell you this, but I lost my heart to him. When I drew near to him, oh, I was afraid!

OFUNE: It was the anger of Yoshioki for the crime against his banner that made me feel faint. But I didn't know, so blinded was I by love. A little while ago I got Rokuzō out of the house and crept to the upper room. While I was there lamenting the turn of events, Yoshimine came and spoke to me. He told me that because I was the daughter of Tonbei, who had murdered his brother, we could never be man and wife in this life, but that if I performed one deed of merit, to show that I was not like my father, then in the world to come he would consent to join me. I was overjoyed at just these few words. But his being in this house made me feel uneasy for his safety. So I confided in him the whole story about us, and then at an opportune moment when the moon was hidden I let them escape in one of the boats.

NARRATOR: When he hears this, Tonbei stamps his feet upon the floor. He grabs the girl's long tresses.

TONBEI: You, you, you dared to fall for a man you don't know, you'd never even seen before! You revealed my plans to a stranger? I had him right in my hands, and you let him escape just like that?! Damn you! Ungrateful wretch! Loathsome creature!

NARRATOR: He shakes his fist and rains blow after blow upon her, thrashing her in spite of her wound. The girl gasps for breath. (*He grabs her by the hair and strikes her mercilessly.*)

OFUNE: Curse me, say I'm ungrateful, but do you think you cut such a fine figure yourself? You are so wicked as to try, by some horrid and vicious trickery, to murder the sweetheart of your only daughter. Now you kill her. Inhuman! Cruel!

NARRATOR: (*Speaking for Ofune*) I don't care if I die but I cannot help worrying about the fate of you who will remain behind.

TONBEI: Ah! Useless drivel! You've let the fugitive escape. How can your father hold up his head?

NARRATOR: He kicks her aside and tries to leave, but Ofune clutches at his sleeve.

OFUNE: Wait, Father, please. I've tried to reason with you, wept over you, but you won't listen to me. If my mother were here, I'm sure there would be something we could do.

NARRATOR: (*Speaking for Ofune*) Say what you will, but when I think that it was my ill fate not to be united in this life with Yoshimine, whom I love with all my heart, then listening to you only makes me love him more. If I die by your hand, proving that I am not like my father,

OFUNE: (*Resuming her lines*) then perhaps in the world to come I will meet this fine man whom I love. I have two requests to make of you.

NARRATOR: (*Again speaking for Ofune*) If your only daughter dies before you do, may the spirit of Buddha arise within you, and may your heart be rectified.

OFUNE: (*Resuming her lines*) With this appeal I die.

NARRATOR: (*Again for Ofune*) Secondly, if you have any pity for your daughter, I beg you to change your mind and help Yoshimine.
She pleads with him, then with a sudden cry sinks down.
Hopelessly her tears of blood battle with the bloody tide—
To call it merely piteous beggars the reality.
Tonbei bursts forth in a mocking laugh.

TONBEI: Even if you told me that the Buddha had returned to the laity to celebrate his coming of age and that he was going to write a formal apology for his misdeeds, it would in no way change me from the man I've been all these years. Since you let Yoshimine escape without giving the signal, I have failed to honor my pledge to Master Takezawa. Oh, yes, the rocket!

NARRATOR: He sends the girl reeling aside and quickly strikes a light to the already prepared rocket.

(*Tonbei rushes down the steps. As he cuts off the top of the Yaguchi marker post, the sound of the rocket is heard.*)

He sets out for the riverbank.

(*As he does so, Ofune tries to stop him, but he strikes her down. Then, posing on the* hanamichi *near the stage, he exits down the runway in a special style of energetic* roppō *movement known as* kumote-takoashi *or "spider arms and octopus legs," consisting of powerful leaps and a vigorous flailing of arms.*)

Ofune struggles painfully to rise.

OFUNE: If Yoshimine is surrounded by that crowd of villagers, how can he be saved?

NARRATOR: In an agony of bewilderment,
She tosses about at her wit's end.
Then through her tears she spies the drum hanging above. (*She poses.*)

OFUNE: A little while ago I heard that when this drum is struck it is the signal that the fugitives have been taken alive. Then the blockade set up by the villagers will be lifted. This is a gift from Heaven!

NARRATOR: (*Speaking for Ofune*) Now I'll show my lord how constant is a woman's heart!

Step by step, she makes her way on tottering legs.
Finally she swings the drumstick trying to strike the drum,
But her hand will not reach. She stands on tiptoe,
Sways and falters, tries again, then leaps up, and
Boom! sounds the drum, as Ofune sinks to the floor.

In runs Rokuzō, astonished by the sound.

(*Musical buildup accompanies the narrator's description. As Ofune strikes the drum, the stage revolves clockwise, bringing the drum pavilion downstage toward the audience. Rokuzō enters from upstage right.*)

[The following is the ending in the kabuki *version of the play.]*

ROKUZŌ: What in the name of . . . ! Who told you you could do that?

NARRATOR: He seizes her, but she struggles and pushes him aside.
Again she swings the drumstick overhead.
"Hold on! Give me that!" cries Rokuzō.
From behind, he snatches at the stick,
But Ofune will not give it up.
Though wounded, she grapples with him furiously
And breaks away.
How resolute a woman's force of will.

(*The two struggle, and again Ofune strikes the drum.*)

In the confusion she pounds the drum,
And pounds upon it again.
No sooner has Rokuzō seized the stick
And thrown it into the river
Than Ofune draws the sword at his waist
And stabs him.
With a sharp cry, he staggers back.

(*During the struggle, Ofune stabs Rokuzō in the shoulder. She poses.*)

He pounces on her, but again she stabs him.
Swinging the empty scabbard, she beats upon the drum.
He tries to stop her, yet she pounds it in a dying frenzy.
But now chill winds of death are blowing over their lives,
And there beneath the swinging drum, they breathe their last.

(*The struggle continues until Ofune's second thrust at Rokuzō, this time his abdomen. They fall dead together.*)

Indifferent to grief, Tonbei calls out.

TONBEI: Hey! Rokuzō! (*The music tempo quickens as Tonbei leaps into a boat and pushes on a boat pole. He moves as stage assistants pull his boat from stage right to center stage, where suddenly a white-feathered arrow flies in and strikes him in the neck. He writhes in agony, and dies as the music rises.*)

NARRATOR: How strange! How terrifying!

(*Curtain, as wave music continues.*)

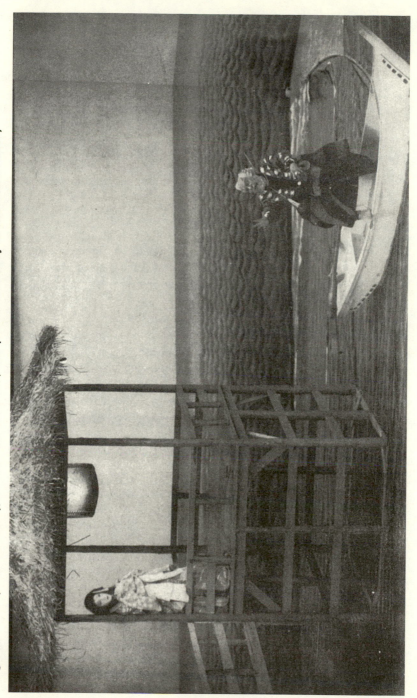

Figure 17.1 Tonbei (Ichikawa Ennosuke II [En'o]), standing in his boat, right, is struck in the neck by an arrow, as his daughter, Ofune (Kataoka Gadō), stands near the drum, left. (Photo: Courtesy of Samuel L. Leiter.)

[The conclusion of the play in the original puppet version follows.²⁵]

ROKUZŌ: Who told you you could do that?

NARRATOR: He grabs her, and as he struggles to push her aside,
Out rushes Tonbei, who nimbly leaps into a moored boat.
He pushes on the sculling oar, and off he rows.
Above, Ofune strains to rise,

OFUNE: Stop! Listen to me!

NARRATOR: In loud tones she calls out, but he is heedless.
Again she swings the drumstick.

ROKUZŌ: Hold on! Give me that!

NARRATOR: From behind, Rokuzō snatches the stick away,
But from his waist Ofune draws his sword and stabs him.
Head over heels from the railing, into the river he topples,
Landing with a splash of spray.
Above him, Ofune grabs the only thing she can
And wildly swings the scabbard Rokuzō has dropped.
Again and yet again she pounds the drum.
Racing against its echoes, Tonbei leans with a grunt upon his oar.
And Rokuzō, ignoring his wound,
And heedless of the current's waves,
Strikes out arm over arm through the familiar water.
Soon now, Ofune is to breathe her last.
Much more her yearning love than that of the serpent of old
Which crossed Hitaka River!²⁶
Far greater her grief at parting
Than that on Scarf-Waving Peak!²⁷
What lingers as her life ebbs away is the drum,
Sounding in ever-slower cadence, to her ears ever more remote.
And far in the distance across the river
Tonbei, rowing with all his might,
Successfully beaches his craft.
He leaps to the sand and breaks into a run.
From the shadows of the shore a loud voice hails him.

YOSHIMINE: Yaaa Ya! Here I am, Nitta Kotarō Yoshimine! Wait a
minute, you!

NARRATOR: Tonbei jerks to a halt. There erect stands Yoshimine.

YOSHIMINE: None of my brother's enemies living today will go unpunished. Nothing can save you now! In appreciation of your daughter's kindness I spared your miserable life, but since you are so reckless as to chase after me, you are beyond my pardon!

NARRATOR: He draws his sword.

TONBEI: Only a fool goes looking for trouble! Since you've told me who you are, your fate is sealed!

NARRATOR: Swords clanging, they clash in heated combat.
Somehow Tonbei stumbles;
Yoshimine seizes his chance and pounces on him.
Holding him down, he prepares to cut off his head,
When in comes Rokuzō, dragging Utena by the hand.

ROKUZŌ: Saaa! Yoshimine! Kill the old man and you'll have only a memory of this woman!

NARRATOR: He tightens his grip on Utena.
Startled, Yoshimine relaxes his hold.
Seeing his chance, Tonbei shifts, leaps up,
Then kicks and beats Yoshimine.

TONBEI: Here, Rokuzō! My daughter's two enemies,[28] these here!
Let's make them die slowly!

NARRATOR: With oar and boat pole they begin to flail the pair.
Yoshimine cries out in anguished desperation.
At the top of her tormented voice, Utena calls upon
The hounds of hell[29] in all their power to rush out
And stop them! But now, just as they are resigned to death,
In an instant, how strange! who can say from where they came!
Two white-fletched arrows shoot through the two men's throats.
Their breath cut short, they die.

UTENA: You weren't hurt?

YOSHIMINE: You're safe? Now who has saved us?

NARRATOR: He pulls out the arrows.

YOSHIMINE: Oh, wait! These are the family treasures, the two arrows called Water Destroyer and Army Destroyer!

NARRATOR: As there he stands astonished,
Utena's keen eyes spy something.

UTENA: It looks like a strip of paper on that arrow.

YOSHIMINE: Yes. Ah . . . hmm. . . . (*reading from paper*) "Since these two arrows were stolen, I have grieved at the decline of the house of Nitta. Through the divine powers generated by my fervent prayers, they have returned from the hands of my enemies. He who sends them to you is Nitta Kotarō Yoshioki . . ."

NARRATOR: Without finishing, Yoshimine bursts into laughter.

YOSHIMINE: Ha ha ha ha ha! So, even though he was killed, it is clear that my brother's ghost still thinks of his family. How can I repay this kindness and compassion for his younger brother? Now that these two arrows are once again in my hands, I will raise an imperial army, crush the rebels, and dispel my brother's grief. These arrows, passed on from generation to generation, are the treasures of our family and stand guard over the fortunes of its warriors. Ha ha ha! Thank you brother, thank you.

NARRATOR: He dances for joy. Even in such dismal days as ours,
People yet make pilgrimages to the Nitta Shrine
For arrows as protective charms; and this is their history.
But now, on the river's distant shore,
Torches and lanterns glitter forth, transforming night to day.

YOSHIMINE: Aha, I see that the enemy constable's men are advancing on us. Let us get away while yet there's time.

NARRATOR: Hastily, together they flee and soon make good
their escape.
Moments later, Takezawa Kenmotsu
And minions by the score crowd on a skiff.

TAKEZAWA: Listen to me, all of you! You've heard the signal drum that I instructed Tonbei to sound, and that indicates that the fugitives have been captured; but we've waited and waited, and no further news has come. I'm sure Tonbei has bungled the job. We'll go after them and stop them! Hurry, men!

NARRATOR: At his command, the men lean with a will
Upon their boat poles and head for mid-river.
Then, strange! Suddenly a wind comes up.
The waves stand on end, and the overcast thickens.
Thunderbolts rend the sky,
While in the heavens sounds a terrible rumbling.

The clouds become more fearsome.
The troops within the boat, as well as captain and crew,
All blanch with terror.
But dauntless Takezawa never flinches.
He pounds the side of the craft and rises up erect.

VOICE: Hold! Hear me, Takezawa Kenmotsu Hidetoki! Know that Nitta Sahyōenosuke Yoshioki, who died through your treachery, appears here now to take his revenge! Mark well!

NARRATOR: Beneath the voice the waves arch high like hillocks,
And the boat is heaved up, pitched down. Even the boastful
Takezawa trembles in every limb, his face pales.
A yet more powerful blast of wind
Now splinters the boat, scattering wide the fragments
And sending its burden of men to the seaweed depths.
But sturdy Takezawa dives beneath the waves and swims on.
Above him a black cloud cloaks the sky,
And from it, girt in armor, fearlessly astride his charger,
Emerges the form of Yoshioki. He stretches forth his hand
And seems to grasp the head of Takezawa.
He splits it at a blow!

YOSHIOKI: Now I am revenged!

NARRATOR: At the sound of his voice, ghosts of the ten soldiers
Who died on board the boat with Yoshioki
Are vivid in the heavens, watching as protectors of their lord.
The thunder subsides, the waves and wind are at peace.
And even unto our own age we revere in gratitude
The shrine of the Ten Horsemen[30]
Whose divine virtues stand as guardians of our fate.

(*Curtain*)

Notes

I would like to register my appreciation to Professor Edward Seidensticker, who read the original manuscript and suggested a number of improvements. Any errors or infelicities that remain, of course, are my own.

1. See Donald Keene, *Chūshingura: The Treasury of Loyal Retainers* (New York: Columbia University Press, 1971), 23–24, 81 ff.
2. Hiraga's age is disputed. I am following Teruoka Yasutaka, *Kinsei Bungaku no*

Tenbō (A view of premodern literature) (Tokyo: Meiji Shoin, 1953), 255–256, who is persuasive in setting his age at death at fifty-two. Since Hiraga's death in early January 1780 is well attested (notably by the famous scholar of Western studies, Sugita Gempaku, who wrote the epitaph for Hiraga's tombstone), this would make his year of birth 1728. For Sugita's epitaph, see Kimura Mokurō, *Gesakusha Kō Hoi* (Thoughts on fiction writers: Supplement):Tokyo: Kunimoto Shuppansha, 1925), 23–25. I have converted Hiraga's dates from their lunar calculation to the Western equivalent.

3. It might be noted, as an interesting sidelight on differing regional tastes in eighteenth-century Japan, that the malevolent character of Tonbei proved too overpowering for playgoers in the Osaka area. When *Yaguchi* was later presented to Osaka audiences, the role was rewritten so that Tonbei repented his evil ways. See Uzuki Hiroshi, "Hiraga Gennai no Gikyoku" (The plays of Hiraga Gennai), *Kokubungaku Kenkyū* (Studies in Japanese literature) 1 (October 1949), 46.

4. The account of Yoshioki's death is in Book 33 of the *Taiheiki*. See Gotō Tanji and Okami Masao, eds., *Taiheiki*, vol. 36 in *Nihon koten bungaku taisei* (Compilation of Japanese literature) (Tokyo: Iwanami Shoten, 1962), 268–271.

5. Interestingly, all of these features found in the original puppet play were successfully incorporated into an English-language *kabuki* production of *Yaguchi* directed by Leonard Pronko and performed in 1967 at Pomona College in Claremont, California.

6. *Shinrei Yaguchi no Watashi*. The text used for the translation of the *kabuki* version is in *Kabuki Meisaku Sen* (Selected *kabuki* masterpieces), ed. Toita Yasuji, 15 vols. (Tokyo: Sōgensha, 1956), vii, 23–45. The best and most helpfully annotated text of the original puppet play is that edited by Nakamura Yukihiko in *Fūrai Sanjin Shū* (Fūrai Sanjin [Hiraga Gennai] anthology), vol. 55 of *Nihon Koten Bungaku Taikei* (Compilation of classical Japanese literature) (Tokyo: Iwanami Shoten,1961), 380–397. Fūrai Sanjin was the pen name Hiraga used for most of his prose writings.

7. Rokugō River is an older name for the lower reaches of the Tama River. It flows into Tokyo Bay along the southern boundary of modern Tokyo, just north of Yokohama. In the early seventeenth century there was a bridge over the river at the town of Yaguchi, but this was washed away during the 1680s. Thereafter, and at the time the play was written, the crossing was made by ferry.

8. Taken from a poem by the noted thirteenth-century poet Fujiwara no Teika and included in his collection *Shūi Gosō* (Meager gleanings) (comp. 1233). In the original poem, the last line reads: "The village along the Tama River." See *Fujiwara no Teika Zenkashū Sakui* (Complete index to the poetry of Fujiwara no Teika), ed. Akahane Shuku (Tokyo: Kasama Shoin, 1973), 37 (No. 1292).

9. In folk tales, the palace of the Dragon King at the bottom of the sea. One of its inhabitants is the beautiful Princess Oto.

10. The unit of gold currency during the Tokugawa period. Though the purchasing power of the *ryō* fluctuated considerably throughout the period, even one of the money packets that Tonbei produces here constitutes a sizable sum.

11. Gambler Tonbei's description that follows of the struggle between Yoshioki and Takauji is couched in gambling terminology. "Big game" and "gambling house," for example, mean, respectively, "major battle" and "battlefield." "Greater resources" means "larger army," and so on.

12. Eda Hangan is an officer serving the enemy forces led by Ashikaga Takauji.

Takezawa is also a member of the enemy camp, but earlier in the play he has become, through deception, one of Yoshioki's trusted lieutenants. It was Takezawa's duplicity that led to Yoshioki's death by ambush at Yaguchi crossing.

13. The oar symbolizes Tonbei's profession as a boatman, though now it is his underling Rokuzō who must handle the ferry; the straw raincoat, typical foul weather garb for peasants, is probably a reminder to Tonbei of his lowly origins.

14. I have translated this line in a straightforward manner. In the original (both for the puppets and *kabuki*), there is a rather indelicate play on the word *fune* (boat), providing a double allusion both to Tonbei's stratagem of scuttling the ferry bearing Yoshioki and to Tonbei's attractive daughter Ofune, who is present on stage during this ribaldry.

15. This is the speech as it occurs in the original puppet version of the play. In *kabuki* the speech is somewhat longer and more erotic, but it does not lend itself easily to translation because of extensive and complicated wordplay.

16. All of these places were unlicensed prostitution districts in the city of Edo. The city's only licensed quarter was the famous Yoshiwara.

17. The daughter of the owner of a teahouse near a shrine in Edo. Osen's beauty won her such fame throughout the city during the 1760s and 1770s that her likeness appeared on everything from wood-block prints and book illustrations to small towels and children's dolls, and people were said to have thronged to the nearby shrine just to catch a glimpse of her. Mention of her name here contributes both to the contemporary sense of the play and to its distinctive Edo flavor.

18. Dōnen was a loyal soldier in Yoshioki's army, who became a priest after Yoshioki's death. In an earlier scene of Act IV, he saved Yoshimine and Utena from ruffians who were attempting to turn them over to their enemies for a reward.

19. The two family heirlooms stolen from Yoshimine in Act I.

20. An adumbration of Ofune's love for Yoshimine, which she expresses shortly.

21. A famous temple in the Asakusa district of Edo dedicated to the goddess Kannon.

22. A variation on a line from the *Genji Monagatari* (The tale of Genji). See Arthur Waley's translation (New York: Modern Library, 1960), 32.

23. A banner bearing the Nitta family's crest: a white disc containing a black bar.

24. An allusion to a passage in the Lotus Sutra, *Hokkekyō Daikōza* (Lectures on the Lotus Sutra), ed. Kobayashi Ichirō, 13 vols. (Tokyo: Heibonsha, 1938), viii, 324.

25. For the original puppet play text on which this translation is based, see Nakamura, *Fūrai Sanjin Shū*, 394–397.

26. An allusion to the nō play *Dōjōji* (Dōjō Temple), in which a woman is spurned by a Buddhist priest with whom she has fallen in love. She follows him, changing into a serpent in order to cross the Hitaka River. In *Dōjōji*, however, the woman in her serpent transformation takes revenge on the priest by killing him. For a translation, see Donald Keene, ed., *Twenty Plays of the Nō Theatre* (New York: Columbia University Press, 1970), 240–252.

27. An allusion to a story and a poem in the eighth-century anthology *Man'yōshū* [Collection of ten tousand leaves. Ed.], which tell of a court lady so saddened by the departure of her lover that she climbed a tall hill and waved farewell with her scarf until his ship was lost to view. See *The Man'yōshū* (Tokyo: Nippon Gakujutsu Shinkōkai, 1940), 261.

28. The meaning of this line is unclear, but it may reflect Tonbei's view that since Yoshimine and Utena set in motion the events that led to Ofune's death (even though at the hands of Tonbei himself), they are her real killers, hence her enemies.

29. In the Japanese text it is Gozu and Mezu upon whom Utena calls. Gozu was a creature with a human body and the head of an enraged bull; Mezu had a human body with the head of a fierce horse. The jailers of the Buddhist hell often had quite specific duties. Thus Gozu's task was to torment those who during their lifetime had eaten beef (a breach of Buddhist dietary laws); the victims of Mezu were guilty of mistreating horses.

30. One of the sub-shrines of Yaguchi.

18

Kabuki and the Elizabethan Theatre

Leonard C. Pronko

There are probably few directors who would want to attempt an archaeological reconstruction in their productions of Elizabethan plays. But we are all interested in finding some style that would give to our performances a spirit as exciting as that the Elizabethans must have found in their theatre. A great deal has been written on the controversial subject of acting styles in the late sixteenth and early seventeenth centuries, but ultimately scholars must admit that there is little that can be proved about that style aside from suggestions that it was indeed stylized or formal (but how?) rather than realistic (in what sense?). Twentieth-century interpretations of these terms, and of others used by writers referring to productions of William Shakespeare, Christopher Marlowe, John Ford, and so on will necessarily be colored by our own understanding—and by half a century of naturalistic bias. [This essay was written in 1967. Ed.] It seems to me that a fruitful approach to the problem might be taken through a living theatrical tradition that arose from historical conditions somewhat similar to those of Tudor England, and—if we can trust reports as they come down to us—that exhibits astonishing similarities to much of what we are told actually took place on the English stage three or four hundred years ago. I am referring, of course, to that form of popular theatre known as *kabuki*, a form that, like Elizabethan drama, mingles hair-raising realism with extreme formalism, low farce with high seriousness.

I am not suggesting that we should follow slavishly the styles of *kabuki*, dressing our actors in Japanese garb, striking the same kind of poses, or using movements that have developed through a way of life utterly different from ours. What I am proposing is that a close study of the *kabuki* theatre can wean us away from a style of presentation that is perhaps more fundamentally realistic than we realize. Taking our cue from a theatre that attempts to appeal to the whole person,[1] we might actually achieve a more "authentic" Elizabethan performance. With this in mind, I should like to point out certain parallels in historical background and some striking similarities in techniques that will, I believe, suggest to the imaginative director fresh and exciting perspectives on the production of Elizabethan plays.

The Historical Moment

Kabuki arose about 1603 and reached its zenith in the late seventeenth and early eighteenth centuries. About one hundred years later than the Elizabethan drama, it reflects a similar historical moment. Tokugawa Japan, like Tudor England, presented a somewhat feudal façade, but there was a sense of change, a bustling activity behind it. It introduced to Japan a long period of unity and peace and brought with it a growing sense of national identity. A vigorous commercial life developed, giving the nation greater economic stability than ever before, but at the same time making the nobility dependent upon the growing merchant class. Indeed, despite clearly defined classes and a wide breach between noble and commoner, the wealthy middle class began to play an important role in the life of the community. It was largely in response to the needs of a wealthy, leisured middle class that *kabuki* developed.

That sense of exuberance that we think of as typically Elizabethan finds its parallel in Japan in the development of popular arts, the importance of the geisha, and the amusement quarters as a part of life and as a central focus in the literature. Although Japan was mostly closed to foreign trade, the Tokugawa period is marked by a growing interest in things foreign, and by 1720 the ban on Western books was lifted. We must not forget these elements, which formed a kind of balance to the highly formalized life we tend to think of as Japanese. It may well be that a dynamic tension created by a pull between freedom and hierarchy, the new and the old, was largely responsible for the flowering of the arts in that most brilliant of Japanese periods known as the Genroku (1688–1704) (figure 18.1).

A similar tension was achieved in Elizabethan England. Elizabethan scholar E.M.W. Tillyard reminds us that Sir Walter Raleigh was a theologian as well as a discoverer, that sermons were as much a part of everyday Elizabethan life as was bearbaiting, and ascribes the greatness of Elizabethan England to the fact that "it contained so much of new without bursting the noble form of the old order."[2]

The blending of the old and the new, the refined and the barbaric, is reflected in the life and theatre of the Tokugawa Japanese and the Elizabethan Englishman: unthinkably cruel punishments for what strike us as rather mi-

Figure 18.1 **Left: Christopher Marlowe's J***ew of Malta* **as produced at Pomona College, Leonard Pronko, director. The messenger of the Turkish prince poses on the *hanamichi* in a defiant attitude. Right: A similar pose struck by the *aragoto*-style *oshimodoshi* (demon queller) character in several *kabuki* works, including one called *Oshimodoshi* and belonging to the famed *Kabuki Jūhachiban* (Eighteen famous *kabuki* plays). (Photos: Courtesy of Leonard Pronko.)**

nor offenses, indifference to the suffering of others, enjoyment of the refinements of poetry and ceremony, often in proximity to the pleasures of bearbaiting and prostitution. Before reaching artistic maturity, the *kabuki* theatre sometimes served as a front to prostitution, while in London the theatres were relegated to the south bank of the Thames, near the infamous Stews. The famous actor Edward Alleyn seems to symbolize the era in England: Creator of Marlowe's major characters, he made much of his fortune by leasing land for bear-baiting, and invested it in the founding of a college.

Prostitution, violence, bloodshed, vengeance, find an echo in many of the major Elizabethan and *kabuki* plays. Refinement and barbarism, both occasionally beyond modern taste, shock us by their juxtaposition in Marlowe, Shakespeare, Ford, and John Webster, as they do in works of Chikamatsu Monzaemon Takeda Izumo. Both theatres are characterized by the historical or legendary raised to the level of the heroic, the encounter between natural and supernatural worlds, insoluble problems ending in death jostled by scenes of the utmost gaiety.

The Actors

The early Elizabethan actor was more versatile than his modern counterpart. Like the *kabuki* actor, he was a dancer and an acrobat as well. "In letters dealing with English players on the Continent in the 1580's," theatre historian Bernard Beckerman tells us, "acting is always linked with dancing, vaulting and tumbling."[3] An Englishman visiting in Germany comments that the Germans, "not understanding a word [the actors] said, both men and women, flocked wonderfully to see their gestures and action, rather than hear them, speaking English which they understood not."[4] Such an attitude suggests that there was something worth watching more than mere walking and handling of objects. As late as 1592, a man writes from Nuremberg, "The English comedians have wonderful music and are so skilled at tumbling and dancing that I have never heard nor seen the like."[5] I have found no indications that Alleyn and Richard Burbage [Shakespeare's star actor. Ed.] were tumblers or dancers, but it is interesting to note that they were part of a theatre which did include dancing and tumbling, and that we may see just such a theatre today, since *kabuki*, unlike modern acting, has not divorced itself from its early traditions.

Whether Alleyn and Burbage and the other major actors of their day tumbled and danced or not, they were at any rate masters of a formal acting style that is lost today. Beckerman characterizes their style as romantic, Alfred Harbage as formal, while Bertram Joseph feels quite certain that they employed the gestures common in contemporary rhetorical delivery, perhaps exaggerating them for the needs of the theatre. A broad playing style must have been demanded by poorly lighted theatres, as well as by the public in the pit. Theatre historian Ashley Thorndike believes that "every means of facial expression and gesture should be employed in the depiction of emotion, making the action somewhat more intense than in the modern theatre."[6] Alois Nagler, quoting a report of a performance of *Othello* by the King's Men at Oxford in 1610, describes how impressed one spectator was by Desdemona's death, especially when she lay in bed, moving the spectators to pity "solely by her face."[7] Such an ability recalls the many occasions on which a *kabuki* actor, for perhaps minutes on end, will register emotions by contraction of the facial muscles and movement of the eyes, achieving effects of great pathos. It was no doubt this gift that caused French audiences in 1900 to rhapsodize over the "dying" of Sadda Yacco [Kawakami Sadayakko (1871–1946), Japanese actress who toured abroad in the early twentieth century. Ed.], who, they claimed, died even better than Sarah Bernhardt.

The *kabuki* actor, using every facet of his body and voice to portray character and emotion, presents himself quite frankly as a theatrical creation on a stage before an audience. Basing all his movements, even the most realistic, on dance, the actor transforms every moment of the drama into a visually artistic experience. The presentational aspect of the Elizabethan actor's performance was underlined by the form of his stage, but in addition to this he might use such techniques as symmetrical blocking or speaking directly to the audience, delivering his lines facing toward the public rather than toward his interlocutor onstage. Moreover, he tended to play not so much *in* a setting as *against* it. All of this might well be said of the *kabuki* actor, who still enjoys a stage structure and type of decor that thrust him toward the audience. The bridge stage, or *hanamichi*, which in important scenes, entrances, and exits brings the actor into close intimacy with the audience, is an acting area of very special strength and emotional appeal. It has not yet been used significantly in the West, despite the advice of French playwright Paul Claudel, who many years ago said of *kabuki*: "It is not without analogy with Shakespearian drama, and the revolving stage and particularly the bridge or *hanamichi,* which traverses the auditorium and permits unusual effects of distance and surprise, give it advantages which we would do well to imitate."[8]

Symbolic Forms and Colors

If the Elizabethan actor gave more importance than we do to the meaning of movement and gesture, it was not simply because he enjoyed picturesque movement—although this is a justifiable reason in the theatre—but because he believed that the inner person was manifested in a visible way. The hunchback was not to be pitied but feared, for a disfigured body was a sign of a disfigured soul. "Man carried the mark of his class and his nature, in his walk, talk, features and costume."[9] Certainly, the twentieth-century theatre is aware of this, but perhaps out of fear of exaggeration or overemphasis it often fails to show such marks in any other way than through speech, and occasionally through makeup and a manner of walking. The *kabuki* stage, harboring no such fears, gives each man or woman (courtesan, peasant, princess, samurai, merchant, demon) a different way of walking, a distinctive makeup (white-face, brown-face, red lines, black lines, purple lines, high eyebrows, no eyebrows, etc.), varying ways of using the voice (falsetto, broken falsetto, deep bass, musical intonations, guttural sputterings, etc.), and diverse colors and forms of costumes to suggest class, character, and feelings.

In an informative study of costume in Elizabethan drama, costume specialist Marie Channing Linthicum describes in some detail the many symbolic values of color used on the Tudor stage. Not only costume color was indicative of character. Beards and hair as well might be changed to show changes in emotions:

If evidence of the dramas may be credited, beards were dyed to harmonize with costumes or to reflect the mood of the wearer, . . . happiness over the return of a favorite might be expressed by dyeing the beard carnation "speckled with green and russet." Catherine-pear-colored beards indicated a wicked disposition, and cane, straw, French crown and Abraham-color beards had each a language.[10] [Costume specialist Rebecca Cunningham suggests that Catherine-pear-colored is yellow-green; cane, straw, and French crown are shades of yellow or brown; and Abraham-color is possibly gray, red, or red-brown. Ed.]

The practice of changing costume or makeup to express changes in character or emotion is a familiar one to the *kabuki* spectator. An actor who has been disguised as a commoner but has finally revealed his true noble identity may turn his back to the audience in order to pencil in the high, thick eyebrows that symbolize noble blood. An even more common practice is that very exciting moment of costume changing known as *hikinuki*. The actor's assistant pulls several threads that basted the actor's top kimono together. At a climactic moment, the assistant grabs the costume at the shoulders or sleeves while the actor steps forward into a pose, suddenly revealed in a completely different costume.

Lavish costumes immediately impress foreigners viewing *kabuki*. Accustomed to the relatively dull clothing worn on the realistic stage, they are unaware perhaps that the Western theatre was once similarly lavish in its use of costume. "No stage ever cared more for fine clothes than the Elizabethans," claims Thorndike, "or lavished on dress a larger portion of its expenses."[11] He points out that authenticity was not sought, but rather display. The Elizabethans would indeed be shocked at some of our modern-dress performances of Shakespeare, for although Elizabethan actors often wore contemporary clothing, it was of a magnitude almost unknown to us: ruffs and farthingales became so wide that they finally had to be regulated by law.

The Women's Roles

Our inability to conceive seriously of boys playing women's roles indicates not lack of imagination but lack of custom. Even as late as the Restoration, men were playing the parts of women in England. Thorndike records Samuel Pepys's opinion that in John Fletcher's *Loyal Subject* the actor Edward Kynaston "made the loveliest lady that ever I saw in my life."[12] And promoter John Downes, Thorndike tells us, declared that "it has since been disputable among the judicious whether any woman that succeeded him [Kynaston. Ed.] so sensibly touched the audience as he." If a man could be lovely, feminine, and touching in a female role, it indicates not only his own skill, but the conventions of an audience that was willing to accept this particular kind of stylization.

While it would seem absurd to advocate the use of men to play women's parts today in the West, I think it is important for us to bear in mind that a stylized performance, such as this kind of impersonation requires, is not necessarily a cold, "alienated" performance that does not involve the audience. Just as the *kabuki* actor of female roles (*onnagata*) can affect his audience, the Elizabethan boy could move his viewers to tears.

The English critic Kenneth Tynan goes so far as to suggest that Lady Macbeth is "basically a man's role" and that "it is probably a mistake to cast a woman [in the part] at all."[13] Whether we would go so far or not, we must agree that the *onnagata* can teach us something about what it means to be feminine, for his movements are more graceful than those of many women in everyday life, even in Japan where women are noted for grace and delicacy. He can also remind us of two Renaissance customs that we have failed to use in our modern productions of Elizabethan plays and that might add to their visual drama: chopines and lead white. Like the high-ranking courtesan or *oiran* in the *kabuki* world, the Renaissance courtesan (and sometimes the "nice" woman as well) would sometimes strut about in chopines, or thick-soled shoes, which added to her height if not to her grace. Rising from six to fifteen inches, the higher variety of chopines necessitated that the lady (like the *oiran*) be accompanied constantly by someone upon whose shoulder she might lean in order not to lose her balance. Again like the women of *kabuki*, the Elizabethan beauty desired nothing so much as a milk-white skin and often destroyed her complexion to achieve it. The standard cosmetic for this purpose was lead white, which soon marked the skin and required ever thicker coats of white paint.[14] The white, highlighted with vermilion lips and rouged cheeks and bosom, might help us today to create some of those theatrical monsters that we have forgotten and that Jean Genet has resuscitated with such effect in his later plays (figures 18.2, 18.3).

Production Techniques

Similar performing conditions bred other resemblances between *kabuki* and Elizabethan drama. The fact that short rehearsal periods were the rule, and a fixed group of actors was used in play after play, meant that scenic conventions developed, a kind of repertoire of devices, which probably would be handled in a similar way from play to play. The manner of handling asides, monologues, disguises, observation scenes, and the like was probably readily understood by the experienced actor so that a minimum of time was needed

Figure 18.2 *Terakoya:* A group pose from the *kabuki* masterpiece. Emotions and attitudes are often suggested through such group poses. (Photo: Courtesy of Leonard Pronko.)

for rehearsing the technical aspects of such a scene. *Kabuki* exhibits a similar repertoire of devices, including the beautifully choreographed murder scene which is both aesthetically satisfying and spine-chilling and the stylized fight scene, once again a kind of dance in which little or no physical contact is made and the visual effect is heightened by an attack on our nerves by sharp wooden clappers. Head-inspection scenes, suicide, recitation of off-stage events accompanied by a pantomimed description of the action, travel-scene dance duets, and pantomime scenes are other devices common to the *kabuki* stage.

A convention arising from the daytime performances of both theatres is that of evoking night by means other than actual lighting: by dialogue in the Elizabethan theatre and by the movements of the actors in *kabuki*. Today, of course, we have recourse to lighting, and even the *kabuki*, in an effort at modernity, will occasionally darken the stage for a night scene.

The two different manners of dealing with this problem are symptomatic of a very basic difference between *kabuki* and Elizabethan theatre: the former stresses movement, dance, gesture, color, music, largely discounting literary

Figure 18.3 *Jew of Malta:* **The governor of Malta threatens Barabas. (Photo: Courtesy of Leonard Pronko.)**

or poetic values of the text, while the latter gives more importance to the text than it does to visual and musical values of presentation. It is possible, however, that scholars largely concerned with literary values of the texts have tended to give them more importance than the Elizabethans did. Since the contemporaries of Shakespeare and Marlowe were often lax in their preservation and handling of manuscripts (to say nothing of their revisions of scripts in performance), we are justified in wondering whether the Elizabethans attached to the texts the importance that we do today. If the acting traditions of Burbage had come down to us in an unbroken line, as the *kabuki* techniques have since the middle of the seventeenth century, perhaps we would be better able to determine whether we are putting undue emphasis on the text (figure 8.4).

Precisely because of this fundamental difference between the literary (as we have been taught to believe) theatre of the Elizabethans and the nonliterary *kabuki* theatre,[15] it seems to me desirable that we attempt to find some way of harmonizing the two perspectives in one "total" theatre. In combining the highly theatrical and sensual techniques of *kabuki* with the more literary virtues of poetry, philosophy, and psychology that are offered by the great Elizabethan texts (to say nothing of their own theatrical and sensual

Figure 8.4 **Left:** *Yoshitsune Senbon Zakura:* **The defeated general Tomomori poses heroically with an anchor before he kills himself by throwing the anchor, which he has tied to himself, into the sea. Right:** *Jew of Malta:* **Friar Jacomo poses with his staff as he is about to strike and kill Friar Bernardine. (Photos: Courtesy of Leonard Pronko.)**

values), we might hope to achieve a maximum of appeal to the senses, the emotions, the imagination, and to our atrophied sense of childish wonder, at the same time arriving at a profound, and perhaps painful, perception of human truth.

Notes

1. *Kabuki* appeals not only to the whole person, but to people of all classes as well. Although it arose as a people's theatre, *kabuki* constantly attracted the nobility, who attended in disguise, had love affairs with the actors, and were reprimanded and even restrained by law.

2. E.M.W. Tillyard, *The Elizabethan World Picture* (New York: Chatto and Windus, 1943+), 8.

3. Bernard Beckerman, *Shakespeare at the Globe, 1599–1609* (New York: Collier, 1962), 123–124.

4. Quoted in Alois Maria Nagler, *Shakespeare's Stage*, translated by Ralph Manheim (New Haven: Yale University Press, 1958), 37.

5. Ibid., 83.

6. Ashley H. Thorndike, *Shakespeare's Theatre* (New York: Macmillan, 1960), 403.

7. Nagler, *Shakespeare's Stages.*

8. "Une promenade à travers la littérature japonaise," in Paul Claudel, *Oeuvres complètes*, vol. IV (Paris: Gallimard, 1952), 406–407.

9. Beckerman, *Shakespeare at the Globe,* 14.

10. Marie Channing Linthicum, *Costume in the Drama of Shakespeare and His Contemporaries* (Oxford: Clarendon Press, 1936), 14.

11. Thorndike, *Shakespeare's Theatre,* 394.

12. Ibid., 372.

13. Kenneth Tynan, *Tynan on Theatre* (Hammondsworth: Penguin, 1964), p. 108.

14. See the enlightening chapters in Elizabeth Burton, *The Pageant of Elizabethan England* (New York: Scribner's, 1958), 235–242, and Carroll Camden, *The Elizabethan Woman* (Houston: Elsevier, 1952), 178–186.

15. Actually it is inaccurate to call the *kabuki* nonliterary, since the plays of the greatest Japanese dramatist, Chikamatsu Monzaemon, possess no mean literary value; but they are the exception rather than the rule.

Part 3

Surveying the Field

19

Kabuki: Changes and Prospects: An International Symposium

James R. Brandon

In the midst of a busy late-autumn season, more than 120 *kabuki* scholars and critics gathered for three days at the Edo-Tokyo Museum to explore the present and future status of *kabuki* as an international theatre art. The occasion was the international symposium entitled *"Kabuki*: Changes and Prospects," sponsored by the Tokyo National Research Institute of Cultural Properties (Tōkyō Kokuritsu Bunkazai Kenkyūjō) and held November 12–14, 1996. This was a unique occasion, and I eagerly made special arrangements to attend all the sessions.

The international significance of the symposium was made clear before the sessions began by the fact that among the eighteen scheduled speakers, nine were invited from abroad, including scholars from France, England, Germany, Switzerland, Austria, New Zealand, and the United States. For these participants it was a very long trip, indeed, a trip they happily embarked upon because of the rare nature of the symposium. This was the first general international meeting on *kabuki* held in Japan. Among important Japanese scholars and critics who spoke were professors Kawatake Toshio, Hattori Yukio, and Watanabe Tamotsu, and critics Nakamura Tetsurō and Ōzasa Yoshio.

In addition to the invited speakers, more than a hundred general participants attended the sessions, completely filling the spacious conference room of the Edo-Tokyo Museum. Highlighting the importance of the conference, some general participants came from as far as Australia. A number were graduate students from foreign countries, studying *kabuki* and other Japanese theatre arts at universities in Tokyo, Kyoto, and Osaka. Presentations were given in Japanese or in English, with simultaneous translation provided in the other language.

Speakers and participants were welcomed at the opening ceremonies on November 12 by Watanabe Akiyoshi, director of the Tokyo National Research Institute of Cultural Properties, who noted that this was the twentieth international symposium on Conservation and Preservation of Cultural Property sponsored by the institute. He observed that while "conservation" and "restoration" are usually used in relation to fine arts and folk crafts, the terms also clearly apply to such traditional theatre arts as *kabuki*. Through its 400-year history, *kabuki* has always adapted to meet the social conditions of its performance. Today, in view of the powerful currents of internationalization that affect all cultural production, the topic of this meeting was especially vital: How will *kabuki* theatre face a changing Japanese culture and a diverse international audience?

Two keynote addresses were given by Kawatake Toshio, professor emeritus of Waseda University and director of the Japan Theatre Association (Nihon Engeki Kyōkai), and by myself. Gamō Satoaki, head of the performance section of the Tokyo National Research Institute of Cultural Properties and chief organizer of the symposium, introduced the two speakers by noting that their talks would raise key issues that would be more closely explored in later presentations and in general discussions. In the first keynote address, "Reflections on *Kabuki* Performance Overseas," Professor Kawatake focused on the vital relation of *kabuki* to its audience. The death of playwright Kawatake Mokuami in 1893 and the Kantō earthquake in 1923 mark, respectively, the beginning of *kabuki* as a "traditional" theatre form and the end of *kabuki*'s plebeian Edo audience. It is common to say that most audiences are attracted to *kabuki* by its spectacle and formal beauty and not the plot or drama, but this is not necessarily so. Today most young Japanese find it difficult to appreciate or understand the traditional, formal aspects of *kabuki* performance. Stated extremely: Japanese and foreign audiences have about the same degree of knowledge about *kabuki*. Audience members who answered questionnaires that were distributed at *kabuki* performances in the United States in 1960 and in Europe in 1965 widely preferred the dramatic plays over the spectacular dances on the program. (In fact in 1960, seventy-nine preferred the play *Kanadehon Chūshingura* (The treasury of loyal retainers; also translated as The forty-seven samurai), while twenty-two preferred the dance *Musume Dōjōji* (The maiden at Dōjō Temple); and in 1965, 561 preferred the drama *Shunkan* (character's name), while 141 preferred *Musume Dōjōji*.) It is necessary today for many Japanese to use earphone guides in order to understand *kabuki*. Workshops, lectures on radio and television, and educational performances for high school and middle school students are increasingly important today to introduce *kabuki* to the general Japanese public.

In the second keynote presentation, "*Kabuki* Performance: Its Value and Use in Western Theatre," I noted that ever since Ichikawa Sadanji II's Russian tour in 1928, *kabuki* has exerted a powerful fascination on Western theatre artists, from Max Reinhardt and Bertolt Brecht before the war to Ariane Mnouchkine in France, and many others, today. Although less well known, small *kabuki* touring troupes had gone abroad nearly thirty years earlier. During the Meiji (1868–1912) and Taishō (1912–1926) periods, these troupes brought *kabuki* to Japanese immigrants living overseas. Small *kabuki* troupes from the Kansai region (Kyoto Osaka) began touring to Hawai'i at least as early as 1893, more than a century ago, and continued through the 1930s. Some actors remained in Hawai'i, establishing a local *kabuki* tradition. In 1924 students of Japanese descent at the University of Hawai'i staged *kabuki* in English for the first time, and since then twenty-six [twenty-seven, as James R. Brandon produced *Summer Festival: Mirror of Osaka* in 2000. Ed.] *kabuki*-style productions have been performed in English by students at the university for large public audiences. The most elaborate production was *The Forty-Seven Samurai* (Kanadehon Chūshingura), directed by Nakamura Matagorō II, which ran for forty performances during a national tour through fourteen states, from Los Angeles, to New York, to Harvard University. Using some of these productions as examples, I noted the characteristics of *kabuki* that appeal to American audiences: powerful, controlled movements and gestures; elaborate stage settings; stunning costumes and makeup; and *kabuki*'s "musicality." Looked at in terms of process, every effort *is* made to replicate classic plays like *Sukeroku Yukari no Edo Zakura* (Sukeroku: Flower of Edo, 1970 and 1995), *Narukami Fudō Kitayama Zakura* (Saint Narukami [often given simply as *Narukami* in English. Ed.], 1973 and 1987), and *Kanjinchō* (The subscription list, 1981), using Japanese performance as models. But even when exact replication is desired, it is not possible. English translation, the bodies and minds of non-Japanese performers, American audiences—all cause the English-language *kabuki* performance to change. Moreover, Western theatre artists may also adapt or "expand" *kabuki*, deliberately altering it. We have written and staged at the University of Hawai'i two "expanded *kabuki*" plays based on *Tōkaidōchū Hizakurige* (A shank's mare tour of the Tōkaidō)—titled *The Road to Kyoto!* (1977) and *The Road to Tokyo!* (1990)—in which story, characterization, and staging devices were handled in new ways. And finally, *kabuki* can be an inspiration to conceive wholly new plays. I wrote the dance-drama *Hoichi the Minstrel* (1981), inspired by the short story *Miminashi Hōichi* (Earless Hōichi, called *Kwaidan* in Lafcadio Hearn's translation). The production was based on general principles derived from *kabuki*—

high energy level, *ma* (pauses), rhythmic cadences, and the division of voice and movement—yet no specific *kabuki* acting techniques were used. Learning *kabuki* acting trains students to value concentration, discipline, and a sense of dedication implicit in the concept of *michi* or *dō* (way). Brief video excerpts from five English-language productions were shown to illustrate these points.

The symposium organizers posed five major issues in separate sessions: *Kabuki*: Its Meeting with the West; *Kabuki* in the Edo Period; Modern *Kabuki*; Present-Day Problems; and Training. Concerning *kabuki*'s meeting with the West, Professor Sang-Kyong Lee, University of Vienna, spoke on the "Influence of *Kabuki* on European Theatre." He drew on a wide range of European documents to illustrate how many seminal twentieth-century theatre artists in Europe turned to Japanese theatre, especially *kabuki*, for inspiration in their own work—Copeau, Craig, Meyerhold, Eisenstein, Dullin, Brecht, Barrault, and Mnouchkine among them. The influences were various: for Craig and Eisenstein, aesthetic principles; for Copeau, dramatic themes; for Meyerhold and Barrault, staging and directing concepts. Since the mid-1960s, Ariane Mnouchkine has drawn on *kabuki* to develop her own style of performance, which emphasizes "body language, acrobatics, visuality, and rhythmic dancelike movements." European theatre artists were strongly attracted to *kabuki*, despite the different social and philosophical backgrounds of the two cultures, because "classical Japanese theatre and modern European theatre have many common characteristics regarding their basic nature."

How could *kabuki* be so influential, Professor Lee asked, when Westerners in the early twentieth century lacked "authentic information"? One answer to this question lies in the four American and European tours that Kawakami Otojirō and his wife Kawakami Sadayakko made in the years 1899–1908. Professor Peter Pantzer, Bonn University, reviewed 200 published accounts in his paper, "Kawakami Otojirō and Sadayakko in Germany, Austria, and Switzerland." These accounts describe the intense interest these performances stimulated in German-speaking areas during four months of 1901–1902. The husband-and-wife team performed at the major theatres in Berlin, Vienna, Budapest, and thirty other cities, drawing more than 100,000 spectators. Day after day they performed standard scenes: Sadayakko danced and died; Otojirō did *tachimawari* (fight scenes) and *seppuku* (suicides). Paradoxically, Sadayakko, who was trained in *nihon buyō* (*kabuki* dance), was praised for the "unbelievable realism" of her death scenes. Other critics saw social and anthropological value, rather than artistic value, in attending the remarkable performances of these rare Japanese theatre artists. One reviewer called their performances "naive" and "utterly lacking in artistry." Regardless of the quality of their stage work, Otojirō and Sadayakko had a strong impact. At the least, their experience in Europe (and, we could add, in America) showed that audiences, critics, and theatre experts were open to this "new" type of theatre from Japan.

Critic Nakamura Tetsurō explored the intersection of Japanese and Western theatre in his presentation, "*Shūzenji Monogatari* as 'Japanese Drama': Reflections on Firmin Gémier's Paris Production of 1927." Nakamura noted that this production, directed by and starring Gémier, was Japanese in "style" and "tone" but was not intended to be a reproduction of Okamoto Kidō's original *shin kabuki* (new *kabuki*) drama. Freely adapted to meet Parisian expectations, it was titled *Le Masque* (Kamen). Gémier incorporated Western music and added new scenes, characters, and dialogue. This is an early example of what theatre scholar Yamaguchi Tarō, in 1929, called *Nihon geki* (Japanese drama). In Nakamura's view, this generic concept includes several types of plays. There are dramas written by foreigners that are about Japan or take their themes from Japanese plays, such as John Masefield's *The Faithful*, based on *Kanadehon Chūshingura,* a German-language *Terakoya* (The village school), David Belasco's *Madam Butterfly*, and Gilbert and Sullivan's *Mikado*. Also, Japanese have rewritten European dramas according to the methods of Japanese theatre, such as Sawada Shōjirō's and Nukada Mutsutomi's 1926 *Shirano Benjūrō*, based on Rostand's *Cyrano de Bergerac*. Then, too, there are performances that "meld together various Japanese stage plots or theatrical arts," of which Denishawn's ballet *Momijigari* and Kimura Kinka's *Jūsansai no Yoritomo* (Yoritomo, age thirteen) are examples. Such intersections occurred at a time when "modern Japan's society reached a certain level and the Japanese could begin to view themselves through foreign eyes." The intersection of Western theatre with *kabuki* during the Meiji and Taishō periods occurred within this overall circumstance. It is clear that the *kabuki* that Chaplin praised as the "greatest theatre art in the world," the *kabuki* which other artists from Europe saw and admired, was not traditional *kabuki* of the Edo period. Was not the *kabuki* that so amazed Western observers in fact a changed, modernized *kabuki,* a *kabuki* that had already absorbed some influences from Western theatre? Discussion followed on these topics guided by session chairpersons Fujinami Takayuki of the Kokuritsu Gekijō (National Theatre of Japan) and Professor Mori Mitsuya.

The session on *kabuki* in the Edo period (1603–1868) was introduced by chairpersons Brian Powell and Takakuwa Izumi. In his presentation, "The Importance of Materials Contained in Western Libraries for the Research of Early *Kabuki*," Professor Thomas Leims, then of the University of Auckland, called attention to three interesting points. Because *kabuki* was born at the turn of the seventeenth century, a time of "intensive Japanese interaction with the Western world," we may reasonably look for some points of contact on both sides, without denying *kabuki*'s "Japaneseness." Leims suggested that the "machines" in the Jesuit Easter play performed in Bungo in 1567, mentioned by brother Ayrez Sanchez to his superiors in Europe, could refer to cylinders painted blue and white to represent waves that were common in theatres in Europe at that time. He noted that the delegates could see almost identical rolling cylinders in the current *kabuki* production of *Imoseyama* (Mount Imo and Mount Se) at the Kokuritsu Gekijo. May this not be one case of early *kabuki* performers borrowing from European stage practice? (In later discussions, it was noted that machines were first seen on *kabuki* stages in the early eighteenth century, nearly a hundred years after Jesuit performances had ceased in Japan.) When Leims examined the original manuscript of Richard Cocks's diary for the latter part of 1616, he found references to weekly, even daily, meetings with female "cabukis" or "caboques" who "played and danced" and often "staid all night." (The latter references are expunged in published editions.) The original manuscript thus shows how numerous were contacts between Europeans and *kabuki* performers in Kyūshū during the *yūjo* (women's) *kabuki* period (1603–1629), thus adding to information for other parts of Japan that are well known to Japanese scholars. A newly discovered love letter to Cocks from the *kabuki* actress Tagano, dated 1619, shows an intimate relationship between the two. Moreover, Leims suggested that Easter and Christmas processions, dances, and plays "provided the ignition for the creation of a new, hitherto unknown, completely different phenomenon within the framework of Japanese performing arts, that is, *kabuki*." In conclusion, Professor Leims showed via photographs the similarity between the body postures, hairdress, and costumes of a seventeenth-century European copperplate and those of the *ayako mai* dance as it is performed in Niigata at the present. How can such a similarity be explained? he asked.

Professor Laurence R. Kominz, Portland State University, spoke on "Parodic Empowerment in *Kabuki*: Playing with Symbols and Icons in *Ya no Ne*." He applied the European concepts of burlesque ("grotesque roughhouse extravagance") and carnival ("destroys any hierarchical distance") to the *aragoto* (roughhouse) play *Ya no Ne* (Arrowhead). In the play, samurai power and strength are parodied by having Soga Gorō wrestle with a *daikon* (large radish) seller who lacks status and, too, through the exaggerated size of the arrow and other properties. *Ya no Ne* is typical of the Ichikawa Danjūrō family line of *aragoto* plays in that it is also a "metadrama"—that is, the audience perceives the "reality" of the actor as well as the reality of Soga Gorō, the character represented by the actor. How can a play like *Ya no Ne*, which Misumi Haruo says is "incoherent and impossible to comprehend," interest audiences? Professor Kominz asked. He suggested that although the plot may be absurd, audiences enjoyed the joking, parodying, slapstick and burlesque, strutting about, and preening that were typical elements of *kabuki* in the city of Edo during the Genroku period (1688–1704).

Professor C. Andrew Gerstle, University of London, addressed the topic "*Kabuki* and the Puppet Theatre: Chikamatsu's *Twins at the Sumida River*." Noting that while puppet texts were regularly published in full at the time of performance, this was rarely true of *kabuki*, for actors wanted to "leave [texts] fluid" and open to alteration. This may be one reason so many puppet texts were adapted to *kabuki* in the mid-eighteenth century (and why *kabuki*, in turn, influenced the puppet theatre). When Chikamatsu Monzaemon wrote *Futago Sumidagawa* (Twins at the Sumida River) in 1720, he placed a *kabuki*-style "outlaw figure," Sōta, in the "moralistic world" of the puppet drama. The emphasis of the five-act history play is thus shifted away from the pathos of a mother searching for a lost child, typical of puppet drama (and of the *nō* play *Sumidagawa* [Sumida River]), to *kabuki*'s outlaw world. Act III is extraordinarily powerful, showing the outlaw's realization of his villainy, his suicide, and his transformation into a *tengu* (a kind of demon). Professor Gerstle showed video clips of this scene as performed in Edo-style *kabuki* (by Ichikawa Ennosuke III), in Osaka-Kyoto-style *kabuki* (by Nakamura Ganjirō III), and by *bunraku* puppets to show their distinct differences in interpretation. The Edo *kabuki* style is the most exaggerated, using many theatrical effects, while the puppet version is the most restrained. Chikamatsu's history plays are sophisticated works; for a successful performance today, the texts need to be looked at "afresh, with respect for their depth, but without fear of innovation." There need to be more experimental *kabuki* revivals of Chikamatsu's plays that will explore the relation between *kabuki* and the puppet theatre.

"Animals in Genroku *Kabuki*" was the topic of the presentation given by Kamakura Keiko of the Tokyo National Research Institute of Cultural Properties. Excellent and numerous illustrations in *kabuki* illustrated *e-iri kyōgenbon* (play texts) of the Genroku era provide a wealth of information on the common "use" of animals in *kabuki* plays. Three issues were of considerable interest. First, Kamakura noted the foreign origin of some animals. Tigers and elephants appear in many play illustrations, but they are not indigenous to Japan. So their appearance in *kabuki* may be seen as a current exotic attraction. (The first tiger was brought to Japan in 1575, and an elephant is recorded as having been imported from Luzon two decades later.) Second, does the term *tsukau* (use), found in the play texts, mean that a living animal was used on stage or that an actor was used to play the role? Perhaps some live animals were brought on stage, but edicts on compassion for living things, in 1691 and 1700, forbade displaying birds, snakes, dogs, cats, and rodents for public entertainment. Live animals would be difficult to handle on the stage in any case, so it seems likely that either the actor played the role or he manipulated a stuffed animal. Third, animals were used according to a play's needs, so that in Edo's *aragoto* plays powerful animals like elephants or tigers would be written into the scripts, while Kyoto-Osaka plays often called for an elegant peacock, a bird introduced to Japan in the Nara period (645–794). The appearance of such animals was extremely appealing to the average spectator who had never seen such creatures in person.

Annegret Bergmann and Hata Hisashi were chairpersons for the session on modern *kabuki*, in which *kabuki* in the Meiji era was examined by three speakers. The first presentation was "Acceptance of 'the Occident' in Modern *Kabuki*" by the critic Ōzasa Yoshio. *Kabuki* is sometimes perceived as a traditional theatre that has come down through several centuries more or less intact, but in fact this is not so: *Kabuki* has had to change. In the Meiji period, *kabuki* shifted direction under the influence of Western thinking, as in 1872 when the Tokyo municipal government ordered managers of the three licensed theatres (the Edo *sanza*) to create a superior theatre that would not embarrass foreign visitors. In the same year, playwrights Kawatake Mokuami and Sakurada Jisuke IV were ordered to write "plays in elegant language that are true to historical fact." In 1872, Morita Kan'ya XII introduced gas lighting in his newly built Morita-za (later renamed the Shintomi-za) and added Western chairs for foreign dignitaries as part of the modernizing of *kabuki*. [This story is told in Takahashi's essay, chapter 1. Ed.] The focus of attention shifted from the actor to the playwright, and new plays came to be conceived as literature, separate from performance, following Western critical concepts. Three acting family lines can be considered important examples. In the 1880s, Onoe Kikugorō V performed new *zangiri kyōgen* ("cropped-hair" plays) about life in the present time. Many were staged at Kan'ya's new Shintomi-za. Kikugorō's son, Kikugorō VI, decried spectacle, such as flying tricks (*chūnori*), and was famous for realistic acting. Ichikawa Danjūrō IX favored *katsureki* (living history) plays in which he abandoned standard *kabuki* role types and played each character as a unique individual. Danjūrō called his quiet and sincere acting style *hara gei* (gut acting), and through it Danjūrō "turned plays of form (*kata*) into plays of the heart (*kokoro*)." Theatrical lies became dramatic truth. The actor most influenced by Western theatre was Ichikawa Sadanji II, who spent eight months observing rehearsals and performances at major theatres in Europe. He also studied acting in London and Delsarte technique [a method of acting. Ed.] on the Continent. It is notable that one aspect of Sadanji's theatrical work encompassed the founding of the Jiyū Gekijō (Free Theatre) in 1909 with Osanai Kaoru as a venue for modern drama.

Professor Kamiyama Akira, Meiji University, further examined the significance of *katsureki* and *zangiri kyōgen* in his presentation, "The Transition of *Kabuki* in Modernization." These two new play forms were part of the *kabuki kairyō undō* (reform movement) dedicated to "modernizing" *kabuki*. They expressed the overall *jidai seishin* (spirit of the times) of the Meiji era. Although it is often said that the restrained realism of Danjūrō living history plays made them uninteresting, his changes toward *shajitsu* (realism/reality) continue to affect traditional *kabuki* even today. On the other hand, the realism of cropped-hair plays conflicted with the traditional elocution used by Kikugorō V, with the result that the experiment ultimately was unsuccessful. It is paradoxical that the idea of "preserving *kabuki*" first appeared in the manifesto of the reform movement that was itself dedicated to changing *kabuki* completely. Modernization is succinctly expressed in the shift from a traditional audience, which "saw" the spectacle of *kabuki*, to the modern audience, which "hears," that is, understands the dramatic content of new *kabuki* plays.

Professor Jean-Jacques Tschudin, University of Paris, considered the specific circumstances of early encounters of *kabuki* with Western theatre in his presentation, "Early Meiji *Kabuki* and Western Theatre: A Rendezvous Manqué." He noted that *kabuki* was in a strong position to resist Western theatre in the early Meiji period: There were popular young actors and good playwrights, audiences were faithful, managers were confident of their abilities, and *kabuki* owned the means of production of plays (the theatres and accoutrements). Further, European businessmen and diplomats living in Japan cared little about theatre and had little influence on *kabuki*. Tschudin viewed the impact of the reform movement and internal changes—such as the new *katsureki* and *zangiri kyōgen*—to have been minimal. He noted that Danjūrō IX's dream of historical accuracy, of pruning away "the frills and fantasies" of *kabuki*, began in 1850, long before Western theatre was known in Japan. Also, European theatre was in fact moving in the opposite direction at that same time, as productions of Hugo and Dumas began utilizing "picturesque sets and exotic costumes" and theatres were installing elaborate stage machinery. The concept of "realism" is extremely subjective. While some Europeans liked *kabuki* and some did not, they all agreed that "the moving, striking representation of real life is indeed the distinctive mark of the Japanese stage"—a view quite opposite to that of *kabuki*'s native reformers. Japanese dignitaries reported back from Europe that opera and ballet—classical, high arts—should be the models to reconstruct *kabuki*. These high government officials did not see the popular theatre of Europe—the bourgeois theatre, vaudeville, melodrama, burlesque, high comedy, and realistic drama—that was flourishing in the late nineteenth century. Consequently, the "meeting of *kabuki* and Western theatre went awry, . . . a case of wasted opportunities, a *rendezvous manqué*." If Japan's early visitors to Europe had reported on popular types of Western theatre, then *kabuki*'s musicalization, use of *onnagata*, and stylized acting might have been seen as acceptable. "In short, they would have seen Western equivalents of what they were being asked to get rid of!"

Professor Brian Powell, Oxford University, carried the examination of modern *kabuki* into the Taishō and Shōwa periods in his presentation, *"Kabuki* in the 1930s: A Decade of Diversity." Looking back at the 1930s from the present, he notes that the genres of *kabuki*, *shinpa* (new-style theatre), and *shinkokugeki* (new national drama), and the productions of the Zenshin-za (Progressive Theatre) troupe, which broke away from commercial *kabuki*, "bear a striking resemblance" to each other. [See Powell's essay on the Zenshin-za, chapter 10. Ed.] Despite uncertain economic, political, and military conditions, the Shōchiku Theatrical Corporation built, in part for *kabuki*, two new theatres, the Tōkyō Gekijō and the enormous Kokusai Gekijō, which seated five thousand spectators. Shōchiku organized *kabuki* for "commercial success," staging lavish, all-star productions of famous scenes. One of the young *kabuki* playwrights encouraged by Ōtani Takejirō, head of Shōchiku in Tokyo, was Mayama Seika. In a score of *shin kabuki* plays, he expressed the varied currents of the times: *Genroku Chūshingura* (Loyal samurai of the Genroku era) upholds nationalist feelings, while *Ōishi Saigo no Ichinichi* (The last day in the life of Ōishi) became a great popular success. He transformed *kabuki* drama in several ways: The dense dialogue of his plays demanded an intellectual engagement from audiences that old *kabuki* plays did not; productions starring Ichikawa Sadanji II at the Tōkyō Gekijō encouraged a more educated audience to attend *kabuki*; and by interweaving elements of the old stagecraft he maintained the interest of traditional *kabuki* fans as well. In all, Mayama Seika significantly developed the style of composing *shin kabuki* drama in the years preceding the Pacific War. Discussions following this session were moderated by Fujinami Takayuki, Kokuritsu Gekijō, and Gamō Satoaki, Tokyo National Research Institute of Cultural Properties.

The fourth session of the symposium offered an extremely enlightening demonstration of the *kabuki* actor training system of the Kokuritsu Gekijō, a demonstration held in the auditorium of the Edo-Tokyo Museum and led by Nakamura Matagorō II. Nakamura Shigeko, Tokyo National Research Institute of Cultural Properties, introduced the training program in her presentation, "Training of *Kabuki* Actors." She produced many useful statistics regarding the National Theatre's *kabuki* training program, which began in 1970 and is now [1996. Ed.] conducting its fourteenth class. The two-year course of instruction includes a minimum of 1,311 sessions of eighty minutes each: scene work 255 sessions, *tachimawari* (fighting) and *tonbo* (tumbling) 169, makeup 104, costumes and wigs 9, dance 206, *gidayū* (puppet-style chanting) 158, *nagauta* singing 115, percussion music 59, *geza* (offstage music) 5, koto music 42, voice production 98, etiquette 19, bodily movement 24, and other subjects. As a culmination of each year's instruction, the students act major roles in recital performances. Although much attention is paid to instilling the basic *kata* (forms) of performance, each student is strongly encouraged to find his personal form for *kata*, such as *mie* (dramatic poses), that conforms to his own features and nature. On the average, seven to ten students enter each course. The program is absolutely vital to *kabuki*'s continuation, for its graduates now fill almost all of the walk-on roles—farmers, servants, attendants, fighting chorus, and animals—in current productions throughout Japan. Among the seventy-two program graduates, however, only fifteen have been awarded *kabuki nadai* (family names), clearly a cause for concern. Nakamura Matagorō II, head of the training school since its beginning, believes the National Theatre must form its own troupe from the graduates. If the troupe performs in the small playhouse of the Kokuritsu Gekijō three or four times a year, the best of the young actors can develop fans and in time might become major stars, but this cannot happen as long as they are merely lent to Shōchiku and the Kokuritsu Gekijō to play walk-on roles. Matagorō then introduced the ten members who make up the present acting class. After briefly describing the method of training, he led the group in a demonstration of the "Kurumabiki" (Pulling the carriage apart) scene from *Sugawara Denju Tenarai Kagami* (Sugawara and the secrets of calligraphy). The scene is an excellent study piece because it provides challenging role types: *wagoto* (gentle leading man), *aragoto* (bravura leading man), and *jitsuaku* (villain). Participants were able to observe Matagorō firmly and carefully correcting body posture, gestures, *mie*, and voice production by demonstrating proper technique himself. Matagorō is known as a "living dictionary" of *kabuki* technique and hence is an incalculable asset to the future of *kabuki*. (In recognition of his importance to *kabuki*, on May 23, 1997, he was designated a Living National Treasure by the Japanese government.)

The final session of the symposium, "Present-Day Problems," was chaired by Professor Thomas Leims and Kamakura Keiko. Hata Hisashi, Tokyo National Research Institute of Cultural Properties, pointed out in his presentation, "Function of Criticism," that special knowledge is necessary to be an effective *kabuki* critic. Most *kabuki* "criticism" consists of rather casual reviews of productions published in daily newspapers and monthly magazines. Unfortunately, much criticism consists of simple, subjective observations that a performance is "beautiful," "skillful," or "interesting" or that an "actor is wonderful" in a role. This type of criticism is particularly insufficient for *kabuki*, a traditional theatre in which acting *kata* are passed on from generation to generation. The critic must be deeply knowledgeable about these traditions. Criticism should relate the actor to the traditions and comment on the actor's strong points, what an actor's major starring roles are, and what an actor is expected to do in the family acting line. The critic should educate the audience as well as guide the performers. Of course, the critic works under difficult conditions—not much space is allotted *kabuki* reviews in newspapers, and the review must be written to a deadline. Why do most reviews flatter the production with praise? As other writers have implied, the power of money, through advertising, influences what critics write, directly or indirectly. Critics and editors do not wish to anger the actors or the large commercial producers.

The important role of the Shōchiku Theatrical Corporation in *kabuki* production was examined by Annegret Bergmann, Bonn University, in her presentation, "*Kabuki* Productions: Art and Commerce." Financial control of *kabuki* production shifted from the individuals of the Edo period—the *kinshu* (backers) and *zamoto* (licensed producers) to stock-issuing corporations during the early Meiji era. In particular, between 1895 and 1930 the Shōchiku Theatrical Corporation, directed by twin brothers Ōtani Takejirō and Shirai Matsujirō, purchased or acquired control over all the large theatres that staged *kabuki* in Tokyo, Osaka, and Kyoto, and they placed all *kabuki* actors under personal contract. They changed many Edo-period management practices in order to create a "profit-oriented modern company": They abolished hour-long intermissions, reduced the influence of *yakuza* (gangster) bosses, and ended the practice of giving gifts to secure tickets. The two brothers cared deeply about *kabuki* and promoted the careers of promising actors such as Nakamura Ganjirō I. Two major challenges to Shōchiku's monopoly of *kabuki* production arose during the Taishō and early Shōwa periods. First were the defections in the 1920s and 1930s of a number of lesser ranking actors—among them Kawarazaki Chōjūrō and Nakamura Kan'emon II, who founded the Zenshin-za in 1931, and Ichikawa Ennosuke II, who started the first actors' union dedicated to "representing the interests of low-ranking actors" in 1930. Second, Shōchiku's theatrical rival, the Tōhō Theatrical Corporation, tried to establish a rival *kabuki* troupe between 1936 and 1939, but in the end its efforts were not financially successful. *Kabuki* is a highly commercial enterprise today, and programs are chosen to enhance revenues. Shōchiku's control is still almost absolute: The Kokuritsu Gekijō must negotiate with Shōchiku each month to borrow actors for its productions. Attempts to create a nonprofit "national theatre" for *kabuki* began in the early Meiji period and continued through the Taishō era: Such a theatre, which is commonplace in Europe, has yet to be created in Japan. [Or in the United States, for that matter. Ed.]

Professor Hattori Yukio, Chiba University, addressed the highly significant issue of "Problems of Repertory in Present-Day *Kabuki*" in his presentation. Despite the collapse of Japan's "bubble economy" of the 1980s and the end of the "Heisei *kabuki* boom" of the early 1990s, *kabuki* production is stable and flourishing. The Kabuki-za recently celebrated its hundredth anniversary, and this year [1996. Ed.] the National Theatre is celebrating its thirtieth anniversary. The *kabuki* system of programming is perhaps unique in the world. From the Genroku period, one all-day play (*tōshi kyōgen*), lasting up to ten hours, was standard in Edo. In the eighteenth century, all-day puppet plays were taken over into *kabuki* almost intact or sometimes abridged.

Under the influence of puppet programming, a third type of program evolved: Crucial scenes were excerpted from long plays and put together in *midori*, a kind of variety program. Puppet-play act finales were commonly excerpted, as well as major scenes from original *kabuki* plays, such as the "Hamamatsuya" scene from Kawatake Mokuami's all-day play, *Shiranami Gonin Otoko* (Five bold robbers, 1862). From the late nineteenth century, a typical program in Kyoto and Osaka had either two plays—a long history play and a short domestic play—or a four-part structure of a history play (*mae* [before. Ed.]), two puppet adaptations (*naka* and *ato* [middle and after. Ed.]), and a closing original domestic play (*kiri* [ending. Ed.]). Theatres in Tokyo at that time followed a similar program made up of three parts: a long history play (*ichibanme* [first piece. Ed.), a puppet excerpt or dance play (*naka maku* [middle act. Ed.]), and a long domestic play (*nibanme* [second piece. Ed.]). Since the 1940s, programs have been divided into morning and evening bills, each lasting four or five hours. Although the total number of hours and the overall structure of a program have hardly changed since the Edo period, modern audiences like variety, so many more pieces are crammed into one day. This tight scheduling exerts strong pressure to shorten plays, thus drastically changing the overall artistic experience of the *kabuki* audience.

It is hard to say what the repertory should be today. (Three short programs per day have been tried experimentally.) When the Kokuritsu Gekijō was founded in 1966, its policy was to perform all-day plays only, to use original texts, and to return to traditional acting forms. That is, "Kokuritsu Gekijō *kabuki*" would be different from commercial, short-play "Kabuki-za *kabuki*." During the first decade, these policies were quite successfully implemented: many all-day plays were revived, beginning with a full production of *Sugawara Denju Tenarai Kagami*, divided into a first and a second half, performed respectively in November and December 1966. But numerous problems have arisen: without a permanent acting company, actors must be obtained from Shōchiku each month; suitable casting is not always achieved; some scenes in all-day plays are boring to modern audiences; rehearsal time is not sufficient; and actors do not, or cannot, contribute fully to the artistic process. In recent years, programs at the Kokuritsu Gekijō have been either bills of excerpts, very much like the Kabuki-za, or revivals a second or third time of earlier, successful all-day productions, such as *Narukami* and *Sakurahime Azuma Bunshō* (The scarlet princess of Edo). Many rare and excellent plays by Tsuruya Nanboku IV and plays in Kyoto-Osaka style that are in danger of being lost could be revived by the Kokuritsu Gekijō, but unfortunately they are ignored. Further, middle-ranking actors could be cast in important revivals in which their talent and energy would shine. Finally, Professor Hattori found much variety among the more than five hundred plays produced at the Kabuki-za over the seven-year period 1989–1995. At the same time, he noted that standard pieces were performed over and over again: *Musume Dōjōji* sixteen times, for example, and *Kanjinchō* and *Fuji Musume* (The wisteria maiden), seven times each. Today *kabuki* is the property of the entertainment industry. "We must hope that producers and actors alike find the will and means to change this situation."

Professor Watanabe Tamotsu, Shukutoku University, raised significant issues in his presentation, "The Passing Down of *Gei*." Transmission of *gei*, or art, in *kabuki* is in crisis. Reading *geidan* (actors' memoirs), Watanabe notes that two stages of transmission are described. First is fundamental training, when skills of dance and various types of musical accompaniment (*tokiwazu, gidayū, kiyomoto, nagauta*) are assimilated into the actor's body through repeated practice beginning in childhood. Second is personal instruction, when the young actor visits a senior or master actor at his home to ask for specific advice regarding a new role the actor has been assigned to perform. What is essential in this instruction is that the young actor must love his senior's acting: It does not matter how often he sees a play on stage; the master's art will genuinely infuse the young actor's body only when he passionately loves that art. Decades may pass, but the body never forgets the art that is loved. This is how the actor "steals" his art. Various problems exist today with both stages of transmission. Concerning the first, today's young actor does not spend enough hours learning basic skills, as did the Edo stars Ichikawa Danjūrō IV or Bandō Mitsugorō VII. Dance master Fujima Kan'emon noted that basic training must begin by the age of six and a half years, before the bones lose their flexibility. Moreover, the young actor's life in modern Tokyo is far removed from the Edo-period customs that underlie *kabuki* acting. Further, Watanabe questions the usefulness of learning from video and audio recordings, as young actors commonly do today. A camera shows only a front view, while in fact art (*gei*) lies in what cannot be seen. Regarding the second stage of learning, there exists a serious misunderstanding. *Gei* is not synonymous with *engi* ("acting" in English), as is often said. *Engi* is a skill that can be systematically transmitted and indeed can surmount cultural and political differences. But *gei*, which encompasses skill and goes beyond it, cannot be taught and cannot be transmitted. *Gei* is a road that never ends. As the actor Nakamura Kichiemon I often said, *gei* is "lifelong study." But today actors treat too lightly their own *ie no gei* (family style), adopting without serious thought the *kata* of other actors. Many young actors do not know how to study and as a result their stage presence is shallow: they have not absorbed *gei* into their bodies. Lacking creativity, they fail to develop *kata* that suit their own *nin* (personality).

Final discussions among participants were moderated by Professor Torigoe Bunzō of Waseda University, Matsui Kesako, and Gamō Satoaki. Questions from the floor to symposium speakers concerned the success of the Kokuritsu Gekijō's training system, methods of teaching *kabuki* to foreign performers, and other topics. The symposium closed with a farewell party. In addition to the symposium proper, participants enjoyed a traditional performance of *Imoseyama* at the Kokuritsu Gekijō on the evening of November 13. With a primarily young cast, the theme of lovers separated was palpably genuine. Professor Kawatake's observation that *kabuki*'s appeal lies primarily in its "formal beauty" could be appreciated in this deliberately paced production. Some participants noted that contemporary *kabuki* performances appear to be slowing down in tempo, just as *nō* performances did during the Edo period, suggesting the gradual movement of *kabuki* toward an increasingly "classic" status in relation to the audience.

In reflecting personally on issues raised at the conference, I was struck by several points. One was Professor Kamiyama's reference to the influence in the Meiji era of Herbert Spencer's theory of the "economy of mental energy." This concept is certainly embodied in most "modern" realistic drama, whether of the West or Japanese *shingeki*, as it is in Danjūrō IX's *hara gei* and use of silence. But highly physicalized, extravagant expenditure of energy is characteristic of traditional *kabuki* performance. Director-theorist Eugenio Barba has noted that all traditional Asian acting techniques require the actor to use "extra daily energy," that is, an excess of energy beyond real life. Spencer was looking for modern "efficiency," but the powerful effect of *kabuki* acting comes from "inefficient expenditure of energy." Today, of course, we can recognize the inappropriateness of applying Spencer's mechanical principle to the art of *kabuki* acting. Moreover, Professor Watanabe, Professor Hattori, and others highlighted the tension that exists between preserving *kabuki*'s various *ie no gei* and the inevitability, indeed necessity, of change. *Kabuki* has always changed in the past; surely it must change in the future. But how much can the art change without losing its identity as "*kabuki*"? That is a great challenge.

The symposium was unusually valuable for several reasons. It brought forward issues of importance to the continuation of *kabuki* in these rapidly charging times. These issues were then discussed in open forum. The symposium provided scholars from Japan and other countries the opportunity to hear new discoveries of research and to test these ideas in public. Finally, it was an occasion to renew or begin personal, scholarly, or artistic contacts among participants of all countries. It was notable that much of the discussion, by both Japanese and non-Japanese participants, was carried out in the Japanese language.

Speaking as one foreign participant, I want to express my appreciation to the organizers of the symposium, the Tokyo National Research Institute of Cultural Properties, for carrying out this important meeting efficiently and in such a warm manner, and to the Bunkachō (Bureau of Cultural Affairs) for its financial support. This symposium laid out basic issues concerning *kabuki* in the international sphere. In the future, it would be useful to hold several additional, smaller-scale symposia, each focusing on one specific issue of concern—for example, the economic reality of *kabuki* as art and as business, the system of artistic transmission in *kabuki*, the contributions and contradictions of the Kokuritsu Gekijō's training program, detailed examination of contemporary audience preferences regarding the repertory, and a study of specific changes in acting techniques. Certainly this successful symposium can serve as an excellent model for future international forums concerned with the place in contemporary culture of other performing arts, such as *bunraku* or Japanese *minzoku geinō* (folk performances). We all owe a debt of gratitude to the sponsors and hosts of this groundbreaking symposium.

[The papers delivered at this symposium were published in and are available from Keiko Kamakura et al., eds., *International Symposium on the Conservation and Restoration of Cultural Property: Kabuki: Changes and Prospects, 1996* (Tokyo: Tokyo National Research Institute of Cultural Properties, 1998). They are printed in either English or Japanese, according to the language in which they were delivered. Each has a page or more of summary attached, including English summaries for the Japanese papers. Ed.]

20

Kabuki as National Culture:
A Critical Survey
of Japanese *Kabuki* Scholarship

William Lee

Although the essays collected in this volume clearly reveal some of the recent advances in *kabuki* research and criticism by Western scholars, this scholarship pales considerably when compared to the voluminous Japanese writing on the subject. In the following, I aim to provide a selective, critical overview of modern Japanese scholarship on *kabuki* as a historical theatrical form. Originally it was my intention to concentrate on postwar scholarship only and to exclude all critical comment dealing with contemporary as opposed to historical *kabuki*. I have become convinced, however, that the most useful context for the understanding of modern *kabuki* criticism and research reflects concern over *kabuki*'s survival as well as its past. I am also convinced that I must begin with Meiji (1868–1912), since it was during this period that Japan, largely as a result of its encounter with the West, embarked on the path of social, political, economic, and cultural change commonly referred to as *kindaika* (modernization). This not only affected *kabuki*'s fate as a viable, living theatre, but also formed the wider ideological context in which the modern scholarly study of *kabuki* was born. Indeed, throughout this survey I have tried to interpret the works and trends examined as varying responses to ideological questions concerning Japan's cultural identity. Thus, while the historical account I have constructed can serve as an overview of some of the most important scholars and their work, it is also designed to show how the modern study of *kabuki* has functioned as a discursive field in which to address broader, ideological concerns and in which *kabuki* itself has been continually constructed and reconstructed as a vehicle to carry the national identity.

While hindsight may justify the conclusion that the Meiji period marks the beginning of the end of *kabuki* as a vibrant living theatre, during the period itself *kabuki* continued to thrive and even reached a historical high point of sorts during the mid-Meiji years when the "Dan-Kiku-Sa" trio (Ichikawa Danjūrō IX [1839–1903], Onoe Kikugorō V [1844–1903], and Ichikawa Sadanji I [1842–1904]) reigned on the stage. This is not to say that these three actors were untouched by the forced end to Japan's seclusion policy and the subsequent wave of modernization that swept early Meiji Japan; indeed, each in his own way tried to make *kabuki* more compatible with the times. Although toward the end of their careers Danjūrō and Kikugorō turned back to the classics, their experiments arguably left a permanent mark on *kabuki*.[1]

It was not actors alone, however, who were responsible for changes in the *kabuki* theatre. To understand the significance of the Meiji period for *kabuki*, one has to look outside the traditional theatre world. If there is one thing that marks Meiji *kabuki* more than any other, it is that the public theatre, long subject to official scorn and regulation, became an object of interest for the educated and governing elite, an interest that itself provided the context for the innovations attempted by those within the theatre world. This change in official and elitist attitudes, moreover, was motivated by an interest in *kabuki* not for what it was but for what it might become. Far from seeing *kabuki* as a traditional theatrical form destined to decline in the modern age, elitist discourse saw only the possibility of a new course for *kabuki*, which would allow it to assume the stature of a national theatre. Thus this discourse was characterized primarily by calls for reform. And since the object of this reform was to create a new national theatre, the direction of reform was itself determined by the conception of the national. In the discourse of the Meiji elite, particularly in the 1870s and 1880s, the national meant a modernized and to a large degree Westernized Japan that would be the equal of the industrialized powers of the West. Reform of the theatre, therefore, meant essentially reform along Western lines. It also meant a rejection of a good deal of the *kabuki* tradition, the recovery of which would form a major part of later *kabuki* scholarship. [For more on Meiji reform, see especially Takahashi and Bach, chapters 8 and 9, respectively. See also Brandon's description of Jean-Jacques Tschudin's 1996 *kabuki* symposium essay. Ed.]

The continuing clamor among the Meiji elite for theatre reform led in August 1886 to the founding of the Engeki Kairyōkai (Society for Theatre

Reform), among whose members and official supporters were the prime minister, Itō Hirobumi, the foreign and education ministers, industrialists, newspaper men, and scholars. According to its prospectus, the three major aims of the Society for Theatre Reform were to put an end to the evil customs of the theatre and foster the development of a better theatre; to make the writing of plays an honored profession; and to construct a theatre building suited to the performance of drama and other stage arts. The prospectus criticizes *kabuki* for being lewd and vulgar. A reformed theatre, it argues, would be one that the upper classes could view without embarrassment. Such a theatre, however, would be dependent on better texts, which would require encouraging scholars and masters of letters to become playwrights. Finally, even with better writers and plays, these reforms would be in vain unless an adequate theatre were built, one to which foreign actors could be invited and at which concerts, too, could be held.[2] Although the prospectus is short on details, the recommendations made elsewhere by members of the society make it clear that what was being proposed was a major change to the form of *kabuki* as theatre. In his 1886 speech "Engeki Kairyō Iken" (Views on theatre reform), for example, the chairman of the society, Suematsu Kenchō, called not only for adherence to Western dramatic principles such as the separation of comedy and tragedy, but also for the abolition of such typical features of *kabuki* as the *hanamichi* (runway), the *seridashi* (traps), the *chobo* (narrative/shamisen accompaniment) used in plays derived from the puppet theatre, and *onnagata* (female-role specialists).[3] Another member of the society, Toyama Masakazu, added to this list the *kurogo* or *kōken* (black-robed stage assistants) and scenes dealing with prostitutes and the licensed brothel district.[4]

Had all of these recommendations actually been implemented, it is difficult to imagine how anything resembling traditional *kabuki* could have survived. As it turned out, the Society for Theatre Reform itself was short-lived and its immediate effects limited. The reform movement did have some long-term effects, however. Whatever their true motives, the interest shown toward *kabuki* by elite members of society helped dispel some of the traditional prejudice against the *kabuki* world. This in turn gave impetus to the serious consideration of *kabuki* as a historical dramatic genre. After all, any attempt at reforming *kabuki* implicitly required first a recognition of what *kabuki* was. It is true that much of what the reformers saw in *kabuki* was rejected, and it would be the task of later generations of intellectuals to recuperate this. Before recuperation could begin, however, *kabuki* scholars had to start with what—in a climate of reform based on Western dramatic models—could be accepted.

What could be accepted was the notion of *kabuki* as a literary theatre. This is already noticeable in the reformers' call for men of letters to take up playwriting. It can also be seen in the work of the man who more than any other was responsible for laying the foundations of modern theatre studies in Japan: Tsubouchi Shōyō (1859–1935). Shōyō was critical of other reformers' emphasis on theatre architecture and questions of morality; in his own contribution to the reform debate, he clearly stated his position that theatrical reform depended above all on improving the texts of the plays, which improvement required recognition of the texts as *literature*:

> The reform of play scripts, this is the essential basis of any theatre reform, and unless this is carried out, all other reform measures will be of no avail. ... Since, fundamentally, the main purpose of the theatre, as of the novel, is to portray the truth (the truth of human emotions, the truth of social conditions), to be so concerned with externals as to kill this truth is a dangerous priority.[5]

Shōyō thus attempted to shift the discussion of the theatre and theatre reform into the realm of literary studies. While drama in the West has a long history of being considered as a literary genre, this was not so in Japan. *Kabuki*, especially, because of the primacy of stage performance, had never enjoyed an independent textual tradition. While Shōyō was able to rehabilitate some Tokugawa-period playwrights—especially Chikamatsu Monzaemon (1653–1725), who wrote primarily for the more literary genre of the puppet theatre and whose *sewamono* (domestic plays) perhaps come closest to resembling Western realist drama[6]—throughout his long career as a theatre scholar, Shōyō's attitude toward *kabuki* continued to be marked by criticism of traditional *kabuki* and by the call for its reform.

A good example of Shōyō's later work can be found in the 1918 essay "Kabukigeki no Tetteiteki Kenkyū" (A thorough investigation of the *kabuki* theatre). This essay not only summarizes Shōyō's approach to *kabuki*, but also defines the directions for future *kabuki* scholarship. Shōyō begins by pointing out that, although much of Japanese culture has been influenced by continental culture, *kabuki* is an exception in that it is an outcome of peculiarly Japanese conditions. However, this alone does not qualify *kabuki* as an object of national pride: "Whether we should be proud of this art or not, depends upon how well we become aware of its weaknesses, and how seriously we endeavor to improve upon it. *Kabuki*, as it is now, is rather a cumbersome burden for us."[7] What makes *kabuki* cumbersome is its lack of artistic unity. *Kabuki*, Shōyō laments, has since its birth held unswervingly to mass appeal, its only principles being popularity, pleasure, and affordability. As a result, it has never hesitated to adopt whatever theatrical device has come along. This hybrid monster, which Shōyō likens to a chimera, embraced all the characteristics ever contrived by artistic talent; it partook of the attributes of an opera, a dance drama and a speech drama. It might even be considered an epic, a lyric or a dramatic poem; it was infinitely varied in its manner of presentation—symbolic, romantic or realistic. Actually, this three hundred year old creature, *Kabuki*, is hardly amenable to human analysis.[8]

This complexity, Shōyō goes on to explain, constitutes both *kabuki*'s strength and its weakness: strength because its versatility and abundance of resources allow it to go on living, adapting to every new situation; and weakness because these same qualities make *kabuki* not only difficult to analyze, but resistant to any attempts at reform. Yet analysis and reform remain Shōyō's only options. For this reason that he praises Ihara Toshirō's *Nihon Engekishi* (History of the Japanese theatre, 1904) and *Kinsei Nihon Engekishi* (History of the premodern Japanese theatre, 1913) as epoch-making achievements. Yet these two books, which deal with *kabuki* in the first and second half of the Tokugawa period respectively, also earn Shōyō's criticism for being little more than compilations of materials concerning plays, performances, theatres, and actors. What is missing, Shōyō argues, is a discussion of the theatre and dramatic literature as a historical record of national culture and literature.[9] This point is emphasized again in his conclusion:

> It is essential that the true character of *Kabuki*, and its inner meaning, along with that of the *Noh* and other related arts, be clearly represented to the people, especially to foreigners and the Japanese younger generation. . . . Merely studying the past, however, may not help much to elevate our theatre either, but as a first step it is important to study what we were in the past in order to prepare the groundwork for building what we will be in the future.[10]

Despite Shōyō's interest in the past, then, his concern for the theatre, like that of the mid-Meiji reformers, is still bound by the broader effort to create a national identity, both for the sake of the Japanese themselves (the younger generation) and as an image to hold up to the world (the foreigners).

While Shōyō's essay thus does not represent a significant ideological development, it nevertheless does reveal how far the study of *kabuki* had come by this time and what directions it would take in the future. Methodologically, he argues for a comprehensive approach, pointing out that the complexity of *kabuki*'s history, repertoire, and formal devices make any attempt to reduce it to an "ism" unproductive. Rather, *kabuki* is characterized by an unparalleled spirit of amusement that resists any formal unification. In order to understand how such a spirit came about and flourished, it is necessary to look at *kabuki* both historically and sociologically. According to Shōyō, the Tokugawa-period conditions that were decisive for *kabuki* were a protracted period of peace following decades of war and social turmoil, and a military government—*bakufu*—that tolerated popular entertainment but held aloof from it, thus denying *kabuki* the benefits it could have received as an art through contact with the upper classes and the intellectuals.[11]

In addition to sociological research on the background of *kabuki*, Shōyō indicates several more areas of historical study which, as he puts it, are part of the necessary preparation for the improvement of the national theatre. These are the study of (1) *nō* and other ancient stage arts that flourished before *kabuki*; (2) stage and acting techniques; (3) play scripts as literature; (4) the puppet theatre (*ningyō jōruri*) as music, literature, and puppet show; (5) the evolution of theatre architecture and organization; (6) dance and its place in *kabuki*; (7) folk and popular song and dance; and (8) other folk and popular entertainments and pastimes.[12]

Because of Shōyō's position at the time as Japan's preeminent theatre scholar, it is not surprising that these recommended areas of study have all become major fields of research. Much of this research, in fact, was started by Shōyō himself and carried on by his disciples. In 1928 a theatre museum was established at Waseda University to commemorate Shōyō's seventieth birthday and the completion of his translation of Shakespeare. The Tsubouchi Shōyō Memorial Theatre Museum became the base for a number of scholars, most notably Kawatake Shigetoshi (1889–1967), a former student of Shōyō's and the adopted son of playwright Kawatake Mokuami (1816–1893). Another important research group was the Engekishi Kenkyū Gakkai (Society for the Study of Theatre History), centered at Tokyo University around the scholar Takano Tatsuyuki (1876–1947). In 1938, Takano's younger colleague, Shuzui Kenji (1899–1983), started a separate *kabuki* research group, the Tōdai Kabuki Kenkyūkai (Tokyo University Research Society).

According to one historical review of theatre research, the Waseda group is characterized by its study of theatre from the point of view of Western dramatic theory, whereas the Tokyo University group under Takano was focused on the study of dramatic texts as part of Edo-period literature.[13] To some extent this is true. Following Shōyō's lead, the activities of the theatre museum and the theatre department later established at Waseda have not been limited to the study of Japanese theatre alone, whereas the work of the Tokyo group fits more easily into the academic discipline of *kokubungaku* (Japanese literature). As far as work on *kabuki* goes, however, in the prewar years both groups took more or less the same approach, namely, the study of texts and playwrights on the one hand, and on the other the compilation and analysis of historical materials concerning theatres, actors, and performances. Both groups were also very active in the editing of *kabuki* and puppet theatre play texts.

While the work of these two groups and other scholars of the period reveals a greater willingness to accept *kabuki* and is thus less concerned with the question of reform, in its basic methodology this work still does not go much beyond the example set by Shōyō. The treatment of *kabuki* as literature, for example, is still noticeable in works such as Shuzui's *Kinsei Gikyoku Kenkyū* (Study of premodern plays, 1932) and *Kabukigeki Gikyoku Kōzō no Kenkyū* (Study of the structure of *kabuki* plays, 1947), as well as in Kawatake's *Kabuki Sakusha no Kenkyū* (Study of *kabuki* playwrights, 1940) and *Nihon Gikyokushi* (History of Japanese plays, 1964); while the emphasis on Chikamatsu is reflected not only in much of the Tokyo University group's critical work, but also in the three complete editions of Chikamatsu's puppet plays produced during this period and Takano's collections of *e-iri kyōgenbon* (illustrated playbooks) of Chikamatsu's and other Genroku era (1688–1704) *kabuki* plays.[14]

If anything, then, although it testifies to a shift in attitude since the days of the reform movement, the study of *kabuki* in an academic setting seems to have legitimized both the literary approach and the collecting of historical materials. For this reason, perhaps, the single most important innovation in prewar *kabuki* studies occurred outside the academic field of theatre research. This came in the form of a book, *Engeki Biron* (Aesthetics of the theatre, 1930), by the artist Kishida Ryūsei (1891–1929). Since the book deals primarily with *kabuki*, it was given the title *Kabuki Biron* (Aesthetics of *kabuki*) when it was republished in 1948, and it was also under this title that an excerpt from the book was published in 1976 in a special issue devoted to *kabuki* of the journal *Gendai no Esupuri* (Today's esprit).

Kishida was an artist whose medium was Western-style oil painting and among whose works are *kabuki* scenes done in a manner reminiscent of European impressionism. This is not to say that Kishida tried to assimilate *kabuki* into the Western artistic tradition. Indeed, what makes his book an innovation in *kabuki* studies is not only that it marks a complete swing away from prejudice and toward acceptance of *kabuki*, but that this acceptance is based on a denial of the Western (that is, literary) quality in *kabuki,* coupled with an unreserved admiration for precisely those features of the traditional theatre that the West-looking reform movement had sought to eliminate. According to Kishida, the charm of the *kyōgeki* (old theatre)—by which he means *kabuki* and *bunraku* as opposed to Western-style *shingeki* (new theatre)—is not only that it is basically aesthetic as opposed to literary, but that its aesthetics are very Japanese: "The old theatre is fundamentally an art that expresses a certain beauty and is not at all meant to be a literary theatre. If one views this theatre with an eye to the literary, one will end up by failing to experience its mysterious and extremely aesthetic charm, which is a product of the Japanese race."[15]

Kishida terms the aesthetic quality with which *kabuki* is endowed a high-class common beauty. By this paradoxical formulation he does not mean a kind of rustic simplicity, but rather a complex type of beauty which he sees as peculiarly oriental. It is a beauty that incorporates not only the usual aesthetic qualities such as sublimity, purity, and tranquillity, but also their opposites. While Kishida sees this kind of beauty as characteristic of Asian and Japanese art in general, it is in the popular theatre of the Edo period that he finds its strongest expression. More than that of any other Japanese art, he writes, the common beauty of the old theatre is vulgar, tinged with evil, the grotesque, the erotic, the anarchic, the worldly, the unlettered, and the nonsensical.[16] Sociologically, he argues, the flourishing of this kind of common beauty in the Edo period is explainable in terms of the rise of the urban nonsamurai class (*chōnin*), who, although uneducated, were not aesthetically unreceptive. It is for this reason, he concludes, that *kabuki* and *bunraku* are the most Edo-like of all Edo-period arts.[17]

Inasmuch as his aesthetic and sociological arguments are able to accommodate and explain those features of *kabuki* that the reformers and even Shōyō found embarrassing and tried to eliminate, Kishida's approach can be seen as a methodological advance in the study of *kabuki*. While on one level this approach represents a complete reversal of the position of earlier commentators, on another level it has in common with both the reform movement and Shōyō's work a concern for the national identity. The beauty of *kabuki*, after all, is in Kishida's eyes precisely a *Japanese* beauty. The ultimate aim of national affirmation is thus the same; it is only the strategy that is different. Whereas the reformers and Shōyō tried to make *kabuki* a suitable vehicle to carry the national identity by forcing it to conform to dramatic and social standards largely gleaned from the West, Kishida takes the alternate course of constructing a particularly Japanese aesthetic system in which *kabuki* not only is the prime example, but also automatically qualifies as a representative national art.

While Kishida's book heralds a change in approach to the study of *kabuki*, it is not necessary to conclude that the inadequacy of the older, literary approach alone provided the motivation for this change. A better explanation, I believe, can be found in the processes of modernization and social change and how these relate to the question of national cultural identity. For whereas in the Meiji period the reformers and Shōyō saw in *kabuki* at best a coarse raw material for creating a new national theatre, by the late 1920s, after several decades of reform and modernization during which *kabuki* had to weather the various reform attempts as well as compete with the new rivals *shinpa* and *shingeki*, Kishida could see in the same theatre a precious part of the national essence threatened with extinction. In short, whereas an earlier generation had looked to the West for an objectification of its national identity, Kishida looked to the past; and what for Shōyō was a slightly embarrassing reminder of what the Japanese *were* became for Kishida a symbol of what the Japanese *are*.

If a note of nostalgic concern for the future of *kabuki* can be detected in Kishida's aesthetic view of *kabuki*, it is only in the postwar period that such concern took on the air of a full-blown crisis. Two reasons for the heightened anxiety over the fate of *kabuki* were the death during and shortly after the war of a number of prewar stars and the censorship of the American Occupation forces; for up to two years, many *kabuki* classics were banned because of their purported antidemocratic sentiments.

One response to the crisis was the so-called *kabuki ronsō* (*kabuki* debate) played out in the pages of the journal *Bungaku* (Literature) over the course of several months beginning in November 1951. It began with a joint article in the form of a letter and a reply by two literary critics, Kondō Tadayoshi and Ino Kenji. Both men sought to defend *kabuki* and hoped, rather idealistically, for its survival as a popular theatre and part of Japan's cultural heritage. Ino pointed to the above-mentioned loss of several of the leading actors as one source of *kabuki*'s problems, but for both him and Kondō the real threat lay in the modern theatre and, more generally, in the influence of Western-based modernization. In order to save *kabuki*, therefore, what was needed, was a clear separation between *kabuki* and the modern theatre and a critical stance that would allow the Japanese to overcome the endemic disease of modernization that was turning them into nationless citizens.[18] A few months after their article appeared, Kondō and Ino were taken to task for their idealism by Kuwahara Takeo, a scholar of French literature. Kuwahara criticized several specific arguments advanced by his opponents, but his major point was that, for better or for worse, contemporary Japan was no longer the Japan that had produced *kabuki*, and therefore *kabuki* would have to either change with the times or cede its place to the modern theatre, allowing the latter to incorporate whatever it could of the best of *kabuki*.[19]

Kuwahara's voice was not the last to be heard, but the debate soon petered out, perhaps because neither the *kabuki* scholars nor members of the *kabuki* world themselves became involved. The end of the debate, however, did not mean an end to the sense of crisis. In the years to follow, the alarm was sounded again and again, perhaps never so loudly as in 1961 when the Nihon Engeki Gakkai (Japanese Theatre Society) issued its "Kabuki no Kiki ni taisuru Yobisho" (Petition concerning the *kabuki* crisis), an appeal, aimed for the most part at the government, calling for support in protecting *kabuki* from vulgar modernization and in preserving it as one of Japan's classical theatre arts.[20] This time the government seems to have listened, for the specific request of the society for a national theatre building as well as research and training facilities was met in 1966 with the opening of the Kokuritsu Gekijō (National Theatre) in downtown Tokyo.

If concern over *kabuki*'s fate and the question of its status as a classical theatre form part of the background to postwar discourse on *kabuki*, an even more important factor for the direction of that discourse, especially during the period of democratization in the immediate postwar years, was the issue of *kabuki's* feudal legacy. As might be expected, one critical position from which this question was addressed was Marxist. Among the most important work in this respect is that of producer, director, and critic Takechi Tetsuji (1912–1988). Takechi is perhaps best known for the series of *kabuki* productions that he mounted between 1949 and 1952 and to which he gave the name Kabuki Saikentō Kōen (Performance of *kabuki* reexamined), although his work is generally known as Takechi *Kabuki*. In the context of postwar *kabuki* scholarship, however, Takechi's importance lies in the series of critical and theoretical works that he continued to write long after his experimental *kabuki* productions came to an end.

As the name implies, Takechi *Kabuki* was very much based on a single individual's view of *kabuki*, a fact not inconsistent with the theoretical position Takechi himself elaborated. At the center of this position is the concept of *enshutsu*, a term that is sometimes translated as "production," but which refers more to the manner of staging or presenting a play, that is, what in the modern theatre would be considered the responsibility of the director. As Takechi argues in "Kabuki no Enshutsu" (*Kabuki* direction), although traditionally *kabuki* has not had a director, this does not mean that the function did not exist. At times this function may have been fulfilled, singly or in a cooperative manner, by the playwright during his read-through of the play with the actors, by a senior actor familiar with the conventions, or by the *zamoto* (troupe leader). Over the course of *kabuki*'s history, however, artistic direction in this sense has often been subordinate to the dictates of the stars, who imposed their personal acting fortes on the production and in so doing founded lines of *kata*, or fixed acting techniques or patterns, for the principal roles in the *kabuki* repertoire. Takechi sees this dominance of stars as the result not only of a feudal ranking system but also of the demands of commercialism. He characterizes the Bunka-Bunsei years (1804–1829), as a period of decadent cultural consumption during which *kabuki* was dominated by arrogant stars such as Matsumoto Kōshirō V and powerful financial backers such as Kubo

Imasuke. This period saw the convergence between feudal and commercial structures achieve the form that would determine the relations of production for future *kabuki*.[21] This broad, historical view of the problem not only enables Takechi to make a connection between feudalism and commercialism, it also provides him with a theoretical justification for rejecting the privileged position given to the actor in *kabuki*. For what today is seen as traditional *kabuki* acting is really only a collection of *kata*, the legacy of past stars; allowing the system to continue will only invite more confusion and artistic chaos. For this reason Takechi can assert that there has never been a greater need in *kabuki* for artistic direction, that is, for the conscious determination of *enshutsu*.[22]

Takechi's criticism of the present state of *kabuki* may seem reminiscent of Shōyō's characterization of *kabuki* as a chimera, and no doubt both are pointing to essentially the same thing, although their explanations as to how such a phenomenon came about may differ. The goal of both Takechi's productions and his theoretical writings, however, is not so much the reform of *kabuki*, at least not in Shōyō's sense of creating something new within the tradition, as it is *kabuki*'s classicalization. He therefore did not reject traditional *kabuki* form or *yōshiki* (stylization) in his own directorial work but sought rather to present formally unified productions. From Takechi's theoretical point of view, however, achieving such unity is again a matter of historical understanding: The possibility of formal unity begins only with the recognition that there is no single, immutable *kabuki* form, but only *historically specific forms*. In another essay, "Takechi Kabuki no Enshutsu" (Takechi's *Kabuki* direction), Takechi breaks down the many different acting and production styles that exist or have existed in *kabuki* into twelve basic types, each one corresponding to a different historical period and/or region. An awareness of the historical specificity of these different forms, and actors capable of reproducing them, are the basic requirements of Takechi *Kabuki*, because for Takechi a formally unified production is one that tries to present the play in its original historic form. Only in this way can the play acquire the historical concreteness that enables us to understand the reality of the age that created it, and only by producing such understanding can *kabuki* obtain the right to be designated a classical theatre.[23]

Against the possible objection that it is the play itself and not its presentation that constitutes the classical, it could be argued in Takechi's defense that since *kabuki* was traditionally not written as literature it is only the performance that can be considered the classical text. This, however, in no way diminishes the very real difficulty of achieving a production even reasonably close to the original. Indeed, one criticism of Takechi has been that for all his fine theorizing his productions did not differ much from the standard *kabuki* fare.[24] Yet there have also been more positive evaluations, especially of the theoretical aspect of Takechi's work. Theatre and cultural historian Moriya Takeshi (1943–1991), for example, ranks Takechi along with Hayashiya Tatsusaburō and Gunji Masakatsu as one of the most important pioneers in the postwar study of *kabuki*, and Gondō Yoshikazu has successfully used Takechi's historical divisions, albeit with some minor adjustments, for his own historical survey of *kabuki* form.[25] Having said this, it must be admitted that Takechi's theoretical and historical approach has not had as great an impact on postwar scholarship as has the work of Hayashiya and Gunji, and most scholars would not be as ready as Moriya to place the three on an equal footing. Yet in light of the tendency in much modern discourse on *kabuki* for dehistoricized essentialism, it is precisely Takechi's insistence on the historical that constitutes the real value of his work.

One other Marxist-oriented critic whose work should be considered before moving on to an examination of the more orthodox trends in postwar *kabuki* scholarship is Hirosue Tamotsu (1919–1993). Although Hirosue's work falls more properly into the category of Edo-period literature rather than theatre history research, he has written perceptively on *kabuki,* and his book *Chikamatsu no Josetsu* (Introduction to Chikamatsu, 1957), if somewhat controversial, is without doubt one of the most important studies of Chikamatsu's work ever produced.[26] For the sake of brevity, I shall restrict myself here to a short synopsis of his 1956 essay "Kabukigeki Seiritsu no Shikata" (How *kabuki* was formed), which provides the essentials of Hirosue's theory of *kabuki*, and to a few remarks on his later work.

Hirosue begins by posing the question whether, despite the undeniable existence of varied historical forms in *kabuki*, there might not be something that is common to all of them, that is, something that is genre-specific and true of *kabuki* throughout its history. If this is the case, he argues, than this more general characteristic must already be present in the Genroku era (1688–1704), since this is the period in which *kabuki* first became a full-fledged, multiact dramatic art. This hypothesis, however, poses a problem in that the Genroku era is also seen, at least in the context of Kamigata (Kyoto/Osaka) *kabuki*, as a period dominated by realism, which is evident not only in the emergence of the *sewamono* genre but also in certain remarks in the *Yakusha Rongo* (Actors' analects) attributed to leading actors of the time. Hirosue, however, argues that an examination of the *Yakusha Rongo* as a whole, as well as of the illustrated playbooks that exist from the period, clearly shows that the realism of Genroku *kabuki* existed alongside other more fanciful or contrived elements. It was, in other words, just one particular acting style and not an overarching structural principle. It is, in fact, on the level of structural composition that Hirosue sees the real weakness of Genroku *kabuki*. To be sure, the plays have multiact plots, but these are little more than devices for stringing together the different scenes of the play. In the absence of a more unified or thematic structure, then, it is the individual scenes that must carry the play—hence the emphasis on affective scenes and on acting style. Hirosue labels as schizophrenic (this disjunction between unequal development of scenic-level expression and overall dramatic structure, and it is this quality, already evident in Genroku *kabuki*, that he sees as characteristic of the genre as a whole.[27]

Although not all *kabuki* scholars may agree with Hirosue's clinical terminology, few would contest the claim that, in *kabuki,* dramatic structure is subordinate to the effectiveness of individual scenes. What sets Hirosue's thesis apart from more orthodox accounts of *kabuki* history is his Marxist interpretation of the reasons underlying this characteristic. Like many others, Hirosue relates *kabuki*'s growth and prosperity in the second half of the seventeenth century to the rise in economic importance of the *chōnin* class. This economic prosperity, he claims, brought about a sense of social optimism, a feeling of liberation, which is reflected in the playfulness and sensuality of *kabuki*. Hirosue argues, however, that already by the Genroku period this prosperity was reaching its limits. Running up against the wall of the feudal order, merchant class optimism itself became disjointed or schizophrenic, clinging on the one hand to the feeling of liberation offered by the theatre and the brothel, while at the same time accommodating itself to the limits of the merchant economy within feudalism. Ultimately, then, this same historical contradiction and the social schizophrenia that it produced are reflected in *kabuki*'s lack of structural development and the compensatory intensification of scenic-level effects.

In several later works, Hirosue explores in greater depth the social contradictions of the Tokugawa period, and the *chōnin*'s schizophrenic search for liberation, through an examination of the function and limits of the twin *akusho* (evil places) in contemporary society, the theatre and the licensed brothel district.[28] Here social contradictions are redefined in spatial or temporal terms, the *akusho* constituting a kind of otherworld that provides temporary liberation from the restrictions of everyday social reality. The opposition between the two worlds is not a simple one, however, for, being spatially contiguous to and only fictionally separate from the real world, the *akusho* is itself shot through with contradictions. [See the essays by Gerstle and Takahashi, chapters 6 and 8, respectively, for more on the *akusho*. Ed.]

Hirosue's analysis of the development of both *kabuki* and Chikamatsu's puppet dramas can be criticized for its literary approach and for ignoring the particulars of the Genroku theatre world. His suggestion, for example, that *kabuki* would have developed in the direction of a more unified structure had the social progress of the *chōnin* not been thwarted is essentially speculative and based on a conception of drama that is largely Western. The Japanese literary and dramatic traditions provide plenty of evidence that formal structure in Japan has always been, if not less important, at least conceived differently than in the West. This, however, does not detract from Hirosue's basic thesis that historical social contradictions have affected the form and development of *kabuki*; his analysis of how these contradictions are reflected spatially in the relationship of *kabuki* and the licensed quarters to everyday life is perhaps the most intriguing part of his work. That this is shown to be a complicated relationship and that the *akusho* is itself seen as the site of a host of contradictions sets Hirosue's work apart from the more common trend in *kabuki* scholarship of viewing *kabuki* and Edo-period popular culture in terms of the simple opposition of *chōnin* spirit and energy against feudal oppression.

While Takechi and Hirosue's work on *kabuki* and puppet theatre can be seen as the fruit of the rehabilitation of Marxism in intellectual circles following World War II, this rehabilitation was short-lived. A number of reasons can be cited for this, not the least of which is a growing anticommunist sentiment fueled by the Cold War and the fact that from about the mid-1950s the Japanese began enjoying the benefits of a high-growth economy. Marxism's foreignness also caused it to be rejected as a critical orientation. In any case, the two approaches that came to dominate *kabuki* scholarship from the late 1950s were not only more Japanese in origin, but also were much more accommodating to the project of constructing a national identity based on an image of the past.

In his own survey of *kabuki* scholarship during the 1950s and 1960s, Moriya defines the approach to theatre history studies established by the cultural and social historian Hayashiya Tatsusaburō (1914–1998) as *kankyō ron*, or environmental studies.[29] Certainly, in light of Hayashiya's emphasis on the social context of the performing arts, this designation is fair and I do not dispute it. I refer to this approach as people's history in order to capture something of the discursive environment in which it first appeared. As a product of the late forties and early fifties, Hayashiya's approach must be seen against the background of the postwar reassessment of Japanese history and—as the preface to his *Kabuki Izen* (Before *kabuki*, 1954) makes clear— of attempts to fully comprehend the feudal legacy of the past:

> Today *kabuki*, *nō*, and *kyōgen*, as well as the tea ceremony and flower arranging, are generally considered to be traditional arts. However, not only does the feudalistic society that produced them still have strong roots in the world around us, but the development of modern and democratic trends opposed to this is not yet general and widespread. At a time like this,

the role played by the so-called traditional arts becomes a very delicate matter. How are we to view this role? No doubt there are aspects of these arts that need to be faithfully continued, as well as aspects that should be discarded. On this question *kabuki* especially has been the subject of lively debate.[30]

The last sentence is a reference to the *kabuki* debate discussed above. Hayashiya's purpose in this and other works, however, was not to enter directly into the debate about the feudal legacy of the traditional arts. Before such a debate could be carried out productively, the calm and thorough study of the history of these arts was necessary, including both their internal development and the social environment in which they evolved, and since the performing arts had always been a part of the life of the people, this history must not only be scientific, it must be a *minshū no rekishi* (people's history).[31]

According to Moriya, Hayashiya's contribution to theatre history lies in his emphasis on three related aspects of the social organization of artistic production.[32] The first of these is the relationship between the producers (the artists themselves), their patrons or economic backers, and their audience. Important for the study of *kabuki* in this connection is Hayashiya's thesis that in the late Muromachi period, that is, just before the dawn of *kabuki*, the social site of artistic creation and reception shifted, in Kyoto at least, to the urban *machishū*, the class of prosperous townspeople who were allied culturally with the lower-ranking samurai and members of the impoverished nobility. The second area of inquiry concerns the origin and social position of the artists themselves. Hayashiya's achievement here lies in tracing the origin of Muromachi and early Edo-period performers to outcast or other social groups of low status in early medieval or even ancient Japan. As regards *kabuki*, this not only provides a perspective through which to view itinerant entertainers such as Okuni, the purported founder of the genre, it also accounts for the continued low social status of *kabuki* performers throughout the Edo period. The third focus of Hayashiya's study of the social environment of the performing arts is summed up in his notion of *yoriai* (coming together, assembly), the structure and organization of performance and performing groups. Starting with ancient shrine associations, Hayashiya traces the development of performance organizations through the medieval *za* (guild) to the *iemoto* (family head) system of the Edo period, together with a parallel shift in performance location from the shrine through the temporary stages of *kanjin nō* (subscription *nō*) performances to the establishment of the permanent *kabuki* stage.

These three aspects of the social organization of the performing arts are the foci not only of *Kabuki Izen* but of many of Hayashiya's other works on the Japanese theatre.[33] What is important to keep in mind, however, is that Hayashiya is primarily a historian of medieval Japan, a fact reflected in all his work. Even his two books on *kabuki* include substantial sections on the medieval period, and in neither does the treatment of *kabuki* proper extend beyond the formative years (roughly the first half-century) of the genre. For subsequent work on *kabuki*, therefore, the value of Hayashiya's work has been chiefly as a methodological model, and it has been up to other scholars to pick up where he left off and apply the approach to later periods of *kabuki* history. At the same time, however, by emphasizing its prehistory and inscribing *kabuki* into a long tradition of performing arts—a tradition traced back to even before the medieval period—Hayashiya's people's history approach suggests that the real significance of *kabuki* lies not so much in the social or ideological role it played in the Edo period as in the tradition itself and whatever communal or ritual functions the performing arts may have fulfilled in an earlier era. The implication of this for the debate about *kabuki*'s feudalism is that, since *kabuki* belongs not only to the people but to a long tradition that predates feudalism in Japan, whatever feudal ideology may be present in *kabuki* can be dismissed as an inessential later accretion.

A similar rehabilitation of *kabuki* in the context of postwar efforts to rewrite Japanese history can be found in the work of Gunji Masakatsu (1913–1998), the critic primarily responsible for the other major methodological innovation in *kabuki* studies. If the distinguishing feature of Hayashiya's approach is its emphasis on the social background and organization of production and reception, Gunji's emphasis is on the cultural background that shaped the plays and their performance. For this reason, Moriya, who dubbed Hayashiya's theatre history environmental study, has labeled Gunji's approach *geitai ron* or study of artistic form.[34] Again, however, other designations are possible, and the one that would be most appropriate is folklore studies.

Although the first examples of Gunji's application of the folklorist's methodology can be found in the essays collected in *Kabuki: Yōshiki to Denshō* (*Kabuki*: Form and tradition, 1954), his first explicit theoretical statements on the subject are contained in two articles published in the journal *Bungaku* in 1956. These articles, "Kabuki to Minzokugaku" (*Kabuki* and folklore studies) and "Kabuki Kenkyū ni okeru Minkan Denshō no Kadai" (The question of folklore in *kabuki* studies), were both later republished as part of Gunji's *Kabuki no Hassō* (The conception of *kabuki*, 1959). Gunji begins the first of these essays with a criticism of previous approaches to theatre scholarship. What goes by the name of theatre history in Japan, he complains, has tended, under the influence of Western dramatic theory, to treat theatre as a literary genre, thus concentrating on the plays alone, or else has been the work of antiquarians for whom theatre history resembles a museum display. Neither of these approaches has been able to answer the basic question as to what is the *honshitsu* (essence) of the Japanese theatre.[35] It is for this reason that Gunji suggests turning to the folklore studies begun in the prewar period by Yanagita Kunio (1875–1962) and Orikuchi Shinobu (1887–1953).

For Gunji, the value of the folklore approach is that it treats the traditional performing arts as living theatre, allowing the researcher to experience them as part of life. As such, it corrects the static image of those arts derived solely from the study of historical documents. This involves looking for living evidence of past forms of the arts in rural survivals. One example of this is Gunji's work on the early history of *kabuki*, in which he sought—and apparently found—remnants of the dances performed by Okuni and other early *kabuki* troupes in certain folk dances still performed in villages on the Sea of Japan coast.[36] [See Tsubaki's essay, chapter 1, for background on the *ayako* and *yayako odori* forms. Ed.]

Even where such living evidence is not available, however, Gunji still sees the methodology of folklore studies as essential to the study of the traditional theatre. In this case it is a matter of looking for keys to understanding particular acting or staging techniques or aspects of the form and content of plays in popular beliefs, rituals, customs, and folk literature. The best example here is provided by Gunji's research on the *aragoto* (rough business) style of acting in *kabuki*. Theatre history in the narrow sense can only conclude that this particular acting style was the creation of the actor Ichikawa Danjūrō I alone.[37] An examination of popular religious iconography, however, reveals that many features of the costume as well as the *mie* (stylized poses) of the actor in *aragoto* roles are drawn from images of Buddhist guardian deities.[38] [See the essays by Kominz and Gerstle, chapters 2 and 6, respectively. Ed.] Moreover, Gunji has argued that the typical *aragoto* hero's superhuman power stems from his identification in the popular consciousness with *arahitogami*, vengeful human-gods, the fear and appeasement of whom formed the core of the popular religious belief known as *goryō*. It is this identification, Gunji claims, that is ultimately responsible for the privileged position accorded in Edo *kabuki* to plays dealing with the revenge of the Soga brothers, the younger of whom (Gorō) is invariably portrayed as an *aragoto* figure.[39]

While the above examples show how the methodology of folklore studies is used by Gunji to illuminate specific aspects of *kabuki* history, plays, and performance, there is also a sense in which folklore studies, as a general approach, inform the whole of Gunji's work and shape his view of *kabuki*. This can be seen in the assumption, often explicitly stated, that *kabuki* represents the historical continuation of the folk theatre. Gunji compares *kabuki* performances to the feasts or banquets that were a part of medieval religious festivals and argues that both share a folkloric quality, which he refers to as *kabuki*'s *kyōensei* (banquet nature).[40] Although he adds that it is a banquet from which the gods have been exiled, he does not always make a clear distinction between religious and nonreligious performing arts and their respective functions. In *Kabuki no Hassō*, for example, he argues that "it is their original conception in the context of *shinji* (religious rites) that has structured the performing arts, and however much they have evolved they are still governed by this conception. Even *kabuki*, which developed furthest in the direction of dramatic literature, could not avoid this basic structure."[41]

For Gunji this banquet-like or folkloric structure manifests itself in a number of features that characterize *kabuki* as a whole. These include the lack of a clear separation between the real world and the theatre, evident in the performance space and resulting in an intimacy between actors and audience; the repetitive, seasonal structure of the *kabuki* calendar, which gives to each new production the atmosphere of an annual festival; the prevalence of the familiar and the typical; and, as an extension of the performing arts' original function as *shinji*, the emphasis on the extraordinary, often taking the form of sudden transformations.[42]

If an emphasis on the folkloric is what characterizes Gunji's work, it is this same emphasis that invites criticism. What is debatable is precisely the extent to which folklore has shaped and remained unchanged in *kabuki*. It could be argued, for example, that folklore stories can do no more than indicate the folkloric origins of certain elements in *kabuki*, for while these elements may still be present, it is doubtful whether in the context of urban Edo-period society they still had the same significance or fulfilled the same function they had in an earlier age or in rural festivals. Seen in this light, Gunji's insistence on continuity only leads back to the ideological dilemma of postwar Japan and the revision of Japanese history. For Gunji, like Hayashiya, has to deal with the problem of Edo-period feudalism and, by extension, the feudal legacy in the militarism of the 1930s and the war period; and like Hayashiya he attempts to clear *kabuki* of any implication in this feudalism by placing it in an alternative tradition. For Hayashiya this tradition is one developed by medieval performers for the people, while for Gunji it is the folk tradition.

There is, however, another ideological factor at work here, both in Hayashiya's people's history and, to an even greater extent, in Gunji's folkloric approach. For if it is important to both Hayashiya and Gunji to absolve *kabuki* of any complicity in feudalism, it is also part of their ideological agenda to show that the performing arts tradition to which *kabuki* belongs is distinctly Japanese. This is why, for Gunji, studying *kabuki* is a matter of determining not only its dramatic or performative features, but also its ethnological characteristics.[43] And if the national character in *kabuki* has been tarnished by the Confucian ideology of feudalism, in Gunji's eyes an even greater danger lies in the processes of modernization and Westernization at work in Japan since the Meiji period. These processes, Gunji warns, not only have alienated the people from their performing arts tradition, but are threatening to turn *kabuki* into a nationless vagrant,[44] while at the same time preventing the development of any new theatrical form that will adequately reflect the national character:

> The influence of the Society for Theatre Reform's imported Western rationalism and superficial dramatic theory has gradually cut *kabuki* off from the real conditions of popular life, resulting in the large gap that exists between the two today. It is not *shingeki* but the scorn and hostility shown to tradition as a result of the importation of Western theatre that has been the great misfortune of both *kabuki* and the modern theatre. If instead of facing this fact we opt for the frivolous solution of simply mixing the East and the West, what can this possibly contribute to the future of the Japanese theatre? A more desirable approach, I believe, would be to confront the modern from the context of the [Japanese] performing arts tradition, that is to say, by first looking at how *kabuki* carries on that tradition, how it spread amongst the people, where its power of entertainment lies, and, above all, by ascertaining what in that tradition is feudal and what is not. Only then can creation begin.[45]

As was true of the Meiji period reformers and Shōyō, then, Gunji too sees *kabuki* as forming the foundation of a new national theatre. However, whereas the reformers and Shōyō saw in *kabuki* a theatrical form in need of much Western-based reform before it could take on such a role, for Gunji it is not a matter of reforming *kabuki* but of preserving it in a pristine form, unsullied by feudalism and modernization. As he suggests in the revised edition of his *Kabuki Nyūmon* (Introduction to *kabuki*), if it is the scholar's task as a researcher to uncover this form, it is his duty as a citizen to demand of *kabuki* today its strict classicalization. [46]

Although Hayashiya and Gunji's work can be termed epoch-making for the way it opened up new research areas that allow for a broader social or cultural contextualization of *kabuki*, it cannot be said that these achievements were immediately followed up by other, equally innovative research. This is a point that Moriya has made in his own attempt to summarize the history of *kabuki* research.[47] In Moriya's view, what was exciting about the appearance of Hayashiya's environmental studies and Gunji's artistic form studies is not so much the new research areas themselves nor these scholars' own work in them, but the fact that the very emergence of new approaches represented an effort at theoretical and methodological advance in the field of theatre history. The problem with later scholarship, according to Moriya, is that rather than carry on this effort most scholars have been content simply to fill in the gaps in Hayashiya and Gunji's research or concentrate on other, isolated problems. As a result, not only has there been little theoretical advance, the methodological questions these approaches raised in the first place have been more or less forgotten.[48] It is for this reason that the scholars who address the larger questions are so noticeable, and it is to these exceptions that I now turn.

One work that could be singled as an exception is *Henshin no Shisō* (The concept of metamorphosis, 1970), by Imao Tetsuya. Perhaps the most interesting part of this book is its introduction. This is basically a theoretical analysis and critique of the modern or bourgeois theatre. Quoting from Diderot and other Western theoreticians of theatre, Imao attempts to show how the rise of the bourgeois theatre with its fourth-wall theory and emphasis on individualized characters at the same time represents a certain impoverishment of the theatre. It was, in other words, not simply a movement away from plays about kings and princes to plays about the ordinary citizens; it was a movement from theatre for and about humankind to theatre for and about the bourgeois individual, a movement from poetry to prose, from collective creation to creation by the author, and, ultimately, from theatre as theatre to theatre as literature. This modern, literary conception of the theatre, moreover, has become dominant in Japan as well and at least since the early twentieth century has also affected *kabuki*. Inasmuch as it is based on Enlightenment and nineteenth-century ideals and values, this literary modernity is already out of date, and thus Imao calls for its rejection. This rejection, however, at the same time opens up the possibility of a return to the richness of theatre *as theatre*, such as existed in the premodern period. For this reason, Imao concludes, the theatre renewal must begin with reflection on the premodern theatre, and it is in terms of such a reflection that he wishes his work on *kabuki* to be read.[49]

Imao thus agrees with Gunji in rejecting the Western-derived modern theatre and in seeing the traditional theatre as a key to going beyond the modern. Yet *Henshin no Shisō* also includes a criticism of Gunji's folklore approach. While Imao concedes that folklore studies have been far more successful than the literary approach in constructing an image of *kabuki* in its totality, their inherent weakness, he argues, is inability to treat *kabuki* in terms of its own historical context and development.[50] The example Imao is dealing with here is the very theme of transformation, which, as has been seen, Gunji points to as evidence of the folkloric world view in *kabuki* plays and performances. Rather than seeing transformations in *kabuki* as a continuation of the performing arts function of fulfilling the people's desire to see gods manifest or miracles performed, Imao views as a kind of entertainment, the pleasure of which lies in witnessing liberation from a closed or suffocating—the feudal structure of Edo-period society itself—reality and the possibility of realizing the utopian reality of what should be.[51] A somewhat similar view of *kabuki*'s social function can be found in the work of Nishiyama Matsunosuke, a widely recognized authority on the history of old Edo and its people. In an article first published in 1960 and entitled "Kabuki no Dentō: Fueki no Ronri" (The *kabuki* tradition and its immutable logic), Nishiyama writes:

> As a theatre by and for the people, *kabuki* was constantly under the oppression of the *bakufu* [military dictatorship]. Under such political oppression, the reason that *kabuki*, a form of commercial entertainment, received the enthusiastic support of the people is that for them it represented the best possible means of liberation. Unable to achieve liberation themselves by consciously confronting their antagonists, the people sought instead other original means. . . . It was this function demanded of the theatre by the people that gave *kabuki* its mission.[52]

Like Imao, Nishiyama is trying to build a case for *kabuki* performances as, if not political theatre, at least something more than simple entertainment or escapism. For Nishiyama, however, this spirit of liberation manifests itself not in transformations but in the *aragoto* heroes of Edo plays such as Soga Gorō and, in particular, Sukeroku, his prime example of the Edoites' proud opposition to their samurai masters. Even if it can be accepted that *kabuki* did serve as a kind of substitute liberation for a politically frustrated people, there is still the question concerning the degree to which this theatre, precisely as a form of pseudoliberation, embodies and is contained within the dominant ideology. That both Imao and Nishiyama fail to deal with this question and instead attempt to read into *kabuki* a form of subdued or indirect opposition to the feudal order suggests that here too an effort is being made to clear *kabuki* of the taint of feudalism, albeit by means of a different strategy. Whereas Hayashiya and Gunji absolve *kabuki* of this charge by inserting it into alternative traditions with roots in the past, Imao and Nishiyama locate *kabuki* within a contemporary popular culture that is distinct from and opposed to the feudal system.

Another criticism that could be made of Nishiyama's assessment of *kabuki*'s role in Edo-period society would be to question whether there is not a contradiction between theatre by and for the people and commercial entertainment. It is interesting that Nishiyama is in fact one of the few *kabuki* historians to have systematically studied the theatre's commercial structure.

In an article entitled "Kabuki no Kōgyōshi" (*Kabuki* entrepreneurs), he argues that what makes the appearance of Okuni *kabuki* at the beginning of the seventeenth century was momentous because it set the pattern for the performing arts to be sold as commodities.[53] This commercialism, however, is invariably given a positive interpretation by Nishiyama. In the passage cited above, for example, it implies that *kabuki* producers' responsiveness to the needs and desires of the audience dissolves the potential contradiction between the interests of the people and commercial entertainment. In a similar way, Nishiyama deals with the restraints of commercial production on *kabuki* as an art by pointing to the positive effects of competition. In "Kabuki ni okeru Ie" (The "house" in *kabuki*, 1971), an essay on the *ie* (artistic school or house) in *kabuki*, he claims that it is precisely competition that has led to the creation of famous plays and acting techniques.[54] This argument not only enables Nishiyama to turn commercialism into a virtue, it allows him to regard the *ie* in *kabuki*, despite its obvious feudal trappings, as a progressive social structure. For since *kabuki* houses were in constant competition with each other, they could not rely on tradition alone but had to go on creating and refining their house arts.

One other critic who should be mentioned and who, like Imao and Nishiyama, attempts to locate *kabuki* within a vibrant, oppositional popular culture is Hattori Yukio. Hattori's first major work, *Kabuki Seiritsu no Kenkyū* (The study of *kabuki's* formation, 1968) is on *kabuki's* history. In his *Kabuki no Kōzō* (The structure of *kabuki*, 1970), however, he attempts to portray *kabuki* in a broader sense, focusing less on historical change than on the structure of Edo-period *kabuki* as a whole. Like Imao, Hattori begins this work with a discussion of the problem of modernity and the possibility of a return to total theatre through the premodern. This helps to explain his emphasis on structure, for Hattori understands structure less as a formal principle than as a framework for creation, a framework that is also an alternative to the author-centered, literary creation of the modern theatre.

For Hattori, this structure can be seen in the *sekai/shukō* (dramatic world/ innovative plot element) dramaturgic method and in the organization of the daily *kabuki* program. In these structures, Hattori argues, playwrights are only following traditional Japanese aesthetics. The *sekai/shukō* technique, for example, in which new twists are given to familiar stories, is an example of the Japanese preference for variation on what already exists rather than radically new creation. [See Kominz and Inoue's essays, chapters 2 and 11, respectively, for more on the *sekai/shukō* method. Ed.] Likewise, Hattori sees the arrangement of the daily program in terms of the *jo-ha-kyū* (introduction, development, climax) structure found both in the ancient court entertainment *bugaku* and in *nō*.[55] Ultimately, however, *kabuki's* structure is defined for Hattori by its actor-centeredness, for it is the actor who carries the performance and it is through his *gei* (art) that both the typical and the novel are expressed.[56] This may have prevented the development of the playwright as an autonomous creator, but at the same time it provides for a different kind of creation, which is more collective, more responsive to the audience, and more theatrical.

This is not to say that Hattori ignores the commercial pressures of *kabuki* production. Indeed, like Nishiyama, Hattori is one of the few critics to consider seriously this aspect of *kabuki* production, and thus in *Kabuki no Kōzō* the first level of structure that he looks at is the organizational one involving financial backers, writers, troupe leaders, and actors. What united them all, he observes, was the desire for full houses and long runs. Achieving this success, however, was primarily the responsibility of the *zamoto* (troupe leader) and the actors. It was their art, in other words, that made or broke the theatre, and thus for Hattori, too, commercial pressure and competition are seen as ultimately beneficial to the development of that art.[57] Elsewhere he suggests that, inasmuch as it provided the energy necessary for developing and refining *kabuki* into a more complex and sophisticated form of theatre, economic pressure was fundamental to the growth of *kabuki* as a whole during its early period.[58]

While it is not difficult to imagine commercialism as the engine that drove *kabuki*'s creation and development, it is somewhat harder to accept that it had only positive effects on *kabuki* as an art. The question could be raised, for example, whether there is any significant difference between the kind of commercial pressure that animated *kabuki* production and that under which producers in the entertainment industry work today. As if to counter this possible criticism, both Nishiyama and Hattori concede a resemblance, but they argue that Edo-period *kabuki* had certain features that distinguish it from modern commercial popular culture. For Nishiyama, *kabuki*'s saving grace is its responsiveness to its audience, its ability to give concrete expression to the people's yearnings. This, he claims, prevented production from falling into the vanity of the star system.[59] In Hattori's view, on the other hand, the danger for *kabuki* was its very emphasis on fixed patterns or types, which could easily have degenerated into the stereotypical and the hackneyed, such as one finds in television drama. He insists, however, that the creative efforts of the producers kept this from happening. Indeed, he argues that it was precisely in not rejecting the typical but in using it for fresh creation that both the difficulty of the *kabuki* producers' art and the value of their achievements should be judged.[60]

What is striking about both these arguments is that modern popular culture is cast in negative terms, as a group of pitfalls into which *kabuki* was ultimately saved from degenerating or falling. The distinction both Nishiyama and Hattori are trying to make, in other words, is between a positive, premodern popular culture and a negative, modern mass culture. Granted, the two are not exactly the same thing, but it is a question whether the difference between, say, the emphasis on stars or the combination of the familiar and the novel in *kabuki* and similar features in modern commercial culture is qualitative or merely one of degree. No doubt commercial production and competition did spur *kabuki*'s early development and were in this sense partly responsible for the mature, multiact dramatic art that emerged by the Genroku era. Even this golden age, however, was not free of crass, economically motivated success formulas and the hackneyed, and what one finds in later periods is an increased reliance on elaborate stage machinery and effects. If commercialism contributed to *kabuki*'s development, it also pushed it in the direction of the formulaic and spectacle, and it is in this context that a reexamination of the question of transformations can be instructive.

As noted earlier, for Imao the prevalence of transformations in plays is proof not of the continuation of folklore but of a shift in the function of transformation scenes from the reenactment of miracles to a form of symbolic liberation. While an intriguing concept, the notion of symbolic liberation would have to be much more rigorously specified in terms of social and ideological relations in order to be convincing. Another criticism that could be made of Imao's argument is that he does not adequately consider the way in which this shift can also be seen as one from transformation as miracle to transformation as spectacle—for the rise in popularity of transformation scenes and transformation dance (*henge buyō*) during the eighteenth century went hand in hand with the development of increasingly sophisticated stage machinery and effects that allowed for more spectacular transformations. In this context, one would have to agree with Imao that transformations in *kabuki* plays were no longer a matter of folklore pure and simple.

Hattori, true to his willingness to acknowledge the commercial aspect of *kabuki*, does not ignore the theatrical nature of transformations, and even points out that *hayagawari* or quick change has been treated by theatre producers as one of *kabuki*'s most salable commodities.[61] In his own work on the subject, *Hengeron* (On transformation, 1975), however, Hattori is equally concerned to distinguish *kabuki* from the modern. In this sense, he takes a line of argument similar to Gunji's, insisting precisely on the popular religious element in transformations. In the chapter entitled "Hitotsu no Dentō Geinō Ron" (A theory of the traditional performing arts), Hattori places *kabuki* within a tradition of religion and play, a tradition which he sees as defining the dynamics not only of the performing arts in Japan but also of the spiritual life of the people. What distinguishes *kabuki* from earlier forms of Japanese theatre is the shift in this dynamic, that is to say, a weakening of the religious function and a corresponding intensification of the play function.[62] For Hattori, however, this in no way implies a complete loss of the religious function, and if there is one point that he stresses in *Hengeron* it is that Edo-period *kabuki*—as well as everyday life—was very much colored by a popular, premodern, religious world view. Thus transformations, however much they relied on special effects and represented a commercially safe part of any play or *kabuki* program, are something more than mere spectacles or techni- cal thrills. In the final analysis, they are indications of a premodern religious consciousness that was all but snuffed out by the modern rationalism of the Meiji period.

In a later book, *Sakasama Yūrei* (Upside-down ghosts, 1989), Hattori gives a similar interpretation to ghost scenes in *kabuki* plays. While acknowledg- ing the tradition of *karuwaza* (acrobatics) in *kabuki*, he tries to show that such scenes in plays from the Genroku period through to Tsuruya Nanboku IV's (1755–1829) great ghost play *Tōkaidō Yotsuya Kaidan* (The ghost sto- ries at Yotsuya on the Tōkaidō) (1825) all draw on the popular belief in and fear of ghosts. In much the same way as Gunji points to the folkloric origins of specific features of *kabuki*, Hattori traces the upside-down ghost pattern back to popular images of murder victims thrown down wells or sinners tumbling headfirst into hell. At the same time, in a manner reminiscent of Imao's interpretation of transformations, Hattori also ascribes a more con- temporary, political significance to the ghost phenomenon. The appearance in *kabuki* plays of vengeful female ghosts, for example, he interprets as a latent feminism, an implicit protest against feudalism's oppression of women. Moreover, in the image of the topsy-turvy he sees an effective weapon against the social order and hierarchy.[63]

In *Sakasama Yūrei*, in other words, Hattori is attempting to have it both ways: *kabuki* as both popular religion *and* political protest. In this sense the work can be seen as an attempt to merge Gunji's folklore studies approach with the more recent trend of seeing *kabuki* as part of an oppositional popu- lar culture. This is understandable since the two approaches serve similar ideological agendas. For just as uncovering the folkloric in *kabuki* is a means of proving *kabuki*'s antimodern character, so seeing *kabuki* as a form of so- cial protest confirms it as antifeudal. Both approaches, in short, serve the need to construct an image of *kabuki* that can provide the basis for a cultural identity free of both Western modernity and the stigma of feudalism.

As mentioned above, one of the examples Hattori draws on in *Sakasama Yūrei* is the famous ghost story play *Tōkaidō Yotsuya Kaidan* by playwright Nanboku IV. The book also contains a separate essay on Nanboku that treats the ghost phenomenon as just one aspect of what Hattori refers to as Nanboku's dramaturgy of reversal and disorder. [64] The whole book, in fact, should be seen against the background of a shift in the focus of *kabuki* studies during the 1970s and 1980s, a shift away from the Genroku period and toward the Kasei (Bunka-Bunsei, 1804–1829) era, the period in which Nanboku dominated the *kabuki* scene. Interestingly enough, it was Gunji who perhaps more than any other scholar sparked an interest in the often neglected *kabuki* of the early nineteenth century. Gunji, for example, was one of the editors of the new complete works of Nanboku that appeared over the years 1971–1974. Even before this, however, he had turned attention to Nanboku with his production of the play *Sakura-hime Azuma Bunshō* (The scarlet princess of Edo) at the Kokuritsu Gekijō in 1967. Earlier scholars had seen the *kabuki* of the Kasei period as "overripe" because of its emphasis on spectacle and on scenes depicting the coarse reality of criminals, prostitutes, and destitute samurai.[65] Gunji's full-length revival of *Sakura-hime*, however, which seems to have been remarkably successful at bringing out the playwright's black humor and penchant for the grotesque as well as the evil energy of his characters, captured the attention of many in both theatrical and academic circles and marked the beginning of what has become known as the Nanboku boom.

At least one critic has attributed the rise in Nanboku's currency to the parallels between the student movement's opposition to an array of government policies in the late 1960s and early 1970s and Nanboku's own cynical and irreverent attitude toward the social order of his day.[66] Certainly a major part of the attraction of Nanboku has been his image as an antiestablishment rebel, an image very much evident in Hattori's claim that Nanboku's plays express an intense satire of and hostility and opposition to the social order.[67] While the politics of protest and opposition may have affected the timing of the Nanboku revival and no doubt had something to do with the interest in Nanboku shown by alternative or underground theatres of the time, the critical attention that has come to be focused on Nanboku's work is by no means inconsistent with more general trends in postwar *kabuki* scholarship. For the development of an enthusiasm for Nanboku's plays, which exemplify the late Edo-period tendency to focus on the grotesque and on reality at its most sordid, is only a further step in the process of rehabilitating *kabuki* as a whole and privileging not only its antifeudal character, but also everything about it which is antirational and, in the last analysis, antimodern. As such, the Nanboku boom represents both the validation of Kishida's aesthetics and the complete and final defeat of the attempted cleansing operation that started with the *kabuki* reform movement.

Although this review has necessarily been selective, it should be sufficient to show that modern Japanese discourse on *kabuki*, wherever it has attempted to rise above a positivist science (itself an ideological position), reveals itself to be governed by a common ideological concern with cultural identity. To be sure, there have been improvements in methodology that have contributed greatly to the understanding of historical *kabuki*. The movements away from reform and toward historical study, for example, and from the conception of *kabuki* as literature to *kabuki* as theatre, have led scholars to explore significant features of *kabuki* and its history that were previously neglected. Yet this same methodological advance has shown itself to be inseparable from a shifting strategy of using *kabuki* as a symbol of the national identity, a strategy that began by seeking that identity in a reformed theatre comparable to that of the West and ended by finding it in a theatre that is both premodern and uniquely Japanese.

By way of conclusion, I would like to make a few comments on the value of the kind of ideological or metacritical analysis I have attempted here, especially for the Western scholar. Whether or not one agrees with my particular reading of the various works and trends in *kabuki* historical research, I would hope that this survey has at least demonstrated that knowledge is never absolute or ideologically neutral. The truth of *kabuki* history, in other words, is not simply out there waiting to be discovered. Of course, we can learn more about it, and Japanese scholars today have a much better understanding of the subject than did the reformers or Shōyō in the Meiji period. But knowledge is always in a certain sense relative, its production directed and shaped in important ways by the researcher's historical and social context. As I have tried to demonstrate, the specific ideological contexts in which Japanese researchers have worked have led to certain weaknesses or blind spots. What this means for the Western scholar of *kabuki* history, I would suggest, is that, despite the voluminous Japanese writing on the subject, there is still important work to be done in many areas. Many Japanese scholars, for example, have seen *kabuki* in terms of opposition to the feudal ideology, but few have attempted to analyze its place within that ideology. There is a need, I believe, for more sophisticated studies showing how *kabuki* plays and production practices, despite their opposition or irreverence, found accommodation (or accommodated themselves) within the limits of their age. Similarly, the tendency to see *kabuki* as a distinctly premodern form of theatre has resulted in a failure to adequately consider *kabuki*'s mode of production and reception as a step in a historical development that leads ultimately to the commercial entertainment industry in Japan today.[68] Of course there are differences between the two, but there are also important continuities and similarities that should be explored. Finally, in their efforts to prove the uniquely Japanese character of *kabuki*, many Japanese scholars have depended on an ideological construction of the West in which Western theatre is invariably seen in terms of realistic modern drama. Thus, while *kabuki* is now generally recognized in Japan as a popular theatre incorporating many folk-loric elements, there has been little consideration of folk or popular traditions in the West as possible objects of comparison. The comparative approach, in other words, still has not been adequately applied to the study of *kabuki* history and has the potential to lead to a better understanding not only of *kabuki* but of theatrical traditions in other cultures as well.

Notes

1. Imao has written of the *kabuki* world's gradual abandonment of Danjūrō's *katsureki* (living history plays) and the return to the Edo-period classics in the 1890s: "People do not understand that this was a recreation of the classics mediated by the experience of *katsureki*. This is what constitutes the establishment of the modern in *kabuki* and which still forms the basis of *kabuki* today." See Imao Tetsuya, *Henshin no Shisō* (The concept of metamorphosis) (Tokyo: Hōsei Daigaku Shuppankyoku, 1970), 313. All translations, unless otherwise noted, are mine.

2. Hijikata Teiichi, ed., *Meiji Geijutsu Bungaku Ronshū* (Anthology of Meiji theories of art and literature), vol. 79 of *Meiji Bungaku Zenshū* (Complete collection of Meiji literature) (Tokyo: Chikuma Shobō, 1975), 407.

3. Suematsu Kenchō, "Engeki Kairyō Iken" (Views on theatre reform), in ibid., 108–109, 105, 110.

4. Toyama Masakazu [Shūichi], "Engeki Kairyō Ron Shikō," in ibid.,146–48.

5. Tsubouchi Shōyō, "Engeki Kairyōkai no Seiritsu," *Meiji Bunka Zenshū* (Complete collection of Meiji culture), vol. 12 (Tokyo: Nihon Hyōronsha, 1928), 252.

6. I have treated elsewhere the Meiji-period critics' preference for the drama of the puppets (*ningyō jōruri* or *bunraku*) over that of *kabuki* and the resultant acceptance of the work of Chikamatsu into the emerging canon of classical Japanese literature. See William Lee, "Chikamatsu and Dramatic Literature in the Meiji Period," in *Inventing the Classics: Canon Formation, National Identity, and Japanese Literature*, ed. Haruo Shirane and Tomi Suzuki, (Stanford: Stanford University Press, 2000), 179–198.

7. Tsubouchi Shōyō and Yamamoto Jirō, *History and Characteristics of Kabuki: The Japanese Classical Drama*, trans. Ryōzō Matsumoto. (Yokohama: Yamagata, 1960), 105.

8. Ibid., 121–122.

9. Ibid., 138.

10. Ibid., 232. Since the translation of the last sentence of this quotation is slightly misleading, I have amended it based on the original as quoted in Gunji Masakatsu, *Kabuki Ronsō* (*Kabuki* debate) (Tokyo: Shibunkaku, 1979), 231–232.

11. Tsubouchi and Yamamoto, *History and Characteristics,* 143, 146–152.

12. Ibid., 153–167.

13. Hayashiya Tatsusaburō et al., "Historical Review of Studies and References," *Acta Asiatica* 32 (1977): 74–76.

14. Takano Tatsuyuki and Kuroki Kanzō, eds., *Chikamatsu Monzaemon Zenshū* (Complete anthology of Chikamatsu Monzaemon), 10 vols. (Tokyo: Shunyūdō, 1922–1924); Kitani Hōgin, ed., *Dai Chikamatsu Zenshū* (Great Chikamatsu anthology), 16 vols. (Tokyo: Dai Chikamatsu Zenshū Kankōkai, 1922–1925); Fuji Otōo, ed., *Chikamatsu Zenshū* (Complete Chikamatsu), 12 vols. (Osaka: Osaka Asahi

Shimbunsha, 1925–1928); Takano Tatsuyuki, ed., *Chikamatsu Kabuki Kyōgenshū* (Anthology of Chikamatsu's *kabuki* plays), 2 vols. (Tokyo: Rokugōkan, 1927); Takano Tatsuyuki and Kuroki Kanzō, eds., *Genroku Kabuki Kessakushū* (Genroku *kabuki* masterpiece anthology), 2 vols. (Tokyo: Waseda Daigaku Shuppanbu, 1925).

15. Kishida Ryūsei, *Kabuki Biron* (Aesthics of Kabaki) (Tokyo: Hayakawa Shobō, 1948), 12.

16. Ibid., 39.

17. Ibid., 40.

18. Kondō Tadayoshi and Ino Kenji, "Kabuki o Mite (Seeing *kabuki*), *Bungaku* 19: 11 (1951): 9–15.

19. Kuwahara Takeo, "Konnichi ni okeru Kabuki" (*Kabuki* today), *Bungaku* 20: 3 (1952): 41–49.

20. Gunji Masakatsu, *Kabuki Nyūmon* (Introduction to *kabuki*) (1954, 1962; Tokyo: Rokuyōsha, 1990), 12–13.

21. Takechi Tetsuya, "Kabuki no Enshutsu" (*Kabuki* direction), *Bungaku* 24: 1 (1956): 60.

22. Ibid., 64.

23. Takechi Tetsuya, "Takechi Kabuki no Enshutsu" (Takechi's *kabuki* direction), *Watakushi no Engeki Ronsō* (Tokyo: Chikuma Shobō, 1958), reprinted in *Gendai no Espuri* 104 (1976): 89–96.

24. Tobe Ginsaku, "Takechi Kabuki Hihan" (Criticism of Takechi *kabuki*), *Bungaku* 24.1 (1956): 104.

25. Moriya Takeshi, "Kenkyū no Tebiki" (Guide to research), *Kabuki*, vol. 8 of *Nihon no Koten Geinō* (Japanese classical performing arts), Geinōshi Kenkyūkai, ed. (Tokyo: Heibonsha, 1971), 340; Gondō Yoshikazu, "Yōshiki no Tenkai" (Evolution of style), 87–132.

26. Hirosue Tamotsu, *Chikamatsu no Josetsu* (1957; rev. ed. Tokyo: Miraisha, 1963).

27. Hirosue Tamotsu, "Kabukigeki Seiritsu no Shikata" (The manner of *kabuki*'s formation), *Bungaku* 24: 1 (1956): 1–11.

28. Hirosue Tamotsu, *Akusho no Hassō* (The conception of evil places) (Tokyo: Sanseidō, 1970); *Henkai no Akusho* (Tokyo: Heibonsha, 1973).

29. Moriya, "Kenkyū no Tebiki," 338.

30. Hayashiya Tatsusaburō, *Kabuki Izen* (Tokyo: Iwanami Shoten, 1954), i.

31. Ibid., 3–4.

32. Moriya, "Kenkyū no Tebiki," 338–39.

33. See, for example, Hayashiya Tatsusaburō, *Nihon Engeki no Kankyō* (The environment of Japanese theatre) (Tokyo: Yashima Shuppan, 1947); *Kabuki no Seiritsu* (Studies in the history of middle-ages performing arts) (Tokyo: Kabuki no Seiritsu, 1949); *Chūsei Geinōshi no Kenkyū* (Tokyo: Iwanami Shoten, 1960).

34. Moriya, "Kenkyū no Tebiki," 338.

35. Gunji Masakatsu, *Kabuki no Hassō* (1959: Tokyo: Nishizawa Shoten, 1978), 4.

36. Ibid., 13–18.

37. Ibid., 8.

38. Gunji Masakatsu, *Kabuki: Yōshiki to Dentō* (*Kabuki*: Form and tradition) (1954: Tokyo: Gakugei Shorin, 1969), 15–31.

39. Gunji, *Kabuki no Hassō*, 40–53.

40. Gunji, *Kabuki: Yōshiki to Dentō*, 3.

41. Gunji, *Kabuki no Hassō*, 24.
42. Gunji, *Kabuki: Yōshiki to Dentō*, 3–14; *Kabuki no Hassō*, 20–39.
43. Gunji, *Kabuki no Hassō*, 20.
44. Ibid., 20.
45. Ibid., 39.
46. Gunji, *Kabuki Nyūmon* (Tokyo: Bokuyōsha, 1990), 15.
47. Moriya, "Kenkyū no Tebiki," 339–340.
48. Of course, work lacking in theoretical or methodological innovation can still represent significant research or scholarly activity. One could point to the research of Ogasawara Kyōko and Hattori Yukio on the birth and early history of *kabuki*, for example, or to Suwa Haruo, Matsuzaki Hitoshi, and Torigoe Bunzō's work on the following period and on Genroku *kabuki*. Perhaps even more important have been the several large collaborative efforts in materials and text compilation and editing. These include: *Kabuki Hyōbanki Shūsei* (Collected *kabuki* critiques) (Tokyo: Iwanami Shoten, 1972–1977), an eleven-volume collection of *yakusha hyōbanki* (evaluations of actors), which was followed by another series (1987–1995) containing a further eleven volumes; the fifteen-volume collection of source materials on popular culture, *Nihon Shomin Bunka Shiryō Shūsei* (Collection of sources on popular Japanese culture) (Tokyo: Sanichi Shobō, 1973–1977); two new complete editions of Chikamatsu's puppet plays, one of which, *Chikamatsu Zenshū* (The complete Chikamatsu) (Tokyo: Iwanami Shoten, 1985–1992), also contains all his extant *kabuki* plays; and a forty-one-volume collection of *kabuki* scripts nearing completion, *Kabuki Daichō Shūsei* (Anthology of *kabuki* scripts) (Tokyo: Benseisha, 1983–).
49. Imao Tetsuya, *Henshin no Shisō* (The concept of metamorphosis) (Tokyo: Hōsei Daigaku Shuppankyoku, 1970), 12.
50. Ibid., 18–19.
51. Ibid., 59–60.
52. Nishiyama Matsunosuke, *Edo Kabuki Kenkyū* (Studies of Edo *kabuki*), vol. 7 of *Nishiyama Matsunosuke Chosakushū* (The writings of Nishiyama Matsunosuke) (Tokyo: Yoshikawa Kōbunkan, 1987), 264.
53. Ibid., 349–350.
54. Ibid., 241–251.
55. Hattori Yukio, *Kabuki no Kōzō* (The structure of *Kabuki*) (Chūō Kōronsha, 1970), 72–73, 187–198.
56. Ibid., 39, 73, 134, 169–170.
57. Ibid., 39–43.
58. Hattori Yukio, "*Kabuki Kōzō no Keisei*" (The formation of *kabuki* structure), *Kabuki*, Geinōshi Kenkyūkai, ed., 50–51.
59. Nishiyama, *Edo Kabuki Kenkyū*, 266–267.
60. Hattori, *Kabuki Kōzō*, 17–18.
61. Hattori Yukio, *Hengeron: Kabuki no Seishinshi* (On transformation) (Tokyo: Heibonsha, 1975), 38–39, 57.
62. Ibid., 21–24.
63. Hattori Yukio, *Sakasama Yūrei* (Upside-down ghosts) (Tokyo: Heibonsha, 1989), 80, 107.
64. Ibid., 50.
65. The term "overripe" (*ranjuku*) is used by both Shuzui and Kawatake. See the

chapter on periodization in Suwa Haruo, *Kabuki no Denshō* (*Kabuki* tradition) (To-kyo: Senninsha, 1981), 188–197.

66. Ōzasa Yoshio, "Chūkindai no Kanōsei: Nanboku-geki no Fukkatsu" (Midmodern possibilities: Reviving Nanboku's plays), *Kokubungaku* (Japanese literature) 31: 2 (1986): 124–125.

67. Hattori, *Sakasama Yūrei*, 64.

68. The major exception is the work of Moriya. While showing an astonishing command of historical detail, Moriya also attempts to place *kabuki* in larger perspective by examining the structure and relations of theatrical production in the Edo period, which he defines as the age in which, by means of the mechanism of *kōgyō* (the theatre business), the performing arts came to function as a kind of commodity. See Moriya Takeshi, *Kinsei Geinō Kōgyōshi no Kenkyū* (Research in the history of performing arts producion) (Tokyo: Kōbundō, 1985), 14.

Selected Bibliography

This bibliography is limited to *kabuki*-related essays appearing in English-language journals and books published after 1945. Several important essays dealing mainly with Japan's classical puppet theatre, generally called *bunraku*, are included because of the close relationship between the puppets and *kabuki*. I have not included reviews of *kabuki* either in Japan or on tour abroad; most of the latter are collected in Shōchiku Company, Ltd., ed., *Grand Kabuki: Overseas Tours 1928–1993* (Tokyo: Shōchiku, 1994). Essays included in the present book are not listed. A good bibliography of mainly pre-1945 essays is given in Margaret H. Young, *Kabuki: Japanese Drama* (Bloomington, IN.: Eastern Press, 1985). This work is an offprint of Young's 1953 Ph.D. dissertation at the University of Indiana, originally titled "Japanese *Kabuki* Drama: The History and Meaning of the Essential Elements of Its Theatre Art Form."

Akimoto, Shunkichi. "*Kabuki* Audiences, Past and Present." *Japan Quarterly* 3 (1962).

Ando, Tsuruo. "The Japanese Theatre." Trans. C. Terry. *Atlantic Monthly* (January 1955).

Armstrong, Ann Elizabeth. "Innovations and Compromises: A Performance History 1924–1995." In *101 Years of* Kabuki *in Hawai'i*, eds. Holly Blumner et al. Honolulu: Department of Theatre and Dance, University of Hawai'i, 1995.

Bach, Faith. "New Directions in *Kabuki*." *Asian Theatre Journal* 6 (spring 1989).

———, trans. and intro. "*Takatoki*: A *Kabuki* Drama." *Asian Theatre Journal* 15 (fall 1998).

Banu, Georges. "*Gesamtkunstwerk* and *Kabuki*." Trans. Marian Schmid. Special issue, "Japanese Theatre and the West." In *Contemporary Theatre Review,* ed. A. Horie-Webber. 1, part 2 (1994).

Bethune, Robert. "Describing Performance in the Theatre: *Kabuki* Training and the Western Acting Student." *The Drama Review* (TDR) 33 (winter 1989).

Bertrandias, Richard. "Fish, Rice and Footlights." *Theatre Arts* 36 (January 1952).

Blakeney, Ben. "Rokudaime." *Contemporary Japan* 18 (October/December 1949).

Blumner, Holly, and Naeko Maeshiba. "*Sukeroku*: A History." In *101 Years of* Kabuki *in Hawai'i*, eds. Holly Blumner et al. Honolulu: Department of Theatre and Dance, University of Hawai'i, 1995.

Bowers, Faubion. "The Japanese Theatre." *Theatre Arts* 32 (October 1948).

———. "*Kabuki* Is Broadway Bound . . ." *Theatre Arts* 37 (September 1953).
———. "Concerning *Kabuki*." *Saturday Review of Literature* (February 27, 1954).
———. "Backstage at the *Kabuki*." *Theatre Arts* 38 (March 1954).
———. "The Past Within the Present." *Dance Magazine* (June 1960).
———. "*Kabuki* in America." *Nation* (July 9, 1960).
Brandon, James R. "Translating *Kabuki* for English Performance." In *Studies on Japanese Culture*. vol. 2. Tokyo: Japan P.E.N. Club, 1973.
———. "*Kabuki*: Japan's First Contemporary Urban Theatre." In *Proceedings of Language, Thought, and Culture Symposium*. Osaka: Kansai University of Foreign Studies, 1978.
———. "Form in *Kabuki* Acting." In *Studies in Kabuki: Its Acting, Music, and Historical Context*. Ed. James R. Brandon, William P. Malm, and Donald H. Shively. Honolulu: University of Hawai'i Press, 1978.
———. "*Kabuki* in English: Toward Authenticity." In *Japanese Tradition: Search and Research*. Ed. Judith Mitoma Susilo. Los Angeles: University of California at Los Angeles, 1981.
———. "The Theft of *Chūshingura*." In *Chūshingura: Studies in Kabuki and the Puppet Theatre*. Ed. James R. Brandon. Honolulu: University of Hawai'i Press, 1982.
———. "Time and Tradition in Japanese Theatre." *Asian Theatre Journal* 2 (spring 1985).
———. "Performance: Edo/Tokyo." In *Tokyo: Form and Spirit*. Ed. Mildred Friedman. Minneapolis: Harry N. Abrams, 1986.
———. "Contemporary Japanese Theatre: Inter-Culturalism and Intra-Culturalism." In *The Dramatic Touch of Difference: Theatre, Own and Foreign*. Ed. Erika Fischer Lichte. Tubingen: Gunter Narr Verlag, 1990.
———. "Text and Performance: A *Kabuki* Perspective." *Modern Drama* 35 (1992).
———. "The Actor's Art: *Ie no Gei* in *Kabuki*." In *Fenway Court 1992*. Boston: Isabella Stewart Gardner Museum, 1993.
———. "Bridging Cultures: 101 Years of *Kabuki* in Hawai'i." In *Performing Arts of Asia: The Performer as (Inter)Cultural Transmitter*. Working Papers Series 4. Leiden: International Institute for Asian Studies, University of Leiden, 1996.
———. "*Kabuki* Performance: Its Value and Use in the Western Theatre." In *International Symposium on the Conservation and Restoration of Cultural Property—Kabuki: Changes and Prospects—1996*. Ed. Kamakura et Keiko al. Tokyo: Tokyo National Research Institute of Cultural Properties, 1996.
———. "Some Considerations of Shakespeare in *Kabuki*." *Theatre Symposium* 6 (1998).
———. "*Kabuki* and Shakespeare: Balancing Yin and Yang." *The Drama Review* (TDR) 43 (summer 1999).
———. "Performance and Text in *Kabuki*." In *Japanese Theatre and the International Stage*. Eds. Stanca Scholz-Cionca and Samuel L. Leiter. Leiden: E.J. Brill, 2000.
Daly, Matthew. "The First Instances: 1883–1900." In Stanca Scholz-Cionca and Samuel L. Leiter, *101 Years of Kabuki in Hawai'i*. Eds. Holly Blumner et al. Honolulu: Department of Theatre and Dance, University of Hawai'i, 1995.
Dubroff, Matthew R. "The People of *Kabuki*: 1900–1940." In *101 Years of* Kabuki *in Hawai'i*, eds. Holly Blumner et al. Honolulu: Department of Theatre and Dance, University of Hawai'i. 1995.

Dunn, Charles J. "The Japanese Puppet Theatre." In *Themes in Drama: Drama and Mimesis*. Ed. James Redmond." 2. Cambridge, England: Cambridge University Press, 1980.

———. "Religion and Japanese Drama." In *Themes in Drama: Drama and Religion*. Ed. James Redmond. 5. Cambridge, England: Cambridge University Press, 1983.

———. "Episodes in the Career of the *Kabuki* Actor Nakamura Utaemon III, Including His Rivalry with Arashi Rikan I." *Modern Asian Studies* 18: 4 (1984).

Enright, D.J. "Japanese Theatre." *Twentieth Century* (August 1955).

Ernst, Earle. "The Influence of Japanese Theatrical Style on Western Theatre." *Educational Theatre Journal* 21 (May 1969).

Gerstle, C. Andrew. "The Sense of History in 18th-Century *Jōruri* Drama." *Maske und Kothurn* (Mask and cothurn) 35 (1989).

———. "The Concept of Tragedy in Japanese Drama." *Japan Review* 1: 1 (March 1990).

———. "Text as Performance: Tragedy in Japanese Drama." In *Recovering the Orient: Artists, Scholars, Appropriations*. Eds. C. Andrew Gerstle and A. Milner. Yverdon, Switzerland: Harwood Academic Press, 1994.

———. "Hero as Murderer in Chikamatsu." *Monumenta Nipponica* 51: 3 (autumn 1996).

———. "*Kabuki* and the Puppet Theatre: Chikamatsu's *Twins at the Sumida River*." In *International Symposium on the Conservation and Restoration of Cultural Property—Kabuki: Changes and Prospects—1996*. Ed. Keiko Kamakura et al. Tokyo: Tokyo National Research Institute of Cultural Properties, 1996.

———. "Heroic Honor: Chikamatsu and the Samurai Ideal." *Harvard Journal of Asiatic Studies* 57: 2 (December 1997).

Gerstle, C. Andrew, and Hiroshi Sakurai. "Margins Between the Real and the Unreal: Bunraku." In *Japanese Theatre in the World*, ed. Samuel L. Leiter. New York: Japan Society, 1997.

———. "The Tragic Hero in Japanese Traditional Popular Drama." *Paolo Beonio-Brocchieri Memorial Lectures in Japanese Studies*, University of Venice. January 1998.

Goodman, David, and Kazuko Goodman. "*Kabuki* from the Outside: Interviews." *The Drama Review* (TDR) 15 (spring 1971).

Green, Paul. "East Meets West." *Theatre Arts* 37 (March 1954).

Guelzo, Carl M. "Transvestite Gentlemen of Japan." *Theatre Arts* 37 (September 1953).

Gunji, Masakatsu. "*Kabuki* and Its Social Background," trans. Andrew L. Markus. In *Tokugawa Japan: The Social and Economic Antecedents of Modern Japan*. Eds. Chie Nakane and Shinzaburō Ōishi. Tokyo: University of Tokyo Press, 1991.

Haruo, Suwa. "The Birth of the *Hanamichi*." Trans. and intro. Samuel L. Leiter. *Theatre Research International* 24: 1 (spring 1999).

Hirosue, Tamotsu. "The Blind Kagekiyo: Beyond the Tragic." *Concerned Theatre Japan* 1 (1970).

———. "Ekin." *Concerned Theatre Japan* 1 (1970).

———. "The Secret Ritual of the Place of Evil." *Concerned Theatre Japan* 2 (1971).

Hirschfeld-Medalia, Adeline. "The Voice in *Wayang* and *Kabuki*." *Asian Theatre Journal* 2 (fall 1984).

Hoff, Frank. "Furyū Odori." In *Studies on Japanese Culture*. Eds. Ohta Saburō and Fukuda Rikutarō. Vol. I. Tokyo: Japan P.E.N. Club, 1973.

————. "Killing the Self: How the Narrator Acts." *Asian Theatre Journal* 2 (spring 1985).

Hyland, Peter. "'A Kind of Woman': The Elizabethan Boy-Actor and the *Kabuki Onnagata*." *Theatre Research International* 12: 1 (1987).

Iezzi, Julie. "Sounding Out *Kabuki*: Music Behind the Scenes." In *101 Years of Kabuki in Hawai'i.* Ed. Holly Blumner et al. Honolulu: Department of Theatre and Dance, University of Hawai'i, 1995.

Imoos, Thomas. "Japanese Themes in Swiss Baroque Drama." In *Studies in Japanese Culture*. Ed. Joseph Roggendorf. Tokyo: Sophia University Press, 1963.

Ito, Sachiyo. "Some Characteristics of Japanese Expressions as They Appear in Dance." *Dance Research Annual* 10 (1979).

Jackson, Earl, Jr. "*Kabuki* Narratives of Male Homoerotic Plays in Saikaku and Mishima." *Theatre Journal* 41: 4 (1989).

Jones, Stanleigh H., Jr., trans. and comm. "Experiment and Tradition: New Plays in the *Bunraku* Theatre." *Monumenta Nipponica* 36: 2 (1981).

————, trans. and intro. "*Moritsuna's Camp*: An Eighteenth-Century Play from Japan's Puppet Theatre, by Chikamatsu Hanji, Miyoshi Shōraku, and Takemoto Saburōbei." *Asian Theatre Journal* 2 (fall 1985).

————, trans. and intro. "Vengeance and Its Toll in *Numazu*: An Eighteenth-Century Japanese Puppet Play." *Asian Theatre Journal* 7 (spring 1990).

Kawatake, Shigetoshi. "*Kabuki* After the Opening of Japan." *Contemporary Japan* 22 (1953).

Kawatake, Toshio. "The Reaction to the Overseas Performances of *Kabuki*." *Maske und Kothurn* (Mask and cothurn) 27: 1 (1981).

————. "A Crisis of *Kabuki* and its Revival Right After World War II." *Waseda Journal of Asian Studies* 5 (1983).

————. "Japanese Traditional Culture and Today's Japan: The Internationalization of the *Kabuki* Theatre and Its Function in Modern Society." In *Contemporary European Writing on Japan: Scholarly Views from Eastern and Western Europe*, ed. Ian Nishi. Woodchurch, Ashford, Kent: Paul Norbury, 1988.

Keene, Donald. "Realism and Unreality in Japanese Drama." *Drama Survey* 3 (1964).

————. "Variations on a Theme: *Chūshingura*." In *Chūshingura: Studies in Kabuki and the Puppet Theatre*. Ed. James R. Brandon. Honolulu: University of Hawai'i Press, 1982.

Kennelly, Paul. "*Ehon Gappō ga Tsuji*: A *Kabuki* Drama of Unfettered Evil by Tsuruya Nanboku IV." *Asian Theatre Journal* 17 (fall 2000).

Kominz, Laurence R. "*Ya no Ne*: The Genesis of a *Kabuki Aragoto* Classic." *Monumenta Nipponica* 38: 4 (winter 1983).

————. "Experiments in American *Kabuki*: Three Performances in the Pacific Northwest." *Theatre Topics* 2: 2 (September 1992).

————. "Ichikawa Danjūrō V and *Kabuki*'s Golden Age." In *The Floating World Revisited*. Ed. Donald Jenkins. Honolulu: Portland Art Museum in association with University of Hawai'i Press, 1993.

————. "Parodic Empowerment in *Kabuki*: Playing with Symbols and Icons in *Ya no Ne*." In *International Symposium on the Conservation and Restoration of Cultural Property—Kabuki: Changes and Prospects—1996*. Ed. Keiko Kamakura et al. Tokyo: Tokyo National Research Institute of Cultural Properties, 1996.

————. "The Power of Fudō Myōo: Ichikawa Danjūrō and His Soga Gorō Character in the *Kabuki* Play *Tsuwamono Kongen Soga*." In *Currents in Japanese Culture*

Translations and Transformations. Ed. Amy Heinrich. New York: Columbia University Press, 1997.

———. "Ganjirō III and Chikamatsu's 'Lost' *Kabuki* Masterpiece." *Asian Theatre Journal* 17 (spring 2000).

Konishi, Gilbert. "*Kabuki*'s Eleventh Danjūrō." *Orient/West* (September 1962).

Laderriere, Mette. "The Technique of Female Impersonation in *Kabuki*." *Maske und Kothurn* (Mask and cothurn) 27 (1981).

———. "The Early Years of Female Impersonators in *Kabuki*." *Maske und Kothurn* (Mask and cothurn) 35 (1989).

Lee, San-Kyong. "Influence of *Kabuki* on European Theatre." In *International Symposium on the Conservation and Restoration of Cultural Property—Kabuki: Changes and Prospects—1996*. Ed. Keiko Kamakura et al. Tokyo: Tokyo National Research Institute of Cultural Properties, 1996.

———. "Edward Gordon Craig and Japanese Theatre." *Asian Theatre Journal* 17 (fall 2000).

Leims, Thomas. "*Kabuki* Goes to Hollywood: Reforms and 'Revues' in the 1980s." In *The Dramatic Touch of Difference*. Ed. Erika Fischer-Lichte. Tübingen: Günter Narr Verlag, 1990.

———. "The Importance of Materials Contained in Western Libraries for the Research of Early *Kabuki*." In *International Symposium on the Conservation and Restoration of Cultural Property—Kabuki: Changes and Prospects—1996*. Ed. Keiko Kamakura et al. Tokyo: Tokyo National Research Institute of Cultural Properties, 1996.

Leiter, Samuel L. "Four Interviews with *Kabuki* Actors." *Educational Theatre Journal* 18 (December 1966).

———. "The Frozen Moment: A *Kabuki* Technique." *Drama Survey* 6 (spring 1967).

———. "Authentic *Kabuki*: American Style." *Theatre Crafts* 2 (September/October 1968).

———. "The Depiction of Violence on the *Kabuki* Stage." *Educational Theatre Journal* 21 (May 1969).

———. "Onoe Kikugorō VII." *Asian Theatre Bulletin* 3 (fall/winter 1973).

———. "Ichikawa Ennosuke III: *Kabuki*'s Most Versatile Actor." Souvenir program, American tour of Ichikawa Ennosuke III and the Grand *Kabuki*, Beacon Theatre, New York City, 1976.

———. "The *Kabuki Jūhachiban*." *Literature East and West* 18 (1976).

———. "*Keren*: Spectacle and Trickery on the *Kabuki* Stage." *Educational Theatre Journal* 28 (1976).

———. *Tachimawari: Stage Fighting in the Kabuki Theatre.* Monographs on Music, Dance and Theatre in Asia, vol. 3. New York: Performing Arts Program of the Asia Society, 1976.

———. "*Terakoya* at Brooklyn College" *Asian Theater Bulletin* 2 (fall 1976).

———. "Ichikawa Danjūrō XI: A Life in *Kabuki*." *Educational Theatre Journal* 29 (March 1977).

———. "*Kumagai's Battle Camp*: Form and Tradition in *Kabuki* Acting." *Asian Theatre Journal* 8 (spring 1991).

———. "The Kanamaru-za: Japan's Oldest *Kabuki* Theatre." *Asian Theatre Journal* 15 (spring 1997).

———. " 'What Really Happens Backstage': A Nineteenth-Century *Kabuki* Document." *Theatre Survey* 38 (fall 1997).

————. "From the London Patents to the *Edo Sanza*: A Comparison of British Theatre and *Kabuki*, ca. 1650–1800." *Theatre Symposium* 6 (1998).

Levine, Norma. "The Influence of *Kabuki* Theatre on the Films of Eisenstein." *Modern Drama* 12 (May 1969).

Lovel, John. "Theatre Audiences of Japan." *Theatre Survey* 5 (November 1964).

Luhrmann, Alice E. "Performer Recollections: A Survey." In *101 Years of Kabuki in Hawai'i*. Ed. Holly Blumner et al. Honolulu: Department of Theatre and Dance, University of Hawai'i, 1995.

Maeshiba, Naeko. "Early Japanese Theatres in Hawai'i." In *101 Years of Kabuki in Hawai'i*. Ed. Holly Blumner et al. Honolulu: Department of Theatre and Dance, University of Hawai'i, 1995.

Malm, William P. "Four Seasons of the Old Mountain Woman: An Example of Japanese *Nagauta* Text Setting." *Journal of the American Musicology Society* 31: 1 (1978).

————. "Music in the *Kabuki* Theatre." In *Studies in Kabuki: Its Acting, Music, and Historical Context*. Ed. James R. Brandon, William P. Malm, and Donald H. Shively. Honolulu: University of Hawai'i Press, 1978.

————. "A Musical Approach to the Study of Japanese *Jōruri*." In *Chūshingura: Studies in Kabuki and the Puppet Theatre*. Ed. James R. Brandon. Honolulu: University of Hawai'i Press, 1982.

Markus, Andrew L. "The Carnival of Edo: *Misemono* Spectacles." *Harvard Journal of Asiatic Studies* 45 (1985).

Matsumoto, Shinko. "Three Codes of the Meiji Theatre." *Maske und Kothurn* (Mask and cothurn) 35: 2–3 (1989).

Maurin, Frédéric. "From *Topos* to Utopia: Is *Kabuki* Bound to Its Cultural Origin?" Special issue, "Japanese Theatre and the West." In *Contemporary Theatre Review*. Ed. A. Horie-Webber. 1, part 2 (1994).

Mezur, Katherine. "Japanese Deconstructions of the Female Body." *Theatre Research International* 24: 3 (Autumn 1999).

————. "Undressing the *Onnagata*: *Kabuki*'s Female-Role Specialists and the Art of Costuming." In *Japanese Theatre and the International Stage*. Ed. Stanca Scholz-Cionca and Samuel L. Leiter. Leiden: E.J. Brill, 2000.

Michener, James A. "*Kabuki* Is a Must for America." *Theatre Arts* 38 (March 1954).

Miner, Earl. "Our Heritage of Japanese Drama." *Literature East and West* 15.4–16.2 (1971–1972).

Mitchell, John D., and E.K. Schwartz. "A Psychoanalytic Approach to *Kabuki*: A Study in Personality and Culture." *Journal of Psychology* 52 (1961).

Mori, Mitsuya. "*Noh, Kabuki* and Western Theatre." *Theatre Research International* 22: 1 (spring 1997). Supplement.

Musolf, Peter. "Bunburying and the Art of *Kabuki*: Or Wilde, Mishima and the Art of Being a Sardine Seller." *New Theatre Quarterly* 12: 48 (November 1996).

Omoto, Lisa Ann M., and Kathy Welch. "*Kabuki* Spectacle." In *101 Years of Kabuki in Hawai'i*. Ed. Holly Blumner et al. Honolulu: Department of Theatre and Dance, University of Hawai'i, 1995.

O'Neill, P.G. "Organization and Authority in the Traditional Arts." *Modern Asian Studies* 18: 4 (1984).

Orita Kōji. "Life Behind the Scenes." *The East* 8: 5 (May 1972).

Ortolani, Benito. "*Nō, Kabuki* and New Theatre Actors in the Theatrical Reforms of Meiji Japan (1868–1912)." In *Acta of the 7th International Congress on Theatre Research*. Ed. Milan Jukes. Prague: University Karlova Prava, 1976.

Ouyang, Yu-Chien. "The Zenshin-za *Kabuki* Troupe." *Chinese Literature* 5 (1960).

Pauly, Herta. "Inside *Kabuki*: An Experience in Comparative Aesthetics." *Journal of Aesthetics and Art Criticism* 25 (1967).

Poulton, Cody. "Drama and Fiction in the Meiji Era: The Case of Izumi Kyōka." *Asian Theatre Journal* 12 (fall 1995).

Powell, Brian. "*Kabuki* in the 1930s: A Decade of Diversity." In *International Symposium on the Conservation and Restoration of Cultural Property—Kabuki: Changes and Prospects—1996*. Ed. Keiko Kamakura et al. Tokyo: Tokyo National Research Institute of Cultural Properties, 1996.

————, trans. and intro. "*Yoritomo's Death*: A *Shin Kabuki* Play by Mayama Seika." *Asian Theatre Journal* 17 (spring 2000).

Pronko, Leonard. "Oriental Theatre for the West: Problems of Authenticity and Communication." *Educational Theatre Journal* 20: 3 (1968).

————. "Freedom and Tradition in the *Kabuki* Actor's Art." *Educational Theatre Journal* 21 (1969).

————. "Learning *Kabuki*: The Training Program of the National Theatre of Japan." *Educational Theatre Journal* 23 (December 1971).

————. "What Is Wrong with *Kabuki*?" *Japan Quarterly* 18 (1971).

————. "*Kabuki* Today and Tomorrow." *Comparative Drama* (1972).

————. "Creating a *Kabuki* Western: *Revenge at Spider Mountain*." *Modern Drama* 35 (1992).

————. "Creating *Kabuki* for the West." Special issue, "Japanese Theatre and the West." In *Contemporary Theatre Review*. Ed. A. Horie-Webber. 1, part 2 (1994).

————. "Boys, Women, or Phantasmal Androgynes? Elizabethan and *Kabuki* Female Representation." *Theatre Symposium* 6 (1998).

Raz, Jacob. "The Audience Evaluated: Shikitei Sanba's *Kyakusha Hyōbanki*." *Monumenta Nipponica* 35 (summer 1980).

Richie, Donald, and Joseph L. Anderson. "Traditional Theatre and the Film in Japan." *Film Quarterly* (fall 1958).

Rimer, J. Thomas. "*Kabuki* at the Time of Kunisada." In *Kunisada's World*. Ed. Sebastian Izzard. New York: Japan Society, 1993.

Samson, Sir George. "The Aesthetics of Japanese Theatre." *Theatre Arts* 38 (March 1954).

Schumacher, Ernst. "Gestic Acting in *Kabuki* and Gestic Acting According to Brecht." *Maske und Kothurn* (Mask and cothurn) 35 (1989).

Serper, Zvika. "Exploration Through a Concept: Japanese Classical Acting as a Model of Harmonic Contrasts." Special issue, "Japanese Theatre and the West," *Contemporary Theatre Review*. Ed. A. Horie-Webber. 1, part 2 (1994).

————. "The *Kabuki* Actor's Manifestations as a Performer." *Journal of the Asiatic Society of Bombay* 75 (2000).

————. "Traditional and Innovative *Kabuki* Elements as Used in Béjart's Choreography of *The Kabuki*." *Studia Choreologica* 2 (2000).

Shively, Donald. "Notes on the Word *Kabuki*." *Oriens* 10 (1957).

————. "Chikamatsu's Satire on the Dog Shogun." *Harvard Journal of Asiatic Studies* 18 (1958).

————. "The Social Environment of Tokugawa *Kabuki*." In *Studies in Kabuki: Its Acting, Music, and Historical Context*. Eds. James R. Brandon, William P. Malm, and Donald H. Shively. Honolulu: University of Hawai'i, 1978.

Soeda, Hiroshi. "A *Kabuki* Stage." *Concerned Theatre Japan* 2 (1971).

Sorgenfrei, Carol Fisher. "Fusing *Kabuki* with Flamenco: The Creation of *Blood Wine, Blood Wedding*." *Theatre Symposium* 6 (1998).

Sugawara, Makoto. "The Drama of Dilemma: *Giri Ninjō* on the Stage." *The East* 7: 2 (1971).

Thornbury, Barbara. "Restoring an Imagined Past: The Kokuritsu Gekijō and the Question of Authenticity in *Kabuki*." *Asian Theatre Journal* 18 (fall 2001).

Torigoe Bunzō. "Edo *Jōruri*." In *18th-Century Japan: Culture and Society*, ed. C. Andrew Gerstle. Sydney: Allen and Unwin, 1990.

————. "The Actor's Art: *Kabuki*." Trans. by James R. Brandon. In *Japanese Theatre in the World*, ed. Samuel L. Leiter. New York: Japan Society, 1997.

Tschudin, Jean-Jacques. "Early Meiji *Kabuki* and Western Theatre: A Rendez-Vous Manqué." In *International Symposium on the Conservation and Restoration of Cultural Property—Kabuki: Changes and Prospects—1996*. Eds. Keiko Kamakura et al. Tokyo: Tokyo National Research Institute of Cultural Properties, 1996.

Tsutsumi, Harue. "*Kanadehon Hamlet*: A Play by Tsutsumi Harue." Trans. Faubion Bowers, with David W. Griffith and Hori Mariko. *Asian Theatre Journal* 15 (fall 1998).

Ueda, Makoto. "Japanese Idea of a Theatre." *Modern Drama* 11 (spring 1967).

Valency, Maurice. "Japanese Theatre: The New and the Old." *Theatre Arts* 43 (February 1959).

Waterhouse, David. "Actors, Artists, and Stage in Eighteenth-Century Japan and England." In *The Stage in the Eighteenth Century*. Ed. J. D. Browning. New York and London: Garland, 1981.

Williams, Henry B. "Shinto-Sponsored Theatre, the Farmers' *Kabuki*." *Educational Theatre Journal* 26: 2 (1974).

Yamaguchi, Masao. "Theatricality in Japan." Trans. E.A. Walker. *Modern Drama* 25: 1 (1982).

About the Editor and Contributors

Editor

Samuel L. Leiter heads the graduate program in theatre at Brooklyn College, CUNY, and also teaches at The Graduate Center, CUNY. He edits *Asian Theatre Journal*, is on the editorial board of *Theatre Symposium*, and has published seventeen books, including *The Art of Kabuki* (revised edition, 1999), *New Kabuki Encyclopedia* (1997), *Zeami and the Nō Theatre in the World* (with Benito Ortolani, 1998), *Japanese Theatre in the World* (1998), and *Japanese Theatre and the International Stage* (with Stanca Scholz-Cionca, 2000), a translation/adaptation of Shiro Okamoto's *The Man Who Saved Kabuki: Faubion Bowers and Theatre Censorship in Occupied Japan* (2000), and *Frozen Moments: Writings on* Kabuki (2001). Forthcoming works include the four-volume *Kabuki On Stage* series (with James R. Brandon). He has twice been a visiting scholar at Waseda University, was a Fulbright Research Scholar to Japan (1974–1975), has held a Claire and Leonard Tow Professorship, was elected in 1999 to the Executive Committee of the American Society for Theatre Research, held a Wolfe Research Fellowship in the Humanities (1999–2000), and was named Broeklundian Professor in 2001.

Contributors

Faith Bach is one of the original earphone guides at Tokyo's Kabuki-za. She teaches at Kantō Gakuen University in Gunma prefecture. Her essays on and translations of *kabuki* have appeared in such publications as *Asian Theatre Journal*, and she is the author of *Burabō e Kabuki Burabō e Japan* (Bravo *kabuki*, bravo Japan, 1993).

Holly Blumner is a doctoral candidate at the University of Hawai'i at Manoa with an emphasis in Asian theatre. Her dissertation is on Sakata Tōjūrō and *wagoto kabuki*. Her translation of *Domo Mata* (Matahei the stutterer) appears in the forthcoming *Kabuki Plays On Stage* series, coedited by James

399

R. Brandon and Samuel L. Leiter. She served as a coeditor of *101 Years of Kabuki in Hawai'i* (1995), which includes her essay "*Sukeroku*: A History," coauthored with Naoko Maeshiba.

James R. Brandon is emeritus professor of Asian theatre at the University of Hawai'i at Manoa. He translates and directs English-language *kabuki* and is the author or editor of *Kabuki: Five Classic Plays*; *Chūshingura: Studies in Kabuki and the Puppet Theater*; *Nō and Kyōgen in the Modern World; The Cambridge Guide to Asian Theatre;* and many other books on Asian theatre. He is the recipient of the Order of the Rising Sun Gold Rays with Rosette from the government of Japan, the Uchimura Prize of the International Theatre Institute, the John D. Rockefeller III Award for contributions to Asian arts, and other awards.

Charles J. Dunn, who taught at the University of London from 1946 to 1982, died in 1995. His books include *Early Japanese Puppet Drama* (1966), *The Actors' Analects* (with Bunzō Torigoe, 1969), and *Everyday Life in Traditional Japan* (1969). A leader in the establishment of Japanese studies in the United Kingdom, he served as president of the British Association for Japanese Studies and of the parallel European Association. The Japanese government awarded him the Order of the Rising Sun.

C. Andrew Gerstle is professor of Japanese studies at the School of Oriental and African Studies, University of London, and director of the new AHRB Research Centre for the Study of Asian and African Literatures. Gerstle's books include *Circles of Fantasy: Convention in the Plays of Chikamatsu* (1986); *Eighteenth-Century Japan* (editor, 1989); and *Theater as Music: The Bunraku Play: Mt. Imo and Mt. Se: An Exemplary Tale of Womanly Virtue* (coauthor, 1990). A volume of translations, *Chikamatsu: Five Late Plays,* will be published in 2001.

Janet E. Goff is a writer and translator. She studied *nō* performance in Tokyo for many years and is the author of the award-winning *Noh Drama and the Tale of Genji* (1991). She has written and translated numerous articles on Japanese theatre and culture. Her essay on *Kuzunoha* in this volume is part of a larger research project, initially funded by a Japan Foundation research grant, on the role of the fox in classical Japanese theatre.

Natsuko Inoue, a native of Osaka, has studied at Brooklyn College, CUNY. Her essay in this volume, adapted from her master's thesis, is her first published work.

Stanleigh H. Jones Jr. is professor of Japanese at Claremont Graduate School, where he teaches Japanese language, pre-1800 Japanese literature in translation, and traditional Japanese theatre. His special interest is the Japanese puppet theatre (*bunraku*), from which he has translated several plays. These include *Sugawara and the Secrets of Calligraphy* (1985) and *Yoshitsune and the Thousand Cherry Trees* (1993). He is currently working on an anthology of translations of puppet theatre plays from the 1730s to the 1870s.

Laurence R. Kominz is professor of Japanese language and literature at Portland State University and director of the university's Institute for Asian Studies. Kominz studies and performs *buyō* (Fujima School) and *kyōgen* (Okura School) and teaches Japanese performance in his classes. Recent books include *The Stars Who Created Kabuki* (1997) and *Avatars of Vengeance: Japanese Drama and the Soga Literary Tradition* (1995). He serves as Japan editor for *Asian Theatre Journal*.

William Lee is assistant professor of area studies at Minnesota State University–Akita in Akita, Japan. His research interests include Japanese theatre, folk performing arts, and popular culture. Lee's translation of the *kabuki* play *Ishikiri Kajiwara* (The stone-cutting feat of Kajiwara) will be published in the *Kabuki Plays On Stage* series edited by James R. Brandon and Samuel L. Leiter. Other recent work includes essays on Japanese TV animation, the formation of the classical canon during Meiji, and Japanese folk theatre.

Susumu Matsudaira who died in December 2000, was a professor at Sonoda Women's University, Kobe, where he taught the history of theatre and did research on *kabuki* history and actor prints. His major publications include *Kamigata Ukiyo-e no Saihakken* (The rediscovery of Osaka prints) and *Moronobu Sukenobu Ehon Shoshi* (Bibliographies of Moronobu's and Sukenobu's illustrated books).

Brian Powell teaches Japanese theatre at Oxford University and has written on *shingeki* and modern *kabuki*, especially the work of playwright Mayama Seika. He is the author of *Kabuki in Modern Japan: Mayama Seika and his Plays* (1990), and is the translator of Mayama's *Death of Yoritomo* (*Asian Theatre Journal*, Spring 2000) and (with Jason Daniel) Kinoshita Junji's *Requiem on the Great Meridian* (2000). In 1994 he was awarded a prize by the Yamamoto Yasue no Kai Kinen Kikin (Yamamoto Yasue Association Memorial Fund) for "outstanding cultural activity relating to theatre."

Leonard C. Pronko is professor emeritus of theatre at Pomona College, where he has directed many *kabuki* plays in English. His various books on European and Asian theatre include *Theatre East and West* (revised edition, 1974) and *Guide to Japanese Drama* (1973). The first Westerner to enroll in the *Kabuki* Training Program of Japan's Kokuritsu Gekijō (National Theatre), he has studied *kabuki* dance for thirty-five years and has presented hundreds of lecture-demonstrations on *kabuki*. He also has used *kabuki* techniques in classic and new Western plays. His honors include the Japanese government's Order of the Sacred Treasure and the Association for Theatre Higher Education's Outstanding Teacher of Theatre Award.

Katherine Saltzman-Li is associate professor of Japanese language and cultural studies at the University of California, Santa Barbara. Her research interests include premodern Japanese drama and literature and Japanese folklore. Her translations of two *kabuki* plays, *Sanemori Monogatari* (The Sanemori story) and *Shibaraku* (Just a minute!), will appear in the *Kabuki Plays On Stage* series edited by James R. Brandon and Samuel L. Leiter. Also forthcoming is her book, *Creating Kabuki Plays: Context for Kezairoku, "Valuable Notes on Playwriting."*

Donald H. Shively is professor emeritus of Japanese history and literature at Harvard University. He also served as Asian librarian at the University of California, Berkeley. His 1953 translation of the classic puppet play *Shinjū Ten no Amijima* (The love suicide at Amijima) was reissued in 1991. Shively is the author of numerous articles in scholarly books and journals, among them his chapter entitled "The Social Environment in Tokugawa *Kabuki*" in *Studies in Kabuki: Its Acting, Music, and Historical Context*, which he coedited with James R. Brandon and William P. Malm.

Yuichirō Takahashi is a professor of performance studies at Dokkyō University in Tokyo. His interests extend from traditional Japanese theatre to avant-garde contemporary performances. His recent writings in Japanese focus on the subject of how a Japanese identity has been fashioned through a variety of forms of cultural performances.

Barbara E. Thornbury is associate professor of Japanese at Temple University. Her recent publications include "National Treasure/National Theatre: The Interesting Case of Okinawa's *Kumi Odori* Musical Dance-Drama" (*Asian Theatre Journal*, 1999). Thornbury's books are *Sukeroku's Double Identity: The Dramatic Structure of Edo Kabuki* (1982) and *The Folk Performing Arts: Traditional Culture in Contemporary Japan* (1997). She is also a contributor to *Japanese Theatre and the International Stage*, edited by Stanca Scholz-Cionca and Samuel L. Leiter. Her translation of *Kiwametsuki Banzui Chōbei* (The renowned Banzui Chōbei) will appear in volume 4 of *Kabuki Plays On Stage*, edited by James R. Brandon and Samuel Leiter.

Andrew T. Tsubaki is professor emeritus at the University of Kansas, Lawrence, where he taught theatre, film, and Japanese. He directed many productions of classical Japanese plays and also experimented with Japanese techniques in Western dramas. Tsubaki also is the author of several important studies of Japanese and Indian theatre.

Index

Abe no Seimei Monogatari, 272–274, 282

Abe Yūzō, 164n

actors (and acting), xxviii; 1837 reforms, 259; actor-spectator relationship, 130, 131, 136 *ff*; affiliation with *mon*, 156–158; apprenticeship system, 168; boys (adolescents, youths, *see wakashu*);breakdown of traditional hierarchy, 160; commercial endorsements, xxiv, 89, 98, 122, 261; costumes, 334; crests, 120; dancers (and acrobats), 248, 332; Danjūrō IX's realism, 350; desertion of major theatres, 157; difference between *gei* and *engi*, 357; difference between *kabuki* and Elizabethan acting, 332; disguising, 235–237; doubling, 235–237; economy of mental energy, 357; Elizabethan conventions, 333; Elizabethan theatre, 329; elocutionary skill, 257; ensemble playing, 183; facial expressions, 332; family

actors (and acting) *(continued)* system, xxii, xxvi, 156,168,182, 189, 192, 264, 265; fan support (*see* fans [audiences]); forfeiture of status, 161, 162; gestures, 53, 73, 243, 248, 248, 249; head coverings, 39; hieroglyphs, 241 *ff*, 247, 252; influence on fashion and manners, 97, 152; *kabuki* conventions, 333; Kansei Reforms, 259; and legal restrictions, xxix, 43, 48, 50, 169, 259, 260 (*see also kabuki*, and legal restrictions); literary groups, 89; literary world, 103; luxurious life-styles, 261; movement, 333; names, xxii, xxix, 79, 85, 233, 262–264, 268; new opportunities of Meiji period,157; performatives, 264; as players of women's roles, 334, 335; power over managers, 259; privileged position in *kabuki*, 369; puppets, 284, 285, 298; regulations against boundary crossing, 161; relationship with roles, 230–232, 234, 235, 237,

ayako odori, 13
Azuma, 36
Azuma-za, 161

Baba Bunkō, 100
Bach, Faith, xxv
bakufu, xxi, 33, 38, 41, 45, 46, 48,
   50, 52–54, 89, 90, 98–101, 106,
   212, 259–261, 364, 379
Balcony, The, 234
Bandō Hikosaburō III, 120, 147*n*17
Bandō Mitsugorō III, xxiii, 79
Bandō Mitsugorō VII, 356
Bandō Mitsugorō VIII, 233
Bandō Muraemon, 155
Banmin Daifukuchō, 255
banzuke, 76, 77, 81, 83, 89, 117,
   164*n*4
Barba, Eugenio, 357
Barrault, Jean-Louis, 346
Baudelaire, 241, 251
Beckerman, Bernard, 332
Beckett, Samuel, 240
Belasco, David, 347
Beni Murasaki Ōsaka Aide Someage,
   77
*Beni Murasaki Ōsaka no Aji. See
   Beni Murasaki Ōsaka Aide
   Someage.*
Benkei, 21, 22
Benten Kozō, 227, 235
Bentley, Eric, 231
Bergmann, Annegret, 350, 354
Bernhardt, Sarah, 332
Bigot, Georges, 145
biwa, 8
Blumner, Holly, xxiii
bon odori, 12
box seats. *See sajiki.*
boys' kabuki. *See wakashu
   kabuki.*

Brandon, James R., xvi, xxx, xxxi,
   107*n*6, 151, 185, 267, 283, 343,
   345, 360
Brecht, Bertolt, 345, 346
bugaku, 10, 380
buka, 4, 5, 6, 14
Bungaku-za, 205*n*4
bungobushi, 100
bunraku. See ningyō jōruri.
Burbage, Richard, 332, 337
bushidō, 214
Butler, Judith, 264
buyō geki, 248

Case, Sue-Ellen, 212, 214, 229
censorship. *See kabuki*, and
   censorship.
chaban, 103, 105, 107*n*12
Chaban Kyōgen Haya Gatten, 107*n*
chabanshi, 105
Chamberlain, Basil Hall, 213, 214,
   218
"Chanson de mal aimé, La," 250
Chaplin, Charlie, 347
characters, in drama, 231–234
chaya, 127, 136, 145*n*3
chigo, 10
Chijimiya Shinsuke, 228
Chikamatsu Josetsu, 370
Chikamatsu Monzaemon, 31*n*10, 52,
   59, 63, 71, 75, 78, 195, 205*n*4,
   206*n*23, 223, 286, 291, 331, 339,
   349, 362, 364*n*, 365, 371,
   386*n*14
Chikamatsu Shibai, 205*n*4
chikara ge, 24
chikara suji, 19, 24
Chikugo no Shibai, 165*n*7
chikushō, 90
Chinen Masabumi, 187, 190, 191,
   205